Crossdressing in Context.

Dress, Gender, Transgender, and Crossdressing

Vol. 4
Transgender & Religion

G. G. Bolich, Ph.D.

Psyche's

Press

Psyche's Press
Raleigh, North Carolina
©2008 G. G. Bolich

Library of Congress Cataloging-in-Publication Data

Crossdressing in Context, vol. 4: Transgender & Religion/G. G. Bolich
     p.   cm.
  Includes bibliographical references and indices.
  ISBN 978-0-615-25356-5
  1. Crossdressing 2. Transgender 3. Religion—Religion and gender
I. Bolich, G. G., 1953-
  HQ77.9 .B65x   2008

Printed in the United States of America

Two are better than one, because they have a good reward for their toil. For if they fall, one will lift up the other, but woe to one who is alone and falls and does not have another to help.

Koholeth (*Ecclesiastes* 4:9-10)

Peacefulness, self-control, austerity, purity, tolerance, honesty, wisdom, knowledge and religiousness—these are the qualities by which the *brahmanas* work.

Lord Krishna (*Bhagavad-Gita* 18:42)

Do not impose on others what you yourself do not desire.

Confucius (*Analects* 12:2)

So speak and so act as those who are to be judged by the law of liberty. For judgment will be without mercy to anyone who has shown no mercy; mercy triumphs over judgment.

Jacob ben Joseph (*James* 2:12-13)

It may well be that God will put good will between you and those with whom you have hitherto been at odds. God is mighty. God is merciful.

The Prophet, peace be upon him.

(*Quran*, Surah 60)

Though especially dedicated to my colleague, Dr. Garry Kenney, this volume is also respectfully and gratefully dedicated to all who believe in and practice a spirituality of tolerance, a religion of diversity, and a philosophy of peace—hallmarks of my friend. Garry, thank you.

Table of Contents

The Questions

Detailed Table of Contents

The Questions

Preface

Can we be honest?

What can you expect?

Let's be candid from the start. The subject matter of this book is controversial. Worse, it is the kind of controversy that often moves beyond mere intellectual disagreement to result in broken relationships and sometimes violence. In preparing this work one particular remark has stayed with me. In a report on violence experienced by transgendered people, the authors wrote, "What is common to most studies of transpeople is their staggering irrelevance to the community at issue."[1]

My intention has been to set forth information that is not irrelevant, either to the transgendered, or to those who find themselves related in some manner to them—which I think is all of us. As the title suggests, this work is about raising questions and offering answers. In the effort to do so, I have drawn both on academic material and on accounts set forth by transgendered people themselves. For example, one question asks how crossdressers describe themselves (Q. 46), while the next offers the results of various formal psychological tests to answer the same question (Q. 47). I have throughout tried to let others speak for themselves. You will find brief quotes from various sources to offer a bit of the flavor of how these other voices sound. In summarizing studies, theories, or personal accounts I have aimed at being concise but fair—and pointed you in directions to follow in order to learn more. Because of the ubiquity of the World Wide Web, whenever possible indication has been made in the endnotes as to where material can be accessed online. At the same time, I have not shied away from offering my own critique of what others have said or my own assessment of the matters about which they speak.

Despite the large number of questions raised, this work barely scratches the surface of transgender realities, including crossdressing. I often refer to 'transgender realities' and I do so quite consciously. I want us to remember that we are examining *realities*—lived experiences that range from very temporary occurrences of minor personal significance to profoundly meaningful matters of per-

1

sonal identity felt and expressed every day. I want us to consider how the *trans* in *trans*gender can mean different things to different people. Nor do I wish us to ever lose sight of how *gender* is basic to trans*gender*. And, because the organizing framework is built around crossdressing, we must also know something about the role clothes play in our lives.

Obviously, I am very ambitious. I hope you are as well. Even something that superficially seems easy enough to describe, like crossdressing, which after all is simply the act of dressing in clothes typically associated with a gender other than the one assigned the wearer, is not really simple when once looked at closely. To understand crossdressing—to begin to truly see transgender realities—takes work. I want to do that work alongside you, serving as a partner in dialog while also offering my modest services as a guide to the vast literature on the subjects considered. Since I am functioning as a guide, you have every right to ask about my qualifications.

Who am I to talk?

One question you may have right away is what my 'position' or 'bias' is on the subject. For example, you might wish to know if I identify myself as a transgendered person. Unfortunately, in my experience, many people screen what they are willing to expose themselves to as they study a controversial topic by using this kind of query. Of course, I know *you* are more fair-minded than that, but the next reader might not be. So, whatever my stance—or identity—may be will have to become a matter of your own judgment (or speculation) as you read the work. I have conscientiously spoken of 'we' and 'us' throughout the book, both when speaking of crossdressers and when referring to noncrossdressers. I wish to convey my conviction that the fundamental humanity that unites us is greater than the differences that we too often let divide, separate, and isolate us. It is a small world we all have to share and a short life we all live.

What I am willing to tell you upfront about myself concerns my qualifications for tackling the subject. I caution you not to infer anything about my being 'for' or 'against' crossdressing from these qualifications.[2] As you know, qualifications do not guarantee people holding reasonable positions or even necessarily knowing what they are talking about! Still, I think you have a right to know relevant portions of my background because they may speak to my level of preparation for talking to you about these things. I don't expect you to take my word on anything from blind trust, but I do hope your confidence in the reliability of my remarks will be strengthened both by my background and by the actual material I set forth.

My background includes more than 30 years working professionally with people, primarily as an educator, but also as a counselor. I hold advanced degrees in the fields of religious studies and psychology, and my teaching and counseling have been in both areas. Because some people view crossdressing as a psychological disorder, my experience in psychology seems relevant. Because

2

some people regard crossdressing as morally or religiously wrong, my experience in religious studies seems relevant, too. In fact, between these two areas, I find most of the questions and concerns about crossdressing that I have encountered from students, clients, and others.

In terms of religious studies, I am seminary trained, holding a M.A. in Theology, and the Master of Divinity—or M.Div.—the degree used to prepare people for professional ministry. My first Ph.D., in Educational Leadership, also focused on religious studies, culminating in a dissertation in the area of New Testament introduction. I am trained in biblical and classical languages (Hebrew, Greek, Latin), and in both traditional and modern methods of translating and interpreting sacred texts. Beginning in 1974, as an instructor at a Bible School, I have taught courses in religious studies at undergraduate and graduate levels in a wide variety of settings, including churches and synagogues, community college, public university, private college, and seminary extension program. These courses have covered matters of ethics, ancient and modern world religions, theology, history, sacred texts, and the relation of religion to psychology. My area of particular interest and specialization has been the religious writings of the period extending from about a century or so before Christ, to the end of the second century after Christ. In addition to scholarly work, I also have been involved in ecumenical work, notably between the Christian and Jewish communities. As a counselor, many people have identified my background in religious studies as an important reason why they chose to come see me.

My second doctorate is in psychology (Ph.D.). I started working with people as a counselor in 1973, while still a college student, on a crisis line. As time passed, my interests began to turn more and more to matters of human development and human sexuality. As a counselor I gradually developed a specialization in Trauma Resolution Therapy, principally working with adult survivors of sexual abuse. Today I teach graduate students in counseling about human sexuality. Both as a teacher and as a therapist I have continually encountered curiosity about crossdressing and transgender people. Because of my additional background in religious studies this curiosity by my students and clients has often extended to specific matters of faith and practice as well as the more specific psychological concerns about whether being a transgender person or engaging in crossdressing is deviant, sick, sinful, or harmful.

Accordingly, this work grows out of many years of interest and experience. I think my background contributes some layers of knowledge that may not be as easily accessible to other professionals whose experience is confined to only one or another of the areas relevant to a full consideration of crossdressing. To these credentials I will add my intention of being fair-minded and honest throughout this work. I intend this work to be educational in nature. At the same time, I am aware that when educating people on controversial subjects it may not be either feasible or even particularly desirable to attempt being completely above the fray and studiously neutral. In truth, I am not neutral on the subject—and I do not know anyone who is. Even scholarly works serve social and political ends, and every work—including mine—must be soberly appraised for fairness. I have every confidence that fair-minded readers who pursue the logic and evidence set down within this work will be able to accurately assess the value of this endeavor.

Introduction

What do you need to know to get started?

Why does any of this matter?

Chances are you aren't looking at this unless you already believe the subject matters. I agree. The fundamental assumption of this work is that transgender realities matter to all of us, whether we are transgendered ourselves or not. They matter because such realities by their very existence pose opportunities for us to explore and expand our sense of sex and gender. In a culture like our own, where sex and gender are so central to the way we define our identities and relationships, such an opportunity must not be missed.

We must also acknowledge from the very beginning that any discussion of these things will generate feeling, and quite often strong feeling. How can it not when the stakes—identities and relationships—are so high? Transgender realities in a culture where sex and gender are rigidly paired at two poles raise a challenge to our sense of what we think and know. But more critically than challenging the narrowness of our perceptions, they prompt questions about our own felt sense of sex and gender. In short, transgender realities matter because they disturb senses of identity and relationship founded and attached to a bipolar duality allowing us only to be masculine men or feminine women.

It seemed to me in framing this work that the most natural and appropriate choice was to mirror what happens in us when we encounter transgender realities like crossdressing. So herein everything is framed by questions. Though 100 questions are used to create what you may think of as 'chapters,' there are literally hundreds of questions raised and considered in this work.

Why this title?

The scope of this work, with all its queries, can be overwhelming—but then sex and gender are precisely that in our culture. You may already feel in over your head just holding this material in your hands. The subject of 'transgender' and 'crossdressing' is perhaps a lot larger than you initially thought—and then 'gender,' 'sex,' and 'dress' are thrown in for good measure! My choice of titles, then, requires a word of explanation.

Crossdressing in Context is meant both to be descriptive and to be implicitly critical of most other works on crossdressing. There are a number of important contexts in which crossdressing must be situated and the separate volume titles indicate these. First and most immediately there is *dress*, especially clothes, without which crossdressing is impossible and by which *gender* is experienced and expressed. Perhaps the greatest failing of studies of crossdressing is the general neglect of the role played by apparel. It is certainly appropriate to focus on gender, but such a focus needs to begin with gender-differentiated clothing. The first volume explores dress and gender, separately and together, in the context of a rich experience and expressive system.

The second volume examines another principal context: *transgender realities*, the actual lived experiences of human individuals. This material opens by introducing basic terminology and provides an overview of crossdressing behavior. The next set of questions considers a variety of possible causes of transgender behavior like crossdressing. Then it moves to a history of transgender realities, revolving around historical depictions of crossdressing, from ancient to modern times. This material also includes special attention to the history of theater, including modern movies and television. The volume then continues with a survey of transgender realities around the world. Collectively, these materials demonstrate that transgender realities like crossdressing have been persistent across times and cultures. The volume concludes by examining contemporary transgender experience from a variety of perspectives, including how transgender people experience it, examined by a variety of psychological tests, understood legally, and regarded by other people.

The third volume highlights the importance of *religion*. Not only is personal spirituality and religious observance as valued by transgender people as by anyone else, the long history of religions around the world show an involvement with transgender realities that make this area of critical value in properly understanding phenomena like crossdressing. Acknowledging the cultural context in which this work is produced, the first religious sphere considered belongs to Western religions. Thus a careful examination of what the Bible says about crossdressing is followed by how biblical material has been commented upon by Christian and Jewish scholars through the centuries. Following this material a survey is made of the principal religions of the world, both East and West. As in volume 2, the evidence documents an awareness and dialog with transgender realities throughout history and around the globe.

The final volume acknowledges the weight of modern *mental health* in discussions about crossdressing and other transgender realities. Since the medicalization of sex has firmly joined crossdressing behavior to sexuality, this volume begins by examining the theories and evidence allegedly connecting crossdressing and sexual behavior. This is followed by a broader examination of the question whether transgender people, especially those who crossdress, are mentally ill. First this matter is explored by providing a broad historical context—the medicalization of sex—and examining how transgender people often come to mental health professionals' attention. Special terminology like 'gender dysphoria' is explained. The possible connection of transgender behavior to various mental disorders is considered. Then follows a review of contributions on the subject by various scholars since the late 19th century. Given the dominant position the American Psychiatric Association's *Diagnostic and Statistical Manual of Mental Disorders* (popularly referred to as DSM) has attained, a careful look at how crossdressing and other transgender realities have been handled by this model throughout its history also is provided. This, in turn, leads to looking at a variety of treatment approaches that have been tried with transgender clients. The issues involved in such treatment lead to a careful consideration about the wisdom of retaining in the DSM model the categories concerning transgender. Finally, the volume—and the work at large—concludes with a last consideration of whether transgender people need to be changed.

Collectively the four volumes represent one sustained approach to placing crossdressing in context. Although this work broadly is about all transgender realities, the focal point has been the behavior most visibly associated with transgender: *crossdressing*. I treat the subject of crossdressing both as a topic of great interest in its own right and as an entrance into transgender realities. As large as the resulting work is, it could be much larger with a more sustained examination of other transgender realities.

What are the goals of this work?

The structure of this work is dialogical in nature. Questions—many, many questions—are raised and considered. The choice of these questions and the way in which they are answered reflects various goals. There are several principal, intentional goals sought by this work, all with the purpose of establishing an understanding in context:

1. to put dress back into crossdressing by situating crossdressing within an experiencing and expressing system built around clothes as the primary vehicle for communicating gender, which is central to our sense of self and relationships;
2. to highlight and explicate the role dress plays both in our affiliations, such as our membership in a gender group, and in our individuality;
3. to explore the basic distinctions between 'sex' and 'gender' in order to better see what transgender is about and how crossdressing is related to each;
4. to use crossdressing—a transgender reality—as entry into other transgender realities, and to see how these realities are similar and dissimilar;
5. to clarify the meaning of terms (e.g., 'transgender,' 'transvestite,' 'transsexual'), while questioning their usefulness;
6. to document transgender realities, especially crossdressing, throughout history and around the world, and to do so with enough depth and

breadth to convince even the most skeptical reader of the pervasiveness and significance of these realities;

7. to broaden our understanding of crossdressing by exploring and illustrating the many various motivations behind it and thereby to simultaneously challenge such narrow and erroneous beliefs as that all crossdressing is done because of disturbed gender identity or sexual perversity;

8. to keep in view always that transgender realities are inevitably human experiences, lived by real people, who are worthy of respect and dignity;

9. to set out and place in context the work of others who have written about transgender realities, especially crossdressing, and in doing so engage in dialog with them;

10. to let transgendered people speak for themselves, especially in addressing matters such as what it is like to live as a transgendered person;

11. to examine basic issues of concern to people, such as the morality of crossdressing, the way in which religious traditions have related to transgender realities, the legal issues connected to transgender experience, the relational aspects of being with a transgendered person as a partner, family member, friend, or helper, and the role of sexuality in the life of the transgendered; and,

12. to address the critical matter of the involvement of mental health professionals, including looking closely at the history of study by professionals about transgender (especially crossdressing), detailing the discussion of transgender in today's dominant diagnostic classification system, reviewing the history of treating transgender conditions, considering whether changes need to be made, and examining new models of therapeutic support.

To meet these dozen goals requires some space; hence the size of this work.

Yet, for all this, there are some things underdeveloped. For example, you should know right off that this book is *not* principally about homosexuality. Because that is the transgender reality that receives by far the most attention this work is organized around a different principle: crossdressing. Yes, some homosexuals (but not all) crossdress. And yes, some crossdressers (but not all) are homosexual. Thus, homosexuals are included within this work. But they are not the focus.

What are 'transgender realities'?

The focus, through the lens of crossdressing, is 'transgender realities.' In choosing the term 'transgender realities' I want to emphasize the multiplicity of expressions that do not fit at the gender poles of masculinity and femininity. A prominent transgender reality—a behavior shared among many transgender people—is crossdressing. I treat all crossdressing as a transgender reality even though not all people whom crossdress identify themselves as transgendered. In other words, just as a self-professed vegetarian may occasionally eat meat, so a non-transgendered person may occasionally enact a transgender reality like crossdressing. In this work I use the broad transgender reality of crossdressing as both entry into other transgender realities and to remind us how pervasive transgender expressions are. But to properly comprehend them they must be retained in their natural contexts.

How is the work structured?

A glance at the questions in the Table of Contents shows an almost bewildering breadth of matters. They are organized into 100 specific questions, each of which entails asking further questions. Yet these questions collectively still by no means exhaust the subject. Instead they aim to reflect a logical organization of reflection based on a variety of the more commonly asked questions related to our interests. Those questions cover all kinds of topics, everything from sex and gender to morals and religion. It takes time to cover so much ground and the length of this work reflects my commitment to taking that time and offering at least enough to cover the basics and point the way to more research. However, this structure allows you to enter wherever you like and get answers quickly.

In truth, this study could be shorter. Part of the length is attributable to the structure. By setting everything as answers to questions and encouraging you to dip in wherever you like, an element of repetition is needed to ensure every answer stays embedded in context with enough detail to make full sense to you. So, in reading through the work in a progressive fashion the effect of this repetition will be felt, though hopefully not in too tedious a fashion. I have tried to be varied in restating matters, but if nothing else the repetition serves pedagogically to reinforce basic concepts and themes.

A significant factor adding to the length is my insistence on fleshing out each context with reason and evidence. Too many people disregard arguments because they only see one or two illustrative cases and fail to recognize them as signifying a vast number of others. I wish to create the sense for you of a phenomenon so common and richly varied around the world and throughout history that it cannot be casually dismissed or superficially examined. Comprehension requires a sense of the complexity and fullness of transgender realities like crossdressing. If you are impatient to press on you can do so, but if you are looking for detail, you will find it here.

I recognize that your interest may not be in all forms of crossdressing, but only a particular kind. You may even only want information on a very specific matter related to that particular kind. As I mentioned above, that is why the organization of this material has been set out as answers to questions. I think this is an intuitive and practical approach that will prove useful to you now with the questions you presently have and later with questions still to come. Hopefully, the net effect will be to also prompt other questions and lead you into a larger, ongoing investigation.

While I like to think the optimal way to use this work is to read it completely from start to finish, it may not be the best way for you at this time. Instead, you might wish to browse it, looking for specific information. This can be done through the questions, a complete list of which is found in the Detailed Table of Contents. Once you locate an interesting question, you can explore it through three levels of interaction. The quickest and most superficial level is 'The Short Answer' provided at the beginning of each answer section. In a few lines you will get a summary answer. Next comes 'The Longer Answer.' This offers a detailed discussion to more fully answer the question. Finally, by using the endnotes for each answer you can find important sources and resources as well as pursue the discussion on some finer points. In sum, the work is organized in a user-friendly manner to meet your needs now and later.

On the use and misuse of this work: Who makes the rules?

A final matter about using this work is important to me. Scholarly work is often proof-texted. In other words, readers pick and choose what conveniently supports the position they want to hold. I don't imagine that any of us entirely escape selective recall or purposeful choosing of 'facts' for presentation, but I ask that you play fair with the material included in these pages. A dialog requires two parties, and fruitful dialog mandates both parties be allowed to speak with an effort to hear them. When once the whole matter is on the table, or as much of it as can be had, then is the time for making a respectful decision based on evidence and reason. I covet for us all making careful judgments and always treating others with respect and charity.

I know—and so do you—that the matters discussed in this work often engage strong feelings in people. None of my goals include telling you how to feel. However you feel about the matters we discuss I will hope you subject those feelings to scrutiny, evaluate the evidence honestly, and behave with respect toward all. This really matters to me—too many people continue to be harmed. Let's think about this matter a moment longer.

One of the curious things about freedom is that most of us demand it in very liberal portions for ourselves, but are less charitable toward others. We want to be left alone to do as we see fit, while often insisting that other folk conform to our personal standards as to what is 'right.' Naturally, we generally have at hand one or another rationale for our judgments. Frequently, our logic centers in an opposition to someone else's behavior on religious or moral grounds. After all, it is unseemly to prioritize the fact that the behavior we condemn makes us personally uncomfortable, so we set that truth in second place and justify it by reasoning that we feel uneasy *because* the behavior is inherently—and to us also *obviously*—wrong. Thus we enjoy the best of all solutions:

moral and/or religious justification for our felt discomfort. If we can get a law passed against the behavior then the justification for our feeling is further strengthened—as may be the feeling itself.

We may even find ourselves justifying unkind remarks, avoidance, harassment, discrimination, or physical violence. Once we convince ourselves something is wrong, it is easy to think whatever is done in opposition must be right. But two wrongs never make a right. No matter how we excuse ourselves, violation of another person's human rights is evil.

Unfortunately, our real motivations often remain unconscious. We don't see that our reasoning is actually just rationalization—a way of thinking that has as its real aim making us less anxious rather than knowing the truth. All we know is that by thinking and judging in certain ways we shield ourselves from uncomfortable feelings. While this may seem useful, when it leads to disruption in our relationships with others and prompts us to words and deeds hurtful to others, then we have become the very makers of evil that we despise.

We are best served in the long run by opening our eyes and trying to see matters as clearly as we can. So let us agree to start in as neutral a position as possible. Instead of assuming that crossdressing is 'right' or 'wrong,' 'healthy' or 'mentally ill,' let us just let it be—and then examine it as best we can. If the subject elicits certain feelings, simply let them be as well. In the privacy of your own reading there is no need to let these feelings be more than they are—one source of information among others. Feelings do not have to motivate you to do anything right now. Simply accept them or set them aside and move on to a sober consideration of the topic.

You can do this—and you *must* if you are to be fair to yourself and to others. I know that it is very likely you are holding this book either because you crossdress or someone you care about does. Your feelings may be clear, or they may be mixed, but they are not facts that by themselves must determine what you think or do. In fact, by learning more your feelings may change. So be patient with yourself and with others.

Ready? Then let's start asking some questions.

Volume 4:
The Context of Religion

The
Questions

Introduction to Volume 4

Though every volume in this set merits its own introduction, such material has been set instead as brief remarks connected to opening each Question Set. However, this volume poses difficulties of such a kind that it seems especially advisable to begin with some remarks of a general nature. The intersection of human sexuality, gender, and religion is perhaps the most dynamic and volatile of all points where matters central to identity and relationship converge. There is no possibility of writing on how these matters may relate without offending someone, no matter how narrowly constrained the focus of the writing or inoffensive the writer's intent.

Complicating factors

No religion belongs so much to the world that it escapes being first and foremost *a personal experience*. As such, for every Christian any remarks on Christianity will be evaluated through the prism of individual belief and experience. The same pertains to every other religion. Indeed, the very word 'religion' is itself objectionable to many people in our society, who not only disclaim belonging to any religion, but who instead proclaim a personal spirituality they believe superior to organized institutions, practices, and doctrinal expressions. In short, to write about any particular religion is to invite criticism; to write about several is to make such criticism certain.

From the standpoint of the writer on religion, the inevitability of criticism is of little import beside the recognition that at least some of the criticism will certainly be valid. All the world's great religions—the subject domain of this volume—are so old, so complex, and so varied that virtually any assertion can be qualified by exceptions. Many critical factors enter in, and any one of them can provide a foundation to stand upon in leveling criticisms.

For example, *religions present themselves as both traditional and folk religions*—formal and informal expressions of the same religion. Like the people who affiliate with them, religions present both a formal, dressed-up appearance for polite society and learned discussion, as well as a more relaxed, informal, folksy side for intimates. Neither display can truly lay claim to being the more authentic. Though scholars are interested in both forms of religion, traditional (or formal) religion gets more attention, especially in textbooks. Religious texts, rituals, and organizations have a relatively fixed form that makes them more readily accessible. Moreover, there is a perception that formal religion, like the man or woman dressed to go out, puts the religion's best face forward and thus is how any religion is most likely to 'look good.' At the same time, though, most adherents of a religion give a polite nod to the traditional aspects while getting chummy with the highly variable expressions of popular religion. All religion, like politics, is local.

Another complicating factor is *time*. History in its inexorable march has a way of stomping into the ground the fine distinctions so readily apparent to former folk. Given enough distance through time, everything ancient can seem to blur together into an incomplete and somewhat formless blob. Scholars do their best to restore the times, drawing out the differences and probing the relations between parts, but the task is almost always one of the educated guess—and thus subject to more than mere quibbling by dissenters. The fact is we rarely know with compelling certainty what ancient folk thought and felt about all they wrote about. We don't always know if they even did all the things they said ought to be done, or that they proclaimed had been done by those who were ancient to them. Finally, even if we knew for sure all that transpired and was thought in ancient times, and in every time since, the facts would remain that there is a gulf fixed between us and that their religion is not our own in many important respects.

A third critical factor is *the difference between insider and outsider*. Expectations—and judgments—concerning those who write on any religion are often shaped by perceptions of whether they stand inside or outside the religion they are writing about. (In the interest of full disclosure, I am a Jew.) Many religious people find it distasteful at best to have outsiders writing about their religion, especially if the outsider claims to have any knowledge about it. There is a sense that only those inside, and perhaps even then only the truly committed, have the kind of knowledge that makes trustworthy what they say. In any work that treats of several religions the writer will be an outsider to most, if not all, of the religions being written about. On the other hand, some people consider that outsiders are more likely to be objective because they have no religious axe to grind, no belief or practice to defend, and an openness to see what those inside cannot or do not wish to see. Yet these views, while they may be accurate with respect to some, hardly capture the essence of the matter. Insiders can be supportive, indifferent, or hostile to their own religion, and the same pertains to outsiders. Just being an insider does not preclude objectivity, nor does being an outsider ensure it. Besides all this, while outsiders may misunderstand certain things in a religion, so may insiders. Accuracy in everything is impossible for us all.

In addition to the difficulties we have named, there are many others. *Language* poses a barrier in many instances. Things truly can be lost in translation. But even if translation difficulties are bridged, whether by intimate knowledge of the original language or by the confidence of an excellent translation, all words and texts exist in a *cultural sphere* that gives them life. And culture—with all its varied elements—is something that no amount of information obtained can equal the experience of inhabiting as a citizen. So wise folk lean on as many voices from within the culture as possible. To be a scholar means to try to hear as openly and well as possible as many voices as one can, all to the point of catching glimpses of how the world looks to an insider. In short, we listen in order to see, and we hear and see in order to know imaginatively what it feels like to be inside what we are studying.

All of this is *absolutely* impossible. But that does not make it *relatively* impossible. In other words, though we cannot get it all right, we can get some of it right. We can initiate a dialog based on respect. In so doing, we who seek to teach both start and continue as learners. True scholarship means a willingness to be wrong—even wrong a lot—in order to get closer to being right. I have no doubt that despite my every effort to be open, fair, and respectful, I will have gotten some things wrong. I trust readers to be discerning, to use this material as but a single step in a continuing process, and to do better than me in their own work.

Aims of this volume

None of the above is meant to excuse inevitable errors or to beg indulgences. What I want is to be honest. While I hope to demonstrate some competence as a scholar, the reality is that I do not know all things equally well. To attempt to discuss accurately how several religions treat of sexuality and gender is so ambitious as to probably merit being called foolhardy. Yet I am not the first to venture on such treacherous ground, and I will be looking often enough to those who have gone before to guide my own steps.

The chief aims of this volume may be summarized in these statements:

❑ Consonant with the intent of this series, this volume uses crossdressing as a focal 'transgender reality' for viewing how sex, gender, and sexuality interact in various ways to express and experience different kinds of transgender identity.

❑ Most especially, this volume examines how the major world religions provide unique spaces and ways for transgender realities to manifest, and how these are variously appraised.

❑ The way religions wrestle with issues of sexuality, and most especially gender, are also considered. This includes exploring how religions discuss any gender related to their deity or deities, as well as to the number and nature of genders among human beings.

Obviously, any one of the matters contemplated here carries with it considerable depth and breadth, so the inevitable character of this volume's discussions must be considered cursory, though some matters get more attention than others. This is an introductory volume, principally written with students in mind, and heavily invested in trying to make a wide range of materials accessible enough to invite the reader to further investigation. In that interest there are many voices listened to, with the hope these voices will not merely inform this work but entice the listener to seek some out for closer and more extended listening.

It may be frustrating to find the coverage of matters discussed uneven, but in some cases this occurs because of a relative paucity of material, and in other cases because of a relative lack in my own capacities. There is simply no sufficient justifying of my choices here, because they reflect ones made in the moment of making this book and would certainly be different if this work had been written at a different time in my life. Put simply, the choices made reflect my own interests, my own comprehension, my judgments as to what matters most in various things, and my access to materials on the subjects considered. This work is less one of original theorizing than an attempt to bring together many materials from a number of disciplines in an effort to present a reasonably sensible introduction to a very large, complex, and difficult subject. My one steadying hope is that readers will look past the flaws because of their own intrinsic interests and find enough within these pages to help them forward in their own individual studies.

Question Set 8

What does the Bible say about cross-dressing?

For many of us the ultimate guide to our judgments about gender, transgender, and crossdressing is found in an authoritative spiritual source reckoned to reveal the mind of God. In Europe, the Americas and elsewhere that source is commonly found in the Bible, whether as understood by individual conscience or as interpreted by the Church or other religious authorities. In this question set our attention will be on the Bible, the collection of documents both Judaism and Christianity look to for direction. However, in order to best understand the interpretation and application of the Bible in its historical and social context, we will also be looking at other Jewish and Christian documents, as well as representative scholars from both faith traditions.

The overarching question for this set is intentionally narrow: what does the Bible say about crossdressing? This specific question will provide entry for us into larger concerns. Inevitably, we wish to also consider the broader idea of gender and the related matter of transgender, but to keep the scope of our treatment manageable we will focus on crossdressing, embedded as always in the expressive and experiencing system of clothes.

What to make of clothes confronts the profoundly devout among us no less than anyone else.[1] As in the population at large, differences of perspective and practice exist—and always have. The sacred texts of Christianity—the Old and New Testaments of the Bible—speak of clothing, both metaphorically and concretely.[2] In the early centuries of Christianity the leading scholars of the church also addressed the matter, though coming to different judgments as to the importance of the subject.[3] Through the centuries Christians have continued to address the matter.[4]

Where specifically religious values and judgments about dress enter in, a new element is contributed to the wider discussion about the role of clothes. Suddenly the sacred is connected with the mundane and clothes take on a higher value. More importantly, this element carries with it the weight many of us assign to religious authority as the decisive arbiter of our own personal beliefs, decisions and acts. Accordingly, many people are concerned about what their religion says about a person's manner of dress. This concern extends to crossdressing.

In those cases where sacred texts or religious authorities say little or nothing, there remains the matter of how the actual practice is tolerated. In this voulme we will look at religions both Eastern and Western. But because the majority of readers of this book will affiliate themselves more with Western traditions (Judaism, Christianity, Islam), these receive more attention. Since Christianity is the religion most likely to affect readers either by virtue of their personal adherence or the influence it exerts on their culture, it receives the most immediate and complete attention, beginning with questions about the Bible and its interpretation and application.

Q. 61 Where does the Bible address crossdressing?

The Short Answer. The Bible is relatively silent about crossdressing. While some folk try to infer from various scriptural texts a base for responding to crossdressing, in fact there is but a single brief text—Deuteronomy 22:5—that explicitly references the subject. The exact meaning of that text, as well as its application, is debated. Because some people place great weight on this text, we must examine it as closely as we can. In this answer the text itself is set forth, both in its original language, and as variously translated in a number of prominent English versions of the Bible. Inasmuch as both Judaism and Christianity share this text, translations associated with each religion are included. Later, the issues involved in interpreting this text, as well as the treatment of it by both Jews and Christians over the centuries, will be considered. Here, even in the relatively simple act of presenting the translation of the text, we discover signs of the difficulties that have presented themselves to Jews and Christians seeking to understand its meaning and apply it to their own circumstances.

The Longer Answer. Christians and Jews share some sacred texts. Jews call them the writings of the Tanakh (Tanach)⁵, or Hebrew Bible, while Christians refer to the same collection as the Old Testament. For convenience I am going to refer to these materials as simply 'the Bible.'⁶ There is only a single text in the Bible that addresses crossdressing. It is Deuteronomy 22:5, originally set down in Hebrew, the text of which is as follows:

לֹא-יִהְיֶה כְלִי-גֶבֶר עַל-אִשָּׁה, וְלֹא-יִלְבַּשׁ גֶּבֶר שִׂמְלַת אִשָּׁה : כִּי תוֹעֲבַת יְהוָה אֱלֹהֶיךָ, כָּל-עֹשֵׂה אֵלֶּה.

Although the Hebrew text is provided, and will be commented on later, most readers will not be conversant in this language. They will rely on one or another version in English. Fortunately, there are many translations to draw upon, some ventured by single individuals, but most by the effort of teams of scholars, as is the case in the versions drawn upon here. The text is rendered below in a selection of translations likely to be familiar to most people, whether Christians or Jews. Representing Christian versions are the King James Version (KJV), dating from the 17ᵗʰ century but still widely used, and some of the most prominent modern translations: the New American Standard Bible (NASB) of 1971 (revised 1995), the 1978 New International Version (NIV), the 1985

21

Catholic translation titled the New Jerusalem Bible (NJB), and the 1989 New Revised Standard Version (NRSV). Representing the Jewish translations are that of 1917 from the Jewish Publication Society (JPS), and more recently the Judaica Press Complete Tanach. The renderings of these translations are:

Christian Translations

King James Version (KJV)

The woman shall not wear that which pertaineth unto a man, neither shall a man put on a woman's garment: for all that do so *are* abomination unto the LORD thy God.

New American Standard Bible (NASB)

A woman shall not wear a man's clothing, nor shall a man put on a woman's clothing; for whoever does these things is an abomination to the LORD your God.

New International Version (NIV)

A woman must not wear men's clothing, nor a man wear women's clothing, for the LORD your God detests anyone who does this.

New Jerusalem Bible (NJB)

A woman must not dress like a man, nor a man like a woman; anyone who does this is detestable to Yahweh your God.

New Revised Standard Version (NRSV)

A woman shall not wear a man's apparel, nor shall a man put on a woman's garment; for whoever does such things is abhorrent to the LORD your God.

Jewish Translations

Jewish Publication Society (JPS) Edition of 1917

A woman shall not wear that which pertaineth unto a man, neither shall a man put on a woman's garment; for whosoever doeth these things is an abomination unto the LORD thy God.

Judaica Press Complete Tanach

A man's attire shall not be on a woman, nor may a man wear a woman's garment because whoever does these [things] is an abomination to the Lord, your God.

These translations offer us, in English, what is *written*. With the text in view, we must now turn to inspection of the issues most pertinent to accurately understanding what is *meant*.

Q. 62 What are the key issues for understanding what the Bible says?

The Short Answer. Understanding any biblical text involves the complementary acts of *interpretation*—understanding what the passage meant to its original audience—and *application*—finding meaning for the contemporary audience. Today these tasks are commonly confused. Many contemporary Christians hear applications of Scripture presented in Sunday sermons as interpretations of the biblical text. As a result some unfortunate consequences result. First, many Christians despair of the interpretive task because they have heard so many diverse statements about what biblical passages allegedly mean. Second, they are discouraged from attending to matters of history, culture, and language by the immensity of each arena and by the sense that such tasks have little relevance to the use of the Bible as they see it put not only on Sunday mornings, but throughout the week. In conflating interpretation and application, each suffers. The former is diminished by too little and often too narrow attention; the latter is hindered by too grand and too varied the claims made in its name. In responsibly handling the text of Deuteronomy, the interpretive tasks must proceed first. It is served by considering literary, historical, and cultural matters, as well as theological ideas pertinent to the original author and audience. Then, based on the acquired understanding, however tenuous or imperfect, the task of application may proceed. In that task the contemporary audience hears itself addressed in relevant fashion. This task is no less daunting than interpretation, for it both depends upon it, and it requires an ability to translate an ancient milieu into today's world in ways that do no injury to either. As we consider the single, short text in the Bible that directly addresses crossdressing, we find ourselves involved in all these tasks. They inevitably lead us into a context of discussion about gender. This broader context shall concern us throughout this volume, and here it is merely introduced in broad strokes. Of specific concern are the words of the text, rooted as much as possible in their own original world. If we can hear them in a manner similar to the first hearers, and grasp the internal logic of them, we can then perhaps translate that logic into words for today. The uncertain nature of certain words, or indeed of a world so far removed from us, cautions us to not be overconfident in our conclusions. A certain reserve in interpretation is not merely sensible scholarship, but ethically responsible. Our applications must not overstep our interpretive grasp of the text.

The Longer Answer. People of the Western religious traditions have sometimes been called 'people of the Book.' It matters not whether the book being thought of is the Tanakh, the Christian Bible, or the Qu'ran, the idea is the same—large communities center themselves with a written text set into an authoritative position. The written word, in turn, is blanketed by oral exposition. A rich legacy of oral tradition links the faithful from generation to generation and keeps the written word alive and relevant. When we come to a text such as Deuteronomy 22:5 it is for millions of believers a living word.

The sense that the text has a life of its own, that in it God's voice is heard, makes hearers of it in every generation conscious of their responsibility to hear it rightly and repeat it truthfully. The weight of this responsibility soon finds company with a realization of how difficult a task may be entailed. Even though God's voice is sought—and heard—it comes conveyed by human voices. Their words belong first to a particular time and place. They come in the form of specific words in one language. They are set down by human writers, and first heard and read by people in specific social settings. As distance in time and space separates this first setting from later ones, a continuing challenge is mounted. How shall this word be faithfully heard anew?

How do we responsibly pursue our task?

Broadly speaking, the answer to this question is found by embracing twin tasks: interpretation and application. They may be said to have one and the same root—the act of translation. So we must begin with what that entails.

Translation

In the previous answer we saw the Hebrew text of Deuteronomy 22:5 and how it has been translated into English. Versions respected within Judaism and Christianity were presented. Despite much similarity, differences in rendering are obvious, though they probably appear minor. Most notably they come in the English choice of words to render certain Hebrew terms. We shall presently examine these original words and ponder how best they should be translated.

First, however, we must address a disturbing lack of confidence among many religious folk concerning translation. We are accustomed to hear people wave aside differences in understanding of a text with the words, 'It's just a difference in translation.' The words sometimes express confusion between *translation*, the rendering of material from one language into another, and *interpretation*, the making sense of the material. Often, though, there is an implicit awareness that the latter depends on the former, and so problems in understanding must stem from errors in translation. Occasionally, someone will also be aware that different copies of the text exist and differences among these copies can complicate translation, leading perhaps to different renderings and different meanings. Rather than wade into the morass, some of us simply resign ourselves to not knowing anything for certain and thus being content to hold whatever opinion we have no matter how shaky its evidentiary grounds.

So let us be clear on some basics. First, the English versions reproduced earlier may be trusted to have adequately rendered into English the Hebrew text. With very few exceptions, virtually all of the passages in the Bible have been competently translated. In truth, errors in translation very, very seldom are an issue. Second, much of the apparent variance often noticed between Bible versions comes from a difference in translation philosophy. Some translations employ a more traditional (or 'classic') manner of rendering word-for-word. The idea is to find the best English word for each foreign one. This one-to-one correspondence style has been long employed and works well. So, too, does a more recent philosophy, often termed 'dynamic equivalency.' Its idea is to render thought-for-thought. The intent is to speak more idiomatically, or naturally, saying in English the thought of the original language even if the words used do not match up one-to-one. Third, the most frequent error stemming from translation has little to do with translation itself. Rather, it occurs when well-meaning people too closely parse the meaning of *English* words as though that captures the sense of the original Hebrew, Aramaic, or Greek terms. This leads us to our next topic.

Interpretation

Translation is the root of interpretation. To understand, for example, what a Hebrew term means for most of us requires a translation into the language we do our thinking in. But merely choosing an English word, or finding a suitable English phrase to capture a thought, just starts a complicated process. Consider Deuteronomy 22:5 in the translations of the last answer. The NIV chooses 'wear men's clothing' where the NJB selects 'dress like a man.' Already in translating a degree of interpretation is involved. Wearing clothing is somewhat more narrow than dressing, an act that can include clothing *and* ornamentation. So immediately we have the potential for differences in understanding that stem from translation, though properly are interpretive issues.

Interpretation in its most comprehensive form entails a set of tasks, each formidable in its own right. It means exploring literary, historical, and cultural matters, as well as theological ideas pertinent to the original author and audience. A thorough interpretation will examine any differences in *textual* traditions (i.e., the copies and copies-of-copies based on the original text) and seek a competent translation of the material. In explicating its meaning it will pay close attention to *literary* matters, like the kind of literature (poetic, historical, legal, etc.) the text is, its immediate and broader literary context, stylistic themes and variances, and so forth. All of these are done while working with the original language—in this case Hebrew. As best it can, the interpretation will take into account the *historical* setting, looking for influences on how something was said, as well as why. The audience and its setting also emerge as significant. Presumably, had the message not made sense to them it would not have been preserved, let alone adhered to in any fashion. Similarly, *cultural* issues will be examined. The social institutions, ideas taken for granted, beliefs and prejudices of people—all may be important to grasp what a text meant for the original audience. In all this, interpretation does not forget that the writer, or writers, or writer and editors, all made their own contributions. In so doing they articulated to a greater or lesser degree what we might call *theology*, their own comprehension of God and things pertaining to God. Yet they were not separated from time and place; they all also were members of faith communities, whose own ideas and practices echo in their writings.

Even such a cursory sketch of interpretation can be overwhelming. We can be sympathetic toward those contemporary Jews and Christians who despair over the possibility of doing adequately at such work. But giving into the temptation to reduce everything to personal opinion, as though all opinions come equally close to understanding the original meaning and as if all that matters is having an opinion, is wrongheaded and dangerous. All interpretations are *not* equal. Poor and wrong interpretions can harm people as applications based on them are put into action.

At the opposite end of stupidity is the notion that there is always only *one* correct interpretation. This view is a fundamental misapprehension of the process and product alike. Even among the original hearers there were degrees of difference in how something was and should be understood. The authors themselves may have meant more than one thing, or conveyed something they did not mean that was nevertheless entirely plausible. Indeed, they might have agreed with this unintended meaning had it been pointed out to them.

However, proper interpretation is always *constrained*. It can be relatively objective as the subjective element is bounded in a disciplined fashion. There are boundaries set by the various factors we considered above, and more. A *limited range* of meaning, or meanings, may be possible, but each is determined by and linked to one or more of the factors an interpretation must manage. For example, a proper interpretation cannot assume the original author, audience, or text to possess an understanding exactly equivalent to that held by a typical 21st century American. To do so is to ignore the real weight and salience of language, context, history, culture and so forth on every person who has ever lived. It is not the task of interpretation to make a text speak to contemporary people. The task of interpretation is to let the text speak again, and be heard again, as it did at the first, including respect for the boundaries of ancient knowledge.

Application

To application belongs the task of making the text speak to a contemporary audience. Another act of translation—that of rendering interpretive scholarship into meaningful terms for ordinary hearers of the message today—marks the transition to application. The work of application is supremely practical and necessary. By it the message first heard as the word of God continues to be heard as such. Sound applications build on careful interpretations. Aiming to capture the original sense in terms sensible to today, applications speak in contemporary words.

But they do something more than translating interpretation into a popular form. Applications, as the word suggests, make those interpretations relevant to today's issues and problems. They offer guidance for how to believe, and how to act. They are often moral in tone, aim, and scope. Applications are frequently the heart of the sermon preached from the pulpit, or at least the part of the sermon a parishioner may be most likely to take away from the service.

Just as proper interpretations are constrained, so also are applications. But the boundaries are more loosely and nebulously drawn. On the one hand, this makes it possible for a wider range of appropriate applications to be drawn from a biblical text. On the other hand, it makes it harder for hearers to be certain the application is genuinely grounded in sound interpretation. Especially where a sermon or lesson is offered with little explicit clarification of how the application was reasoned out from a sound interpretation the hearer will have difficulty knowing if the application is trustworthy.

Having considered translation, interpretation, and application in general, we must now attend to the text of Deuteronomy 22:5. In the remainder of this answer and in the ones immediately following, these important tasks are shown in various ways. Part of our effort is to do them ourselves. However, part of our effort is also to indicate how others have done them.

We will begin with the translation and interpretation of the text by focusing on its key elements. In the Hebrew text certain terms have garnered the most attention. These linguistic terms must be placed in the appropriate setting, which includes the cultural background, the historical setting, and the author's own use and understanding (so far as they may be obtainable). In this biblical text, three terms have garnered most of the attention. Each merits a separate investigation as well as attempting to see them in relation to one another.

What does "abomination"/"abhorrent" (*to'ebah*) mean?

One term that punctuates the whole discussion and arrests attention is the Hebrew תּוֹעֵבָה, translated as 'abomination' or 'abhorrent,' and which may be transliterated as *to'ebah*. Though our modern sense of a word like 'abhorrent' carries strong moral and/or aesthetic connotations, we must remember we are bridging both time and culture in trying to recapture the sense meant by the writer for his own audience. This term in the author's time and culture is commonly found in connection to matters of ritual purity; something 'abhorrent' was ritually unclean—inadmissible for religious purposes.[7] However, meaning is context dependent and sometimes *to'ebah* is found attached to matters other than religious observance, including the infamous passages of Leviticus 18:22

and 20:13. In Deuteronomy, as biblical scholar P. J. Harlan points out, all of the occurrences are concerned with the purity of the religion.[8]

Exactly what this means here is unclear, but two matters do seem likely. First, it probably acts as a precaution against falling into pagan ways where crossdressing occurred in a religious context for what Jews regarded as immoral purposes (i.e., sexual liaisons as a form of worship). Second, it apparently did not carry any grave penalties—no sanction is specified, such as fines, casting such people out of the camp, or stoning them.[9] Applications that stress a contemporary understanding of 'abomination' or 'abhorrent'—both connoting profound detestation of what is seen as morally objectionable so that strong punitive action should be taken—are therefore misguided. A more appropriate application that stays closer to a sound interpretation would be to stress a warning that even ordinary practices like dress carry religious weight and can be used to signify a group's peculiar relationship to God. Therefore members of the group should be careful to dress consonant with their group's identity and not misuse their dress so that it becomes associated with immoral purposes.

What is meant by "clothes" (*keli*)?

Two other key terms pertain to what men and women wear or carry: כְּלִי (*keli*) appears first; the second is שִׂמְלָה (*simlah*). The former of these is a very versatile term, capable of being translated as "accessory," "armor," "bag," "clothing," "jewelry," "weapons" and various other words. *Simlah* has a more limited range, but can be translated as "cloak," "clothes," or "garment." The variation in terms contributes to the different ways this deceptively simple text has been rendered.

In the opening phrase—"A woman shall not wear . . . *keli*"—the Hebrew *keli* can be translated by different words *and* be variously interpreted. Thus, one can use the generic "clothing" and still interpret it as referring to specific clothing, as in the male clothing associated with warfare (armor and weapons). Or, one can opt to both translate and interpret the word along such lines by rendering something like, "A woman shall not wear the martial dress of a man," or simply, "the armor of a man." Along these lines we find a translation like that of religious scholar Cyrus Gordon: "The instrument of a man (i.e., a man's weapon) shall not be upon a woman . . . ."[10] On the other hand, since the Hebrew word is so versatile, it can be translated and interpreted as meaning "clothing" in a broad sense—everything associated with men's style, from accessories to armor to weapons to any and all form of male-styled garment.[11]

So how do we decide what is the proper translation and figure out what the original writer meant? The determinants as to how this is best translated are context and word usage. Since this text is an individual entry in a list, the context is principally itself. This list is a legal one, with the cluster of items here apparently linked by a concern not to mix things belonging to different kinds. The author of the entry for this term in the *Theological Dictionary of the Old Testament* says that it is only in legal texts that *keli* means 'clothing.' Unfortunately, no other instances are offered of such use and this conclusion thus appears more theological than empirical, especially given the abundant examples provided for the far more common alternative renderings.[12]

The clause beginning "A woman shall not wear . . ." is balanced by the clause "neither shall a man wear . . ."; they are clearly intended to stand in juxtaposition. One might suppose the term *keli* to be understood, then, as a synonym for *simlah*. In this case, the interpretation is straightforward: neither sex should wear the garb of the other. However, since the writer could have used the same word in both places and chose not to do so, the suggestion that the difference was intentional and is meaningful has some weight. Thus, *keli* and *simlah* are to be understood—and translated—differently. If this is the case, then the ordinary usage of *keli* in biblical Hebrew becomes important. Such usage suggests that "implements" (e.g., the implements of war: armor and weapons) would be a more apt choice than "clothing."[13]

What is meant by "clothes" (*simlah*)?

That still leaves the problem of what to make of *simlah*. Of its nearly 30 occurrences in the Hebrew Bible, the King James Version (KJV) translates it as follows: raiment (11 times), clothes (6), garment (6), apparel (2), cloth (2), and clothing (2). The meaning would seem rather straightforward: what one wears. Once more, though, we encounter the same dilemma as with *keli*. We can try to view *simlah* as roughly synonymous to *keli* or decide that the writer meant something different by choosing a different word. If we adopt the former course, treating *simlah* as an equivalent and starting from our best guess as to what *keli* means, then the sense might be: as women are not to wear the distinctive implements of war put on by men, so men are not to wear the distinctive ornaments (such as jewelry) worn by women. On the other hand, if we opt to see *simlah* as some kind of counterpoint to *keli*, and different in meaning, we might arrive at: as women are not to wear the military garb of men, so men are not to wear . . . what? What is the distinctive garb of women? Especially in a time and culture where men and women wore what today we might call a 'unisex' garment the question is hard to answer.[14]

If a particular garment, or style of dress, or practice is meant by *simlah*, then determining what it is becomes the problem to be solved. What may have been obvious to the original audience about what *simlah* refers to is not obvious to us. Yet we are not without clues. We already have debated how it stands in relation to *keli*. We must also remember that the key term *to'ebah* ("abhorrent") is important. Its presence indicates a religious connection that ought not to be overlooked. Thus, cultural and historical factors enter into the discussion of deciding how best to render and comprehend this verse. *Simlah*, whatever it may exactly mean, should be seen as referring to some kind of dress in a specifically religious setting. Having done that, responsible application can follow.

What conclusions can be drawn?

Obviously, the matter of translating and interpreting this text is not so easy as it might first appear. Should *keli* and *simlah* be seen as synonymous, or as intentionally referring to different things? How should *keli*—so versatile a word—be translated? How does *to'ebah* factor in? What cultural practices might give us the key we need to solve the mystery of the text's meaning? Is there a greater principle that provides the context?

Each time we make a decision, it impacts subsequent decisions. Unfortunately, we don't have the original writer to question. But there have been plenty of experts down through the ages to try to think along the original writer's lines and thus discern the original intent. These experts have wrestled with the questions we have raised. It is time we look at some of their conclusions and assess them.[15]

Q. 63 What do Jewish commentators say?

The Short Answer. Though Judaism is a smaller religion than Christianity, it is substantially older and a source for Christianity; Deuteronomy 22:5 comes from the Hebrew scriptures. Thus it is appropriate to consider what Jewish commentators have said about this text before turning to Christian commentators. The prohibition in Deuteronomy is variously understood both in ancient Jewish texts and by modern writers. The Dead Sea Scrolls, in a fragmentary document, preserve the text imperfectly, but with an interesting modification. The Targums, ancient translations or paraphrases, render the text in a variety of ways. The differences all reflect interpretive efforts to clarify the inherent ambiguity of the Hebrew. Ancient commentaries, known as Midrashim, expand the interpretive effort. Perhaps the most notable of these is Midrash *Sifre*, which reflects the ancient Hebrew desire to keep different kinds of things separate and removed from one another. Over the centuries a complex body of literature grew up around an earlier core of oral tradition. First codified as the Mishnah in the 2nd century C.E., it continued to grow through Gemara, interpretive layers on the Mishnah. Collectively, this vast body of text and commentary accrued across centuries as the Talmud. A passage in tractate *Nazir* offers the most extensive treatment of Deuteronomy 22:5. It is a legal discussion and proceeds as such. After establishing that the prohibition in Deuteronomy is not merely a product of earlier scribes, the rabbis probe what it is that constitutes an 'abomination.' They conclude that since the mere act of crossdressing does not merit such a label something else must be in mind. What is forbidden is crossdressing that results in some objectionable mixing of the sexes. The Medieval scholar Rashi, most authoritative of later commentators, follows this line of logic. He sees in the prohibition a practice of crossdressing pursued for immoral purposes. This approach is found in other documents of the era, such as the 13th century *Sefer HaHinukh*, or the mid-16th century *Shulhan Arukh*. More recent commentaries draw upon modern scholarship as well as the older Jewish texts. In the middle of the 20th century, the famed rabbi Joseph Hertz provided continuity with the traditional interpretation by seeing in the prohibition a warning against an improper mixing of the sexes such as happened in the worship of the pagan nations around ancient Israel. Even more recent comments continue this thinking.

The Longer Answer. Judaism is arguably the oldest of the world's major religions. Throughout its long history the religion has been characterized by the preservation of multiple points of view, allowing the minority report to stand honorably alongside the prevailing judgment on various matters. Guiding these diverse views is Torah, the instructed way of living set forth by the Divine One. Both the Hebrew Bible and the Talmud provide this Torah along with its interpretation and application.

The foundational body of sacred literature is the Hebrew Bible, also referred to as the Tanakh (for its three constituent parts: *Torah* ('Law'), *Nevi'im* ('Prophets'), and *Kethuvim* ('Writings')). Although somewhat differently ordered, its contents are the same as those found in the Christian Old Testament, which we considered earlier (in the answer to Q. 61). Only one biblical text explicitly references crossdressing: Deuteronomy 22:5. The Hebrew text is rendered by the Jewish Publication Society (JPS) version into English as follows:

> A woman shall not wear that which pertaineth unto a man,
> neither shall a man put on a woman's garment; for whosoever
> doeth these things is an abomination unto the LORD thy God.

More recently the Judaica Press Complete Version renders it:

> A man's attire shall not be on a woman, nor may a man
> wear a woman's garment because whoever does these [things]
> is an abomination to the Lord, your God.

This text already has been examined (in the answer to Q. 62). Rather than repeat that material here, we shall attend to how the Judaic tradition has treated the passage. To do so we shall briefly examine the Qumran documents (Dead Sea Scrolls), targums (ancient paraphrastic translations), midrashim (ancient commentaries), and talmudic texts, alongside more modern literature. As with the Christian tradition, the difficulties posed by Deuteronomy 22:5 produce some variety in interpretation.

What do the Dead Sea Scrolls say?

In the years following the Second World War, a series of startling finds occurred in the Judean Desert. Many of these were associated with a community that had settled at Qumran, near the Dead Sea. A great many of the 'Dead Sea Scrolls,' as they came to be called, survive only in fragments. One such document bears the code 4Q159 (or 4QOrd^a) and is comprised of a partial collection of laws that paraphrase and modify those found in the Hebrew Bible.

One of the fragments that has survived echoes the Deuteronomic text: "A woman is not to wear the clothes of a male; every[one ... and he is not] (7) to put on a woman's cloak, and he is not to dress in a woman's tunic, for it is an [ab]omination."[16] The incomplete nature of the text and a lack of certainty over the text's social context make much speculation ill-advised. The first clause, with reference to women, seems unremarkably similar to the biblical text. The second clause, presumably with reference to men, appears to expand upon the biblical text. The use of the referents 'woman's cloak' and 'woman's tunic' are more specific than the ambiguous phrasing of the biblical text. Given a setting in the Hellenistic/Roman period, the woman's cloak and tunic would have been readily identifiable articles of clothing. However, the prohibition is no more forthcoming than the biblical text in offering a rationale for its prohibition, specifying any context, or setting out a specific penalty.

What do the Targums say?

The targums were ancient translations of the biblical Hebrew into the vernacular for use in synagogue services.[17] Various targums render the text as follows:

> A woman must not wear a man's armament, nor shall a man put on woman's clothing; for whoever does these things is remote before the Lord your God. (*Targum Onkelos to Deuteronomy*)[18]

> A woman shall not wear *the armor* of a man, nor shall a man put on a woman's garment; for whoever does these things is *detestable and* abominable *before* the Lord your God. (*Targum Neofiti to Deuteronomy*)[19]

> A woman should not wear *a fringed cloak or phylacteries,* which are male *ornaments,* and a man *shall not shave his armpits or his pubic hair or his face to appear as a woman* for it is an abomination before the Lord your God. (*Targum Pseudo-Jonathan to Deuteronomy*)[20]

What these targums share in common is a refusal to see the first phrase—"A woman shall not wear that which pertaineth unto a man"—as having a general, all encompassing character. Where they differ is in what specific kind of male clothing is envisioned: whether war dress (*Targum Onkelos* and *Targum Neofiti*), or religious dress (*Targum Pseudo-Jonathan*). The second phrase—"neither shall a man put on a woman's garment"—is only expanded upon by *Targum Pseudo-Jonathan*. It understands the text in such a manner that clothes seem a moot point. The objection is to men trying to pass as women. The 'clothing' or 'covering' is body hair, of which men have more than women. This understanding is important in the Talmud, to which we shall soon turn.

What does the Midrash *Sifre* say?

Early in the Common Era, the commentary on Deuteronomy known as *Sifre* states:

> This is the general principle in this matter: a woman may not dress like a man and go among men, and a man may not adorn himself with women's finery and go among women. R. Eliezer ben Jacob says: Whence do we learn that a woman may

not arm herself with weapons and go out into battle? From the verse *A woman shall not wear that which pertaineth unto a man*. And (whence do we learn) that a man may not adorn himself with women's finery? From what follows, *neither shall a man put on a woman's garment*.[21]

The commentary is explicit in enunciating a general principle: forbidding the mixing of the sexes. This is in keeping with the character of many of the laws in Deuteronomy around the one found in 22:5. These different laws reflect the Hebrew aversion to mixing elements from different categories, or kinds of things. Perhaps the most obvious and general example of this way of thinking is the desire to keep the Hebrew people apart from the ways of other people, and especially their religions. This desire is reflected in the Torah in numerous laws meant to preserve them as a 'holy' people—one kept apart for God's own special purposes and marked in visible ways as different from other peoples. But since the sexes must inevitably mix at some times, a specific form of mixing of male and female must be in mind. The natural tendency would be to conclude that what is referred to is a mixing through disguise in order to have illicit sexual relations.

Sifre appeals to a famous Rabbi, Eliezer ben Jacob (2nd century), who understands Deuteronomy 22:5 as forbidding specific behaviors that would inappropriately mix the sexes: women dressing in armor and going with men into battle, and men putting on "women's finery," presumably to gain access to them sexually. Rabbi Eliezer ben Jacob's opinion also figures in the discussion in the Talmud.

What does the Talmud say?

Alongside the written Torah of the Hebrew Bible is the Oral Torah set down in written form in the Mishnah, which occurred at the end of the 2nd century C.E. To it was later added Gemara, a comprehensive commentary on the Mishnah, with both legal (Halakah) and non-legal (Aggadah) materials. The Mishnah and Gemara together comprise the Talmud, which exists in two forms, the more authoritative Babylonian Talmud and the Talmud of the Land of Israel, known as the Jerusalem Talmud. The critical Talmudic text is in *Nazir* 59a, the relevant portion of which follows:

> Others say [that the above argument took the following form]. R. Hiyya b. Abba, citing R. Johanan, said: One who removes [the hair of] the armpits or the private parts is to be scourged because of [infringing the prohibition] *neither shall a man put on a woman's garment*. An objection was raised. [We have been taught:] Removal of hair is not [forbidden] by the Torah, but only by the Soferim?—That statement [of R. Johanan] agrees with the following Tanna. For it has been taught: One who removes [the hair of] the armpits or the private parts in-

fringes the prohibition, *neither shall a man put on a woman's garment*.

What interpretation does the first Tanna put on [the verse] *'neither shall a man put on a woman's garment'?*—He requires it for the following that has been taught: Why does Scripture say, *A woman shall not wear that which pertaineth unto a man* [etc.]? If merely [to teach] that a man should not put on a woman's garment, nor a woman a man's garment, behold it says [of this action] *this is an abomination* and there is no abomination here! It must therefore mean that a man should not put on a woman's garment and mix with women, nor a woman a man's garment and mix with men. R. Eliezer b. Jacob says: How do we know that a woman should not go to war bearing arms? Scripture says, *'A woman shall not wear that which pertaineth unto a man.'* [The words] *'Neither shall a man put on a woman's garment,'* [signify] that a man is not to use cosmetics as women do.[22]

The textual dialog in *Nazir* 59a reflects understandings seen in the targums and in *Siphre*. The debate at hand concerns whether a man may shave certain parts of his body. In forbidding it, Rabbi Hiyya b. Abba follows the teaching of Rabbi Johanan I, finding the prohibition of shaving in Deuteronomy 22:5. An objection is then raised: wasn't this teaching actually something the scribes of earlier days (i.e., the Soferim) forbade, rather than it really being the Torah that condemns it? The reply is that Rabbi Johanan's teaching is consistent with the Tanna (Mishnaic Rabbi) who appeals to the Torah text. So, a man who shaves his armpits or private parts merits a whipping.

The dialog then turns to figuring out why this conclusion is necessary in light of the Torah's text. This means noting that the phrase in question—'neither shall a man put on a woman's garment'—follows the prohibition of a woman putting on 'that which pertains to a man.' At once the observation is made that what Deuteronomy says cannot be simply understood as a general prohibition of men wearing women's clothes or vice versa, because the Torah is talking about something that is an "abomination" and such behavior does not qualify. Therefore, something more specific must be in mind. The conclusion reached echoes *Sifre*: an inappropriate mixing of the sexes is what is meant. The Deuteronomy text, it is argued, has two parallel clauses intended to be understand in light of one another. Both phrases refer to specific *ornamentation*—men's armor worn by a woman, or women's cosmetics put on by a man.

What does Rashi say?

The general sense set out above has endured in mainstream deliberations about Deuteronomy 22:5. Thus we find in Rashi (1040-1105 C.E.) the following notes on the Torah text:

35

5. <u>That which pertaineth unto a man shall not be upon a woman</u>

In order that she shall resemble a man, in order that she should go among men; for this is only for the purpose of immorality (Siphre; Nazir 59).

Neither shall a man put on a woman's garment

In order to go and sit among women.

Another interpretation: He should not remove the hair of the genital region nor the hair of the armpits (Naz. 59).

For an abomination

The Torah forbids only a garment which leads to abomination.[23]

Among Talmudic and biblical scholars, Rashi stands in the first rank. His understanding of the text has wielded great influence. Here he notes prior judgments but gives preeminence to the idea of crossdressing used for disguise to perpetrate sexual immorality.

What does Maimonides say?

Moses ben Maimon (1135-1204), more familiarly known as Maimonides (or among Jewish scholars as Rambam), emphasized both the legal context and the theological concern. As to the former, he observed that the law of שַׁעַטְנֵז (*sh'atnez*)—the 'mixing stuff' prohibition (see Deuteronomy 20:23)—offered a general commandment aimed at keeping Israel from following the practices of its Canaanite neighbors.[24] This informed the theological concern in 22:5 (the 39th and 40th of his famous listing of the Torah's 613 commandments): a desire to keep away from pagan worship practices. In his renowned *Mishneh Torah*, and elsewhere, Maimonides advances more than one point about the text. In appealing to history, he pointed to the practice of men dressing as women in their worship of Venus, while women put on the martial garb of men in praise of Mars, the Roman god of war, as instances of pagan practice that the text has in mind. He proposed as a general rule that men avoid dress practices (including the use of cosmetics and ornamentation) that in the person's location were exclusively associated with women. This logic is consistent with his reasoning that the point is to keep the Jewish people a separate people, one whose identity and religious practices were distinct from the Gentiles around them. But he also advances the idea that crossdressing may promote lust and sexual immorality.[25]

What do other commentators say?

The 13th century *Sefer HaHinukh* also weighs in on the matter. This text took as its task explaining all 613 of the *mitzvoth* (commandments) of the Torah. Its alleged author, Rabbi Aharon Halevi of Barcelona, concurring with the sense in Rashi, comments that the root of the *mitzvah* in Deuteronomy 22:5 is the concern that crossdressing will lead to sexual sin. The text remarks, "There is no doubt that if men and women's clothing were the same, they would mix and the earth would be filled with impropriety."[26] In other words, an inability to distinguish between male and female by means of appearance in any society that segregates the sexes allows the sexes to mix freely and thus sets up scenarios where improper sexual conduct can occur.

Another, later text, returns to the reasoning expressed in the Talmud. The authoritative halakhic (legal) text, *Shulhan Arukh* (*The Set Table*), was the work of Rabbi Joseph Caro, a Sephardic scholar of the mid-16th century. He interprets crossdressing as either the shaving of underarm hair, or shaving of the genital region—unless local custom allows it.[27]

What do modern Jewish scholars say?

In the middle of the 20th century, Joseph Hertz (1872-1946)—Chief Rabbi of the British Empire—noted briefly, "An interchange of attire between man and woman would promote immodesty and, in consequence, immorality. This law is probably directed against rites in Syrian heathenism, which included exchange of garments by the sexes and led to gross impurities."[28] This interpretive comment continues the tradition noted in Rashi and others.

In the latter half of the 20th century, commentator W. Gunther Plaut, in his likewise brief interpretive remark on the verse, directs his attention to the word 'abhorrent.' He writes, "The Hebrew term suggests that transvestism was considered not so much a sexual deviation as an idolatrous practice."[29] This note succinctly displays the Jewish interpretive mind: what is 'abhorrent' is whatever makes ancient Israel like the idolatrous nations around it. An 'abomination' destroys the intended purity for God's people when he chose to set them apart. Crossdressing, in this logic, is wrong to the extent it incorporates the Jewish people into the style of worship of pagan peoples, who mix men and women in immoral activities as part of their religious devotion.

Robert Alter, acclaimed scholar of the Hebrew Bible, follows this same interpretive tradition. He focuses on two matters. First, he observes, "What is 'abhorent' about the practice of cross-dressing could be an association with pagan orgiastic activities or even with pagan magic (a Hittite text prescribes crossdressing as the first stage in a ritual for curing impotence."[30] Second, he reminds us of the need to observe the context. This prohibition is in a list sharing in common the forbidding of mixing members from different binary categories. In addition to human male and female—the kinds of Deuteronomy 22:5—there is, for example, the prohibition of 22:11 that forbids mixing wool (which comes from an animal) with linen (which is derived from plants). The two points cohere in the ancient Hebrew logic noted earlier: God's order intends keeping different kinds apart, at least within the community of Israel.

In a more expansive treatment, Rabbi Jon-Jay Tilsen, of the Masorti-Conservative tradition, reviewed the Jewish tradition of commentary on this text. He notes the lack of consensus in how the unusual structure of the Hebrew text has been interpreted. A minority of scholars view the clauses on men and women as parallel, while most argue that the use of different terms suggests a lack of parallelism. After examining the various texts of pervious commentatots, Tilsen concludes that the scope of the Torah's prohibition was limited and "designed especially to prohibit men and women from misrepresenting themselves as the other gender with the aim of illicit heterosexual activity." The key, in his mind, is the concept of deception for illicit purposes. Thus the Torah does *not* prohibit all crossdressing, such as the practice of crossdressing for Purim.[31]

Jeffrey Tigay perhaps sums up the situation best with his comment:

> Several plausible reasons have been suggested for this commandment. Some think that it is directed against disguising oneself as a member of the opposite sex since this would facilitate mingling with them and hence fornication. Others think that transvestism is inherently abhorrent, either because it blurs the sexual differences that God created (see Gen. 1:27 and compare the laws of forbidden mixtures below, vv. 9-11), because it is a perverse means of sexual stimulation or homosexual role-playing, or because it was a part of certain pagan rites and magical practices. Pertinent to the suggestion that it was a pagan practice is a Babylonian adage, according to which a person who is apparently an Amorite says to his wife, 'You be the man and I'll be the woman,' but there is no indication of what act this refers to. . . . The halakhah combines both views: women may not wear armor or clothing, hairdos, or other adornments that are characteristic of men, nor may men wear what is characteristic of women (what is characteristic of each sex is defined by local practice.[32]

In all of these interpretive comments the aim is to understand the prohibition of Deuteronomy 22:5 in its literary, historical, cultural, and social contexts. The 'theology' of the original writer and audience stresses the necessity of Israel's separation from the ways of its neighbors. The underlying logic for this theology resides at least in part in a view of God's creation, especially with respect to a particular people. That view in the Torah privileges the role and responsibility of the Hebrew people as set apart. As a separate, and separated 'kind' of people, they are not to be improperly mixed with others in manner or practices, especially with respect to religion. In this light, crossdressing pursued for immoral purposes is doubly damned: it not merely mixes two kinds of people—men and women—but does so expressly for illicit reasons. Thus application of this text attempts to apply this logic to contemporary Jewish practice.

Q. 64 What do Christian commentators say?

The Short Answer. The Christian interpretation of Deuteronomy 22:5 shares some commonality with Jewish commentary. Notably, this has meant attention to literary, historical, cultural, theological and other matters relevant to understanding the text in its context. At times, Christian commentators even have shown an awareness of the logic and treatment by Jewish scholars. Nevertheless, Christian treatment has been more diverse and the line between interpretation and application often more blurred. The origin of this fuzzing of the line between the two tasks is probably due to a preeminent concern with theology. The history of comment on this text reveals an early preoccupation with theology that only gradually gave way to more attention to literary and historical context. An example of the earlier treatment is found in the Puritan writer Philip Stubbes. His remarks focus on crossdressing by women—a social preoccupation of his day, and hence already an application of the text. Like the *Geneva Bible*, Stubbes' interpretation locates the prohibition of crossdressing in its presumed violation of God's created order. The early 19th century Protestant scholar Adam Clarke represents his era's shift to critical concerns with matters like language, history, and culture, while retaining a theological forcus. Though in time the attention of biblical scholars more carefully distinguished between interpretation and application, even today one can find commentaries relying more on general doctrinal convictions to guide contemporaries than on historical and literary evidence to comprehend the original meaning. This situation, coupled with a widespread lack of distinction between biblical interpretation and application among the laity, causes confusion for many Christians when they seek help from scholarly or pastoral professionals. Modern scholars, like the esteemed Gerhard Von Rad, tend to stay close to the interpretive aims of setting the text among its original audience. Von Rad, and others, emphasizes the ancient community's need to define itself in distinction to the other nations and their religions. Modern interpreters may draw the context more narrowly or widely, but they typically note how the prohibition is situated in a very particular religious, cultural, and historical context. This guides how the prohibition of a specific use of crossdressing should be understood, rather than how crossdressing in general should be comprehended. Unfortunately, many applications do not base themselves on sound interpretation.

The Longer Answer. The sheer size and diversity of Christianity makes it impossible to say with any real force what Christians believe about most things, including matters far more theologically substantial than crossdressing. In simple fact, Christians as individuals believe and practice whatever they personally accept as true. Still, most look to certain sources for authority to guide their faith and practice—or at least confirm their opinion. These sources may include their local priest or minister, Church tradition, prominent theologians, or others. But preeminent among authorities for most Christians is the Bible. That means the texts of the Bible have drawn much attention and over the millennia numerous commentaries have been written to help Christians better understand the biblical message.

What are biblical commentaries like?

Because Christianity looks to the Bible as authoritative in matters both of faith and practice, it is fitting to start with a brief examination of how the text of Deuteronomy 22:5 has been handled by various Christian commentators, both past and present. In both older and more recent commentaries we often meet a curious blend of theology, critical analysis based on historical and literary knowledge, and contemporary social values. Thus, one important task in reading any commentary is sorting out what remarks owe more to the attitudes contemporaneous with the commentator and which observations represent a more objective presentation of factual matters that any student of history and literature can verify or refute. While any commentator is welcome to espouse his or her own theological conclusions, and while none of us can entirely escape the influence of our own culture, the most valuable information remains that which sets out historical and literary evidence and invites us to make up our own minds as to its pertinence and weight. We should bear that in mind while examining the comments found below, which are followed by some remarks aimed at making even clearer what the commentators are doing in their writings.

What do older commentators say?

First, let's see how some commentators at earlier times have treated this text. Since we elsewhere examine the writings of the Church Fathers, our starting point here is much later in Church history. The sources used here are mostly well-known and some are often referenced. Since the long history of Christianity has been marked by a few decisive events, the starting point for our brief examination is the Protestant reformation, when Christianity assumed its division into the three great traditions (Eastern Orthodoxy, Roman Catholicism, and Protestantism) that still mark it today. Inasmuch as other materials in this volume afford an opportunity to look at Roman Catholic scholarship, the emphasis in these selections has been on Protestant writings. Illustrative of the diversity available, some of these writings appeared as brief notations in editions of the Bible, while others were part of scholarly commentaries, whether as stand-alone volumes or in respected collections.

Philip Stubbes: A Puritan Perspective

More often than not comments on the text of Deuteronomy 22:5 have been in the context of making an application to a specific situation. Although most of the materials included in this answer are from general biblical commentaries, and not applied texts, it seems important to include at least one instance of this latter kind to remind us of the polemical use to which biblical texts were—and are—often put. In early modern England a Puritan commentator on the dress of his compatriots appealed to the Bible to support his contention that a number of dress practices violated the will of God. Prominent among the abuses Philip Stubbes discovered were incidences of crossdressing. In appealing to Deuteronomy 22:5, after detailing an example of female crossdressing (discussed in the answer to Q. 46), Stubbes wrote:

> Now, whether they be within the bounds and limits of that curse, let them see to it themselves. Our apparel was given us as a sign distinctive to discern betwixt sex and sex, and therefore one to wear the apparel of another sex is to participate with the same, and to adulterate the verity of his own kind. Wherefore, these women may not improperly be called *Hermaphroditi*, that is, mothers of both kinds, half women, half men.[33]

Stubbes presumes a purpose to dress, which is to identify the sex of the wearer. Given the questionable assumption that sex determines gender, men and women are thereby separated into their respective kinds through dress. So, anyone crossdressing 'participates' in the sex/gender group signified by the clothing. But to do that means to violate the truthfulness of their own sex/gender kind. Yet Stubbes goes beyond calling crossdressing women self-deceivers. He castigates them by proclaiming crossdressing has made them monstrosities.[34] In violating the ordinance on dress they not merely have defied the proper order of things, they have defiled it, and pay the penalty in becoming grotesque—for this was how their critics viewed their crossdressed bodies.

Geneva Study Bible

The 1599 *Geneva Study Bible* is succinct, offering a single note on the biblical text: "For that alters the order of nature, and shows that you despise God."[35] This brief remark makes a theological argument. The contention—one of the most common made when rejecting crossdressing—is that the practice disturbs the 'order of creation.' This idea is prominent in the Reformed tradition within Protestantism. It posits two important 'orders' (i.e., patterns or arrangements) established by God: creation and redemption. These ideally should mirror one another. Within both, men and women have their assigned places (see, for example, 1 Corinthians 11:3-16). Perhaps tellingly, the placement of the notation mark next to the word 'woman' suggests a primary concern with female cross-dressing, which represents a usurpation of male privilege.

Crossdressing, the argument runs, blurs the delineation of the genders and thus demonstrates disrespect for the arrangement established in creation. Because it contravenes the divinely established pattern it constitutes, at least implicitly, an arrogation of divine prerogative to the person who does so. In thus setting oneself up in God's place, deciding what is or is not 'natural,' the cross-dresser—in the words of the *Geneva Study Bible*—"shows that you despise God." Hence, the argument concludes, crossdressing must be opposed as sin.[36]

This interpretation is by no means confined to older commentators. Some modern writers mirror it. For example, P. J. Harland, in a 1998 review of the text, concluded that the prohibition here constitutes "a rejection of actions which might confuse or mix sexual identity." In the spirit of the *Geneva Study Bible*, Harland contends that, "all the regulations on marriage and sexual conduct point to a distinction in the creation of male and female." Though they belong together, they stand in contrast; abnormal sexual practices, Harland warns, can sever the unity of person intended by God.[37]

Adam Clarke's Commentary

With the Enlightenment, biblical scholars turned more attention to seeing texts in their historical and literary contexts, although theological concerns remained prominent. This trend is evident in the early 19th century commentary by Adam Clarke:

> The woman shall not wear that which pertaineth unto a man] *keli geber*, the instruments or arms of a man. As the word *geber* is here used, which properly signifies a strong man or man of war, it is very probable that armour is here intended; especially as we know that in the worship of Venus, to which that of Astarte or Ashtaroth among the Canaanites bore a striking resemblance, the women were accustomed to appear in armour before her. It certainly cannot mean a simple change in dress, whereby the men might pass for women, and vice versa. This would have been impossible in those countries where the dress of the sexes had but little to distinguish it, and where every man wore a long beard. It is, however a very good general precept understood literally, and applies particularly to those countries where the dress alone distinguishes between the male and the female. The close-shaved gentleman may at any time appear like a woman in the female dress, and the woman appear as a man in the male's attire. Were this to be tolerated in society, it would produce the greatest confusion. Clodius, who dressed himself like a woman that he might mingle with the

Roman ladies in the feast of the Bona Dea, was universally execrated.[38]

Clarke's comment demonstrates the important distinction between *interpretation*—understanding what the text meant in its own time—from *application*—understanding the text so that it has value for the commentator's time. Clarke's interpretation has the virtue of joining literary analysis (the meaning of key terms like 'adornment') with historical knowledge (the practices of ancient neighbors to the Jews) to produce a conclusion driven by evidence and logic: the crossdressing of the woman was the putting on of the apparel of war worn by men, a practice contemporary in some groups at the time Deuteronomy 22:5 was written. Clarke points out that the cultural conditions of the time—the close similarity of male and female garments and the near universal wearing of beards by men—make a simplistic reading of crossdressing as "a simple change in dress, whereby the men might pass for women, and vice versa" impossible. However, Clarke continues, the application of the text makes using this text as a general principle valuable because it serves to protect the need to distinguish between the genders. To this he adds the historical illustration of a Roman aristocrat whose crossdressing caused a great scandal.[39]

Jameison-Fawcett-Brown Commentary

A subordination of historical evidence to theological concerns is illustrated in the following comment from the venerable Jameison-Fawcett-Brown commentary (late 19th century):

> Though disguises were assumed at certain times in heathen temples, it is probable that a reference was made to unbecoming levities practised in common life. They were properly forbidden; for the adoption of the habiliments of the one sex by the other is an outrage on decency, obliterates the distinctions of nature by fostering softness and effeminacy in the man, impudence and boldness in the woman as well as levity and hypocrisy in both; and, in short, it opens the door to an influx of so many evils that all who wear the dress of another sex are pronounced "an abomination unto the Lord."[40]

This commentary recognizes that historical context matters, but implies that because more than one historical situation is possible (i.e., either crossdressing 'in heathen temples' or in 'unbecoming levities practised in common life'), the one chosen should be the one that best fits the commentator's sense of a general biblical principle. In this case it is one we have seen before: the order of creation. Hence the commentary argues that crossdressing is 'properly forbidden,' as 'an outrage on decency,' because it 'obliterates the distinctions of nature.' Dire consequences follow: men become soft and effeminate while women become bold and impudent; both sexes increase in levity and hypocrisy.[41] This conclusion relies on gender stereotypes reflecting a certain ideal in masculinity and femininity. Whether these stereotypes accurately reflect biblical views of men and women is not addressed, but does seem to be assumed.

What do modern commentaries say?

'Modern' commentaries for our purpose are those from the 20th and 21st centuries. These are mostly, but not universally, distinguished by keen concern for interpretation along the scholarly lines earlier identified. Many add to the interpretive task some attention to application, either to aid preaching or to assist the reader in Christian practice. Our selections represent some of the most noted commentaries of this time period.

International Critical Commentary (ICC)

A new standard in scholarly biblical work was reached at the beginning of the 20th century with the appearance of the renowned *International Critical Commentary* (ICC) series. The volume on Deuteronomy, by noted Old Testament scholar S. R. Driver appeared in 1901. This volume accented historical and literary evidence, drawing together a number of examples of crossdressing from the ancient world and scrutinizing the Hebrew terminology to place the biblical text in context. Driver notes:

> No doubt the prohibition is not intended as a mere rule of conventional propriety—though even as such, it would be an important safeguard against obvious moral dangers,—but is directed against the simulated changes of sex which occurred in Canaanite and Syrian heathenism, to the grave moral deterioration of those who adopted them.[42]

This remark stands in the line set by Clarke's commentary. What distinguishes Driver's work from that of Clarke is his far more extensive appeal to both linguistic and historical evidence. Those materials are still commonly referenced when scholarly considerations of Deuteronomy 22:5 occur. Academic volumes of interpretive work continue to follow this kind of procedure.

Gerhard Von Rad

Most recent commentaries generally reflect a greater reliance on historical and cultural factors in explaining the text because they view the task of scholarly commentary as first interpretive in nature, and then subsequently as providing contemporary application. For example, one of the most distinguished Old Testament theologians of the 20th century, Gerhard Von Rad, noted on this text: "[S]omething more is involved than mere observance of what is seemly, or obedience to a rule prescribed by nature. The reason offered makes use of a very weighty argument ('an abomination to Yahweh'), which suggests some cultic offense."[43]

Von Rad appeals to evidence within the text—the formula at its end—to argue that whatever the prohibition means it must be understood with this formula in view. The idea that the behavior prohibited is an "abomination" (תּוֹעֵבַת, *to'ebah*—discussed above in Q. 63), must govern the interpretation of the behavior. If this key term references a "cultic offense" (i.e., a religious violation), then the 'crossdressing' must be viewed as something affecting religious practice. Given the nature of the wider context, this makes sense. Von Rad's principal interest is in seeing that the text is not improperly handled by negligence of its unique setting.

Cambridge Bible Commentary

Similarly, Anthony Phillips also wants to remain rooted in the *cultus* of ancient Israel. He demonstrates this focus in his succinct treatment:

> This is another example of anti-Canaanite legislation and reflects certain sexual practices in the cult. Its purpose is then not to prohibit what is considered improper from the secular standpoint, but rather, as the phrase *abominable to the* LORD *your God* indicates, what might contaminate the purity of the Israelite faith.[44]

Phillips, like Von Rad and any number of other scholars, finds the most pertinent context for understanding the prohibition of Deuteronomy in a very specific—we might even say 'limited'—religious milieu. Recognition of this context should dissuade believers from too grand of claims in making proper application.

New Interpreter's Bible

Of course, there are dissenting voices. Ronald Clements offers the following observation:

> It is possible that some forms of transvestism were practiced in cultic ceremonies of which the deuteronomists disapproved, so that they are here outlawed as idolatrous and non-Isrealite. However, the overall context of the ruling shows that it was concerned to uphold what were perceived to be given boundaries of the natural order, rather than being a further ruling to outlaw acts of apostasy from the Lord God.[45]

It is noteworthy to see that Clements, like Von Rad, starts close to the text and its historical setting. But he thinks the context is wider than a specific historical concern. For Clements, the wider religious context takes precedence. He writes, "These rules prohibit the practice of transvestism as a forbidden crossing of one of the foremost distinctions established at creation (Gen. 1:27)."[46]

Whether this text actually constitutes an appeal to what Clements views as a broad literary context or is merely his own reading of the theological context is unclear. It may be that in his comments the theological interest of contemporary application has encroached on the interpretive task, or it may be argued that the theological interest of the original author is the most proper way to interpret the text. The latter way of conducting interpretation is riskier than giving priority to matters of language, history, culture and so forth, because it is harder to substantiate with much confidence the theological mind of the writer. Yet this approach is popular among Christians who prioritize theology to the degree they are willing to risk overstatement rather than refrain from speculating on the theology of the author.[47]

International Bible Commentary

Today, even brief comments like that set out in the conservative *International Bible Commentary* display the tendency to focus on literary, historical and cultural matters relevant to interpretation, while not neglecting application:

> Within living memory, this verse has been cited against the wearing of trousers by women; yet there has been no corresponding refusal to wear ray-on/cotton or terylene/worsted mixtures (see Deut. 22:11). The practice referred to may have been thought to have magical effects. There is certainly evidence of transvestism and simulated sexual inversion being associated in the ancient world (as well as today) with sexual license—and in a religious context.[48]

This short comment starts with recognizing the role of culture: our own history has seen this verse applied against a practice now common among Christians—women wearing jeans. It then points out that other prohibitions near this text are routinely ignored. Having thus pointed out two pertinent contemporary cultural matters, the comment turns to the text's historical context. It very briefly summarizes this evidence as perhaps involving magic and sexual license, and noting its connection with a religious context. Much is left to the reader to conclude from this brief commentary, which succeeds both in giving caution against arbitrary singling out of this text for application and simultaneously sanctioning applications that connect crossdressing with illicit sexual practices.

IVP Bible Background Commentary Genesis-Deuteronomy

The equally conservative *IVP Bible Background Commentary Genesis-Deuteronomy* offers a more expansive comment:

> Just as clothing served as a status marker in the ancient world, it also distinguished gender. In classical contexts, cross-dressing occurred in the theater, where women were not allowed to perform, and was also an aspect of homosexual practice. Most instances in which cross-dressing or transvestism are mentioned in ancient Near Eastern texts are cultic or legal in nature. For instance, when the Ugaritic hero Aqhat is murdered, his sister Paghat puts on a male garment under her female robes in order to assume the role of blood avenger in the

absence of a male relative. An Assyrian wisdom text contains a dialogue between husband and wife who propose to exchange their clothing and thus assume each other's gender roles. This may be a fertility rite or perhaps a part of a religious drama honoring a goddess. It may be this association with other religions that made transvestism an 'abomination' in Deuteronomy, but the issue may also be the blurring of gender distinctions. Hittite texts use gender-related objects as well as clothing in a number of magical rites used to influence one's sexual status or diminish or alter the gender status of an adversary. The objects of the female were mirror and distaff; those of the male, various weapons.[49]

This sophisticated comment succinctly produces several possible historical contexts in which Deuteronomy 22:5 might be best understood. Rather than telling the reader what to conclude, the evidence is set out and the reader is left to make her or his own judgments—or to suspend a final judgment because no evidence is so conclusive as to carry the field. What is offered here fits the volume's title—it provides background. This background serves efforts for the interpretive task, but can contribute as well to the work of application.

Bruce Oberst

However, among the many commentaries available today some are intended not as scholarly interpretations but as pastoral reflections, devotional guides, or doctrinal illustrations. And some modern commentaries still represent an older social view. About the time the social sciences were catching up to empirical reality about homosexuality, some biblical commentators were still making over-generalized assertions like this from Bruce Oberst: "Transvestism has historically almost always been practiced by those who exemplified the characteristics of the opposite sex; and these were often homosexuals. To wear clothes of the opposite sex immediately labels one in his community."[50]

It is hard to imagine a more contemporary commentator making such a sweeping statement. But this example does serve as an instructive reminder that commentaries vary in intent, scope, and scholarship. If we like, we can almost always find someone writing what we want to read; commentaries can be used to support almost any conclusion a modern reader wishes to make with regard to crossdressing. However, serious, fair, and responsible dialog relies on appeal to evidence of a more objective character, evidence that all participants can appeal to as they talk. In light of this need, commentaries that clearly and carefully distinguish between the interpretive and application tasks are especially valuable. We need both to understand Deuteronomy 22:5 in its own right, as a product of its own time, and as something that still speaks in some way today. Christians are not put in a position of having to choose doctrine over historical and literary study, or vice versa. They are partners in a holistic and comprehensive conversation.

Perhaps a sensible course of action is to consult more than one commentary, compare them, and reflect on the two-step process (interpretation first, then application based upon it), *before* coming to a conclusion about the meaning of the text. Even after drawing a conclusion we might be wise to exercise caution in how vigorously we apply it, restrained by our sense of the difficulty of the text. Such considerations lead us to consider more closely what truly constitutes a 'reasonable position'—the matter to which we now turn.

Q. 65 What constitutes a "reasonable" position to take?

The Short Answer. A reasonable position on any matter is a matter of logic and evidence. To that it seems sensible to add a specific moral dimension: humble civility. Whatever position we take on the interpretation and application of Deuteronomy 22:5 will serve us best if it flows from reason plus evidence, liberally mixed in the restraint produced by an awareness of our imperfect knowledge and presented with humane civility toward all. In that light, it seems reasonable to propose that a sound interpretation of the text will stay close to the matters most apprehensible (e.g., language) and refrain from over dependence on things less clear (e.g., theological mind of God). Given those strictures, it seems reasonably clear that Deuteronomy 22:5 is best understood as specifying a religious setting in which objectionable crossdressing by both men and women was taking place. Crossdressing is thereby forbidden as a legitimate means of enacting worship. The reason seems to be because such practices are like those of people who do not share Israel's position in a unique and holy relationship with God. Applications that stay close to this sense will stress contemporary boundaries in dress meant to facilitate a proper focus in worship by a people with a special sense of relationship to God, rather than general prohibitions or condemnations that have nothing at all to do with maintaining a religious identity and decorum in worship.

The Longer Answer. As we have found, a number of significant issues are at play in understanding Deuteronomy 22:5 (see Q. 62). Because of these matters Jewish and Christian commentators find themselves presented with a range of possible meanings (see Q. 63-64). We could continue at some length examining comments long and short on Deuteronomy 22:5. But what we have seen so far does permit us to draw some reasonable conclusions:

1. We profit from distinguishing *interpretation* (understanding what the text meant to its original audience) from *application* (understanding what the text has to say to us).
2. In addition to theology, we need to consider literary, historical, and cultural evidence.

3. The *theological* point generally appealed to is the distinction of the genders in conformity to the order of creation, though this position is more debatable than other interpretive matters.
4. The literary considerations tend to hinge on *linguistic* issues concerning three Hebrew terms: *keli, simlah,* and *to'ebah.*
5. The *historical* and *cultural* evidence appealed to generally reflects pagan practices, specifically religious ones, where crossdressing accompanied religious practices rejected by the author's faith community.
6. How all of the above strands are woven together constitutes a commentator's stance. But none of these stances can claim universal assent.

The best one can ask is for *a reasonably argued hypothesis.*

Given all we have considered, one explanation makes more sense than the alternatives. It seems reasonable to propose that the term *to'ebah* ("abomination") must govern how we understand what precedes it. This technical term, used in a religious context, keeps us from separating the condemned practice from religious and moral considerations. Since the purpose of this restriction, and others in this Deuteronomic code, is to separate the Israelite community from its neighbors, the practices of those neighbors must be relied upon to see what the Hebrew community was to avoid. Thus, the pagan use of crossdressing in illicit worship practices appears the most likely object in the original writer's mind. The readers were to keep themselves from dressing as members of the opposite sex for religious purposes that the writer found abhorrent.

Now, this conclusion does not mean one cannot argue that additional concerns were also at play. For example, the author might also have had a wider theological precept in view, such as a divinely intended separation of the sexes. In this light, crossdressing is wrong when it blurs the division of the sexes. However, because of the manner of dress of the author's own culture, this most likely did *not* refer to clothes as such, but to other items worn or carried that served to distinguish the genders (such as weapons of war and female adornments). At any event, inferring a theology of creation is risky even based on much more evidence than this slender text provides.

To interpretation—which aims at understanding what the message was for its original audience—we can add application, which seeks the contemporary message. In doing so, one can argue that in our culture, where dress is relied on to distinguish the genders, crossdressing now violates the biblical admonition in a way similar to what happened millennia ago when women put on armor. However, to do so is to risk making an inappropriately broad application. An application that stays closer to a solid interpretation would instead stress ways in which contemporary Christians can use dress to reflect their identity within the community called the Church. They can also legitimately warn against dress practices that in the place and context of worship would be too much like the dress and worship practices of other religions. The point is the same: dress is meant to mark a special religious identity and not to serve irreligious ends in worship.

On the other hand, one could also argue that this text has no true application for today, either because the Old Testament law has been set aside for Christians, or because crossdressing today rarely (if ever) has any relation to a sacred act in public worship. Some do take this stance, but it seems as overly broad as an application that sees in this prohibition anything that resembles crossdressing in the eye of the beholder. To simply give up a text as irrelevant—which seems to have happened to much of the Bible—might make us wonder why Christians don't spare a lot of forests and simply publish a more slender Bible. Of course, such a proposal will fetch objection, but why should these have more weight than the objections of those who wonder why so much of the Bible seems not to matter at all?

We can legitimately be bothered by the convenient selection of this text to be applied today when others nearby, such as Deuteronomy 22:11—"Do not wear clothes of wool and linen woven together"—are completely ignored and routinely violated. There has been some ingenious reasoning to justify using this text while others are set aside, but it all seems to serve as an excuse to indulge in contemporaneous prejudices. For instance, this same text at an earlier time was used to condemn women wearing jeans, while today it is principally reserved for men wearing women's clothing. This utter arbitrariness in application confirms to many of us that contemporary social mores, rather than the 'abiding biblical principles' often appealed to, are at work.

Some may not concur with these conclusions. But perhaps we can agree that the task of properly comprehending Deuteronomy 22:5 is a difficult one. Perhaps, too, we can agree that while we may never be able to claim to have the final word on the subject, if we are careful and respectful of the evidence we can mount a reasonable position. Finally, maybe we can agree that given the nature of the situation we will be charitable towards those who see the text differently from ourselves.

We can disagree without being disagreeable.

Question Set 9:

What does Christianity say about transgender realities like crossdressing?

As we did with the previous question set, and for the same reasons, our scope in this material is focused by our attention to crossdressing. Because our work ultimately concerns gender and transgender realities, we will remark on more than crossdressing, though that behavior always anchors us. There have been, especially in recent years, a wonderful proliferation of learned books and articles specifically addressing matters like gender in one or another connection with Christianity. There also have been several worthy entries attending to homosexuality. But this present work redresses the relative lack in a comprehensive treatment centered on the behavior of crossdressing and the wider phenomena of transgender.

Where specifically religious values and judgments about dress enter in, a new element is contributed to the wider discussion about the role of clothes. Suddenly the sacred is connected with the mundane and clothes take on a higher value. Importantly, this element carries with it the weight many of us assign to religious authority as the decisive arbiter of our own personal beliefs, decisions and acts. So, many of us are concerned about what our religion says about our manner of dress. This concern extends to crossdressing.

In those cases where sacred texts or religious persons say little or nothing, there remains the matter of how the actual practice is tolerated. In this question set we will look at the history of Christian thinking as it relates to dress and crossdressing. We will begin with the foundational documents of the New Testament. These offer some material on dress that helped shape Christian thinking, though none say anything about crossdressing. That subject seems of no interest to Jesus, Paul, or any of those who wrote the New Testament, even though they all must have been aware of such practices, both in the secular world and as part of various foreign religions.

From the New Testament era we proceed through the Church Fathers of the first few centuries, a time often called the Patristic Age, though today more commonly refered to as Late Antiquity. The volume of material from this pe-

53

riod is much greater; our selections are meant to identify the most famous voices across a range of time and with specific reference to matters crucial to our concerns. As is true also of the New Testament materials, the information obtained from the Fathers of Late Antiquity is drawn upon in more than the one answer specifically dedicated to them. The material touches upon subjects ranging from the creation of the sexes, to the Fall, to speculations about the nature of gender, to issues surrounding dress, and finally to crossdressing.

Of course, discussion of gender, dress, crossdressing and other relevant matters did not cease with the Church Fathers. We take time to investigate subsequent Church pronouncements, drawing upon Church councils and other voices of authority—especially the Popes—down to the present time. The Catholic Church especially lends itself to our interests because of its Episcopalian structure, its historical prominence, and the fact that it commands more allegiance than any other single Christian body. The long history of the Church and its hierarchical structure make for ready identification of authoritative sources, and their relative weight. As elsewhere, all we can do is sample materials, but those selected offer a sense of the logic maintained by the Church, both past and presently.

Finally, we work our way forward to contemporary voices, both of those in opposition to crossdressing and others tolerant or accepting of the behavior and supportive of transgender people. Each side gets an entire answer, though the answer for supporters is longer for a number of reasons. Chief among these is that opponents tend to rely more on slogans and briefly stated objections than on lengthy and carefully articulated arguments. It is left to the minority—transgender people and their supporters—to respond to the vocal critics, and to do so with a depth not expected of their critics. This section of material also takes time to examine resources available for transgender Christians.

Along the way through these various answers we will also consider particular experiences, both of so-called 'transgendered saints' and of other notable men and women of Christian faith. In addition we will look at the wider social context afforded by considering religious festivals where crossdressing has been practiced. While we can scarcely exhaust the subject, we can attain a broad and useful perspective from a multitude of Christian sources.

We start at the foundation.

Q. 66 What does the New Testament say?

The Short Answer. There are no texts in the New Testament that speak explicitly about crossdressing, or even make oblique reference to the text in Deuteronomy. In that respect, then, we might wonder why we should consider the New Testament at all. However, the New Testament does speak about dress and does offer ideas (or 'principles') that many Christians have used to articulate a position with regard to crossdressing. That makes some attention to this primary source essential. Perhaps the most salient text for such purposes is found in Paul's Galatians 3:27-28, which reads: "As many of you as were baptized into Christ have clothed yourselves with Christ. There is no longer Jew or Greek, there is no longer slave or free, there is no longer male and female; for you are all one in Christ Jesus" (NRSV). This text, as we shall see in a later answer, set a high standard that occupied much of the thinking of theologians in the period after the close of the New Testament. But we begin not with Paul, but with the figure he followed: Jesus of Nazareth. His words, as recorded in the Gospels, provide teaching that Christians have looked to with special reverence. Jesus offers some thinking on clothing, but it is his use of the figure of the eunuch that has particularly drawn attention down through the ages. The 'eunuch for the sake of the kingdom of heaven' has been an inspiration from the early Church to the present—and is seen by some as a model for transgender Christians. When we turn to Paul, the aforementioned text has drawn by far the most attention. The particular Greek terms selected by Paul are of interest, because alternatives exist he might have used instead. That these terms are the ones he used may be key to understanding his meaning. It may be that Paul has in mind social constructions of gender and is proclaiming that gender is transcended through Christ. There are other voices in the New Testament who have things to say about dress that have been influential in Church history. In another writing attributed to Paul (though most scholars believe it was written in his name by another person), 1 Timothy 2:9-10, the subject of dress is mentioned with particular reference to women. This is true as well in 1 Peter 3:3. These texts initiated a special concern over women's dress that persisted in following centuries. Finally, we come full circle with words attributed to Jesus in the Gospel of Thomas, a document dated to the period of the New Testament but not included within that body. Its final 'saying' also has exerted influence.

The Longer Answer. What to make of clothes and how to dress confronts the profoundly devout among us no less than anyone else.[51] As in the population at large, differences of perspective and practice exist—and always have. The sacred texts of Christianity—the Old and New Testaments of the Bible—speak of clothing, both metaphorically and concretely, though they are silent about crossdressing *per se*.[52] Yet because there are materials that speak about dress, and do so at times with respect to gender, we must examine them. They have been used to develop principles of thinking then applied to matters such as crossdressing.

In the early centuries of Christianity the leading scholars of the church picked up where the New Testament left off. They also addressed the matter of dress and gender, coming to a variety of judgments as to the importance of the subject.[53] Through the centuries Christians have continued to address the matter.[54] Here our focus will stay to the New Testament texts and not the use to which they were later put—a matter later addressed.

In addition to remarks about dress and gender, the New Testament offers at least one other matter of special interest to us. In Jesus' teaching he speaks about a eunuch who has made himself such 'for the sake of the kingdom of heaven.' This particular figure has always exercised a degree of fascination and continues to do so. Since Jesus is the preeminent figure in Christianity, it is with his words that we begin.

What Did Jesus Say?

Christianity locates its origin in the person and work of Jesus of Nazareth, a historical figure whose association with the title of 'Christ' ('anointed one,' i.e., Messiah) became so powerful that it now functions virtually as a name. A number of teachings and sayings are related in Jesus' name in the four canonical Gospels. For convenience, Jesus' remarks on matters relevant to our consideration are grouped topically, beginning with comments pertinent to dress.

On Apparel

The most extended discussion on clothes offered by Jesus in the Gospels comes in Matthew 6:25-33, part of the famous 'Sermon on the Mount.' In this portion the issue at hand is confidence in divine providence. Jesus addresses himself to the matter of anxiety, about life and the matters of living, such as food and drink—and clothing. He exhorts his listeners not to be anxious, instead retaining confidence in a beneficent God. In regard to dress he reminds his audience that though the lilies of the field neither toil nor spin, God clothes them in radiance. He asks rhetorically if God would expend less effort on people than he does the grass of the field. Later, in Matthew 25: 36-44, Jesus hearkens again to the mundane need for clothes and tells his disciples that in their providing clothes to those in need they are ministering to him, and on the path to eternal life.

For the most part, Jesus' references to clothing are incidental and illustrative. The above texts suggest that he both recognized the human need for clothes and saw attention to meeting this need as concrete religious action. At the same time, the sense of his words relegates clothing to a practical matter to which basic attention and no more is merited. As we shall see (in answering Q. 67), the Church Fathers of the first few centuries elaborated the proposition that Christians not preoccupy themselves with what they wear, preferring modesty in appearance to match a modest and moral life. This was the 'principle' they deduced, and that general idea has been persistently followed.

Clearly it would be inappropriate to interpret any of Jesus' thoughts on dress as having crossdressing in mind. But although Jesus' words do not address crossdressing, he does speak of a figure that often crossdressed. In doing so, his thoughts are pertinent to the modern discussion about transgender.

On Eunuchs

In a remark found only in Matthew's Gospel, Jesus says, "For some are eunuchs because they were born that way; others were made that way by men; and others have renounced marriage because of the kingdom of heaven. The one who can accept this should accept it" (Matthew 19:12; NIV). The saying is appended to Jesus' teaching on divorce, which he forbids "except for unchastity" (19:9). The disciples' response is that if marriage is so binding, it may be better not to marry, to which Jesus then adds this saying. The sequence of discourse in Matthew has influenced the interpretation of this saying such that traditionally the eunuch has been connected to the idea of celibacy. Alternatively, some see the context with the disciples as implying this saying was Jesus' response to critics of his loyal followers, who had embraced a chaste single life—like eunuchs—rather than follow the social demand to be married.

In either case, the use of the word 'eunuch' draws attention; it heightens the stakes. Eunuchs were well known in the ancient world. Unlike other men, they had no beard; their faces were smooth like a woman's. By virtue of their infertility they were permitted more freedom among women. As people who were considered 'between' the ordinary statuses of male and female[55] they were also uniquely positioned in a religious sense. Eunuchs were commonly involved in religion, as priests or attendants (see the answer to Q. 76). But we should avoid assuming that any uniform view on them adhered across time and different places. Similarly, we should avoid assuming that Jesus had one or another view inherited from either his predecessors or his contemporaries.

Though ancient Judaism opposed castration, it was well aware of intersex individuals and of others castrated voluntarily or otherwise. The Deuteronomic code specified that, "No one whose testicles are crushed or whose penis is cut off shall be admitted to the assembly of the Lord" (Deuteronomy 23:1; NRSV).

Yet eunuchs were known among the royal entourage of the Jewish court (Jeremiah 34:19) and the religiously faithful among them are promised "a monument and a name better than sons and daughters" (Isaiah 56: 5; NSRV). Rabbis of the Talmudic period distinguished between *seris chamma* ('born eunuch') and *seris adam* ('man-made eunuch')[56]—both terms derived from an Akkadian phrase, *sa resi*, referring to royal attendants.[57]

The world of Jesus' day was well-acquainted with eunuchs. Throughout the Roman world there were eunuchs attached to religious sects, often serving as priests. Some had voluntarily undertaken castration as a sign of their devotion. There were also eunuchs in the secular world, many involved in the administration of state affairs. It is such a person that the New Testament offers a text (Acts 8:26-40) about—an Ethiopian eunuch to whom the Holy Spirit expressly directs Philip. This individual gladly embraces the Gospel and no objection is anywhere expressed over the inclusion of this 'transgender' figure.

In this saying Jesus acknowledges the same distinction as the rabbis, but allegedly extends the thought to embrace celibacy. Yet if there is a pairing of celibacy with eunuch status, Jesus seems to be suggesting we see celibacy in a way somewhat different from mere self-restraint. After all, the Wisdom tradition had employed the figure of the eunuch as the symbol of frustrated sexual yearning: "He sees with his eyes and groans as a eunuch groans when embracing a girl" (Wisdom of Sirach 30:20; NSRV). A eunuch may be infertile but not without desire. Perhaps, then, the emphasis is less on celibacy and more on intense yearning and devotion.

In fact, there is no compelling reason to view the figure of the eunuch as asexual. Scholar of hermeneutics and rhetoric David Hester argues that our available evidence argues against such a depiction. "The eunuch," Hester contends, "was a figure perceived to be neither celibate nor morally chaste." The eunuch's gender formation entailed an ability to navigate the worlds of the gender conforming, and was the source of the eunuch's ambivalent social status.[58] With respect to Matthew 19:12, Hester sees the saying as authentically the word of Jesus, and not merely a redaction by Matthew. His interpretation of its original social context highlights the role of ritual castration by the religiously zealot—a phenomonen well-documented in the religions of the time, including Christianity.[59] Over time, a more symbolic reading was adopted that led away from actual castration to the practice of self-restraint: celibacy. However read, the self-made eunuch 'for the sake of the kingdom of heaven' was a figure to be esteemed, someone so devoted to exclusive spiritual focus that personal sexuality was sacrificed (either through castration or chastity).

As neither male nor female, neither masculine nor feminine, a eunuch is 'sexless' (though not asexual) and between genders. This condition puts the eunuch in a unique position. In honoring the eunuch who is so 'because of the kingdom of heaven' Jesus also recognizes this person as outside the normal sphere. Eunuch religious persons were understood in Jesus' era as inhabiting a place between this world and a divine one, just as their sex and gender status placed them 'between' the human genders. Is it impossible to imagine that a eunuch for the sake of the kingdom of heaven becomes someone independent of the male/masculine and female/feminine duality without castration?

Among Jesus' own disciples, the beloved disciple John is treated by the tradition as a eunuch (Greek εὐνοῦχος; Latin *eunuchus*) in the sense of this text.[60] Here the notion of celibacy might be pertinent. John may represent a voluntary celibacy joined to devotion so complete that the person becomes something different.[61] A new status is obtained. But that raises another question—one faced by every religion where eunuchs have a role.

How is such an individual to be visibly marked? For instance, a man who castrated himself to serve a deity needed some way to show that condition to others since superficially he still looked like an ordinary male, though he was no longer sexually male, or female, but between the sexes. Religious eunuchs were commonly crossdressed, either in part (i.e., by a single distinctive item) or wholly. At a later date, the so-called 'crossdressing saints' were women who disguised themselves as men and acted as such in their pursuit of the kingdom of heaven. These women were often mistaken for eunuchs. Both the literal eunuchs and the crossdressed women thus 'preformatively' (to use Judith Butler's term) constructed a distinctive gender. In fact, Christian historian Stephen Davis argues that, "In late antiquity, eunuchs occupied a unique social position—one that was culturally constructed as a 'third gender.'"[62] Might this also be what metaphorical 'eunuchs for the sake of the kingdom of heaven' do?

While it is apparent that contemporary Christians see the self-made eunuch of Matthew as celibate, it should be just as apparent that had Jesus meant celibacy *only* as voluntary self-restraint, while remaining fully identified with a sex and gender, he could have said us much and avoided the idea of a eunuch. That he does not suggests an intentionality inviting the kind of speculation just engaged in. In fact, in Christian history this occurs metaphorically in the Roman Catholic priesthood. Though they do not practice castration, they do dress in distinctive garb, take on perpetual celibacy, and occupy a place that might fairly be termed between the sexes and genders. They are, in sum, eunuchs for the sake of the kingdom of heaven.

What did Paul say?

Probably the most salient text from the Pauline corpus with regard to the relation of dress and gender is one in which clothing is used figuratively. The passage in mind appears in an early letter the apostle Paul most likely wrote some two decades after Jesus' death. In Galatians 3: 27-28 the following words ring out in a clarion call echoed throughout Church history: "As many of you as were baptized into Christ have clothed yourselves with Christ. There is no longer Jew or Greek, there is no longer slave or free, there is no longer male and female; for you are all one in Christ Jesus" (NRSV).

The metaphor of Christians having 'clothed yourselves with Christ' is striking. The Greek verb root (ἐνδύομαι) carries the ordinary sense of wrapping oneself in a garment, such as a cloak. Just as putting on and wearing clothes expresses the self, and embodies an experience of the self, so the Christian in 'putting on' Christ expresses an identity and embraces an experience. Conjoined with the metaphor of baptism, an initiating into Christian identity through a public presentation, the clothing of the individual with Christ signifies an ongoing identity and presentation. The idea seems to be that having clothed the self with Christ, no other garment (i.e., experience and presentation of self) is needed. If this is correct, then the literal clothing a believer wears can be regarded as mostly superfluous because wearing Christ trumps wearing anything else—a conclusion some Christian theologians reached. Or, the idea can be interpreted as believers needing to in some manner concretely reflect their metaphorical clothing, such as in the distinctive apparel of priests, nuns, or monks, or perhaps in a simple modesty of dress—a conclusion other theologians reached.

In either reading, the question of crossdressing is left unresolved. If what we literally bear on our skin is inconsequential, then a freedom and egalitarianism in dress may be said to parallel that promised in the remainder of the text. In that case, crossdressing can be said to be neither 'good' nor 'bad' since it really doesn't matter if the focus stays on experiencing and expressing Christ. An application of this interpretation might suggest that becoming absorbed in how ourselves or others dress distracts attention from what really matters and we ought rather to keep our focus on Christ. Doing so helps us overcome the artificial distinctions drawn along lines of race, ethnicity, religion ('Greek or Jew), social class ('slave or free'), sex or gender ('male or female').

On the other hand, proponents of the other view remind us that we still must put on literal clothes and that such clothes also carry experiences and expressions. Just as the redeemed order of the Church is to mirror the order of creation, so might literal clothing seek to mirror being clothed with Christ. But what manner of dress best displays Christ? The answers to that question—all applications of this interpretation—have varied widely, though 'modesty' probably has been the most popular response. Yet crossdressing need not be excluded if one finds in Christ a figure who, as the text puts it, eliminates the distinctions between genders. An androgynous Christ, or even a metaphorically crossdressing Christ (see the answer to Q. 76), can be signified in literal crossdressing—a confounding of prevailing gender distinctions in which the world puts so much stock. Crossdressing for Christ could be construed as a profound proclamation of Paul's text.[63]

If the Greek verb for clothing oneself in Christ leaves open possibilities for transgender realities, what of the nouns for gender used by Paul? The terms for male (ἄρσεν, *arsen*) and female (θῆλυς, *thelus*) are the same as those used by Jesus (Matthew 19:4) when citing the creation of text of Genesis 1:27. These studiously neutral terms are an interesting choice for a number of reasons. First, they can refer to *either* sex *or* gender—which in Greek thinking are closely linked—though mostly to sex, and if gender, to gender-based-on-sex. Second, they both can be understood as neuter forms grammatically, leaving open the possibility of androgynous or transgender realities. Third, with the creation text as a backdrop, they represent human 'kinds' originally intended to be equal and joined together (however that might be understood), which in Christ Jesus again happens. To be clothed with Christ, then, means the restoration of 'male and female' to their original status, with the division, separation, and status rankings that arose after creation overcome. Certainly it can be argued that transgender realities accomplish this more successfully than the Church at large ever has.

It is possible the apostle meant to convey 'maleness' and 'femaleness' with gender (i.e., masculinity and femininity) predominantly in mind, rather than sex. Yet there are Greek words that more clearly and regularly convey gender, for either 'man' (ἄνθροπος, *anthropos*, or ἀνερ, ἀνδρός *aner, andros*) or 'woman' (γυνή, *gyne*). It seems reasonably clear here that Paul is drawing on the connection to the creation text and intending his readers to draw the conclusion that the common divisions and distinctions drawn between the sexes and the genders paired with them are obliterated when Christ is put on. In such a context, how could any objection to transgender realities be raised?

Are there other sources we should consider?

Although Jesus and Paul are the best known and most often cited figures of the New Testament, other voices should be noted at least in passing. For example, James 2:15-16 echoes the sentiment of Jesus in the practicality and proof of faith in providing clothing to those in need. However, especially noteworthy for their influence on later Christian thinking about modesty and dress are two texts, one attributed to Paul (though its authenticity is disputed and commonly rejected), and the other to the apostle Peter (in a text also sometimes debated for its authenticity).

We begin with the former text, found in 1 Timothy 2:9-10—"I also want women to dress modestly, with decency and propriety, not with braided hair or gold or pearls or expensive clothes, but with good deeds, appropriate for women who profess to worship God" [NIV]. This sentiment is echoed in the other text, 1 Peter 3:3—"Your beauty should not come from outward adornment, such as braided hair and the wearing of gold jewelry and fine clothes" [NIV]). Both of these texts are directed at women. Neither envision crossdressing. However, they express a sentiment that was strongly endorsed by influential (male) Church leaders (see the answers to Q. 67 & 72). Each can be read theologically with Paul's Galatians text in mind. The point is clear: Christians—especially Christian women—should be noted not for clothing that draws attention but for a demeanor and deeds that draw praise. Dress behavior is subordinated to other acts viewed as better showing Christianity.

The matter of dress also surfaces with explicit connection to public assembly for worship. Important for its influence on regulations regarding dress at church is 1 Corinthians 11:3-10, a portion of which (vv. 4-5) reads: "Every man who prays or prophesies with his head covered dishonors his head. And every woman who prays or prophesies with her head uncovered dishonors her head--it is just as though her head were shaved" [NIV]. In our own time where hair length and beards are less important to gender distinctions we are apt to take little note of such a text. But in the Apostle's time hair on head and face mattered to gender differentiation. The specific gender marker in view here is a head covering; men are to not use one, while women should.[64] Perhaps paralleling the Galatians text, the justification here is the created order, which the redeemed order being realized in the Church is supposed to show (see 1 Corinthians 11:7-9; cf. vv. 14-15 on the issue of hair length).

Extracanonical Texts

Other very early Christian ideas of note come from texts that did not gain inclusion in the New Testament canon. In early documents outside the New Testament known collectively as 'Gnostic' (from a Greek word for 'knowledge') texts, a notion relevant to our study is found. This idea is that women must—and shall—be made 'like men' for the sake of salvation. Thus, the *Gospel of Thomas* (late 1st—early 2nd century C.E.) concludes with Jesus saying, with reference to Mary: "See, I shall lead her, so that I will make her male, that she too may become a living spirit, resembling you males. For every woman who makes herself male will enter the Kingdom of Heaven."[65]

This text may bring to mind Paul's words in Galatians, considered above, although the difference between them seems dramatic. Paul's words would seem to relegate gender-based differences to no consequence, at least in terms of being a Christian. The words attributed to Jesus in the Gospel of Thomas strongly preserve a gender hierarchy, surmounting it for women by making them like men. Various movements in the Church's first few centuries took such ideas in one or another way, including trying to obliterate social distinctions between the sexes (see the example of the Eustathians, in the answer to Q. 72), or singling out women who succeeded in performing masculine piety as well as or better than the holiest of men (cf. the answer to Q. 68).[66]

Women themselves could reason in this manner, as in the following saying preserved from the lips of a woman who was a notable desert recluse, Amma Sara: "I may be a woman in body, but not in spirit."[67] Ironically enough, the women who best exemplify the spirit of Galations 3:28 are those who by their 'making themselves male' demonstrated the senselessness of gender-based distinctions that preserved a male-dominated gender hierarchy. In short, crossdressing female saints illustrate Paul's Gospel.

Q. 67 What did the Church Fathers say?

The Short Answer. While the Church has had plenty to say about gender roles, curiously Christianity has generally not been overly concerned with crossdressing. This is seen from the beginning in the indifference of the New Testament and the scarcity of comment in the voluminous writings of the Church Fathers. The remarks of Christianity's most prominent writers in its first half millennium generally treat crossdressing as something adjunctive to a more substantial interest under consideration. That interest, often enough, is gender. As always, crossdressing must be kept in the context of gender, and thus how the Fathers of the Church treat gender matters. There is some fairness in the argument made by various scholars that patriarchalism, incipient at the Church's founding, becomes well-established in the next few centuries. Consistent with the character of the biblical voices, there is both a certain consistency of theme and a measure of variability among the Church Fathers that means while we can draw broad strokes of similarity, we must also recognize meaningful degrees of difference. In general terms, discussion of dress tends to focus on two groups within the Church (ecclesiastical figures and women), and one outside it (actors). Perhaps the most prominent idea about dress is the importance of modesty. In this respect, women are especially admonished to dress modestly, and much of what is presented has to do with what one should *not* wear. One of the more interesting aspects of how the Church Fathers handle the subject of gender is the disjunction between their feelings about actual gender distinctions and their freedom to employ gender metaphorically. With respect to the former, the Church Fathers both speak well of women, while setting out strictures that from a practical standpoint ensured they remained subordinate. Metaphorically, they could employ gender images with more freedom, relying on a biblical tradition that pictured the Church as the Bride of Christ, or the Christian as clothing him- or herself in Christ. Thus, although they could express unease at actual gender variant behavior, they weren't reluctant to employ a gender variant voice to articulate theology. With respect to gender differentiated dress, and crossdressing, a prominent issue is deception—a matter that makes criticism of actors attractive to some theologians. The Church Fathers display no discernible interest in what today we would call 'gender identity.' For them, what matters is how dress is used. If it is employed as an artifice for some unseemly gain, then it is wrong. By this logic, though, we might wonder if they would find objectionable dress meant by the wearer to convey a truthful gender sense.

The Longer Answer. Christianity can hardly be called gender blind; its historic inequities with respect to gender are not merely well-documented, they are patently obvious to even casual observers. For many centuries the Church has been a bastion of Western culture's entrenched gender hierarchy. To be sure, some Protestant groups have mounted mild challenges to the hegemony of a larger body like Roman Catholicism, which continues to exclude women from the priesthood.[68] But even among those denominations that permit women in the clergy, the power both nationally and locally has almost entirely resided with men. Defenders of this patriarchal structure often point out that Jesus' own twelve disciples were men, and the founding Apostles of the Church—Peter, James, Paul—likewise were men.

Those who decry the gender inequality in the Church respond to such thinking by pointing to a long line of prominent women figures in the Bible, including some in leadership positions like Deborah the prophetess (Judges 4:4). They note that in the New Testament women were among the followers of Jesus even unto his crucifixion (Matthew 27:55-56), when his 'masculine' disciples had deserted him (Matthew 26:31). In fact, women were the first witnesses to his resurrection (Matthew 28:1-10). Between the resurrection and Pentecost, women waited alongside the men (Acts 1:14). They were included fully in the outpouring of the Holy Spirit, as had been prophesied (Acts 2:17-18). Some, like Tabitha of Lydda, were greatly honored for their good works (Acts 9:36-42). It appears that a woman like Priscilla (or Prisca), wife of Aquila, worked alongside him in Christian ministry (Acts 18:2; Romans 16:3; 1 Corinthians 16:19). Women held key roles in the faith community, such as being deacons (Phoebe, in Romans 16:1-2), and even apostles (Junia, 'prominent among the apostles,' Romans 16:7). In sum, it seems there is no intrinsic reason women should not be permitted all the same opportunities and avenues of service as men. But they have not been.

How do the Church Fathers talk about gender?

Gender lines and distinctions organized in a hierarchical fashion always seem to have mattered in the Church. The period of the Church Fathers, extending from the end of the New Testament period over the first few centuries of the Common Era (C.E.), wrestled with such distinctions despite their allegiance to Paul's declaration, "There is no longer Jew or Greek, there is no longer slave or free, there is no longer male or female, for all of you are one in Christ Jesus" (Galatians 3:28). This text put the Church Fathers in a bind. As historian Jo Ann McNamara remarks, "patristic writers were committed to the doctrine that with God there is neither male nor female. Thus, despite the personal proclivities of many of its formulators, the logic of Christian doctrine required a commitment to sexual equality."[69] Yet that commitment was qualified by just as much fervor for other ideas, like Paul's teaching on the subordinate role of women in the Church (1 Corinthians 11:3-16). Moreover, models with respect to gender roles could be interpreted in different ways. There also always was the pressure of the wider societies in which Christians dwelled. To cope with the varying tensions confronting them the Church Fathers had to engage their creativity, and did so. As they struggled to articulate ideas on gender and gender relations they sought to be honest with the reality of a fallen creation while aspiring to a redeemed one.

Figurative Gender Language

Their efforts were aided by metaphor. Gender language can be used both literally and figuratively. For example, the biblical precedent of referring to the Church as the bride of Christ (Ephesians 5:25-33) justified later writers employing feminine terms to refer to themselves, as Origen of Alexandria did in the early 3rd century,[70] and other writers—men and women—would do in later centuries (see the answer to Q. 76). Allegory—a particularly strong reliance on symbolic meaning for interpreting and applying biblical texts—became a prominent tool in late antiquity among Christian writers. This use of language offered ways not merely to say things about God, but about human beings as well, including things about the nature of gender itself. Historian Peter Brown suggests, for example, that Origen's rejection of sexuality was about more than repression of sexual drives: "It meant the assertion of a basic freedom so intense, a sense of identity so deeply rooted, as to cause to evaporate the normal social and physical constraints that tied the Christian to his or her gender."[71]

This radical vision could not only make figurative gender crossing a reality, but inspire action in life as well. Though our interest here will focus on the literal, practical exigencies of gender, we must be aware that the Church Fathers freely employed symbolic uses of gender to address lived realities, as we shall see shortly.

Gender Realities

However gender inequality in the real world might be explained, its existence was irrefutable and the Church Fathers had to reckon with it. In so doing they both decried inequities and often supported practices that perpetuated them. McNamara observes that the Church Fathers were cognizant of what women *could* do, but tended to be restrictive in saying what women *should* do.[72] Some degree of the evident duality about women may be attributed to a desire to combat what they saw as extremists who championed radicalism of one or another kind. An example or two should illustrate the dilemma they faced and how a way between the extremes was sought or fashioned.

Seeking a Way Between Extremes: Clement of Alexandria

Near the beginning of the period of the Church Fathers, Clement of Alexandria (late 2nd-early 3rd century) in his *Stromata* (*Miscellanies*) wrestled with the conflicting tensions about gender relations among those who called themselves Christians. On the one hand were libertines, like the Carpocratians. Clement decried the teaching of Epiphanes, proponent of the Carpocratian heresy,[73] as set forth in a book titled *Concerning Righteousness*. The Carpocratians strenuously advanced a notion of equality that purported to eliminate artificial distinctions between males and females, such as those instituted by monogamous marriage. They advocated an equality that permitted men and women to have sexual relations freely with one another (*Stromata* III.2.6-8).[74] Clement rejected this position as making a mockery of the biblical regulations on marriage.

On the other hand, Clement was barely more sympathetic to the ascetics who advocated a renunciation of marriage. Their position was that they were faithfully following the example of Jesus. In fact, some taught that marriage is the invention of the devil and marital relations mere fornication. Clement accused such folk of hiding beneath a pious cloak as they blasphemed both the Creator and his creation by their words and works (*Stromata* III.6.45-49).

Yet renunciation of heretics is a *via negativa* theologically. What about a *via positiva*? Negotiating such a path was not easy. Much discourse in the Church Fathers centers on the practical problems connected with marriage and divorce—the male-female relationship *sine qua non* for humanity. Clement, for example, addresses Jesus' saying about the eunuch in Matthew 19:12 as referring to the question whether a man is free to remarry after having divorced his wife for fornication (*Stromata* III.6.50; on the eunuch, cf. III.15.98-99). He explains the example of the apostles as demonstrating marriages that were in accordance with their particular ministries. In order not to be distracted from their work, Clement says, "they took their wives with them not as women with whom they had marriage relations, but as sisters, that they might be their fellow-ministers in dealing with housewives."[75] Is this, for women, equality or subordination? Clement does not say.

He advances his position as one of gender relations characterized by freedom from desire through control of the will. That will, he says, should be directed only toward that which is necessary. A man who enters marriage to have children ought to love his wife—but not desire her. Procreation should proceed with a chaste and controlled will (*Stromata* III.7.58).

It is in the context of disputing the ascetics who refrain from marriage altogether that Clement cites the *Gospel of the Egyptians*:

> Those who are opposed to God's creation, disparaging it under the fair name of continence, also quote the words to Salome which we mentioned earlier. They are found, I believe, in the Gospel according to the Egyptians. They say that the Saviour himself said "I came to destroy the works of the female," meaning by "female" desire, and by "works" birth and corruption.[76]

Clement does not deny the words attributed to Jesus are authentic, but he interprets them as meaning that humanity under sin shall continue to struggle with desires until the full redemption and restoration of God's elect is accomplished.

A number of things are worth noting here. First, clearly there was in circulation a teaching attributed to Jesus that sounds hostile to women. Second, and equally clear, this saying was interpreted in more than one fashion. It could, for example, be understood along the lines of the last *logia* of the Gospel of Thomas, so that the destruction of the works of the female parallels the act of becoming male and so achieving salavation—both aspects being understood metaphorically. Or, it might be seen as reflecting a line of logic that identified women with the flesh (always at war with the spirit), flesh with the world, and the world with the devil.[77] But Clement seems to understand it (noting later that it is not a saying found in the four canonical gospels) in a way that makes 'female' symbolic of an inherent and very real process—the cycle of birth and death. If she is the bringer of death, she is also the author of life (*Stromata* III.9.64-65). He seeks a middle path by which a person of self-control may either choose marriage or refrain from it.

Rethinking Gender: Gregory of Nyssa

In the 4th century, Gregory of Nyssa wrestled with gender in a somewhat different manner. Not quite forming a theory, he nevertheless managed to articulate ideas in service of a new vision of gender realities. Religious scholar Michael Nausner writes, "To me it is clear that Gregory, in spite of his repeated recurrence to gender stereotypes, aims at a community that transforms lives in resistance to communal life that is structured in accordance to fixed gender identities and erotic roles."[78]

Nausner sees the key in Gregory's eschatology, which views the terminus of history in a restoration of the original state of creation. In accord with other scholars, he points out that Gregory believed that the original creation of humanity was without sex differentiation.[79] Gregory's comment in *On the Creation of Man* states his position clearly:

> Thus the creation of our nature must in some way have been double; that which renders us like God and that which establishes the division of the sexes. And indeed such an interpretation is suggested by the very order of the account. Scripture says in the first place, "God made man; in the image of God, he made him." Only after that is it added, "He made them male and female," a division foreign to the divine attributes.[80]

Any gender hierarchy thus established on Eve being taken from Adam's side is thereby voided if the end of all things is a return to our original state. Such a view, by the way, predates Gregory of Nyssa; it is a notion found in earlier literature such as the pseudepigrapha.[81]

Whether Nausner is correct or not in his surmise of Gregory's aim, he is surely right in observing that the Father's treatment of gender is both complex and ambiguous. In terms of our own discussion, Gregory both employs figurative use of gender language and offers models of real people who in their personal traits and behavior escape the gender expectations of their society. When these two characteristics of his work come together they leave an impression that in the here-and-now it is possible for God's people to live such that they anticipate an ultimate reality beyond the confines of gender roles and expectations. Precisely by working with the real roles and expectations of his own time and place, Gregory points out the possibility of gender transcendence.

Nausner observes that Gregory uses both himself and his sister Macrina the Younger as examples.[82] The latter model is the one that has drawn the most attention. In his praise of Macrina, Gregory writes:

> As often happens at such times, the [960 B] talk flowed on until we came to discuss the life of some famous person. In this case it was a woman who provided us with our subject; if indeed she should be styled 'woman' for I do not know whether it is fitting to designate her by her sex, who so surpassed her sex.[83]

How did Macrina surpass her sex? She did so by embodying characteristics associated with men. She exhibits a rationality and intelligence that leads Gregory to describe her through an unconventional use of gender language as 'the [feminine article] teacher [masculine noun]' (*he didaskolos*—ἡ διδάσκολος).[84] In his biography of her, *De Vita Macrinae* (*Life of Macrina*), Gregory again combines gender in applying to her the titles both of 'mother' and 'father' [Greek πατήρ] in her care of her youngest brother, Peter, after the death of their parents.[85] In light of his treatise *On the Soul and the Resurrection*—a treatise based on a dialog with Macrina as she lay on her deathbed—it seems reasonable to suppose he had her in mind as the kind of person who in this life resembles one who in the resurrection will be restored to an original nature transcending binary gender.

Gender Stereotypes: The Promulgation of a Gender Hierarchy

Both Clement of Alexandria and Gregory of Nyssa in their own ways sought a path between the lofy ideal expressed by Paul and the cold reality of gender relations in their worldly experience. They could ignore neither, but finding a true path—one honoring a gender ideal but practical—was elusive, too. The difficulty of a middle way may be especially obvious in how the Church Fathers depict masculine and feminine attributes. McNamara points out that while they might proclaim that 'man' used in a general manner refers to both men and women, their actual gendering of 'man' presents masculine attributes as higher than feminine ones.[86] Hearkening back to the New Testament voice, women could not escape being "the weaker sex" (1 Peter 3:7). All too often in the Church Fathers we encounter such disparaging remarks about women as that of Ambrose, who could casually equate unbelief with women[87]—a remarkable judgment in light of the biblical stories mentioned earlier.

As for the traits associated with masculinity and femininity, we might follow others in offering a short accounting of both positive and negative traits distilled from patristic writings. If we put these in Table form we have the following short list:

Table 67.1 Gender Stereotypes[88]

Feminine Positive	Feminine Negative	Masculine Positive
Compunctious (tender conscience)	False	Intelligent
Full of faith	Garrulous (chatty)	Strong in action
Humble	Given to drink	Powerful in the public sphere
Intuitive	Irrational	Possessing great endurance
Nurturing	Morally depraved	Rational
Obedient	Ostentatious	Virtuous
Pure	Quarrelsome	
Sensible	Weak	
Submissive	Wicked	

Lynda Coon, Katherine Haldane, and Elisabeth Sommer maintain that, "through the patristic definition of masculine and feminine, late antiquity set the stage for future differentiation of gender roles."[89]

As we know, the unfolding of this legacy led slowly to an ever more sharply drawn sense of gender duality. Women remained relegated to subordinate status, diminished rewards, and fewer opportunities in life. Within the Church, when they proved their spiritual mettle they were liable to be praised as strong members of their weaker sex, or as transcending their feminine nature, even perhaps earning praise as having become 'male.'[90] Yet women who took such words as authorization to actually emulate men in their manner and appearance more often earned rebuke (cf. Jerome's words, below), despite the multiple accounts of crossdressing saints. It is this reality that leads us closer to gender crossings—or transgressions as they were apt to be viewed—and the intrinsic role played by dress.

Gender Differentiated Dress

Where gender matters, gender lines must be marked. Gender differentiated dress does that. Not surprisingly, then, some attention has been given this matter off and on throughout Church history. Our attention here is limited to the so-called 'Church Fathers'—the most prominent Christian theologians of the first few centuries of the Church. Their influence helped entrench and justify a patriarchal structure to the Christian community. They spoke both praise and condemnation of women, leaving plenty of strands for latter writers to select for their own use. Overall, the balance struck seems to settle in efforts to keep women controlled. Thus, with respect to gender differentiated dress, more attention is given to what women wear and how they appear than to the dress of men. Much of what is said concerns what a woman should *not* do or wear. Along those lines, it is paramount that she should refrain from appearing like a man. To appear like a man may be construed as a disruption of the natural order, but it mostly seems to bother objectors as an effort to usurp a superior status.

Crossdressing

Though attention to dress is unsurprising, it perhaps may be surprising how relatively little attention is specifically given to crossdressing by the Church Fathers. Yet, this practice occurred with some regularity among those who called themselves Christians as well as in the wider cultures of which Christians were a part. The reasons for the practice varied, and some recognition of this occurs in various writings both religious and secular. The weight attached to crossdressing by different theologians is in part a function of the general regard for the role of clothes in the life of the Christian, and on this point ancient thinkers differed. It is in light of this larger consideration that our brief survey starts.

As the Church struggled to find a common voice (a struggle still ongoing), various writers and groups adopted considerably different stances on the role played by apparel. Many saw it as a relatively minor issue; most urged simplicity and modesty in dress. In fact, as we shall presently see, the connection of clothes to modesty became the general thread by which most later theological documents connected themselves to crossdressing. It is, however, rare to find a Christian writing of any kind preoccupied with the practice. Instead, it is most often mentioned incidentally and used as an illustration in service of some larger point (like modesty).

It also can be said that not all clothing or groups are equal. Relatively more attention is given to two groups: *religious officials* and *women*. The former held offices distinguished, in part, by their garb. The latter had been addressed by biblical texts and, in a male dominated hierarchy, were an obvious and easy target in the struggle against carnal temptations. Like clergy, women receive a good amount of attention in terms of what is seemly or not to wear. A third group—*actors*—also merits attention, as they are those most directly discussed as crossdressing, a common practice for many centuries because men played all the roles. Some selections from ancient texts will illustrate these matters.

What did Clement of Alexandria say?

In the late 2nd and early 3rd century C.E., Clement of Alexandria set forth a simple, rather austere philosophy regarding Christians and clothes:

> I say, then, that man requires clothes for nothing else than the covering of the body, for defence against excess of cold and intensity of heat, lest the inclemency of the air injure us. And if this is the object of clothing, see that one kind be not assigned to men and another to women. For it is common to both to be covered, as it is to eat and drink. The necessity, then, being common, we judge that the provision ought to be similar. For as it is common to both to require things to cover them, so also their coverings ought to be similar; although such a covering ought to be assumed as is requisite for covering the eyes of women. For if the female sex, on account of their weakness, desire more, we ought to blame the habit of that evil training, by which often men reared up in bad habits become more effeminate than women. But this must not be yielded to. And if some accommodation is to be made, they may be permitted to use softer clothes, provided they put out of the way fabrics foolishly thin, and of curious texture in weaving; bidding farewell to embroidery of gold and Indian silks and elaborate Bombyces (silks), which is at first a worm, then from it is produced a hairy caterpillar; after which the creature suffers a new transformation into a third form which they call larva, from which a long filament is produced, as the spider's thread from the spider. For these superfluous and diaphanous materials are the proof of a weak mind, covering as they do the shame of the body with a slender veil. For luxurious clothing, which cannot conceal the shape of the body, is no more a covering. For such clothing, falling close to the body, takes its form more easily, and adhering as it were to the flesh, receives its shape, and marks out the woman's figure, so that the whole make of the body is visible to spectators, though not seeing the body itself.[91]

Clement here assumes the purpose of clothing is protection against the elements and, since both men and women need similar protection, similar garb is warranted. He attributes women's "weakness" for the desire to have more in dress. But he notes how evil training and bad habits can entice men, too, into craving such luxury in clothing that they are rendered effeminate by it. While Clement urges not yielding to such desire, he does grant a concession: women can be permitted softer clothing, as long as it remains simple rather than luxurious. The latter is no longer a covering, but reveals the shape beneath—and that can be the occasion for sin.

Interestingly, when Clement hearkens back to the Deuteronomic code, he treats it not in a concrete way with reference to clothing, but in a metaphorical manner: "What reason is there in the law's prohibiting a man from 'wearing woman's clothing'? Is it not that it would have us to be manly, and not to be effeminate neither in person and actions, nor in thought and word?"[92]

In this way Clement remains consistent. Clothes are not what matter, except as they either cover and protect us, or expose us and make us vulnerable to sin. What does matter is strength of character. The legal precept with regard to clothes, then, is a matter of being strong. Men are to be "manly"—strong in character, acts, thinking and speech. For a man to wear clothes associated with women is to also associate with their presumed weakness.

What did Tertullian say?

Another familiar idea is seen in a later text: truth in advertising. Prominent in the early 3rd century, the vigorous theologian Tertullian invokes Deuteronomy 22:5 in service of his condemnation of actors:

> The Author of truth hates all the false; He regards as adultery all that is unreal. Condemning, therefore, as He does hypocrisy in every form, He never will approve any putting on of voice, or sex, or age; He never will approve pretended loves, and wraths, and groans, and tears. Then, too, as in His law it is declared that the man is cursed who attires himself in female garments, what must be His judgment of the pantomime, who is even brought up to play the woman![93]

Tertullian makes no pretence about what he is doing. The appeal to Deuteronomy is not interpretive in nature. He is applying the text, adding logic to his understanding of a general purpose to reach his conclusion. *If* God hates what is false, and *if* actors practice falsehood (in voice and action as well as in dress), *then* God must surely detest actors! Tertullian is principally interested in condemning the pretence practiced by actors; crossdressing is just one aspect of this pretence, albeit an aspect for which a biblical text is conveniently at hand. But it would be a mistake to view Tertullian as starting from Deuteronomy. Rather, he starts from a general principle and uses Deuteronomy to support his point.

What did Cyprian say?

A lengthier diatribe against actors occurs in the mid-3rd century, when the Bishop of Carthage, Cyprian, wrote the following in a letter:

> 1. Cyprian to Euchratius his brother, greeting. From our mutual love and your reverence for me you have thought that I

should be consulted, dearest brother, as to my opinion concerning a certain actor, who, being settled among you, still persists in the discredit of the same art of his; and as a master and teacher, not for the instruction, but for the destruction of boys, that which he has unfortunately learnt he also imparts to others: you ask whether such a one ought to communicate with us. This, I think, neither befits the divine majesty nor the discipline of the Gospel, that the modesty and credit of the Church should be polluted by so disgraceful and infamous a contagion. For since, in the law, men are forbidden to put on a woman's garment, and those that offend in this manner are judged accursed, how much greater is the crime, not only to take women's garments, but also to express base and effeminate and luxurious gestures, by the teaching of an immodest art.

2. Nor let any one excuse himself that he himself has given up the theatre, while he is still teaching the art to others. For he cannot appear to have given it up who substitutes others in his place, and who, instead of himself alone, supplies many in his stead; against God's appointment, instructing and teaching in what way a man may be broken down into a woman, and his sex changed by art, and how the devil who pollutes the divine image may be gratified by the sins of a corrupted and enervated body.[94]

Cyprian's argument may appeal to the same biblical text used by Tertullian, but his reasoning is different. He condemns the actor for a crime "much greater" than merely crossdressing: teaching—or rather, corrupting—boys by his "immodest art." The true seriousness of the crime in Cyprian's eyes lies in how this art teaches males to appear as females—"his sex changed by art." This can only lead to sin. The Church continued to struggle with the deceptions of the theater, though without marked success either in curbing the staging of plays or in keeping the faithful from watching them.

What did Ambrose of Milan say?

Ambrose of Milan, in the 4th century, provided an important link between two figures today better known than himself: Origen before him, and Augustine after him. A master of allegory, Ambrose employed gender language figuratively and, says Kim Power, an expert on his work, helped shape the gender stereotypes so influential in the Church.[95] Interestingly, while it was self-evident to him that men were superior to women, he did not hesitate to employ feminine ascription to such vital matters as the human soul. Power sees this use accomplishing two ends: it demonstrates the soul's moral fragility, and it establishes the soul's submissive subordination to Christ the Bridegroom.[96]

73

Embracing an already well-established tradition of thinking on the matter, Ambrose envisions a godly woman as one possessing virile traits. Yet despite any spiritual achievements, she was to remain visibly feminine in every way. Her hair was to be worn long, and her dress both modest and unambiguously feminine. Virginity was especially prized, and Ambrose wrote extensively about virgins—female virgins, that is. As the epitome of womanhood, a virgin is one "in whom modesty adorns their age, and silence commends their modesty."[97]

Dress, for Ambrose, is crucial to gender differentiation. In a letter to Irenaeus, he responds to a question concerning those who disguise their sex. After citing Deuteronomy 22:5, he asks a series of rhetorical questions, followed by a general premise:

> Now, if you will consider it well, that which nature herself abhors must be incongruous. For why do you not wish to be thought a man, seeing that you are born such? why do you assume an appearance which is foreign to you? why do you play the woman, or you, O woman, the man? *Nature clothes each sex in their proper raiment.* Moreover in men and women, habits, complexion, gestures, gait, strength and voice are all different.[98]

Ambrose especially can scarcely credit any male not wanting to be seen as a man, though he addresses both sexes. For him, Nature has fixed a gulf marked by natural differences, not merely in body, but in manner as well. Still, he is aware of cultural differences, such as among the Greeks. This example, in fact, elicits an admission that he can grasp why a female might wish to appear as a man. But he remains baffled as to why any male might want to be seen as a woman. "Be it allowed however that they should imitate the nature of the more worthy sex," he writes of women, "but why should men choose to assume the appearance of the inferior?"[99]

It is a query for which he has no answer. Instead, he resorts immediately to the core iniquity: "A falsehood is base even in word, much more in dress." Like the ancient Hebrews did, he links crossdressing to heathen religious practices. "It is there considered holy for men to assume women's garments, and female gestures" he notes, and then declares this is the reason for the biblical prohibition.[100]

Bad as merely donning the apparel of another gender is, even worse is assuming their manner. It is our habits and actions that especially matter, says Ambrose. A certain kind of act befits men; another kind is fitting for women. To support this assertion he appeals—as he often does elsewhere—to Paul's instructions for order in the Church (1 Corinthians 14:33b-35). There the Apostle forbids women to speak in the assembly of Christians. This is buttressed with the even stronger language of 1 Timothy 2:11-12.[101]

Ambrose proceeds to use sarcasm to underscore his point: "As for those who curl their hair, like women, let them conceive also, let them bring forth." His logic remains that of the Essentialist; it is the very nature of things that men

74

and women wear their hair differently and dress differently. In fact, for Ambrose, Nature trumps culture. In a blatant use of gender stereotyping, Ambrose declares, "the one sex wears veils, the other wages war."[102]

Finally, Ambrose proclaims that such inappropriate habits of dress, which include not merely clothing but also ornamentation, endanger chastity. Where a clear and unambiguous distinction between men and women is lost, sexual impropriety cannot be far behind.[103]

What did Jerome say?

The problem of deception through dress and manner was also on the mind of another prominent figure. Jerome, perhaps the greatest biblical scholar of the 4th century C.E., in his famous letter to Eustochium, touches upon the problem within Church circles. His context concerns the use of an altered appearance by Christians for duplicitous purposes. He speaks of both women and men who change their dress and their demeanor to appear differently than they are and thus gain attention. For example, he cautions against exchanging costly garb for simple attire as a means of winning favor (i.e., for piety), or disfiguring the face so as to appear to have been fasting. In this same vein he describes women who dress as men:

> Others change their garb and assume the mien of men, being ashamed of being what they were born to be—women. They cut off their hair and are not ashamed to look like eunuchs. Some clothe themselves in goat's hair, and, putting on hoods, think to become children again by making themselves look like so many owls.[104]

But women are not alone in such deceptions. Immediately afterward he writes:

> But I will not speak only of women. Avoid men, also, when you see them loaded with chains and wearing their hair long like women, contrary to the apostle's precept, not to speak of beards like those of goats, black cloaks, and bare feet braving the cold. All these things are tokens of the devil.[105]

From this remark he then proceeds to speak of those Christian men who seek the offices of the church (deacon and presbyter) for improper reasons. Jerome says of them that their only purpose is ease of access to women and their only thought is for their dress, by which he also means their use of perfumes and the curling of their hair. In all these things, Jerome is not concerned with clothes *per se*, but with their misuse to perpetuate deception in religious guise. In short, Christians misuse clothes when they try to portray themselves as more pious than they are in fact.

We should note, on the other hand, that Jerome did not oppose the kind of gender crossing that a woman might do in seeking salvation—providing it was done 'properly.' Jerome proclaimed, "As long as a woman is for birth and children she is as different from man as body is from soul. But when she wishes to serve Christ more than the world, then she will cease to be a woman and will be called man."[106]

What did John Chrysostom say?

Another prominent figure returns to the notion of preserving distinctions in dress as part of keeping a 'proper' order between men and women. In the late 4th—early 5th century C.E., John Chrysostom, Archbishop of Constantinople and revered as one of the greatest of the Church Fathers, wrote:

> Symbols many and diverse have been given both to man and woman; to him of rule, to her of subjection: and among them this also, that she should be covered, while he hath his head bare. If now these be symbols, you see that both err when they disturb the proper order, and transgress the disposition of God, and their own proper limits, both the man falling into the woman's inferiority, and the woman rising up against the man by her outward habiliments.
>
> For if exchange of garments be not lawful, so that neither she should be clad with a cloak, nor he with a mantle or a veil: ("for the woman," saith He, "shall not wear that which pertaineth to a man, neither shall a man put on a woman's garments:") much more is it unseemly for these (Deuteronomy chapter 22, verse 5) things to be interchanged. For the former indeed were ordained by men, even although God afterwards ratified them: but this by nature, I mean the being covered or uncovered. But when I say Nature, I mean God. For He it is Who created Nature. When therefore thou overturnest these boundaries, see how great injuries ensue.[107]

Chrysostom upholds the assumption of his world: men are established above women. A symbol of this is women having their heads covered, while men's heads remain bare—an injunction found in the New Testament (1 Corinthians 11:4-10). Regardless of whether it is the man or woman who does otherwise, the act constitutes a disturbing of "the proper order." Chrysostom portrays this in a dire manner: when a man does such he is "falling into the woman's inferiority," while a woman so transgressing is "rising up against the man." Deuteronomy 22:5 is advanced as an inferior case of the same kind; *if* men and women wearing the garments of the opposite sex is "not lawful," *then* how much more "unseemly" is violating the ordinance on coverings.[108] In either case, garb is relevant to the higher cause of preserving the order of the sexes.

As has been true throughout Christian history, the Church Fathers were generally more active in applying Scripture than interpreting it in a historical-literary fashion. They were apt to attach biblical texts to a variety of contemporary matters, thus both proving the continuing relevance of the Bible and appealing to its authority. In this way they used the text of Deuteronomy 22:5, borrowing its power to make points about such matters as actors and acting—though there is no evidence such a concern was at all in mind for the writer of Deuteronomy. Theologically, their interest in clothing was largely twofold: first, to maintain a modesty in dress that would not detract attention from Christian behavior (an idea consistent with the apostolic thinking of the New Testament), and second, to preserve some form of boundary between the genders, largely to maintain a social order where males enjoyed preeminence. The Church Fathers appear indifferent to such modern preoccupations as crossdressing as sexually fetishistic.

Q. 68 Are there crossdressing saints?

The Short Answer. The creative tension reflected in the writings of the Church Fathers was mirrored in the lived reality of gender relations in the Church. Women, in particular, struggled to realize in their own lives the promise of Paul's Gospel that in clothing themselves in Christ Jesus there would no longer be artificial lines drawn between male and female, meaning an equality of opportunity for Christian service. Yet the practices of the Church continued to exclude them from coveted avenues of devotion. Not all women accepted the limitations put upon them. Some found that to clothe themselves in Christ meant the literal putting on of masculine apparel and the assumption of a man's identity and role. For some this was only for a temporary period in their lives; for others the assumption of manhood lasted the remainder of their lives. Regardless of duration, and irrespective of the immediate stimulus for such radical action, all distinguished themselves by the purity and zeal of their devotion. In both Orthodox and Catholic traditions many such crossdressing women became recognized as saints. Such figures can be found throughout Church history, starting with early accounts of a woman named Thecla, said to be a companion of Paul. Nearly three dozen women who gained sainthood can be grouped under the heading of 'crossdressing saints.' For most, crossdressing was connected to one or another issue associated with marriage. For some, crossdressing was pursued to protect their virginity—highly valued in the Church for a very long time—when compulsorary marriage looked imminent. Their history, spanning more than a thousand years, perhaps climaxes with the most famous female crossdresser of all, Joan of Arc. Few today realize how seriously both her accusers and Joan herself regarded her appearance in masculine martial dress. Collectively, these women had various motives for crossdressing, but none of their reasons had anything to do with immorality. In fact, crossdressing was an aspect of behavior associated with exceptional piety in lives recognized as truly saintly. Though rare, and of a different character, there also have been male saints associated with crossdressing. Serge and Bacchus were military men noted for their devotion to Christ and to one another. Their crossdressing was forced upon them, in order to shame them, but it did not deter their witness. In fact, they used it to proclaim themselves brides of Christ. Like the female crossdressing saints, being clothed in Christ meant their literal apparel paled in importance and derived significance only to the degree it facilitated their Christian service.

The Longer Answer. There are saints, both male and female, who cross-dressed. In fact, crossdressing is integral to their stories. However, the women saints who crossdressed far outnumber their male counterparts. There are other differences as well, reflecting the differing status of men and women in both church and world. Thus, the most famous example of crossdressed male saints features two men forced to crossdress in an attempt to humiliate them; no parallel to this motive exists among the female saints. Since most of our attention in this answer will be on these women, we shall begin with some general remarks.

Christian tradition from the beginning has consistently favored modesty in women's dress, though exactly what constitutes modest dress has been variously interpreted. However, for the most part one aspect of such modesty, meant to reflect the different place women have been assigned from men, has been a gender-based differentiation in clothing. However contextually understood, Christian women in every time and place generally have been expected to look different from men. This distinction in dress has paralleled a distinction in roles and status in the Church.

Accordingly, as a rule, Christian authorities have not looked with favor on women who crossdress because in crossing gender lines they threaten the order that religion preserves. So it may come as a surprise to learn that a number of crossdressing women have been viewed as especially pious, and many of them have gained sainthood. Curiously enough, the very women who proved exceptionally adept at passing as men escaped lasting censure despite most seriously violating jealously guarded male prerogatives, such as various venues of Christian ministry and leadership, and habitation among monks. Put most bluntly, their success at doing what men most feared—passing as one of them—was instrumental to realizing their devotion to Christ, and led ultimately to their recognition as saints. The acknowledgment of the importance of crossing gender lines to their attainment of sainthood resides in their being called 'crossdressing saints.'

These women chose to live as men because only in so doing could they realize a spiritual vocation they recognized as coming from God. While pursuing their vocation could and did mean different things for various of them, often enough it entailed entering a world set apart for men—the religious monastery. As Lynne Dahmen observes, their putting on men's clothing offered them a chance to join in "a realm inherently masculine," a cloistered religious life.[109] Their drive and complete devotion to the service of their Lord proved far weightier than their crossdressing. Such piety amazed other Christians, eventually winning for these women dispensations of acceptance and respect unexpected in the face of their gender violations. In fact, the tolerance of the Church is notable in the number of crossdressing women who came to be recognized as saints. Valerie Hotchkiss has identified 34 so-called crossdressing female saints.[110]

The stories of these saints stretch across centuries. However, nearly a third of these were published during a particular stretch of time. Christian historian Stephen Davis notes that 11 *vitae* ('*Lives*') of female crossdressing monastic saints appeared from the late 5th century through the 7th century. He contends these stories exhibit subtle variations on a theme: crossdressing empowers the woman to enter monastic life liberated from the normal constraints of family expectations or social prejudice. Davis views these lives as simultaneously endorsing a bipolar view of gender and ultimately destabilizing it. He places the transvestite saint in the biblical context of the apostle Paul's declaration in Galatians 3:28 (cf. the answer to Q. 66); both, he argues, overturn the traditional binary conception of gender identity.[111]

Davis also highlights the history of interpretation of the lives of these saints. He observes that the few scholars of the late 19th and early 20th centuries to look at them tended to relegate them to a place of little historical value, seeing them as romantic studies designed to teach Christian piety with roots in classical literature and mythology. When more recent scholars turned new attention to these stories a decided difference in perspective emerged. These new studies sought to see the lives as shedding light on their context of early Christian thought and practice. Various avenues were used to explore them, including psychological, anthropological, and sociohistorical as well as literary and theological approaches. Each, in their own way, highlights the Church's struggle with gender and sex-based distinctions.[112] The crossdressing saint thus illuminates for us provocative and important notions that challenge the conservative instinct to preserve a gender dichotomy and gender order that work against the highest values of the Christian faith (cf. the answer to Q. 66).

With these thoughts in mind, it is to such individuals we now turn, using examples sequentially drawn across several centuries. By inserting the story of male saints who crossdressed at the appropriate place the contrast with the stories of these women should be even more starkly apparent.

Who was St. Thecla?[113]

Crossdressing behavior by saints starts in the era of the early Church. In the late 1st- to early 2nd century emerges the story of Thecla (or Thekla). Told in the New Testament Apocrypha,[114] Thecla was a young woman whose story was joined to that of the Apostle Paul. She attained such renown in her own right that she came to be regarded as saint, protomartyr, and "equal-to-the-apostles."

Thecla was a young virgin of 17 years of age when the apostle Paul visited Iconium, where she became the unwitting agent of trouble for him. It so happened that her mother was betrothed to one of the leading men of Iconium. When Thecla spent day after day in enraptured listening to this stranger, her mother was beside herself. Turning to her betrothed for aid, he made an inquiry that eventually led to Paul's arrest and imprisonment. Thecla bribed the guard to visit Paul in prison, where her new faith was strengthened. But when her mother found out where she had been, there was a great uproar. Both Paul and Thecla were brought for judgment and when she proved unrepentant, Paul was whipped and cast out of the city while Thecla was ordered to be burned.

Stripped naked, Thecla was presented for punishment. She made the sign of the cross, the fire was lit—and no harm befell her! Instead, a great cloudburst quenched the fire and Thecla was saved. She immediately followed after Paul and finding him presented herself to accompany him. She offered to cut her hair, but Paul, who saw her beauty, worried that she might later fall to temptation. Yet Thecla persisted in her devotion and accompanied him to Antioch.

In that city a powerful man named Alexander became infatuated with her. His lust got the better of him and he forced himself upon her in public. Thecla resisted and made him an object of ridicule. Thus shamed, he had Thecla brought to trial and after she confessed what she had done, she was once more condemned to death, this time by being fed to wild beasts. Though this judgment scandalized the local women, who cried out against its unfairness, Thecla was in due time put into the arena to die. Once more she was stripped and set out for public spectacle. However, divine intervention again spared her. Having made her Christian confession before the governor, he ordered her clothed and released. Only 18 years old, she already had twice escaped death.

Thecla then went seeking Paul again. Mindful of her previous experience, she made her garment into that of a man and went to the town of Myra in Lycia. Thus disguised she traveled safely to reach Paul. Thecla declared to him all that had happened to her and then announced her intention to return to Iconium. With his blessing, she did so, visiting her mother before retiring to an ascetic life. She lived in a cave outside Seleucia for some 72 years. At an advanced age she was again saved by miraculous intervention from trouble and went to Rome, where Paul had been martyred. There, aged 90 years, she died.

Who was St. Eugenia?[115]

In the mid- to late 3rd century, a lady of high birth sacrificed her social standing and life of privilege for the sake of Christ. Eugenia, daughter of the Roman governor of Egypt, desired to convert and serve Christ. According to Syriac and Armenian versions of her life, Eugenia possessed a copy of the *Acts of Paul and Thecla*; the example of Thecla inspired Eugenia to action and imitation.[116] With the aid of two servants, she disguised herself as a man and escaped the palace at Alexandria. Her ability to pass as a man proved remarkable. First, Eugenia made her way to Helenus, bishop of Heliopolis, who baptized her. The bishop sent her to an abbey, where she devoted herself to such good works as evangelism and caring for the sick. In time, she became the abbot in charge of the abbey.

However, one of the women who had recovered from illness under her ministrations, thinking her a man, made advances toward Eugenia. Rebuffed by the abbot, the scorned woman accused Eugenia of adultery. The trial was held before Eugenia's unsuspecting father. He believed the accusation and sentenced Eugenia. In prison, she managed by her testimony to draw her father to the Christian faith. Also, her true identity was revealed and she was freed. Later, in the company of her mother, who had also been converted, Eugenia went to Rome. There, both she and her mother were martyred. Her father became a bishop and also suffered martyrdom. Because Eugenia, while an abbot, had written a book, she became a patron saint to women writers.

Who were St. Serge and St. Bacchus?[117]

A remarkable story of two crossdressed male saints is placed at the turning of the 3rd into the 4th century, during the reign of the Emperor Maximian. These two Gentiles were officers in the Roman army. Serge was a friend of the emperor. Together with his constant companion, Bacchus, the two presented a Christian witness. This invited their enemies to denounce them as Christians, a charge with potentially serious consequences. The emperor, reluctant to believe the charge, asked them to accompany him as he went to the Temple of Zeus to make sacrifice. Serge and Bacchus remained outside. When forced to come in they refused the imperial order to offer sacrifice.

The emperor was greatly angered. As punishment Serge and Bacchus were stripped of all military insignia and clothing. Next they were dressed as women and, in chains, paraded publicly so as to shame them. This kind of compulsorary crossdressing was sometimes used to humiliate men who had shown cowardice and the public association with femininity for a military man was as calculated an insult as could be made. But the punishment was ineffective; the pair sang praise declaring they had been dressed as brides, and proclaiming that they were clothed in salvation and righteousness. After again making confession of their faith before the emperor they were reassigned to a remote province. However, they were promised that should they change their minds and make sacrifice to the gods their previous rank and wealth would be restored to them. This they were unwilling to do and following more Christian confession the unrepentant pair were imprisoned. Bacchus was flogged until he died. Not long after, following torture, Serge was beheaded.

Who was St. Pelagia?[118]

In the early 4th century lived a woman whose story has become entwined with legend to the extent that separating fact from fiction has long been problematic. What seems to have happened is that a Christian writer who named himself as 'James, Deacon of Antioch,' built upon the name of a young virgin girl named Pelagia who had been martyred in Antioch much earlier. He attached her name to a story told by the Church Father Chrysostom of an actress of Antioch. Thus joined these disparate accounts were further elaborated by the author to afford us the 'life' of a crossdressing saint.

St. Pelagia the Penitent (a.k.a. Margaret or Marina) of Antioch—patron saint of actresses and penitents—was noted for beauty, wealth, and a dissolute life. Called the chief actress of this great city, she was in some accounts depicted also as a harlot. In the account by James, Pelagia was one day riding a donkey, dressed only and completely in gold, pearls and precious stones used artfully to conceal parts of her body, but leaving both arms and legs completely exposed. Her retinue of followers consisted of merry-making boys and girls, all surrounded by music and the sweet smell of perfume. This procession suddenly competed for attention with a gathering before a church door where Bishop Nonnus (or Nonnos) of Edessa stood preaching.

As Pelagia passed by, her appearance prompted Nonnus' fellow bishops to avert their eyes, hiding their heads in their robes. Not Nonnus though. He fixed his eyes on her and used her as an object lesson, declaring that her zealous attention to her beauty and lovers put to shame himself and his fellow Christians, who had not shown at all such devotion. These words caught Pelagia's attention so that the next day she for the first time entered a church in order to hear him again. That day Nonnus preached a sermon on judgment and salvation. His words arrested her and she was convicted in spirit. She sought him out, asking for baptism. The good bishop was understandably reluctant. But Pelagia persuaded him through tears of her sincerity, weeping as prostrate she clutched his feet. She converted, was baptized, and gave her wealth to the care of the poor and widows, and freed all her slaves.

Thus abandoning her former manner of life, Pelagia took on male dress, exchanging her lavish outfits first for a baptismal robe and then for some clothing of the Bishop himself, at her request. The articles she received were a hair shirt and wollen mantle. She modified her name to the masculine form of 'Pelagius,' and traveled to Jerusalem. There she took up residence as an ascetic hermit in a cave on the Mount of Olives. Over time she became renowned as 'the beardless monk,' being perceived by others as a male eunuch. Pelagia's strictness toward her way of living took its toll. She became emaciated and weakened in body even as her spirit proved strong. After a period of about three years her self-imposed discipline finally claimed her life. Her true sex was only rediscovered at her death as her body was being prepared for burial.

Who was St. Athanasia?[119]

In the 5th century, St. Athanasia embarked on a remarkable course of action. A native of Alexandria in Egypt, she had married a local silversmith named Andronicus and had two children with him. He was a pious man who gave most of his earnings to the care of the poor and the ministry of the Church. The couple took up residence in Antioch, where an unfortunate turn of events (perhaps a plague) resulted in the death of their son and daughter on the same day. Where her husband bore his grief more stoically, Athanasia was beside herself, refusing to leave the church where they were buried, resolved to remain until she also should die. But a vision of St. Julian the martyr, for whom the church was named, persuaded her otherwise. This prompted Athanasia and Andronicus to decide to dedicate their lives to God's service. They first freed their slaves, sold everything and gave away their wealth, then departed to take up religious lives of solitude, separated from each other. He became a monk; she either a nun or a hermit.

Different versions of her story account variously for her decision to cross-dress. As a hermit in the Egyptian desert it would make sense to disguise herself as a man to be left alone. If a nun in a convent there would be no need to do so for safety unless leaving the convent to journey alone somewhere. So, one version has it that more than a decade after separating from her husand, Athanasia determined to make a holy pilgrimage to Jerusalem. For her own safety, she took on masculine garb, calling herself 'Athanasius.' Along the way to Jerusalem she accidently met Andronicus, who did not recognize her, so altered was she by a dozen years of ascetic life. They continued to Jerusalem together, cementing bonds of brotherhood. Subsequently they journeyed back to Egypt together and took up residence in the same monastery, sharing a cell and a vow of silence. For twelve years the only words they spoke in each other's presence were their prayers. When she died after being stricken by a fever, a note she had left revealed her true identity to him. By another account, she confided on her deathbed her secret to the abbot of the monastery, who in turn revealed it to Andronicus when a short time later the same fever brought him also to life's edge. After his death the couple were buried side by side.

Who was St. Euphrosyne?[120]

Also in the 5th century, St. Euphrosyne of Alexandria followed a course similar to some of the other saints. Euphrosyne was something of a miracle baby, having been born when her parents were aged, after the intercession of a monk. Paphnutius, her father, wished to marry her to a wealthy man, but Euphrosyne preferred to devote herself to Christ alone. During an absence of her father, she gave away her possessions and became a nun. In this station she became a student of the very monk who had prayed for her birth.

But Euphrosyne, fearing her family's intervention, took on the manner and appearance of a monk. Calling herself "Smaragdus," she established a reputation as a wise teacher. Her own father sought her out as a spiritual teacher, never recognizing her. Only at her deathbed did Euphrosyne confess the truth to him. Paphnutius' response was to take upon himself the same life of a monk and to reside in the cell where his daughter had lived for the remainder of his life.

Who was St. Apollonaria?[121]

The 5th century saint Apollonaria was the eldest of two daughters of Anthemius, who served as regent at Rome during the youth of the emperor Theodosius the Younger. Apollonaria had no wish to marry, desiring instead to devote herself to Christ. She persuaded her father to permit her a pilgrimage to Jerusalem. There she sent all but two of her attendants home. Having given away her possessions, she went with her two companions into Egypt. As they neared Alexandria, Apollonaria left her attendants and escaped into the wilderness. After some years, she went to a well-known desert monastery. Disguised as a man, she called herself "Dorotheus," and was accepted into the monastic community.

Meanwhile, her father was advised to send Apollonaria's younger sister, who suffered from insanity, to the monks for their intercession in prayer. So it happened that Apollonaria—known only as the monk Dorotheus—came to pray for her sister. After some time, the sister was healed and returned home. However, she was discovered to be pregnant and suspicion naturally fell upon the monk who had cared for her. Apollonaria/Dorotheus was ordered to Rome. There her astonished family learned the truth of the monk's identity. They agreed to keep her secret and Apollonaria returned to the monastery, where she lived out the remainder of her life. Only at her death did her brethren at the monastery discover the truth.

Who was St. Mary?[122]

Perhaps also in the 5th century, St. Mary followed in her father's footsteps by disguising herself so that she could enter the same monastery he was in as a monk. Her father, a pious man named Eugenios, had raised Mary by himself, instructing her in godly ways. After she was raised, he announced his intention to enter a monastery. But she would not be parted from him, declaring, "I shall first cut off the hair of my head, and clothe myself as a man, and then enter the monastery with you." So Mary persuaded him to permit her to put on the guise of a man and accompany him into the monastic life. She called herself "Marinos" and the two of them entered the monastery.

Mary's deception proved greatly successful. Obedient, humble, and ascetic, other monks came to regard her either as a eunuch, or as particularly severe in her habits, for she grew no beard and continued to have a feminine voice. She remained as a monk even after her father died, becoming noted for healing the sick. However, her disguise proved too perfect. While in service for the monastery, she was accused of having impregnated a young woman—a charge Mary did not contest. Instead, she accepted the judgment against her and was cast out. She took up residence outside the gates, exposed to the elements. More remarkably, she took the child she was accused of fathering and raised him as truly her own.

After three long years, the other monks interceded with their leader on her behalf. Mary, with the child, was readmitted to the monastery, where she was assigned the lowliest tasks, as well as having still to take care of the child. Her true gender was discovered only at her death. Then she was justified in the eyes both of her superior and her accuser.

Who was St. Hilaria?[123]

In the late 5th- early 6th century, St. Hilaria, daughter of the Emperor Zeno, ruler of the Eastern Roman Empire (474-476 C.E.), forsook her life of privilege for one of humble service. Hilaria was the older of Zeno's two daughters. Well-schooled and raised in the Christian faith, Hilaria yearned to remain a virgin and devote herself to the monastic life in the Egyptian desert wilderness. However, she hesitated because her position as the emperor's daughter complicated matters; her parents had more mundane hopes for her and her rank might mean refusal from a monastery fearful of the repercussions from admitting her. So she sought God's counsel and was reassured that her desire was proper. In fact (according to the Arabic version), God himself instructed her how to proceed.

Hilaria disguised herself as a man and boarded a ship to Alexandria, Egypt. Once there, again guided by the voice of God through the words of scripture, she firmed her resolve and departed into the valley of Scetis in the desert to the monastery of Abba Macarius. There, still in the guise of a man, calling herself 'Hilarion,' she gained access to the monastic life. The Presbyter in charge was fooled by her manly dress and her darkened complexion from her journey. So she was given a cell in which to dwell and joined the monastic community. Hilaria's self-renunciation and pious endurance in prayer vigils and through fasting won her great respect, but after some three years there the monastery's leader discerned her actual sex and confronted her.

Yet Hilaria was permitted to remain. Her beardless condition—a sign that might cause others to question her masculinity—was interpreted as signifying that she was a eunuch. And so a decade passed. Meanwhile, Hilaria's much younger sister fell ill. The emperor was counseled to send her to the pious monks of Hilaria's monastery, who would pray for her recovery. The emperor did as he was bid and so the girl came to the monastery and into the presence of Hilaria, whose own body had become greatly emaciated from her life of self-denial.

Hilaria was overcome at the sight of her sister, throwing herself upon her with many tears. The other monks were impressed with this show of caring and, when the sister had recovered a little, she was placed under Hilaria's care. During this time, Hilaria demonstrated her affection for her sister with kisses and sometimes by sleeping beside her. When the sister recovered, returned home, and related this to her father, he was disturbed by the monk's behavior. So Zeno summoned the monk named 'Hilarion' for questioning.

After her father expressed his concerns, Hilaria revealed her true identity to him and recounted her story. She returned to the monastery where she lived another twelve years. Only after her death was her true sex made known to the other monks, who wondered at such a matter, but who also praised God for Hilaria. Similarly, her parents, though they grieved, praised such a pious and holy daughter.

87

Who was St. Matrona?[124]

Also in the late 5th- early 6th century, St. Matrona of Perge in Pamphylia, distinguished herself over a long life that was filled with travel and adventure. Having been well-educated by her parents, when she was of eligible age they married their beautiful daughter to a distinguished townsman by the name of Domitianus. The couple had a daughter, Theodote, who was dedicated to God from infancy. In her early twenties, Matrona persuaded her husband to move to Byzantium, where she spent much time in the churches and in Christian service. But Domitianus was a jealous and suspicious husband. He tried to confine Matrona to home. Through sheer persistence she wore her husband down and was permitted to go to church.

There, one day as the church closed for the evening, she found an elderly woman named Susanna, who gave her refuge for the night. The next morning, after consulting with a teacher named Eugenia, Matrona gave over the care of her daughter to Susanna and committed herself to the life of an ascetic. In a dream she saw a vision of herself being rescued by monks from her pursuing husband. Taking this as a sign, she cut her hair close to the scalp, put on the garb of a eunuch, called herself by the name of Babylas, and presented herself to the monastic community under the leadership of Basianus.

Accepted by the monks, Matrona excelled at their labors. They began to observe her more closely, seeking to imitate her zeal and virtue. But this almost led to her being discovered as a woman. A new monk, named Barnabas, had been an actor and he noticed Matrona's pierced ears. She was able by her quick wit to answer him such that he put away his suspicion. But Matrona herself was troubled by this, remembering how Eugenia had warned her of the difficulty there would be in trying to pass as a man, and how she would eventually be caught.

And so it came to pass. Basianus, the leader of the monastery, finally confronted her. He inquired about matters such as how she could take Holy Communion without her head being covered. Matrona told him how she would feign illness at such times so as to have an excuse to present herself with covered head and so not violate the apostolic ordinance requiring such for women. Basianus was impressed both by her virtue and her wisdom. He offered her counsel and support as she left the monastery to take refuge again with Susanna.

Meanwhile, Domitianus had been seeking Matrona and piecing together what had happened since she disappeared. He went from monastery to monastery looking for her. When he came to the one under Basianus, he made a spectacle of himself in his anger. The monks misled him and he turned away. Basianus, still wanting to help Matrona, heeded the advice of a deacon and arranged for Matrona to be put on a ship to a nunnery in Emesa, far from her searching husband.

Matrona's excellence in Emesa caused her fame to spread. The persistent Domitianus tracked her there and tried to disguise himself as someone she would receive. However, Matrona put on her own disguise and escaped. She made her way to Jerusalem. But Domitianus was not one to give up. He followed her and she only narrowly avoided him. She finally took refuge in a pagan temple, preferring to contest with demonic spirits rather than her husband.

Her pious virtue eventually cleansed the temple and brought other women to serve with her. Once more she grew in renown. But now she felt the desire to go to Constantinople that she might see Basianus again. Though she feared being discovered by her husband, she undertook the journey and took up residence in the city. There she lived to reach 100 years of age, her life filled with good works.

Who was St. Papula?[125]

Gregory, Bishop of Tours in France, in the 6th century recounted the life of the pious St. Papula of Gaul, whom he praised as *vir inter viros* ('a man among men'). As a girl she wished to become a nun, but her parents could not bear to be parted from her. So desiring the religious life of singular devotion she would not be put off, Papula cut off her hair and put on masculine apparel. She went to the diocese of Tours and presented herself successfully as a man. Though her distraught parents searched for her, they never found her. Papula spent some thirty years at the monastery there, eventually winning such respect from her fellow monks that on the abbot's death they sought to have her assume his place. Only at the end of her life was her true identity exposed.

Who was St. Mary of Egypt?[126]

Another story probably first told in the 6th century is that of St. Mary of Egypt. Mary's story differs from those of most of the other female crossdressing saints in two regards: her formerly dissolute life (cf. the story of St. Pelagia, above), and her situational use of male clothing to hide her nakedness (cf. the story of St. Theoktiste, below).

Mary had, in her own words, rejected her parents' love at age 12 and gone to Alexandria, where she relentlessly pursued casual sexual encounters for the next 17 years. Then, on a whim, she joined a crowd going to Jerusalem for a festival—financing her passage with her body. In Jerusalem she continued her same practices before the festival commenced. On the day it began, Mary joined with the throng seeking entrance to a church, but her way was blocked by a force greater than men. She retreated to a corner of the churchyard, where she experienced conversion. After going inside the church to worship, she departed the city, crossed the Jordan River, and took up residence in the wilderness.

For 17 years she struggled with temptation, but persevered. She had lived in the wild for 47 years when a monk named Zosimas encountered her. Because she had long been naked, she begged of him a covering, and he gave her his cloak. Then she told him her story. At its conclusion, she swore him to secrecy while she still lived, and asked that a year from then he would come again, bringing her the holy sacrament, but not crossing the Jordan. A year later, he did as requested, and Mary crossed the Jordan, walking on the water. When she had joined him, she received communion and set a date for the following year when he should meet her again at the place of their first encounter. The following year, Zosimas did again as asked, and discovered Mary dead. So he buried her there, miraculously aided by a lion that dug her grave; Mary was clad only in the masculine cloak he had provided her two years previously.

Who was St. Anastasia the Patrician?[127]

In the 6th century, St. Anastasia the Patrician used crossdressing as a means of escape from a paramour. Of high birth, Anastasia of Egypt caught the eye of the Emperor Justinian (reigned 527-565 C.E.), when she became a lady-in-waiting at the imperial court in Constantinople. Seeking to avoid the pursuit of the married emperor (and his wife Theodora's understandable animosity), she journeyed to Alexandria, Egypt. There she used her wealth to support a convent in the nearby village of Quinto and gave herself over to good works.

She thus succeeded for a time in escaping Justinian, but when the emperor's wife died he made it known he still desired her. He had begun a search for her and when this news reached the virgin Anastasia, she fled into the desert of Sceta. There the abbot Daniel heard her story and helped her find refuge. Taking on the guise of a hermiting monk, complete with a false beard, and identifying herself as "Anastasios the Eunuch," she spent more than two decades as a recluse, devoting herself to prayer. As she found herself dying, she sent a signal to the abbot, who hurried to her side accompanied by a younger monk. She begged the abbot's permission to be buried in the clothes she had worn as a monk and to keep her secret even in death. After being buried, when the monk asked if the abbot had known 'Anastasios' was really a woman, the entire story was disclosed.

Who was St. Theodora?[128]

A rather different experience from that of Athanasia happened in another marriage. In the 8th century, St. Theodora of Alexandra took on crossdressing as part of her penance for adultery. While her husband was absent for an extended period of time, another man sought to court her. Her resistance was overcome when she was deceived by the claim that her act would be covered by darkness and not seen by God. At once filled with remorse after the act, Theodora embarked on a remarkable course. Rather than face her husband, she cut her hair, put on some of his clothes, and journeyed some 18 miles to a monastery. There she presented herself as "Theodorus" and was accepted into the company of monks. Years passed as she lived a life of asceticism and service.

But her trials were not over. Falsely accused of impregnating a woman, Theodora kept silent and accepted disgrace and removal from the monastery. Even more remarkably, Theodora took the child and raised him! After dwelling seven years in a cave, continuing steadfast in faithful devotion, Theodora and the child were received into the monastery. Not long after, Theodora died and her true sex was revealed. Her husband, who had never ceased loving her, took up residence in the same cell of the monastery where Theodora had lived and remained there until his own death. The child raised by Theodora grew up to become the abbot of the monastery.

Who was St. Anna?[129]

In the late 8th- early 9th century, St. Anna of Constantinople undertook the life of a monk. Anna had been married and had children, who were lost to tragedy. Taking on the dress and manner of a eunuch, she became a monk known as "Euphemianos." Although her true gender was discovered, Anna persisted in a live of ascetic piety. At Constantinople she became a famed wonder worker.

Who was St. Theoktiste?[130]

The story of St. Theoktiste of Lesbos is known from the 9th century, placing her life then or somewhat earlier. Her story differs from many of the other crossdressing saints in a significant fashion: while she voluntary adopted men's clothing, it was in a limited circumstance when modesty prompted borrowing such clothes to cover her nakedness. Theoktiste, orphaned in childhood, was placed by her relatives in a nunnery. At about age 18, while visiting a relative, she was captured by enemy raiders. The prisoners were taken to an island to be appraised, and Theoktiste was able to escape. The others departed the next day and for some 35 years she lived alone on the island. When a hunter by chance surprised her in the church where she took refuge, she was naked and solicited him for his cloak, which he gave to her. Theoktiste then told him her story and begged him that he should bring to her on a return visit some communion wafer. The hunter did so, finding her again at the church, wearing the cloak he had given to her. She took the eucharist from him and he departed. When he came again a few days later, he found her dead.

Who was St. Uncumber?[131]

Likewise we might place here St. Uncumber, whose story perhaps belongs somewhere between the 7th and 11th centuries, although the legend about her seems to first appear in the Netherlands at the beginning of the 15th century. Also known in various other lands by the names Liberata, Liberdade, Liverade, Kümmernis, Ontkommer, Ontkommena, or Wilgefortis, this legend presents a striking picture of a dramatic change. Uncumber was the beautiful daughter of a king who intended to marry her to another ruler for political purposes. But Uncumber, a pious girl, had taken a vow of chastity in order to serve God as the bride of Christ alone. In this unequal contest of power, Uncumber seemed to have lost when her father put her in a cell until she should give in. But she fasted and prayed, petitioning God that he might take away her beauty so that she would not be the desire of men's affection. Her prayer was granted. When they came to take her from her cell they discovered Uncumber had grown a beard and body hair. She had, in fact, become like a man—a bearded saint. Her father, outraged, put her to death by crucifixion that she might die like the Lord she preferred over other men.

The sudden, miraculous appearance of a beard—that signal marker of masculinity—draws much attention when Uncumber's story is told. Religion scholar Alison Jasper observes that it seems to function in the tradition about her as a symbol of virility, perhaps along the lines of assuming the masculine qualities often presumed to make one more like Christ.[132] But Jasper also finds that examination of the various names by which the saint is known to be revealing of key ideas. Uncumber, Ontkommer, Ontkommena, and Kümmernis, Jasper notes, derive from the German word *Kummer*, a word signifying grief and bondage, and the name variations suggest liberation from an en*cumbr*ance [Jasper's emphasis]. The name Wilgefortis, Jasper suggests, is perhaps derived from the Latin *Virgo fortis*—'strong virgin'—though it is also possible it comes from a medieval religious tradition of *hilge vratz*, 'holy face,' and reflects a connection to popular depictions of the face of Jesus.[133] The names Liberata, Liberdade, Liverade may simply represent translations of Uncumber; 'Liberata' is a Latin name of similar meaning.[134]

Once popular in many places in central Europe, the veneration of St. Uncumber diminished after the 16th century. Jasper observes that since the reforms of Vatican II in the early 1960s, efforts by the Catholic Church to control the veneration of this saint have increased. Yet, as Jasper points out, the figure of the bearded saint retains a certain appeal in this day of reexamination of gender. She does, in some sense, reflects Jasper, exemplify what feminist theology has proclaimed in recent decades: that Christian theology does not need to be wedded to a masculine-dominated gender hierarchy and all it entails.[135]

Who was St. Hildegund?[136]

St. Hildegund of Germany, in the 12th century, was born in the diocese of Cologne to pious parents who had been for many years childless. They had sought the favor of heaven by good deeds and the promise that any children born to them should be dedicated to God's service. In due time, their prayers were heard and they had twin girls, whom they named Agnes and Hildegund. Both girls were raised in the care of a nearby convent.

Their parents had resolved a pilgrimage to Jerusalem, but their mother fell ill and died before this could be accomplished. Their father selected Hildegund to take her mother's place. But, fearing for her safety on the trip, he dressed her as a boy. Her hair was cut short and she was given the name 'Joseph.' In the company of some crusaders they made their way.

Unfortunately, Hildegund's father fell ill and he, sensing the imminence of death, warned her to strictly guard her secret. Henceforth known as Joseph, the youngster and a servant who served as guardian completed the pilgrimage. In the city of Acre in the Holy Land, the servant deserted, taking horses, money, and baggage with him. This was but the first of a series of adventures and misadventures. These included joining the Knights Templar, among whom he spent a year and traveled throughout the Holy Land. Then a pilgrim from Cologne arrived. 'Joseph' joined him in returning to Europe. This good man died before they reached home, leaving 'Joseph' all his money as an inheritance.

Retaining disguise as 'Joseph,' Hildegund reached home. There a canon of the local cathedral took him into his home. A local dispute involving this man's sister's claim on ascension to the position of abbess meant the canon needed to travel to the Vatican. He persuaded 'Joseph' to accompany him. Along the way they became separated and 'Joseph' was mistaken for a thief. After being beaten by those arresting him, he was sentenced by the magistrate to immediate execution, being permitted only to make confession beforehand. But this confession persuaded the priest who heard it of the youth's innocence. A reprieve was won, his accuser caught, and the two of them made to undergo a literal ordeal by fire. Each was made to walk across red-hot iron. The real thief was burned; 'Joseph' was not. Thus vindicated, 'Joseph' resumed the journey.

Unfortunately, the hanged thief's relatives came upon him in the wood. Vengeful, they made 'Joseph' share the same fate as their kinsman. They hung him on a tree and left him for dead. Spotted by some passing shepherds, the nearly dead Hildegund was cut down and cared for. Having been rescued again from death, the youth hurried to overtake the canon, and the two went on to Rome. The case was referred to the Bishop of Spire, and there 'Joseph' remained while he pondered what to do with his life. His parents had been joined in death by his sister Agnes and bereft of family Hildegund considered a life in religious seclusion.

While taking instruction with respect to such a life, 'Joseph' lived with a female recluse named Matilda. This soon raised suspicion. A man recently committed to becoming a Cistercian monk tried to persuade 'Joseph' to join him at the monastery near Heidelberg. Though filled with doubts and fears of discovery, Hidegund joind the monastery as 'Brother Joseph.' There Hildegund/Joseph lived successfully as a man, despite acts that jeopardized her secret. At last, 'Brother Joseph' fell ill and died shortly after Easter. Only then was the truth of her sex discovered. Publicity and the piecing together of bits of information eventually led to reconstructing her remarkable story.

Who was St. Joan?[137]

Arguably the most famous of the female crossdressing saints is St. Jeanne La Pucelle of the 15th century, better known as Joan of Arc. In her own lifetime she was accused both of crossdressing and witchcraft, among a laundry list of other crimes against both Church and State. The charge against Joan read, in part:

> It is well known how for some time a woman calling herself Jeanne the Maid, putting off the habit and dress of the female sex (which is contrary to divine law, abominable to God, condemned and prohibited by every law), has dressed and armed herself in the state and habit of man, has wrought and occasioned cruel murders, and it is said, to seduce and deceive the simple people, has given them to understand that she was sent from God and that she had knowledge of His divine secrets, with many other dangerous dogmatizations most prejudicial and scandalous to our holy faith.[138]

What seems to have particularly disturbed her accusers was that Joan's actions had been so public. Unlike the other women we have discussed, Joan of Arc made no pretence of being a man. She simply was openly herself—the "Maid of Orleans"—a woman dressed in men's clothes. Repeatedly her accusers demanded to know why she acted in such a manner. Repeatedly Joan defended her action:

> Asked if God ordered her to wear a man's dress, she answered that the dress is a small, nay, the least thing. Nor did she put on man's dress by the advice of any man whatsoever; she did not put it on, nor did she do aught, but by the command of God and the angels. Asked whether it seemed to her that this command to assume male attire was lawful, she answered: "Everything I have done is at God's command; and if He had ordered me to assume a different habit, I should have done it, because it would have been His command."[139]

After some time, Joan agreed to give up male dress in order to celebrate Mass, but then 'relapsed.' This occasioned a new round of interrogation:

> Now because the said Jeanne was wearing a man's dress, a short mantle, a hood, a doublet and other garments used by men (which at our order she had recently put off in favor of woman's dress), we questioned her to find out when and for what reason she had resumed man's dress and rejected woman's clothes. Jeanne said she had but recently resumed man's dress and rejected woman's clothes. Asked why she had resumed it, and who had compelled her to wear it, she answered that she had taken it of her own will, under no compulsion, as she preferred man's to woman's dress.[140]

Interestingly, the final verdict made no explicit mention of Joan's crossdressing. It was invisibly incorporated by vague reference to her many misdeeds and she was found guilty of having verbally, but not truly, recanted earlier. Condemned, she was burned at the stake (1431 C.E.); she was not yet 20 years old. A generation later, the pope overturned the verdict. History has since proven indifferent to her crossdressing and she is one of the best-known and most popular figures of Christian history.

What can these saints teach us about crossdressing?

What might we learn from these crossdressing saints? We have seen enough of each story to be able to substantiate some very general observations. The two broadest are these:

1. These women did not all crossdress for the same reason.
2. None of these women crossdressed to satisfy an immoral urge, but rather to accomplish a virtuous life otherwise beyond their reach.

Let's start with the first observation, which may not be obvious. At one level, we can say they crossdressed for the same reason: to have access to a kind of holy life not otherwise open to them (hence observation #2). But while this desire may have been the ultimate cause for their action, the proximate—more immediate—cause was generally a specific situational need. Thus, while the similarities among these stories have often been remarked upon, the differences seem just as interesting and important.

Often the crossdressing had something to do with marriage. Some of the women were virgin singles, some married or widowed. Of those who were virgins (e.g., Anastasia the Patrician, Apollonaria, Eugenia, Euphrosyne, and Uncumber), crossdressing or other male signifier was pursued to protect that virginity when marriage looked imminent. Of those who were married, crossdressing was pursued either to escape marriage (e.g., Matrona), or to be close to one's husband while remaining chaste (e.g., Athanasia). A married woman might take up crossdressing as part of penance for adultery (e.g., Theodora). Even a widow might crossdress (e.g., Anna). Of course, not only 'respectable' women might crossdress; the formerly dissolute might do so as well, as they escaped their former life (e.g., Pelagia and Mary of Egypt). Interestingly, crossdressing proved instrumental in establishing their innocence when some were accused of impregnating others (e.g., Apollonaria, Eugenia, Mary, and Theodora).

There were other practical purposes served by crossdressing. In some cases it was modesty that prompted a naked saint to borrow a man's garment to cover her (e.g., Mary of Egypt and Theoktiste). Sometimes crossdressing was for staying safe from predatory men through disguise, especially when traveling (e.g., Thecla and Hildegund). Only one of the women was openly, ostentatiously crossdressed: Joan of Arc. But her reason for her crossdressing—the beckoning of God—was not unprecedented; Hilaria and Matrona, too, had received divine instruction that led to their behavior.

The second observation, obviously related to the first, merits some individual attention because of Deuteronomy 22:5. As indicated in the answers to question set 8 (Q. 61-65), a number of different explanations for the biblical prohibition of crossdressing have been offered. One line of reasoning argues that the prohibition is meant to prevent a blurring of the sexes, which of course is exactly what happens when these women crossdress so that they successfully pass as men. Yet even when discovered, this fact seems not to be of much concern.

Another way of viewing Deuteronomy 22:5 emphasizes that the prohibition is aimed at crossdressing in the service of immoral sexual activity, especially under the guise of religiousness. This element certainly plays into several stories where the crossdressing saint is accused of a sexual impropriety she could not have accomplished. In this manner, the stories of these saints appears to support more the latter understanding of the biblical prohibition than does the idea that a blurring of the genders is at stake. Adding more credence to this conclusion is the current in the Church—springing from Paul's theology—that in Christ "there is neither male nor female," or, as others in the Church saw it, the woman may become a man (or like him) in order to be saved. Thus the order of redemption trumps the order of creation even as it restores it.

How did these women successfully pass as men? The stories concern themselves with this query relatively little. They cut their hair and dressed as men. Also, some of them were assumed to be eunuchs—a convenient and plausible explanation for not having beards. In addition, they pursued manly spirituality; the notion that women would do so apparently seemed so preposterous to most of their contemporaries that it was easier to find reasons to accept the deception than to question it, although as a general rule at some point the disguise was questioned and, of course, eventually the truth always came out.

That 'truth' is what matters—and the fact of their anatomical sex being at variance with their gender presentation is at the heart of that truth. The historicity of the lives of these saints is secondary to what they teach anyone who reads them. But what, exactly, do they teach? What is the central truth such stories aim at? As indicated earlier, a variety of answers have been proposed, all of them agreeing that whatever exactly a writer may have intended, the meaning resides in the Christian context in which the stories originated and were passed on. These stories were preserved because they matter. They say things needing to be heard, and anxious to be heard by many, then and also today.

Whatever else they communicate, the lives of these crossdressing saints certainly proclaim that anatomical sex is not the basis for Christian piety, nor its boundary. Women who *trans*gress the so-called gender 'order' can *trans*cend gender discrimination through *trans*vestism. In putting on male clothes they embraced a perceived masculinity that was all society permitted as the vehicle for certain forms of spiritual expression. In performing masculine piety these women—*because* they were women—exposed the falsity of notions of any spiritual privilege based on sex or gender. Simultaneously they exposed the ludicrousness of the proposition that either sex or gender pose legitimate divisions for establishing a hierarchy of spiritual worth or work in the worshipful service of God.

Q. 69 Are there notable Christian cross-dressing women?

The Short Answer. Other than those who have attained sainthood (see Q. 68), a number of prominent Christian women have crossdressed. Some of these figures may be largely or entirely legendary, but others are undeniably authentic historical figures. Like the crossdressing saints, these women proved themselves exemplars of faith. Their reasons may also recall the saints previously discussed. Women, much more than men, have historically had reasons for gender crossing in a religious context. Christianity long has endorsed the reigning gender hierarchy, limiting women in important respects. Today, Christian women use different strategies to cope with the persistent inequalities presented within the Church. In former times, however, gender crossing through crossdressing and the adoption of a masculine identity was more attractive—and feasible. The social lines between the genders were more rigidly drawn and the opportunities for important paths of spiritual devotion less available. Coupled with an arguably greater role of religion in both personal and social life, the incentives for women to cross gender lines seems to have been greater in prior historical periods. Hence the illustrative examples presented here are drawn largely from a long vanished past. Contemporary examples of female crossdressers are more likely to reflect transgender realities such as transsexualism—a reality in which the very notion of 'crossdressing' can reasonably be challenged as an inaccurate label. What remains true across the reach of history is that persons born female, and assigned at birth to be girls who will become women, have for one or another reason crossed the socially drawn gender lines to stake a claim for themselves elsewhere. Whether the initial or primary motivation has been one of personal gender identity, or spiritual zeal, the effect has been to produce persons who violate social norms but nevertheless stand out as exemplars of Christian faith and service. Although the figures recounted here are among the most well-known, they are best understood as prominent examples drawn from a much larger population for whom little if anything is known about most of its members. Historical accounts leave scarcely enough room for the famous and most of us vanish entirely. The same inevitably proves true for gender variant women of faith who in other respects lived such ordinary lives their difference in gender identity or behavior proved historically unremarkable. Perhaps that is an important lesson in itself.

The Longer Answer. Not all of the stories of Christian crossdressing women feature saints, though the lady in question may have been a prominent figure. A variety of notable Christian women are briefly profiled here. However, we need to note the context in which others could view such behavior as praiseworthy. Valerie Hotchkiss may have offered a key rationale in pointing out that female crossdressing could be seen as demonstrating the power of Christian faith to transform believers.[141] Certainly, in light of the early Christian idea—arguably originating with Jesus himself (cf. the last saying of *The Gospel of Thomas*)—that one must 'become male' to join the coveted ranks of high discipleship, the incentive to seek gender transformation has been substantial. But that observation raises the question of what the experience of being a woman in a patriarchal structure entails.

What is it like to be a woman in the Christian Church?

Christian women throughout Church history have had to contend with a gender hierarchy privileging masculinity. Indeed, it has long been an intriguing question why women invest so much in a religion that through its social institution of the Church so persistently and systematically devalues them. Research has shown that in addition to such obvious markers of discrimination as more limited access to professional ministerial roles, women face obstacles ranging from worship centered in language and symbols about a deity almost exclusively considered in masculine terms, to strong gender stereotypical expectations about dress and participation in religious activities both ordinary and special. It would seem women would find great incentive to abandon an institution so unfavorable toward their gender. Yet most not only do not do so, but continue to invest much of themselves despite little apparent recognition or reward.

How Women Cope with the Church's Gender Hierarchy

In researching this puzzle among contemporary Christian women, psychologist Elizabeth Weiss Ozorak interviewed 61 women between the ages of 18-71. She explored how these women responded to the patriarchal aspects of their religious experience, considered whether such responses are like those used in other similar experiences of potential dissonance and internal conflict, and wondered if such responses demonstrate an orientation toward relationship rather than individuation. Some of these women (7%) denied there was any gender inequality in their religious community, while some (16%) agreed there was such inequality, but felt it was appropriate. Of the remaining more than three-quarters of the women, all of whom both saw injustice and believed it inappropriate, several different coping responses could be distinguished. A few (8%) rejected their religious tradition; a few (8%) coped behaviorally, such as by asking for equal treatment and/or involving themselves in proactive social groups (e.g., a woman's group within their church). A majority of the rest (43%)

relied on cognitive coping strategies—reframing their experience so as to interpet it more favorably—while a good number (18%) integrated both behavioral and cognitive coping. These kind of strategies include focusing on things the woman likes, rather than on inequities, comparing her religious group with others she sees as less desirable, optimistically finding indications that things are changing for the better, or creatively substituting her own images, words, and personal interpretations for the dominant masculine ones. Ozorak found such strategies similar to those women use to reduce discomfort in other circumstances. She also found that the women did orient toward relationship, rather than individuation, evaluating their religious experience by their sense of community and connectedness.[142]

One way this data can be viewed is that some contemporary Christian women continue to transform themselves—as some Christian women always have—but perhaps in rather different ways than in the past. As has always been the case, some women accept their subordinate status and may even justify it. Many cope with the discomfort this inequality produces by adjusting their own thinking, a kind of transformation internally that permits them to not only remain within the Church, but also offer much to it. However, a small group of women both past and present have embraced stronger transformations. In the past, recognizing the futility of changing the patriarchal structure, they changed themselves to become recognizably masculine in appearance and manner. In that fashion they could pursue religious activities and spiritual experiences reserved for men. Today, probably because of some success by women in other social spheres, a few women embrace other transformational paths. On the one hand, some succeed in transforming themselves into traditionally masculine roles like becoming clergy. On the other hand, some seek the transformation of the Church itself, propogating feminist theology, agitating for structural changes, and in some cases joining together to fom new, more egalitarian faith communities. Of course, a few women find ways to join both personal transformation with the pursuit of a transformational social justice within the Church.

The Value of Female Crossdressing in the Past for Today's Christian Women

What may be difficult for most women (and men) to see is how such contempory transformations have anything in common with female crossdressing in the past. Yesterday's crossdressing women used a socially important and recognizable device to pursue valued spiritual and religious ends. To a greater or lesser degree they succeeded individually, but regardless of personal success they prepared the soil for subsequent generations of women. First, they showed to both men and women that the zeal of faith can and will impel individuals to cross even lines as basic and critical as gender. Second, they proved the artificiality of lines drawn by gender with respect to spiritual identity, roles, and experiences. In so doing they demonstrated that, given the chance, female bodies possess personas as suitable for anything the Spirit or Church may offer as do male bodies. Third, they offered evidence that transformations come in many forms, but the form whereby change comes is less important than the change itself.

In sum, gender transformations have played an important role in indicating both the wrongness of inequality in the Church and the genuine possibility of change. It is worth our noting that such gender transformations—what we today might call transgender realities—not only have been present from the beginning, but they have exercised a degree of power continuously throughout Church history. Part of that power comes from the hope offered to women that they might indeed enjoy all a man does. Part of that power also comes from the sense men have that women might successfully breach the gender gap. Some men want that; others resist it. The power of gender transformations reaches beyond actual historical incidences of them to imagined instances. Let us begin with one such imagined transformation—of a woman into the most powerful of men.

Who was the female Pope?

There is a story of 'the female Pope,' a woman named Joan alleged to have posed as Pope John VII Angelicus, in the mid-9th century (853-855 C. E.). 'Pope Joan' is widely regarded today as a fiction, and various accounts of her story exist. One holds that she disguised herself as a man (taking the name 'John') out of love for a monk vowed to celibacy. She resided near him, her passion unquenched, until his death. A gifted scholar, she moved up through the ranks of the church hierarchy until finally becoming pope. Then she came to love another monk, with whom she became romantically involved, resulting in a pregnancy. At giving birth her secret was discovered and she was immediately deposed. Various accounts then have her either executed at once, or placed with her child in a convent, or sent into exile to die in disgrace.[143]

Here we have a transformational story sure to evoke the anxiety of defenders of the gender hierarchy. The Catholic Church is patriarchal in structure and philosophy; the spectre of a female rising to the seat of St. Peter unthinkable. Yet the imagination of an earlier people thought exactly such a thing. The story has elements similar to those of some of the crossdressing saints. But there are important differences. This is a cautionary tale. The story ends with exposure leading not to praise and sainthood, but to disgrace and removal. Like many gender transformation stories, this one presents a complex message containing seeds of hope (A female could become head of the Church!) and despair (The masculine powers will never let the hierarchy be broken!). Like so many stage plays where crossdressing occurs, this story both challenges gender conventions and reinforces them.

Who were the 'Desert Mothers'?

But we don't have to rely on just the sensational story of 'Pope Joan' for a challenge to gender conventions. The example set by the female saints we saw in the answer to the previous question was repeated many times in less spectacular fashion by a substantial number of women through the ages. Margot King, for instance, has called attention to the widespread phenomena of what she terms the 'Desert Mothers.'[144] These women were recluses, like Theodora, who lived a life of religious devotion. King notes:

> Perhaps the most interesting facet of the life of the Desert Mother was her assumption of male clothing. This would appear to have been not only a reflection of the male orientation of the early Church, but also a prudent course of action in the desert where a lone female could easily be mistaken for a demon and summarily thrashed or killed. The disguise did, however, have its dangers for there are many cases reported where "the female man of God" was accused of seduction by another woman, who would then produce a child as proof of the saint's sin.[145]

The Middle Ages' fascination with crossdressing has often been noted and extensively studied.[146] Many of the stories preserved about the practice contain a number wherein a religious motif is central. The spirit of the 'Desert Mothers' described by King for women of an earlier age remained strong in Medieval Europe, where female recluses continued to be 'manly' in spirit and, often, in dress.[147]

However, the religious crossdressing woman is not a phenomenon confined to the pre-Modern world. She has persisted even down to our own time. A few portraits can show how women across time have transgendered themselves as part of their religious experience. Two American examples, one from the 18th century and the other from the 19th century illustrate the engagement of transgender realities in strikingly different ways.

Who was Jemima Wilkinson? [148]

The early American case of Jemima Wilkinson (1752-1819) reflects a distinctive religious identity in which crossdressing engaged the explicit end of serving her self-representation of having *no* gender—a *trans*cending attempt at realizing the Pauline proclamation of Galations 3:28. Raised as a Quaker in Rhode Island, Jemima moved to Connecticut after the death of her mother. At age 24 she joined a New Light Baptist church—a Christian group arising out of the Great Awakening of the 18th century, particularly the preaching of George Whitefield. Two months later, in October, 1776, an event happened that shaped the remaining course of her life: she fell ill, lapsing into either a trance-like or comatose state, and finally appearing to have died.[149] Indeed, in her own eyes she had died and then been returned to life. In this resurrected state she now lived as a Second Redeemer. Asking her followers to refer to her simply as 'the Friend,' she disavowed gender and chose a life of celibacy.

The twin gestures of disdaining recognition of gender and disavowing a sexual life can be seen as radical personal applications of Paul's claim that in Christ Jesus there is neither male nor female. Or they can be viewed as a zealot's effort to eliminate the traditional limitations placed on a woman within Christianity to deny her spiritual leadership. By setting aside gender and sexual activity Jemima defied convention and expectation and could lay claim to a higher purpose for living than what her culture held. But while celibacy could be enacted by chaste behavior, finding a way to demonstrate a transcendence of gender required something obvious and dramatic. Crossdressing without pretense of being a man could exactly fit that requirement.

Whatever her intent in how she dressed, Jemima's choice of apparel was widely perceived as masculine—a striking contrast for an attractive young woman previously known for her passion for clothes.[150] A witness in 1787 described her as wearing in public a light cloth cloak with a cape like a man's, a man's shirt with a handkerchief or cloth tied round her neck in masculine fashion, her hair short and worn like a man's with a man's hat on top. At the same time, observes historian of American religion Catherine Brekus, "she ridiculed men by implying that their power lay in the trappings of dress rather than in their natural superiority."[151] Her appearance, manner and message all made her controversial—and exciting. She was invited to speak in many churches, often attracted considerable crowds, and by 1790 had made more than 250 converts with whom she established the colony of Jerusalem in northwestern New York State.

Though Jemima was unconventional in some respects, her actual teaching and the Christian practices she espoused were largely conventional ones. She taught mostly what she already knew and believed, and likewise largely practiced what was familiar to her. Thus her sect looked much like the Quakerism of her day, although her un-Quakerlike sermons featured a mix of ideas from the different Christian theologies she had been exposed to, all filtered through her own unique sensibility. Her fellowship, 'The Society of Universal Friends,' was remarkably egalitarian for its day. Though celibacy was held up as a higher way for the faithful, marriage was not forbidden. The group's social values were anti-war and anti-slavery. But the community did not long survive the passing of its founder; by the end of the 19th century it was just a memory.

Who was Emma Edmonds?

Emma Edmonds (1841-1898) combined crossdressing with religious ministry in mid-19th century America. Calling herself "Frank Thompson," Emma put on male clothes and traveled selling Bibles. In 1861, when war between the states broke out, she was in Flint, Michigan. Emma promptly joined the volunteer Company F of the Second Michigan Infantry. Not long after, she was in Virginia serving in an army field hospital. For two years she successfully passed as male. Ironically, among the duties she performed, Emma volunteered to serve as a spy, adopting among her disguises that of a female Irish immigrant! Thus she was for a time a woman—pretending to be a man—pretending to be a woman. Weary of war, she deserted in 1863, resuming full-time life as a woman. Under the name "Sara Edmonds," she became a member of the U. S. Christian Commission and served as a war nurse. At war's end she wrote her autobiography. In 1884, Emma was granted a veteran's pension.[152]

Are there others?

The very brief biographies presented here are the tip of the iceberg. There are other women, noted in their own day, whose stories are almost forgotten today. Any number might have been selected for these pages. Many more less public female crossdressers also lived lives dedicated to Christianity. There also have been a few public figures about whom there has been speculation about crossdressing or other gender variant behavior. In the examples below we find women whose exhibition of certain assumed masculine traits led to speculation about their sex or gender.

Mother Julian of Norwich

The medieval saint Mother Julian of Norwich (1342-c. 1417) is the first indisputably certain woman writer in English.[153] In her 30s she experienced visions that became the basis of her famous *Showings*.[154] In later life she entered the religious vocation of an anchorite—a devotee who voluntarily enters seclusion in a solitary place and style of life in order to fix attention on spiritual matters. Among the most famous of Christian mystics, she sometimes has been identified as either a crossdresser or transgendered. This identification, rather suspect, probably derives from two things: her name, and her gender mixing writings. The former is likely the result of her having lived in a cell adjacent to St. Julian's Church in Norwich. As for her writings, these we have discussed elsewhere.

Sor Juana de la Cruz

The Mexican nun Sor Juana de la Cruz (Sor Juana Ines de la Cruz de Asbaje y Ramirez) is another woman who has been subject to rumor. A noted 17th century writer (1648 (or 1651)-1695), she has been called the last great figure of Spanish literature's Golden Age. Some allege that she crossdressed in order to attend an all-male school and thus further her learning. That seems unlikely, but her desire to pursue an education motivated her to beg her mother to send her disguised as a boy to study at the university in Mexico City. She also listed among historical exemplars who provided her inspiration Queen Christina of Sweden, as famed for her crossdressing as for her support of education.[155]

Mother Ann Lee

In 18th century America, Mother Ann Lee (1736-1784) of the pacifistic and celibate Shakers was the object of rumors that she was a man in disguise—a rather ridiculous charge as she not only had been married, but she had given birth to four children, who all died in infancy.[156] We know from a variety of accounts that rumors and baseless accusations swirled around the Shakers because of their unconventional beliefs and lifestyle. These included charges that Shaker males were castrated and that the Shakers danced naked at night and engaged in perverted debauchery. As the most visible personage, Mother Lee drew disproportionate attention. She was labeled a 'virago' (a derogatory term for an unladylike woman) by some, while others charged she was a crossdressed man. To prove the case one way or another a band of men assaulted her and her followers more than once, finally succeeding in kidnapping her. Shame and fear of prosecution, however, kept them from fully accomplishing their intent. On another occasion, she was assaulted in court by a judge, who struck her breast with a staff, apparently aiming to discover her true sex, and leaving her with a scar for life. [157] Although she exhibited qualities associated by most of her contemporaries with masculinity—and hence can be said to have at least bent the gender lines—Mother Ann Lee made no pretence of being a man.

These exemplars merely sample the long, rich history of female crossdressing by deeply religious individuals. Though they may never have attained recognition as saints, in that respect they stand closer to the many religious women unknown to history who employed crossdressing at one time or another, in one way or another, for one purpose or another. Crossdressing proves not to be irreconcilable with religious devotion in the lives of many, many people.

Q. 70 Are there notable Christian cross-dressing men?

The Short Answer. It seems especially important, in an age when women are permitted to look like men while male crossdressers are often scorned, that we should look at the experience of a few Christian men. Though not as easy to find, their stories do exist. Unfortunately, verifying stories of crossdressing by prominent Christian men is often difficult. Because male crossdressing so often in Western history has been associated with unacceptable effeminacy—a perverse loss of male privilege and status—sometimes enemies of public figures have charged them with crossdressing when they actually did not do so. At other times, men who liked and could don exquisite finery inaccessible to most other men were termed crossdressers simply because such ostentatious manner of dress was deemed the domain of women, not of men. Still another factor is that some religious men dressed in distinctive garb that can be viewed as placing them outside masculine conventions of dress. In other words, with respect to their religious clothing, such men could be said either to be dressed effeminately (as has on occasion been said about priests), or actually to stand apart from gender, perhaps as a third gender (as has been said about monks). Yet after all such factors are accounted for, there remain at least some instances of notable Christian men who practiced what we would today recognize as crossdressing. At least one Pope—Paul II—has been alleged to have crossdressed, although the case is far from a certain one. An indisputable case of a prominent Christian male who crossdressed was Francois Timoleon, Abbe de Choisy. In late 17th century France he was active in the spheres of religion, state, and literature. Even more famous was his 18th century countryman, Chevalier d'Eon, arguably the most famous male crossdresser in history. Among his many accomplishments was service in the King's Secret, a network of royal spies for Louis XV. D'Eon succeeded so well as both a man and a woman that a frenzy of betting occurred over whether this remarkable person was truly male or female. Another religious man who used crossdressing to assist his work was the modern martyr, Father Miguel Augustin Pro of Mexico. Such disguise facilitated ministry in difficult times. Finally, Leo F. Heller, Jr. was a recent Christian crossdresser who dedicated the last years of life to ministry with fellow male crossdressers. These men, each distinguished by Christian service, are only a few of many men who have combined both Christian identity and transgender realities.

The Longer Answer. We have seen throughout this multivolume work that in Western culture, at least in recent centuries, crossdressing has been typically viewed with suspicion at best, and often with outright hostility. Correctly or incorrectly, pronouncements about crossdressing in a culture where Christianity is the dominant religion have frequently sought to apply perceived Christian values to the matter in order to render moral judgments. Although diversity of view characterizes Christians on crossdressing and other transgender realities (see the answers to Q. 73-74), the negative voices have tended to drown out others. Thus the general public perception is that crossdressing has been condemned by Christianity and that crossdressers are therefore either not Christians at all, or are Christians caught in sin.

Undoubtedly more so for men than for women—for whom justification is often made that their crossdressing was reasonable given their circumstances— judgment may occur that professing Christian men who crossdress only masquerade as Christians. Their crossdressing often has been presumed to be purposefully deceitful in order to engage in illicit sexual activity, especially homosexual behavior. While there is little doubt such instances have occurred, there also seems little reason to doubt they have been comparatively rare among the occasions and rationales for crossdressing. The reasons for this behavior are manifold and only infrequently intended for immoral or illegal activities. As best we can discern, those crossdressers who have proclaimed the faith have been as sincere, dedicated, and moral as any other Christian.

The judgment that one cannot both be a Christian and a crossdresser seems unfairly harsh in light of the evidence from both the Bible's teachings and the stance of ecclesiastical authorities (as described in answering other questions). While the actual nature of their devotion to the Christian faith must remain best known to these men themselves and to their contemporaries, it seems unreasonable (to say nothing of uncharitable) to assume they were all charlatans. The following brief biographical sketches scarcely represent all the Christian men who have crossdressed through the ages. Rather, these individuals are among the better known figures and display some of the diversity characteristic of men who crossdress. As in all discussions of crossdressing, we must situate it in a broader context of gender. Here we may do so with a very focused question.

Have gender and religious dress interacted?

Do gender and religious dress interact in any significant manner? There is some evidence that they do, and logically we should expect they would. So, before we look at specific figures of crossdressing Christian males, this matter needs at least a cursory look. We should note that the religious dress of men, and the voluntary changes many make in the practice of their lives—especially sexually—also constitute relevant matters. Obviously, religious garb worn by officiants is meant both to convey status and present a certain symbolism. In

Western culture such garb has, as Catholic priest Donald Cozzens puts it, constituted an "intentional gender blurring" with dress that has "for centuries fostered an androgynous cultural milieu."[158]

To understand how gender and religious dress can matter to our discussion we must recall the essential nature of gender in Western culture. Gender is a matter of sorting people into kinds, and does so with special reference to sex and sexuality. Dress serves as a principal marker of gender differentiation. Religious officials like priests and monks—the two male groups we shall consider here—have distinctive dress that is paired with a distinctive presentation of sexuality. Combined, these elements place them into a gendered space outside traditional masculinity. Given the way priestly functions such as mediation and healing are coded culturally as more feminine than masculine, the union of dress, celibacy, and priestly functions all serve to move these male bodies in the direction of femininity without making them either female or women. In effect, priests and men can be said to be gendered as 'androgynous,' or perhaps even as a 'third gender.'

The gender status of Christian priests and monks has historical precedence. The ancient world offered models that the Church could draw upon. Especially the figure of the religious eunuch provided a kind of template. As the Church developed, the nature of the priesthood and the various monastic orders took on more clearly defined shape. By the time of the Catholic Church's dominance in the Middle Ages, the various forces at work in culture—including the relatively fluid ideas about gender—made it inevitable that religious figures would be seen to some degree as 'different' in kind.

Priests

Priestly garb is meant to be distinctive. That it can be so with reference to gender is unquestionable in some instances. However, it might be argued that even where no conscious statement about gender is intended, enough of a message is sent in the elements of dress, the silhouette, and the context to also constitute a discernible gender text. Examples for each type are warranted.

In the ancient world the *kurgara*, priests of the Sumerian deity Inanna (or Inana, identified with the Akkadian Ishtar, or Astarte of the Semitic peoples of the Mideast), dressed so as to conspicuously incorporate mixed gender elements in their public processionals. They wore masculine elements on the right side and feminine ones on the left.[159] The priests of ancient Baal—that deity so inimical to the early Hebrew people—also appeared in a manner different from other males of their society. The famed 19th century scholar Paul Lacroix (writing under the synonym of 'Pierre Dufour'), depicted them as unbearded, with depilated bodies and fragrantly perfumed.[160] The classical world was familiar with priests whose dress not only marked their religious office but also made a gender statement. Perhaps the best known example would be the *Galli*, eunuch priests of Cybele,[161] though a number of other priestly groups are known and remarked upon by ancient authors.[162]

Roman Catholic priests provide a more readily accessible example. They dress and behave in distinctive ways that separate them in important respects from the masculinity of Western culture. At an earlier time in European history, this could lead to criticism of priests, who were seen as effeminate in the garb of their vestments.[163] In the United States, anti-Catholic rhetoric by Protestants liked to picture Catholicism as effeminate and point to the dress of clergy as an exhibit.[164] But such observations occurred outside Christian circles as well. The early 20th century economist Thorstein Veblen used priests as an example of men whose dress incorporated 'womanly elements' that placed it outside the cultural norms for masculinity.[165] The unbifurcated outer garment often worn presents a silhouette more associated with women than with men in recent centuries. As the division between genders sharpened in Western culture, the sense of the priest occupying some space outside the conforming genders waned. It became more important to locate them within the bounds of masculinity. Not surprisingly, then, dress reform of religious officials took place. The Second Vatican Council, in the second half of the 20th century, simplified clerical dress and in some respects moved it more clearly back within the boundaries of masculine fashion.

Monks

Christian monks of various religious orders have been a distinctive part of Church history. Like priests, monks achieve a distinctive status, one that has important gender implications. Anthropologist Bettina Arnold, after referencing female crossdressing saints, succinctly remarks:

> Monks as well as priests, with their long flowing robes, represent another version of this costume-based de-sexing through transvestism. By wearing what is in effect a form of dress, a costume ordinarily associated with women, they enter a zone between the sexes in which, as an institutionalized third gender, they are protected from sexual interaction with women.[166]

Daniel Boyarin, scholar of Talmudic culture and the development of Jewish sensibilities of gender, agrees that in the Middle Ages Christian monks effectively formed "a distinct gender within Christian society, one that is removed from the paternal and sexual order."[167] The monk, by the practice of 'escaping' sex and sexuality,[168] thus becomes someone outside the order and rules pertaining to the conforming genders. It is not merely their dress, but their apparel *and* celibacy that set them apart.

Priests and monks clearly share a certain gender status. Although typically male (remembering the numerous instances of crossdressing females passing as males), these 'men' were men of a different sort—and clearly regarded as such. In fact, it was precisely because of their presumed distance from the needs, desires, and practices of gender-conforming men that they were accorded proximity and opportunities for intimacy with either conforming gender. That some did so sexually is irrefutable. We certainly know this situation has persisted in the modern Church.[169]

Although our brief remarks here barely scratch the surface, they should be sufficient to indicate that gender and religious dress do, indeed, interact. If, as seems plausible, one such interaction has been to carve out a distinctive gendered space for some Christian males, then how far removed can be the phenomenon of crossdressing? It is to that we next turn, offering select examples of notable figures.

Who was Pope Paul II?[170]

Italian Pietro Barbo (1417-1471) became Pope Paul II on August 30, 1464. Nephew to Pope Eugene IV, whose position made his own rise through the ecclesiastical ranks rapid, he was a unanimous choice to succeed Pope Pius II. Despite this support, Pope Paul II proved a controversial figure, and not merely for decisions related to church politics.

His critics called him vain. Pope Paul II apparently regarded himself a handsome man and one story claimed he had to be talked out of choosing for his papal name 'Formosus' ('well built'). He loved splendor, providing lavish public spectacles, and liking to dress in the full richness of ecclesiastical finery. To him has been attributed the introduction of the scarlet color for the 'royal purple' of the College of Cardinals. His style of dress may have been seen by some as effeminate, as likely was his penchant for crying in times of stress. Also alleged by some to prefer the love of men to that of women, Pope Paul II was either a transgendered male or a man whose enemies sought to emasculate him, perhaps precisely because of his pride in his manliness.

These days it is not uncommon to find brief references on the internet to Pope Paul II as a crossdresser. This attribution seems to rest on two things: a notation that after his death it was suggested he be called 'Our Lady of Pity,' and his reputation for preferring elaborate priestly garb—which has occasionally been regarded as effeminate. But historical evidence lacks that Pope Paul II either dressed in what his contemporaries regarded as women's clothing, or tried to present himself as a woman. Perhaps he was a transgendered male, perhaps not—but any representation of him as a crossdresser is more fanciful than historical.

Who was Francois Timoleon Abbe de Choisy?[171]

Among notable individuals, the French writer—and priest—Francois Timoleon, Abbe de Choisy (1644-1724) was dressed as a girl throughout childhood. This ended briefly when he left home at 18 for studies at the Sorbonne. However, only a year later—freshly granted an abbacy—he secretly appeared on stage as an actress. Continuing to crossdress as an adult, he would refer to himself as 'Comtesse des Barres.' When he married, de Choisy selected Mademoiselle de Charlotte, who also loved to crossdress in the identity of 'Monsieur de Maulny.' Apparently, none of this prevented his pursuing activities with the blessing of the Church. In 1676, he accompanied Cardinal de Bouillon to witness the coronation of Pope Innocent XI; he appeared at the subsequent ball dressed as a woman. In 1685, he was part of a mission to Siam, where he appeared in woman's garb and apparently made quite an impression on the locals. Admitted to the French Academy in 1687, de Choisy enjoyed a long and distinguished career, contributing to literature numerous works, mostly religious, including a well-regarded, multi-volume history of the Church (written between 1703-1723). He continued his crossdressing until the end of his life.

Who was the Chevalier d'Eon?[172]

Arguably the most famous crossdressing man of history is Chevalier d'Eon (1728-1810). This is due in no small measure to the influence of the pioneering British sexologist, Havelock Ellis, who chose to term crossdressing behavior as 'Eonism.'[173] The Beaumont Society, a United Kingdom support group for transgendered people, is named after him.[174]

Charles-Geneviève-Louis-Auguste-André-Thimothée d'Eon de Beaumont[5] was born into 18th century France's upper class. His father, Louis d'Eon de Beaumont, was an advocate in the High Court of Justice, and his mother was Lady Françoise de Chavanson, of a wealthy aristocratic family. This granted d'Eon social privileges and advantages, but also helped ensure his later life as a very public figure.

Chevalier d'Eon's childhood was marked by excellence in school. Later, it was also the subject of speculation. His 1779 book of memoirs, *La Vie Militaire, politique, et privée de Mademoiselle d'Eon* (*The Military, Political and Private Life of Mademoiselle d'Eon*),[175] makes the extraordinary claim that d'Eon had actually been born female, but reared as a boy, only later reverting to 'her' true identity as a woman. In fact, he was biologically male.

In 1749, having completed his studies, d'Eon became a secretary in the Paris office of finance, where he wrote his first book—on government finance. It marked the beginning of a long literary career. Perhaps his most famous book is his 1764 volume *Lettres, mémoires, et négociations particuliéres* (*Letters, Memoirs, and Private Negotiations*). A 13-volume work, *Les Loisirs du chevalier d'Eon de Beaumont* (*The Leisure Activities of the Chevalier d'Eon de Beaumont*), appeared in 1774. His last intended book was a never published autobiography entitled *La Pucelle de Tonnerre* (*The Maiden of Tonnerre*).

However, Chevalier d'Eon lived more than a life of quiet contemplation. Though comfortably surrounded by books as a royal censor, in 1756 he entered the King's Secret, a network of royal spies for Louis XV. That same year, the king sent him on a secret mission to Russia's Empress Elizabeth I. Though he was ostensibly a secretary attached to the French secretary Chevalier Douglas, d'Eon met with the empress, while in disguise as a woman, as the King's envoy. The negotiations he conducted were successful; in 1757 France and Russia renewed formal diplomatic relations.

Back in France, in 1762 d'Eon was appointed a captain of the renowned Dragoons, and saw action in the Seven Years War. He distinguished himself in combat while receiving wounds in both thigh and head. At the war's end he was part of the negotiations that led to the treaty adopted. By age 35, he had earned the Cross of Saint-Louis and was raised to noble rank with the title 'Chevalier.'

In 1763 he was appointed Plenipotentiary Minister to England. It began a long association with the British. Alongside his official duties, d'Eon continued to operate as a spy for the King, who was planning an invasion of England. But d'Eon's lofty status proved short-lived. In October of the same year he was ordered back to France. Fearing the outcome, he refused to return and spent the next fourteen years in voluntary exile. He published the aforementioned *Lettres, mémoires, et négociations particuliéres* (1764) and began amassing a large personal library. Despite whatever concerns d'Eon had about going home, in 1766 the king granted him an annual pension for his previous services.

Interestingly, during his years in England, d'Eon became the subject of rumors and betting concerning his true gender. Though he regularly dressed as a man—and a military one at that—speculation swirled that he was actually a woman masquerading as a man. The betting on his gender became widespread, even reaching the London Stock Exchange. The wagering reached hundreds of thousands of British pounds—a truly staggering volume for the time. The Court of the King's Bench finally had to resolve who were the winners and who the losers—all without recourse to proof one way or the other. The matter would not be finally resolved until an autopsy after his death in 1810.

After the death of France's Louis XV in 1774, d'Eon began negotiations for his return to his homeland. The new king, Louis XVI, was eager to reclaim documents in d'Eon's possession. In their settlement, a startling announcement was made: the Chevalier d'Eon was really a woman! Having lived a very public life as a man, d'Eon in middle age now fully took on the life of a woman—in which he remained the rest of his days. The king ordered d'Eon be publicly recognized as a woman and dress as one—and even granted funds for purchasing a wardrobe. So, in 1777, the now 'Mademoiselle' d'Eon returned to France. There he dressed regularly as a woman, though proudly wearing the Cross of Saint-Louis prominently on the left breast. In such garb he even participated in fencing matches. Through it all, the public accepted the declaration that d'Eon was, in fact, a woman whose earlier life as a man had been the fiction.

But Chevalier d'Eon did not long enjoy the king's favor. In 1778 he was briefly imprisoned, then spent the next six years mostly at the family home in Tonnerre. During this period Christian faith became ever more important to d'Eon. But France was no longer proving a satisfactory home. In 1785 he left again for England. There he lived the rest of his life. However, when the French Revolution occurred in 1789 he lost his annual pension, introducing him to financial difficulties that persisted from then on. He was forced to sell his beloved books and to participate in fencing tournaments to earn money. After a serious fencing wound in 1796, he retired from such contests and his last years were marked by poverty. He died in 1810.[176]

Why did d'Eon give up the life of a man for that of a woman? Biographer Gary Kates finds more than a single reason at work. In part the 'transformation' seemed to be a response to his own life events—a public career in decline. But Kates also finds motivation in d'Eon's convictions about the genders. Utilizing the unpublished autobiographical materials d'Eon penned, Kates suggests that the Chevalier gradually came to the conviction that man is as inevitably tied to sin as woman is to virtue. Thus, personal salvation lay in being as like a woman as possible.[177] In this respect, d'Eon pursued a radical but sensible course. Yet having embarked on this life, d'Eon seemed guided by a particular vision of the ideal woman. As Kates remarks, "d'Eon did not simply want to be known by his public as a woman; he wanted to be known as a certain kind of woman: Amazonian, pious, virtuous, patriotic; a woman in the mode of the Maid of Orléans, Joan of Arc."[178]

Kates also finds an element of both motivation and support for d'Eon's remarkable transformation in his Christian thinking. The Chevalier had in adulthood become ever more attached to Christianity and, in Kates' words, "d'Eon's Christianity became an armor to protect and justify his new gender identity."[179] Specifically, Kates thinks d'Eon reached the conclusion that men are associated with sin, while women are associated with virtue. In such a scheme, his crossdressing and identity as a 'mademoiselle' was a religious choice of virtue.[180]

Who was Miguel Augustin Pro?[181]

Father Miguel Augustin Pro (1891-1927) was a Mexican Catholic priest. Like many others, Father Miguel's alleged crossdressing was not for sexual satisfaction. Nor was it a reflection of homosexual or transsexual urges. Rather, if he crossdressed it was to have a disguise that permitted him greater freedom of movement as he ministered to people. Traveling by bicycle, Father Miguel utilized a number of disguises, allegedly including that of an old woman. These were necessary because the Church was facing a wave of persecution in 1920s Mexico. In defiance of his enemies, Father Miguel steadfastly continued to minister even after his capture. Condemned on false accusations of an attempted bombing, he was sentenced without trial to execution by firing squad. Forgiving his enemies and confessing Christ with his last words, he was martyred in 1927. Pope John Paul II beatified him in 1988, a critical step toward sainthood.

Who was Leo F. Heller, Jr.?[182]

Leo F. Heller, Jr. (1919-2000) is better known today by the name Lee Frances Heller. Born a biological male, Heller joined the Marines and served in World War II. Following the war, Heller became a resident at Good Shepherd Mission in Patterson, New Jersey. There a life-changing commitment transpired. Heller became chaplain at the mission and served two decades as resident director, until retiring in 1985. Moving to Jackson, Mississippi, Heller at age 67 finally came to terms with a long-standing life issue: being transgendered.

At a time in life when many are devoted to pursuing retirement leisure, Heller crossed over in a myriad of ways into a new life. Having come to terms with being both a Christian and a crossdresser, Heller now determined to help others in a similar situation. In 1990, *The Grace and Lace Letter* began, an ongoing series of writings about living as a transgendered Christian. This work survived Heller, whose poor health meant ceasing to write for it in 1997, and it continues as an online project. In 1998, hoping to be able to manage a more modest effort, Heller started the *Christian Love Letter*. This work was an ongoing occupation until Heller's death. Not long before her death, Heller became confirmed in the Episcopal Church.

Heller's message of encouragement and acceptance was widely dispersed through many articles in the aforementioned projects. Additionally, various writings were collected together in a book, *By the Grace of God*.[183] Heller was honored and revered by the transgender community for open, persistent, articulate and charitable spiritual service.

Who are more recent examples?

Interviews with crossdressers reported in any number of books and articles include those with members of the clergy, ranging from Baptist preachers to Episcopalian priests. Increasingly, crossdressing ministers are making themselves publicly known. Some of these are folk who acknowledge being 'transvestite,' while others declare themselves 'transsexual.' By whatever label they offer to others, their behavior involves previously hidden crossdressing.

While it may be premature and misleading to characterize what is happening as a movement, it is an event capturing attention in some ecclesiastical circles. A minister here or there who suddenly confesses to being transgendered is one thing; disclosure of a larger group within a denomination draws more scrutiny. In 1998, for example, it was reported in the London *Sunday Times* that nearly two dozen Anglican clergy considered themselves 'transgendered' (see Q. 20), with more than a dozen identified as 'transvestites.'[184] Such numbers garner attention—and for some, concern. But though some Christians worry over what the presence of crossdressers in the Church means, others embrace the transgendered as brothers and sisters in the faith (cf. the answer to Q. 75).

113

The contemporary Christian Church is discovering a surprising number of the transgendered in their midst. Rather than interpret this as a modern phenomena, the more likely explanation is that crossdressers feel more emboldened by changes in society to openly express their transgendered status. The evidence available to us from history shows crossdressers—male and female—have always been part of Christendom. But in previous eras, for many reasons, all but the most powerful, the most marginal, the most desperate, or the unluckiest kept their crossdressing secret. Even today the majority of Christian crossdressers keep their behavior hidden. Yet the signal being sent by clergy courageous enough to disclose their own transgendered nature may open the doors both to more openness by crossdressers and to greater acceptance by noncrossdressers.

Q. 71 Are there Christian festivals where crossdressing is permitted?

The Short Answer. As we have seen, the Church has struggled to reconcile lofty ideals of gender equality with the practice of masculine privilege. All people feel the pressures of the gender hierarchy, and some feel them most particularly within the Church. The Church has responded to this situation in a number of ways, some of which we already have discussed. One important response has been the use of certain Christian holidays ('holy days') for social celebrations where gender pressures can be eased temporarily through sanctioned gender crossings. Throughout Church history there have been festive occasions where crossdressing has been both common and unremarkable. During such times the normal restrictions on gender behavior are loosed, though within certain boundaries. At some places and times gender reversals were actually encouraged. Even clergy might participate in the ensuing, often ribald behavior. Three holidays in particular—Carnival, the Feast of Fools, and Halloween—became associated with gender crossings. Of these, Carnival and Halloween still enjoy widespread acceptance. Carnival, practiced for centuries and remaining popular in many places around the world (including the American Mardi Gras), features crossdressing as a kind of social play—an experience shared with others— and offers an important safety valve to relieve cultural pressures concerning gender. But there may be more than just that involved. Given its roots in ancient Saturnalia, perhaps Carnival recalls and celebrates a sense that original human nature was androgynous rather than differentiated by sex and gender. Even more dramatic in its 'transgression' were the activities of the Feast of Fools. The 'Fool' at the center became the personification of the folly of inverted roles. Accounts tell of priests dancing in the sanctuary dressed as women. Though condemned more than once by Church councils, it persisted for centuries before finally passing from the scene. In part, its passing was eased by its elements being transformed into secular counterparts. Americans are especially familiar with Halloween, another occasion where even grownups can play at being a different gender. This holiday, however, has lost its religious ties for many people. Another largely secular holiday in American life is Thanksgiving. Contemporary Americans are likely to be surprised to find that this holiday, too, has been associated with crossdressing. Because it also has association with religious sentiments it is added to this discussion.

The Longer answer. For centuries crossdressing has featured in various festivals associated with Christianity. Crossdressing itself has been either supported or tolerated, depending on the time and participants being considered. In answering this question we will focus on three religious festivals—Carnival, the Feast of Fools, and Halloween—as well as the quasi-religious holiday of Thanksgiving.

What is Carnival?

One festive Christian holiday stands well above the others in its ongoing association with sanctioned gender crossings. Known around the world as 'Carnival' (Mardi Gras in the United States), the name is derived from the Italian *carnevale* (itself from the Latin *carnelevarium*) and refers to the 'removing of meat' characteristic of the Lenten period. It was known by this form—'Carnival'—as early as the 13th century, but centuries earlier as 'Carne Levale.' In 1091 C.E., the Synod of Benevento formally established Ash Wednesday at the conclusion of Carnival, thus joining the festival to the season of Lent. Christian missions spread the festival everywhere Catholicism prospered so that it became a fixture in many societies, from Brazil to Trinidad to the United States. Carnival customs include feasting, games, parades, costumes—and crossdressing. Role reversal is a fixture of Carnival practice, including gender reversal through crossdressing.[185]

In his influential exploration of Carnival, philosopher Mikhail Bakhtin elucidated the idea of this festival season as a clearly defined period in time when normal social rules and conventions are suspended, when "life is subject only to its own laws."[186] The natural liberty of life, freed from social constraints, allows movements and changes otherwise unknown or disapproved. Both physical realities and social constructions can be given freer reign. Thus the sexed body and gender representations in dress and manner become things open to manipulation. That these manipulations occur in a festive context gives them the character of play—and play is a serious matter.[187]

Carnival & Play

Typically, when considering Carnival scholars regard the comedic spirit of gender crossing as something needed to discharge any anxiety over the behavior involved. While this is plausible enough it depends on the idea that if it is play it need not, perhaps *cannot* be taken seriously. Play is all too often relegated to childhood, though by whatever other name it is called (e.g., 'leisure' among adults), play persists throughout life. Festival occasions where gender crossing behavior occur help remind us that such activities, whatever they may signify, are enjoyable.

Play is pleasurable in itself. Indeed, the nature of gender crossing during Carnival *as play* may be the very key to best understanding it. Though Freud viewed play as determined by wishes, Erik Erikson probably offers a richer explanation. He understands play as an activity both of childhood and adulthood. His comments on its purposes in childhood may be pertinent to comprehending elements of gender crossing play. Erikson proposes play as a way of mastering and remastering experience through "meditating, experimenting, planning, and sharing."[188] Few experiences in life are more demanding than gender with its expectations for identity and role behavior imposed from birth to the grave. Carnivalesque periods afford uniquely suitable ways of 'meditating, experimenting, planning, and sharing' different explorations and expressions of gender. Given their sanction in the festival season, and guided by Carnival conventions, an individual can safely stretch or cross boundaries in public while aware of the safety net below. Such play enriches gender experience even as it provides release and relief from the rigid work of ordinary gender performance.

Psychologist Raymond Cattell's observations about play also seem highly pertinent. He posits that play exists because "the cultural pattern has to allow for escapes from its psychologically more exacting (long-circuited, highly discriminating) tasks."[189] In his view, play increases when cultural pressures mount; play provides a safe release and aids adjustment.[190] Cattell's thought about play's general functions is in line with his logic that play responds to cultural demands. It does so in three ways: play helps prepare us for facing the world's demands, offers relief from the stresses of such demands, and discharges our excess energies.[191]

Consider these ideas with reference to festive crossdressing. As noted a moment ago, sex and gender matters are invested in Western culture with much significance and surrounded with persistent expectations, some of them contradictory, which exert pressure on everyone inhabiting Western societies. Yet comparatively few sanctioned outlets exist for individuals *within community* to escape these pressures. Private diversions, however useful they may prove to an individual, are not the same as experiences shared with others. But experiences that involve crossing important boundaries require the weight of long sanction for most people to engage in them. Festivals like Carnival provide this needed authority.

Crossdressing as *social* play—experiences shared with others—offers an important safety valve opened by Carnival to relieve cultural pressure.[192] But it may do more. Such play, by showing the fluidity and artificiality of things like gender role expectations, may make them easier to endure on reentering the mundane world. In this manner they are as preparatory as the early experiences of childhood when all the expectations were being learned. Finally, the simple discharge of tension, physical and psychical, is highly pleasurable. Whether crossdressing is itself dressed in the thrill of tasting forbidden fruit, vicariously experiencing 'the other side' of sex and gender, fulfilling a wish, or simply indulging the senses in the experience of clothes with a different look and feel, crossdressing is pleasurable. Were it not, the behavior would long ago have been discarded.

Daniel Burlyne offers another perspective we may profit from. He connects the purpose of play to the satisfaction of our inherent need to explore. He sees play as satisfying this need by offering possibilities of novelty, complexity, uncertainty, surprise, and incongruity.[193] Clearly, cross gender activities like crossdressing excel in providing all five of these. Perhaps that helps explain why it can provide such pleasure. Remember, too, that this pleasurable experience is a communal one: both actors and observers participate in the gender crossing regardless of who is crossdressing.

Alan McGlashan's Psychology of Carnival

British psychiatrist Alan McGlashan views Carnival as an ongoing mechanism in society used to channel—and to try to control—impulses human nature insists on expressing but which society resists giving general sanction. He traces the festival back to the ancient Greek Dionysiac revels, which the Romans imported, modified, and made into the winter solstice festival of Saturnalia. The triumph of Christianity in the Empire meant further efforts at change. Saturnalia was gradually transformed into Carnival. But the Church proved more successful at spreading the festivities than in controlling them. The spirit of Carnival unleashed the myriad forms of the human unconscious in the spectacles of Carnival—and kindred festivals such as the Feast of Fools (see below), and the Feast of Asses.[194]

Noting the strong association of Carnival with public crossdressing, McGlashan offers the following explanation:

> The interchange of clothes between the sexes is part of the essence of the Carnival spirit and reveals a curious link between Carnival and one of the earliest ideas to enter the mind of man. For in many primitive societies the primordial gods and the first human beings were believed to be androgynous, and only after the fatal separation of Heaven and Earth – the Fall of Man – were the sexes set apart. Primitive festal rites were often designed to undo this "inferior" arrangement and restore the original state of completeness, in order to make possible a new beginning, a transcending of one's everyday self. Many centuries later this strange concept was still alive, and still related to festive occasions. Plutarch recorded with astonishment that in Argos a bride wore a false beard for the marriage night, while in Cos it was the husband who put on woman's clothes to receive his wife. In the fragment of a lost play by Aeschylus, the bisexual god Dionysus is greeted by cries of *"Where have you come from, man-woman? What is your country? And what is that garment?"* – questions which incidentally might well be addressed to a contemporary teenager. This deliberate confusion of sexes is also part of the basic aim of Car-

nival which seeks, however crudely, a dissolution of the stiffened traditional order, a reversal of all accepted values, and a reactivation of the boundless power and creativity of the Beginning. [195]

We can easily see that Carnival is subject to varying interpretations—each of which might in its own way capture a part of the whole. Bakhtin's notion of the festival as a time when social artifice is relaxed to let natural laws exercise their own sway is hardly incompatible with McGlashan's idea that society uses this temporary substitute for its normal rules as yet another social effort to control basic human impulses. In either reading society and nature collaborate and that collaboration results in a fluidity of gender. Similarly, the importance of play as an element actualized in Carnival through crossdressing fits with the perception that the festival offers us an opportunity to explore, experience, and even escape various aspects of gender. However understood, Carnival persists as an attractive and popular Christian holiday with gender crossings at its heart.

What was the Feast of Fools?

Although popularly remembered as 'the Feast of Fools,' the original occasion and intent of the Church was to celebrate 'The Feast of the Circumcision of Our Lord.' This celebration, which seems to have been popular from the 5th–15th centuries C.E., had its roots in older pagan ceremonies (notably the Saturnalia) and represented a new way of continuing them. The 'Fool' at the center became the personification of the folly of inverted roles, such as the preeminence of the feminine over the masculine. Males in this role dressed like women and acted like children, thus associating the image with persons of lesser social status.[196]

The festival was condemned by the Council of Toledo in A.D. 635. An account written in 1445 by the Dean of the Faculty of Theology at Paris describes clergy dancing in the sanctuary dressed as women. The Council of Basle, a decade earlier (1435), strongly condemned it, but its popular power was such that some time passed before the festival lost its force and was discontinued.[197]

Certain alternatives like the French *Société Joyeuse* ('fool-societies') provided a creative response to the condemned Feast of Fools by constructing a secularized counterpart. There were many such societies throughout France, such as the *Enfants sans Souci* ('Children without Worries') in Paris, from the 16th century forward. The ceremonies of the *Société Joyeuse* were led by a man—sometimes a member of the clergy—dressed in women's garb. This fellow, the *Abbé de Maugouvert* ('Abbey of Misrule'), portrayed the patriarchal interpretation of feminine nature—unruly, chaotic, disordered. The Abbey presided over other men who enacted roles such as 'princesses' or 'grand ladies' or even 'mothers.' In Dijon, France, where the *Société Joyeuse* was called the *Mère Folle,* a crossdressed *Mère Folle* ('Foolish Mother') served the leadership role and cheerfully maintained a scandalous running account on the sexual activities of his minions.[198] In such guise the Feast of Fools continued into the 17th century.[199]

What about Halloween?

For most Christians in the United States, Halloween (All Hallows Eve) is the best known Christian festival where crossdressing may occur. While this is completely unremarkable when small children are dressed in costumes so that little boys might become witches and little girls Harry Potter, it draws little comment even when it is adolescents or adults crossdressing. Halloween offers a rare and limited period where public crossdressing is sanctioned because it is not going to be taken as a serious or enduring statement about gender.

Halloween, observed on October 31st each year, is observed on the eve of All Saints Day (November 1st). The Catholic Church established All Saints Day in the 9th century and in the following century established All Souls Day (November 2nd), which answered to pre-existing pagan festivities concerned with the dead. Halloween capitalizes on both holy days, though is more readily associated with the latter. The manner in which it is known today has its most immediate roots in the 18th century, brought by immigrants from Europe and molded into its distinctively American form.

Donning costumes is a popular aspect of Halloween. While the most often chosen reflect the theme of departed souls and the supernatural, adults especially may select costumes that satirize one or another aspect of culture—like gender distinctions. Most of those who crossdress for the holiday do so only for the holiday. Still, some crossdressers take advantage of the opportunity for annual forays into public, though they would not any other time. Therapist Gianna Israel, though, has noted that even a holiday like Halloween can prove dangerous for the transgendered if they publicly crossdress in an unfamiliar environment.[200]

In sum, at least two widely observed Christian festivals—Carnival and Halloween—still offer socially accepted occasions for crossdressing. Though it may be argued that these festivals have become so secularized that their religious character has little if any influence, that does not mitigate historical reality. Past and present, whether 'religious' or 'secular,' these festivals have known crossdressing without significant or widespread protest. As other lines of evidence have suggested, within Christianity crossdressing is simply not typically viewed as a serious offense, even where it is not welcomed.

What about Thanksgiving?

Although Thanksgiving in the United States is a secular holiday Christians have long attached it as a quasi-religious occasion. Historian Elizabeth Pleck aptly terms it a holiday of American civil religion.[201] Prayers of thanks and other religious acts, such as giving to others in the name of Christ, are common. Most Christians view the holiday as perfectly fitting a Gospel where the ultimate gift from God of His Son provides the greatest bounty imaginable. Further, Christians regard all good things as coming from above and can point to many scriptural texts enjoining the giving of thanks as well as the sharing of what one has been blessed to receive. For all these reasons it does not seem inappropriate to consider Thanksgiving in this place.

Although the national holiday was birthed by Presidential declaration from Abraham Lincoln in 1863, the actual observance of such a day is much older. The story of the Pilgrim celebration with American Indians in 1621 provides the seminal root for the tradition. Pleck points out that no less than three Presidents before Lincoln—Washington, John Adams, and Madison—all had issued *ad hoc* national days of thanksgiving. Yet, she notes, prior to the mid-19th century the holiday was more regional than national, with greatest observance in New England.[202]

Prior to assuming its present shape, Thanksgiving was less domestic—or domesticated. Pleck recalls the 1907 observation of William Dean Howells that among the poor Thanksgiving was treated as a variant of Carnival, a day for mischief and merrymaking, where men and boys escaped domestic duties.[203] Pleck relates that, "groups of men, crossdressing, who called themselves the Fantastics or Fantasticals, masqueraded on Thanksgiving beginning in the 1780s."[204] The Fantastics also paraded on other holidays, such as New Year's Eve and Day, Washington's birthday, and the 4th of July. This practice, in New York City and in Pennsylvania, persisted more than a century; Pleck points to its acceptance, even support, into the mid-1880s. This social approval declined in the last decade of the century and by 1910 the Fantastics had disappeared.[205]

Today there remain remnants of earlier practices in the costumes sported in various Thanksgiving Day parades. However, the contemporary practice of the holiday with respect to gender strongly tends to reinforce stereotypical gender roles, with the women spending the day cooking a grand meal while the men engage in masculine boasting and competitive sports. If anything, the secularization of the holiday has only intensified gender expectations.

Q. 72 Has the Church said anything 'officially' about crossdressing?

The Short Answer. Eastern Orthodox and Roman Catholic traditions give more weight to the judgments of collective bodies and ecclesiastical leaders than is generally true in Protestantism. Therefore it is not surprising to find relatively more influential Church documents outside Protestantism. Crossdressing itself has remained a very minor matter. Historically, official attention by the Catholic Church to dress, however brief or tangential, dates back to the era of the Church Fathers. Propriety in dress mattered and entailed gender distinctions. The 4th century Council of Elvira offered two disciplinary edicts concerning dress. Women were particularly targeted. In the same century, the Council of Gangra in an epistle and canon also focused on them. Although the dress and manner of men was never ignored, until modern times more attention was given women in terms of dress violations. In the pre-Modern period, gender presentations in dress and other forms of gender behavior were often discussed in terms of a presumed 'natural order'—a tendency that persists to the present. The 1917 Code of Canon Law, which prevailed until 1983, set forth explicit dress expectations for both men and women. Modesty in dress, a concern from the New Testament onward, remained a focal point. The Sacred Congregation of the Council explicitly addressed modesty in feminine dress in 1930 by setting out directives for proper wear. Various Popes also weighed in on matters of dress and gender behavior. For example, in 1921, Pope Benedict XV addressed women in an encyclical, enjoining on them the need for modesty in dress. At mid-century Pope Pius XII wrote about 'the modern girl' and cautioned that her interest in fashion must not become an occasion for sin. Other, lesser authority figures also have spoken, such as Archbishop of Genoa, Giuseppe Cardinal Siri, who explored the relation of dress to gender identity. Vatican II issued in reforms, including the 1983 Code of Canon Law. While strictures on dress lessened overall, the Church retained its commitment to gender distinctions and its opposition to any significant gender nonconformity. In recent years, with the more prominent visibility of transgender people, the Roman Catholic Church has addressed itself to transgenderism. Although not all Catholics agree with the official stance of the Church, the Vatican's position has been in opposition to transgender people serving in religious orders.

The Longer Answer. Though the Christian Church always has been aware of the role and importance of clothing in human affairs, specific concern over crossdressing has been intermittent and relatively insignificant. Of far more importance to the Church has been the role of modesty, which might be summarized as the desire to not let the believer's manner of dress draw attention away from Christian faith and behavior. The overarching theme has been to not let clothing have more importance than is due it. When crossdressing has been attacked it often has been for its presumed link with homosexuality. To the degree that religious officials have appointed themselves the guardians of a rigidly bipolar gender scheme, to that same degree they have been likely to speak out against male effeminacy or female masculinity in any and all respects, including crossdressing.[206] Although contemporary Catholic authorities show little interest in crossdressing *per se*, they continue to offer negative judgments on homosexuality and on transsexualism.

What did the Council of Elvira say?

Early in the 4th century (c. 300-309 C.E.) the Council of Elvira met in a town near Grenada, Spain. This was the first such council on Spanish soil and there were 19 bishops and 26 priests in attendance. Of the 81 canons allegedly issued by the bishops in the acts of the council, many are today suspected of having been added at a later date. Regardless of whether this is the case or not, the canons constitute a wide-ranging set of disciplinary edicts, many of them concerning acts of sexual immorality. Two of the canons are of modest connection to our interests:

> 57.   Women and men who willingly allow their clothing to be used in secular spectacles and processions shall be denied communion for three years.
> 67.   A woman who is baptized or is a catechumen must not associate with hairdressers or men with long hair. If she does this, she is to be denied communion.[207]

The first of these concerns the clergy's opposition to theater and other gaudy public affairs. Participation in these was immodest at best, a consorting with worldly, pagan people and acts that jeopardized Christian witness. The curious aspect of this canon is the prohibition against allowing one's clothing to be used, even if the person him- or herself was not involved. This is reminiscent of Jewish ideas on purity, but may simply serve as warning against any kind of involvement with such affairs, no matter how seemingly innocuous.[208] The seriousness of the offense in the minds of the council is signified by the sanction— a denial of communion. In those days this was a much more serious penalty than many might regard it today.

The latter canon has a similar bent; attention to hair is addressed in the New Testament (see 1 Corinthians 11:6, 14-15; 1 Timothy 2:9; 1 Peter 3:3). Men with long hair could be presumed to not be under Christian discipline. Whether the canon has in mind that such men were effeminate is unclear, but certainly any number of Christians in various times and places have made such a judgment.

What did the Council of Gangra say?

Some may argue that the most germane document for our study from the first half millennium of the Church's history is the Synodal letter and canons of the Council at Gangra, held in the mid- to late 4th century C.E. This Synod of Catholic bishops condemned the followers of a prominent figure, ostensibly Eustathius of Sebaste. The severe asceticism of this group included opposition to marriage and separation from the worship of other Christians. But what is relevant to us is that they apparently also adopted what for the times was a very radical view of the equality of the sexes, even granting women the freedom to don the monk's attire, an act reserved by other groups for men alone—hence "crossdressing." Relevant excerpts are as follows:

[*From the Letter*]: They were found, moreover, fomenting separations from the houses of God and of the Church; treating the Church and its members with disdain, and establishing separate meetings and assemblies, and different doctrines and other things in opposition to the Churches and those things which are done in the Church; wearing strange apparel, to the destruction of the common custom of dress; making distributions, among themselves and their adherents as saints, of the first-fruits of the Church, which have, from the first, been given to the Church; slaves also leaving their masters, and, on account of their own strange apparel, acting insolently towards their masters; women, too, disregarding decent custom, and, instead of womanly apparel, wearing men's clothes, thinking to be justified because of these; while many of them, under a pretext of piety, cut off the growth of hair, which is natural to woman . . . .

[*From the Canons*]: Canon XIII. If any woman, under pretence of asceticism, shall change her apparel and, instead of a woman's accustomed clothing, shall put on that of a man, let her be anathema.

[*From the Epilogue*]: [W]e commend plainness and frugality in apparel, [which is worn] only from attention, [and that] not over-fastidious, to the body; but dissolute and effeminate excess in dress we eschew. . . .[209]

This condemnation must not be overstated. It fits a context and, as we have seen in answering other questions, there were exceptions to the anathema[210] pronounced on female crossdressers. The Eustathians were ascetics met with opposition by others who were also ascetic, though in a different manner. The

Gangra Synod's opposition to women dressing as men stemmed less from the crossdressing itself and more from what was viewed as a prideful usurpation by women of male prerogatives. Their taking on men's clothes symbolized their seizure of men's roles and offices, which was generally unacceptable in both Church and society.[211]

What was being said during the pre-modern period?

In Europe, before the modern age, the Church enjoyed an extended period of authoritative social influence. Christianity religiously unified Europe's culture and lent it a more conservative bent in fashion. Both sleeves and hemlines lengthened as the Christian emphasis on modesty expressed itself in dress. Although both sexes were admonished to be modest in dress, the emphasis was particularly placed on modesty in women. Accordingly, their dress became more restrictive in showing less of the body, both flesh and form. Women's tunics in the early Middle Ages were longer, while bifurcated garments (e.g., trousers) were reserved for men. The liberalization of dress made possible by events such as the disillusionment following the passing of a millennium since Christ's ascension to heaven, and the development of the means for more diversity in fashion, made things more challenging for ecclesiastical authorities (see Q. 45).

The Church continued to develop its ideas about what constituted proper distinctions and relations between the genders. Sociologist David Greenberg documents for feudal England and Normandy that some Christian clerics in the 11th-12th centuries viewed gender variant behavior as 'unnatural'—literally a violation of Nature. As keepers of order, both religious and otherwise, clergy sometimes sought to check what they viewed as threatening the ordained and natural order between the genders. Of course, this gender order kept masculine males firmly entrenched at the top of society. Males exhibiting feminine traits or behavior thus represented an undermining of natural and social order—especially when those males were members of the royal court.[212]

Men were not the only ones under pressure to conform to gender expectations. Women were not uniformly content to be subordinate. In fact, the 13th century Dominican friar Albertus Magnus (aka St. Albert the Great), in his *Quaestiones de animalibus* (*Inquiry Concerning Living Things*), probably reflects a common sentiment with his remark, "There is no woman who would not naturally want to shed the definition of femininity and put on masculinity."[213] That some women did so through crossdressing was certain—as was the Church's response, which sometimes veered into hysteria as gender nonconforming women were proclaimed witches.

The prevailing Christian ideology viewed women as especially prone to the wiles of the Devil—and crossdressing suggested to some folk that a woman seeking what was not 'hers by nature' must be bedeviled. In the *Malleus Maleficarum* (*The Witch Hammer*) witches were attributed with the ability to work glamour spells—illusions that could make a man believe he had no penis, or otherwise change someone's appearance. By the work of the devil, a girl was alleged to have been transformed into a boy. No wonder, then, crossdressing at times might be connected with witchcraft. Even where it was not so linked, a connection might be drawn between dress violations and dire consequences. Renaissance scholar Kate Chedgzoy refers to a 1560 broadsheet entitled *The True Description of a Child with Ruffles*, in which the birth of a child 'with ruffs' is attributed to the mother having worn them in violation of her proper social place.[214]

Both the Church and various states made efforts to regulate dress. Sumptuary regulations (*sumptuariae leges*) for clergy were in place in the high Middle Ages. These were eventually accompanied by regulations aimed at various groups, especially religious minorities (e.g., Jews and Muslims), but also others, including heretics, harlots, and those afflicted by various diseases like leprosy. Among European states the best known such laws emerged in the 14th-15th centuries, the period immediately preceding the Protestant Reformation, in England, where they continued into the 17th century. But England was not alone in its efforts to regularize dress to maintain distinctions of gender or class. The same was transpiring elsewhere, and everywhere it seemed women were the special target.[215]

As Protestantism grew, it for the most part shared Catholicism's concern to carefully maintain the prevailing gender hierarchy. Gender appropriate dress continued to matter—and crossdressing continued to occur. The persistence of the practice was such that by the early 17th century, England's King James I commanded London's pastors to speak against the practice of women dressing in mannish attire.[216] And still it persisted, both among women and men. Terry Castle, a leading scholar on 18th century English life and literature, writes of the time that, "Transvestite costume was perhaps the most common offense against decorum. Women strutted in jack-boots and breeches, while men primped in furbelows and flounces."[217] In their masquerades, men appeared as old women, witches, bawdy women, nursery-maids, and shepherdesses, while women disguised themselves as soldiers, sailors—and clergymen!

What did the 1917 Code of Canon Law say?

The Church addressed increasing secularization in the states of Europe in a variety of ways. In 1917, the Catholic Church, under the direction of Pope Benedict XV, promulgated a Code of Canon Law (*Codex Iuris Canonici*) that remained in effect until 1983. This code, based on an earlier one, contained a provision specifically addressing the appearance of men and women when receiving Mass. Canon 1262, § 2, reads: "Men should attend Mass, either in church or outside church, with bare heads, unless approved local custom or special circumstances suggest otherwise; women, however, should have their heads veiled and should be modestly dressed, especially when they approach the table of the Lord."[218]

This canon reflects the New Testament text of 1 Corinthians 11:3-10, especially the following two verses (vv. 4-5): "Every man who prays or prophesies with his head covered dishonors his head. And every woman who prays or prophesies with her head uncovered dishonors her head—it is just as though her head were shaved [NIV]." To this textual foundation might be added others in the New Testament addressing the general theme of modesty and dress, such as 1 Timothy 2:9-10 and 1 Peter 3:3 (see the answer to Q 66).

What did Pope Benedict XV say in *Sacra Propediem?*

Reflecting the ecclesiastical temper of the times, Pope Benedict XV made the following remarks in his 1921 encyclical *Sacra Propediem*:

> From this point of view one cannot sufficiently deplore the blindness of so many women of every age and condition; made foolish by desire to please, they do not see to what a degree the indecency of their clothing shocks every honest man, and offends God. Most of them would formerly have blushed for those toilettes as for a grave fault against Christian modesty; now it does not suffice for them to exhibit them on the public thoroughfares; they do not fear to cross the threshold of the churches, to assist at the Holy sacrifice of the Mass, and even to bear the seducing food of shameful passions to the Eucharistic Table where one receives the heavenly Author of purity. And We speak not of those exotic and barbarous dances recently imported into fashionable circles, one more shocking than the other; one cannot imagine anything more suitable for banishing all the remains of modesty.[219]

These remarks reflect the Church authorities ongoing struggle with the secularization of society. The triumph of modern fashion could be viewed as the death knell of modesty. While the latter continued to be extolled, a shrinking number even among the faithful seemed to find it as worthy a goal as the celibate leaders of the ecclesiastical hierarchy. But the Church persisted.

What did the Sacred Congregation of the Council say?

During this time, the emphasis on modesty in dress was put into specific instructions. In 1930, under Pope Pius XI, the Sacred Congregation of the Council set out the following directives:

> We recall that a dress cannot be called decent which *is cut deeper than two fingers breadth under the pit of the throat,* which does not cover the arms at *least to the elbows,* and scarcely reaches a bit beyond the knee. Furthermore, dresses of transparent material are *improper.*
>
> *Let parents keep their daughters* away from public gymnastic games and contests; but, if their daughters are compelled to at-

tend such exhibitions, let them see to it that they are fully and modestly dressed. *Let them* **never** *permit their daughters to don immodest garb.*[220]

Despite such exacting pronouncements, modern Catholics—especially in Europe and the United States—tended to dress in a manner more consistent with the general culture.

What did Pope Pius XII say in *Counsel to Teaching Sisters?*

The concern of the early 20th century was still evident at the beginning of the second half of the century. In 1951, Pope Pius XII, commenting in an encyclical on 'the modern girl,' wrote:

> The modern girl! You can measure better than many others the still unsolved problems and the grave dangers resulting from recent changes in the woman's world from her sudden introduction into all walks of public life. Was there ever such a time as the present when a girl had to be won on and trained interiorly, according to her convictions and will, for Christ's cause and a virtuous life, remaining faithful to both despite all temptations and obstacles, beginning with modesty in dress and ending with the most serious and distressing problems of life?[221]

In both of the instances above, the Popes' concerns are directed at women. This is consistent with the general tendency of Christian tradition, always more preoccupied with the dress of women than of men. The focus is modesty, both in dress and behavior. Another remark, offered by Pope Pius XII in 1948, shows the general concern: "style must never be a proximate occasion of sin."[222]

While crossdressing as such is not explicitly addressed by these documents, it is not hard to imagine papal opposition to women adopting masculine dress. The fashions of the time often incorporated masculine elements into feminine styles. Moreover, there was a growing popularity among women of bifurcated garb—notably pants. There continued to be an expectation that modestly dressed women, especially when attending church, would be dressed in distinctly feminine apparel, and that did not include pants, no matter how feminized.

What did Giuseppe Cardinal Siri, Archbishop of Genoa say?

The growing discrepancy between common practice and Church protocol proved a continuing tension in the Church. In 1960, for example, the Archbishop of Genoa, Giuseppe Cardinal Siri, issued a notification on 'Men's Dress Worn By Women.' In it he sought to articulate a stance that would constitute a 'balanced moral judgment.' He began by acknowledging that women wearing men's trousers was *not* in itself a grave offense against modesty, though wearing too tightly fitting pants was immodest. What concerned the Archbishop was the chain of events set in motion by such dress behavior. First, he believed, the wearing of men's dress by women affects the woman's feminine psychology. Secondly, it affects the relationship between the sexes. Thirdly, it harms her dignity in her children's eyes.[223]

Cardinal Siri argued that clothing exerts an influence such that it "imposes" a particular frame of mind. For women wearing pants it creates a masculine frame of mind and indicates a reaction against her femininity as though it were inferior. At the same time, by diminishing diversity between the genders it weakens the "normal psychological structure" the sexes depend on for attraction to one another. One aspect of that is a diminishing of the sense of shame accompanying the wearing of properly modest dress. Since this sense of shame helps hold people in check, reducing it yields more degradation into sensuality. Finally, the Cardinal argued, such dress diminishes the mother's dignity in the sight of her children. In sum, then, women wearing men's dress damages her psychology and her relations and ought to be considered a factor "tearing apart human order."[224]

What was evident in manner of dress was no less obvious in other matters concerning gender. These various tensions eventually led to the progressive vision of the modern Catholic Church articulated in the Second Vatican Council (1962-1965).

What did Pope Paul VI say in *Ecclesiae Sanctae?*

Vatican II, under the leadership of Pope John XXII, initiated substantial changes. Reflecting the spirit of the Council, canon 6 of the 1983 Code of Canon Law specifically ended all the provisions of the previous code unless particular earlier canons were directly incorporated into the new code. Among the canons that thus passed from ecclesiastical potency was Canon 1262 (cited above). Instead, the Church hierarchy issued statements such as the following one from Pope Paul VI in his *Ecclesiae Sanctae*, issued in 1966: "As far as the religious condition is concerned (No. 18), care should be taken lest more attention be given to exterior forms (such as gestures, dress, the arts, etc.) than to the religious dispositions of the peoples which are to be adopted and the evangelical perfection which is to be assimilated."[225]

In essence, the Church tried to shift attention away from outward forms back to inward states. If these were properly attended to, outward forms—including dress behavior—would take care of themselves. At the same time, Vatican II did not eliminate concern over outward forms, despite the opinion of some within the Church that it had gone too far in its 'concessions' and 'modernizations.' Predictably, there was some opposition.

What does Bishop Antonio de Castro-Mayer say?

Although the new Code of Canon Law might have discarded earlier canons, there remained sectors of the Church resistant to the changes. Our Lady of Fatima, for instance, continued to champion a conservative notion of modesty. Their ongoing resistance to some contemporary fashion styles is relevant to our consideration. Bishop Antonio de Castro-Mayer wrote in 1998: "Indeed, the styles of dress of the women and girls of today such as: very tight clothing; dressing like men, including slacks and tights; low necklines; skirts with hemlines or slits which do not cover the leg below the knee - are absolutely contrary to the norms of Christian modesty."[226] They have sought to remain in continuity with what they regard as the true and constant thread of Church tradition.

What does Father Robert Auman say?

Of course, there also have been a variety of less formal pronouncements issued at various levels of hierarchy. While space limitations prohibit looking at these across history, we should note that the contemporary diversity of thinking within Roman Catholicism, coupled with today's ease of publishing one's thoughts, has made it easier than ever to access varying opinions. For example, at the beginning of the 21st century, Catholic priest Father Robert Auman addressed the issue of crossdressing on the *Catholic Online Forum*:

> Simply dressing in clothes that are normally worn by the other sex is morally neutral, that is, neither morally good nor morally bad in itself. It derives its morality or immorality from the purpose for which it is done and how and where it is done. For instance, to put on a stage performance or an amusement performance, there would be nothing sinful for a man to dress as a woman or for a woman to dress as a man. But if either were to crossdress in order to work some deception for immoral purposes, obviously that would be gravely sinful.[227]

This comment reflects Church tradition with a certain modern sensibility. Unlike the Church Fathers and ecclesiastical authorities down into the modern period, Father Auman shows no anxiety over theatrical crossdressing. However, in keeping with an emphasis in the Church since its founding, Father Auman desires to keep Christian use of dress connected to propriety. Crossdressing intending the blurring of gender lines in order to conduct immorality remains objectionable. But the mere matter of crossdressing is neutral.

In sum, gender distinctions in dress have been a constant concern to the Church, though it is easy to exaggerate that concern. The Church traditionally has upheld the use of clothing to preserve gender distinctions. A major motivation in maintaining a gender divide has been the hierarchical nature of church authority. Especially in the Roman Catholic tradition, male and female roles have been carefully marked out. Crossdressing, as we have seen (cf. answers to

Q. 68-69), has been used on occasion by women to gain access to roles reserved for men. The concern, then, has been to forbid masquerades that create improper role-playing within the religious community. Yet this concern must be tempered by remembering how many crossdressers have been recognized as saints; their very crossdressing testified to their religious fervor.

Has anything been said about other transgender realities?

We cannot pass from this question without some consideration of the transgender realities commonly associated today with crossdressing. Even as the present Church has little to say on crossdressing as such, it has some pointed words about other pertinent matters. The contemporary Roman Catholic Church has not been friendly toward transgender people in its official remarks. Especially in light of clergy sex abuse scandals the Church has reinvigorated homophobic and transphobic positions in the ranks of authority, especially in more socially restrictive societies. Some laity in many of these societies, and some of the clergy, have opposed these developments. At the present time there exists significant tension within Catholicism with respect to transgender realities, and especially with respect to homosexuality.

The Catholic Church's Stance on Homosexuality

As this is being written, the Roman Catholic Church under Pope Benedict XVI is in the process of issuing clarifying directions on the status of homosexuals in the clergy or admitted into any of the offices of the church, or even permitted as students in seminaries preparing for ministry. If anything, restrictions are certain to increase. When still known as Cardinal Joseph Ratzinger and Prefect of the Congregation for the Doctrine of the Faith (CDF), the present pope was the author of the 1986 *Letter to the Bishops of the Catholic Church on the Pastoral Care of Homosexual Persons*. Noting the increasing debate over homosexuality and how it should be evaluated morally, the document aims to set down the Church's official position. It hearken's back to the 1975 *Declaration on Certain Questions Concerning Sexual Ethics*, which noted a distinction between 'the homosexual condition or tendency' and 'individual homosexual actions.' [228]

Ratzinger notes that some utilized this distinction to draw what he characterizes as "an overly benign interpretation" of homosexuality itself. He writes, "Although the particular inclination of the homosexual person is not a sin, it is a more or less strong tendency ordered towards an intrinsic moral evil; and thus the inclination itself must be seen as an objective disorder."[229] He especially warned against succumbing to pressures brought by some both inside and outside the Church to accept homosexuality and to condone homosexual activity.[230]

The current Pope's thinking also can be seen in his 2003 *Considerations Regarding Proposals to Give Legal Recognition to Unions Between Homosexual Persons*, also written while Prefect of the CDF. He began that document by reaffirming his view that, "Homosexuality is a troubling moral and social phenomenon. . . ."[231] He contends that Scripture condemns homosexual acts as "serious depravity."[232] However, he reiterates his earlier stance that despite the immorality of homosexual behavior, homosexual persons should not be subject to "unjust discrimination."[233] Yet he does not see denial of marriage to same-sex couples as discriminatory and, in fact, calls for Christians to oppose laws permitting such unions. This stance he seeks to support on various grounds.[234] Ratzinger concludes, "The Church teaches that respect for homosexual persons cannot lead in any way to approval of homosexual behavior or to legal recognition of homosexual unions."[235] As pope, he has continued to view the matter in the same way, declaring in 2005 that same-sex unions are "pseudo-matrimony."[236]

The present pope's position notwithstanding, the relationship of Roman Catholicism to homosexuality has been long and complex—far outside the reach of this work. What can be said is that the relationship has not been as simple and straightforward as some have sought to represent it. The work of scholars like historian John Boswell[237] makes it clear that claims that the Church has always resisted, opposed, and condemned homosexuality and same-sex unions is at best historically short-sighted and at worst a malicious caricature of history. The current statements made by various Catholic scholars and leaders makes it plain that there is no more unanimity on this matter than pertains among other Christian groups. For example, a Catholic priest writing on biblical teaching about homosexuality has maintained it is not condemned in holy writ,[238] and a number of clergy, like those who issued the so-called 'Phoenix Declaration' have spoken out against Church teachings that they perceive as intolerant, discriminatory, and encouraging of violence.[239] However, the Vatican's recent apparent tying together of homosexuality and the sexual abuse of children by clergy represents an extremely disturbing development.

The Catholic Church's Stance on Transsexualism

With regard to transsexualism, the Vatican's Congregation for the Doctrine of the Faith under Pope John Paul II defined the reality in accordance with prevailing mental health diagnostic systems. Thus it is regarded as a mental disorder. In 2000 this body issued a confidential (*sub secretum*) memorandum to leaders of religious orders directing them to report instances of transsexualism and to respond to such cases by either prohibiting applicants from admission into the order or by disciplining those already in the order by suspension or expulsion if they pursued sex changes. According to reports confirmed by Vatican officials, the document directs that, "When, from clear external behavior and the testimony of those assigned to formation, there emerges the prudent doubt about the presence of transsexuality, the superior should arrange for a careful medical and psychiatric exam." Confirmation of signs of transsexuality leads to the responses indicated above. This document only became more widely known in 2003.[240]

The alleged principal author of this secret document is Father Urbano Navarette, a Spanish Jesuit canon law scholar, retired from duties at the Pontifical Gregorian University. A specialist with respect to issues of marriage and family, in 1997, he authored an article on transsexualism published in a journal on canon law. His position is that transsexualism does not change a person's gender, nor does sex reassignment surgery change their sex. Therefore, marriage by a transsexual person to a member of the same genetic sex is a same-sex union and forbidden. Navarette appears to be the person most looked to by the Vatican in these matters; he was used as a consultant by the CDF when the present pope was Prefect there. In 2007, Pope Benedict XVI elevated the 87-year-old Navarette to the rank of Cardinal—the highest rank except for the papacy itself.

The Church forbids sex-change operations. These are regarded as contravening God's creation. The *Catechism* covers the matter indirectly, under the dictum that "directly intended amputations, mutilations, and sterilizations" are forbidden except when performed for "strictly therapeutic medical reasons."[241] Though the text could be construed that sex reassignment surgery fits this qualification, it is clear from the Church's reasoning that it does not.

Pope John Paul II's successor, Pope Benedict XVI, has continued the Church's stance on homosexuality and transsexualism. Though not all Catholic clergy support this position, most do. One put the matter on sex changes this way:

> When examining this moral issue, once must not simply focus on the gravity of the physical mutilation. Rather, one must also focus on the devastating impact this act has on loved ones — parents, spouses, children — as well as friends and the community at large. Couldn't a child say in this story, "My father killed himself to be someone else?" Therein lies the tragedy of this heinous act.[242]

At present, then, transgender realities are not welcomed nor positively regarded by the Roman Catholic hierarchy at the Vatican. Yet it would be an error to assume that all Catholic clergy concur in this stance. Nor do all Catholic religious scholars. Nor do all Catholic believers. Whatever the declaration of the Church, which is subject to clarification and revision at any time, there will persist differences of opinion. Nevertheless, the vast majority of Catholics can and do agree that in such matters a spirit of charity should prevail so that differences are met with acts of kindness rather than violence in the name of piety.

Q. 73 What do Christians today who oppose transgender realities say?

The Short Answer. What little attention given within the Church today to transgender realities is usually focused on homosexuality. Second to that is some concern over crossdressing, which tends to be joined to the stereotype that all crossdressing males are gay. Because of the little excitement generated by women who crossdress, most attention with respect to crossdressing is directed toward males, who typically are perceived as employing gender confusion for sexual purposes. While it is true that Christian groups and individuals reflect the diversity both of Christianity and society in the various responses they make to transgender realities, it is also true that Christians collectively generally share in the wider cultural biases. They mostly support as 'natural' and 'God given' that sex, gender, and sexual orientation should line up in the manner they do for the majority of people. Thus, those who are neither heterosexual masculine males nor heterosexual feminine females are often regarded as outside the divine plan, folk who reflect in one degree or another a state of sin. Most Christians are not outspoken on the matter, but their silence should not be construed as tolerance, a term often loosely used when it is employed. In fact, the silence of the majority often reflects passive acquiescence to the culture. Probably a majority of Christians have not pondered whether their culture's gender scheme reflects the best of Christian values and thinking. The value of 'tolerance' comes under special scrutiny. Are many Christians as tolerant as they suppose themselves to be? The most common form of a supposedly tolerant response is found in the oft-heard expression, 'Love the sinner, but hate the sin.' This idea permits many Christians to denounce transgender realities that they personally detest while salving any unease about their harshness through reminding themselves that they 'love' the person whose acts they hate. With this manner of rationalization as a backdrop, those Christians who have been especially vitriolic in their opposition to transgender realities, especially homosexuality, are the ones who have gained the most public attention. Such voices remind all of us how conflicted our society is on such matters because the stridency of their positions often clashes with other cherished cultural values and proves distasteful even to many who generally agree with them. However, even those made uneasy by the rhetoric of hate often continue to support the opposition to transgender realities, though with only the barest of arguments.

The Longer answer. Transgender realities are arguably more visible in the world today than perhaps ever before. Their visibility has extended into the world of religion. Christian people, both individually and collectively, have found themselves discussing transgender realities. By and large this has meant sympathy and support for intersex people, but controversy concerning other transgender populations. Nowhere has controversy been more intense than concerning homosexuality.

What is the argument against homosexuality?

Because this present work has elected not to focus on homosexuality, less attention is given to this debate than it merits. But it is too large and important a controversy to pass over in silence. Accordingly, a brief treatment of the debate is offered in this and the following answer. In this answer we examine the broad context of the modern controversy and the contours of the argument against homosexuality. Unfortunately, often 'contours' are all that opponents provide. The comfort of operating from within a majority, one enjoying cultural support, means less of a need being felt to supply carefully reasoned and supported contentions. However, for more information on either side of the debate any number of scholarly resources are available.[243] We begin here with homosexuality since it is where opponents to transgender realities usually start.

Christian Traditions & Authorities

The Christian world is diverse, with three distinct major traditions (Eastern Orthodox, Roman Catholic, Protestant), and many expressions within each. There is no consensus on many matters, from the role of the Holy Spirit to the manner of baptism to whether homosexuality is sin. While every individual believer forms a personal answer to each matter of faith and practice, most look for guidance in coming to that answer. For some that guidance principally or entirely comes from a sense of their own relationship with God. Others rely on the authority of those they accept as called to ministry, such as pastors and priests. They trust these authorities to have studied the matters in question, to have formed answers consistent with their faith tradition and its sources of knowledge, and to have no personal axe to grind. Still others turn first and foremost to the Bible, seen as Holy Scripture and trusted as a Living Word of God. Commonly multiple sources of guidance are looked to in the effort to formulate an answer on difficult questions.

All of these forces are brought to bear in the debate over homosexuality. There are individuals, both lay and ministers, who stand on either side. The same holds true for groups, including churches and denominations.[244] Even though the parties on one side may agree in their broad conclusion, there are generally significant differences in how they got to that conclusion, how strongly they affirm it, and how they carry it out in policy and practice.

The general character of the argument as usually advanced is relatively simple. It typically appeals to the Bible, though often adds appeals to certain moral arguments,[245] ecclesiastical authority[246] or other sources, such as a particular view of Nature as God's created order. The biblical outline of the argument against homosexuality generally runs something like this: God created male and female, commanding them to 'be fruitful and multiply' (Genesis 1-2). However, sin entered and disrupted both the Natural order of creation and humanity's relationship with God (Genesis 3). Some consequences were spelled out with regard to reproduction: a woman's desire would be for her husband and the children she delivered him would be brought forth through pain (Genesis 3:16). The picture thus created is of two sexes with sexual desire for each other in service of God's command but complicated by the reality of sin.

The Bible recognizes complications of sin in sexual life by laws set out to constrain human sexual behavior and relationships. These include, for instance, laws prohibiting incestuous relationships, sexual intercourse during the menstrual period, bestiality, and adultery (e.g. Leviticus 18:6-23; 20:10-21; Deuteronomy 22:22-30). One particular set of statements occasions much comment: "You shall not lie with a male as with a woman; it is an abomination" (Leviticus 18:22, NSRV); "If a man lies with a male as with a woman, both of them have committed an abomination; they shall be put to death; their blood is upon them" (Leviticus 20:13, NSRV).

To these verses are often added the story of the fate of Sodom and Gomorrah (Genesis 19), about which a New Testament text remarks they "indulged in sexual immorality and pursued unnatural lust" (Jude 7, NSRV; cf. 2 Peter 2:4-10). Further 'proof' is added by appeal to the Apostle Paul's logic that unbelievers who exchanged truth about God for a lie, worshipping and serving the creature rather than the Creator, were given over by God to degrading passions; "Their women exchanged natural intercourse for unnatural, and in the same way also the men, giving up natural intercourse with women, were consumed with passion for one another. Men committed shameless acts with men and received in their own person the due penalty for their error" (Romans 1:26-27, NSRV). As a kind of clincher one or another 'list' text is often thrown in, such as, "Do not be deceived! Fornicators, idolaters, adulterers, male prostitutes, sodomites, thieves, the greedy, drunkards, revilers, robbers—none of these will inherit the kingdom of God" (1 Corinthians 6:9-10; cf. 1 Timothy 1:10). In this last text, the words translated 'male prostitutes' and, especially, 'sodomites' have been variously translated, but are often popularly construed as referring to homosexuals.

The sum of the picture thus drawn is that the Bible condemns homosexual behavior. Those who practice it are sinning. If unrepentant, they are judged by God and experience negative consequences, either in this world or the next, or both. Some Christians regard HIV and AIDS as one such consequence (though this view is no longer as popular as it once was). Others see it as appropriate that homosexuals are shunned, shamed, or otherwise 'correctively' mistreated. Many draw a distinction between the sinner and the sin; homosexual behavior is wrong but being a homosexual is not. Others make no such distinction, arguing that homosexuality is as homosexuality does: a homosexual is someone who does homosexual sex, either in the flesh or in their hearts (cf. Matthew 5:27). If they stop the behavior and renounce their lustful passion for same-sex people, then—and only then—forgiveness is possible.

The Appeal to Theology

Commonly the biblical texts are placed in the context of more general theological arguments. Typically these stress the nature of God's original intention and design—the created order—and the exclusive (or at least preeminent) place of reproductive sex. Since reproduction requires male and female, heterosexuality is natural; homosexuality is thus unnatural. The unnatural reflects sin. The redeemed order established in the Church resists, condemns, and overcomes sin. There is no place in this 'new creation' for old brokenness—nonreproductive sexual behavior like homosexuality has to go.

Obviously the degree of sophistication of the argument mounted varies considerably. Some simply spout, 'God made Adam and Eve, not Adam and Steve,' and let it go at that, as though the matter were so simple and obvious any dissenter must be a moron. Others are more respectful, acknowledging that issues involved in interpreting each text and relating them to one another are complicated by historical, linguistic, and cultural matters besides theological ones. However, those who make an argument against homosexuality agree in one matter: it is sin, a 'missing of the mark' for what God intends, and should be responded to accordingly.

What is the argument against transsexualism?

Compared to the roar that is the ongoing debate over homosexuality, other transgender realities are barely a whispered conversation. This appears to be true even if we grant Cambridge religious scholar Fraser Watts' arguable contention that people are "instinctively" more unsettled by the transgender reality of transsexualism.[247] A principal part of the reason that other transgender realities receive less individual attention is because they are generally attached to the conversation about homosexuality. Thus, crossdressing in general, and transsexualism in particular, are typically regarded as serving some deviant sexual instinct or aim, and that aim is usually regarded as homosexual in character.

Argument 1: Transsexualism is an Excuse for Homosexuality

We have seen repeatedly how many people link transgender realities with homosexuality. Nowhere is this more true or pronounced than with transsexualism. One objection raised by Christian opponents to transsexualism is that it is a psychological maneuver by the individual to justify as heterosexual what is really a homosexual orientation. In other words, a transsexual deceives him/herself by claiming that changing the sexual appearance of the body makes having sexual relations with a different appearing body heterosexual, and therefore all right.

According to this view, what transsexualism is really about is sexual desire, not some sense that one's body sex and gender disagree. The perceived disagreement between two things that *cannot* disagree is a fiction. The person who adopts this fiction is mentally disturbed in a literal sense—they have disordered the natural logic of sex and gender because they are unwilling to face their homosexuality. The elaborate artifice of becoming transsexual is a radical effort to deny their sinful sexuality.

Argument 2: Transsexualism is Satanic

Some Christians view the contemporary fascination with transsexualism as a sign of Satanic influence. One perspective on this is that Satan aims to controvert every form of order God establishes. Since God has established two sexes with corresponding genders, any change in this arrangement is a rebellion. Those who aim to overthrow this divinely established order thus prove themselves the allies of Satan, 'the Adversary.'

Regardless of whether some Christians see Satanic influence as a point of origin for transsexualism, they can point to what they perceive as religion-like aspects. They may reason that, like Satan, transsexuals (and other transgender people) are trying to set up a rival world order. Within the transgender community there might be seen a kind of fervor that may seem to others religious in character, but which establishes a different center of attention than Christ. Similarly, Christian opponents to gender variant people recognize a growing transgender community—and worry about it. Like the Church, this community shares a central, defining experience, offers mutual support, and affirms its validity. Might they also be like the Church in proselytizing? Some believe that homosexuals, crossdressers, and transsexual people seek to make other people not only accept them, but join them in their behavior.

Argument 3: Transsexualism Despoils God's Creation

Christian opponents to transsexualism further argue that the very fact that someone is being actively supported to modify the body God gave them is thereby being encouraged to sin. Body transformations, whether through hormones or surgery, state openly a belief that the body given at birth is *wrong*. Christian opponents respond that what is wrong is altering what God has made. They may point to Bible verses such as Psalms 139:13f., addressed to God:

> For it was you who formed my inward parts;
> you knit me together in my mother's womb.
> I praise you, for I am fearfully and wonderfully made.
> Wonderful are your works; that I know very well.

139

Similarly, the Roman Catholic Church's *Catechism* states:

> Everyone, man and woman, should acknowledge and accept his sexual identity. Physical, moral, and spiritual difference and complementarity are oriented toward the goods of marriage and the flourishing of family life. The harmony of the couple and of society depends in part on the way in which the complementarity, needs, and mutual support between the sexes are lived out.[248]

What disturbs many Christians is what they see as an implicit hubris in transsexualism. It seems that the individual acts as though they know better than God how they should be made, and claim an authority to make changes that usurps what only properly belongs to God. Thus, in addition to being sinful for changing God's creation, transsexualism is sinful for its overweening pride.

Argument 4: The Bible Condemns It

Much of the biblical argument against transsexualism found by its opponents is circumstantial, appealing to texts in line with the three arguments advanced above. Thus, transsexualism when linked to homosexuality is thereby brought under the condemnation of homosexuality that opponents find in various scriptures. By linking together verses perceived as presenting a normative view of creation—which in opponents' eyes is a *hetero*normative one—a calculated impression is made that anything other than gender conforming heterosexuality is outside divine intention. In short, based on a particular understanding of what *is* written, assumptions are made about things for which *nothing* is written. In this manner, the biblical argument advanced by opponents is primarily a theological (rather than exegetical) one.[249]

However, a particular New Testament text is sometimes advanced as referring to transgender, though most often it is enlisted in the opposition to homosexuality. This text is one we quoted earlier, which bears repeating: "Do not be deceived! Fornicators, idolaters, adulterers, male prostitutes, sodomites, thieves, the greedy, drunkards, revilers, robbers—none of these will inherit the kingdom of God" (1 Corinthians 6:9-10). The key term here is the Greek word μαλακοί (*malakoi*), rendered in English in the New Revised Standard Version (NSRV) as 'male prostitutes.' When used against transgender people, the translation preferred by opponents is 'effeminate.' The Greek μαλακός (*malakos*) can be rendered in English as either 'soft,' or 'effeminate.' In fact, this is the translation offered by the King James Version (KJV), an older translation still preferred by many Christians.

The masculine form of the Greek word makes it clear that males are being referred to by μαλακός. If the meaning is 'effeminate men,' then it is easy to see that transgender males are ranked alongside a host of other undesirable characters. The impression that transgender males are in view here may be strengthened by the way the *Interlinear Greek-English New Testament* translates the word,

140

using an entire phrase: "abusers of themselves as women."[250] It is easy to envision this as a picture of crossdressed males masquerading as women.

What is the argument against crossdressing?

As has been characteristic throughout Church history, Christian theologians, scholars, and ecclesiastical leaders mostly have had other matters on their mind; crossdressing has excited relatively little attention. That does not mean, though, that it is today widely embraced as an approved practice. For the most part Christians everywhere reflect the cultural biases of the societies they live in. Religion's predominant social function is as the conserver of the dominant culture. Religious scholars and leaders are hardly the only ones who can be vocal on a subject. Many lay people voice their thoughts and feelings as well.

Not only do such voices reflect the value Christianity gives to individual conscience, they also often display the recognition that religious judgments made on the matter impact the lives of real people. Not surprisingly, many of those who write on the topic do so from a particular stance, whether vigorously opposing transgender realities like transsexualism or crossdressing, or appealing for tolerance. Among the former, it is common to find lines of argumentation similar to those employed against homosexuality: an appeal to the Bible, a reliance on Church authority, and a use of theological reasoning.

1. The 'Appeal to the Bible' Argument

It is common for Christians to begin and end their objections to crossdressing with an appeal to Deuteronomy 22:5, which reads simply: "A woman shall not wear a man's apparel, nor shall a man put on a woman's garment; for whoever does such things is abhorrent to the LORD your God" (NRSV; see the answers to Q. 61-65). This single verse is typically treated as a self-evident and complete answer. When it is sometimes bolstered by reference to other texts, the effort seems to be to justify the acceptance of this particular Old Testament text as it stands, while not being bound by many other Old Testament prohibitions.[251]

The appeal to the Bible is given pride of place because most Christians regard the holy text as a final authority in matters of faith and practice. If the Bible says crossdressing is wrong, then crossdressing is wrong. Because the words in the English translation are so straightforward, there is little interest in expanding or expounding them. Simply repeating them seems to be enough to make the opponents' point. They regard this text as 'proof' that their opposition to crossdressing is correct.

2. The 'Appeal to Personal Experience' Argument

Other opponents write from personal experience, recounting how they came to renounce what they once practiced. Especially within Protestant Evangelicalism there is a long history of favoring the authority of a personal witness capable of stirring feelings and changing the will. Two examples, one with respect to transsexualism and the other in regard to transvestism, illustrate the nature of such arguments.

Testimony of a Converted Transsexual

For example, the conservative *Journal of Biblical Counseling* carried a testimony from an anonymous man who claimed to have been a transsexual rescued from his condition by the grace of God. 'Anonymous' offers a fairly straightforward and common account of transsexual experience: he recalls from early childhood a persistent desire to be a girl, an identification with them, feminine mannerisms and behavior, and crossdressing that began about age 6 and developed in extent over the years. By college he owned his own wardrobe of feminine clothes, was regularly crossdressing in secret, and was appearing in public as a woman once or twice a week. The crossdressing was not associated with sexual arousal. "I never masturbated because I was not at all after a sexual thrill. The experience felt to me to be one of freedom. I felt like 'myself.' It was a liberty and a release that was absolutely exhilarating. There was tremendous joy, and yet I would sometimes weep with relief when I was dressed."[252] All this represents elements of experience common to transsexuals.

So, too, does his growing sense of alienation and isolation. He relates experiences of being mocked and becoming increasingly lonely. In adolescence he began to experience same-sex desires. He also learned about transsexualism and saw himself in what he learned. A longing for sex reassignment surgery grew in him. A late developer, he began thinking about taking female hormones as his body changed and became more masculine. While still finding crossdressing a deeply satisfying experience, it was accompanied by persistent feelings of loneliness and a fear of being discovered and ridiculed. Like most crossdressing males he occasionally made efforts to stop the behavior by getting rid of his feminine clothes. Despite the satisfaction that life as a woman offered, his loneliness and fears kept him in a state of longing for relationships that did not ever develop.[253]

Then he met some people who showed an interest in him and persuaded him to join their Christian fellowship. 'Anonymous' became a Christian. This introduced him to satisfying relationships and led him to share in a partial, distorted fashion his transsexual experience. A discerning male friend recognized that he was actually still crossdressing and confronted him. 'Anonymous' now became aware of a new feeling, one that told him his desire to be a woman was wrong. A series of frightening experiences, including discovery of his biological sex by the police when stopped one night while crossdressed, now added to a mounting distress. That same night he went to a Christian friend's place and confessed to God that his crossdressing and desires to be a woman were sins.

Henceforth he undertook a different perspective on his feelings and behavior. He interpreted the feelings as jealousy of women and his longing as reflecting an emptiness now filled by Christ. He believed his transsexualism had made him self-absorbed; as a Christian he could now serve others. He felt his biggest error had been not recognizing he was in rebellion against God as his Creator. He now became convinced he was created to be a man—a *Christian* man. Though he continued to struggle for years, he eventually mastered both his desires and behavior. Support by friends, and later his wife, helped him prevail. Today, he relates, he occasionally has a cross-gender dream but no longer struggles with crossdressing or cross-gender desire and identification.[254]

This kind of approach—long on testimony, short on evidence or clear reasoning—unfortunately characterizes most first person appeals on *both* sides of the debate. 'Anonymous' never offers any reason for the feeling his previous desires and behavior were wrong save his claim that conversion awakened in him his conscience.[255] On this side of the argument testimonies often proclaim that what contemporary secular therapy cannot—or will not—do can be accomplished by the power of God.[256] The point of such testimony is to deflect attention away from the perceived muddled thinking characteristic of sinful humans and toward the clear power of God's grace. Hence looking for reasons beyond a recognition of falling short of God's perfect standards is fruitless; the emphasis is not on why something is viewed as wrong, but on the remedy for all things: salvation by God through Christ.

Testimony of a Converted Crossdresser

A similar testimony is offered by Randall Wayne, a formerly crossdressing man but not a transsexual. Wayne's confession is very direct:

> I was typical of many male to female cross-dressers in that in all other areas of life, I was masculine in appearance and actions. I also had absolutely no desire for relations with other males, so homosexuality was not part of my problem. [257]

However, he realized he had a clear-cut decision he must make: either to choose the ways of the world or follow after God. Since, he concluded, he loved the Lord more than he loved the urge to cross-dress, he made a decision—get Christian-based help.

This latter caveat was motivated by his experience of finding that the resources he consulted indicated crossdressing could not be 'cured.' Then he encountered First Stone Ministries, an internet presence that addressed crossdressing as a sin. He underwent Christian counseling. With time he began to triumph over the temptation to crossdress. Wayne reached what he considered an important conclusion:

> I realized that cross-dressing was like playing the childish game of "dress up" like I used to with my cousins when I was a child. Cross-dressing also tends to be self-centered, with the cross-dresser expecting others to accommodate their behavior even to the detriment of their families. I could either stay in a

childish condition or I could move on and be a man. I chose to be the man God wanted me to be.

Learning to be a man patterned after God's plan was a matter of learning the truth and modeling after Jesus. I realized that a lifetime of being raised and taught by women had unknowingly feminized me. Actually, I think many men today share this condition. I don't mean to be sexist, because certainly both male and female models are needed for a balanced upbringing. The problem is that males and females approach life from different perspectives and being exposed to largely the female perspective, I developed a gender confusion.[258]

Eventually Wayne reached a point where he felt free. In essence, Christian counseling masculinized him, liberating him to become the man God intended.

Based on his experience, Wayne offers five reasons why he believes crossdressing is a sin:

❑ Crossdressing constitutes deception.

❑ Crossdressing violates God's established gender role for the person.

❑ Crossdressing fathers present a confusing role model to their children.

❑ Crossdressing is typically self-centered.

❑ Crossdressing tends not to be healthy for the marriage relationship.

Wayne sees the conflict that crossdressing Christian men experience as a form of spiritual bondage. He urges turning to the Holy Spirit for discernment of the truth. Wayne believes that despite what secular psychologists maintain change is possible. It requires repentance and a commitment to follow "the Lord's way" rather than that of the world.

There are similarities between the testimonies of 'Anonymous' and Wayne. Both view behaviors like crossdressing as self-centered and contrary to the order God created. In that order, both men believe, biological sex is meant to determine gender. Dress and behavior that do not conform to the pairing of male sex with masculine gender are thus unnatural. Men faced with desires to crossdress need to repent of these unnatural desires and choose through faith to become the men God-as-Creator intends. However, the point of a testimony is not to develop a sophisticated theological position. Testimonies aim at proclaiming how personal experience is transformed by encounters with God and thus stir feelings that will prompt others to a change in their own will. For explicitly theological arguments we must look elsewhere.[259]

3. The 'Appeal to Theology' Argument

In our society, by far the two largest Christian groups are Roman Catholics and Protestants. Though they share more in common than some of their adherents would like to admit, they also have important differences. In theology, these differences tend to be about matters of authority relied upon to guide the believer, views of the sacraments, and certain doctrinal emphases. With respect to transgender realities, though, opponents tend to present similar perspectives, whether Catholic of Protestant. An example from each tradition may be useful, although it must be remembered that theologians often vary greatly from one another and these examples do not necessarily represent the views of all opponents.

A Catholic Argument

We have already considered a number of Catholic thinkers ranging across the two millennia of the Church. The ones we have thus far considered have been 'professionals' in the sense that they hold offices within the Church. But there are many learned members of the laity who share a keen interest in theology. One such person is Ronald Conte Jr., a Catholic lay theologian. He articulates a theological argument within the framework of his understanding of the Church's position. Conte first presents his conclusion about appropriate behavior: women should wear unbifurcated garments like skirts and dresses, rather than pants. Accompanying such clear gender-differentiated dress, women should have longer hair than men—and that should be worn in a distinctively feminine style. Indeed, in all respects of grooming and appearance they should be obviously feminine. Why? Conte's reasoning to justify these contentions is succinctly stated: "Women should dress and groom themselves in a feminine manner, to show that they accept the place God has given women in Creation, in society, in the family, and in the Church."[260]

Interestingly, Conte separates this position from the issue of modesty. He contends that the wearing of conservative pants by a woman is not a lack of modesty but a crossdressing offense. "The offense of a woman wearing pants," he argues, "is an offense against the very order which God built into Creation and humanity." Though Conte indirectly references the Bible, he depends more on the theological premise that God established an order into both creation and human nature. For a woman to dress like a man—especially when attending Mass—is an 'abomination' because it violates this divinely created order. This situation is different in kind and degree from the offense of a woman who wears an immodest feminine garment such as a short skirt or tight dress. While offending modesty, such dress "does not contradict or rebel against the fundamental order which God gave to Creation and humanity."[261]

As seen elsewhere (see, for example, the answers to Q. 64, 67, 72), a central theological argument mounted against crossdressing is that it violates God's intended order, which separates the sexes. Implicit to this position is the acceptance that gender is predicated on sexual anatomy. God's order is viewed both as divinely ordained (since God created it) and natural (since it generally occurs in Nature the way they find it). While appeal can be made to the Bible for specific textual support, the more important thrust is to abstract general ideas or principles from the sense of the whole Bible. Despite the risk that such efforts can be highly individualistic and contentious, this approach typically remains optimistic that Christians can agree on broad and generally stated theological positions. In fact, most Christians do appear to endorse the notion that God created a sexually differentiated order in creation and that gender should conform to that. Where they may depart from Conte is in the conclusions for practice drawn from such a position.

A Protestant Argument

On the Protestant side such theological appeals also appear. For example, Baptist ethicist Daniel Heimbach adopts a line of reasoning that shares some common ground with Conte's. Heimbach's interpretation of the biblical prohibition is that the moral issue involved is the intentional confusion of gender differences, and acting as though such differences are inconsequential. He appeals to the creation story (Genesis 2:18) to justify his contention that God intends only two genders (man and woman) joined in a heterosexual relationship. He acknowledges a cultural element: "clothing associated with one gender in a particular culture might not be so paired in another culture," but insists that this is not significant because it is the *intentionality* of the dress behavior that matters. Crossdressing, then, is the intentional use of clothing to confuse the proper gender order and relations.[262]

The prohibition of such conduct, he maintains, is universal across cultures and time. Heimbach connects crossdressing with sexual prohibitions. "Gender confusion by cross-dressing," he writes, "does not necessarily involve having sex with another person, but it does stir up sexual thoughts and desires that lead in the direction of homosexual activity. And since homosexual sex and lust are prohibited regardless of culture or time, then prohibiting intentional gender confusion has to apply broadly as well." Heimbach believes that the most obvious role served by forbidding crossdressing is its protection of the difference between bodies that underlies heterosexual relationships. He views crossdressing as sending a wrong message—namely, that a sex and gender difference between sexual partners does not matter. For him, the prohibition of Deuteronomy 22:5 sends the clear message that such difference does matter.[263]

What does it mean to 'love the sinner, but hate the sin'?

Although variants on the appeal to theology can be found that are articulated with as much elaboration as those described above, they remain less common than another kind of theological position: 'love the sinner, but hate the sin.' Some Christians characterize this formula as the heart of what they call 'tough love,' an exercise of Christian charity that wields a stick for the punished one's own good. Some would claim a parallel between this and the discipline administered by parents in rearing righteous children. Others would appeal to the notion that one's eternal state is more consequential than their temporary state in this world, and thus acts designed to secure a favorable eternal state jus-

146

tify harsh warnings and even punitive acts in this present life. Such thinking is not arbitrary. It rests on an old intellectual tradition.

The idea of 'love the sinner, hate the sin' relies on a basic philosophical distinction between personal identity and behavior. *Who* one is must be distinguished from *what* one does. Where the former is relatively stable, consistent, and enduring, the latter is highly variable. The dualistic split between act and identity relies on the older division between body (external source of acts) and soul (internal source of being), or to put it more pertinently, between imperishable spirit and perishable flesh. The soul is prized above the body (e.g., Matthew 10:28; Luke 12:4), so that it seems truly gracious to secure the destiny of the soul even if that requires the sacrifice of the flesh (cf. Matthew 5:29-30), as was the logic in the Inquisition.

Of course, few among today's Christians favor anything remotely approaching the tactics of the Inquisition. Yet they would agree that Christian love mandates doing what one can to secure another's eternal wellbeing. They believe that just as God disciplines those he loves (Hebrews 12:5-11), the Church has a responsibility both to discipline those who would be part of the community of faith (cf. Colossians 1:28), and to warn those outside the faith of their need to repent and be saved (Mark 16:15-16). In this light, warnings to turn away from transgender behavior (e.g., crossdressing, sex changes, or homosexual acts) place the soul (or identity) above flesh (or transitory actions). Christians, many would remind us, are called to hate sin (Romans 13:9), and calling sin what it is can hardly be construed as hateful.

Got Questions Ministries, an internet service answering questions for Christians, affirms the formula 'love the sinner, hate the sin,' though they acknowledge it as a cliché. They maintain only God can do this perfectly, but that it is right for Christians to try, despite the reality that human beings can only love imperfectly and cannot hate without malice. In attempting to explain the 'mystery' of how God can do both perfectly, they offer that God is able to love the sinner as someone he created who is redeemable, "as well as hate them for their unbelief and sinful lifestyle."[264]

Unfortunately, the phrasing here underscores a significant problem many find with the formula: it is not all that easy to separate act and identity. The explanation just cited has God both loving and hating the *person*. All that is different is the motivation for the duality in feeling—love based on having made a creature worth being saved and hatred based on that person being a sinful unbeliever. In a world where, as Jesus himself declares, 'You will know them by their fruits' (Matthew 7:15-20), how can what one *does* be separated from who one *is*?

Despite such quibbles, the formula remains widely espoused. We shall return to it in answering the next question, but here we must turn our attention to how it can be put into practice. Most simply put, the answer is that Christians seek to change the changeable—the behavior of a person that puts her or his soul at risk—in order to secure the imperishable soul its place in the grace of

God for eternity. So the focus is on ending transgender behavior—regarded as sin—as part of the repentance accompanying true conversion, or if the person already espouses belief, as part of ongoing sanctification.

Are there ministries to change transgender people?

Christian practice, as well as Christian belief, is the intended aim of various ministries that exist to change transgendered individuals in order to bring about conformity to ideas like those expressed above. Typically the first step is a confession that transgendered realities are sinful ones. A transgender person persuaded that his or her gender reality is sinful may desire spiritual help. Often the aid they seek is from like-minded believers who share their ideas about Christian faith and practice.

In one remarkable case, a 21 year-old MtF preoperative transsexual, who had crossdressed since before age 5, who had a feminine gender identity since early childhood, and who had been taking female hormones while preparing for sex-reassignment surgery, was persuaded to visit a conservative Christian physician. This doctor believed the patient's transsexualism resulted from evil spirits. Accordingly, the doctor conducted an exorcism. In a session lasting almost 3 hours, through prayers and exhortations, with laying on of hands, some 22 demons were named and expelled between the patient's fainting spells. The physician told investigators that he had showed the patient that his life was a fake, that Jesus could redeem him, and that through an application of Scripture readings the 'spirit of the woman' inside the patient had disappeared. Immediately after this conversion experience, the patient disavowed the wish for any sex change and began to express gender-conforming behavior. When, a short time later, doubts surfaced, alongside cross-gender yearnings, he was taken to a faith healer's revival meeting where once more he experienced laying on of hands and prayer as he repeatedly fainted over the course of about a quarter of an hour. After this healing he reported his female breasts were suddenly gone. The patient's new gender identity and behavior was still in evidence more than two years later.[265]

This case study is unique in the literature, and even many conservative Christians are skeptical about such things as exorcisms and faith healings.[266] Not many would suggest that such transformations are likely to become routine. However, many Christians share the belief that something *can* be done and *should* be done. In what follows we shall briefly examine a few of the ministries operating on this belief.

CrossOver Ministries

One figure prominent in the ministry of helping end transgender behavior in Christian believers is Jerry Leach, former Director of CrossOver Ministries in Lexington, Kentucky, and now a counselor. Leach presents as his credentials not "some academic title," but "the gut-wrenching 'school of hard knocks!'"[267]

His appeal to his own struggle with "gender confusion," is buttressed with claims to what he learned through years of personal therapy and self-education. His eclectic approach combines use of personal experience, testimony from others, and theological reasoning.

Leach and his wife Charlene, who partners in ministry with him, express the desire to avoid "judgmentalism," aiming instead to provide "an honest and candid look at the underlying reasons for such activity and its resolution."[268] They intend to provide both sound biblical and psychological insights. Their approach begins with an effort to expose what they see as the 'lies' ensnaring the transgendered. Such 'lies' a transgender believer might embrace include: 'I should have been born a girl,' 'God made a mistake and has given me permission to be a woman,' and 'Cross-dressing is showing who I really am—a woman.'

The Leaches advocate a plan of ministry that includes confronting such lies, but in a safe place. By 'safe' they mean a place where healing can occur through speaking the truth, focusing on guilt, depending on God and offering hope. They advise caregivers to "prepare for spiritual conflict" using education and meeting weekly for at least a year with the person. They also urge securing the aid of a professional Christian therapist. But they see as even more important keeping the individual "daily immersed in the loving acceptance of others who are grace-filled and able to tell the truth in love." They urge focus be placed not on matters such as the desire for sex reassignment surgery, or crossdressing, but on the matter of who will rule the heart—Christ or the self? At the same time, they think it important to delve into issues such as why the person feels inadequate in the assigned gender, what is behind their rage and anger, and what was the relationship like with the parents. Because they see deception as such an intrinsic aspect of transgender conditions, they urge, "never accept the story given as the entire truth." Finally, they remind the caregiver to consider and support the person's family, offering aid and resources for them as well.[269]

True Freedom Trust

In the United Kingdom, True Freedom Trust is active in providing what they term a "Christian support and teaching ministry." Founded in 1977 by Canon L. Roy Barker and Martin Hallett, the ministry maintains a website, sponsors support groups, and publishes a newsletter. Though the ministry historically has focused on homosexuality, it also addresses other transgender realities such as transvestism and transsexualism. Strongly endorsing the idea of a rigid dualistic division between two sexes and genders, the True Freedom Trust believes this division exists by the mandate of God. Through its publications, including its website, testimonies are offered by individuals who declare their struggles and triumphs over the sin they believe transgender reality is.[270]

The above ministries are only a few among a number that offer services intended to end transgender behavior. Most such ministries focus on combating homosexuality. Ministries aimed at crossdressing transvestites or transsexuals tend to be much less visible. This situation reflects the greater prominence the issue of homosexuality has in the culture and in the Christian community. Deep divisions persist among Christian groups, not only about homosexuality, but about all transgender realities. Generally speaking, the more conservative religious groups tend to oppose such realities and to advocate ministries designed to confront and change transgender people.

Conclusion

Christians who oppose transgender realities such as homosexuality are much more visible than those who oppose transsexualism and crossdressing. Whether the latter constitute a majority of Christian laity or clergy is unknown, but it may be assumed that they in general mirror the attitudes of the society at large. Those who oppose transgender realities generally take one or another of very popular and longstanding approaches to controversial matters: they either offer personal testimony of redemption from a state they now regard as sinful, or they present a theological case against the subject. In either event, what most often happens is that those who already agree find these approaches reassuring evidence (known as 'preaching to the choir'), while those who disagree either ignore them or respond in kind.

Q. 74 What do transgender Christians and their supporters today say?

The Short Answer. At no other time in Church history have there been so many outspoken and visible transgender Christians. As a minority within a majority that has trouble offering them acceptance, they find themselves faced with many challenges. Among these are answering to harsh judgments made about them by other Christians. Male or female, heterosexual or homosexual, transgender believers and their supporters, including many in professional ministry, have constructed strong replies to those Christians they perceive as standing in wrongful judgment about transgender realities and transgender people. Their responses tend to parallel the types found among opponents. Thus we find many witnesses to the grace of God and experience of God's love as a transgender person. Some testimonials distinguish between a personal faith experience of an accepting God and the rejecting experience they have found within religious organizations. In fact, the hostility of gender-conforming Christians in some congregations has prompted many transgender people to develop an individual spirituality where a communal faith experience has been denied them. Positive faith responses matter because negative religious experiences can have a deleterious affect on health, while affirming experiences promote wellbeing. In the quest to develop their own Christian identity, transgender believers today can draw upon a number of models, including the biblical figure of the eunuch, as well as historical and contemporary people. Transgender people also respond to the contentions made that transgender realities are condemned in the Bible. Such responses show how responsible readings of the biblical texts might lead people to a different, more favorable conclusion. They dispute claims that the Bible clearly condemns homosexuality and argue that the prohibition of crossdressing is generally misunderstood and should not be applied to most of the crossdressing behavior found in today's world. They especially challenge the presumption that being transgender is wrong in and of itself. There are arguments also along more general theological lines, arguing, for instance, that opponents emphasize ideas contrary to grander themes of Christianity, such as love, forgiveness, and restraint from passing judgment. Transgender Christians find particularly troubling the reliance of some fellow believers on the 'Love the sinner, hate the sin' argument. They observe that not only is the logic problematic, but that in actual practice there is much more hate than love being shown.

The Longer answer. The previous answer made apparent what all of us already know: many Christians oppose the existence of transgender realities and have no desire to welcome transgender people into their midst. Speaking with respect to the Church's ill-handling of sexual issues, theologian Robert Hamilton Simpson pinpoints the problem as the holding of a 'one size fits all' view that oversimplifies and thus distorts and denies real life experiences. In effect, an unrealistic stance by the Church has forced sexuality to be repressed. "Subsequently," he says, "the Church's theology and pastoral care has often been disconnected from the sexual reality of the lives of the people who compose church membership, and this has had detrimental consequences."[271] Although Simpson speaks with sexual minorities in mind, all the same things could be said with respect to gender variant Christians.

Make no mistake about it: transgender realities pose a challenge to many Christians. But, then, at one time so did the propositions the world is not flat or the earth does not stand at the center of the universe. Many believers at the time felt that challenges to such assumed truths were defiance of God and biblical truth. Some believed that the very existence of the Church depended on continued allegiance to these ideas. Such convictions rested on simple, appealing logic that simply did not fit the facts. But while contemporary Christians laugh at their predecessors they are blind to their own similar foibles. We all have a tendency to confuse our cultural beliefs with religious truth and to cling to what we think we know rather than carefully examine evidence we find emotionally unsettling or threatening. We may find it hard to accept in practice that simply because many believers regard something as wrong, or sinful, does not make it so. Of course, the reverse proposition is also valid: simply believing something is right and moral does not make it so either.

Every debate and controversy requires two sides. This debate has two increasingly vocal sides. The danger in raising voices is that too often more heat than light is shed in the ensuing discussion. For transgendered people there has been the double threat of rejection and, occasionally, violence in either word or deed. Our task here is understanding, not provocation. To attain it we need to start with the situation as it may be viewed from within the transgendered community. Even there two sides matter: how transgender people relate to Christianity and how Christianity relates to them.

Much of the discussion already in this volume has been pertinent to this latter concern. As we have seen, there are good grounds for agreeing with theologian Fraser Watts' claim that, "There are indications that transgendering has sometimes been valued in the Christian tradition."[272] Inasmuch as that material is discussed elsewhere, here our focus will be on the other side: how transgender people relate to Christianity. It is an interest slow to come to researchers' attention, but increasingly studies are being done on this very matter.

We may begin by noting that research indicates transgender people, like the wider population, tend to be religious or spiritual. As early as the mid-1960s, with respect to our own society, researcher Wardell Pomeroy found transsexuals often are actively religious when young.[273] In the early 1980s a study reported that transsexuals depict their parents as more religious than did a comparison group of homosexuals, and the study's authors speculated that growing up in such a home, combined with homophobia and early developmental issues with gender identity might contribute to the development of transsexuality—a provocative idea unlikely to be embraced even by most of those who think transsexualism is environmentally caused.[274] Aside from such considerations, one matter is clear, as mental health practitioners constantly discover: issues of religion and spirituality matter to transgender clients. "In working clinically with transgender individuals to combat shame and isolation and to facilitate their coming-out process," write psychologist Walter Bockting and Episcopal priest Charles Cesaretti, "spiritual questions and experiences are common."[275]

Put broadly, transgender Christians look to their faith for help in coping with life and the question of meaning it poses, but in so doing face certain issues and obstacles that gender conforming Christians do not. We will not be wrong to say that Christians who also happen to be transgender individuals face all of the same issues as nontransgender believers, as well as certain issues related to their unique reality. Among these distinctive issues we must especially consider the way in which other believers respond to transgender Christians.

What are religious issues transgender believers may face?

The response of others who also claim to be Christian can lead to a sense that the majority—gender conforming Christians—have staked out a proprietary claim on the Church: 'This is *our* community!' In many cases this leads to intolerance of transgender believers; in come cases a touted 'tolerance' comes at a cost. Seldom is there outright celebration of gender variance of any kind, let alone something as dramatic as transsexualism. This situation has an adverse impact on the well-being of many transgender Christians and may lead them to adopt an approach emphasizing more of an individual spirituality rather than an affiliation with a congregation. It may also prompt them to look for creative ways to express their own religious identity or to seek role models to emulate.

Intolerance in the Church

Let us begin with the problem of intolerance. "Most anti-LGBT religious groups," writes religious scholar Melissa Wilcox, "consider minority sexual or gender identity to be a false identity, brought about through bad influences, misperceptions, poor upbringing, or even demonic intereference."[276] Though it commonly presents itself in the guise of 'hating sin, not the sinner,' it is rarely clear whether the thinking behind the intolerance follows from a reasoned application of purposeful bible study or mere cultural prejudice. Given the role religion takes in supporting cultural norms, it is easy enough to confound cultural beliefs with religious ones.

Transgender realities can elicit anxiety among gender conforming people, and efforts to fight that anxiety can lead to unhappy consequences for transgender people. An irrational anxiety over transgender people is called 'transphobia' and that anxiety typically discloses itself in defensive behavior of one kind or another, whether subtle and covert, or overtly hostile. Verbal or physical aggressiveness is often self-justified because it follows from this defensiveness. The aggressor views him- or herself as merely being self-protective, or protecting others.

Transphobia & Homophobia

Transphobia in the Church is both similar to homophobia and most likely connected to it. It can spring from homophobia because transgender realities are often stereotypically linked to homosexual orientation. This link can have significant repercussions. As Suzanne Lease, Sharon Horne and Nicole Noffsinger-Frazier observe, there persists a common perception that people with sexual orientations other than heterosexual cannot have a religious identity.[277] As we have seen, this often ill-formed and even unconscious idea stems from a certain sense of what is God-intended, right, orderly, and natural. For many believers, to be a Christian is to be philosophically an Essentialist in thought and practice.

Biblical studies scholar William Countryman and his colleague, historian and Episcopal priest Mary Ritley, comment on a certain irony residing in the contemporary Church:

> Oddly enough, in a church increasingly aware of the need for sensitivity to the cultural contexts of other groups it seeks to minister to, there is a peculiar blindness to gay cultural contexts, as if they had neither legitimacy nor respectability, and could therefore safely be ignored while a version of Christianity approved by the majority was superimposed on this minority. Such a strategy in dealing with any other minority would be horrifying to mainstream churches nowadays, a legacy of nineteenth-century cultural imperialism. It may take a significant amount of education to convince the churches that, just as they should not treat Asians, Africans, or Native Americans as defective Europeans, neither should they pretend that gay and lesbian Christians are defective heterosexuals.[278]

There remarks, though offered with only homosexual Christians in mind, are just as pertinent to all transgender Christians. Heteronormativity—the idea that heterosexual sexuality and conforming gender identities are Nature's standard for society—is rarely examined within the Church, let alone actually questioned or challenged.

Intolerance often focuses upon sexual orientation with outspoken rejection of minority orientations. But it also often identifies body transformations as specific points of objection (see the answer to the previous question). This poses a significant problem for those transgender individuals who seek internal harmony by modifying their body presentation to more closely match their gender sense. In essence, from the transgender person's point of view, they are being asked (or required) to renounce any effort to reduce disequilibrium and to live with their body no matter how flawed it seems. This creates a dilemma: choose personal congruity and face rejection, or live with incongruity by preserving the body one was born with in order to satisfy others. Put another way, the person can choose to live with the intolerance of their body experience or the intolerance of their fellow congregants.

Religious 'Tolerance'

While intolerance born of transphobia, with its attendant hostility, is a significant concern, so too is the less often discussed 'tolerance' of some congregations. Countryman and Ritley remark that many 'tolerant' Christians treat the 'tolerated' as creating a problem by their mere presence, and "the classic fantasy of toleration is that the tolerated ought to be so grateful for that status that they meekly submit to whatever lingering indignities may go with it."[279] The 'tolerant' often give little consideration to the implicit judgment in the 'minor concessions' (e.g., no crossdressing at church services, or no public signs of affection among homosexual couples) that they may require in the name of 'Christian harmony.' As discussed in a previous volume in this series, 'tolerance' covers a spectrum that ranges from highly conditional and easily able to slip into rejection, to unconditional and open to moving to celebration. It is quite clear a greater number of 'tolerant' congregations are closer to the former end of this spectrum.

Spirituality & Health

We have cause to be concerned about this. A number of studies demonstrate a link between faith and health, and a great many people count their faith as important to coping with life.[280] In short, the resources provided by faith and the faith community may be very beneficial to a person's mental health. Unfortunately, as investigators Lease, Horne and Noffsinger-Frazier observe, a positive relationship of religion and spirituality to mental health is not so clear among nonheterosexual believers. In fact, some evidence suggests both that such individuals are less involved in organized religion and that when they are the participation may actually be detrimental to their mental health.[281] Thus an important resource for well-being is at stake for these Christians. Fortunately, these same researchers in a study involving 583 gay, lesbian and bisexual people, found that when these persons experienced the presence of a faith group affirming their identity there was a reduction in internalized negative messages and an enhanced spirituality.[282]

Given the lack of welcome often experienced in the Church, the incentive to distance oneself from other believers can be great. As we just heard, and as Wilcox reminds us, the message transgender people often hear is that one cannot be both transgendered and a Christian.[283] The conflict such a belief brings is often more than a mere difference of opinion between people of differing views—it penetrates deep inside the minority person told such bad news and raises serious questions about the presumed 'Good News' ostensibly being offered by Christianity. As documented by some researchers, gay, lesbian and bisexual persons may internalize such messages in a 'homonegativity' that parallels others' homophobia, and which may be associated with internal conflict, shame, depression and other undesirable outcomes.[284] Thus, minorities may conclude that to retain a Christian identity they must do so outside of the institutional Church and without the support of the community of believers. In essence, they may feel compelled to strike out alone on their spiritual course.

Religion or Spirituality?

However, we should not assume that such a step means transgender Christians simply choose to believe whatever suits them. Rather, like a great many people who are nontransgender they may find more meaning in a personal relationship with God than in the observance of religious rituals or attendance at Church. A majority of contemporary Americans draw a distinction between *religion*, the institution of the Church and activities associated with it, and *spirituality*, a personal, individualized relationship with God. The preference for spirituality is all the more likely when a gender conforming majority marginalizes transgender believers within the Church, or ostracizes them altogether.

The transgendered person of today, in step with many other folk who profess to be Christians, can self-define exactly *how* they are Christian. Wilcox, in a study over four years that involved interviews with over 70 transgender people ('transgender' in the broad sense, including homosexual, bisexual, transsexual, et al.), reports that these believers "sifted through the 'practices and attitudes' of Christianity in order to assemble a Christian identity that could be integrated with their LGBT identity."[285] In constructing such an identity most transgender Christians also may rely on the Essentialist argument that they were born the way they are, or even more strongly, that God created them so. Among those adopting this strategy Wilcox found two very different approaches: some saw being made transgender as a trial or test, while others viewed it as a gift. The former perception results in the stance that being transgendered is something to be endured; the latter sees being transgendered as something to be celebrated.[286]

Wilcox found among her interview respondents that they overwhelmingly agree that God's most important characteristic is love. Many also emphasize God's immanence—a sense of the Divine Presence being near. To such theo-

156

logical convictions they add an approach to the Bible that relies on historical and cultural contexts to answer the use of scriptural texts against them. In choosing to 'come out,' they respond to rejecting experiences by changing their attendance to places where they are welcome. Wilcox concludes that, "For those whose identities collide sharply with official religious doctrine, the growth of congregational, denominational, and religious shopping and switching, can be of critical importance—and from their experiences there is a great deal to be learned about contemporary forms of religiosity."[287]

Reframing: Transgender and Grace

The resilience of spirit exhibited by many transgender people prompts a creative response that can ameliorate the kinds of negative effects mentioned earlier. Developing a personal spirituality is one such response. But whether outside of or within a congregation, transgender Christians can reframe the thinking they may have received and transformatively develop a message of transgender in the context of God's gift of grace. This may take different forms. At its most fundamental level this entails receiving God's grace as a divine acceptance of transgender realities—it is *all right* to be transgender.

Position 1: Transgenderism as Inherently Neutral

While many Christians believe transgender realities reflect a broken Nature and a sinful humanity, others regard transgender as a neutral state, one no more or less available than any other for receiving God's gift of grace. Advocates of this position argue that transgender people—like gender conforming ones—are born that way, and therefore the matter of their origin is natural and ethically neutral. They view transgender people as loved and accepted by God, and worthy of the same response from God's people. Some of those holding this view have not been silent. Faced with occasionally virulent intolerance from other professing Christians, these believers have spoken out vigorously on behalf of true Christian charity and genuine tolerance if not outright acceptance. Among their number are both transgender people and many supporters, including some in the ministry.

One bearer of this message—a role model and inspiration to many—was Lee Frances Heller, who in the latter years of life edited a quarterly newsletter entitled *Grace and Lace Letters*. This publication's theme, as the title suggests, is that the grace of God extends also to crossdressers, and it is all right to be transgendered.[288] Heller sums the matter nicely in a letter:

> *Grace and Lace* is published to encourage Christian cross-dressers and to convey to them and others that God loves you. Those who are in the closet are not seen of others but are seen of God. We are prisoners in our own darkness and when we come to the Light of Lights, the divine essence shining on our

being, our souls, we find we are loved exactly as we are. The
force of God's grace comes to you where you are.[289]

Heller, and many others, wants to make of transgender realities a nonissue in the Church. This response to opponents who call transgender realities sin is a modest one, arguing in reply that being transgender is like anything else—neutral in itself. It is what one does with what one is that matters.

Position 2: Transgender Is a Gift of Grace

Some transgender people embrace a more provocative notion: *being transgender is itself a gift of grace.* An important difference between this position and the former one is the perspective on how one comes to be transgender. Rather than argue that all people are born the way they are—an argument that sidesteps the controversy over the role of the Fall—proponents of this position take a definite, proactive stand. They contend that being transgender is God's intention; that transgenderism is part of God's creation. Wilcox is correct in reflecting that, "a claim to have been created lesbian, gay, bisexual, or transgender by God is much stronger than a claim simply to have been born that way."[290]

What most distinguishes this position, though, is the conviction that being transgender is not merely okay, it is itself a boon from God to humanity. As created by God, and therefore good, it is meant to benefit not only those made that way, but all people. Being transgender itself is a gracious gift to the Church. Seen this way, a lack of welcome of transgender people is a spurning of God's grace. This perspective proclaims transgender realities as occasions for celebration. Implicitly, it warns those who reject transgender realities and people that they are rejecting what God has made and called good.

The possibility of such a faith response is amazing because it is so implausible. It requires extraordinary fortitude in the face of opposition within the Church. The jolting discrepancy between the biblical promise of inclusion and the experience of rejection can prompt seeking solace and support from a number of resources. First among these are *sacred texts*. One such is 1 Peter 2:4-10, wherein Christians are called to be built into a spiritual house, becoming a spiritual priesthood offering spiritual sacrifices. Like Jesus—rejected by people but precious to God—transgender Christians claim the promise (2:6), that "whoever believes in him will not be put to shame." Like Jesus, they may be the stone the builders reject, and one that makes others stumble, but they know themselves to be part of a holy house.

Even more positively, advocates of this stance can look to texts such as Paul's discourse in 1 Corinthians 12. There the Apostle speaks of persons not only having spiritual gifts, but of themselves *being* gifts (12:28-31; also see Ephesians 4:11-13). In his extended metaphor of the Church as a body (12:12-27), Paul expounds on the value of diversity. *Every* part of the body has its valued place, whether esteemed much or little by other parts—and every part is as God chose (12:18). No part of the body can say to another that it has no need of it

(12:21). Transgender Christians may even draw special comfort from Paul's words (12:22), "the members of the body that seem to be weaker are indispensable." Though some other Christians might not welcome them, or esteem them, transgender Christians know they have a place, that they are gifts to the Church, and that God values them.

Beyond drawing on biblical ideas, transgender Christians can look to *biblical examples*. They know that from its very roots there have been divisions in the Church. Merely being in the minority does not make one either wrong or rejected by God. Paul himself faced opposition from other believers (see Acts 15; cf. Galatians 2:4-5), and on one occasion even felt compelled to rebuke the Apostle Peter (Galatians 2:11-14). Paul did not let the fact that he was regarded by some as an outsider, and by others with suspicion, deter him from articulating the message God had given him. As the Apostle felt compelled to speak out, so today are some transgender Christians who desire for the Church to be renewed and strengthened by inclusion of *all* God's gifts and people.

They also have *models throughout Church history* to point to. Transgender Christians can point with righteous pride to gender variant individuals whose love of Christ led them to risk all, braving every danger, and even facing martyrdom for his sake. Though looked upon with less favor in their own lifetimes, later the spiritual quality of such lives won respect and sometimes even acclaim as saints. Ironically, some of the very Christians who oppose today's transgender Christians regard past saints such as Thecla, the companion of Paul, or the warrior maiden Joan of Arc with approval, despite their gender variant behavior. Advocates of the position that transgender persons are God's gift to the Church can point out that such gifts do not need to be set aside for later generations to be appreciated but can be embraced and celebrated now.

Finally, transgender Christians can draw upon a growing *body of empirical evidence* suggestive of the benefits such people offer simply by being who they are. Uniquely blessed with a different perspective on life from their place along the boundary between conforming genders, transgender people commonly develop creative responses to life and others that translate into lives of service through priestly functions, healing ministries, and intermediary roles. Societies around the world, both past and present, have recognized this. In letting transgender people be who they are, and granting them a space and socially sanctioned roles, such societies have benefited from their gifts. There is no reason the Church cannot do likewise, save for its choice not to.

Obviously, for some people this position is controversial. This answer to opponents moves as vigorously in affirming the goodness of transgender realities as opponents move strenuously to proclaim them as sin. Unlike the first position described, advocates of this one do not seek to make transgender a nonissue. Rather, they think it a matter of importance and seek to confront the Church with the stakes of rejecting what God has offered.

The creation of a positive spiritual self-image is facilitated by recognition of role models. But to whom might transgender Christians look? The answer may seem surprising: from the earliest days of the Church to the present there have been figures that might serve as role models. Some of these we mentioned a moment ago, and some we have examined elsewhere in this series of books as well as elsewhere within this volume. Here they will only be briefly touched upon again.

Biblical Model of the Eunuch

The most salient biblical role model is the eunuch. We already have devoted some attention to this figure. We noted how well-known they were in the ancient world. We saw that Jesus extolled the self-made eunuch, 'for the sake of the kingdom of heaven.' We noted that some early Christians practiced ritual castration to become like this figure. We also saw how various saints identified with the eunuch. The present has some continuity with the past.

Watts notes that some contemporary Christian transsexuals identify with the figure of the eunuch.[291] He points to the influence of biblical texts such as Matthew 19:12 ("For there are eunuchs who have been so from birth, and there are eunuchs who have been made eunuchs by others, and there are eunuchs who have made themselves eunuchs for the sake of the kingdom of heaven. Let anyone accept this who can."). The eunuch—viewed in the ancient world as one between the sexes and genders—might be such because of biology ('eunuchs from birth'), because of the environment ('made so by others'), or by personal choice ('for the sake of the kingdom of heaven'). It should be noted that such a choice is a *spiritual* one, an act of deep devotion. Watts relates the New Testament text to the prophet Isaiah's conveyance of God's promise (Isaiah 56:4-5):

> For thus says the Lord:
> "To the eunuchs who keep my sabbaths,
> who choose the things that please me
> and hold fast my covenant,
> I will give, in my house and within my walls,
> a monument and a name better than sons and daughters;
> I will give them an everlasting name that shall not be cut off."

Certainly, as Watts points out, the early Church had space for a gender variant person like a eunuch, as the story of the Ethiopian eunuch (Acts 8:26-40) demonstrates. Nor is this person the only available biblical model; Daniel—that paragon of faith and courage—was most likely a 'eunuch made by others.'[292]

We must offer, though, an important caveat. Despite pressures from some Christians for transgender people to render themselves asexual, the model of the eunuch does not presuppose such a condition. A eunuch may be chaste and celibate, or sexually active. Religious scholar David Hester, in deconstructing how the church arrived at a tradition of seeing the eunuch of Matthew as a celibate figure, documents how in the context of Jesus' own time the eunuch was widely known as a sexually vigorous being. "In fact," he writes, "eunuchs were universally characterized by the frequency, ease and adeptness with which they performed sex acts with both men and women."[293]

Transgender Christians in adopting pertinent role models may find that others try to shape their perception of these models. In the case of the self-made eunuch this might mean pushing on the transgender believer the necessity of perpetual celibacy. Such an injunction more likely proceeds from a cultural bias than from an interest in biblical scholarship. Like anyone else, the transgender person has both the right and the responsibility to determine how best this figure and the biblical text should be understood and applied.

Historical Figures

The popularity of the self-made eunuch of Jesus' saying is not a new phenomenon. There were Christians in the early Church who took such texts very seriously. Watts offers as an example the prominent early Church father Origen (c. 185/6-254/5). The 4th century Church historian Eusebius, for whom Origen is such an admirable figure he devotes most of an entire book to him, writes:

> At this time while Origen was conducting catechetical instruction at Alexandria, a deed was done by him which evidenced an immature and youthful mind, but at the same time gave the highest proof of faith and continence. For he took the words, "There are eunuchs who have made themselves eunuchs for the kingdom of heaven's sake," in too literal and extreme a sense. And in order to fulfill the Saviour's word, and at the same time to take away from the unbelievers all opportunity for scandal,—for, although young, he met for the study of divine things with women as well as men,—he carried out in action the word of the Saviour.[294]

Moreover, Watts is right in remarking that it is unlikely this was an isolated case.[295]

Though the figure of the eunuch may have provided inspiration for some, there are no lack of other figures who stepped outside conventional gender norms in pursuit of righteousness and because of their devotion to Christ. As we have seen earlier in this volume, many women followed a path that transgressed gender boundaries. They were gender variant in behavior, and perhaps sometimes in identity as well; we remember them as saints—the so-called crossdressing saints (see the answer to Q. 68). Such figures span more than a millennia of Church history, ranging from St. Thecla, companion of Paul in the 1st century, to St. Joan of Arc, martyr in the 15th century. Though many are female, male figures like Serge and Bacchus became influential figures in a variety of contexts, including Church ceremonies blessing same-sex unions.[296]

Indeed, it can with some justice be argued that priests, monks, and nuns all serve in their own ways as models of gender variance. As we discussed earlier (the answer to Q. 70), priests and monks, by both dress and manner (especially as sexually celibate), separate themselves from conventional notions of masculinity. Various scholars have argued that for all intents and purposes they functioned as a 'third gender' analogous to eunuchs of an earlier period. Nuns also carved out gender space apart from traditional femininity. Women's studies and foreign language scholar Stacey Schau points out with respect to nuns of the 16th-18th centuries that both male clergy and female colleagues identified them as models of 'virility.'[297] "In some very concrete ways," she argues, "nuns projected themselves as a 'third gender,' which functioned as a safety valve for women."[298] These devoted persons—male and female—stepped outside the ways of gender conforming Christians in order to serve Christ. Transgender people already exist outside the conventional gender boxes, so why should their Christian identity or devotion be suspect? If they are in some respects more like priests, monks, and nuns than other Christians, how is that a bad thing?

Throughout Church history there have been any number of notable gender variant Christians (see the answers to Q. 69-70). These have included figures at the highest reaches of the Church, such as Pope Paul II in the 15th century, and Francois Timoleon, Abbe de Choisy (1644-1724), who among other accomplishments wrote well-regarded volumes of Church history. The deeply religious Chevalier d'Eon of France made notable marks in many fields of endeavor, especially as a diplomat, and did so while presenting as a woman. Among females, we saw earlier the diverse social roles, including religious ones, played in the mid-19th century by Emma Edmonds (1841-1898). Early in the 20th century, Father Miguel Augustin Pro (1891-1927) unashamedly crossdressed to facilitate a ministry that ultimately led to his martyrdom. In the later 20th century, Sister Mary Elizabeth, a nun in the Order of the Sisters of Saint Elizabeth, was a very public advocate for transsexual rights. During this same period Leo/Lee Frances Heller (1919-2000) served in ministry, acting for decades as chaplain at a Christian mission and in later life editing *The Grace and Lace Letter*, a publication celebrating transgender realities. In the 21st century an increasing number of transgender Christians, both male and female, have proclaimed their identity *and faith* in very public ways. Today there are no lack of positive role models for transgender people of faith.

How can one respond to 'love the sinner, hate the sin'?

Role models who have shown creative and prosocial ways to respond to the negativity of some believers are needful, and perhaps nowhere more so than in dealing with those who allege they love the transgender person but hate his or her sin. In the last answer we saw that a popular theological argument marshaled against transgender realities is to distinguish between person and deed in exactly this way: 'love the sinner, hate the sin.' Although this phrasing is nowhere found within the Bible, it makes sense to many Christians and seems to them to fit ideas that are found within Scripture.[299]

However, this logic often vexes transgender people. They are baffled at how selective some Christians can be in the scriptural texts that are used to justify a stance that seems contrary to the predominant spirit of the Bible, especially the teachings of Jesus. Transgender believers also find it troubling that so many who use the 'love the sinner, hate the sin' argument *assume* being transgender is a sin without ever bothering to question how sound that assumption is. Finally, the argument may leave them wondering whether they are truly loved or actually hated, since in their personal reality it seems impossible to distinguish between *who* they are and *what* they do. Moreover, it typically feels to them like what the Christians who use such language are doing is focusing more on hating what they do than ever getting around to loving who they are. These concerns lead to specific objections.

1ˢᵗ Objection: Scripture Teaches Otherwise

Transgender and nontransgender people who object to this formula often seek to address it in the same terms as its advocates, by appealing to the Bible and using theological reasoning. Most often this takes the form of another popular formula, 'God tells us not to judge others, but to love everyone.' In support of the former clause they cite Jesus' words, 'Judge not, lest you be judged' (Matthew 7:1; cf. James 2:13). In support of the latter clause they appeal to Jesus' words both to 'love your brother' (John 13:34-35) and to 'love your enemies' (Matthew 5:43-48). They might point out that not only does Jesus not make the distinction between hating the sin and loving the sinner, but instead boldly tells his followers to focus on their own behavior (Matthew 7:1-5), and to be so focused on avoiding being angry with others or insulting them (Matthew 5:21-22), that they should seek out anyone who has something against them and be reconciled to them (Matthew 5:23-26). They argue that the tenor of the New Testament favors words of loving-kindness over those of condemnation, reconciliation over estrangement, and good deeds over punitive ones. In sum, they reject the formula 'love the sinner, hate the sin' as true neither to Scripture nor to Christian love.

2ⁿᵈ Objection: The Initial Presupposition About Transgender Is Wrong

Others point out that the formula's application to transgender people relies on the presumption that transgender behavior is sinful—an arguable proposition. In tackling the matter in this way, such people argue that before you can use the formula you must determine if it is applicable. Simply assuming something is sinful does not make it so, no matter how personally offensive one might find it. After all, a good many folk find proselytizing Christians offensive! So the grounds are shifted to challenging the too often unexamined premise that transgender realities like crossdressing are wrong. That kind of debate we consider elsewhere, at length, so here we may turn to another form of resistance to this formula.

3rd Objection: The Proposed Distinction Is More Apparent Than Real

Disciples of Christ minister Rev. Kenneth Collins remarks knowing many people who invoke the formula's principle, but finds that none of them prove able to maintain the fine distinction; they inevitably wind up hating the sinner. "In fact," Collins writes, "I have never met a person who sighed soulfully, 'That minister hates my sin, but I know he really loves me.'" In Collins' estimation, this way of thinking is a tool of Satan that ends up chasing off the very people the Church is meant to minister to. He asks why Christians would waste time hating sin when there are sinners who need to be loved.[300]

Women's studies scholar Janet Jakobsen and religious studies scholar Ann Pellegrini also wrestle with the (il)logic of this formula, though in a different manner. They argue:

> Love the sinner, hate the sin means that when Christians like Rev. Jerry Falwell or media personalities like Dr. Laura denounce homosexuality, they are not being hateful. They are simply taking a moral stand about a particular act or set of acts. In practice, however, love the sinner, hate the sin allows people to take positions that are punitive toward their fellow citizens, while at the same time experiencing themselves as being not simply ethical, but compassionate and even tolerant of difference.[301]

Jakobsen and Pellegrini wonder if it is truly possible to 'love the sinner, but hate the sin.' They ask whether the so-called 'compassion' and 'tolerance' espoused by holders of this position feels like that to those on the receiving end. "Does it really feel any different from contempt or exclusion?" they ask.[302] In the final analysis, they contend, court cases such as *Bowers v. Hardwick* (1986) and *Romer v. Evans* (1996) show that the sinner-sin distinction is no distinction at all.[303] In fact, the line fixed between *whom* we are supposed to love, and *what* we are supposed to hate proves not to be fixed at all; it moves in baffling and even contradictory ways. Though the formula espouses tolerance (at best), Jakobsen and Pellegrini remind us that tolerance, though an improvement over outright hate, is not the same as freedom. Rather than proving a sign of openness, this kind of tolerance proves hierarchical, exclusionary, and undemocratic.[304]

What are answers to concerns over homosexuality?

By far the largest debate within Christian circles with reference to transgender realities concerns homosexuality. Countryman and Ritley observe that, "To many people, gay and straight alike, it seems that little else has taken center stage at church conventions, councils, or synods in the last decade, so that for many genuinely engaged gay and lesbian Christians, these meetings have become what one gay man, with more imagination than delicacy, called the 'annual faggot-flaying.'"[305] As such a comment indicates, more heat than light is often shed in discussing the subject.

The debate hinges on whether homosexuality itself, or sexual behavior associated with it, is sin. To answer that question much attention has been given to a few texts condemning allegedly homosexual behavior. While this work is not focused on homosexuality, this debate is too large and hotly contested to pass over in silence. In answering the previous question we briefly examined one side of the debate; now we shall consider the other side.

Those who do not regard homosexuality as a sin are as diverse as those who disagree with them. Some find it uncomfortable to be around homosexuals and personally view homosexual behavior as distasteful—but not sinful. Others think God has more on his mind than what two consenting adults do together in their bedroom regardless of the sex of the participants. Still others feel that not only is homosexuality not sinful, it is both natural and as desirable as heterosexuality. Like their counterparts, they come to their conclusions by various paths. However, much of their argumentation is framed as a response to opponents rather than as a positive position set forth on its own. Here we will look briefly at both avenues of argumentation.

1st Objection: Opponents of Homosexuality Use Selective Reasoning

The more common approach to argument has been to contest and refute those who say homosexuality, or homosexual behavior, is sin.[306] Certain lines of defense are common. One is to point out that opponents are inconsistent. They apparently value some sins more than others because many of the things the Bible condemns they either overlook entirely or regard with less vehemence. The selection of homosexuality for special attention suggests a homophobia unrelated to the actual weight of biblical prohibition.[307] Similarly, opponents often justify disregard of inconvenient laws in the Old Testament by arguing that the New Testament declares the Law 'dead' or null (see Romans 7) because Christ fulfilled it (Matthew 5:17b). If so, then why are some laws, like the one ostensibly directed against homosexuality, retained? To their opponents' response that some portions of the Old Testament represent 'abiding principles,' they counter with two queries: who gets to decide what constitutes such a principle? Why is this principle weightier than others with much more biblical support, such as the kindness, love, and acceptance of God, or the injunction not to pass judgment on others?

Since homosexuality is often resisted as a threat to marriage, why are obvious and strongly worded passages like the divine judgment against adultery (Deuteronomy 22:22; Malachi 2:13-4; Matthew 5:31-32; 1 Corinthians 6:9), or God's abhorrence of divorce (Malachi 2:16; Mark 10:2-9; Matthew 5:27-30) given more attention? Neither of these threats to marriage seems to energize gender conforming, heterosexual Christians quite like gay-bashing does! No wonder, then, some decry the opponents of transgender Christians as hypo-crites who would be better to look first to their own sins before searching out questionable faults in others.

2nd Objection: The Bible Does Not Condemn Homosexuality

A second line of defense consists in examining each biblical text alleged to condemn homosexuality. This may take either the form of a general line of rea-soning about how the Bible deals with sex and sexuality, or a case-by-case analy-sis of specific texts. Consistent with the former approach, it is often pointed out that 'homosexuality' as we conceive it is a modern notion, not one in the minds of the biblical authors, and that reading modern ideas into ancient minds does both a disservice. This basic point is arguably the most important one. The an-cient authors did not think about sexuality like we do and the concept of 'sexual orientation' would be foreign to them. This invention largely of the medicaliza-tion of sex belongs to the world of the mid-19th century and since, not to the ancient world.

Nevertheless, because most people are ignorant of history and naively as-sume that the biblical authors believed and think as they themselves do, the lat-ter approach of parsing biblical texts remains popular. With respect to this ap-proach we can offer a few examples of how various commonly appealed to texts may be addressed to refute those who loudly claim homosexuality is con-demned in the Bible.

1st Example: The Misuse of the Creation Story

'God created Adam and Eve, not Adam and Steve.' This old witticism seems to be repeated more often than the actual words of Genesis—and to some opponents seems to carry more weight than the biblical text itself. The most often cited verses are Genesis 1:26-27 (NSRV), here edited to focus on the relevant portions: "Then God said, 'Let *us* make humankind in *our* image, ac-cording to *our* likeness . . . . So God created humankind in *his* image, in the im-age of God he created them; *male* and *female* he created them." The italicized words are ones that both sides appeal to as critical.

Opponents of homosexuality highlight the phrase, 'male and female he cre-ated them.' They conjoin this phrase to the following verse (1:28): "God blessed them, and God said to them, 'Be fruitful and multiply. . . .'" They may also add reference to Genesis 2:18-25, an account of how God created woman for man, which culminates in the words (2:24) often used in marriage ceremonies: "Therefore a man leaves his father and his mother and clings to his wife, and they become one flesh." Pieced together in this fashion it seems obvious to many Christians that God created only two sexes (with corresponding genders), that these sexes are meant for sexual union only with each other, and that pro-creation is the divine intention for sexual behavior.[308]

A traditional way to put these elements together has been to follow the 4th century theologian Augustine of Hippo. He argued that the original creation was of two physical sexes who were each asexual in practice! In other words, there was a male and a female, and each was chaste. Augustine thus paved the way for sexual activity to be associated with sin as the Fall (Genesis 3)—precipitated by the female—brought sexual desire into the world. Interestingly enough, for Augustine it was not her role in the Fall that relegated the woman to a subordinate status, for that he believes was the divine intention all along. In commenting on the phrase 'male and female' in Genesis 1:28, Augustine remarks, "For there was first the chaste union of male and female, of the former to rule, of the latter to obey. . . ."[309] Here, then, we have the reigning Essentialist view: a fixed two sex/two gender system that entrenches men at the top and views women principally as sexual objects for men in a heteronormative world.

Certainly the text can be theologically used in such a manner. But is this use of Genesis the *only* possible one, or even the *best* one? Regardless of whether one thinks homosexuality is morally acceptable or not, it is plain the creation account does not directly address it. Roman Catholic priest and theologian Daniel Helminiak points out that, "the Adam-and-Eve-not-Adam-and-Steve argument depends on a logical fallacy—the *ad ignorantiam* argument, argument by appeal to the unknown, argument based on assumptions about what was *not* said."[310] In short, opponents speak as though *if* the creation story does not explicitly say God created homosexuality, *then* he did not create it and thus it is the product of the Fall (Genesis 3)—clearly fallacious reasoning. In any event, the most obvious conclusion—the 'plain sense' of the text ostensibly being the goal of opponents—is that the account says nothing about homosexuality at all.[311]

Rather than read things into what is *not* written, we would do well to understand clearly what *is* written. Yet that may not be as easy as we often presume. At least two other plausible interpretations of the creation of 'man' (in the generic sense) can be advanced. Both seek to address an often overlooked issue: God, who has no sex, creates 'man' in God's own image and likeness, yet the end result is 'male and female'—two sexes. How could this be?

The first possibility is that God originally fashioned האדם (*ha-adam*, 'the man') as an androgynous, sexually undifferentiated being. In short, 'man' originally was neither 'male' nor 'female,' and neither 'man' nor 'woman'—or the first human was both, if one prefers. Contemporary biblical scholar Phyllis Trible, in her influential book *God and the Rhetoric of Sexuality*, supports this solution. "Until the differentiation of female and male (2:21-23), *'adam* is basically androgynous: one creature incorporating two sexes."[312] At least two ancient documents also represent the picture in this manner. As we saw earlier (the answer to Q. 67), Gregory of Nyssa, one of the so-called 'Fathers of the Church,' interpreted this text as saying the original creation was of an androgynous person. Even earlier, the *Apocalypse of Adam* (written sometime in the 1st-4th centuries C.E.) presumes an original state that is changed when, "God, the ruler of the

167

aeons and the powers, divided us in wrath." This text also pointedly notes a resemblance to "the great eternal angels."[313] That thought leads to another way to understand how sexually differentiated humans came to be.

This second possibility represents a different way to cope with the awkwardness of an asexual deity creating sexual beings. Consider the curious switch between plural ('us,' 'our') and singular ('his') pronouns in the creation account. Christians often read into the plural pronouns God's Trinitarian essence, with the singular pronoun emphasizing the unity of God's nature. Whatever one thinks of this theologically, it is less interpretively plausible than reading the words in light of their origin in an ancient Hebrew community rather than a centuries later Christian one. Thus the conclusion of the 1st century Jewish scholar Philo of Alexandria was that 'us' refers to God and heavenly assistants.[314] Many contemporary biblical scholars think the 'our' refers to heavenly beings constituting God's court—beings mentioned in a number of other places in the Hebrew scriptures (e.g., Job 1:6, 2:1; Psalm 89:5-8; 1 Kings 22:19; Revelation 4; cf. Psalm 86:1, 6).

It seem plausible that the 'our' refers to God *and* those in the heavenly court. This resolves the problem of how human beings with sex and sexual interest could be made in '*our* likeness.' At least some heavenly beings are sexual, as the text in Genesis 6:1-2, 4 (NRSV), a kind of postscript to the creation narrative, pointedly says:

> When people began to multiply on the face of the ground, and daughters were born to them, the sons of God saw that they were fair; and they took wives for themselves of all that they chose. . . . The Nephilim were on the earth in those days—and also afterward—when the sons of God went in to the daughters of men, who bore children to them.

The 'sons of God' (Hebrew *bene elohim*) named here may be the heavenly beings alluded to in Genesis 1:26. These beings are clearly sexual, in that they mate with human women and have children (the Nephilim) by them. Though the encounters here are avowedly heterosexual—heavenly male (allegedly) to mortal female—that does not mean all sexual encounters between heavenly beings and people are heterosexual; once again we cannot infer anything certain from silence. The reason their heterosexual behavior is noted here is because of the interest of Genesis to explain how certain things came to be—in this case, the Nephilim.

What we know is intriguing: only presumably *male* heavenly beings are mentioned. It would seem logical to reason that *if* the heavenly beings are all male, *and* have sexual natures, *then* they must be at least bisexual since there do not appear to be any female heavenly beings. *If* they are bisexual, *then* human beings created in their sexual likeness might have desire for either same-sex or opposite-sex beings—an outcome that would explain not only Adam and Eve's desire for one another, but also for the actual occurrence in the world of homosexual people (especially since this is not said to be an outcome of the Fall).

Obviously, all this is highly speculative. Yet it is at least as logical—and certainly closer to what the Bible actually says—than the 'God made Adam and Eve, not Adam and Steve' argument. It might also be worth mentioning that, as seems typical in biblical considerations of sexuality gone astray, this story of *heterosexual* behavior displays something deemed improper and contrary to God's intention in creation—a point made explicitly here (Genesis 6:4).

Let us return to the creation story proper. Opponents of homosexuality argue that Genesis 1:28 proves God intended two sexes for heterosexual activity in order to produce offspring.[315] Interestingly, what they confound as a single command—'be fruitful *and* multiply'—might be better seen as *two* commandments, both offered in the context of a blessing.[316] In the spirit of ancient Judaism, we can argue that God would not waste words or be repetitious; the compound phrase thus has two distinct elements. The relation of these two is marked by their union. So 'be fruitful' (הרפ, *parah*) is different from 'multiply' (הבר, *rabah*) but should be interpreted in light of it. Accordingly, since the latter refers to sexual behavior, so must the former. What does 'be fruitful' mean in a sexual sense, if it is different from 'bearing fruit' in producing children? 'Be fruitful' can be construed as a command—and blessing—to be sexually active. It is the first commandment and precedes 'and multiply' because it makes procreation possible, just as 'and multiply' then makes keeping all other commandments possible. Simply put, the enjoyment of sexuality comes before the procreation of children. Seen in this light, the emphasis on procreation as the be-all and end-all of human sexuality is incorrect, as is the assumption that we are created sexual beings *only* for reproductive purposes. If nonreproductive sexual behavior is a positive command, then why must it only be heterosexual?

2nd Example: The Case of Sodom

Each text brought forward as condemning homosexuality is not as straightforward or as obvious as opponents would like people to believe. To understand the text properly requires attention to context, the actual words used and their relation to each other, matters of history and culture, and so forth (see the answer to Q. 62). For example, the infamous story of Sodom (Genesis 19) is often used to prove that the city was destroyed for practicing homosexual acts. In support of this interpretation Jude 7 (and 2 Peter 2) are brought forth. But what about Ezekiel 16:48-49 (cf. Wisdom 19:13), which says the fall of Sodom was because of pride and a failure to be hospitable to strangers? What about Jesus' echoing (Matthew 19:5-15) of this same sentiment? Many other texts at least allude to Sodom and Gomorrah, and there are many sins listed, including adultery (presumably a heterosexual sin). Even Jude 7, with its link to the angelic beings of verse 6, suggests that the sexual sin of Sodom was like that committed by the angelic beings—a flagrant taking of sexual liberties with folk who should have been off-limits to them. In the case of Sodom and Gomorrah, the emphasis is on the contemptible disregard for the fact these were strangers depending on hospitality; the sexual act itself, or the sex of the strangers, is downplayed in the story, which has Lot offering his virgin daughters to the rabble outside in order to protect the strangers within his house (Genesis 19:5-8). To see this as a condemnation of modern homosexuality is a remarkable stretch.

3rd Example: The Levitical Code

The material in Leviticus also presents difficulties for those who would use it. To refresh our memories, the relevant texts read: "You shall not lie with a male as with a woman; it is an abomination" (Leviticus 18:22, NSRV; the Hebrew text: ואת־זכר לא תשכב משכבי אשה תועבה הוא); "If a man lies with a male as with a woman, both of them have committed an abomination; they shall be put to death; their blood is upon them" (Leviticus 20:13, NSRV; the Hebrew text: דמיהם יומתו מות שניהם עשו תועבה אשה משכבי את־זכר ישכב אשר ואיש בם:). The contexts are roughly parallel in the manner they present their contents, so both may be considered together.

First, the context suggests that the audience is both men and women, presumably heterosexual (to use our contemporary way of viewing them). After all, most of the condemned acts are clearly heterosexual, explicitly discussing male-female forbidden relationships (Lev. 18:6-18; 20:10-12, 14, 17-21), having sexual relations during the woman's menstrual flow (Lev. 18:19; 20:18), and heterosexual adultery (Lev. 18:20; 20:10). Why should 18:22 (20:13) be seen as suddenly, intrusively, *not* addressed to the same folk, especially since what follows it once more appears to have the heterosexual population in view? To presume such an abrupt shift in audience is both illogical and unnecessary. The burden of proof is on those who read this as aimed at homosexuals.

Second, the impression that the men involved are those we today know as heterosexual is also strengthened by the actual wording. The Hebrew construction 'lies with a male as with a woman' is awkward because no word for homosexual exists in Hebrew. Centuries later, in light of prolonged contact with the Greek world, words for males who had sex with other males were coined to avoid having to use such a cumbersome Hebrew expression. The 'as with a woman' is a superfluous phrase if homosexual males are intended but quite pointed if the men in view are heterosexual. Homosexual men would not be thinking about how their sexual behavior is like that of heterosexuals. But heterosexual males engaging in sex with another man like they would with their normal female partners would readily grasp the point. They are acting *as if* the partner who takes the feminine passive role is like an actual woman, their normal partner.

Third, with respect to same-sex sexual acts—regardless of the sexual orientation of the one performing them—it is curious that no mention is made of *female* same-sex acts. This does not mean the ancient Hebrews had no knowl-

170

edge of people we today call lesbians. Rabbinical sources make it quite plain that such people were known then. So why are only *male* same-sex acts condemned? After all, the next verse (Lev. 18:23; 20:16) explicitly refers to both men and women in condemning the practice of bestiality. So the omission of female same-sex behavior is curious, but hardly accidental. To read into the text an unwritten parallel to female homosexuality can only be a theological decision, not an exegetical one. Add in a knowledge of how the ancient rabbis looked at things and it becomes clear that they did not find here a condemnation of what we call lesbianism.[317]

Finally, even if this prohibition is (incorrectly) seen as referring to homosexuals, it is perhaps curious that it receives far less attention than other sexual matters found here, such as adultery, incest, or bestiality—all of which are discussed elsewhere in the Bible more often than male-with-male sex. If there is a heterosexual/homosexual split in attention in Leviticus, it seems clear that the majority heterosexual readership has decided to spend most of its attention on the condemnation not aimed at itself. We may be reminded of Jesus' question: "Why do you see the speck in your neighbor's eye, but do not notice the log in your own eye?" (Matthew 7:3; cf. verses 4-5).

Paul's Argument in Romans

There is also a concern with the manner in which opponents wrest biblical texts out of their context. A passage often cited to proclaim biblical opposition to homosexuality is Romans 1: 26-27, which reads:

> For this reason God gave them up to degrading passions. Their women exchanged natural intercourse for unnatural, and in the same way also the men, giving up natural intercourse with women, were consumed with passion for one another. Men committed shameless acts with men and received in their own person the due penalty for their error.

We need no recourse to Greek to grasp the logic of this material. The context in Romans 1 is part of a more general argument across the first three chapters that aims to demonstrate God's righteousness. Paul contends that all people are without excuse concerning knowledge of God and the divine nature (1:19-21). But they have chosen to suppress the truth and place others before God (1:18, 22-23). God's righteous judgment is to permit them to suffer the consequences. In acting against what Nature teaches concerning God, they corrupt their own nature—and God lets this play out.

One way to understand this is to say that by virtue of the 'Fall' of humanity (Genesis 3) all human nature has been corrupted, with the result that all sorts of impurity and degrading passions have entered in. Those who read the text this way often argue that homosexuality then constitutes one form of such degradation—that it is a *choice*—and thus condemned in verses 26-27. The emphasis on free will fits a general theological construct they may have, but it is debatable that such is the emphasis here.

Another way to understand this passage is to point to the obvious emphasis throughout on the concept of 'nature'—a point the early Church Fathers were quick to grasp. Nature writ large reveals God's nature. Human nature, meant to follow in the image of God's nature (Genesis 1:27), is corrupted when people willfully 'exchange the truth about God for a lie' (Romans 1:25). Since Paul elsewhere (Romans 8:19-23; 1 Corinthians 11:2-16) seems to argue that God intends the natural order of creation and the redeemed order of the Church to parallel one another, presumably this entails individuals seeking to adhere to their essential nature in the confidence that it is God-given, redeemed in Christ no matter how imperfect, and subject to the hope of perfection one day. If sexual orientation is *given*, being an internal and reasonably steady disposition, rather than *chosen*, then it is part of human nature. It is disengenious of heterosexuals to contend their own sexual orientation is part of their nature, an essential component given by God from the start, but deny the same for others (homosexuals and bisexuals). If they wish to appeal to biology, there is plenty of evidence to contend that any and all sexual orientations are derived by the same general dynamics of development.

In this framing of the logic of the argument, then, whom are the people acting against nature? If sexual orientation is a matter of nature rather than choice, then apparently it is people we today call 'heterosexual' being addressed in verses 26-27. If giving up natural inclinations for unnatural ones is the point, then heterosexuals indulging in same-sex intercourse *must* be what is condemned. The 'exchange' of 'natural for unnatural' by both men and women makes no sense unless there has been a willful movement from heterosexual desire and activity to homosexual desire and activity. This seems to be the way the Church Fathers understood the text: it was heterosexual people willfully giving away their natural sexuality—a relinquishment God permits when he 'gives them up' to the folly of their choices.[318] Those who are by nature homosexual presumably would not be making such an exchange, since their desire all along has been for partners of the same sex. Thus, as a corollary of the logic, if homosexuals engage in heterosexual sex they are acting against Nature.

Paul's List in 1 Corinthians

One text that opponents of homosexuality use is a list found in Paul's first letter to the Corinthian Christians. "Do not be deceived! Fornicators, idolaters, adulterers, male prostitutes, sodomites, thieves, the greedy, drunkards, revilers, robbers—none of these will inherit the kingdom of God" (1 Corinthians 6:9-10). Such vice lists are common in ancient literature and more than one appears in the Bible. While it is used against homosexuals, since it is also the principal text specifically employed against transgender people we will discuss it a little further on.

Just as biblical texts can be used in a defense of homosexual Christians, so similar defenses are possible by appeals made to Church authority or tradition. Historian John Boswell, for example, presents a veritable mountain of evidence demonstrating that the ecclesiastical record is not so one-sided as opponents often try to represent. In his book *Christianity, Social Tolerance, and Homosexuality*, Boswell sums up his research by noting that, "Moral theology through the twelfth century treated homosexuality as at worst comparable to heterosexual fornication but more often remained silent on the issue."[319] Though intolerance may have grown in the late Middle Ages, and may have persisted to modern times, it was not always so blatant. The historical record, as Boswell shows in his later book, *Same-Sex Unions in Premodern Europe*, abounds with liturgies to bless same-sex unions. Consider, for example, the following excerpt from a Greek service to bless a same-sex union. In it, the priest says:

> Forasmuch as Thou, O Lord and Ruler, art merciful and loving, who didst establish humankind after thy image and likeness, who didst deem it meet that thy holy apostles Philip and Bartholomew be united, bound one unto the other not by nature but by faith and the spirit. As Thou didst find thy holy martyrs Serge and Bacchus worthy to be united together, bless also these thy servants N. and N., joined together not by the bond of nature but by faith and in the mode of the spirit, granting unto them peace and love and oneness of mind. [320]

Selective use of hate speech by ecclesiastical figures can be counterbalanced—and countered—by other texts, if one knows where to find them. The ignorance of Church history—or the willful misconstrual of it—does not change the record. Despite some horrific intolerance and persecution, the Church has also known laity and clergy who have been indifferent toward, or accepting of homosexuals—and not a few who were themselves what we today call 'homosexual.'

The Positive Case

Thus far, all of the material has been in response to opponents. Yet it would be wrong to conclude that the best supporters of homosexual people can put forward is a defensive case. A spirited defense has been necessary against the accusations, particularly in light of the gullibility of many Christians, who presume their cultural biases are biblically supported and who flock to listen to only the voices proclaiming what they want to hear (cf. 2 Timothy 4:3-4). In the homophobic atmosphere of the contemporary Church a classical apologetic approach has been warranted. But it is more and more being accompanied by a positive theology.

The positive case put forward for homosexuality typically runs along these lines: God is the author of creation, which he called 'good' (Genesis 1-2), and this extends to the making of *all* people. Increasing scientific evidence supports that homosexuality occurs throughout Nature, is thus 'natural,' and accordingly comes under God's authorship and blessing. Though sin entered creation, and placed it in bondage, it did not ruin creation or spoil its essential character; assuming homosexuality is the result of the Fall denigrates God's work. In any event, no matter how the Fall is interpreted to affect human sexuality, all human beings remain made in the image of God and every one is worth respect. Further, love in any manner or relation is godly and to suggest that love between two people of the same sex is ungodly is contrary to the dominant theme of the Bible about God. In embracing and acting according to the way they are made, homosexuals honor and praise their creator. Their sexual expressions of love should be evaluated in exactly the same way as heterosexual expressions, according not to which body parts do what, but according to personal dimensions of affection, care, respect, and so forth.

The handling of sacred texts is also of great concern to supporters of homosexual Christians. Simpson points out that when the Bible is read without the filter of heterosexual expectations, that non-heterosexual eyes see many stories otherwise left untold. The recognition that such other stories exist to be seen, says Simpson, constitutes the first step in finding the Bible a resource for a praxis of sexual justice. But Simpson doesn't underestimate the size of the challenge: the long history of using the Bible as a club against sexual minorities requires for most people a dramatic re-thinking about how to approach the text.[321]

Just as heterosexuals may look to biblical models of loving devotion between men and women (e.g., Jacob and Rachel), so too homosexuals can find evidence of the same between members of the same sex (e.g., Ruth and Naomi, or David and Jonathan), regardless of whether any sexual behavior was actually involved. Of course, many heterosexual Christians object to viewing any biblical couples as having homoerotic qualities. But such objections don't erase the evidence that leads to seeing a 'friendship' like David had with Jonathan as more than common male comradery. The biblical text says Jonathan loved David "as his own soul" (1 Samuel 18:1), and David reciprocated such intense affection, saying at Jonathan's death, "your love to me was wonderful, passing the love of women" (2 Samuel 1:26). Of course, nothing in the biblical account *demands* we find here an instance of homoerotic attraction or same-sex behavior, but by the same token nothing *forbids* it (see, for example, 1 Samuel 20:41). Their culture lacked our homophobia and, like some modern societies, embraced strong same-sex relationships, with or without a sexual component.

Yet if opponents find themselves free to treat biblical figures as though they were contemporary Americans, why shouldn't sexual minorities enjoy the same liberty? After all, bad handling of biblical texts is bad handling no matter who does it. But if we exercise careful scholarship, as many have done, there remain tantalizing possibilities. Given historical and cultural factors, a reading of same-sex erotic attraction is at least plausible in some places. If nothing else, the intense emotional closeness indicated between Ruth and Naomi, or between Jonathan and David (or, indeed, between Jesus and his 'beloved disciple' John) stands as a rebuke to the homophobic shunning of anything remotely like such close affection between people of the same sex today.

Conclusion

In sum, however we arrive at it, and whatever exact shape it takes, both homosexual Christians and their supporters have reasonable grounds for asserting that homosexuality is not a sin. If it is not a sin, condemnations of it are wrong. Worse, efforts to change the homosexual through what is generally called 'reparative therapy' actually constitutes harm—and thus violates the most basic premise in the helping professions. From a Christian perspective the matter is succinctly expressed by Rev. Mel White, himself raised as an Evangelical, who writes, "The notion that homosexuals can and should be 'changed' is an insult to God, who loves variety in all things, including sexual orientation."[322]

What are answers to concerns over transsexualism?

As we saw in the last answer, although some Christians are disturbed by both homosexuality and transgenderism, the former has gotten more attention. When opposition has turned to those most often called transgender people, it has focused on transsexualism and crossdressing. We shall consider the objections to transsexualism first. As we do so, we might note that many Christians assume that there are no theologians or theological ideas in the Church actually supportive of transgender realities as positive things. In fact, so identified is Christian theology with opposition to transgender realities that this presumption poses no insignificant obstacle to most transgender believers. Religion scholar Alison Jasper gets the matter exactly right in musing that, "It might be thought then, at first glance, that, being part of the problem, Christian theology would have little positive to offer to a discussion of transsexualism."[323]

Yet there has developed an entire body of theological thinking that is often labeled 'Queer Theology.' The term 'queer' here is not used derisively, but as a self-descriptor that owns in an affirming manner a word used by some as an accusation. This adoption is in the same spirit as the early followers of Jesus who took the label 'Christian,' intended to mock them as 'little messiahs' who thought they could save the world, and made it into a self-affirmation. This theologizing aims to reinvigorate Christian thinking by challenging Essentialist presuppositions, reexamining biblical figures and texts, and recasting ecclesiastical language in ways that are more inclusive, egalitarian, and liberating.[324] In fact, Queer theology is seen by some as a theological hope for overcoming a deep-seated dishonesty within the Church about the sexual and gender lives of many of its members. Counterbalancing the prevailing but narrow view about sex and gender might reinvigorate pastoral practice and promote deeper connections with and among parishioners.[325]

Asking opponents to consider something like Queer theology is likely to be rejected out of hand. Therefore, a more modest and frequently applied tactic is staying to the methods and manners familiar to opponents. This 'fighting fire with fire' approach yields a substantial body of arguments refuting their opponents' contentions. To some of these—ordered as they appeared in the previous answer—we must now turn.

Counter to Argument 1: Transsexualism Is Not an Excuse for Homosexuality

Transgender people and their supporters often find it frustratingly wearying that many people persist in forging an unbreakable bond between gender identity and sexual orientation. The notion that all transsexuals are homosexual, and that people claim transsexualism in order to justify a sex change to cover their homosexuality is pernicious nonsense. As typically advanced the opponent's position has some major flaws.

First, there is no basis logically to associate *gender* variance with *sexual* variance. Despite the close tie forged in our culture between sex and gender, they are different things. Similarly, gender identity (our sense of being masculine, or feminine, or otherwise) is distinct and separate from sexual orientation (our pattern of erotical arousal). Majority members of a population have a tendency to lump minorities together, and given our society's confusion over how gender and sexuality relate, linking gender variance to homosexuality is hardly surprising, even if illogical. The evidence from actual lives is that some gender variant people also identify as homosexual, and some as heterosexual. Likewise, some homosexual people identify as gender variant, but many do not, seeing themselves—and being seen by others—as either masculine men or feminine women.

Second, opponents generally assume that sexual orientation is determined by *genetic* sex, rather than by either body sex or gender. This is a very convenient position, especially since it is never applied to themselves. In other words, they assume that as heterosexuals they must be genetically male or female, though none of them are likely to confirm that through genetic testing! Rather, they confirm their genetic status by appeal to their body presentation—the very appeal they deny to post-operative transsexuals.

Transsexuals have two ready answers to this hypocrisy. On the one hand, if what really matters in practice is how a body appears and how its parts fit together with bodies of a different sex, then a post-operative male-to-female transsexual having intercourse with a man looks and acts like any other woman, regardless of genetics. Opponents to transsexuals are being unfair applying one standard to themselves (i.e., how the body looks), and another to transsexuals (i.e., what the genetic origin was). On the other hand, the whole debate thus

176

framed is simply wrong-headed. Sexual orientation is not determined by the genitals, but by the brain.

This gets at the crux of the matter. *Gender*, not *sex*, determines sexual orientation. What resides between the ears has more power than what rests between the legs. If one's gender sense is of being a woman, and one is attracted to men, the attraction is heterosexual. Similarly, if one experiences the self as a woman, and is attracted to women, the attraction is homosexual. Whether pre- or post-operative, a female-to-male transsexual who is attracted to women is heterosexual because from first to last the attraction is to a different gender. Add to this reality an actual change in body appearance and sexual function, and the post-operative transsexual achieves exactly the same kind of internal and external consistency that a heterosexual has all along and takes for granted. Seen thus, the opponent's position amounts to a petty resentment of transsexuals attaining to what heterosexuals always have had.

Can transsexuals experience a change in sexual orientation because of the way in which the body is altered? Absolutely. But heterosexuals ignore that the same possibility exists for them. Homophobia is one blatant attempt to guard against this happening—and an implicit acknowledgment that it can. We know today that sexual orientation is a *relatively* fixed erotic attraction pattern. Accordingly, we might venture to warn heterosexuals that 'those who live in glass houses shouldn't throw stones.'

Counter to Argument 2: Transsexualism Is Not Satanic, But Holy

The essence of opponents' charges that transsexualism is Satanic embraces two notions: Satan is the author of gender confusion and transsexuals sow that confusion by encouraging others to join them. This is a theological argument that has no reference to specific biblical texts, though opponents may try to reason it out by appeal to ideas they find in Scripture, such as the general notion that Satan is God's adversary and has an agenda that sets up a counterfeit structure to the Church. The latter, derived from the New Testament's book of Revelation is highly debatable, but not uncommon among some Christian fellowships.

Aside from pointing out the inherent weakness of this argument, we might point out that almost universally transgender people are viewed as holy rather than unholy. To be 'holy' means to be 'set apart' for a special purpose. Transgender people are typically seen as placed by their transgender reality in a place between the conforming genders and between all people and transcendent realities. They are, in short, in the valuable and valued position of *mediators*. They are commonly seen as possessing special insight into both conforming genders, and into the divine. This may be one reason that some theologians see Jesus—the greatest mediator (see Hebrews 9:15, 12:24)—as a kind of transgender figure (see the answer to Q. 76). Apparently, throughout history and around the world people have found it more plausible to see transgender people as uniquely placed for contact with the divine than inspired by evil to tear down holy communities.

As for a desire to convert others into the transgender (especially transsexual) experience, perhaps the testimony of one transsexual best answers the charge. In her autobiography, male-to-female transsexual Cindi Jones mentions that when she was contemplating going to California, "I was admonished several times before I made my trip . . . that there was a religion of transsexualism. I was told that groups of people would get together and talk each other into making the transition; to talk each other into castration." Jones observes how preposterous such an idea is: it imagines that the support offered by others for a process of self-help somehow has the power to "induce an individual to play the role of the opposite sex for a full year, embarrass himself and his whole family, financially bankrupt himself, and then castrate himself. . . ." As Jones puts it, such an idea is "beyond belief." [326] Whatever else one may imagine, it is hard to see much appeal or power for most people in the 'message' opponents allege is being spread.

Counter to Argument 3: Transsexualism Does Not Despoil God's Creation, It Redeems It

Opponents claim that transsexualism despoils creation because hormones, surgery, and other means alter the body one was born with. Such acts are often depicted as an arrogant usurpation of what properly belongs to God. Once again, opponents are typically selective in their reasoning and application. Few are the sermons against other body alterations, including purely cosmetic changes like breast implants or reductions, or a wide array of plastic surgeries. Opponents do sometimes draw a distinction between surgeries to promote health and well-being as opposed to unnecessary ones to improve appearance. Sex reassignment surgery—covered as medically necessary by many insurance companies—is viewed by a majority of medical and mental health professionals as justified in promoting psychological health and well-being.

Rather than usurp God's role, transsexuals can be viewed as working alongside God to redeem a creation in bondage because of the Fall (see Romans 8:19-23). Instead of blaming God for creating an imperfect match between gender sense and body sex, a transgender Christian can attribute the mismatch to a Fallen creation and claim that efforts to restore an orderly peace between mind and body is exactly what God wants. To the objection that it is the mind, rather than the body, that is disordered, a transgender believer can respond that as God is without a body, being made in the divine likeness must refer to the inner essence. The gender sense is a more fundamental and meaningful psychological reality; further, there are good reasons to believe God has made some of us to stand between the genders and between all people and the divine. So it makes better sense to see the internal self as God-created and the body as defective.

To argue otherwise is to use a logic that suggests God intends what human beings commonly see as birth defects and handicaps. If we regard those as products of the Fall, why not see a body that disagrees with the person's gender sense as flawed? Or perhaps better, why not find in imperfect bodies an occasion for redemptive work to occur through transformation of that body? In this we have biblical precedent, as in this story about Jesus: "As he walked along, he saw a man blind from birth. His disciples asked him, 'Rabbi, who sinned, this man or his parents?' Jesus answered, 'Neither this man nor his parents sinned; he was born blind *so that God's works might be revealed in him.*'" (John 9:1-3 NRSV, italics added.) Having said this, Jesus healed the man.

We should note that sin is detached from the man's condition; why should we not do likewise for transsexualism, since evidence supports it has a biological foundation? Positively, Jesus finds in the man's condition a potential—that God's works might be revealed in him. But those works are only revealed in him by a transformation of the body. It is hard to see why this should not be said of the transsexual, who seeks transformation 'that God's works might be revealed' in becoming a whole person—as God intends. Neither the condition at birth, nor growing up, need be seen as due to sin (or sinful), but the occasion of change becomes a spiritual as well as physical act. The transsexual's body modifications are not despoiling creation but restoring it to the glory of God.

Counter to Argument 4: The Bible Does Not Condemn Transgender People

The argument that the Bible condemns transgenderism advances one specific key text, typically used in conjunction with a more general logic. That broader logic, theological in character, we have addressed in the first three counterarguments. To refresh our memories, here is the focal text: "Do not be deceived! Fornicators, idolaters, adulterers, male prostitutes, sodomites, thieves, the greedy, drunkards, revilers, robbers—none of these will inherit the kingdom of God" (1 Corinthians 6:9-10).

As discussed in the last answer, the key term in this text is the Greek word μαλακοί (*malakoi*; pl. of μαλακός [*malakos*]), rendered in English in the New Revised Standard Version (NSRV) as 'male prostitutes.' When used against transgender people, the translation preferred by opponents is 'effeminate,' the translation of the King James Version (KJV). The masculine form of the Greek word makes it clear that males are being referred to by the word. Thus—consistent with our present culture's obsessions—the chief anxiety is over male sexuality.

That it is cultural anxiety rather than sound biblical scholarship that is the engine driving the opponent's argument is the thrust of Christian writer Elisabeth Anne Kellogg's critique. She points out that the early 17th century translation embodied in the KJV had a different conception of male effeminacy than we presently do. She argues that then it was used with reference to heterosexual males who were notorious womanizers.[327] Similarly, Helminiak contends that the tendency to translate μαλακοι consistent with reigning cultural prejudices has been persistent in Church history. He notes that, "until the Reformation in the 16th century and in Roman Catholicism until the 20th century, the word *malakoi* was thought to mean 'masturbators.' It seems that as prejudices changes, so have translations of the Bible."[328]

So what does the text mean? Even with an effort to set aside cultural baggage the answer is not clear. More than one problem besets us. First, as we can see, the meaning of the word is unclear. In Classical Greek when μαλακός is used for a person, the general sense is of someone who is 'soft,' 'mild,' or 'gentle.' It also can be used negatively, as of someone who is cowardly, or morally weak (e.g., lacking in self-control), or pathetic, or physically weak or ill.[329] Since the list before us is one of vices, we can safely infer the μαλακοι are not people we want to be like. But that doesn't tell us who they are or why they are objectionable.

That leads us to a second problem. Scholars find themselves divided on whether μαλακοί should be seen as a separate item on a list of distinct items, or joined with the preceding term, ἀρσενοκοίται (*arsenokoitai*). Those who join the two terms are thereby able to find the active (ἀρσενοκοίται) and passive (μαλακοί) partners in same-sex sexual relations. This is the approach taken, for example, by Fritz Rienecker in his *Linguistic Key to the Greek New Testament*. The word μαλακός is therein called a technical term for the passive partner in homosexual relations, and ἀρσενοκοίται is viewed as naming a male homosexual.[330] The problems with this approach are both logical and lexical. Logically, we should expect them to be treated as unrelated items since all other items in the list are disconnected from one another. Moreover, in the only other place in the New Testament where ἀρσενοκοίται occurs, another vice list (1 Timothy 1:10), it is both disconnected from other items and appears without μαλακοί.

This issue leads to a third problem. Lexically, ἀρσενοκοίται is a very rare word. It may actually have originated in use in the New Testament and only a handful of instances of it are known. Though the meaning of its separate parts are clear (ἀρσενο- pertaining to males, and ᾽κοίται, pertaining to sexual relations), what happens when they are placed together is less certain. If we interpret the former part by the latter part of the word, it suggests the male as the active partner in sexual relations. It might, in fact, be parallel with the idea of 'a man who lies with another man as with a woman' (Leviticus 18:22; 20:13).[331] On the other hand, it might refer simply to males who are sexual aggressors (like rapists). On the other hand, if we interpet the latter part of the compound by the first part, it might suggest males who are the object of sexual activity, rather than the initiators of it. In this case, we still might think it means men who are passive objects of same-sex sexual behavior. But we could also speculate it is any male in the 'unmanly' sexually passive role, regardless of the sex of the partner. Since the New Testament's use of the word in both instances is simply as an item in a list, we cannot be sure what is meant.[332]

Finally, a fourth problem ensues even if we accept that the terms are both sexual, linked, and actually pair a passive partner with an active one in a same-sex encounter. Even under all these conditions it is unlikely the text is referring to what we today know as homosexuality. In our modern context we typically construe homosexuality as same-sex behavior between consenting adults. If one is unconsenting it is rape; if one is a minor, it is child sexual abuse. But in the ancient Greek world there was a practice called *pederasty* that formed between an older male (ἐραστής [*erastes*], the 'lover'—the active partner in any sexual encounter) and a younger male (ἐρόμενος [*eromenos*], 'the beloved'—the passive partner). Though erotic in nature, and not unusually with a sexual component, this highly social relationship was far more than a merely sexual one and did not have sanction merely to satisfy an adult male's lust. Outside of Greek culture, pederasty was typically seen negatively. Though it is simplistic to do so, our modern culture would reduce it to child sexual abuse—within our cultural framework an entirely appropriate judgment since the younger partner would be judged incapable of giving informed consent and the inherent inequality in power being the parties would always possess the potential for misuse. Though it is common to see pederasty as what is named in this list, that practice is manifestly *not* equivalent to the adult homosexual relationships condemned by some Christians using this text.

So we are led back to the puzzle of μαλακοί. We know it is construed negatively. But we don't know how. Given the apparent sexual nature of the words before and after it, it seems more likely than not to refer to something sexual. To be 'soft' sexually might mean any of a number of things—which is why it has been construed as referring to masturbation ('soft' as 'self-indulgent'), or to male prostitution ('soft' in giving one's self up for money), or to being the passive partner in sex relations (which conceivably could be with either another man or with a woman). We do not know what is the most likely case, and so the easy certainty of opponents who read the word as either referring to homosexuals or to effeminate transgender males is unwarranted and irresponsible.

What are answers to concerns over crossdressing?

The overwhelming majority of Christians acknowledge that a person can be a crossdresser *and* a Christian believer. Of course, those who regard crossdressing as a sin think that those who crossdress need to repent and change their behavior (see the answer to Q. 73). Many others, however, simply give the matter little, if any, attention. Very few ever consider how widespread the phenomenon might be or whether there might even be a connection between crossdressing and religiousness.

1. Countering the 'Appeal to the Bible' Argument

Opponents appeal to Deuteronomy 20:5 ("A woman shall not wear a man's apparel, nor shall a man put on a woman's garment; for whoever does such things is abhorrent to the LORD your God"), often without any further elaboration. They see the message as so plain as to be indisputable.

The issues surrounding this text have been treated at length earlier (see the answers to Q. 61-65), so we shall not repeat what was said there. However, we should note that opponents generally resist any effort to get beyond a simple recitation of the English words. Regarding them as 'self-evident,' they disparage as sophistry any effort to examine the text further. So scholarship regarding the words, the literary context, the historical culture, and so forth, is seen as unnecessary at best and, at worst, an effort by religious liberals to undermine the 'plain sense' of the Bible.

Those who crossdress, and their supporters, find the opponents' stance difficult to counter, not because the facts are against them, but because the opponents often aren't open to discussion on the matter. They regard the matter as 'case closed' and efforts to reopen it as proof that the person is trying to tear down a truth they don't like. In such a climate, dialog is impossible.

Nevertheless, for those fairer-minded, the facts are such that simplistic judgments are impossible. No one can dispute that the text condemns crossdressing. What is at issue, though, is what is meant by crossdressing here and whether its context applies to Christians today.[333] In those respects, there are plenty of grounds to argue that the Bible is *not* condemning crossdressing as it is principally known today. Crossdressing as an expression of gender variant identity does not seem at all what the Bible has in mind.

2. Countering the 'Appeal to Personal Experience' Argument

There are far more testimonies to the experience of feeling loved and accepted by God *as* a transgender person than there are testimonies, as in the preceding answer, claiming to have been rescued *from* transgender realities. In fact, as Lee Frances Heller illustrates, there are even accounts of transgender individuals pleading for years to be changed before coming to a realization that it is okay to be who one is.

1st Testimony: Coming to Terms with Crossdressing (Lee Frances Helle)

Heller, born in 1919, struggled with crossdressing throughout much of life, only becoming a public advocate on behalf of crossdressers after retiring. Heller writes that *sie*[334] threw herself "into a pink tizzy spiritually" for 39 years, from conversion in 1947 until coming to terms with being a crossdresser in 1987, at age 67. Heller says, "In those years I asked God many times to 'deliver' me from it so that I could be more comfortable. He didn't do it. Period. Now I know that he didn't need to."[335] For Heller the resolution came in finally concluding that for God crossdressing was a nonissue. "No," Heller remarks, "God does not approve of crossdressing, because that is not the issue. He has no need to approve."[336] The bottom line is simple: "Pants or skirts don't make the difference. Our heart's attitude toward God does."[337] Heller emphasizes faith and forgiveness, but that does not mean *sie* regards being a crossdresser something sinful. Rejecting the idea that God makes mistakes,[338] Heller maintains that crossdressers "come out of the womb" as that kind of person.[339] Though different, or 'unorthodox,' a crossdresser is like Jesus in an important respect: he, too, was 'unorthodox' and misunderstood by others.[340] Finally, Heller advises other crossdressers to accept who they are in the grace of God. "To ask for deliverance from the very nature God gave us and from the way He made us," Heller says, "is an unreasonable expectation."[341]

2nd Testimony: Answering Critics (Lacey Leigh)

Crossdressing Christians often directly address opponents' criticisms of what they wear. For example, Lacey Leigh in an online piece entitled, "Speaking of Crossdressing," uses logic to answer critics who quote the Deuteronomy text. If women are permitted to wear trousers made and sold as 'women's pants,' then by the same token men should be permitted to wear skirts and dresses tailored for them. Leigh points out that stylistically the difference between a 'shirt' and a 'blouse' is that they have buttons on different sides and the latter is often a more colorful fabric. Leigh asks, "Is God so petty He would deny me entrance to heaven over button placement and fabric color?" But, recognizing the futilitely of trying to talk to someone whose mind is already made up, Leigh advises crossdressers to simply remind the critic of the Christian's obligation to love others and leave the judging to God. [342]

3rd Testimony: Journey of a Christian Transsexual (Rebecca Anne Allison)

Christian transsexuals often have a particularly difficult time because both world and Church can be hostile. It can be bad enough to be viewed as a crossdresser though one is merely dressing to fit what society says is appropriate for the gender the person identifies with. But when talk of body altering surfaces, the negative attention can drastically escalate. Male-to-female transsexual Christian and physician Becky Allison echoes the struggle articulated by Lee Frances Heller to come to a self-acceptance based in believing in God's acceptance. Like Heller, Allison upon becoming a Christian and first being exposed to Deuteronomy 22:5 assumed her crossdressing was a sin and prayed for deliverance. Like Heller, closer study of the Bible provided release from a false guilt.[343]

Coming to terms with being transsexual took longer than accepting her crossdressing; she was in middle-age when it happened. But the process yielded great significance. "Next to my own personal relationship with Jesus Christ," Allison says, "this acceptance is the most basic and profound experience of my life."[344] It was hard won—and not shared by some of the important people in Allison's life, like her spouse. In her journey of self-discovery, Allison has had to find answers and face the questions of others. Allison writes:

> How do I know I am a woman? I have the anatomy of a man.
> But just as surely as I know my anatomy, I know my soul—my
> spirit. And I have the soul of a woman. I did not arrive at this
> knowledge hastily. It comes from hours of study, prayerful

meditation, and prayer. And I know I have the assurance of the
Holy Spirit and the peace that passes all understanding.[345]

That peace, though, did not mean her transitioning was easy. Allison drew upon biblical models like David and Paul to cope with rejection and struggle.[346] She found that sacrifice was needed; she voluntarily gave up her professional position as she began transitioning and went months without employment. She also gave up her home, moving to another state to begin her new life. Friends were another sacrifice as most could not see beyond how the change in Allison's life impacted on themselves. Even harder was the loss of family. Yet this time was met with hope. Allison found a new home, new friends—and new personal strengths, gaining in self-confidence, patience, and the blessing of giving with no thought of receiving in return.[347]

Eventually Allison located suitable employment. Sex reassignment surgery went without complications. Allison sees such surgery as correction of a birth defect, and counts it as the answer to her prayers across many years. Candidly, Allison speaks of her transsexualism as a 'dilemma,' but emphasizes that it had a solution—one reached by seeking God's will.[348] Now, post-surgery, she says, "Truly, my life's dreams are coming true. I praise God for allowing me to live a life of fulfillment and joy."[349] Yet even so, her life remains marked by some of the consequences of being transsexual. She still experiences misunderstanding, rejection, even hostility from others. Even after years living as a woman, Allison still finds the need to draw upon the love of Christ to turn the other cheek and offer forgiveness to opponents. In that same love she seeks to set an example that will win others to acceptance of herself and other transsexuals.[350]

4th Testimony: A Female-to-Male Transsexual ('Lisa'/'John')

Lest the impression be that such stories only come from those born biologically male, consider the story of one of Walter Bockting's clients. 'Lisa,' a biological female, was a staunch Roman Catholic who even spent time in a concent. She struggled with identity issues. She wondered if God wanted her to be a man, or a lesbian—though her masculine gender identity was apparent in many ways. Having explored life as a lesbian, which she found was not who she was, she adopted living as 'John,' a heterosexual man. Yet John's body remained an obstacle, one pitted against a belief that God had made his body and altering it would bar him from heaven. Fortunately, John found support not only in therapy and a therapeutic support group, but within a congregation that welcomes transgender people. Remarkably, his deeply conservative birth family also expressed acceptance. In this climate John continued to develop his spirituality, staying active in church and prayer. He also drew upon his priest for support and guidance. Although John elected not to pursue surgical changes, he did find living as a Christian man more fulfilling than life as a woman.[351]

The literature today is full of such examples. The point is worth repeating: there are far more of these kinds of witnesses than of those who renounced being transgender and found fulfillment within their birth assigned sex and gender. In fact, evidence suggests reparative therapy does not typically result in long-term change.

3. Countering the 'Appeal to Theology' Argument

For opponents, the primary theological objection to crossdressing is the claim that it violates God's intended order, which separates the sexes. Implicit in this position is the acceptance that gender is predicated on sexual anatomy. As we have seen elsewhere, to the link between sex and gender is also joined an assumption about sexuality, especially sexual orientation. Thus, on one side are the God-intended masculine men and feminine women, comfortable in their gender conformity and heterosexuality, and on the other side are the deviant gender variant homosexuals.

Consider again the argument made by Daniel Heimbach. He fears that crossdressing sends the wrong message, that it inevitably stirs up homosexual thoughts and often leads to same-sex lust. What is striking in this thinking is how crossdressing itself is subordinated to the real concern: safeguarding heterosexual sexuality. It is hard not to see in the background the old psychoanalytic assumption that crossdressing and homosexuality (even if only 'latent') are intrinsically bound to each other. Heimbach's view with regard to crossdressing narrows the behavior to one motivation—intentional gender confusion—and suggests that motivation either serves or awakens another one: homosexual lust. We are left to wonder what amendment, if any, he might give were he to find evidence of other motivations for crossdressing. In the context of his argument as given it appears that all that really matters is the prohibition of any behavior that might endanger what he regards as mattering most: heterosexual sexuality.

Let's look further at the argument that crossdressing challenges God's intended order. The opponents' argument assumes that God intended only masculine men and feminine women, with each desiring the other. As we have seen, this is a selective and not particularly astute reading of the Bible, especially the creation account of Genesis. The text does say God created 'male and female' (Genesis 1:27; Hebrew: זכר, *zachar*, 'male' and נקבה, *nekeva*, 'female'). Pope John Paul II affirmed in his Apostolic Letter *On the Dignity and Vocation of Women (Mulieris Dignitatem)* that this text declares male and female are human beings to an equal degree and both are created in God's image.[352] Yet, neither the text in itself, or even the Pontiff's elaboration of it, are terribly helpful since we can and do use the words to refer to all people, regardless of their genetic coding. In other words, even intersex people—those who aren't 46-XY or 46-XX—are called male or female depending on their apparent body sex at birth. Mere sex designation does not say anything about either sexual orientation or gender identity.

Of course, opponents link body sex ('male,' 'female') to gender ('man,' 'woman'). They appeal to Genesis 2:23-24 (". . . this one shall be called Woman, for out of Man this one was taken. Therefore a man leaves his father and his mother and clings to his wife, and they become one flesh.") as affirming *only* two genders, and *only* heterosexuality as God's intention. Apart from being a lot to read from so little, nothing directly connects the sex designations of Genesis 1 with the gender names of Genesis 2. The gender labels 'Woman' (אשּׁה, *ishshah*) and 'Man' (אישׁ, *ish*) are linguistically related somewhat the way our English terms are. 'Woman' in English originally meant 'man's wife'; *ishshah* in the Genesis account is literally taken from the man and the Hebrew term is often used to mean 'wife.' Yet the ancient rabbis never presumed that all women must or would marry, even though that was normative practice.

Opponents might reply that since there originally were only two people, and the second was taken from the first and then given to be his sexual partner, that this proves sex and gender are reliably paired and heterosexuality presumed. Any number of difficulties might be pointed out about this reading of the text. First, most scholars understand that Genesis 1 and Genesis 2 present two creation accounts. Reading them together as one seamless story thereby does each an injustice and can lead to seriously wrong conclusions. Second, most scholars also regard the story of Adam and Eve as symbolic rather than historical. But, third, even if we presume a literary unity, and even if we presume that originally there was actually and exactly one male and one female, who mated to produce children, that in no way compels us to see a statement about how *all* people must henceforth be and act. If we think the first man and woman present a model for all men and women, why not conclude all brothers should act like Cain and Abel? As it turned out, the pairing of Adam and Eve was hardly flawless; the first couple managed to get themselves booted out of Eden for disobedience—hardly a shining example to emulate!

The creation account in Genesis 1 depicts God creating living beings "of every kind" (Genesis 1:11, 12, 21, 24, 25). Certainly it is appropriate to find in this a reference to all the diversity *of* species, but why not also all the diversity *within* species? The Hebrew word translated 'every' (כּל, *kol*) is a robust term that might fit both kinds of diversity. The Hebrew word translated 'kind' (מין, *miyn*) is exactly the sort of word used for gender—it references a 'sorting out' that can apply equally to species or to genders within species. Since we have abundant evidence of multiple genders among animals (see the answer to Q. 21), why not recognize the same among human beings and see in them all the verdict rendered again and again after this sorting is accomplished: "And God saw that it was *good*" (Genesis 1:12, 21, 25, 31; emphasis added).

Conclusion

Not surprisingly, those most likely to speak out in behalf of transgendered Christians are either themselves transgender people or those who minister to them. The former have firsthand experience of the obstacles often placed in their way by other Christians, but also have experience of the support many

186

fellow Christians offer. The latter, too, know what it is like to face hostility for ministering to a marginalized community, but they also know the reward of seeing transgender people as human beings like themselves, hungry for fellowship, struggling with the demands of life, and eager for the grace of God. We shall soon turn to the people who minister to transgender Christians, but first we would do well to consider a too little asked question.

Is there a need for conflict?

In light of the fact that not all Christians regard crossdressing in the same way, is conflict inevitable? Probably. The issue touches culturally sensitive and personally value laden matters, which typically generate more heat than light in discussions. Those who see crossdressing as sin may feel the need to confront it, and those who do not see it as sin may feel the need to defend against the confrontation. Is there a way out?

Perhaps we can appreciate the nuanced appraisal of Christian writers like Stephanie Paulsell, who addresses a theme close to the heart of the Christian Gospel: freedom:

> "Is not life more than food and the body more than clothing?" Jesus asks in Matthew's Gospel. Like my mother, wishing me to be unencumbered enough to travel quickly and lightly toward the most important destinations, Jesus urges us toward freedom. "Why do you worry about clothing? Consider the lilies of the field, how they grow; they neither toil nor spin, yet I tell you, even Solomon in all his glory was not clothed like one of these." Are your habits of adornment a burden or a pleasure, a source of anxiety or confidence? Do your clothes free you to be yourself, or do they constrain you by forcing you into an identity that, however fashionable, you would not have chosen? Did the production of your adornments constrain the freedom of another? These are questions that might guide us in our clothing and our adornment, to help us develop our own ideas of what is beautiful, and to allow the daily practice of getting dressed remind us that we are children of a God who desires our freedom.[353]

She makes good sense by reminding us all of where our priorities could better lie.

There is a degree of irony that in the Land of Liberty, where Christians glady embrace cultural values of freedom of expression and individuality, so many of them seek within the Church to enslave others to their own manner of gender conformity and sexual practice. Apparently, for them Christian freedom extends only so far as compliance to their own ideas and practices. Interestingly, in line with this theme of freedom, Vern and Bonnie Bullough, a pair of expert researchers on crossdressing, make the following observation about the Christian response to the Deuteronomy text:

> In spite of this prohibition, Christianity has always tolerated transvestism at festivals such as Halloween, or under certain conditions as in the theater. Christianity has also generally looked with favor upon women trying to be like men and even dressing like men, providing they removed all sexual connotations from such cross-dressing.[354]

So, perhaps, regardless of local conflicts or personal disputes the historic drift of Christian practice has been largely benign and tolerant. Though the weight of this verdict rests largely on the Church's treatment of crossdressing women, perhaps the same will prove true, in time, for male crossdressers. As has been observed by others, Christians are often better than their words, and most seem to prefer charity to judgment, especially when they can find grounds for liberality. Perhaps transgender Christians and their supporters, if they are listened to, can offer them such grounds.

In many matters prohibited by ecclesiastical authorities, or looked down upon in former times, there has proved to be a historical movement from seeing things as *sin*—often punished civilly as crimes—to removing them from courts to receive counseling as a matter of *sickness*, only to eventually accept them as variant forms of *sanity* in a world none of us find easy to navigate.[355] We may be in such a process with respect to transgender right now.

Fortunately, born of goodwill and Christian charity, there are important resources available to today's transgender believers. It is to these we must next turn.

Q. 75 Are there resources for trans-gender Christians?

The Short Answer. As we have seen, the members of the Christian faith are divided in their regard of transgender realities. Some adopt a stance that ostensibly aims to 'love the sinner, but hate the sin.' Others do not regard transgender realities as sinful expressions of a fallen nature but rather as reflections of God's varied creation and grace. Depending on whether a Church or Christian organization condemns or accepts transgender people and practices like crossdressing determines whether its resources intended for such Christians are used to try to change the people and their behaviors or instead support them as they try to exist within an ignorant society. In truth, both sides recognize a problem exists: the one sees it residing in the gender variant person, the other in the wider society. Inasmuch as a previous answer (to Q. 73) examined ministries trying to change transgender people, this answer focuses on those ministries accepting and supportive of transgender people as they are. Today more than 1500 Christian churches and ministries in the United States publicly affirm their acceptance of members of the transgender community. However, this number, which is growing, still represents only a small percentage of the faith communities in the U.S. and many transgender people find themselves without such supportive resources. The responses made in the face of rejection and isolation by other Christians proves varied. Some transgender people react by concluding that Christian intolerance reflects so poorly on the religion that they no longer wish to be associated with it. Many turn from allegiance to formal religious organizations to all they see left to them—the cultivation of an individual spirituality. In one manner or another, perhaps the majority of transgender believers, no matter how poorly treated by their fellows, cling stubbornly to their faith and seek, often in highly creative ways, to give expression to it and to find for themselves some sense of community. Aiding them in this effort are both other transgender believers, engaging in a ministry of outreach and fellowship, and nontransgender Christians who believe that the character of Jesus and the nature of their faith points them to an openness, compassion, and acceptance that is proactive. Such believers are seeking to move their congregations to take stands on behalf of the transgender community, make themselves known as welcoming congregations, and establishing ministries sensitive to the unique needs of transgender people.

The Longer Answer. Whatever judgment we might make about cross-dressing behavior, virtually all Christians agree that a person can be a Christian and crossdress. The real issue is whether it is 'sin.' On that point there is disagreement. This difference leads to two conceptions about resources for crossdressers: one stressing the conversion of the crossdresser from the behavior (cf. answer to Q. 73), the other not seeking such change. In this answer, we shall consider resources supportive of the Christian crossdresser as well as Christian sexual minorities and gender variant believers.

How do transgender believers seek support?

Before we look at resources available to transgender Christians we must acknowledge that not all transgender people easily find such resources, or having found some, then determine they are sufficient. We would be incorrect to think that transgender Christians can *easily* find support for their faith. As the answer to a previous question (Q. 73) suggests, many congregations are not open to the visible presence of the transgendered in their midst. Many Christians are openly hostile to transgender realities. The visibility of supportive Christians in our society remains far less than that maintained by those who oppose them.

In such a climate a degree of despair is likely. Many transgender Christians struggle with whether they can even consider themselves Christian when there seem to be so many voices telling them they cannot be Christian unless they conform to our culture's normative matched set of sex, gender, and sexual orientation. In short, there is often a deafening chorus shouting that unless one is a heterosexual masculine male or heterosexual feminine female, the individual stands outside God's will and plan, cannot be a Christian without renouncing their mismatched nature, and must actively conform to the cultural expectation placed on them at birth. Put most simply, this expression of Christianity upholds vigorously—if generally uncritically—the cultural notions about sex, gender and sexual orientation established by the medicalization of sex.

Growing up in this culture it is extremely difficult for transgender people not to accept this way of looking at things, no matter how poorly it fits their own experience. When joined to seemingly authoritative proclamations by prominent religious figures, the judgment seems certain and true. Accordingly, transgender people often feel themselves desperately desiring a faith they cannot be sure of without rejecting the very self they hope that faith is intended for. In such a no-win situation they may try to live a double life—pretending publicly to be the kind of person who finds acceptance within the Church while privately living as transgender. If they cannot or will not live such a double life they may feel forced to deny one of two equally potent realities, their belief in Christ or their sense of self.

Fortunately, creativity is often born of desperation. Sociologist of religion and gender studies scholar Melissa Wilcox reports that her research with transgender women shows they may craft a religiosity of their own through one or more of at least six distinct ways: leaving their religious tradition before coming out; staying in their tradition as they come out; switching to another congregation or denomination; struggling with a homophobic, bi-phobic or transphobic tradition; seeking a new religiosity among alternative or new religious movements; and/or relying on divine assistance.[356] Sometimes the path chosen is pursued mostly in solitude. But increasingly there are resources a transgender Christian can draw upon.

What kinds of written resources are available?

At present, a number of different kinds of resources exist to support those who identify both as Christian and as transgender. These range from the material to the ministerial. What they have in common is a refusal to regard transgender realities as inherently evil, together with a welcoming approach to the incorporation of transgender people into the community of faith. We begin with written resources.

Books

Surprisingly few books deal at any length with crossdressing from a religious perspective. Of those that do, most tend to be historical reviews. A Christian crossdresser looking for material explicitly about his or her kind of experience will have some difficulty acquiring materials. But persistence can pay off. Here are some of the books relevant to a Christian crossdresser:

❑ Gerald Larue, *Sex and the Bible*—published in 1983, this book by a professor of Biblical history and archaeology at the University of Southern California offers a scholarly review of biblical materials. Cultural context, literary factors, and historical matters are also examined. This volume offers a solid orientation to the wider context in which discussion about Christianity and crossdressing may take place.[357]

❑ Vanessa Sheridan's short *The Cross and the Crossdresser*—an effort to present a conscientious Christian spirituality, in the space of just 48 pages the author discusses the Bible and theological sources, and offers counsel on living the Christian life as a crossdresser.[358]

❑ Vanessa Sheridan, *Cross Purposes on Being Christian and Crossgendered*—a longer work (93 pages) this book considers various spiritual issues, including dealing with religious institutions and fundamentalists. The volume also includes an autobiographical section.[359]

❑ *Religion and Transvestism*—a collection edited and published by International Foundation for Gender Education (IFGE), it uses materials that first appeared in *TV/TS Tapestry Journal*.[360]

❑ Lee Frances Heller and Friends, *By the Grace of God: Writings for Families, Friends, and Clergy*—this is a compendium of writings by the founder of

The Grace and Lace Letter (see below on internet resources), and by others.[361]

❑ Pat Conover, *Transgender Good News*—covering a wide number of topics, chapter 9 (pp. 199-270), and the appendices, are especially relevant to religious issues. Conover, a sociologist and for 35 years a minister in the United Church of Christ, holds a Master of Divinity (M.Div.) degree from the University of Chicago, and a Ph.D. from Florida State University.[362]

❑ Justin Tanis, *Trans-Gendered: Theology, Ministry, and Communities of Faith*— a scholar and minister, graduate of Harvard Divinity School, Tanis covers both cultural and religious issues in a work sponsored by the Pacific School of Religion's Center for Lesbian and Gay Studies in Religion and Ministry.[363]

❑ Virginia Mollenkott, *Omnigender: A Trans-Religious Approach*—the author is a respected theologian whose writing here avoids a narrow approach to spirituality by looking at other cultures as well as our own. Her intent is to present an 'omnigender' construction that breaks down the rigid binary gender system typifying our culture.[364]

Because most chain bookstores carry few, if any, materials helpful to crossdressers, the best place to look for help or to order materials is the internet.

The Internet

In most respects a chief resource for Christian crossdressers is the World Wide Web. The internet has a variety of sites providing not merely information with reference to a Christian stance on the behavior, but offering opportunities to make connections with other Christian crossdressers. A few listings may suffice to indicate the kind of material available:

❑ *Emergence*—a comprehensive site, this place provides a web community for the transgendered. Its features include Bible study materials, essays, profiles, resources, and chat.[365]

❑ *The Gender Tree*—another comprehensive website with material about Biblical passages, various essays, and links.[366]

❑ *TransFaith On-line*—this website provides various transgender Christian resources together with articles, bibliography, and links.[367]

❑ *Welcoming Ministries*—an online resource for the network of more than 1500 faith communities in 10 religious traditions committed to welcoming gay, lesbian, and transgendered people.[368]

❑ *Whosoever* online magazine—this internet periodical is for Gay, Lesbian, Bisexual and Transgendered Christians.[369]

❑ *The Grace and Lace Letter*—founded and edited by Lee Frances Heller (1919-2000), and maintained by Becky Allison, M.D., this site features articles on Christian spirituality of pertinence to Christian crossdressers, the transgendered, and transsexuals.[370]

Unfortunately, because the internet is such a fluid medium, websites appear, move, and disappear with enough frequency that any listed today may very well be gone by the time this is read. Patient persistence using a search engine will yield one or more websites right for whatever is being sought.

Conclusion

While written sources are valuable, and ones like internet sites often lead to human contacts, the importance of direct human support cannot be underestimated. Yet this can be problematic given the divisions among Christians. In recent decades, as transsexualism has gained more attention, this specific transgender reality has become more a focus by both opponents and supporters within the Church. The question of transsexuals within the Church has caught the eye of social scientists, too.

At the 10th World Congress of Sexology, held in Amsterdam, The Netherlands, in 1991, the first major conference on the relation between sex and religion convened. Transgender realities were among the matters discussed. We may profit from drawing upon some of that discussion, particularly work offered by two scholars in attendance, Woet Gianotten and Harris Brautigan. In their contribution, subsequently published in the volume on the proceedings of this conference, they wrote, "Transsexualism is neither a sin nor a kinky aberration." Given this starting point, it follows that, "Neither praying nor psychotherapy will cure this condition nor will it eliminate the craving for the other body." However, they do not thereby conclude such things are without value. They remark that both prayer and counseling can help alleviate pain and the anxieties a transgender believer may experience.[371]

Gianotten and Brautigan also squarely address a matter key to our present interest:

> Few pastors will be confronted with a transsexual person amongst their believers. For those pastors who are, the question arises: what could or should the Church or the pastor do? If the person wants to stay in the community (and the Church could help him/her to do so!) a religious ritual of transition could be of much value both to the persons involved and to the community.[372]

Of course, in the years since 1991 an increasing number of ministers and churches have been 'confronted' with the need to address transsexualism. Ministers, whether priests or pastors, exercise tremendous influence in their faith communities as transgender realities are faced. To see what some ministers have done on behalf of transgender people is our next task. As we turn to it, though, we should remember that religious officials are not alone responsible for the actions of churches. All Christians share in the responsibility of determining appropriate ministry to the transgender people among them.

What do supportive ministers provide?

While flamboyant opponents with loud voices and inflammatory words have received more media attention, ministers supportive of transgender people have been by no means silent. In addition to noncrossdressing clergy who minister to crossdressers, there are crossdressing clergy who minister to crossdressers and others as well. If nothing else, such individuals by the courage of their testimony serve as role models to other transgender believers. One such person is Rev. Becky Edwards, married with children and grandchildren, and a minister for more than a quarter century. Edwards has attempted to answer the query, 'How can I be a minister and still crossdress?' Edwards' answer is a traditional one that appeals to personal conscience and to leaving the matter to God to judge as to who is right in their behavior.[373]

Yet being openly transgender as a member of the clergy is not easy. Periodically, news articles recount 'coming out' occasions for members of the clergy.[374] In the Anglican Church, in particular, attention has been raised over transgender members of the clergy. An article published in the *London Sunday Times* in 1998 claimed that at least 21 clergy in the Church of England considered themselves transgendered, with 14 of them transvestites.[375] Across the Atlantic, the United Methodist Church wrestled with how to handle the request by the former Rev. Richard Zamostny, now Rev. Rebecca Steen, to lead a congregation as its pastor. Zamostny had taken a voluntary leave of absence in October, 1999, to undergo sex reassignment surgery. When the request for reinstatement met resistance, the church scheduled a hearing, but Steen resigned from the denomination instead.[376] That difficult decision is only one way a transgender minister might respond to the controversy and conflict that can arise. Others have taken different paths, though as Rev. Edwards remarked, each path must answer to personal conscience.

The ways in which ministers have spoken out have been varied. Here we offer only a few examples of some of the myriad ways their voices have been pressed into the service of the Christian community. The following ministers include both transgender and nontransgender folk, though the former have been emphasized because they show that it is possible to be both a transgender person and called to Christian ministry. The examples here have been listed alphabetically by denominational affiliation.

1. Rev. David Horton (Anglican Church)

Rev. David Horton, an Anglican priest who ministers to the transgendered community, is among the best known and most well-respected members of the clergy among transgender Christians. He first became involved with the issue of crossdressing in 1987, shortly after his ordination, when approached by a married couple. This initial encounter led to his interest in learning more, which in turn led to a booklet entitled *Crossing Channels*, published in 1994.[377] His research and involvement eventually led to his becoming honorary chaplain to the Gender Trust (a charity for transsexuals) and GENDYS Network.[378]

Through a number of venues, including both writings and personal ministry, Horton has very publicly supported the full inclusion of transgender believers within the Church. Among other things, he has dedicated himself to educating other Christians about transgender realities, helping to refute myths and dispel fears. Horton is a voice for reasoned tolerance. He observes about Deuteronomy 22:5 and other texts sometimes used against crossdressing that, "the few biblical statements are a very weak foundation for a theological and pastoral judgement!"[379] Specifically with reference to Deuteronomy 22:5 he writes:

> The verse clearly prohibits cross-dressing, with women as the primary case, and men as the corollary. In itself this poses a major problem for our society since cross-dressing in masculine styled or men's clothes is very common in women, while the converse is much rarer. It would be a brave person who stood up to condemn women in this way, so to attack men for the same thing seems unjust.[380]

In fact, based on his own careful consideration both of the scriptural and theological arguments on the one hand, and the scientific evidence on the other, Horton concludes that "to be transgendered is a human variation and is not in itself wrong."[381] He finds neither biblical nor scientific support for condemnation. Indeed, he writes that, "I have been amazed and blessed by the many faithful, believing, transgendered people I have encountered down the years, from ministers through to ordinary church members. It seems to me that they are following successfully in the tradition of the Ethiopian in Acts 8."[382]

Horton thinks it no accident that so many transgender people are drawn to Christianity. He has remarked, "There seems to be a higher proportion of Christian believers among transsexuals than the general population, not unreasonable when the condition pushes the person to look for answers to meaning and existence."[383] Horton finds many of these Christians active in their churches, with some in leadership roles, including pastoral ministry.[384]

Yet, Horton observes, these believers often meet with problems. He writes:

> I have also found that evangelicals seem to have a worse reception, which saddens me. It was my failure when first confronted on my doorstep by such a person which led me to become involved in this whole area. Sadly, society as a whole seems to show more willingness to suspend judgement than we manage. If it is a sin to be this way then that is fair enough, although I know people who have repented, sought deliverance, and still been thrown out. If it is a prenatal variation then ultimately it will have to be accommodated in some pastorally sen-

sitive way. . . . A Christian viewpoint is desperately needed, provided it is biblical and thorough.[385]

Rev. Horton himself has contributed to such a viewpoint and continues to do so.

In light of the situation pertaining for many crossdressing Christians, it is easy to see how they—and their supporters—might object to the reasoning employed by their opponents. Specifically, they often raise the objection that most Christians pick and choose which biblical prohibitions they view as binding today.[386] In light of this tendency, these writers appeal for both tolerance and more honesty by their opponents. Rev. Horton, again with reference to the chief biblical text wielded by opponents, points out:

> Then there is Deuteronomy 22 verse 5 - which says God abominates women who cross-dress and men too. But if you had seen some of the things that the cross-dressing fertility priests of Canaan got up to, you would be angry too. If this is taken as a rule for today then women would be in a lot more trouble than trannies! The Bible used this way can be very hard on the transgendered. Society gives them enough grief without them having to cope with an angry God as well! As far as God is concerned we are all sinners, and Christ paid for our sins in full. We don't eat solely kosher food, sacrifice animals, or throw our wife out of the house while she has her period. So why consider the cross-dressing references as rules?[387]

Horton raises issues that, unfortunately, comparatively few congregations have intentionally wrestled with.

2. Rev. Erin Swenson (Presbyterian Church U.S.A.)

Rev. Erin Swenson knows firsthand the pain of being at the center of controversy when a faith community wrestles with the transgender reality of transsexualism. Swenson, born male and named Eric Karl Swenson, was ordained by the Presbytery of Atlanta in 1973. In the mid-1990s, Swenson made news by becoming the first known mainstream Protestant minister to change sex while remaining in ordained office.[388]

But the process was not without a struggle within the church. A committee considering removing her ordination because she was a transsexual person subjected Swenson to a lengthy interrogation. That committee put 52 questions to Swenson. One of these was the following: "How do you answer the charge that you are living a life of public deceit contrary to Holy Scripture and our Constitution?—that your behaviors are deceitful and a denial of your creation?—that your behavior will bring shame on the Church and offend many of 'the least of these?'" Swenson's answer addressed the anger she heard in the questions, an anger she said was hers as well. She recounted to the committee her long struggle to suppress the truth about herself and how in finally facing that truth she now found herself facing such questions. "And so I am now before you," she said, "bewildered that I am being charged with deceit now when my experience is that I have, at great cost, ended my deceitful life and devoted myself to living in the light of the truth."[389]

Swenson confessed coming to the sobering realization that having never been a man, she could also never be a woman. Instead, she was transgendered and would remain so. But she was also persuaded that the Church itself has a transgendered nature and might in acknowledging it discover more completely God's love for people has nothing to do with their sex or gender, but exists simply because one and all they are God's children. Therefore, Swenson concluded, being openly transgender was living a truth the Church was struggling to understand not just about people like herself, but also about itself.[390]

By a divided vote, the Presbytery of Greater Atlanta, on October 22, 1996, voted to sustain Swenson's ordination. She continues to serve in Atlanta as a pastor. In addition, Swenson is a licensed Marriage and Family Therapist. She is also active in More Light Presbyterians, an organization devoted to facilitating full inclusion in the Presbyterian Church of sexual minorities and gender variant people. In 1999, Swenson and Raja Qasim founded the Southern Association for Gender Education, Inc., a nonprofit organization committed to educating not only faith groups, but also medical professionals and institutions of higher learning about gender diversity issues.[391] Through these and other activities Swenson has been both a model and a support to transgender Christians—and to everyone else.

3. Sister Mary Elizabeth (Roman Catholic)

Sister Mary Elizabeth is a nun in the Order of the Sisters of Saint Elizabeth. Sister Mary is also a male-to-female (MtF) transsexual. She has been active helping other transgendered people in the United States receive legal protection. In the 1980s she acted as Chair of the Transsexual Rights Committee of the Southern California chapter of the American Civil Liberties Union (ACLU). She lobbied for legislative changes in California that now make life easier for the transgendered in such practical matters as driver's license identification information and the amending of birth certificate information after sex reassignment surgery.[392]

4. Rev. Lauren Renée Hotchkiss (Unitarian)

Rev. Lauren Renée Hotchkiss, the administrator of the Berkeley Fellowship of Unitarian Universalists, has tried to help others understand transgender realities by authoring a piece entitled, 'Is Transgenderism Wrong?" Hotchkiss, as a transgender Christian, has a particular stake in wanting others to see what matters to members of the transgender community as they struggle with issues of faith. Fortunately, Hotchkiss has found a home in the Unitarian Church, a fellowship of congregations that has been especially welcoming of transgender Christians.

Hotchkiss addresses the issue of crossdressing and the problem posed by the text in Deuteronomy by offering the following interpretive translation of the text: "No man shall put on a dress to enter the women's tent (fear of rape), nor shall a woman wear an article of men's clothing for the purposes of entering the holy temple (from which women were prohibited by ancient Judaic law)."[393] In this manner Hotchkiss hopes to bring attention to the issue of the motivation behind the behavior—crossdressing meant to deceive to gain illicit access to something (whether sex or worship) is wrong. As for other motivations, such as to express gender, Hotchkiss believes the real issue is not how God feels about it ("I mean c'mon, God 'could care less'"),[394] but how *we* do. That is where attention needs directing.

5. Rev. Christina Hutchins (United Church of Christ)

Among those who have helped a congregation face squarely the reality of nonheteronormative Christians is Rev. Christina Hutchins. In the early 1990s, she pastored a congregation during a two year process of self-study that eventually resulted in a congregational vote to become an affirming church that openly welcomes gay, lesbian, and bisexual people. Hutchins comments about the process leading to this decision that, "While I in no way want to minimize the resistances, pains and trepidations involved in such processes, I have repeatedly noticed that churches in the midst of these difficult conversations display a kind of spiritual intensity, a liberatory energy and purpose."[395]

For herself, Hutchins found the experience also led her to wonder why Christians get so energized over the issue of inclusion of sexual or gender minorities. From her perspective, the resulting 'ferment' is good, with the potential benefit to facilitate self-examination about otherwise obscured philosophical assumptions held within the Church. In particular, she thinks the conversation about 'queer' lives "destabilizes the metaphysics of substance." In short, the commonplace view most Christians hold about the way people are—or *should* be—with respect to their bodies and relations with one another, particularly sexually, needs discussion. Opening up such discourse affords opportunities to reconsider ideas that do not well serve the Church.[396]

Hutchin's examination takes place squarely in the wider debate on gender and sexuality taking place in societies around the world today. The worldview she questions we have elsewhere termed 'Essentialism.' This perspective views the world as easily divisable into discrete categories with members inside that are stable and fixed in nature. Philosophically appealing for its simplicity and orderliness, it suffers from a fatal flaw: it does not well represent the actual facts on the ground. What excites Hutchins is the realization that in the ferment of dialog on real people a congregation has the chance to itself experience *becoming* a church, rather than *being* one in some fixed fashion. In this dynamic process people can be freed from the stifling confines of a worldview reliant on Essentialist principles.[397]

It can be easy to overlook such musings when talking about the support rendered to transgender Christians by clergy. Yet Hutchin's efforts to challenge the easiness with which so many Christians hold worldviews they assume are intrinsically 'Christian' benefits both transgender and nontransgender believers alike. After all, many transgender Christians suffer from holding the same Essentialist ideas as their Christian opponents. Helping to free the thinking of all Christians from philosophical ideas that actually harm others is an invaluable service.

6. Rev. Drew Phoenix (United Methodist Church)

Just as Rev. Eric Karl Swenson transitioned from male to female, and remained a professional minister, so the Rev. Ann Gordon transitioned from female to male and has continued as a United Methodist pastor named Drew Phoenix. The transitioning occurred while the then Rev. Gordon was minister of a small Baltimore church. Gordon/Phoenix, ordained in 1989, had been pastor at the church for five years when the transition took place. At age 46, after a lifetime reckoning with an experience that Phoenix later described as being like having a homeless spirit, sex reassignment surgery brought body and soul into line and gave his spirit a home at last.[398]

In addressing his congregation concerning the change, Phoenix discussed a lifetime of struggling with an identity imposed by society but not corresponding to his own sense of himself. He explained that in choosing to transition from the gender assigned at birth, to the one experienced persistently inside himself, he was both being true to himself and honoring his spiritual transformation and relationship with God. About the latter Phoenix remarked, "Jesus' central message is that God's love and grace extend unconditionally to all of us, not because we look a certain way or have a particular identity, but because we are all children of God created in God's image. Each of us is a beloved child of God. No exceptions."[399]

While the local church Phoenix served proved accepting of the change, not all Methodists were so agreeable. Within the Baltimore-Washington Conference of the denomination some other pastors questioned whether a transsexual should be permitted to serve as a professional minister. Although the Bishop of the Conference reappointed Phoenix, the denomination's Judicial Council took that reappointment under review. In the autumn of 2007 that body affirmed the Bishop's reappointment of Phoenix, though it explicitly stated it was not ruling on the broader question of a transsexual serving in ministry.[400] That issue was addressed in May, 2008, at the denomination's General Conference meeting in Fort Worth, Texas. A number of resolutions to ban transgender people from pastoral ministry were defeated. Remarkably, not one of these made it to the floor for general debate; each was defeated in committee.[401]

199

The response—or perhaps we should say, the *lack* of response—to the situation of Drew Phoenix by his denomination's General Assembly may be a sign of growing acceptance (or at least tolerance). Certainly it is true that a growing number of churches and Christian organizations have decided that being transgender does not preclude being welcome.

Are there churches that minister to transgender people?

Because Christian opponents to transgender realities have been more vocal than supporters, and have received more media attention, an impression may be formed that there are no supportive Christian ministries for transgender people. On the contrary, a number of efforts exist to minister to transgender people without trying to change their gender identity or behavior.

Welcoming Ministries

There is a growing network of Christian churches and other ministries that are welcoming of members of the wider transgender community (gays, lesbians, bisexuals, transsexuals, transvestites; the latter two groups are sometimes embraced in the term 'transgender' in abbreviations like GLBT). A partial list of such organizations (in alphabetical order) includes:

❏ *Association of Welcoming & Affirming Baptists*—an association that includes churches, organizations and individuals of the American Baptist denomination "willing to go on record as welcoming and affirming" as well as advocating "for the full inclusion of lesbian, gay, bisexual, and transgender persons within Baptist communities of faith."[402]

❏ *Brethren Mennonite Council for Lesbian, Gay, Bisexual and Transgender Interests*—founded in 1976, the council works to provide support, promote dialogue, and offer accurate information.[403]

❏ *DignityUSA*—an organization for gay, lesbian, bisexual and transgender Roman Catholics.[404]

❏ *Gay, Lesbian and Affirming Disciples (GLAD) Alliance*—the alliance describes itself as "a presence working for the full dignity and integrity of gay, lesbian, bisexual, transgendered and affirming people within the Christian Church (Disciples of Christ)."[405]

❏ *Integrity*—founded in 1974, this organization describes itself as "a witness of God's inclusive love to the Episcopal Church and the gay, lesbian, bisexual, and transgender community."[406]

❏ *More Light Presbyterians*—an organization "seeking the full participation of lesbian, gay, bisexual and transgender people in the life, ministry and witness of the Presbyterian Church (USA)."[407]

❏ *Open and Affirming Program*—sponsored by the United Church of Christ Coalition for LGBT Concerns, the program was established in 1987 and by 2004 had enlisted some 500 churches.[408]

❑ *Reconciling in Christ Program*—a program begun in 1984 by the Lutherans Concerned/North America to welcome GLBT (gay, lesbian, bisexual, transgendered) people.[409]

❑ *The Reconciling Ministries Network*—a national grassroots organization that exists to "enable full participation of people of all sexual orientations and gender identities in the life of the United Methodist Church, both in policy and practice."[410]

❑ *Unitarian Universalist Office of Bisexual, Gay, Lesbian, Transgender Concerns*—the Church went on record in 1970 as supportive of gay, lesbian, and bisexual people, and opened this office in 1973. No less than 14 resolutions in support of GLBT people have been adopted. Today its website proclaims '436 welcoming congregations, 1 welcoming organization.'[411]

The spirit of the Welcoming Churches is captured in the 'Affirmation of Welcome' adopted by accepting churches following the Reconciling in Christ Program. They offer the following sample affirmation:

As a community of the people of God, we are called to minister to all people in our world, knowing that the world is often an unloving place. Our world is a place of alienation and brokenness. Christ calls us to reconciliation and wholeness. We are challenged by the Gospel to be agents of healing within our society.

We affirm with the apostle Paul that in Christ "there is neither Jew nor Greek, there is neither slave nor free, there is neither male nor female" (Galatians 3:28). Christ has made us one. We acknowledge this reconciliation extends to people of all sexual orientations and gender identities.

Because gay, lesbian, bisexual and transgendered persons and their families are often scorned by society and alienated from the Church, we wish to make known our caring and concern. It is for this purpose that we affirm the following: that people of all sexual orientations and gender identities share the worth that comes from being unique individuals created by God; that people of all sexual orientations and gender identities are welcome within the membership of this congregation* upon making a common, public Affirmation of faith; and that as members of this congregation*, people of all sexual orientations and gender identities are expected and encouraged to share in the sacramental and general life of this congregation*.

* synod or organization[412]

The work of these ministries extends beyond simply welcoming attendance. For example, the Unitarian Universalist 'welcoming congregations' aim at realizing a number of goals. These include acknowledging GLBT concerns at every level of congregational life; celebrating and supporting same-sex or same-gender relationships; nurturing communication among all people to build trust and sharing; advocating for justice, freedom and equality for GLBT people; and speaking out when the rights of GLBT people are at stake.[413] Similar commitments can be found among other welcoming congregations.

Within these ministries are thousands of dedicated clergy and lay people, some of whom are themselves transgendered, and many more who are not. The claim that one may occasionally hear that the only ones accepting of crossdressing Christians are other crossdressers is not only ludicrously untrue, but a form of hate speech. We do not have to directly experience another person's life in order to imaginatively put ourselves in their place ('walk a mile in their shoes'). Nothing more is required in fulfilling the Golden Rule than the *will* to do so. The facts are that many non-transgender Christians are accepting of transgender believers, even when those transgender individuals are in ministry. As recounted earlier, in 1996 the Presbytery of Greater Atlanta (Presbyterian Church USA) voted in favor of a MtF transsexual pastor retaining ordination.[414] In 2007 a United Methodist judicial council did the same. While it remains true that many congregations and church leaders are not accepting of transgender people, we must acknowledge that some are—and their numbers are growing.

Though many matters remain controversial, the basic instinct of most Christians and their organizations has been to extend grace and acceptance to members of minority groups. While there remain those resistant to welcoming LGBT people (apart from their willingness to see themselves as engaged in sin and seeking change), such folk increasingly seem to be on the wrong side of history. On balance there appears to be a growing spirit of acceptance as Christian ministers and laity become better informed about LGBT issues, including crossdressing. With better knowledge the inherent charity of the Christian religion seems to become ever freer to shine.

Question Set 10:

What do other religions say about transgender realities, including crossdressing?

To this point we have spent all our energy looking at the major world religions historically dominant in Europe and the Americas, namely, Christianity and Judaism. As explained previously, our choice has been to keep our focus on the behavior of crossdressing, while permitting that focus to serve as a limited entry into broader consideration of transgender and gender. The latter, in particular, remains a necessary backdrop. We also have persisted in viewing crossdressing in its context of the experiencing and expressive system centered in clothing. With these same parameters in place, we now shall turn to examining other religions.

Various materials in the extant literature on gender, transgender, and crossdressing examine the connection of each separately to religion. A few do so broadly, offering summary views or select examples to illustrate a matter in various religious contexts. Many more are focused on very particular aspects or on a single religious tradition, group, or experience. Our aim is to accomplish a broad survey of transgender realities, especially crossdressing, in the major religions found around the world, with some limited examination of various indigenous religions. As we do so, we will investigate various ideas, examine history, look briefly at specific examples, and try to establish a multifaceted picture reflective of the diversity found in the world.

Another aim in these answers is finding transgender people's experiences with religion. On the one hand, this is an easier task than identifying relevant religious texts because many transgender folk are willing to talk about their religious identities and how others have received them. On the other hand, this is a harder task in terms of relevant academic literature. As Ramona Oswald observes, "the intersection of family and religion has not yet been explored with reference to gay, lesbian, bisexual, and transgender (GLBT) people."[415] In fact, materials even more broadly constructed, such as exploring the religious identities of transgender people or detailing the resources available to them, or even enumerating the obstacles they face are all scarce, save with specific reference to gays and lesbians. But we shall make do as best we can.

For the most part this has meant relying mostly on studies of groups rather than of particular individuals, save for a few of special significance. In using sacred literature the aim has been both to draw forth some general ideas and to use specific texts to illustrate those ideas. At the same time, mindful of the distance between what is set down in sacred writings and the actual religious life of the people who esteem them, our goal must always be to not confuse the former for the latter. At the same time, we shall also seek to understand lived religion as typically aspiring to actualize the lofty ideals found in scripture. The ongoing dialog between adherents of a particular time and place and their scriptures is impossible to adequately capture in writing. Yet we must remain mindful of this dialog if we are to make sense of what we encounter.

If in what follows more space seems given to sacred texts, it is because these are stable and fixed in comparison to the fluidity of belief and practice in different times and places. But as we shall see, a 'stable and fixed' writing is neither 'stable' nor 'fixed' when it comes to transmission, interpretation, and application. Although we cannot deal exhaustively with any religion, let alone all of them, we can trace lines of dialog between texts and people that serve to show at least a little of how religion, gender, and transgender realities intersect. If in so doing we accomplish nothing more than to demonstrate such things do intersect, and matter, we shall have done something valuable.

Everywhere the religions of the world wrestle with gender. Everywhere they also recognize the existence of gender variance. How they understand gender and gender variance works itself out in the context of a peculiar religious sensibility. That sensibility inevitably is not uniform for individuals shape it, and so do communities. As a result, there is far richer diversity and depth than a brief survey can do more than hint at. But if we start by trying to tease out how transgender realities exist within these religions, we shall both extend our reach and broaden our grasp of matters important to making our world better for all of us.

Q. 76 How did crossdressing figure in ancient and premodern religions?

The Short Answer. This answer paints a broad picture in various religions against which specific treatment of transgender realities, especially crossdressing, may make better sense. To create a proper backdrop it is necessary to depict by overview various ways divine beings can and have been regarded with respect to gender. This entails both the question of whether (or how) such beings possess gender, as well as how divine gender crossings affect mortals. With respect to the former question, religions may depict their divine beings as gender ambiguous (i.e., without gender), as androgynous, or as gender altering—but gender always remains an aspect that must be accounted. With regard to gender crossings, these may occur in many ways and for different purposes—but they do occur. If gender crossings are possible for divine beings, they are also possible for the mortal beings devoted to them, for whom divine figures serve as both models and guides. Indeed, in certain religious offices, acts, and events, such crossings are expected. Although our discussion focuses upon ancient and premodern times, the fact is that modern religions have significant continuity with their pasts. Therefore, our discussion ranges from the ancient past to contemporary reflections. With a backdrop in place our attention can turn more productively to transgender realities, especially crossdressing in its various manifestations. Crossdressing is recorded around the world from the ancient past up to the present. Crossdressing did not always serve the same function in various religions, but it often mirrored gender crossing actions of a deity or deities. In a number of religions officials such as priests crossdressed. Obviously, in such contexts crossdressing not only was tolerated, it was supported as an aspect of religious devotion. On the other hand, some religions (e.g., ancient Judaism) opposed crossdressing for religious purposes precisely because it was practiced in other religions as part of religious service; not crossdressing then became a way of being different from a rival religion. In some manner, then, many religions had to reckon with sacred gender crossings regardless of whether such were an integral part of themselves or not. In Western culture, one uneasy compromise might be seen in religious festivals where gender crossings were permitted while also being carefully circumscribed. Such festivals, like Carnival, have roots in older times. Appropriated for new religions they persist to our own time, even if relatively secularized.

The Longer Answer. In answering other questions we have looked often to the past. Now it is time to give direct attention to religion in a broad historical context. The material covered here reaches from the dawn of civilization more than 4,000 years ago up to the modern period. Our goals will be to understand something about the nature of religion that facilitates divine and human gender crossings, and offer relevant illustrations. These are drawn from around the world and a variety of time periods. But the appropriateness of the examples depends on the underlying rationale for selecting them. So we must start with some general reasoning.

Religion provides ways for human beings to explore and connect to transcendent realities. Because most of us believe there are realities both greater than our own limited existence and to some extent removed from us, many of us turn to religion for a bridge to such realities. But bridges reach both ways. Even as we may seek what lies on the other side, whatever is there may be reaching out toward us. Thus religion is a two-way avenue with our portion involving both giving and receiving sacred actions. In either instance some act of gender crossing might be involved, and of all the ways to cross gender boundaries crossdressing remains the clearest and easiest.

On our side, the task is complicated by certain factors such as our relative inability to see or understand realms beyond our own, and by our corresponding need to draw upon things in our realm to comprehend and represent divine realities. One of the basic problems concerns sex and gender. Do deities have bodies? Are they sexed and gendered? What roles do sex and gender play in transactions between mortals and immortals?[416]

Complicating the situation is cultural variety in conceptions of sex and gender—particularly the latter. While our modern Western culture is only just beginning to reconsider the idea that there are more than two sexes and genders, an openness to a wider range of alternatives for human beings can be found throughout history (including that of the West), and around the world today. Our problem in modern Western societies is that limited notions of gender have particularly hindered our comprehension of all that might be entailed in sacred gender crossings.

Indeed, with respect to gender crossings in general, Lisa Penaloza got it exactly right when she remarked, "Gender crossings remain misunderstood if left within a dualist conceptualization of gender."[417] As she points out, gender crossings as such pose a problem for gender schemes like that embraced in the modern West—their very existence poses a challenge to Western assumptions. At the very least we should be left open to the possibility we have gotten things wrong with our insistence on a two sex/two gender framework, with rigid pairing of masculinity to maleness and femininity to femaleness.

As we mere mortals have wrestled with how such matters apply not merely to ourselves but to divine beings, a number of ideas have emerged. How divine entities have or express sex and gender, and how these things enter into divine-human interactions, has been variously conceived—much like corresponding ideas about human beings. In fact, whether taking a cue from realities seen in this sphere or trying to start from knowledge of a sacred realm, once these things have been figured out about deities, then we can fashion appropriate human responses. On the human side, gender crossings have proven time and again to be instrumental in this process of responding to the divine. Antiquities scholar Margaret Miller writes, "It has been observed that the transformation of gender is often associated with the process of coming closer to divinity by breaking down the categories of ordinary experience."[418] And that is where crossdressing often enters. Crossdressing frequently has played a role in sacred transactions.

Why? The reasons vary. Sometimes it is a case of *imitation*. The manipulation of dress is the most visible and convenient way for human beings to do what divine beings accomplish by other means, including crossing gender. Sometimes crossdressing is not an imitation of divine behavior, but imitation of divine being. In this sense, crossdressing is imitation through *transformation*, with the result of becoming more like the deity being worshipped. In other circumstances, crossdressing is not imitative at all, but pursued as a way of sacred *transgression*. The transgression often is against artificial boundaries that keep our realm and the divine realm apart. By breaking down these barriers crossdressing itself becomes a bridge between deity and humanity. But because this bridge is constructed by transgressing a boundary set either on our end or the divine end, it stirs some controversy. In any event, all these reasons and others are meant to serve a religious purpose.

We should be wary in light of all this to assume that crossdressing, when it occurred, was deviant religiosity. In our culture, if we are aware of any connection between crossdressing and religion at all, we are likely only to have heard that the Christian Bible condemns it (see the answers to Q. 61-65)—an oversimplified generalization that has unfortunately colored and complicated our understanding of transgender realities in religious contexts. Miller reminds us, with reference to practices in the ancient Greek world, that crossdressing was not only condoned, but in certain ritual contexts *required*.[419]

The advantages presented by religious crossdressing have figured in numerous religions. In fact, religions both modern and ancient have made a place for sacred crossdressing. In the ancient world crossdressing served various functions such as those described above in a range of religions found both East and West. Because crossdressing intends a human response to divine realities, we must spend some time looking at how these divine realities have been viewed. Only by comprehending the broader context of sacred gender crossings by both human *and* divine figures can religious crossdressing make full sense.

What are sacred gender crossings?

Sacred gender crossings reflect human violation of normal gender boundaries for sacred reasons or by deities for their own reasons, whatever those may be. The ancient world offers numerous instances of which various examples are offered below. In general, sacred gender crossings typically fall into one or the other of the following broad categories:

❏ Divine or other sacred nonhuman beings appearing in unexpected gender manifestations;

❏ Human beings pursuing sacred roles or tasks in a gender performance different from the gender identity and role assigned them at birth; and,

❏ Sacred festivals, where divine and human interact, *and* where an aspect of that interaction involves gender crossing.

These are all explored in what follows.

Sacredness

The key element in sacred gender crossings is not the gender crossing itself. It is that it is *sacred.* The gender crossing is an act set apart from ordinary acts. Things become holy by being removed from mundane occurrence or use, and in sacred gender crossing it is gender conformity thus removed. The individual—whether divine, semi-divine, or human—sets apart (or aside) normal gender presentation for the express purpose of some kind of interaction (e.g., human with divine, or divine with human). Just as food becomes holy and wholly different by being offered to a deity, so gender becomes holy and wholly different in sacred gender crossings.

Divine Gender Crossings

Though best known in the West through stories coming down from the ancients, divine gender crossings persist in religious traditions kept alive today in various parts of the world. Such crossings exist in various forms and may be placed into certain categories. A simple division concerns the separation of divine figures and their gender acts into the manifestations by certain divinities on the one hand, and that by characters found within the pantheon of non-human religious figures (e.g., demons and demigods) on the other. This division between kinds of divine figures is often used but may not be as helpful as another.

A different way to categorize divine gender crossings is by the nature of the figure's gender manifestation. This approach is equally useful for deities, demigods, and others. What matters is whether we are able to classify a figure by a characteristic or distinguishing feature with respect to gender. It turns out this can be done by utilizing three distinct classes. Viewed this way, it matters relatively little whether a figure has been *assigned* gender. Whether gender is assigned or not, many divine figures manifest gender outside their assignment. Divine manifestations that confuse or confound gender may be divided generally into three kinds:

- ❑ Divine figures appearing as *ambiguous* in gender (i.e., neither clearly male nor female, usually because they are absent gender);

- ❑ Divine figures appearing as *androgynous* (i.e., with both male and female characteristics), such as hermaphroditic deities; and,

- ❑ Divine figures appearing in an *altered* gender, one different from the one they are traditionally assigned (e.g., a female deity appearing in masculine guise), and thus engaged from the human standpoint as emasculated, masculinized, or in a gender masquerade.

These are not mutually exclusive. A deity may appear in more than one category, as Artemis does by exhibiting both androgyny and gender altering. Moreover, the kinds themselves may mix as happens when Hermaphroditus, originally male, is altered in gender to become androgynous. Also, strictly speaking, one could argue that only the last kind (gender altering) represents 'gender *crossing*.' And to these we might add curiosities like the crossdressed Heracles, a demigod figure (see the answer to Q. 42). These three general types are relevant to our discussion because all three confound in some way the dichotomous scheme most of us find so comforting and in so doing raise gender questions and issues pertinent to a broad examination of religious crossdressing.

Table 76.1 Examples of Gender-Crossing Deities

Gender Ambiguous	Gender Androgynous	Gender Altering
'Unities': *Allah* (Islam) or '*God*' (Christianity, Judaism); *Cghene* (Nigeria/Isoko); also possibly *Tlaltecuhtli* and *Tlaloc* (Aztec)	'Assigned gender deities': *Aphrodite, Artemis, Athena, Dionysus* (Classical Greek); *Inanna* (Sumerian); *Jesus* (Christianity); *Shiva* (Hinduism)	'Emasculated gods': *Mahadeva* (Hinduism); *Odin* (Norse); *Quetzalcoatl* (Aztec) *Ra* (Egyptian); *Uranus* (Classical Greek); *Amaterasu* (Shintoism)
'One-as-Many': *Brahman* (Hinduism) 'Dual Gender': *Ometechutli* (Aztec)	'Either gender deities': *Agni* (Hinduism); *Asgaya Gigagei* (Cherokee Nation); *Atutahi* (Polynesia); *Atum*? (Egyptian); *Nyame* (Ghana)	'Masquerading deities': *Athena* (Classical Greek); *Vishnu* (Hinduism); *Zeus* (Classical Greek)
'Spirits': *Kami* (Shintoism)	'Hermaphroditic deities': *Agdistis* (Classical Greek); *Ardhanari* and *Ayyappan* (Hinduism); *Hermaphroditus* (Classical Greek); *Inle* (W. Africa/Yoruba)	'Tricksters': *Hermes* (Classical Greek); *Loki* (Norse)

Some brief remarks with examples drawn from this table for further elaboration should make clearer these different types.

What are some examples of gender ambiguous deities?

Many deities, especially the greatest figures, are conceived as possessing no inherent gender—and perhaps no body either. Such beings can, however, assume any gender shape they wish. Even if they do not do so, their followers can use gender language to metaphorically speak about them. Such divine figures are found around the globe, both in major world religions and in smaller indigenous ones.

The Monotheistic God of the West

In this manner the God of the Western traditions (Judaism, Christianity, Islam) can be spoken of using either masculine or feminine attributes since the deity is beyond any gender. This is one of those universally acknowledged facts that in practice carries little weight. For all intents and purposes, for most Christians, Jews, and Muslims, God remains resolutely masculine, if not outrightly male. Nevertheless, the essential lack of sex and ambiguity of gender remain important ideas in all three relgions regardless of common practice. Let us quickly examine each, beginning with the Western root, Judaism. Both Christianity and Islam claim descent from this root and both borrow at least portions of its religious logic.

Judaism

There is, in principle at least, a freedom in Judaism with respect to how God is referred to with gender terms. As we shall see in looking at Christianity, and in our later review of Judaism, God in Jewish sacred texts can be spoken about using either masculine or feminine terms. Though the dominant pronoun used is masculine, one name especially preserves a sense of the feminine: the 'Divine Presence' (*Shechinah* or *Shekhinah*; the *-ah* ending is a feminine form). Daniel Matt, an expert on Judaism's mystical traditions, has expressed the judgment that "the rabbinic concept of *Shekhinah*, divine immanence, blossoms into the feminine half of God, balancing the patriarchal conception that dominates the Bible and the Talmud."[420] This counterbalance is especially felt in the mystical tradition of Kabbalism.

In Kabbalah the Eternal and Infinite One (*Ein Sof*), though a transcendent unity, manifests as a personal God through divine emanations (*sefirot*). Some of these are masculine, some feminine. Thus, for instance, 'Malkhut' ('Mouth')—the Oral Torah, which expounds the Written Torah—is feminine.[421] So, too, is 'Binah' ('Understanding'); conversely, 'Hokhmah' ('Wisdom') and 'Tif'eret' ('Beauty') are masculine. The interplay of various sefirot express divine characteristics metaphorically, as the following text makes plain:

Hokhmah and Binah are called man and woman, father and mother. Just as human sexual union requires the medium of genitalia, so above, these two qualities unite by means of Da'at, which mediates between father and mother. . . .

This manner of union may be found in Tif'eret and Malkhut, who are male and female, groom and bride, lower father and lower mother, son and daughter of the upper couple, king and queen, the Holy One, blessed be He, and *Shekhinah*. All these are metaphors.[422]

The reminder that 'these are metaphors' underscores two important facts: God remains without sex or gender, but God's ways of being, acting, and relating can be usefully understood using gender. Later, we shall examine nonkabbalistic ways within Judaism of speaking about God using gender metaphors.

Christianity

The Christian New Testament makes the case about God's gender explicit when Jesus declares, "God is spirit" (John 4:24, RSV). The point is that lacking a body, God lacks sex and therefore cannot be assigned a gender such as is done with human children. Instead, gender attributions are always metaphorical, or to use the language of theologians, 'analogical.'[423] Though masculine pronouns, attributes, and metaphors abound, feminine ones are not unknown. Thus, for example, the Christian Bible incorporates the Hebrew Bible, which has the prophet Isaiah's utterance from God picturing a woman in childbirth: "Now I will cry out like a woman in travail, I will gasp and pant" (Isaiah 42: 14, RSV). Again, there is the same prophet's message wherein the deity is identified with motherhood: "As one whom his mother comforts, so I will comfort you" (Isaiah 66:13, RSV; cf. Psalm 131:2-3). This anthropomorphic way of speaking of God relies on analogical thinking, but the compelling power of gender in human existence makes of it in respect to discussions of God more than mere poetic speech. In human imagination, at least, God is incomprehensible apart from gender. If God cannot *have* gender, then God must *do* gender. To hearken back to Judith Butler's ideas (see the answer to Q. 5), gender is performed by God rather than possessed as an aspect of divine being.[424]

Christianity, like Judaism, has had those who have kept alive a sense of the feminine in God. Even as Kabbalism presents a mystical tradition within Judaism, Christian mystics have perpetuated a similar tradition rich in gender metaphors for the Church. Especially notable are the writings of Mother Julian, a Christian mystic of the early 15th century. She wrote in her *Showings* (chapter 52) that God both enjoyed being Father, and also being Mother. The truth of the Trinity is 'father,' but the wisdom of the Trinity is 'mother' (chapter 54). Even Christ can be depicted as mother, in whom the believer is endlessly born (chapter 57). In fact, the second person of the Trinity is especially singled out for use of metaphors of the feminine (see chapters 58-62).[425]

We shall examine this further in the next section. But what is critical here is grasping that all such language is *metaphorical*, not literal. The mystics employ gender metaphors to enrich an experience of a God without gender, not to render that deity into gender duality. The effect is that by employing both masculinity and femininity with respect to God, the deity's essential gender ambiguity is preserved in a manner impossible by relying on one gender only to speak about God.

Islam

The youngest of the major Western religions shares with Judaism and Christianity a conviction that there is but one God and that deity is without sex or gender. As with its Western predecessors, both masculine and feminine gender terms can be used precisely because of this gender ambiguity. In Islam, Allah is variously referred to as 'He' (*huwa*) or 'She' (*hiya*), though the masculine form of reference predominates as it does in Judaism and Christianity.

Again parallel to its predecessors, it is especially in Sufism—Islam's mystical tradition—that the feminine expressions are emphatically given voice. In Sufi texts Allah can be depicted as feminine (cf. Jalal al-Din Rumi's *Masnavi*, I.2437), the Beloved One (the *ma'shûq*), and even the Divine Mother (cf. *Masnavi*, V.701).[426] The Muslim mystic, like Jewish and Christian counterparts, aims to attain a deeper felt experience of the deity. By escaping the limited character of overdependence on the masculine gender to contemplate the deity the mystic may be better able to approach the genderless divine essence.

Despite the mystics, though, the mainstream in each of the major Western religious traditions almost exclusively relies on male gender terms and the masculine pronoun with reference to God.[427] Though in practice the result may be for many believers to imagine God as male and masculine, most realize intellectually that God has neither sex nor gender. The Western tradition's conception of a gender ambiguous deity is not unique, however.

African Deities Without Gender

The peoples of Africa also know of deities without inherent gender. For example, in southern Nigeria the Isoko religion extols Cghene as Supreme Being. Cghene is "beyond human comprehension, has never been seen, is sexless, and is only known by his actions, which have led men to speak of Cghene as 'him,' because he is thought of as the creator and therefore Father of all the Isokos."[428] Thus, Cghene, having no gender being, performs gender through acts assigned a gender connection by the faithful. If Cghene is referred to as 'he' it is only because the deeds then being spoken about are like those associated with human men. Apparently, the Isoko have little difficulty keeping gender performance separate from gender as a possession of being.

A traditional Pygmy song about a genderless Supreme Being (Khonvoum) includes this praise:

In the beginning was God,
  Today is God
  Tomorrow will be God.
Who can make an image of God?
He has no body.[429]

These are words any member of a Western major religion could easily claim. A Supreme Deity is found in many African religions, and whether designated by a masculine or feminine pronoun, a characteristic of such deities is that they are beyond gender. Gender designations are a matter of human convenience rather than an intrinsic property of being.

Eastern Deities Without Gender

Deities ambiguous in gender (or absent gender) are found in the East as well. This is especially important to note because many Western Christians construct their view of the world's religions in such a way as to emphasize the uniqueness and superiority of Christianity. If they can dismiss Eastern religions as polytheistic, an orientation which they believe both primitive and inferior to monotheism, then they feel secure in a sense of religious superiority.[430] The apparent 'polytheism' of some Eastern religions is the result of a working out of certain ideas stemming from a conception of a basic unified reality.

Hinduism

Such is the case in what is arguably the world's oldest religion. Hinduism's Brahman is described in an Upanishad as "Soul alone, in the shape of a Person."[431] Though English translations use the pronoun 'he' for Brahman, Hindus understand *Nirguna Brahman* (the impersonal Ultimate Reality) as genderless and *Saguna Brahman* (the personal aspect of Ultimate Reality) as capable of being worshipped as either gender. The independence from sex and gender has had important repercussions thoughout Hindu representations of deity. Even those figures assigned sex and gender, because they are manifestations of a supreme reality independent of such illusory things, show remarkable freedom from both.

Shinto

The *kami* of Japan's Shintoism, described by eminent religious scholar Mircea Eliade as "omnipresent manifestations of the sacred,"[432] may also be called ambiguous deities, though only with qualification (some, for example, are venerated ancestors). The original, heavenly *kami* are spirit-beings, shapeless in their own domain, but able to take shape in our world. The kami Omononushi-no-kami offers an example of how one of these spirits can utilize either masculine or feminine gender. In the *Nihongi (Chronicles of Japan)*, the tale is told of how this *kami* possessed Princess Yamatototohimomoso and spoke to the emperor. Upon learning the identity of the *kami*, the emperor offered veneration. That very night, in the emperor's dreams, Omononushi-no-kami appeared to him again, this time as a noble man.[433]

These genderless deities *use* gender rather than possess it. Though we can term them 'ambiguous' with reference to gender, it might do as well to call them 'absent gender.' A preference for the term 'ambiguous' reflects the practical reality that human beings insist on using gender referents when talking about divine beings, even those they insist are without gender. The gender absence creates an ambiguity for people who cannot conceive of any being-without-gender. This difficulty is resolved by using various gender pronouns, especially by using mulitple gender pronouns, a practice perhaps especially amenable to helping devotees remember the real state of affairs.

In making sacred crossings to interact with their followers these deities can shun any gender presentation or use whatever gender performance suits them. Similarly, human beings attempting to describe them, or have contact with them, can avoid gender terms or employ those they wish to metaphorically express one or another divine trait or action. In many respects, gender ambiguity permits the maximum flexibility for both human and divine.

What are some examples of androgynous deities?

Another group of divine figures express more than one gender simultaneously—another way of solving the problem posed by the limitations of dichotomous gender. Androgyny in divine figures was explained by Eliade as existing "to express—in biological terms—the coexistence of contraries, of cosmological principles (male and female) within the heart of the divinity."[434] For those of us raised in Western societies where the ambiguous deity—routinely rendered by masculine pronouns reflective of our patriarchal heritage—is the norm, the idea of an androgynous deity can be challenging.

Androgynous Deity in the Western Religious Tradition

Mark Matousek has cogently observed that, "an appreciation of divine androgyny is difficult to grasp in a hemisphere dominated by a church in which women cannot be ordained as priests."[435] Others have echoed this observation. The need for an androgynous Christ is obvious to thinkers like theologian Rosemary Radford Ruether, who observes that ideas locked into the maleness of God "threaten to undermine the basic Christian belief that women are included in the redemption of 'man' won by Christ."[436] Too pronounced an emphasis on the masculine Christ—of Jesus as a masculine male—marginalizes if not outrightly excludes women. Whether or not such a consequence is intended, the actual results are clear enough in a Church where women still are subordinated in myriad ways, with such subordination theologically argued as appropriate. Allegiance to an androgynous Jesus would obviate the power of such arguments.

Accordingly, a number of contemporary Christian scholars have concluded that the Church would profit from more robust ways of considering Jesus. Toward this end theologian Elizabeth Green asks, "Can Jesus be seen in terms of a non gender specific identity which subverts and 'plays with' gender constructs?"[437]

Jesus

The answer has been a resounding 'Yes!' Although controversial—even blasphemous to some—the quest to comprehend Jesus in ways that escape the limitations of traditional popular images has borne fruit. Such ways have included an androgynous representation of Jesus. To understand the appeal of such a depiction we need a touch point. History readily provides one—and it is theological in character.

Definition of Chalcedon

Jesus, revered as the Son of God in orthodox Christology, has been 'officially' viewed as both wholly divine and wholly human since the 5th century (cf. the Definition of Chalcedon, 451 C.E.). The key in this formulation is *wholly*. Both sex and gender are intrinsic to the experience of being human. Yet, as theologian David Hamilton Simpson observes, "Dualist tendencies have fractured the possibility of Jesus being both sexual and divine, as if such a combination is inherently antithetical."[438]

Is the matter much different with respect to gender? Can Jesus, in our present dualistic gender trap, be freed to be both masculine and feminine? Gender experience also is intrinsic to humanity as we know it, and gender markers are used in speaking of God. How can the gender differentiation of masculine and feminine be applied to understanding Jesus as *wholly* divine and human? As we might expect, more than one answer has been proposed—and such proposals are implicit within the New Testament.

Jesus' Feminine Identity in the Gospels

Although Jesus is today almost universally assigned masculinity and referred to by masculine pronouns, in his Passion he played the traditionally feminine role of passive victim, the recipient of God's wrath on behalf of his children. Culture scholar Steven Connor argues that this is "status as feminized victim—God would be fatally compromised" should the suffering Jesus be portrayed in bifurcated garments like breeches or trousers.[439] Judaic and gender scholar Lori Hope Lefkovitz believes that Christian culture historically sought to balance an omnipotent God of patriarchy with a more feminine male son.[440]

The Early Christian Church

Against the weight of most contemporary depictions of a masculine Jesus, Christian New Testament and Early Christian History scholar Stephen Davis reminds us that, "among different early Christian communities, Christ was viewed as an androgynous or gender-ambiguous figure: he was variously identified as the incarnation of the female, divine Wisdom, pictured in eschatological visions as a woman, and depicted in early Christian art in the form of Orpheus, the androgynous figure of Greek myth."[441]

The visionary appearance of Christ that Davis particularly has in mind is recorded in the *Panarion* ('the breadbasket' against heresies) of Epiphanius, 4th century Christian bishop at Salamis, Cyprus. In the relevant text, a Christian woman speaks as follows: "'In the form of a woman,' says she, 'arrayed in shining garments, came Christ to me and set wisdom upon me and revealed to me that this place [= Pepuza] is holy and that Jerusalem will come down hither from heaven.'"[442] But Epiphanius—and the weight of Christian tradition—judged such utterances 'madness' and their speakers heretics.

Hildegard of Bingen

Nevertheless, such visions of Jesus never entirely disappeared and have on occasion resurfaced dramatically. For example, Hildegard of Bingen (12th century) wrestled with the relation of the second person of the trinity to divine and human nature, and explained the matter thusly: "man signifies the divinity of the Son of God and woman his humanity."[443] Her formulation preserved a place for both dominant genders *and* for the gender hierarchy.

On the other hand, it also was not unknown to link Christ to the *feminine* in God. Since contemporary Christians are all too familiar with the masculine Jesus, the link to femininity requires more attention here.

Bernard of Clairvaux & William of St. Thierry

Historian and late medieval period expert Caroline Walker Bynum points out that any number of medieval Christian writers—like Bernard of Clairvaux and William of St. Thierry—used the image of Jesus as a mother in their writings.[444] As early as the 2nd century, she notes, Clement of Alexandria referred to Christ as 'mother,' drawing an analogy between Christ's giving of his blood in the Eucharist and a mother nursing her infant. Later, when male writers depicted the motherhood of God they sometimes used the imagery of the soul suckling at Christ's breast. Moreover, both men and women employed the image of drinking from the breast of Christ—an image sometimes received through religious vision. Walker Bynum refers to Catherine of Siena, among others, who used such imagery and remarks, "by the thirteenth and fourteenth centuries the image of the nursing Jesus regularly stressed blood more than milk as the food of the soul."[445]

Mother Julian of Norwich

Some writers excelled in an even more robust use of gender metaphors. The medieval saint, Mother Julian of Norwich (1342-c. 1417), among the most

216

famous of Christian mystics, depicted Jesus as 'Mother.' To Jesus such attributes as childbearing and nurturance were ascribed. Mother Julian imagined Christ as a pregnant woman who, after sustaining Christians in his womb, brings them forth safely through the travails of childbirth. Mother Julian sustained the idea of the maternal Jesus as she further depicted Christ as a mother raising a child.[446]

Henry Suso

Meister Eckhart's disciple Henry Suso, a Dominican friar and 14th century mystic, was famed in his own time for his devotion to the suffering Jesus and his ministry to women. He extolled the figure of Christ/Sophia ('Wisdom'). Barbara Newman comments that in his *Horologium Sapientiae* (*Wisdom's Watch Upon the Hours*), Suso plays with gender—both human and divine—referring to himself at times as a feminine soul longing for Christ the Bridegroom, and at other times imagining himself as a masculine disciple in love with Christ the goddess. Similarly, Jesus is imaged both as male and female, as an excerpt from his autobiographical *Life of the Servant* makes clear when talking about his beloved Eternal Wisdom: "The minute he thought her to be a beautiful young lady, he immediately found a proud young man before him." In his use of gender Suso offered male believers a way to spiritually embrace a heterosexual marriage to God, with the added benefit of retaining their own masculinity. Newman quotes Suso's depiction in the *Horologium* of coming from the royal wedding where "the supreme King and divine Emperor himself has given me his only beloved daughter, Eternal Wisdom, as a bride." Far from proving scandalous and resulting in Suso's rejection as a heretic, his work was warmly embraced; the *Horologium* was one of the most widely read devotional works of the Medieval period.[447]

Contemporary Feminist Theologians

The depiction of Jesus in terms of feminine gender does not emasculate. Rather, the juxtaposition of such imagery with more familiar masculinity creates androgyny in the strong sense—as a figure embracing the best of both men and women. Jesus is not neutered but balanced. The androgynous Jesus is a figure as fully feminine as masculine because Christ is *wholly* human.

This inclination to re-envision the gender of Jesus persists, showing up sporadically in Christian expressions, especially artistic ones, right down to our current era.[448] Feminist theologians, for example, have sought to rework Christology using androgyny as a way to rebalance Christian thinking. The androgynous Christ also can be figured in more radical ways through drawing upon metaphors and images that transcend the limitations of our dichotomous gender system. To those who might object that such efforts have no biblical roots, someone like Green can respond by pointing out episodes in the gospels which portray Jesus as transgressing the boundaries which separate men from women and

217

episodes showing Jesus performing functions more commonly associated with women (e.g., serving food, washing feet, ministering to the sick). Pre-eminently, of course, Green indicates Jesus' occupation of the role of victim—key both to the Christian idea of salvation and the real experience of women around the world and across history.[449]

In fact, theologian Eleanor McLaughlin has gone so far as to suggest the notion of *a transvestic Jesus*—Jesus the crossdresser, a "destroyer of dualities." She is not arguing for an effeminate Jesus but an appreciation of a Jesus who "is like a 'cross-dresser,' one not 'caught' by the categories" but free to express feminine ways of love, sacrifice, and forgiveness. McLaughlin's goal is to weaken the association of Jesus to masculinity that has so often and forcefully been used to support inequality, even oppression, in the Church. She likens Jesus to a Trickster figure, who can open us to new understandings, *if* we are freed from "a merely male Jesus," who she regards as "a violation of the scandal and transgression which is the Gospel."[450]

Contemporary Queer Theologians

Alongside feminist constructions of an androgynous Christ are queer theorists' efforts to see a Jesus who can relate to them. Religious studies scholar Robert Goss observes that queer constructions of Christ question the dominant heterosexual perspective that conveniently dresses Jesus as a heterosexual (if celibate) man. Goss regards their experiences and efforts as planting seeds for 'a larger Christ,' one not confined to our culture's heteronormativity, but enlarged beyond our society's binary gender system. He points to the work of theologian Marcella Althaus-Reid, author of a provocative work entitled *Indecent Theology*. She believes Christ can be movingly portrayed in ways that challenge conventional notions of gender and sexuality. Thus, in words Goss approvingly quotes from her:

> Christ can be represented very movingly as a young woman holding another woman tightly, as they stand at closed door of the church amidst voices within the church shouting 'stay out' to the young lesbians. Or we can envisage a transgendered Christ, taking on the Christself the oppression and injustice that a person suffers when gender and sexuality are dislocated.[451]

The point in all this is to shake up those entrenched ideas about Jesus that more probably reflect cultural convention than divine truth. No one disputes that the historical Jesus frequently challenged and crossed boundaries set by his society. No one disputes that the figure of Christ shattered boundary lines separating divine from human. Yet most of us struggle to extend our image of Christ Jesus to one who *tran*scends gender—a transgender person. The provocative efforts to depict an androgynous Jesus, or a 'transvestite' Christ may at least remind us of a central Christian truth—that Jesus belongs to *all* people.

Atum

Androgynous deities are found in many places. Most are more obvious than the ambiguity surrounding divine gender in Christianity. In ancient Egypt, for example, the god Atum could be depicted androgynously, as in the following coffin text:

I am Atum, the creator of the Eldest Gods,
I am he who gave birth to Shu,
I am that great He-She . . . .[452]

Yet Atum also presents a feature common to the androgynous deities. Though encompassing traits and sometimes even physical characteristics of more than one gender, these beings are almost invariably associated with a particular gender. Atum is regularly regarded as male, as is Dionysus. Aphrodite, Artemis, and Athena are all ordinarily regarded as goddesses. As with mere mortals, immortal beings find it difficult to escape gender assignment even when the choices offered by a dichotomous scheme fit poorly.

Inanna

Perhaps less obviously androgynous was the Sumerian deity Inanna (or Inana), identified with the Akkadian Ishtar, or Astarte of the Semitic peoples of the Mideast. Assigned femininity—indeed, extolled as the very embodiment of femininity and idealized as the goddess of female sexuality—Inanna uses androgyny to bridge heaven and earth.[453] Herself capable of either gender presentation ("When I sit in the alehouse, I am a woman, and I am an exuberant young man"[454]), Inanna also holds gender-altering power: "To turn a man into a woman and a woman into a man are yours, Inana."[455] Her cultus included priests, the *kurĝara*, whose dress, as we noted earlier, conspicuously incorporated mixed gender elements in their public processionals.[456]

Dionysus

The Greeks excelled at the idea of androgyny among divinity. Hans Licht, in his famous *Sexual Life in Ancient Greece*, remarks that "the Greeks possessed a really astonishing notion of the double sexual (hermaphroditic) nature of the human being in the embryonic condition and of the androgynous idea of life generally."[457] He enumerates a variety of instances in which this idea surfaces through stories and practices. For Licht the 'androgynous idea of life' is rooted in the very subconscious of the ancient Greeks.[458]

In the Western classical tradition, perhaps the best known example of a divine gender-blender was Dionysus. The god of vibrant fertility, especially associated with wine, Dionysus came by his androgyny quite naturally. Another of his names, Dithyrambos ('double entrances'), tells the story—Dionysus was borne by both his mortal mother and then, after her death, by his immortal father Zeus, who sewed the fetus in his thigh until he was ready to be born.[459] Greek literature scholar Albert Henrichs once noted of him: "Perceived as both man and animal, male and effeminate, young and old, he is the most versatile and elusive of all Greek Gods."[460] Among his other associations are those of impersonation and the theater [461]—both fitting for a crossdressing god.

Just as there are many legends about him, so there are varied depictions. Sometimes he is shown bearded, other times with a smooth chin. Many statues represent him as "a youth of soft and feminine shape, with a dreamy expression, his long, clustering hair confined by a fillet or crown of vine or ivy, generally naked, or with a fawn or panther skin thrown lightly over him."[462] Camille Paglia notes other artistic representations of Dionysus: "Archaic vases show him in a woman's tunic, saffron veil, and helmet. His name Bassareus comes from the Thracian *bassara*, a woman's fox-skin mantle."[463]

Aphrodite/Venus

Another well-known deity who expressed both maleness and femaleness was Aphrodite (Venus). Though ostensibly female, and best known as a goddess, Aphrodite was depicted in various places as an androgynous deity. The Roman writer Lucian (2nd century) referred to "Aphrodite, who had two natures and double beauty."[464] Macrobius (early 5th century), in his *Saturnalia*, reported concerning Venus that, "there is in Cyprus a bearded statue of the goddess with female clothing but with male attributes, so that it would seem that the deity is both male and female."[465] The deity in this form was known as *Venus Barbata* ('Bearded Venus'). As *Venus Castina* the goddess defended her temple at Ascalon by transforming the attacking Scythian men into women. By this name she was also the patron deity of men who have feminine souls caught in male bodies.[466] Yet Venus was not a deity merely for men to adore; women also crossed gender lines to worship her. Macrobius observed that, "Philoshorus, too, in his *Atthis* says that Venus is the moon and that men offer sacrifice to the moon dressed as women, and women dressed as men, because the moon is thought to be both male and female."[467] Another possible representation of the androgynous deity may be the *Venus Calva* ('Bald Venus'), whose images show a woman as bald as any man might be. But while one scholar might see in this particular image an analogy to the priests of Isis, another finds in it reference to the lock of hair Roman women dedicated to Venus on their wedding day.[468]

Interestingly, though imaged in some places as an androgynous deity, for most of Western history Aphrodite—especially in the Roman form of Venus—has been known as the most feminine and sexually alluring member of the Greek and Roman pantheon. As a goddess, she was associated with beauty, love, marriage, and birth. Yet, her connections with androgyny are more than a few isolated representations and a couple odd names. In many ways Aphrodite is perhaps the patron deity for the transgendered.

Of particular importance is her link with androgynous Dionysus. Together they head a powerful transgender family. By Dionysus she had as son the god Priapus, who was especially associated with Roman sexuality. Another of their reputed offspring was Hymen, a deity both beautiful and bisexual, and celebrated as the god of marriage. Finally, our term 'hermaphrodite' conjoins her name with that of Hermes. By him she had a son who while bathing in a pool became joined with the spring's nymph so that they became one body with the characteristics of both sexes. All of the potency, mystery, and multidimensional character of sex, gender, and sexuality are represented in this family.

Artemis

Two other deities regularly called goddesses exhibit strongly androgynous characters. One, Artemis (the Roman Diana), twin to Apollo, has been called the most complex of the Greek deities.[469] The deity's principal associations include things strongly associated with females (e.g., the moon), but other things with males (e.g., hunting). Although Athenians revered Artemis as protector of women-in-childbirth, Spartans connected her with warfare. Such things would seem to fit Eliade's idea of divine androgyny.

Classics scholar Christiane Sourvinou-Inwood observes that as Artemis Brauronia, the deity was associated with the transition of girls into marriage-eligible young women. As Artemis Tauropolis, she was connected to a boy's initiation ceremony, and as Artemis Orthia the boys of Sparta were under her watch as they grew up to become citizens and warriors. Sourvino-Inwood speculates that at the core of Artemis' personality might lie a concern "with transitions and transitional marginal places . . . and marginal situations"[470]—certainly appropriate for transgendered people. Predictably, some artistic representations catch, at least partially, Artemis' duality. In Ephesus, the virgin deity is presented as a fertility deity in statues depicting a female form with bull testicles.[471]

Athena

Athena, too, may be grouped among the androgynous deities. Though, like Aphrodite and Artemis, Athena was designated a goddess and represented in female form, she exhibits an androgynous character. Like Dionysus, Athena's birth was by a manner that incorporated both male and female: Zeus, the father, had swallowed whole Metis, the mother; Athena emerged—in some accounts fully armed for battle—from the head of Zeus. Athena, the divine author of weaving, also invented the chariot. As Homer put it in the Iliad (V.733-737), she who had made her own robe cast it off in favor of armor and weapons of war during the Trojan War. It was Athena's idea to build the Trojan horse and Athena in armor is how she is best remembered in art. In stories, Athena stands foremost among the gods as the helper of heroes. For example, in Homer's Odyssey she takes on the guise of the man Mentor in order to aid Telemachus, son of Odysseus.[472] As historian Robert Christopher Towneley Parker puts it, Athena "unites in her person the characteristic excellences of both sexes."[473]

Agdistis

The most noticeable way to unite characteristics of male and female is to be hermaphroditic. A number of deities possess both male and female sexual parts. In Classical religion among the most notable hermaphroditic deity is Agdistis. This deity's origin occurred when Zeus, chief of the gods, had a nocturnal emission ('wet dream') and impregnated Gaea ('Mother Earth'). Agdistis was born with the sexual anatomy of both a male and a female—a potent and dangerous combination in a deity. So Agdistis was emasculated. In time, Agdistis became identified with one of the most prominent deities of the classical world: Cybele. One story relates that from the severed male organ of Agdistis grew an almond tree. One day Nana, the daughter of a river god, masturbated using one of this tree's almonds. She was impregnated and bore Attis (or Atys), who as an adult castrated himself and became an example to later followers of Cybele, whose priests voluntarily became eunuchs in her service.[474]

Hermaphroditus

The very notion of a hermaphroditic deity comes from Hermaphroditus, offspring—as the name suggests—of Aphrodite (an androgynous deity) and Hermes (a trickster deity). Hermaphroditus is routinely pictured by ancient artists as possessing female breasts and male genitals. But this was not a mere matter of birth. The story is told that as a youth Hermaphroditus was male, and very comely. He attracted the attention of Salmacis, a nymph, who desired him, and all the more when she glimpsed him naked as he went to swim in her pool. The Roman poet Ovid (32 B.C.E. – 17 C.E.) described what then happened:

'I've won, for he is mine,'
She cried, clothes torn away and naked, as she
Leaped to follow him, her arms about him fast,
Where, though he tried to shake her off, she clung,
Fastening his lips to her, stroking his breast,
Surrounding him with arms, legs, lips, and hands
As though she were a snake caught by an eagle . . . .
The heir of Atlas struggled as he could
Against the pleasure the girl desired,
But she clung to him as though their flesh were one,
'Dear, naughty boy,' she said, 'to torture me;
But you won't get away. O gods in heaven,
Give me this blessing; clip him within my arms
Like this forever.' At which the gods agreed;
They grew one body, one face, one pair of arms
And legs, as one might graft branches upon
A tree, so two became nor boy nor girl,
Neither yet both within a single body.[475]

222

The figure of Hermaphroditus, in Licht's estimation, reveals "a being that has its root in the dim consciousness of the androgynous idea of life, artistically perfected by sensually aesthetic longings, who was worshipped as the good spirit of the house and private life, more than as a divinity who was the object of public worship."[476]

What are some examples of gender-altering deities?

Deities do not always retain the gender presentation they started with, or are best known by. While gender alteration may happen by gender masquerade, other alterations are possible. A deity might change dress without also affecting a masquerade, as the Greek river god Acheloös does in donning the feminine *peplos*. In dramatic instances a male deity may emasculate himself. Barbara Walker has cited examples from various parts of the world: Ra in Egypt, Mahadeva in India, Quetzalcoatl in Mexico, Uranus in Greece, and Odin in Northern Europe, among others.[477]

Deities in Masquerade

Deities often take disguises. When the disguise involves appearing as a gender different from the one typically associated with that deity, then a gender masquerade has happened. Athena, for example, in Homer's *Odyssey* disguises herself as Mentor, the male friend of Odysseus.[478] Though we have placed Athena among the androgynous deities, the appearance as Mentor is clearly not meant to represent the divine presence and it does involve a change in gender from that typically associated with 'her'—and so qualifies as an instance of gender masquerade.

Other Greek gods also masqueraded. Zeus, first among the gods, disguised himself to appear like Artemis. His aim was one of those familiar to gender-crossings: to gain an access he would have otherwise lacked. In this case, it was to the nymph Callisto. Masquerades are characterized by gains sought through duplicity.

In the East, Vishnu—that popular deity of Hinduism—is viewed as a male god. Nevertheless, when he takes form among mortals it can be however he wishes—human or otherwise, male or female. He has famous *avatars* who are male: Krishna, Rama, Buddha. Yet he also is famed for a female presentation. Vishnu took the form of an enchantress named Mohini in order to distract some demons (*asuras*).[479] The ruse succeeded. On another occasion, Vishnu utilized the same guise to rescue the god Shiva by again distracting a demon. Later, Shiva also was enamored of the masquerading god when he encountered Vishnu-as-Mohini in a garden. Shiva and Vishnu engaged in a sexual encounter that left Vishnu-as-Mohini pregnant. Their child was the hermaphroditic deity, Ayyappan (or Hariharaputra).[480] Vishnu's use of gender is utilitarian, and his employment of masquerade bends gender to a purposeful deception. Although we tend to see deception as immoral, Vishnu's artifice to save Shiva is noble.

A common figure in many religions, both ancient and modern, who may employ a gender masquerade is the 'Trickster.' Such a figure is not always a deity; it may be an animal, as in various Native American religions, or a quasi-divine figure, such as Satan in Christianity. But tricksters can be deities, as Loki (who spent years in female form) is in Norse mythology,[481] or Hermes in Classical religion. Though the essential nature of the trickster may be characterized as male or female, the trickster has the ability to change shape and gender. This 'gender-bending' being plays a vital role in many mythologies, often involved in creation or reshaping creation, posing temptations or challenges, and being a vehicle for driving home moral lessons in stories.[482]

Gender Altered Deities

The case of Amaterasu (or Ohirume-machi) presents a different situation. Amaterasu today is known as a female deity, goddess of the sun and progenitor of the Japanese imperial line. However, the name itself is gender neutral. Some evidence suggests that Amaterasu originally was a male deity, or perhaps ambiguous in sex. More than one plausible explanation for the deity's altered status has been offered. Religion scholar Brian Bocking writes that in Pre-Meji images of the deity the depiction is of a Buddhist masculine figure or person of indiscriminate gender. The present image (since the Muromachi period) may derive from the influence of the Buddhist figure of Uho Doji, a young male bodhisattva. He was depicted in a form resembling that of Amaterasu today—a standing figure with long hair dressed in simple white garb and bearing certain ornamentation. At the Buddhist temple near the Ise shrines, Amaterasu was venerated in the form of Uho Doji.[483]

Matsumae Takeshi, an expert on Japanese mythology, traces a different linkage of Amaterasu to maleness. Takeshi points to early sun worship among the Japanese. A number of Amaterasu shrines, like that on Tsushima Island in the medieval period, worshipped Ameno-himitama, believed to be a male deity. Similar instances are found elsewhere, all sharing in common that the Amaterasu shrine venerated a male deity, by whatever name. Takeshi remarks, "I have come to the conclusion that almost all Amaterasu and Amateru-mitama shrines were dedicated to the same deity, 'Amateru Kuniteru Hoakari' or Heaven and Earth Shining Fire." Takeshi is persuaded that originally Amaterasu was a male deity named Amateru, worshipped by the fishermen of Ise, but who became in perhaps the 5th or 6th century identified by the royal family as its ancestral deity. Over time, the gender characteristics associated with the deity changed from masculine to feminine and the god became a goddess.[484]

Whichever explanation we might adopt, if Amaterasu was originally a male god, then we possess an example of a deity who is gender *altered* rather than gender *altering*.

What are some examples of human sacred gender crossings?

In addition to figuring out the nature of divine figures and how best to relate to them, ancient folk also had to determine the role of sex and gender in their own lives, and how these fit into the religious sphere. Answers differed radically. Some viewed sex and gender as those aspects of human experience most directly relevant to religion, particularly because they involve relationships and the renewal of life. Others thought human sex and gender were those parts of human existence that most interfere with connecting to the divine because they are distracting and deluding powers. In fact, some regarded humanity's division into male and female as a fall from an original androgynous state. Many others took one or another position in-between the extremes, finding a place for sex and gender without making it central or excluding it as evil.

One creative answer was to remove sexuality from the literal world of fleshly practices into a realm of metaphor. In this way, a degree of gender crossing could be done without raising eyebrows. Christianity affords numerous examples of this practice from the Church Fathers onward. On the one hand, as we have seen, this made possible new discourses about and with the figure of Jesus. But it functioned as well to free Christians to imagine themselves in different gender roles—a symbolic realization of the Apostle Paul's declaration that in Christ Jesus there would be neither male nor female (Galatians 3:28). Bernard of Clairvaux, for instance, in the early 12th century could speak of Christian men as siblings of Christ whose identity was as sisters rather than brothers: "Living in the Spirit of the Son, let such a soul recognize herself as a daughter of the Father, a bride or even a sister of the Son, for you will find that the soul who enjoys this privilege is called by either of these names."[485]

In a great many of the varying religious responses crossdressing played a part. As indicated earlier, it might be done for a variety of reasons, such as imitation of the divine, for transformation, or as an act of transgression. Ancient expressions of sacred gender crossings are discussed in their geographical and religious tradition contexts in answering other questions in this work, so here we only shall explore briefly various ways of utilizing cross-gender religiously, retaining our focus on crossdressing. Among the more notable avenues for transcending gender—or at least crossing culturally dominant gender conventions—are these:

❑ *Shamanism*—perhaps the religious phenomenon most famously associated with gender crossings;

❑ *Priests and priestesses*—religious officials serving deities who themselves play with gender crossings often follow suit;

❑ *Eunuchs*—transgendered either by nature or by human hand, eunuchs have long had special roles in different social institutions, including religion;

225

- ❑ *Disciples*—devoted followers who imitate their leaders will defy social conventions of gender if their master has done so; and,
- ❑ *Gender artifice in social relations*—where gender conventions are crossed or transcended in order to serve some particular social relation.

We shall briefly consider each of these.

Shamanism

Shamanism is a phenomenon found around the world, albeit in various forms and under different names (e.g., the 'medicine man (or woman)' of Native Americans). One unifying matter, though, is the religious character of the shaman. Another aspect very common among shamans is gender crossing of one kind or another. Most often this takes the form of crossdressing.

Shamanism utilizes crossdressing as part of the transformation by which a shaman not only mystically transcends the boundaries of mundane reality, but also the artifice of gender. Shamans thus can be interpreted as masters of deconstruction who transgress social convention in the service of a higher end. "Shamans break down categories; confound boundaries, especially those between worlds; and specialize in ambiguity."[486] Certainly in this regard crossdressing by a shaman proves a deconstructive act. Like crossdressers in mainstream society, shamans represent those of us who are marginalized by society. Their exhibition of "ambiguous sexuality"[487] confounds norms while opening up new possibilities.

Mircea Eliade, using a history of religions approach, notes that shamanism, in its purest sense, is a phenomenon rooted in Siberia and central Asia. Starting with and focusing upon Siberian shamanism, Eliade finds connections to shamanism elsewhere in the world, both East and West. The shaman as a religious figure is one who bridges the mundane and sacred spheres. Shamans are also masters of religious ecstasy. But of importance to us, Eliade cites shamans as an example of 'ritual androgyny.' They unite, or 'reconcile,' opposing principles such as masculinity and femininity.[488]

The androgyny achieved by uniting male and female in one's own person is frequently represented in the clothing the shaman wears. The Siberian shaman, for example, dons a caftan (a unisex garment) adorned with iron disks, bars, and other things that symbolize various aspects of nature, such as the human body, including two orbs for breasts. Anthropologists early in the 20th century observed that among the Siberian Yakut the male shaman, when not in his costume, wore as his ordinary wear a woman's dress fashioned from the skin of a foal.[489] In Korea, female shamans wear male clothing; "the rare male shaman in Korea (*paksu mudong*) performs *kut* wearing women's clothing, down to the pantaloons that hide beneath his billowing skirt and slip."[490] In the Philippines, the Spanish conquerors encountered both female shamans and male shamans—the *Bayog* (aka. *Bayoc*, *Bayoguin*, or *Asog*)—who appeared as women in dress, hairstyle and effeminate behavior.[491]

226

Comparable examples come from Africa (see the answer to Q. 83), and the Americas. In the United States, for example, about two dozen Native American societies have shamans (commonly referred to as 'medicine men' or 'medicine women'), with male shamans predominating in about two-thirds of these. An expert on gender variant Native Americans, Sabine Lang remarks about these 'women-men':

> Where men were the primary healers or medicine men, the women-men moved partly within the domain of the masculine gender role, both with respect to their status as medicine "men" and also with regard to acquisition of the necessary supernatural powers. Women's clothes and components of the feminine gender role appeared there as the expression of the personal "medicine" of a woman-man. In such cases, women-men were not healers in the framework of the feminine gender role, but—despite their ambivalent gender status—they were males with a special kind of supernatural power.[492]

Notable in these and other instances that might be mentioned is the lack of sexual fetishism in the crossdressing connected to shamanism. Instead, the crossdressing is an aspect of costuming, ritual in character, and highly symbolic. Through crossdressing a tangible manifestation of a spiritual embracing of male and female together occurs. In this manner it matters little whether we style the shaman as 'male' or 'female' for doing so misses the point that the shaman's appearance creates a point of integration (or, if you prefer, 'reconciliation').

Appraisal of the gender effect of the shaman's presence and work varies. A shaman can be an individual whose gender is as a man, a woman, or a member of a 'third gender' (e.g., a Native American 'two-spirit' person). Accordingly, appraisal of the gender status of the shaman will affect how the dress and the behavior of the shaman is interpreted. As we have seen, we may view the shaman as breaking down gender lines, or as achieving androgyny. But although this has symbolic power for all the shaman's people, the actual effect on the community sense of gender is not necessarily the same everywhere. Some observers contend that the crossdressing associated with shamanistic ritual may actually enhance gender differences rather than neutralize them as the shaman manifests different gender qualities.[493] If so, this also can be variously appraised as to any alleged benefit it accrues to different gender groups. Precisely because shamans exist at the boundaries and actively engage mysteries they defy either easy categorization or summary judgments with respect to gender and crossdressing.

Priests & Priestesses

Priests and/or priestesses also are often involved in sacred gender crossings and crossdressing. At the dawn of literature, in ancient Sumeria, we find references to crossdressing priests called the *kurĝara*, whom may have been a template for later gender-crossing priests, such as the effeminate male *assinnu* of Ishtar, or the "male shrine prostitutes" referred to in the Jewish and Christian sacred literature (1 Kings 12:24).[494] We might count among their figurative descendants the 'Galli,' priests of Cybele, famed throughout the classical world (see above). They not only crossdressed, but sometimes castrated themselves. These acts represented their imitation of a revered figure (Attis) and constituted a transformative action whereby the priests became acceptable to the deity they served.

In northern Europe, crossdressing was also a part of the worship of the Alcis, twin deities whom 1st century Roman historian Tacitus identified as equivalent to the Roman deities Castor and Pollux. According to Tacitus, the presiding priest of the Alcis dressed in women's clothes.[495] It is worth noting that the Alcis have also been identified with the *Haddingjar*—'they of womanly hair.'[496] Perhaps, then, the priestly crossdressing indicates something about how the duality of the gods was understood by those who followed them.

Eunuchs

Eunuchs occupied a unique and often privileged place in many ancient societies. Their infertility made them a logical choice for sensitive positions, such as service among the women of a ruler's harem. Many of these eunuchs were intersex individuals—eunuchs 'made by nature.' Others were eunuchs 'made by man,' sometimes voluntarily, often by the choice of another. However they arrived at this state, it was generally viewed as placing them in a border state between sexes.

Of course, they were not the only denizens of this space. Dominic Montserrat, in considering gender in the world of the Roman Empire, remarks that the Roman patriarchy constructed its notions of sex and gender in accordance with priority on procreative ability. Eunuchs, lacking this power, thus existed outside the conventional gender categories; they were 'third gender' people. But they were not the only ones. Montserrat numbers among other 'third gender' members genetic intersexed people, medically castrated men (e.g., the Galli), and celibates such as Rome's Vestal Virgins.[497]

The eunuch's position *between* sexes and gender statuses also was ideal for religions. Richard Gordon observes that castration placed an individual 'between worlds' and was parallel to other acts of devotion such as voluntary poverty or homelessness. Some way was needed to mark out such persons and things like face whitening or crossdressing served such a purpose admirably. Gordon distinguishes two forms of religious eunuchs: senior priests (perhaps even as High Priest), or religious attendants who remained outside the priesthood.[498] We already noted the eunuch priests of Cybele. But eunuchs involved in one or another aspect of religious service were common. They were known in both the East and the West.

228

Perhaps the most famous eunuchs are those of the Byzantine Empire (5th-15th centuries C.E.). Roberta Gilchrist comments, "The eunuch is now widely regarded by Byzantine scholars as a third gender, neither male nor female, although the precise physical definition of this category is insecure."[499] Gilchrist notes the reports of such individuals as mixing physical characteristics of male and female. Whatever their physical nature, in terms of gender they were a third gender by virtue of a set of distinct mannerisms and accompanying social perception that combined to create for them a separate gender class. Their high social status carried with it political, religious, and ceremonial duties, which can be generally described as mediating and supervising life boundaries (e.g., that between healthy and ill, alive and dead).

Gilchrist perceptively notes that social—not sexual—concerns were central in the construal of the Byzantine eunuch as a third gender. Whether by nature or by choice, the eunuch came to occupy a place between genders. In this respect, applying a term like 'crossdressing' may be meaningless—though it has not been uncommon when the genetic sex of the eunuch was male and feminine dress was adopted. What we need to recognize here is that eunuchs cross gender conventions, willingly or not, and once between the gender poles are often called upon to perform religious, or quasi-religious, roles and functions. These range from priestly duties, to those of sacred healers, to social mediators in conflicts between gender (and other) groups.

Disciples

The faithful following of a special figure—in the Judaeo-Christian tradition termed 'discipleship'—entails a keen observation and imitation of the beloved master. Interestingly, some early Christian literature suggests that becoming a follower of Jesus means changes with gender implications. At least, that is a contention made by biblical studies scholar Richard Valantasis with reference to the *Gospel of Thomas*. He writes that the new person envisioned by Jesus in the sayings of this document "has become in essence a third gender"—a person outside the cultural categories of masculinity and femininity. This new individual, Valantasis declares, "makes concrete and defines the new third gender that replaces the former dual-gender paradigm."[500]

Gender Artifice in Social Relations

Gender artifice within a religious system can arise as a way of constructing a particular social relation. In the religious/philosophical system of China's Confucianism, social relations in general are central and carefully proscribed. Among the most fundamental relations are those of husband to wife and of ruler to ruled. In both instances, the relationship is vertical; the latter is subordinate to the former. Moreover, Confucianism is a rigidly patriarchal system where females occupy a limited and inferior position. The male ruler stands alone, in a special class, and must be treated as such in social discourse. Thus, in the *Analects* of Confucius, we find the wife of the emperor accorded a special ritual etiquette:

> The wife of the ruler of a State is referred to by the ruler as 'That Person.' She refers to herself as Little Boy. The people of the country call her 'That person of the Prince's.' When speaking of her to people of another State the ruler calls her 'This lonely one's little prince.' But people of another State likewise call her 'That person of the Prince's.'[501]

Arthur Waley, the translator of the above passage, notes that the phrase *Hsiao T'ung* ("Little Boy") refers to a pageboy and is exclusively masculine. Waley remarks that "the sovereign's wife may not be referred to (either by himself or anyone else) by any term that is feminine in implication and must in referring to herself use a term that is definitely masculine."[502] In short, the inflexibility of social relations mandates a flexibility in gender designation in order to protect the social order.

Yet the *yin/yang*, feminine/maculine divide was bridged by at least one Chinese ruler. In the late 7th century, during the T'ang Dynasty, Empress Wu Zetian (624-705) declared herself 'Son of Heaven' and emperor (690 C.E.).[503] In Confucian China this was not only unparalleled, but unthinkable—*yin* had usurped *yang*! Even prior to her attainment of supreme power, Wu had occupied the role of an advisor to the throne, even sporting a beard like her male advisors.[504] In the hands of a capable and ambitious woman like Wu, the social artifice of Confucian China could be employed to transcend gender rather than transgress it.

What are some examples of sacred festivals involving gender crossings?

In sacred festivals divine figures interact with human ones. Frequently this interaction is a solicited *meeting* of the parties. Often this is construed as a passive act on the part of the deity, who may merely hear a prayer or accept an offering. But in some instances the deity takes a more active part, typically through a representative human figure, who may be a priest (or priestess) in a priestly role or masquerading as the deity. In meetings between divine and human beings one or the other may engage in gender crossing. The deity may do so for any number of reasons, including putting the worshippers to the test, seducing a person, or utilizing a masquerade for some other purpose, such as mixing among the faithful. A human may also gender cross, because such is suitable for the worship of the divine being, or perhaps because the human is attempting a subterfuge to trick the deity for some reason.

In other instances, the human participation in the festivities may involve actions to *avoid* a divine, semi-divine, or demonic figure. In such cases the person may cross gender as a way to deceive a wrathful deity or a malevolent one. Through successful deception the person escapes harm until the danger is past.

Rarely, the divine figure might be portrayed as gender crossing to avoid being met by human pursuers. In such a case the idea is to effect a disguise in order not to have to yield some benefit.

While the above ideas are not exclusive to sacred festivals (i.e., they can occur in individual experience outside any religious structure), they take on special meaning in a festival. The occasion of the festival adds regularity and fixes the contextual form and process for the gender crossing. It has a sacred character by virtue of being set apart from ordinary action. The gender crossing is *not* typical of ordinary, mundane experience. Instead, it exists in a special time and place for a concrete and sanctioned reason.

The easiest way to convey a gender crossing is through dress. It is not the only way, however. Dramatic and extreme steps might also be taken, as among eunuch priests who self-castrate and undertake a life of gender crossing that sets them apart from others. Obviously, for the majority of the faithful this is not a course that will be taken. Festivals offer a way to do something similar, though limited in time and extent. In a festival a male can become female, or a female male in order to effect a meeting with a deity or, perhaps, to avoid a meeting with one, or with a malevolent spirit.

In ancient religious festivals both male and female crossdressing occurred—though not necessarily in the same festival, nor for the same reasons. Since crossdressing inherently represents a transition, it often was connected to rites of transition such as initiation. "In many initiatory rituals, novices wear opposite sex clothing, signifying a ritual transformation into the other sex, a state of androgyny."[505] In other cases—such as in what has been term 'ritual transvestism'—it represented a temporary gender role reversal or (more rarely) a permanent gender role change.[506] No matter the aim, motivations might vary and appraisals by others certainly did.

Finally, humanities scholar Camille Paglia, in a rather striking assertion, contends: "Ritual transvestism, then and now, is a drama of female dominance. There are religious meanings to all female impersonation, in nightclubs or bedroom. A woman putting on man's clothes merely steals social power. But a man putting on women's clothes is searching for God."[507]

This is putting the matter rather too strongly in light of the evidence (even her own), but it does prompt us to regard crossdressing in a way we might not have done before. To whatever extent crossdressing may or may not reflect connection to an eternal feminine, it certainly had—and can retain—a sacred connection to deep and abiding forces. The ancient festivals understood this reality.

Ancient Eastern Religious Festivals

In southern India, at the festivals of Kuvakkam and Pillaiyarkuppam, a re-enactment of a story from one version of the *Mahabharata* occurs. That story is of Vishnu appearing as Mohini to honor and fulfill the condition of a princely warrior fated to die the following day. The hero, Aravan, did not wish to die without having married. Thus he was wed to Vishnu-as-Mohini. The Tamils know a group of male devotees of Vishnu-as-Mohini, called the 'Ali,' who crossdress and whose principal religious ritual has this story at its center.

A variety of other occasions and manners existed by which to honor Mohini. The Hindu Mohini Attam—the dance of the enchantress—commemorates the story of Vishnu's cross-gender appearance as Mohini in order to distract the demon Bhasmasura and thus save fellow deity, Shiva. Also, on the fifth day of the festival of the Brahmotsavams of Tirumala, 'Mohini Avatarotsavam,' the same story of Vishnu-as-Mohini is honored, with the divine lord dressed as Mohini and taken in a procession.

Ancient Greek Religious Festivals

As we might expect, deities associated with gender bending or gender blending might also have followers who followed their example. This is indeed the case. Devotees of Dionysus crossdressed in connection with different sacred occasions. Dionysian festivals, as Henrichs has observed, frequently featured role reversals such as crossdressing.[508] In the festival of *Oschophoria*, for example, young, wealthy noblemen dressed as women and led a sacred procession from the Temple of Dionysius to that of Athena.[509]

Saturnalia

As noted in another place (cf. answers to Q. 41-43), ritual crossdressing occurred in a number of religious contexts, especially where rituals of reversal were involved. The best known example of these is Saturnalia, a festival rooted in the worship of the Roman deity Saturnus, but which persisted long after the religious tones were well-subordinated or even forgotten. The Saturnalia might last from 3-7 days (depending on the era), and was characterized by role reversals such that, for example, slaves dined before their masters did, and leisure wear was donned when formal wear could be expected.[510] Crossdressing was part of the amusements of the festival, a practice that persisted in later festivals such as Carnival (see the answer to Q. 71).

Conclusion

This very brief exploration into sacred gender crossings only hints at the manifold ways they have played a part in the world's religions. Human devotees, seeing themselves as taking their cue from divine models, have often crossed gender boundaries in order to express and experience something important. Now that we have looked at this matter through a broad historical review, we must look at a number of religions in more depth.

Q. 77 What stance does Judaism take?

The Short Answer. Judaism is arguably the oldest of the world's major religions. Distinctive in its own right, Judaism also is significant for laying the foundation of the Western religious tradition, thus providing a key contribution to both Christianity and Islam. Though having fewer adherents than either Christianity or Islam, Judaism is hardly monolithic; it has a long tradition of preserving diverse viewpoints, including the minority opinion on various matters. Similarly, it offers diverse appreciations of and approaches to God. Most people are aware that Judaism's unrelenting monotheism regards God as without sex or gender. However, a substantial patriarchal tradition means a long history of conversing about God in masculine terms. Yet Judaism also includes a mystical tradition that extols the feminine aspect of divinity, the Shekinah. With respect to human gender, although Judaism has embraced a strict dualistic gender system within its patriarchal structure, there still has been surprising flexibility. Biblical stories offer examples of decidedly nonstereotypical men and women, like the patriarch Jacob and the judge Deborah. In Europe, under the influence of the Talmud, the construction of the Jewish man within the broader cultural context left room for males who were accepted within the Jewish community as gender conforming men but could be easily seen by outsiders as effeminate. Transgender realities have been a subject of some comment since biblical days, with a frank acknowledgement of their existence but—like everything else—subject to regulation. In addition to the famous text in Deuteronomy 22:5, there are references to crossdressing in Josephus, the Jewish historian of the 1st century, and the Talmud. The latter set of writings also discusses intersex individuals, sexual minorities, and others who today might be called transgender. Always preoccupied with preserving a purity central to being a holy people, transgender expressions are interpreted and regulated with respect to this overriding concern. Crossdressing is forbidden in specific religious situations (cf. the answer to Q. 63), yet in other contexts it escapes censure. Indeed, some religious authorities permit it in the religious observance of Purim. This does not mean, however, that Judaism presents an unambiguously welcoming community for transgender people. Homosexuality, intersexed conditions, and transsexualism are all variously regarded by different traditions within Judaism. The Reformed tradition has been the most accepting, while Hasidic Orthodoxy continues to sit at the more rejecting end of the religious continuum. Overall, it is perhaps the most tolerant of the Western religions with respect to transgender religions.

The Longer Answer. Judaism is perhaps the oldest of the world's major religions. Throughout its long history the religion has been characterized by the preservation of multiple points of view, allowing the minority report to stand honorably alongside the prevailing judgment on various matters. Guiding these diverse views is Torah, the instructed way of living set forth by the Divine One. Both the Hebrew Bible and the Talmud (cf. Q. 61 and Q. 63) present this Torah along with its interpretation and application. The resulting religious tradition is both broad and deep. It even has a mystical wing, represented in Kabbalah.

In its religious documents, practices, and the life of its people, transgender realities are acknowledged, though variously assessed. There are numerous texts that refer to intersexed people, some that may be relevant to homosexuals, and a few pertinent to crossdressing. With reference to the last named, perhaps the dominant interpretation of the biblical prohibition of crossdressing has been that it exists to counter an *improper* mixing of the sexes, leading to sexual sin or inappropriate religious practices. The prohibition, however understood, seems to be a limited one since crossdressing in secular situational contexts has long been unremarkable.

In other answers we have examined transgender realities in the past and present of Israel (see Q. 53), with relation to how God can be viewed (see Q. 76), and specifically with reference to the one specific text on crossdressing in the Hebrew Bible (see Q. 61-63). Repetition is kept to a minimum here; our present goal is to attain a broad overview of how Judaism has interacted with transgender realities, both as seen in various texts, but also with respect to actual religious practice. A logical place to begin is with the general idea of gender crossings in relation to sacred matters.

How has Judaism regarded divine gender?

As the foundation for the Western religious tradition, Judaism exercised influence on the later development of both Christianity and Islam. Ideas expressed in the Hebrew Bible, as well as actual Jewish practices, contributed important sources to help shape Western cultural sensibilities on a number of things, including gender. Though Christianity became the dominant member of the Western religions throughout Europe and the Americas, and Islam in the Middle East, both were indebted to Judaism and to classical thinking. Christianity, for example, creatively wove Greek philosophy with Jewish theology. Basic convictions in Judaism about gender and gender crossings in a religious context helped mold later thinking on these matters in Christianity and Islam, but even had they not they would remain significant as a distinctive set of answers about questions raised by human experience. To comprehend those answers we must try to grasp the logic behind them.

In Judaism, everything starts from God. To understand gender, then, means starting from God's revelation. That disclosure is only partially a *self*-disclosure, since what God reveals is primarily intended to regulate relationship between the deity and all that exists by the divine will. Much of that will is focused on relationship with human beings, especially a people separated from the nations to be the vehicle for the divine revelation. Therefore, the nature of God's revealing is not an egotistical self-portrait, but a careful setting out of what people need to know in order to practice a relationship with God—*Torah*.

Accordingly, Jewish thinking works out matters with an eye to the moral and practical, that is, with respect to how one ought to live in light of knowledge. This logic extends to all things sacred and mundane. Gender is not an abstract matter for speculation, but an aspect of creation intended to reflect God's created order and thus to help regulate human affairs, especially with respect to marriage and family.

Gender crossings are intrinsically problematic because they contravene an established order, and whenever that happens there should be a compelling reason. In a religion where holiness is a matter of setting apart people, things, times and places so that they can be dedicated to special purposes in service of relationship to God, anything that sets itself apart from the ordinary will be subject to special consideration. Only some things are chosen to become sacred, and in Torah those things chosen collectively mark out a separated people. That requires choosing differently than other people and rival religions. So, in a relevant example, crossdressing for religious purposes—a practice employed by its immediate rivals—was shunned by Judaism.

We shall consider the working out of this logic as we proceed, but first we must pause to consider how Judaism wrestled with gender—typically a mundane matter—in connection with the highest reality of all, God. This is important since the aspect of Torah that is self-revelatory of God does more to hide the divine being (*Deus absconditus*) than to disclose it (*Deus revelatus*). In light of this we can hardly be surprised that Jewish 'theology' is rather sparse. Unlike other religions that try to take their cue about gender, gender relations, and gender crossings directly from what they know of their divine being (or beings), Judaism has been forced by the nature of Torah to take a more indirect approach.

Representations of Divine Gender

Judaic theology centers in one idea: the unity of one God, expressed in the six foundational Hebrew words of the Shema: *Shema Yisrael, Adonai Elohaynu, Adonai echod*—"Hear O Israel, the Lord our God, the Lord is one" (Deuteronomy 6:4). But what is the nature of this Being? The great Jewish scholar Moses ben Maimon (Maimonides) was of the view that we are better saying what God is *not* than trying to specify what God is.[511] The reluctance to speculate on such matters flows logically from the nature of the divine name: יהוה (YHWH) is essentially a declaration of complete independence from the controlling knowledge of human beings. God will be who God will be, and no one can say who that *must* be. Recognition of this basic fact is accompanied by a reverence that leads the Orthodox Jew to shun any direct reference to God, instead using terms such as 'Adonai' ('Lord') or 'Ha-Shem' ('the Name'), or G-d. Consistent with God's name, the deity cannot be said to possess either sex or gender. From the Bible forward there is an acknowledgment of this independence from gendering by referring to the deity using both masculine and feminine images.

Images of God in the Bible

In the Tanakh (the Hebrew Bible in its three parts: *Torah* ('Law'), *Nevi'im* ('Prophets'), and *Khethuvim* ('Writings')), God is commonly depicted by masculine imagery, a culturally influenced choice reflecting a desire to establish before the other nations the Jewish God as the one, only, and supreme deity. In a world where men ruled, a masculine image for God was an understandable choice. Yet occasionally God was also talked about using feminine images.[512] Thus, in the prophetic literature, God is likened to a woman giving birth (Isaiah 42:14): "Now I will cry out like a woman in travail, I will gasp and pant" (Isaiah 42: 14, RSV). Again, there is the same prophet's message wherein the deity is identified with motherhood: "As one whom his mother comforts, so I will comfort you" (Isaiah 66:13, RSV; cf. Psalm 131:2-3). Arguably, though, the most important feminine image with respect to God is found in the third part of the Tanakh.

Wisdom

In the writings, particularly the wisdom literature (e.g., Proverbs 1:22-33; 8:22-31), Wisdom (*hokma*) is both feminine and so closely linked to God that, as biblical scholar Mary Joan Witt Leith puts it, "the dividing line between Wisdom the woman and God can grow hazy."[513] Leith also observes the similarities between Wisdom and various goddesses of the region, including the Canaanite Asherah. This deity was often worshipped alongside YHWH in Israelite popular religion[514] and for some it may have been a small step to see Wisdom—or even Asherah—as the feminine aspect or expression of the Hebrew God.

The post-biblical Wisdom literary tradition continued to personify Wisdom in suggestive ways. Jewish writings collected in the Apocrypha, representing generally a period after the composition of the Hebrew Bible, further develop the connection between Wisdom and God. Baruch, for example, locates her place as heaven (3:29), though she appears on earth to live among people (3:39). Wisdom of Solomon extols her in praise customarily associated with divinity, calling her "radiant and unfading" (6:12), a law-giver (6:18), present from the beginning of creation (6:20), and "the fashioner of all things" (7:22). The distinction of Wisdom from God (7:25-8:4) underscores their intimate connection. So, too, in Sirach, who says Wisdom was created before all things (1:4). That Wisdom enjoys a preeminent and intimate connection with God is clear; whether Wisdom at any point represents God-as-feminine is debatable.

The Qumran community's Dead Sea Scrolls also preserve a Wisdom tradition. In it we find echoes of earlier ideas. For example, God is likened to both parents: "For Thou art a father/ to all *the sons* of Thy truth,/ and as a woman who tenderly loves her babe,/ so dost Thou rejoice in them;/ and as a foster-father bearing a child in his lap/ so carest Thou for all Thy creatures."[515] Wisdom is again extolled: "By thy wisdom *all things exist from* eternity . . . ."[516] Still, as in earlier literature, though the relationship between God and Wisdom is a close one, and Wisdom might be said to express something divinely feminine, it is too great a stretch to firmly state that Wisdom *is* the Divine feminine.

Shechinah

A better candidate, the term most expressive of the divine feminine, is *Shechinah* (or *Shekhinah*; the *–ah* ending is a feminine form), the 'Divine Presence.' *Shechinah* is a key figure in the mystical writings of Kabbala, such as *Sefer Bahir* (*The Book of Brightness*) and *Sefer Zohar* (*The Book of Splendor*). In Kabbalah the Eternal and Infinite One (*Ein Sof*), though a transcendent unity, manifests as a personal God through divine emanations (*sefirot*). Some of these are masculine, some feminine (cf. the answer to Q. 76); the most immediate of these is the *Shechinah*. God above (masculine) yearns to be united with the Divine Presence below (feminine). Or, in other kabbalistic representations, God's left (feminine) side seeks reunification, harmony, and balance with God's right (masculine) side. This unification is a process in which human beings play an ongoing and critical role. The *Tikuney Zohar*, seventy chapters explicating portions of the biblical text of Genesis, speaks of the devotee's concentration in 'unifying' the 'Holy One, Blessed be He,' with the *Shechinah*—seeking thus the union of the masculine and the feminine elements of God. The fulfillment of this unifying is then regarded as either the assumption of the feminine into the masculine, or a balancing of the aspects—a gender equality in God.

How are human gender and gender crossings regarded?

The discussion thus far demonstrates that at least a strand depicting God using feminine images has existed from the time of the Bible. The most dramatic expression of God as feminine is found in Kabbalah in the figure of *Shechinah*, who serves as a bridge between divine transcendence and divine immanence. This Presence dwells among people and, as we shall see, can even be said to depend upon them. Yet it would be a mistake to characterize the dominant view of God in Judaism as gender fluid, or even gender neutral. For most Jews, though God is recognized as beyond either sex or gender, the primary gender association is with masculinity and the most common pronoun is 'He.' Thus, in considering human gender crossings, while there are religious texts we can draw upon to free the image of God from a unipolar gender constraint, the dominance of the patriarchal image commonly poses an obstacle to transgendered Jews.

However, there may be human examples in the Tanakh that shed helpful light on a Jewish sensibility about gender capable of embracing transgender people. These may be rooted in the sense that the original human creation was of a being, Adam, who was without sex or gender. The first century philosopher Philo of Alexandria, for example, notes in Genesis that human beings are first labeled by the generic term 'man' and only afterward assumed distinct form in the sexed bodies of male and female.[517] An originally genderless or androgynous humanity offers a foundation for later gender crossing because it both demonstrates the artificiality of gender divisions and their distance from the original creation. Crossing gender so that the social presentation is at odds with that expected for a particular body reproduces, to some degree, the original state of humanity.

But whether we impute such thinking to anyone, the Tanakh still offers examples of identity presentation that entail elements of masquerade, another aspect of transgender realities. Gender and Judaic scholar Lori Lefkovitz points to the biblical narratives of Jacob, Joseph, Moses and Esther as stories including an element of identity masquerade. Moreover, these masquerades, she believes, are relevant to how Jewish masculinities have been conceived since the 19th century. "Identity performance, it turns out, is central to the myths of the Hebrew patriarchy and matriarchy, both in biblical narrative and in the narrative traditions that elaborate on Hebrew Scriptures."[518] In short, masquerades are a part of conforming gender realities as well as nonconforming ones.

Jacob offers a particularly salient example. He is described in the Bible as "a quiet man, dwelling in tents" (Genesis 25:27)—a trait and a sphere associated with women—and he is his mother's favorite (25:28). Levkovitz reads Jacob's disguising of himself to pass as his brother Esau (Genesis 27) as a masquerade to pass as a man capable of inheriting the patriarchy. Similarly, Joseph, Moses, and Esther also engage in masquerades—each poses as a non-Jew at some point in their stories. Levkovitz sees in these narratives a playing with identity categories ('man,' 'woman,' 'Jew,' 'queer'). For example, she is convinced that Jacob's masquerade contributes to the later stereotype of "compromised Jewish masculinity"—the overbearing mother, the blind father, and a son with a confused identity—the elements also associated in the modern world with the gay male.[519]

Lefkovitz sees in these narratives images of crossdressing, too. Jacob, she says, performs a kind of crossdressing in putting on animal skins and becomes "a man in drag enacting masculinity."[520] Joseph, she notes, was seen as 'queer,' a 'crossdresser' by some Jewish commentators.[521] Women, too, 'crossdress'; she points to Tamar, Yael, Delilah, Judith, Esther, and perhaps Ruth as enacting "femininity in drag" by performing a heightened—and false—sense of femininity.[522]

While we can err in reading into ancient narratives modern ideas, it isn't inappropriate to read those materials in light of contemporary concerns and thought. In that respect, Lefkovitz offers us substance plausible in context and eminently applicable to today. Historical study depends on the premise of a very basic continuity in human nature and experience; otherwise, we would be unable to understand what we read. There is no reason not to think that the world of the Bible was one where people had multiple gender identities, crossed gender lines, and otherwise wrestled with gender issues. Though they may have comprehended those issues differently than we do, and articulated them in different ways, does not mean we cannot find in them experiences similar to our own.

The utilization of biblical personages as models has been a staple for gender conforming people. Why shouldn't gender nonconforming folk do the same? All of the figures just named—and more besides—exhibit qualities or perform acts that offer resources for transgender people to glimpse themselves. In fact, the Tanakh would be less useful if it did not provide an instructed way of living for transgender Jews as well as gender conforming ones.

Construction of the Jewish Man

Over the centuries after the destruction of the Temple in 70 C.E., the rabbis of the Talmud resculpted Judaism. The resulting construction of a Jewish culture was one adaptive to the many foreign lands a displaced people found themselves a part of. The richly complex and diverse Talmud provided resources helpful for all aspects of life, including gender. Of course, their principal concern rested on the conforming genders, particularly masculinity. Daniel Boyarin, professor of Talmudic culture and active in gender studies, argues that a deepseated ambivalence about masculinity can be found among the Talmudic rabbis and thus within the culture they shaped. "The ideal male," he writes, "seems to be feminized in this culture, but since that very ideality is openly marked as effeminate, the text—and presumably the culture—seems hopelessly ambivalent about male identity."[523]

Boyarin also contends that, "Although rabbinic Judaism also provides an array of male ideals and modalities, it fell to Ashkenazic Judaism to furnish European culture with the possibility of a male who is sexually and procreationally functioning, but otherwise gendered as if 'female' within the European economy of gender."[524] Such a man challenges the stereotype of an aggressive masculinity. Rather, this Jewish man was a gentle scholar and a family man. Thus, according to Boyarin, the very Talmudic culture that could—and did—construct a patriarchal world offered a way for men to coexist with women in a nondomineering fashion.

Gender Crossings

Of course, this also opened possibilities for gender crossing. They are attested from the biblical period onward, down to our own time. As we might expect from what we find among other religions and cultures, some of these gender crossings are transient and situational. Others are more enduring markers of gender identity.

Ancient Judaism

Inasmuch as we earlier devoted substantial attention to the issues regarding the Tanakh's prohibition of crossdressing within the Deuteronomic Code (see answers to Q. 61-63) we shall not revisit that material. Gender crossing involving crossdressing appears again in a report by the Jewish historian Josephus during the 1st century C.E.[525] Jews remained concerned not only with gender crossings in their own community but those in the world around them. For example, also in the 1st century, Philo of Alexandria denounced the Roman world's use of slave boys whose appearance yielded a calculated femininity.[526] Talmudic passages reflect the presence of transgender realities—as we saw in their wrestling with the meaning of Deuteronomy's prohibition.

The Middle Ages

The Middle Ages saw the Jewish community continuing to be dispersed thoughout the Mediterranean world and other places. A sizable and active Jewish presence grew throughout Europe. As we shall see later, gender crossing through crossdressing became a popular part of the holiday of Purim. Yet there were other gender crossings. Some of these at least hint at the presence of deeper, more abiding transgender realities than the occasional and situational crossdressing associated with festivals.

For example, there is a curious text from a medieval Jewish author noted by scholar Tova Rosen. The importance of the text lies in its transgender expression; the curiosity factor resides in our uncertainty as to whether transgender is being played for laughs or constitutes a more serious matter for the author. In the early 14th century, Qalonymos ben Qalonymos' *Evan bohan* (c. 1322) set out passages that describe a man's yearning for a woman's life. Rosen, while noting the often cursory dismissal of these texts as comic fodder, contends that a closer look shows an exploration of "the boundaries of Jewish masculinity," one that "investigates the assumptions of Jewish gender and produces a subversive critique of fundamental issues in Jewish life, the life of the man as well as the life of the woman."[527]

Among the remarkable passages in *Evan bohan* is Qalonymos ben Qalonymos' prayer to the Almighty in which, after reciting a number of miracles, he petitions, "if only you would turn me from male to female!" But this startling plea is immediately followed by a comic twist: such a divine grant would spare the petitioner from military service. However, the author also yearns, "If only the craftsman who created me would have made me a decent woman!"—and follows this wish with a recital of female activities ranging from spinning wool and cooking to gossiping with friends. Moreover, in an earlier place in the book, the author expressed his passion for fine clothes, referencing women's clothing and declaring, "O my heart, you seduced me [to desire . . .] precious attire . . . and . . . fine linen of the kind that virgin princesses wear."[528]

So what should we make of this material? At the very least, Rosen is correct in stating that the work opens up gender conventions and boundaries for consideration. Humor is often used to soften the impact of matters people are unaccustomed or uncomfortable examining. We all know that things said in jest can convey very serious messages. Also, it seems unlikely that such provocative material came from nothing in the social context to which the author's audience could relate. As seen elsewhere (cf. the answer to Q. 45), the times in which Qalonymos ben Qalonymos lived were no stranger to questions about gender. Readers likely had little difficulty identifying in the *Evan bohan* the kind of character they either knew firsthand or had heard about. The author's fantasies would have been mirrored in realistic enough fashion in his world for such words to strike a ready chord no matter how an individual reader might respond to them.

Given all we know about such matters, it is far less likely that no Jews before modern times ever had what we today call transgender identities than that some did. However, accessing such lives is complicated by numerous factors. In addition to the difficulties posed by historical distance and differences in language, culture and custom, there remain the peculiar problems associated with Jewish experience. Many representations of Jews are tainted by anti-Semitism. Those expressions arising from within the Jewish community had to keep in mind the perceptions of the majority populations around them. This meant a certain care in what they said about themselves, a tendency to put their best face forward, which would mean appearing as 'normal' and 'conventional' as possible, save for those distinctives that preserve a Jewish identity. In societies where gender nonconformity is not celebrated—a situation pertaining throughout Western culture—it isn't likely a Jewish author or community would go to any effort to point to gender variant Jews.

However, some Jewish religious authorities showed little reluctance to comment on the wider culture within which Jewish communities were embedded. In the 17th century, for instance, Rabbi John Selden (1584-1654)—chief rabbi in Renaissance England—weighed in on gender crossings. In a 1616 letter to playwright Ben Jonson he addressed the use of Deuteronomy 22:5 to justify efforts to shut down the theatrical practice of crossdressing players. Following Maimonides, Selden argued that the text refers to women wearing the martial dress of men for worship purposes, and men dressed as women for the veneration of Venus.[529] A scholar of immense reach, Selden wrote at some extent on the nature of sex and gender with respect to conceptions of deity, arguing that throughout the ancient world the gods were seen as both male and female.[530] English scholar Jason Rosenblatt, an expert on Selden, argues that Selden's ideas about the fluidity of both gender and identity have important bearing on our own day's questions on these matters.[531]

In a tradition rich in identity masquerades that illustrate, among other things, the malleability of gender, surely there is room for today's transgendered Jews. Indeed, there are some who argue that Judaism occupies a place in the first rank of world religions offering acceptance to at least some people placed under the wider transgender umbrella—notably gays and lesbians. But perhaps that is an easier step in a religious system where rituals and obligations are based on the Western pairing of gender with sex, with the former dependent on the latter. In other words, a homosexual orientation that does not disturb this sex-gender pairing also does not pose the kind of problem prompted by gender variance. As long as a male body with a masculine presentation does what it is supposed to, and a female body with a feminine presentation stays to its pre-scribed sphere, all may be well. At the very least, a 'don't ask, don't tell' philoso-phy can prevail. But manifest gender crossings in a religious context are prob-lematic, as we will see.

However, there are voices within contemporary Judaism proclaiming an op-timism about the contributions of transgender Jews to Jewish life today. For example, historian and Jewish studies scholar David Sneer and sociologist Caryn Aviv maintain that despite the particularly complicated relationship transgender Jews have with "the binary mode of Jewish gender/sexual politics," their very questioning of the established constructions is "inherently liberationist." They add that, "we see the special place transgender people have in bringing together the transformation of existing structures and the simultaneous liberation from them."[532]

There are other matters pertinent to this idea, other forces at play. Like all major religions, Judaism has been faced with modern social movements toward greater gender egalitarianism in both secular and religious matters. These exert a pressure on those whose interpretation of the spirit of Judaism depends on a gender hierarchy. Rabbinic Judaism—the core of Orthodox and Conservative traditions—sets out a gender order that typically relegates femininity second place in a two-gender system. This is more than a merely formal matter of divid-ing religious duties. As Sarah Benor shows, in Orthodox circles the very con-struction of a masculine identity incorporates sex-based distinctions in religious education and language.[533]

Shaul Magid remarks, "The problem of gender inequality in Jewish law is not only about particular issues, such as synagogue rituals, women serving as witnesses, or marital law; it goes to the very core of rabbinic Judaism."[534] Magid contends that the problem is philosophical as well as a matter of religious juris-prudence. For modern Jews to embrace gender equality *and* remain within rab-binic Judaism, the challenge is not simply finding rabbinic precedents, but to engage the issue of gender philosophically in order to create new 'dogma' within the *halakhic* (legal) tradition. The problems faced by anyone who is not a con-forming, expressing masculine male can be considerable.

Halakhah, whether found in the Tanakh or rabbinic tradition, assumes a gender dualism despite the many musings of Rabbis on gender and sex variance. The setting forth in religious law of prescribed behaviors and prohibited ones, when gender distinctions are drawn, sets them down in terms of masculine males and feminine females. Thus, for example, eunuchs are described in the Deuteronomic code in terms of disturbed maleness (Deut. 23:1). The rabbis distinguished between *seris hamma* (eunuchs born that way) and *seris adam* (eunuchs made by human action),[535] but in either instance what matters is the same as in the Torah—the person is a nonprocreative male. In a religious tradition where an esteemed sage such as Rabbi Eliezer can proclaim, "Any Jew who does not have a wife is not a man,"[536] the inferior status of the eunuch is ensured. Unlike surrounding societies, in Judaism the eunuch has no special place, no unique ritual role.[537]

In contemporary Judaism, transgender people—especially transsexuals—replace the attention once given to eunuchs, just as today's intersex stand in for yesterday's hermaphrodites, about whom the rabbinic tradition has much to say. We shall examine these situations more in a moment, but first we need to underscore the *halakhic* reality: Jewish law and ritual as traditionally formulated relies on a sex and gender dualism. For transgender Jews this is an uncomfortable truth but not a hopeless situation. The genius of the *halakhic* tradition always has been its flexibility in interpreting and applying Torah to fit contemporary situations not in sight when the Law was first being set down in written form. The Oral Torah's very existence depends on the conviction that God gives an instructed way of living to every generation. Contemporary rabbinic efforts to apply Torah to today's situations continue the past's process of debate within the community to ascertain and conform to God's Torah. In this debate transgender people are not without supporters.

Gender Crossings & Contemporary Judaism

However, whether in terms of Jewish law and tradition, philosophy, or some other approach, many modern Jews—including religious leaders and scholars—are wrestling anew with gender and sexual issues. These contemporary considerations include questions related to sexual orientation (e.g., can homosexual people be ordained rabbis?) and matters of transgender.[538] The former represents a modern matter related to the issue of sacred gender crossing. The latter represents an even broader reappraisal of gender, a matter taken for granted by most Jews in a long entrenched dualism.

As noted before, the matter of sexual orientation may be less a problem than, say, transsexualism because homosexuality *per se* does not necessitate gender crossing. One can be a masculine male or feminine female and possess a relatively fixed erotic attraction pattern for members of the same sex. On the other hand, transsexuals, transvestites, and transgenderists confound expected sex-gender pairings. Rabbi Alon Levkovitz correctly points out that despite some midrashic tales of changed sex, neither the biblical nor rabbinic traditions offer a logic about transgender realities that make contemporary discussion easy. But it isn't impossible to reason out matters like transsexualism. Levkovitz offers the example of Rabbi Eliezer Waldenburg, head of Israel's Supreme Rabbinical Court, who argues that while sex reassignment surgery may violate established *halakhah* (e.g., forbidding castration), the higher law of preserving life may cast such acts in a different light—and one consequence that serves *halakhic* interest is that such surgery aligns sex and gender, making fitting into a recognized sex-gender pairing possible.[539]

As this example illustrates, for many Jews whatever answer they come to must come in the context of one or another Judaic text tradition. The rabbinic tradition offers a rich, even bewildering collection of documents, with a variety of texts that might be considered more or less relevant to questions of gender and transgender. Rabbinical student Danya Ruttenberg observes that the Talmudic rabbis distinguished as many as seven genders, debating matters of status, religious obligations and roles for each, yet still failed to describe the kind of gendered realities seen in our world today.[540] Their approach presents a strictly hierarchical gender order, though it acknowledges exceptional realities.[541]

On the other hand, the Kabbalah's interest in dualities unifying allows more play for both main genders—and thus potentially for variant genders. In fact, gender transformations may be seen as critical to Jewish experience and to the hope of redemption. Religious scholar Talya Fishman, who specializes in Jewish intellectual and cultural history of the medieval and early modern periods, remarks:

> A recent study of sefirotic dynamics within zoharic Kabbalah sheds light on the process of cosmic gender transformation which underlies the historical experience of exile, redemption, and revelation. The separation of male and female aspects of Divinity is responsible for the unredeemed state of the Jewish people and reflects that condition.[542]

But, Fishman observes, reunification of the masculine (right side) and feminine (left side) aspects of Godhead is not something that can be accomplished in one grand gesture. The experience of exile is one of imbalance between feminine (the left side of judgment) and masculine (the right side of love) attributes. Though the latter, through the onset of redemption, enfolds the former within itself, thus effecting a kind of reunification, it does not thereby achieve harmony and balance. Instead, the feminine aspect is present, but hidden. A balance must be achieved between the sides and attributes. This ongoing process is symbolized in Jewish ritual practice, as the *Sefer HaKanah* explains women's obligation to eat *mazzah* the first night of Passover. The act participates symbolically in the onset of redemption. The feminine *mazzah* undergoes an apparent transformation into an 'unblemished male lamb.' Thus the feminine gender symbol (*maz-*

zah) becomes the masculine gender symbol (male lamb). In this way the participant actively initiates desired change in the Godhead.[543]

Just as God is both masculine and feminine, and strives to unite them, so also ought human beings—made in God's image—to follow the divine example. The *Zohar* advises, "It behooves a man to be 'male and female,' always, .../ in order that the Shekhinah may never leave him./ Moreover, it is his duty, once back home,/ to give his wife pleasure, inasmuch as it was she/ who obtained for him the Heavenly Union."[544] Here we see that the goal of uniting the genders is placed in the practical context of sexual union between a man and woman (cf. Genesis 2:24).

Still, the mystical tradition can be patriarchal, too. The masculine aspect of God is transcendent, like a Father gone off to work, while the maternal presence of the *Schechinah* remains on earth, pining after Him. In the same way, a man being 'both male and female' can mean much less than expressing his feminine side if simply getting married and having sex will do the trick. Yet the language and imagery in Kabbalah have been appropriated by some Jews as an aid in facilitating movement toward gender equality. Likewise it may provide resources for transgendered Jews.

How does crossdressing enter into Jewish religious life?

Historically there has been no place for literal gender crossing in specifically ritual matters, though some symbolic gender crossings have a place, especially in the mystic tradition. We see the exclusion of gender crossings in religious matters through the regard of gender variant people in traditional Judaic injunctions and prohibitions. Some have understood Deuteronomy's prohibition of female crossdressing to be aimed at preventing women from usurping male privilege in the Temple (which was segregated such that women were literally left on the outer margins). Intersex people—'hermaphrodites'—were relegated to a position below women.[545] Eunuchs, prominent in some ancient religions (see answer to Q. 76), had no official religious role in ancient Judaism, though they are not uniformly excluded (see the answer to Q. 66). Ancient Judaism, unlike many of the religions around it, eschewed gender crossings by its priests. In short, in light of this history, gender crossings as specifically religious acts are easily interpreted as a foreign idea that Jews ought to resist.

The same sentiment prevails in contemporary Judaism. Crossdressing has no place *ritually*. Yet that does not divorce it entirely from religious concerns. While it would be an exaggeration to say that crossdressing is at all a prominent religious concern in contemporary Judaism, the issue does occasionally arise. When it does, it is typically in connection with one or another of these three questions:

- ❑ Are some items of religious dress exclusively reserved for males?
- ❑ Is crossdressing permissible in any festive holiday setting?
- ❑ How shall crossdressers be regarded?

We shall grapple with each of these in order.

Religious Dress

Traditionally, certain religious clothing items have been worn only by Jewish males. These include the *kippah* (or *kippa*; Yiddish *yarmulke*), used to cover the head, the *tallith* (or *tallis*; prayer shawl), and the *tefillin* (phylacteries—two square black boxes, fastened together, containing Torah sections and worn like an amulet). The *halakhah* (or *halachah*) exempts women and children from so-called 'positive' commandments (i.e., things one ought to do), such as the obligation to wear these items. For the most part, it is women wearing the *kippah* that generates comment as an alleged instance of 'crossdressing.' Wearing of the other items by women is much rarer.

Scholar Suzanne Baizerman asks what would seem to be logical questions: "Are the *kippa* and *tallis* distinctly male items of attire? Does the donning of a *kippa* or a *tallis* violate the biblical injunction against cross-sex dressing?"[546] Certainly, with respect to what seems to be the sense of Deuteronomy, women wearing religious items reserved for men constitutes the very kind of violation the text prohibits. If we should protest that *kippah* are gender neutral articles, we face two problems: first, that in itself would not obviate an act of dress behavior by women in a religious context where the article in question is supposed to be worn only by men. Second, Baizerman, a museum curator and textiles scholar, demonstrates that items like the *kippah* (specifically the *kippa sruga*, one crocheted and multicolored) are used in the construction of gender. If, as she observes, the making, giving, and wearing of this item of dress reinforces gender categories within a group where gender distinctions are important, than the implicit answer is obvious—yes, such dress behavior would be crossdressing.

And yet . . . being *exempt* from the performance of a commandment is not the same as being *forbidden* to undertake it. Neither does custom have the force of ordinance. The fact is that some women, particularly in the United States, do put on *kippah* (and sometimes other religious apparel). They would doubtless be mortified by the suggestion that in voluntarily performing a *mitzvah* they might be construed as violating the Torah's prohibition of crossdressing. Yet, as we have seen, that prohibition is by no means clearly applicable to much of what the contemporary world views as crossdressing. So the matter remains open.

With respect to other instances of crossdressing in a religious context, such as males in feminine apparel or females in masculine wear attending synagogue, there is no answer that fits all situations. In an Orthodox synagogue, where men and women are separated, the issue has more salience than in a Reform synagogue where the sexes mix. The Orthodox would likely see crossdressing in this setting as an improper mixing of the sexes rather than as appropriate because of the crossdressing individual's gender identity. Where body sex is given priority over gender, such a conclusion is rather certain. Conservative and Reform congregations are likely to take a more relaxed stance, especially if the religious acts being performed by congregants do not depend on status as a man or woman. In Reform synagogues women wearing *kippah* is generally a nonissue. It seems unlikely a crossdressed person would be seen as violating any religious precept, though some might apply the prohibition of Deuteronomy. Most who would object, regardless of being Orthodox, Conservative, or Reform, probably would do so based on cultural values rather than religious ones.

Purim

As might be expected from the variety of ways the Torah's presentation of crossdressing is understood (see the answer to Q. 63), Jewish practice tolerates some diversity in practice. We just saw that as a possibility with regard to some religious dress, though we noted a number of factors that come into play. Jewish religious settings can be construed to include the home, especially on Shabbat. Even just with respect to the synagogue, in broad strokes the occasions involved would include Shabbat services, bar and bat mitzvah ceremonies, weddings, funerals, and the like, and various religious holidays.

We already considered in a general sense how crossdressing might be construed in a synagogue. But we need to devote particular attention to one special situation: the holiday of Purim. Just as Christianity has Halloween, where costumes are put on and crossdressing occurs, so Judaism has Purim as a festive occasion where such behavior might occur. This is definitely a religious observance, even though much in connection with it seems very secular.

The Role of Reversals in Purim

For centuries in the festivities of Purim—a holiday celebrating the events recounted in the biblical book of Esther—some Jews have practiced crossdressing. Given the story, this is not surprising. Judaic scholar Monford Harris notes of the biblical book that it is full of "amazing reversals." This 'topsy-turvy' quality, Harris remarks, from the first has been understood by the Jewish people. It is expressed in the popular view that at Purim the Jews become *goyim* (Gentiles), and the *goyim* become Jews. The holiday custom of wearing costumes is rooted in the biblical account, where changes of clothing (e.g., Mordecai's dressing in royal robes) are highly significant. Not only may a celebrant dress as Mordecai or Esther (both Jews), but also as Haman (a Gentile). Moreover, they may cross genders in their costuming. Harris quotes the hasidic rebbe Abraham Joshua Heschel of Apta, who wrote, "As we see in the days of Purim: when a man changes his garments and dresses in the garments of a woman, pleasure and joy result from this. Truly, the essence of pleasure comes about because of a change of a thing to its opposite."[547]

Though crossdressing is not explicitly rooted in the text, Harris believes it is an important aspect of the holiday. He roots his conclusion in biblical reasoning. The Tanakh concerns itself with human beings as reproductive creatures who continue on—they generate themselves. Generations (*toldot*) create both

Israel and Jewish history under God's dominion, even though the book of Esther lacks both God's name and emphasizes a threat to the generating of the Jewish people. The story is about the potential end to Jewish history. Harris contends this threat to continuing as a people is why the Jews of Eastern Europe adopted crossdressing as part of the festival. They were enacting the denial of *toldot* in the scroll. The crossdressing means an exchange of social roles, but Harris argues it also implicitly entails an exchange of *biological* roles. A man stops being male and a woman ceases being female. This means the end of family—and that means the end of history. Harris comments, "Wearing the clothes of the opposite sex, Jews opt out of *toldot*, and become *goyim*, strangers, representatives of the dangerous outside world." Crossdressing thus captures something essential and intrinsic to the Purim story.[548]

Purimspiel

Regardless of whether we view crossdressing as having the importance Harris finds, it is clear that in practice it had a very visible role through the *Purimspiel*, a Jewish folk festival celebrating Purim in early modern Europe (15th century onward). By the 18th century, *Purimspiel* performances were drawing sizable Christian crowds alongside the Jewish celebrants.[549] Israeli theater scholar Ahuva Belkin contends that both Purim and *Purimspiel* served to express the pent-up feelings of folk whose ordinary lives were spent under the dominance of the wealthy, powerful, and privileged. "The theme of the reversal of fortunes of the strong and weak, as found in the original stories of the Biblical canon," writes Belkin, "became a salient theme in the Purimspiel, expressing the frustration of the community's poor and underprivileged."[550]

Belkin views the practice of *Purimspiel* as influenced by the Christian practices found in Carnival (see the answer to Q. 71). In the Jewish version, the male celebrants would don masks—many also dressed in women's clothes—and parade through the streets, stopping now and again to bargain entertainment in exchange for food and money.[551] The acting out of the biblical story was done with male actors in all the parts, and the *Purimspiel* frequently utilized ribald jokes about women, misogynous songs, and lewd remarks. "Throughout," says Belkin, "it is the male characters who establish the 'nature' of the female characters—and women in general—by their comments about them."[552] The crossdressing added to the exaggerated qualities of *Purimspiel*. Clothes might be on backwards or upside-down. The men in female garb wore rags in contrast to the masculine finery of those playing male parts. Judicious padding with pillows, donning a wig or scarf, and adding other feminine elements all conveyed the appearance of a woman, but a highly exaggerated one. No effort was made by the men playing women to appear as real women. In intent and effect, the crossdressing supported the dominance of men in the gender hierarchy.[553]

Given the purposes to which crossdressing was put in the *Purimspiel* it is little wonder Jewish religious authorities might have differing feelings about it. But irrespective of the festival, the broader question of the practice in celebrating Purim remained. At least some rabbis concluded it was acceptable. For example, in the late 15th century, scholar Rabbi Yehuda Mintz of Padua permitted the practice, writing in a *Responsa*:

> Great and righteous ones of blessed memory, in whose surroundings I was brought up, [who] saw their sons and daughters, sons-in-law and daughters-in-law wearing such masks as well as switching clothing from men's attire to women's and vice versa. And if, heaven forbid, there had been the slightest transgression involved, heaven forbid, that they would be silent and not protest—surely they had proofs and authoritative sources that demonstrate that this [practice] is absolutely permissible.[554]

This was a ruling not universally endorsed by his colleagues.[555] Some worried over behavior that might accompany successful masquerades (unlike those of the *Purimspiel*). Over time a rather informal line came to be drawn: obvious crossdressing—the kind where the real sex of the celebrant is never in doubt—could pass as unobjectionable. The drawing of a distinction between crossdressing done for 'gaity,' as at Purim, and that pursued in order to gain improper access to members of the opposite sex, has been widely embraced, though not all Jews accept it.

What is religious life like for contemporary transgendered Jews?

Today, transgender Jews are an increasingly visible part of Jewish life,[556] and that inevitably includes the sphere of religion. Varying views reflect the pluralism of modern Jewish life, even among religious scholars. Homosexuality, for instance, is variously appraised even by the Orthodox.[557] The dilemmas for a religious transgendered Jew typically focus around the gender identity they must express to fulfill religious obligations without censure. For example, when standing at the Western Wall (Wailing Wall) of the Temple in Jerusalem, on which side—the one represented by their gender or the one matching their genetic sex—shall a transgendered person stand to pray?[558] But dilemmas extend everywhere religion does. How does one respond—or does one?—when a Rabbi, upon learning a guest at a wedding identifies herself as a lesbian and introduces her partner of a quarter century, quickly withdraws his hand, turns, and walks away?[559] A multitude of similar dilemmas could easily be produced.

Orthodox View on Sex Reassignment

Various religious scholars have chimed in with their views on matters related to transgender realities. For example, Rabbi David Bleich, a Talmud scholar and teacher at Yeshiva University, surveyed Orthodox religious opinions on the permissibility of sex change operations. He found a consensus from the Orthodox position that sexual reassignment surgeries are not religiously permitted for either sex. In this view, gender and sex are irrevocably fixed and paired at birth. For males the operation is forbidden because castration occurs (see Leviticus 22:24 or Deuteronomy 23:2 in the Tanakh); for females it is forbidden because it results in sterilization (see Shabbat 110b in the Talmud).[560]

Reform View on Transsexualism

But not all religious Jews are Orthodox (and there are divisions even within Orthodoxy). The Reformed tradition is the most liberal in Judaism. The Central Conference of American Rabbis (CCAR) addressed the question of transsexualism in the context of a MtF transsexual's petition to convert and be married within Judaism. The CCAR noted the Torah prohibition of admitting into the assembly one whose testicles have been crushed, but pointed out that injunction was already being mitigated in biblical days (see Isaiah 56:3ff.), and was understood in rabbinic tradition to prevent marriage but not Jewish status. Therefore, they do not object in principle to conversion by a transsexual person. With respect to sex reassignment surgery, the CCAR acknowledges the Halakhic prohibition in general, while noting that even so some exceptions have been affirmed in the case of intersexed infants. The CCAR, however, goes further in affirming that *"Reform also would accept the findings of modern science, which holds that external genitalia may not reflect the true identity of the individual"* (italics in original). In at least one instance of local practice a Reform Rabbi has permitted a transsexual to marry (*kiddushin*), and a CCAR Responsa Committee has allowed sex reassignment surgery and marriage.[561]

Congregation Beth Simchat Torah

There are Jewish religious communities that have proven especially welcoming to transgender people. Congregation Beth Simchat Torah (CBST) in New York, which is not affiliated with any Jewish movement or denomination, is the largest of these. At its website, CBST declares it is "dedicated to the proposition that gay, lesbian, bisexual and transgender (GLBT) Jews are wholly legitimate members of the Jewish People, are equally legitimate members of civil society, and have a unique and essential contribution to make to the life of Judaism and to the larger society in which we live." Founded in 1973, CBST is located in a metropolitan area that they estimate has 200,000 GLBT Jews. The congregation has grown to include over 800 households and maintains a visible presence in the life of New York City and beyond.[562]

Transgender Dilemmas

Still, many Jewish religious communities (Synagogues or Temples) find interacting with transgendered Jews difficult because their culture's bipolar masculine/feminine gender order leaves no room for them. Cole Krawitz, a female-to-male transgendered person writes eloquently of the practical and emotional difficulties in trying to remain religiously faithful in such an environment. Raised in a deeply religious family, Krawitz' gender identity means longing to wear the *kippah* ('cap') and donning the *tallith* ('prayer shawl')—items reserved for men in conservative religious circles—in a place where the gender presentation, and attendant privileges permitted must strictly pair with genital sex. When dressed in masculine presentation to attend services with family, Krawitz must explain why *kippah* and *tallith* are not put on, thus "requiring me to erase myself each time to appease my parents."[563] Other religious experiences, like participating in a weekend retreat, can also prove alienating and dehumanizing. Even when Jewish people banded to move Judaism toward greater inclusiveness, Krawitz found that meant only *some* (notably gay, lesbian and bisexual people) of those within transgendered communities. In Krawitz' view what is needed is an openness among Jewish leaders to let transgendered people—of every kind—define themselves and their own liberation. Krawitz writes, "I call for a day when halakhah will not have been changed to 'prove' our worth, because halakhah never reflected our worth in the first place."[564]

Welcoming Congregations

There has been some movement in Judaism to respond to transgender Jews. For example, at the beginning of the 21st century there were over two dozen synagogues in North America that identified as LGBT (Lesbian, Gay, Bisexual, Transgender).[565] Among the major traditions, Reform Judaism has taken the lead. In 2000, the CCAR, leading Reform Jews, approved rabbis officiating at 'rituals of union' for same-sex couples.[566] In March, 2003, the Reform Commission on Social Action passed a resolution entitled 'Support for the Inclusion and Acceptance of the Transgender and Bisexual Communities.' After briefly reviewing the state of transgender and bisexual people in the modern culture, then citing the Torah's affirmation that *all* human beings are created *b'tselem Elohim* ('in the image of God'), and placing it alongside the Torah's injunction 'Do not stand idly by while your neighbor bleeds' (Leviticus 19:16), the committee resolved:

- ❑ First, that the 1977 policy on 'Human Rights of Homosexuals' be fully applied to transgender and bisexual people.
- ❑ Second, that legislation opposing discrimination based on gender identity should be supported, as should also allowing individuals to be treated under the law as the gender by which they identify.
- ❑ Third, that congregations adopt inclusive policies.

❑ Fourth, that the CCAR and the American Conference of Cantors be invited to discuss how transgender Jews might participate ritually.[567]

In the first years of the new millennium both Reform and Reconstructionist seminaries held symposia on the subject of transgender Jewish concerns.[568] In 2003, FtM transsexual Reuben Zellman became the first openly transgender Jew to be accepted into a Jewish rabbinical school.[569] Internationally, the World Congress of Gay, Lesbian, Bisexual and Transgender Jews: Keshet Ga'avah consists of some four dozen member organizations from more than a dozen countries.[570]

But the reality for many transgender Jews remains more like that described by Cole Krawitz. Religiously inclined transgender Jews are likely to find obstacles everywhere. Even mental health circles can pose a problem. A transgender Jew who wants a counselor who identifies as a religious Jew may find that counselor refusing to offer treatment on the grounds that Jewish law forbids it.[571] What the future holds for transgender people within Judaism is uncertain, but it will likely reflect both the persistence of transgender Jews in seeking inclusion and efforts to understand the *halakhic* tradition in such a manner that synagogues and temples become more welcoming places.

Q. 78 What role has crossdressing played in Islam?

The Short answer. Islam is a major world religion rapidly growing in the United States and influential throughout the world. With respect to gender and dress, Islam traditionally has supported both rigid gender distinctions and formal, gender-differentiated dress codes. Nevertheless, like the older Western religions of Judaism and Christianity, Islam's experience of transgender realities is complex. In its extensive and varied texts and traditions, Islamic theology preserves a sense of divine femininity alongside the dominant sense of divine masculinity because Allah transcends gender. The religious legal tradition acknowledges transgender realities and distinguishes, for example, among intersexed individuals, homosexuals, transsexuals and transvestites. Throughout its history Islam has known crossdressing practitioners. More often than not this practice has been tolerated, if not officially approved. However, those who oppose transgender identity and presentation often do so forcefully; those in power in Islamic societies sometimes have sanctioned strong penalties against transgendered people, especially homosexuals. The intersexed, by contrast, have fared better, enjoying certain protections under Islamic law. The religious law (*Shari'ah*) draws upon not only the sacred text of Islam's holiest book, the Qur'an (or, Koran), but also from other sources, most notably accounts relating a narration of a saying or act of the Prophet (*hadith*). The *Shari'ah* is a 'living' body in that it continues to be interpreted and applied to contemporary situations. Particularly of interest in this respect are the learned opinions (*fatwas*) issued in response to questions and petitions. These rulings offer some insight into how Muslim authorities today regard various transgender realities. Despite the common perception by many non-Muslims that Islamic thought is uniformly censorious, the actual reality is that Islamic scholarship displays breadth and vitality of discussion and view. Further, Muslim societies also vary in their adherence and expression of Islam. The result is that transgender people have varying experiences in different parts of the Islamic world. But, as elsewhere and as under other forms of religion, Muslims who experience and express transgender realities of one kind or another somehow carve out for themselves some space in which they continue to live both as transgender, or third gender people, and as Muslims.

The Longer Answer. In lands like the United States, Islam too frequently receives cursory and biased attention. In truth, Muslims are as diverse in their habits and views as adherents of other religions, and Islamic society is neither as rigid nor uniform as often depicted. For example, Islam is typically pictured as a male-dominated religion—a representation that generally is superficial even if it is accurate. Some Americans view all Muslim men as bullies and all Muslim women as passive and submissive, hidden behind veils and layers of clothing. However, despite the patriarchal character of the religion as expressed in the Islamic world today, there are many Muslim men who respect and advocate greater rights for women, there are Muslim women who identify themselves as feminists, and there are groups of 'gender-bending' people—all of whom claim for themselves legitimacy as followers of Allah and his blessed Prophet. So, while it is fair to claim that modern Islam embraces a generally rigid dichotomous view of gender, both in its conception of Allah and in the world of Muslim practice, actual expressions of gender among the faithful still can prove remarkably fluid. Indeed, if Allah can encompass and express gender traits associated with both males and females, then Muslim people can do so, too. Some have done so through transgender identity, including behavior such as cross-dressing.

How does gender figure in Islamic thinking?

In our effort to understand Islam and to be fair to its complex realities, we must seek to avoid either demonizing what we do not like or fantasizing that things are better than they are. The evidence of contemporary Islamic life is that the robustness and fluidity in how gender can be conceived is often overshadowed by the more common reality of a relatively rigid patriarchalism in Islamic societies. Yet it does not require much looking to find expressions of a deep awareness about the uncertain nature of both sex and gender in human reality. Indeed, like most religions, Islam also extends gender fluidity to descriptions of the divine. It is with theological musings about the nature of Allah that we must begin, because Islamic thought seeks always to submit itself to the divine nature and will.

Gender & the Divine

Monotheistic, Islam proclaims that Allah is the only God. According to some, the Arabic word *Allah* is the equivalent to the English word 'God.' Others regard the term 'Allah' as a unique name that neither should be translated into any other tongue, nor perceived as a synonym for the perhaps generic term 'God.' Various authors differ, too, on how the relation of Allah to gender ought to be conceived. Islamic scholar Iftikhar Ahmed Mehar remarks, "The important fact to observe is that the word 'Allah' cannot be made plural, nor can it be associated with a masculine or feminine gender."[572] Yet, the early 20th century Western scholar Mohammed Marmaduke Pickthall wrote in his translation of the Qur'an, "The word *Allah* has neither feminine nor plural and has never been applied to anything other than the unimagineable Supreme Being."[573] Of course, from a grammatical point of view this may be a fact, but it is an unremarkable one. The common practice has been to refer to Allah using this grammatical gender. Thus, the pronoun most often found with Allah is 'he.'

Early 20th century scholars, in particular, sometimes looked to history to explain the name 'Allah'; their research may help explain why Allah came to be predominantly associated with masculinity. In pre-Islamic Arabia, the polytheistic society included tribal gods both masculine and feminine. Allah was a name associated with a masculine god during this time, and by the advent of Islam already had attained a stature above the local tribal gods. Among the feminine deities, al-Uzza (sometimes identified with Venus), Manat, and Al-Lat (or, Allat; the name has been reckoned to be the feminine form of 'Allah'), were sometimes identified as the 'daughters of Allah,' another indication of Allah's pre-eminence over them—and perhaps indirectly also of the subordination of the feminine to the masculine. [574] The history of the word, conjoined with its grammatical gender, and added with common practice, all add up to the easy impression that Allah is a masculine deity, despite any formal declaration of gender transcendence.

The above considerations thus suggest that Allah cannot be connected to the feminine. But the easy impression is not a completely accurate one. Islamic scholarship recognizes that because Allah transcends gender, in theory either grammatical gender is equally logical for use—and such has sometimes been the case. Ibn al-'Arabî, author of the *Fusûs al-hikam* and the *Tarjumân al-ashwâq*, is among the Muslim writers who have proclaimed it permissible to refer to Allah as either *huwa* (masc., 'He') or *hiya* (fem., 'She'). After all, both masculine and feminine (e.g., 'wise,' 'merciful') qualities belong to Allah. Particularly in Sufism, Islam's mystical tradition, Allah is depicted as feminine (cf. Jalal al-Din Rumi's *Masnavi*, I.2437), the Beloved One (the *ma'shûq*), and even the Divine Mother (cf. *Masnavi*, V.701).[575]

Finally, we should remember that Muslims do not depict Allah in any visual manner, thus shunning any image that would suggest a bodily form. Allah is neither male nor female in sex, and by Muslim gender logic accordingly neither masculine nor feminine. Any and all gender designations are metaphorical in nature. But that does not render them unimportant, both because metaphors are essential to human thinking and because using gender language forms is inescapable. The gender of pronouns and words attached to Allah *do* matter. Perhaps, then, we would do well to heed the observation of Indian writer V. A. Mohammed Ashrof: "It should also be noted that while 'Allah', the name of God revealed and worshipped, is grammatically masculine, the name of the unknowable and inscrutable divine essence, *Dhat*, is grammatically feminine. This provides to theological discourse in Arabic a sort of gender counterpoint and dialectic."[576]

Therefore, it is not entirely beyond the realm of possibility to suggest that Islamic vocabulary offers a way to see the transgendered, too, as reflections of the divine. If Allah transcends the gender of human masculinity and femininity, so carefully circumscribed and set apart from one another, no less do transgender Muslims. Or, if Allah can with appropriateness be referred to by both masculine and feminine words, why not also transgender people, who in their experience and identity connect to the dominant genders in ways that make it no easier to pin them to one or the other than is proper to do so with Allah? In short, there seems no compelling reason for transgender Mulims not to claim an affinity with the nature of Allah any less than any other gendered person. Yet, in Muslim thinking such conclusions have been avoided. Nevertheless, because Islam is a living religion, there remains hope among transgender Muslims that further consideration may discover more room for them within the community.

Genders

As we have remarked, in general practice Islam seems to support a rigid gender dualism with the conforming genders (masculinity and femininity) dominant. Modern Islam, much like the other Western religions, statically pairs masculine gender with male sex and femininity with female sex. Islam, generally more so than Judaism or Christianity, continues to prescribe a number of social markers to identify individuals as belonging to one or the other of these two genders, and for using those markers to keep them apart. Each gender is accorded a sphere of primary activity, and each is given expectations for when and how contact with the other gender is to proceed.

We shall return to these markers in a moment, but first we should caution that once more the matter is not as simple as a first look might suggest. Islam is not as inflexible as it might appear at a casual glance. The adherence to a two sex/two gender scheme proves not to be exclusive of other possibilities. Within Islamic culture gender statuses other than merely 'masculine' and 'feminine' can be recognized, and are. Malaysian scholar Yik Koon Teh contends that Islam recognizes four distinct gender groups:

- ❑ Masculine male;
- ❑ Feminine female;
- ❑ *Khunsa* (hermaphrodites); and,
- ❑ *Mukhannis* (male transsexuals) or *Mukhannas* (male transvestites).

The last group, though recognized as a distinct gender presentation, is often socially discouraged from acting feminine through crossdressing, use of makeup, or seeking to enhance a feminine form through taking hormones or surgery.[577] Even though labels exist to identify some groups, their members are pressured to exhibit a gender conformity consonant with their body sex.

Before we attend further to the *khunsa* and *mukhannathun* (i.e., *Mukhannis* and *Mukhannas*), we must offer a very brief consideration of masculinity and femininity—the dominant genders. These are conveniently refered to as the 'conforming genders' because they are defined by the expectations of a society for the personality characteristics, gender identities, and gender roles associated with becoming and living as socially approved 'men' and 'women.'[578]

Muslim societies exhibit the same kind of gender hierarchy as found throughout the Western world. Men hold higher status and exert more power than do women. Even Turkey, arguably the most liberal Muslim land, shows recognition of this hierarchy in multiple ways. Parents there—by a 86% to 14% margin according to one study—strongly prefer having boys to girls. Division of labor falls along gender lines; a man who does 'woman's work' (e.g., domestic or child-rearing activities) is seen as shameful. Stereotypes about personality differences between men and women remain widely embraced. Women are commonly viewed as more childlike, emotional and dependent, while men are regarded as stronger and more active. Some evidence does suggest such stereotypes may be weakening, at least among the young adults attending universities. A study reported in 2005 finds evidence for more endorsement of traits like 'independent,' 'assertive,' and 'self-sufficient' for both men and women.[579]

Our concern here, though, is the extent to which conventional stereotypes of masculinity and femininity reflect an intrinsic Islamic perspective. Does the religion itself endorse such views?[580] The typical manner in which this question is addressed is by focusing on women since they are commonly contended to be in a disadvantageous position. However, an Islamic conception of masculinity needs also to be considered, because Islam regards the genders as made relationally so that any discussion of one proceeds with the other in mind. Whichever gender is the focus, Muslims appeal to the Qur'an and to the *Sunnah* (the Prophet's sayings and deeds) and *ahadith* (reports, or narrations, by others of the Prophet's sayings and deeds). These texts rank in authority in the order just presented. As we might expect, the nature of the texts, together with the distance between ourselves and the texts' original context, results in varying appraisals of what is said about men and women.

Although it is beyond our scope here to explore this problem at any length, we can offer an example of the nature of the difficulty facing us. The Qur'an in its fourth Surah presents materials that have been utilized by different Muslims in varying ways. The Surah begins:

> Men, have fear of your Lord, who created you from a single soul. From that soul He created its mate, and through them He bestrewed the earth with countless men and women.[581]

On the one hand, the text extols the origin from Allah of both genders. On the other hand, it is men who are addressed, and it is they who have precedence; from the masculine soul comes 'its mate.'

The Surah proceeds to deal with a number of familial matters. For instance, mothers are to be honored. Any woman who is married must be treated equably and her dowry bestowed to her as a free gift. Women have a right to inherit. They also have a right to trial if accused of sexual impropriety. Likewise, they are afforded protection if divorced. These positive matters are all in a context, though, that presumes the woman's identity within roles as wife and mother. Her orbit is around a man—and other women may share it. A man may have more than one wife, and he may divorce a wife at will. A female inherits only half of what a male does.[582] The entire presentation suggests a preeminence for men, and subordination of women, that is then made explicit:

> Men have authority over women because God has made the one superior to the other, and because they spend their wealth to maintain them. Good women are obedient. They guard their unseen parts because God has guarded them. As for those from whom you fear disobedience, admonish them and send them to beds apart and beat them. Then if they obey you, take no further action against them. God is high, supreme.[583]

Much later in the Surah we are told that, "the believers who do good works, both men and women, shall enter Paradise. They shall not suffer the least injustice."[584] Women, no less than men, can earn the reward of Paradise. Like men, Allah protects them from injustice. Yet the context of their righteousness is construed in their roles adjacent and subordinate to men.[585]

To most American eyes the state of affairs described above seems terribly sexist if not outrightly misogynstic. They might decry the practice of multiple wives and the apparent constraints placed on women. Yet many Muslims have a different take on the matter, as explained by a historian of Islam, Yvonne Yazbeck Haddad: "Defenders of Islamic traditionalism believe that in a genuine Islamic society current inequities will disappear. Islamic laws, they argue, guarantee the woman's control of her household."[586] So what if a woman's sphere is different from a man's, if her role within it matches or exceeds his?

In this respect, defenders of the gender hierarchy might point to the Prophet Mohammed's own household, where a woman like his remarkable wife A'isha apparently enjoyed a companionate relationship within a traditional gender role for women, while she pursued spiritual education. A *hadith* in Al-Bukhari's *Book of Knowledge* (part of *Sahih Bukhari*) relates that, "Whenever A'isha heard anything she did not understand, she used to ask again till she understood it completely."[587] Her own commitment to religious learning led her to admire women like herself, as we see in this praiseful remark from another *hadith*: "A'isha said 'How excellent the women of the Ansar are! They do not let shyness intercede in the pursuit of learning sound religious knowledge.'"[588] Here, then, is a model of a Muslim femininity that resembles the love of learning and zeal to be educated that is typically associated with Muslim men.

Inevitably, the role of Islam in constructing gender as it appears in societies today is obscured in part by other forces of culture and by the difficulty of outsiders to see matters in the same manner as insiders. The task is further complicated by differences of interpretation among both outsiders *and* insiders! However judged ideologically, the facts on the ground show in the public sphere a general public deference by women to the status of men. To the extent there is a gender hierarchy, men hold a higher place than women; masculinity is prized above femininity.[589]

If so, the next question that springs to mind concerns the status in this hierarchy of any who exhibit a gender identity other than as a man or a woman. After all, as one Muslim woman put it, "I am very often left with the uneasy and unpalatable notion that as a female, I am the 'Other' within the house of Islam."[590] If a woman feels that way, how much more might a transgender Muslim? To get at that question, we must now return to the markers relied on to differentiate and separate the dominant, conforming genders. In short, it is time to discuss the relation of gender to dress, a matter that will in turn lead us to the role of crossdressing.

Gender & Dress

Islam's regard of dress veers from the monodimensional austerity and plainness often associated with early Christianity's sense of modesty. Muslims, too, are to be modest in dress. But clothes are positively extolled as a God-given gift for adornment—a crucial element that adds dimension to Muslim reflection and practice. The Quran's 7th Surah captures succinctly the intended sensibility about dress: "Children of Adam! We have given you clothes to cover your nakedness [modesty], and garments pleasing to the eye [adornment]; but the finest of all of these is the robe of piety."[591] The same Surah, shortly thereafter, urges the faithful to 'dress well' (or 'attractively') when attending the Mosque. An accompanying reminder warns that, as the gift of Allah, modest finery in dress is never to be forbidden.[592]

Sunan Abu Daoud (or, *Sunan Abu-Dawud*) preserves a number of *ahadith* related to clothing. In Book 32, *Kitab Al-Libas* (*Clothing*), the narration of Abu Sa'id al-Khudri recounts how the Prophet enacted the spirit of the Quran's teaching whenever he put on a new garment by naming it and thanking Allah for the gift of it.[593] Numerous *ahadith* describe the Prophet's dress practices and sketch out at least a partial logic then developed by his followers.[594] Certain of his remarks concern dress differences between males and females.

Dress is an important gender marker in Islam. Befitting their status at the top of the gender hierarchy, the rules for dress are principally formulated with men in mind. These are sometimes more restrictive, as in a *hadith* noting that a garment dyed in a manner making it unsuitable for a man might be suitable for the women of his household.[595] The sacred texts offer instances of things forbidden (*haram*), such as both silk and gold for boys and men.[596] In fact, one narration of Jabir ibn Abdullah pointedly comments on the practice of taking silk away from boys and leaving it for girls—an early indication of gender socialization at work.[597]

Women are distinguished in large part by how dress is used to conceal the body. Veils, for instance, are prominent markers.[598] There is an awareness of how dress can be used seductively, as in a *hadith* in *Sahih Muslim* that names as a type of person found in hell those women "who would be naked in spite of their being dressed, who are seduced (to wrong paths) and seduce others with their hair high like humps."[599] In some other respects, there seems to be a preference for what we might call 'natural beauty.' In *Sahih Bukhari* the Prophet curses both women who give tattoos and those who receive them, as well as those who alter their smile by manipulating their teeth, and "such women as change the features created by Allah."[600] This appears to extend to acts such as plucking the eyebrows. Artificial lengthening of the hair is also forbidden.[601] Yet, at least one *hadith* perhaps permits women to dye their hair or clothing in saffron, though the same is forbidden to men.[602]

Dress gender differentiation extends beyond clothing to other adornments. For example, *Sunan Abu Daoud* records the narration by Imran ibn Husayn that the Prophet declaimed the perfume of men should have odor without color, while that of women should have color without odor. This was qualified by the interpretation that the distinction was meant to be a *public* one; in private the woman could use any perfume she wished.[603] In fact, this example underscores a vital point: gender differentiation matters more in the public sphere. In the privacy of the household, certain restrictions are relaxed or abandoned.

Dress, in general, has for centuries functioned in multiple critical roles in Islamic societies.[604] Given its attention in the Qu'ran and other authorities this is unsurprising. Dress has constituted an important aspect of Muslim culture since its beginning. In the long stretch of prominence enjoyed by the Ottoman Empire (14th-early 20th centuries) "clothing laws maintained and reinforced gender, religious and social distinctions . . . ."[605] Despite changes in the nature and social roles governed by dress codes, gender-differentiated dress remains an important influence in the modern Muslim world alongside the other roles dress plays.

Gender & Crossdressing

Under Islamic thinking, the genders are based on sex and the sexes are kept carefully separate. Gender-differentiated dress is a strong instrument to enforce the distance between the genders. But the symbolic marking power of dress means it has potency for gender crossings. *If* certain dress stands for a particular gender, *then* donning such dress is a gender claim. The power this entails transcends mere pretence. *Sunan Abu Daoud*, in discussing clothing, remarks the Prophet's declaration, "He who copies any people is one of them."[606] Betül Ipsirli Argit translates thusly: "If a person of one group puts on a dress associated with another group he thus deviates from the accepted order and he will be regarded as a member of the other group (*"men tesebbehe kavmen fehüve minhüm"*).[607] Though the target of the dictum is religious distinction in dress, its logic potentially could be extended to other dress-differentiated groups, such as genders.[608] Crossdressers are, after all, staking an identity claim when copying the dress of a different gender. [609] In this manner it is conceivable that the text could be applied to modern transgender people.

Yet crossdressing itself seems forbidden, as in a *hadith* narrated by Abu-Hurayrah: "The Apostle of Allah (peace be upon him) cursed the man who dressed like a woman and the woman who dressed like a man."[610] Similarly, the contemporary Egyptian religious scholar Yusuf al-Qaradawi, in his book *Al-Halal Wal Haram Fil Islam* (*The Lawful and the Prohibited in Islam*), views crossdressing as a rebellion against the natural order.[611]

This way of thinking has had real world implications with harsh consequences for some transgender people. For example, *The Guardian* reported that the Kuwaiti parliament at the end of 2007 amended its penal code to make "imitating the appearance of a member of the opposite sex" a crime punishable by fine and imprisonment of up to a year. This followed an open proclamation in September, 2007, of the government's intention to crack down on the transgendered. The paper noted that Human Rights Watch had reported at least 14 males had been arrested in Kuwait City alone in the first few weeks after the law went into effect. None of these individuals were provided access to legal representation. Imprisoned in a 'special ward,' their heads had been shaved; some were alledgedly beaten.[612] This, though, is only the latest eruption of oppression and violence toward transgender people under the guise of law found in Muslim societies. The problem has been a persistent one.[613]

It might seem the issue of Muslim opposition to crossdressing specifically, and transgender generally, is an open-and-shut case. But we shall see that the matter is by no means as straightforward as it appears. Much like the text in the Hebrew Bible, this *hadith* must be regarded in context. Crossdressing was and remains a potent transgender reality among Muslims. Islamic religious tradition has a number of sources pertinent to understanding how this reality and the possibilities for modern paths derive from ancient texts. These we shall turn to shortly. One thing is certain: gender-variant individuals, born male, female, or intersexed, have been known and discussed in Islamic literature for a very long time.

Who are the *mukhannathun?*

The presence of crossdressing Muslims is documented from early in Islam's history. Whether these crossdressers were predominantly what we today might designate 'transvestites,' or 'transsexuals,' is impossible to know. What is known is that both women and men were known to engage in the practice. It is also clear that it was controversial, enjoying more acceptance in some times and places than in others. The legal status of crossdressers within the Islamic community is also controversial and impossible to separate from the experience of Muslim crossdressers throughout history.

Undoubtedly the most authoritative treatment on the so-called 'effeminate males,' the *Mukhannathun*[614] (sing., *Mukhannath*), comes from Islamic scholar Everett Rowson. He notes the derivation of the word is uncertain, though the verb *khanatha*—to fold back the mouth of a waterskin to drink—provides the source for derived terms that develop the basic idea in the direction, for instance, of languidness, tenderness, or delicacy. The 9th century Muslim scholars Abu 'Ubayd and Ibn Habib attributed it to the idea of languidness (*takassur*), a trait that when found in males links them to femininity. On the other hand, al-Khalil b. Ahmad, in the late 8th century, derives the label from *khuntha*, 'hermaphrodite.' Rowson himself notes that lexicographic evidence supports that irrespective of its root source the term *Mukhannathun* only refers in general to 'effeminate' males and not to crossdressing. The latter idea comes from the actual context in which the word is used in Islamic literature.[615]

In considering the *Mukhannathun* of early Islam, Rowson draws the following major conclusions:

❑ *Mukhannathun* in pre-Islamic and early Islamic Arabian society were publicly recognized as an institutionalized form of male effeminacy that included crossdressing.

❑ One important, and controversial, aspect of their social functioning was as an intermediary between men and women.

❑ They played a key role in the development of Arab music in Umayyad Mecca and Medina.

❑ The persecution they experienced was not because of their sexuality, but as corrupters of society because of their music and mediating activities.[616]

These ideas shall be explored in what follows.

The *Mukhannathun* of traditional Islam are, as we have seen, today commonly divided into two distinct groups, though they share at least one chief feature in common. Both groups are comprised of males whose behavior is like that associated with women. On one side, the *Mukhannas* are effeminate men who nevertheless retain a masculine gender identity despite their feminine behavior. On the other side, the *Mukhannis* claim a gender identity different than the one assigned based on their body sex. They correspond to the West's transgender males who live as women without seeking sex reassignment surgery or, especially, to transsexual males who desire body change to conform to their gender identity as women. Both *Mukkhanas* and *Mukhannis* dress such that others commonly label them as crossdressing.

Islam's religious texts speak of the *Mukhannathun*, though not always in ways as unambiguously clear as some interpreters suggest. The principal texts with respect to these males deserve close attention. As is our focus, we shall examine texts with respect especially to crossdressing. Although our work here is not an Islamic legal parsing of the original language, it does rely on sound Muslin scholarship.

What do Islamic sacred texts say?

The *Qur'an* (or *Koran*), the holiest of Islam's sacred books, is silent on the question of crossdressing as such. However, there is a Surah (chapter) that is pertinent to our consideration. Though it does not concern itself with cross-dressing, it does address a group of people whom today would be considered transgendered. The text of Surah 24:31 refers to male attendants who, to put it politely, 'lack in natural vigour.'[617] These men in a Muslim household are permitted to see the women in ways not permitted to other male non-relatives. These men may have been eunuchs, or hermaphrodites, or effeminate men. Whatever their exact nature, they appear to be the object of a number of brief pronouncements or discussion in other sources.

Outside the Qur'an there are a number of *ahadith* (or, *hadiths*; cf. *hadith* (sing.): a narration of a saying or act of the Prophet) pertinent to our topic. Rowson remarks of the *ahadith* about the *Mukhannathun,* that the relevant texts essentially number seven. It is his contention that while the most famous of these texts—the Prophet's cursing of the *Mukhannathun*—does not specify the cross-gender behavior being condemned, the evidence suggests crossdressing was at least an aspect. [618] We shall examine some of these texts in the hope of following in Rowson's effort to establish a context for understanding them, though our interest lies in seeing the connection to gender and religion, and we shall not expend the space he does in considering the *Mukhannathun* role in Arabian music or the specific musicians he discusses.

As we might anticipate from remarks already made, and consistent with an identification with people we today call transgendered males, the *Mukhannathun* are linked to feminine traits in both dress and presumed personality characteristics. Thus, from *ahadith* in *Sunan Abu-Dawud* we hear that such males dressed as women,[619] and had a lack of sexual interest,[620] and/or ability (e.g., to sustain an erection).[621] The notion of sexual inadequacy—the opposite of masculine potency—can connect the *Mukhannathun* to women, or to hermaphrodites. Modern Muslim scholar Abdelwahab Bouhdiba, in his discussion of Islamic sexuality, describes one way of comprehending the *Mukhannathun*:

> Al-Washtani defines the hermaphrodite thus: "He resembles women in his moral qualities, his way of speaking, his way of walking. The name comes from the word *takhannuth*, which is a way of associating gentleness and a break. Indeed the *mukhannath* is gentle of speech and broken of walk. It may be as a result of creation, but it may also be a mode of behaviour deriving from a perversion."[622]

Though this text understands the *Mukhannath* as a hermaphrodite—a common interpretation—as we have seen in considering the derivation of the term it is by no means necessary to draw this conclusion. Such people may have represented more than one sexual or gender reality.

Ibn Qudaamah preserves the following description:

> Ibn 'Abd al-Barr said:
>
> "The *mukhannath* is not only the one who is known to be promiscuous. The *mukhannath* is the one who looks so much like a woman physically that he resembles women in his softness, speech, appearance, accent and thinking. If he is like this, he would have no desire for women and he would not notice anything about them. This is one of those who have no interest in women who were permitted to enter upon women. Do you not see that the Prophet (peace and blessings of Allah be upon him) did not prevent that *mukhannath* from entering upon his wives at first, but when he heard him describing the daughter of Ghaylaan and realized that he knew about women, he commanded that he should be kept away."[623]

This last text encapsulates a complex of related events, portions of which are preserved in various accounts, which we need to understand. Other accounts elaborate that the Prophet heard this *Mukkannath*, in the presence of a woman, offer some 'matchmaking' advice that revealed his unseemly awareness of sexual matters. Thus these apparently harmless, effeminate men became the object of censure by Mohammed.

A brief record of his response is found in slightly different forms in a number of places. One such is a *hadith* by Muhammad Ibn Ismail al-Bukhari (810-870 C.E.) in the *Al-Sahih* (*The Genuine*, aka *Sahih Bukhari*)—a collection of the Prophet Mohammed's sayings and deeds which, in the Sunni tradition, enjoys a place second only to the *Qur'an*. There we find the following:

> Narrated Ibn 'Abbas:
>
> Allah's Apostle cursed those men who are in the similitude (assume the manners) of women and those women who are in the similitude (assume the manners) of men.[624]

Another rendering has it the following way, which highlights our concerns:

> Abu Hurairah (May Allah be pleased with him) said:
>
> The Messenger of Allah (PBUH) cursed a man who puts on the dress of women, and a woman who puts on the dress of men.[625]

This text, and others, raise important questions.

What place did the *Mukhannathun* have in early Muslim society?

Why should these people be cursed, and what should be done with them? To answer this requires understanding the roles played by such folk. As noted above, these men-who-imitated women, sometimes referred to as 'effeminate men,' were known as *Mukhannathun*, and the women who 'assume the manner of men' were known as *Mutarajjulat*. Their indeterminate sex and/or gender posed challenges for their society. This is because Islamic culture keeps males and females apart except under specific conditions. Those folk somewhere in-between might be useful as go-betweens, but they also posed a problem: what if they were using this in-between status as an artifice to gain an illicit advantage?

The *Mukhannathun* played public roles in various places in the Islamic world. In the birthplace of Islam they were known from the earliest days of Muslim Arabia. In fact, Rowson maintains that for a period of some two generations in the first century of Islam they held "a position of exceptional visibility and prestige."[626] Yet this came to an abrupt end early in the 8th century, under the caliph Sulayman. To understand why this happened we must look beyond our modern assumption of a homophobic or transphobic response without losing sight that then, as now, being differently gendered poses a significant cultural quandary in a predominantly bigendered society.

Although these men were feminine in manner and dress, apparently only a few were homosexual. Yet despite an overwhelmingly heterosexual orientation, by virtue of their gender status they were trusted to mingle freely with women—a right not enjoyed by most males. It meant they were often allowed to serve the female members of a man's harem.[627] This unique privilege of the *Mukhannathun* made them ideal brokers for marriage. Indeed, such a person could even be found in the Prophet's own household, among his wives.[628]

But, as is the case in the modern Western world, the crossdressing male presented a set of challenges for society. In a patriarchal society where rigid divisions are set between the gender roles, a feminine male represented a troubling specter for authority, because what male would want to lower his social status? It was easy to suppose that if he did so he might have an ulterior motive, such as gaining greater sexual access to women. One solution was to see such people as neither male nor female but as a 'third gender' (or 'third sex'), and while this solved some problems it introduced others. Among them was the possibility of a *Mukhannath* who uncharacteristically showed sexual interest, knowledge, and/or ability.

And that brings us back to our earlier query: Why should these people be cursed, and what should be done with them? In another place in *Sahih Bukhari* we find:

> Narrated Ibn 'Abbas:
> The Prophet cursed the effeminate men and those women who assume the similitude (manners) of men. He also said, "Turn them out of your houses." He turned such-and-such person out, and 'Umar also turned out such-and-such person.[629]

Variants of this saying are more or less exclusive in scope. Some add, or substitute, the admonition to keep the *Mukhannathun* from their presence—an obviously more far-reaching action than being thrown out of the household. In fact, Abu Dawud adds the tale that the *Mukhannuth* in question was banished to the desert, allowed only to enter the city twice a week to beg for what he needed to survive.[630]

But the question of why Mohammed first tolerated their presence and then denounced them and, further, urged them to be expelled requires further scrutiny. More than one answer is possible. Perhaps, given the example that he turned one such person out, the individual had done more than shown knowledge he should not have had. Perhaps he was under suspicion of having used his guise as an effeminate for attempted immorality.[631] Other, related sayings indicate that the expelled individual displayed a sexual awareness and interest inconsistent with one privileged to be in such a position.[632] In such a case, maybe the edict originally was limited in scope. Then, perhaps, it was thought better to err on the side of caution and keep all such people away from the women.

Against this interpretation of events is the testimony in other materials that the *Mukhannuthun* were not accused of immoral acts (*fahisha*). The early presumptions about *Mukhannuthun* sexuality appear to be that they were perceived as either uninterested or incapable; later, they were viewed as homosexually inclined.[633] It seems unlikely, then, that it was their sexuality that was generally in question, even if it might be an issue in specific cases. If this explanation does not well suit a broad edict of censure, what does?

It may have been a concern that the *Mukhannathun*, by virtue of their intermediary role between the sexes, were viewed as uniquely poised to corrupt weak-willed women—a possibility perhaps enhanced by any perceptions about their character arising from association with music, frivolity, and a certain measure of irreligiosity.[634] Thus the Prophet's concern may have been sparked less by the knowledge the *Mukhannath* displayed then by the fact he revealed it as he did. In the careless utterance of the *Mukhannath* the Prophet may have found confirmation of others' suspicions about the manner of such people—and judged them an unacceptable risk to a pious household.

Or, perhaps the saying attributed to Mohammed did not originate with him. It has been suggested that later measures enacted against the *Mukhannathun* may have motivated putting such a saying on the prophet's lips to justify the action taken. This interpretation of things suggests an opportunistic crafting of a saying perhaps made plausible by a real incidence of the Prophet expulsing some person from his household, on whatever grounds. In this reading, the particular expulsion of one person from one household becomes a more general banishment from any possibility of contact with women, including ultimately an exclusion from society.

In any event, no further sanction is set forth here than that they should be separated from the household. This penalty requires some consideration. Maybe all this meant was a simple separation, a sort of distancing that kept the *Muk-*

hannathun marginalized but nothing more punitive, such as imprisonment, exile, or death. On the other hand, in the culture of the time the idea may be more ominous. Besides the shame attaching to such an action, the repercussions of being denied a place in a household, and perhaps by extension the rule of hospitality in a culture where this cornerstone moral value often meant life or death, is no slight penalty. Certainly there is other evidence that being accused of being a *Mukhannath* was no little matter. Rowson notes a specific penalty is set forth for those who falsely accuse someone as being *Mukhannath*. In the 9th century Ibn Maja and al-Tirmidhi offer that the penalty is twenty lashes—the same penalty, says al-Tirmidhi, for falsely accusing someone of being a Jew.[635] So however else we assess the situation, the *ahadith* present the *Mukhannuthun* as a stigmatized group.

Rowson points to one further *hadith* in Abu Dawud pertinent to the matter of penalties:

> Abu Dawud, on the authority of Abu Hurayra:
> A *mukhannath*, who had dyed his hands and feet with henna, was brought to the Prophet. The Prophet asked, "What is the matter with this one?" He was told, "O Apostle of God, he imitates women." He ordered him banished to al-Naqi. They said, "O Apostle of God, shall we not kill him?" He replied, "I have been forbidden to kill those who pray."[636]

This *hadith* presents the banishment of one person, but suggests both that such a penalty may have been an option for others and, perhaps, that any *Mukhannuthun* who proved not religious might be executed.

This latter possibility apparently proved the case in an example preserved of the hostility of at least some in the ruling class. Yahya b. al-Hakam (late 7th century), uncle to Umayyad caliph 'Abd al-Malik and a senior member of the ruling house, gained a reputation for his hatred of the *Mukhannathun*. Though himself perhaps relaxed in his religious practice, he used intolerance based on religion to suppress the *Mukhannathun*.[637] When governor of Medina, he had brought before him a suspicious-looking person—suspicious in that the individual was a male in feminine dress, with coiffed hair and henna upon his hands. Identified as Ibn Nughash, a *Mukhannath*, the governor challenged Ibn Nughash's allegiance to Islam. When the fellow made an irreverent reply, al-Hakam ordered him executed and set a bounty on other *Mukhannathun*.[638]

So it would appear that the answer to our earlier query is that these people are cursed on some moral grounds and the penalty, whether physically mild or not, was attached to shame and marginalization. And yet the *ahadith* may not tell the whole story. As we noted earlier, Rowson relates that for the space of two generations the *Mukhannathun* enjoyed prestige as well as visibility. Obviously, not everyone was hostile to them. Rowson tells us *Mukhannathun* musicians were especially popular among young men and patrons included even members of the aristocracy, such as Ibn Abi 'Atiq, a great-grandson of caliph Abu Bakr.[639]

The *Mukhannathun* figured prominently in the development of Arabic music and their role in this aspect of culture probably provided them a visibility, respect—and measure of protection—not unlike that enjoyed by esteemed performers in other times and places, including our contemporary world. Especially in Medina music occupied a vital and highly regarded role. One of the great early musical masters of Medina, noted as the creator of *al-ghina' al-mutqan*, was Tuways (632-670 C.E.)—perhaps the first *Mukhannath* known in the region.[640] Yet the same things that may have made them visible and popular to some made them an eyesore to others, especially since they also came to be associated with male prostitution.[641] Because their alleged activities in music, in marital arrangements, and in the sex trade were viewed by some as corrupting social morality the *Mukhannathun* were subject to intermittent persecution by the state. Especially harsh measures under the Caliph Sulayman (in 717 C.E.) spelled an end to their prominence in the Islamic Mideast, but not to their existence.[642]

What has been the place of *Mukhannathun* since the early Muslim period?

The *Mukhannathun* have persisted. The exact form of their manifestation may have changed from time to time and place to place, but these third gender people have continued. We can resume our account of their story in the Middle Ages at a time when both their status and their reputation had changed.

Mukhannathun in the Middle Ages

Rowson contends that after the calamity of the early 8th century, the *Mukhannathun* were not only less prominent, but their association with music became less than their fame as clever wits, noted especially for their skill at imitation and role-playing. In this respect, Rowson offers the example of the 9th century court entertainer 'Abbada, famed during the reign of Caliph al-Mutawakkil (847-861 C.E.).[643] The *Mukhannathun*, rightly or wrongly, continued to be associated with a sexual desire for other males, especially male youths. The assumption seems to have been that their identity with femininity would naturally produce such a desire.

A different development, one that impacted Europe during the Middle Ages, should also be mentioned. It, too, concerns the link made between crossdressing males and sexual behavior. The Crusades acquainted European Christians with a practice found among the Muslims of Persia: sexual relations with feminized, crossdressed boys. The response of the Europeans may have had ripples inside Christian societies of great consequence for their own gender variant people. Cultural anthropologist Anne Bolin views the beginning of the Christian Church's 13th century campaign against gender and sexual variations—a campaign then carried out by the powers of the State—with opposition to this practice, which was viewed by the Church as accepted Islamic practice and therefore pagan.[644] The existence of crossdressed male youth engaged in the sex trade and patronized by male clients apparently continued to shock visitors well into the 20th century.[645]

Modern Transgender Muslims

The modern Islamic world has continued to recognize the presence of the *Mukhannathun*, though increasingly under the influence of European and American culture in more negative ways. We cannot hope to trace thoroughly that presence down through time or in all of the various societies where they are found. But we must at least offer a general summary on the situation for contemporary transgender Muslims and indicate a few of the more prominent instances in lands outside the birthplace of the religion.

Islam today remains divided into two major traditions (Sunni and Shiite), with the former larger and generally more liberal in their teachings. Transgendered people are not all treated alike. Intersexed individuals, for example, are permitted to undergo surgical body alteration in order to unambiguously present as male or female. On the other hand, transgendered behaviors like crossdressing, using hormones for body alterations, or seeking sex reassignment surgery are not sanctioned.[646] However, in an unprecedented court decision, a Kuwaiti court legally recognized the female identity of a Male-to-Female (MtF), postoperative transsexual. In so doing they were following a *fatwa* (edict) issued by Sunni Islam's highest legal institution, Al-Azhar, which permits gender changes through sex reassignment surgery when medically substantiated.[647] We shall examine the role of *fatwas* presently, but first we shall look at a few examples of *Mukhannathun* in various societies outside the Middle East.

The Mukhannathun in Islamic Asia: The Hijra

In India under the reign of Muslim rulers (11th –mid 19th centuries) a Hindu sect of eunuchs called the *Hijra* (see the answer to Q. 52 in volume 3) proved to be *Mukhannathun* of a somewhat different kind. Skilled in song and dance, the *Hijra* were welcomed at the royal court. The *Hijra* combination of a female-oriented spirituality, and ritual song and dance, shared similarities with Islam's Sufi tradition. Certain Sufi holy men may also have become members of the *Hijra* community. At any rate, the *Hijra* prospered under Islamic rule and in the north some *Hijra* adopted Islam, undertaking the Five Pillars and even becoming religious teachers. The *Hijra* today occupy a more marginalized role in contemporary Pakistani society, but they still persist. While some among them are self-made eunuchs, others are not; some are transsexuals.[648]

The Mukhannathun in Islamic Malaysia: The Mak Nyahs

Malaysian people have terms for different transgender realities: effeminate men are called either *pondan* or *bapok*; transsexual men refer to themselves as *Mak Nyah* (*mak* being the word for 'mother'); and transgendered females are variously called *abang* ('brother' or 'man'), or *Pak Nyah* (*pak* being the term for 'father'). While these people have received attention elsewhere in this set (see volume 3, the answer to Q. 52), some focused remarks on Muslim *Mak Nyah* are in order. The *Mak Nyahs* ('men who are like women') are probably the best-known Malaysian transgendered population, variously estimated at 10,000-100,000 people (with the latter estimate representing about .5% of the population). The Western category that seems to come closest to the *Mak Nyah* is 'transsexual.' Such individuals not only dress and act like women, they desire to be anatomically female. In fact, Yik Koon Teh's 1998 study of 510 *Mak Nyahs* found that almost all of them saw themselves as women and described themselves as soft and feminine.[649]

The identity for most of them is shaped in the context of Islam. However, anthropologist Michael Peletz observes that this situation has not always existed for Malaysia's transgender people. "While women and transvestites (the majority of whom seem to have been male) were highly regarded as ritual specialists throughout much of Southeast Asia during the early part of the period between 1400-1680," Peletz writes, "they experienced a marked decline in status and prestige during the latter part of this period, owing to the development of Islam and other Great Religions. . . ."[650] In contemporary times, significant developments related to Islam stem from the mid-1980s.

The name *Mak Nyah* is a self-chosen descriptor whose origin has been traced to 1987. Khartini Slamah,[651] a *Mak Nyah*, explains the twin hopes of those who adopted the name: "first, a desire to differentiate ourselves from gay men, transvestites, cross dressers, drag queens, and other 'sexual minorities' with whom all those who are not heterosexual are automatically lumped; and second, because we also wanted to define ourselves from a vantage point of dignity rather than from the position of derogation in which Malaysian society has located us."[652] That 'derogation' occurs in an Islamic context that forbids males to seek body modifications to become like females.

In 1983, the Islamic Conference of Rulers in Malaysia issued a *fatwa* prohibiting sex reassignment surgery (SRS) for Muslims. Other restrictions and penalties also apply. For example, males caught in feminine dress can be arrested and fined substantially. Muslim males are referred to the Jabatan Agama Wilayah (Muslim Religious Department).[653] Inasmuch as most *Mak Nyahs* are financially unable to afford surgery, the restrictions on dress prove the more constant obstacle. Slamah remarks, "The prohibition on cross-dressing assumes greater significance in our daily lives, since we are not allowed to pray in mosques dressed as women. We are often forced to worship at home, even though for Muslims it is more meaningful to pray in groups."[654]

The opening years of the 21st century have not brought the relief sought by *Mak Nyahs* in respect of any significant change in Islamic thinking. However, they do have advocates for social changes via the national law. In 2005, Member of Parliament Ms. Chong Eng petitioned to amend existing law so that persons having undergone SRS be permitted recognition of their new status on their National Registation Identity Cards (*My Kads*). At the same time, court cases were being decided both for and against transsexual applicants seeking recognition of their sex change.[655]

Nevertheless, despite the fact that SRS is legal in Malaysia, as is gender reassignment therapy (GRT, which may include hormone administration), the individual who has completed such work remains unable to obtain official recognition of the resulting change on legal identity documents. Muslim *Mak Nyah* continue to be forbidden by Islamic authorities from seeking such services. However, it has been reported that in a few cases the National Fatwa Council (Majlis Fatwa Kebangsaan) has allowed SRS after considering the surrounding circumstances.[656]

The Mukhannathun in Islamic Indonesia: The Waria

Mukhannathun exist in Indonesia, too, where a distinct group of transgendered men are known as *Banci* ('hermaphrodites') or *Waria* ('feminine men'; cf. the answer to Q. 57). Anthropologist Tom Boelstorff has observed that Islamic influence in Indonesia, with its strongly dichotomous view of gender, serves to marginalize transgendered people. Yet, while many *Waria* have struggled with whether their condition is a sin, most eventually reconcile their gender identity with their religion; some even come to regard being *Waria* as fated by divine decree (*takdir*). Many draw a distinction between sinful deeds, such as prostitution, and God's wish for them to exist in a state of being as *Waria*. In this light, it is even possible for some to perform their daily prayers wearing female garb, or to make the pilgrimage to Mecca in female guise. They regard themselves as males with female souls.[657]

What do contemporary *fatwa* say?

Contemporary transgender Muslims, as we have seen, are known by various names in different societies. But Muslims everywhere are guided by *fatwas*, statements issued by religious authorities that have roughly the weight of judicial opinion. In other words, for purposes of Islamic law, a *fatwa* has as much authority as the expert issuing it and the people receiving it accord to it. Thus, *fatwas* have much less importance than do *ahadith* at all times, though particular *fatwas* have assumed significance because of the respect accorded the issuer and through compliance by a powerful group or sizable body of followers.

Sunni Fatwa

Earlier we mentioned a *fatwa* issued by Al-Azhar, the most revered body of Islamic legal authority in the Sunni Muslim world. Al-Azhar, a university located in Cairo, Egypt, constitutes the Supreme Council for Islamic Affairs. The head of Al-Azhar is the Grand Imam; since 1996, this has been Shaykh (or 'Sheikh,' 'Sheik'—an honorific) Muhammed Sayid Tantawi. In 1988, before assuming this highest post, Grand Mufti Tantawi issued a *fatwa* to the Giza Doctors General Syndicate authorizing sex reassignment surgery (SRS) for a patient.

The case involved Sayyid 'Abd Allah, in 1982 a medical student at Al-Azhar University. Presenting to a psychologist with depression, 'Abd Allah was subsequently diagnosed with a disturbed gender identity, treated for three years, and referred for sex reassignment surgery, which was completed in 1988. Sayyid submitted a petition for a name change to Sally. The University's position was that the surgery was impermissible on the grounds it had proceeded to permit unlawful homosexual conduct under the guise of heterosexual relations. The investigation by the Doctors Syndicate concluded the surgeons had failed to establish just cause for the operation before proceeding. They petitioned Mufti Tantawi for a legal opinion. On June 8, 1988, Mufti Tantawi issued his *fatwa*.[658]

Tantawi's 1988 Fatwa

In the *fatwa*, which appeals to various *ahadith* (e.g., *Muntaqi l-Akhbar wa Sharhan nayl al-Awtar*, v. 8, p. 200, and *Fath al-Bari bi Sharh Sahih al-Bukhari*, by al-cAsqalani (29), v. 9, p. 273, in the chapter on those who imitate women), Tantawi draws a careful distinction:

> As for the condemnation of those who by word and deed resemble women, it must he confined to one who does it deliberately [*tacahhada dhalika*], while one who is like this out of a natural disposition must be ordered to abandon it, even if this can only be achieved step by step. Should he then not comply, but persist [in his manners], the blame shall include him, as well—especially if he displays any pleasure in doing so.
>
> The person who is by nature a hermaphrodite [*mukhannath khalqi*] is not to be blamed. This is based on [the consideration that] if he is not capable of abandoning the female, swinging his hips in walking and speaking in a feminine way, after having been subjected to treatment against it, [he is at least willing to accept that] it is still possible for him to abandon it, if only gradually. But if he gives up the cure with no good excuse, then he deserves blame.[659]

This distinction appeals to the *hadith* we examined earlier with respect to a *Mukhannath* being permitted entrance to the women's quarters until and unless displaying unseemly knowledge of them. Shaykh Tantawi then states:

> That being so, the rulings derived from these and other noble *hadiths* on treatment grant permission to perform an operation changing a man into a woman, or vice versa, as long as a reliable doctor concludes that there are innate causes in the body itself, indicating a buried [*matmura*] female nature, or a covered [*maghmura*] male nature, because the operation will dis-

close these buried or covered organs, thereby curing a corporal disease which cannot be removed, except by this operation.[660] Finally, then, opines Tantawi:

> To sum up: It is permissible to perform the operation in order to reveal what was hidden of male or female organs. Indeed, it is obligatory to do so on the grounds that it must be considered a treatment, when a trustworthy doctor advises it. It is, however, not permissible to do it at the mere wish to change sex from woman to man, or vice versa.[661]

Tantawi's ruling was worded in such a fashion that all parties claimed it supported them. In brief, two key points emerged. First, sex change was not allowable under Islamic law if only motivated by individual desire.[662] Second, such operations were permissible if there was established a medical condition for which such surgery was the only cure. In Sayyid/Sally's case, the issue was one of 'psychological hermaphroditism.' Thus, in the subsequent investigation by the Attorney General, expert physician testimony was that Sayyid was a biological male, but psychologically a woman. Although the Doctors Syndicate rejected this opinion, the Attorney General declined to prosecute. In November, 1989, Sally was legally certified a woman.[663]

The subsequent application of this *fatwa* has been interesting. Mufti Tantawi's ruling typically has been utilized in the Sunni world for approving SRS in the case of petitioning intersexed persons, but *not* transsexuals. Thus, a 2004 article reported that in Saudi Arabia five siblings of one family all were transitioning from female to male through SRS. The justification for the SRS was that medical examination had determined all of them had more male than female hormones.[664] As the presiding physician, Dr. Yasser Jamal, explained, the sisters were designated intersex rather than transsexual—the latter a condition associated with homosexuality in the society.[665]

Yet Dr. Ezzat Ashamallah, the plastic surgeon who performed the sex change on Sally, remarks, "Contrary to what people think, I wasn't the pioneer of these operations. . . . I can't claim the honor of the breakthrough when the procedure has been in the books for years; similar surgeries were performed here in Egypt as early as 1920."[666] Today, though Sunni Muslims under the Al-Azhar *fatwa* are generally eligible for SRS only if judged as intersex, the practical reality is that transsexuals may also obtain it *if* they can find a sympathetic medical professional, who will certify they meet the conditions of the *fatwa*. In other words, transsexual or not in reality, the certification must be as intersex for the surgery to be approved.

The logic can look confused to an outsider. For example, in a *fatwa* from a lesser authority, issued in 2001 (1422 by the Muslim calendar), scholar Abdullah Al-faqih remarks that an 'effeminate man' who imitates women commits a great crime—one made much greater through a sex change. On the other hand, "If he has now changed completely to a woman by having woman's genitals and woman's breast, he is no longer a man. Indeed he is a woman."[667] As such, all the Islamic rules and regulations pertaining to women are in full effect.

Tantawi's 1996 *Fatwa*

The consequences of a sex change are the object of a second important *fatwa* issued by Tantawi. In 1996, now Shaykh Tantawi issued another *fatwa* with respect to cases where a sex change had transpired. This *fatwa* was applied to a case where inheritance rights were at issue. Hasan, the eldest of two sons to a deceased Egyptian man, had undergone SRS after his father's death and adopted the feminine name Jilan. Hasan's younger brother contested his sibling's share of the estate. Under Egyptian law, sons inherit more than daughters—the latter being the status assumed when Hasan became Jilan. However, Tantawi's *fatwa* had ruled that for inheritance purposes the status of the inheriting person is established by the sex at the time of the bequeather's death. Thus, Jilan inherited as a son because at the time of the father's death Hasan had been male.[668]

This Al-Azhar *fatwa* has applied in other Sunni lands. A Saudi court ruled in favor of a woman who had previously been a man concerning an inheritance dispute. The Saudi woman's magazine *Sayidaty* (*My Lady*) reported the story of 'Ahmad,' who told the magazine of growing up a male but identifying with females. Sent abroad to the United States for college, Ahmad began crossdressing and developing feminine bodily features. His request for SRS funding from his father met with a threat of disinheritance. However, his wealthy father died before Ahmad underwent SRS. So Ahmad inherited as a son. He then had SRS and lived as a woman in the U.S. After 9/11, though, Ahmad returned to Saudi Arabia, now presenting as a man. When the family learned of the sex change, a sister and her husband sought in court to have the inheritance reapportioned, which would have cut Ahmad's share in half. However, the judge indicated at a preliminary hearing that the suit would not prevail and it was dropped.[669]

Azza Khattab, writing for *Egypt Today*, maintains that these and other medical cases ultimately hinge on how one interprets a key phrase in Surah 30 of the Qu'ran: "There is no changing God's creation" (*la tabdeel lee khalq Allah*).[670] One stance uses the text to argue not only against SRS but a host of other medical procedures that alter the body. Another stance counters that such logic can lead to ridiculous extremes and thus frustrate physicians' efforts to bring relief to their patients. For some, SRS is understood as a medically justified, morally appropriate response to human suffering and consistent with Allah's intentions.

Fatwa on Intersex Issue

The *fatwa* issued from Al-Azhar may be the best known, and carry the most weight, but they are hardly alone. Many *fatwa* have been issued on questions touching transgender realities. Some concern intersex matters, as in a *fatwa* issued by Abdullah Al-faqih in response to a Canadian Muslim, who desired a ruling to address concerns held by the family of his fiancé. At birth this 39-year old engineer had appeared female and been gender assigned to be a girl. Despite this assignment the person had always felt himself male, dressed and acted in a masculine fashion, and welcomed changes at puberty that diminished female function while promoting male development. As an adult he had sought and obtained surgeries to correct his appearance as a male, though he was infertile. Dr. Al-faqih answered by noting that only Allah can determine one's sex and that sometimes the male and female genital organs are combined. But in such cases, he maintained, "the judgment will be for the dominating organ." In this case it is clear that maleness and masculinity dominate, so the rules pertaining to a man are in effect. The *fatwa* recommends the prospective bride's family support the young man, relieving his grief, easing his anxiety, and assisting his purity and chastity.[671] This *fatwa* is in the general tenor of Islamic thought on such matters.

The same authority, in another *fatwa*, offers guidance on distinguishing two types of 'bisexual' (i.e., intersex) person: one possessing both male and female genitalia, and the other possessing neither, but only a 'hole' through which urine passes. Four characteristics are set forth with respect to the first type. These aim to determine whether the person can be classified as either male or female, or as a true 'epicene' with a balance of male and female characteristics. The first test, as it were, is with respect to the flow of urine, whether it proceeds only from the male organ or female one, or from both. In the latter case, if the urine stops from both organs simultaneously, but started first from one, the one it started from determines sex assignment. If the urine starts simultaneously from both, but comes longer from one, then that organ determines assignment. If in all respects the urinating is the same from both organs, then the person is an epicene—at least until the time of puberty. The second characteristic is tied to puberty: if the person emits semen several times, then he is male; if there are several menstrual cycles, then she is female. The third characteristic—appealed to only if the first two fail to resolve the matter—concerns sexual orientation. Since homosexuality is disavowed, heterosexuality is assumed. If the person desires a male, then that proves she is female; if a female is desired, the person must be male. In the event that both sexes are equally desired, the person is an epicene. Finally, the last characteristic appeals to observable physical markers. Growth of a beard shows the person is male; breast swelling indicates a female. Similar signs are used with respect to the second type of intersex person.[672]

Shiite Fatwa

In the Shiite Muslim world a somewhat different course has been established. Iran's Ayatollah Ruhollah Khomeini, when head of state as well as the supreme religious figure, granted a petition by a transsexual compatriot to issue a *fatwa* supporting a sex change.[673] The authorization granted by Khomeini to one individual has become by extension a grant to other similar individuals. SRS can proceed with the permission of the government. While it remains common for Iranians to actually procure SRS outside the country, many cases are known to have occurred within Iran. One physician, Dr. Mir-djalali, conducted more than 300 over a decade's span.[674] Yet, as *New York Times* correspondent Nazila Fathi observes in a 2004 article, growing tolerance among clerics and doctors does not equal acceptance among the general populace, where prejudice remains strong.[675]

What about crossdressing females?

As noted above, the practice of crossdressing was not limited to males. Though they did not receive the same attention as crossdressing males, at least a few different instances of crossdressing females merit our attention.

Mutarajjulat

During the same century the effeminate male *Mukhannathun* were gaining prominence, there were so-called 'masculine women' (*Mutarajjulat*) too. However, this term—stemming from the 9th century—harbors uncertainty as to how best it ought to be understood. Some today interpret the term to refer to lesbians, and that may be the case, but it is not certain. Others render the term's meaning as 'women who want to resemble men,' an ambiguous rendering that can admit of either transvestism or transsexualism. Some have even rendered it 'female eunuch.'

Whatever the best translation, apparently the *Mutarajjulat* adopted masculine dress as one aspect of their assumption of masculine manner. The modern Islamic scholar Bouhdiba observes that such women were common in the Arabic world, and did not cease to be so even after the revelation to Mohammed. Bouhdiba regards the need of these women to dress as men to be "a more or less satisfied revolt" against femininity and its associated lower status in society.[676]

Ghulamiyat

Another kind of crossdressing female were the *Ghulamiyat* ('boy-like'; sing., *Ghulamiya*), slave girls in the Islamic world during the Middle Ages who at their owner's command were made to look like adolescent boys. Rowson explains the term as an adjective meant to call to mind a pubescent or pre-pubescent boy. However, he notes its root, *ghulam*, could be used in reference to a male slave of any age or used euphemistically for a eunuch.[677] It is this latter connection that provides a link to the origin of the term.

Rowson writes that the *Ghulamiyat* emerged in early 9th century Baghdad under the Caliph al-Amin (reigned 809-813 C.E.). He quotes the historian al-Mas'udi, who explained the origin of the *Ghulamiyat* as owing to an act of the Caliph's mother Zubayda on behalf of her son:

When Zubayda saw how entranced he was by the eunuchs, and how he spent all his time with them, she took some of the slave girls who were well-built and had beautiful faces, and put turbans on their heads, arranged their hair in bangs and side-curls, and cut short at the back, and dressed them in *qabas* [a close-fitting robe], *qurtaqs* [a close-fitting tunic], and *mintaqas* [a sash]; this attire gave them a svelte carriage, and emphasized their buttocks.[678]

The act won the Caliph's approval, who proudly displayed them in public. This encouraged copying of the act, and the practice spread. The *Ghulamiyat* probably are the ones historian John Boswell has in mind when he mentions an "unusual form of transvestism" in which it was "the practice in many areas of the Muslim world (especially Spain) of dressing pretty girls to look like pretty boys by cutting their hair short and clothing them in male attire" in the early Middle Ages.[679]

Rowson notes there was no attempt in the appearance of the *Ghulamiyat* to actually pass as male, though their artifice was compellingly persuasive. For example, they made no effort to bind their breasts. In Rowson's estimation, the popularity of the fad depended on their being seen as *really* female, though they *appeared* male.[680] They were employed at the caliphate's court, and probably elsewhere by those who could afford it, to serve as musicians, singers, and dancers. [681] If we can judge from the poetry written about them, they also were objects of sexual attraction. Historian Ruth Mazo Karras seems to put it adroitly in remarking that, "their appeal lay in their gender-crossing, the fact they allowed men to have sex simultaneously with a woman and a boy."[682]

Contemporary Crossdressing Muslim Women

Crossdressing women still occur in the Islamic world today, though how often is impossible to determine. Certainly it is regarded within Muslim societies as extremely rare regardless of how accurate such a declaration might be. One case, reported in Malaysia in the mid-1990s is illustrative. In 1996, Azizah Abdul Rahman, then 21, successfully impersonated a man in order to marry her lover (a woman named Rohana). According to published reports, "The accused Azizah Abdul Rahman was said to have fooled her bride, the local imam (religious leader), the district registrar of marriages, and the witnesses at her wedding by successfully passing herself off as a man." This was hailed in the press as the first such case in Malaysian history. An ostensible 'news' report in 1997, based on an interview with Azizah's mother, used this incidence to offer a warning to Muslim parents on the importance of good guidance and a religious upbringing to secure their children's future.[683]

Conclusion

Islam is a religion both idealistic and practical. Through religious law it aims to provide Muslims guidance on how to submit to the will of Allah. Recognizing from the very beginning the existence of sexual minorities and gender variant people, Islam has found ways to simultaneously endorse an ideal of a two sex/two gender system while accommodating the obvious transgender realities in its midst. Thus, both crossdressing males and crossdressing females are discouraged from gender expressions at variance from what is expected for their body sex. But at the same time, in one way or another, Muslim lands of both the past and the present have found ways to allow such people to exist. Though often marginalized, there have been occasions when they have been more tolerated, and in a few instances perhaps actually celebrated. Islam is realistic. The adherents of the religion understand that transgender realities persist. Some of these realities in many Islamic lands they continue to actively persecute; others are largely ignored. The intersex fare the best, because they have proved the easiest to fit within Islamic legal logic. Yet as time progresses there are some indications that other transgender people may yet find greater acceptance within the religion.

Q. 79 How does Hinduism regard crossdressing?

The Short Answer. Hinduism presents us with one of the oldest, largest, and most diverse of the world's religions. The sprawling and complex character of the religion, together with its manifold cast of strange and wondrous personalities, make it an especially elusive religion for most Westerners. We may be helped by thinking of Hinduism as a religion that recognizes reality itself as grandly complex and susceptible to a variety of appropriate paths through life. Although reality is unified, it manifests in various forms, all of which are illusory to the extent they can mask our awareness of the ultimate unity among all things. We are aided in remembering and seeking this unity by things that show us how transitory, ephemeral, and inconsequential are many matters we take for granted, such as sex and gender. To our limited vision, gender and sex seem paired and permanent. Yet if we accept this as reflecting the ultimate nature of reality we deceive ourselves. Such ignorance gives rise to passions that overvalue illusions and leave us separated from one another and from God. Hinduism seeks to promote a larger, more accurate comprehension, one that sees the essential unity that diversity manifests. If all things are essentially united, then all forms are not merely impermanent, but also malleable. The Hindu universe is one accustomed to changing shapes. Divine beings and others change appearance often. Sex and gender for such beings often seems more a matter of convenience than necessity. Among human beings, too, sex and gender are subordinate to higher, unchanging realities. Neither ought to prevent us from seeking and eventually finding release from the cycle of birth and rebirth that confines us to a world of illusory forms. Sex and gender are not aspects of the true Self. In this way of thinking, just as gender can become a trap as one grants its illusory nature greater weight than warranted, so conversely gender crossings can aid in penetrating to the heart of reality. Both sex and gender can be used, crossed, or transcended in service of one or another divine manifestation. Accordingly, crossdressing can and often does serve a positive function in Hinduism. It can prove devotion to a deity, remind of the arbitrary and fluid nature of gender, and/or mark an androgynous or third gendered alternative. Whether an individual is assigned to being male or female at birth, both in this life and across lives both sex and gender prove forms that can be changed and subordinated to a greater reality.

The Longer Answer. Hinduism is one of the world's oldest religions as well as one of its biggest and most influential. It comprises a large and varied body of thought that has informed a complex culture for millennia. While we shall explore that thought throughout this answer, we may begin by stressing the Hindu theme that a fundamental and permanent unity constitutes the reality that manifests itself to our senses in so many diverse forms. The Hindu goal is to pierce and surmount the limitations of these forms in order to perceive and be joined to this ultimate reality.

In India, Hinduism exists alongside other religions, such as Buddhism, Jainism, and Sikhism. Hinduism takes on somewhat different shapes in the various regions of the country, which each have their own stories and rituals. This situation makes it impossible to say anything that can be truly accurate for all Hindus—a reality much the same in discussing any large and ancient religion. Nevertheless, we can say enough to indicate that transgender realities are as well-known in the Hindu world as they are in other religions we have considered.

Indeed, we may go further in contending that such realities are better documented within the reach of Hindu-dominated India than any other place. For example, speaking of 'transsexualism'—i.e., the changing of body sex—Sanskrit scholar Robert Goldman writes, "Few cultures have accorded this phenomenon so prominent a place in the realms of mythology and religion as that of traditional India."[684] Indeed, we may be tempted to find in this ancient culture a fascination paralleling our own. But historian Vinay Lai cautions, "The history of Indian literature and sexual practices suggests . . . that certain premodern civilizations may have presaged the postmodern enchantment with transgendering and multiple sexualities without either the debilitating anxieties attendant upon such enterprises in our times or the much-vaunted celebration of supposed pluralisms."[685] Perhaps, then, we might profit from examining this culture, if only in the hope of easing our own cultural anxieties.

To get at this ancient Indian sensibility, however imperfectly we might in our limited space, requires two efforts. First we must aim to get a broad perspective on the role of gender and gender crossings in Hinduism. Second, we must at least offer some nods to local views and practices. This latter step is necessary to avoid falling into the misperception that Hinduism is some monolithic entity that everywhere looks the same. We may begin by trying to capture some wide sense of Hinduism's thinking on gender.

What is 'gender' in Hinduism?

Unfortunately, most of what Westerners know with respect to Hinduism and gender concerns what Westerners see as an overvaluation of male children. It has been well-documented how many Indian families use modern technology to facilitate their desire to only bring to full term male offspring. Those who know a bit more realize this modern trend continues a centuries old view that esteems boys and men far more than girls and women. Indeed, the announcement of the birth of a girl has often been met with the disdainful announcement, "Nothing was born."[686] Traditionally, the highest role—arguably the only valued one—a girl could aspire to was to become a wife and bear him sons. No one was more desolate than a widow. The old practice of *suttee*, where a wife suicidally threw herself on her husband's funeral pyre in an act esteemed as pius if done out of true devotion, has only grudgingly given way.

Certainly, outright misogynistic texts are not hard to find. Goldman offers a verse from the Sanskrit poem *Subhasitaratnabhandagara* on the perils a woman carries for a man: "The sight of her carries off your mind, her touch your fortitude. To have sex with her is to lose your manhood. Truly, a woman is an ogress in the flesh!"[687] Yet we would be overreaching to think such sentiments universally predominated. Rather, they form an undercurrent that still exercises influence.

There is some evidence that the pronounced domination of masculinity in the gender hierarchy has not always been so, but originated in the Vedic period (c. 1500-500 B.C.E.). The *Manusmerti* (*Laws of Manu*) codified the subordinate place for girls and women:

> 147. By a girl, by a young woman, or even by an aged one, nothing must be done independently, even in her own house.
>
> 148. In childhood a female must be subject to her father, in youth to her husband, when her lord is dead to her sons; a woman must never be independent.
>
> 149. She must never seek to separate herself from her father, husband, or sons; by leaving them she would make both (her own and her husband's) families contemptible.
>
> 150. She must always be cheerful, clever in (the management of her) household affairs, careful in cleaning her utensils, and economical in expenditure.
>
> 151. Him to whom her father may give her, or her brother with the father's permission, she shall obey as long as he lives, and when he is dead, she must not insult (his memory).[688]

Of course, as is so often the case, the impression left by such texts can be weightier than it need be. Life on the ground often defies religious edicts, and even among sacred texts there are varying representations. Sanskrit and Indian Studies scholar Stephanie W. Jamison and her colleague Michael Witzel point out the Vedic literature such as the *Upanishads* offer clear evidence of learned activity by women, and a prominent woman like Maitreyi is said to have been so schooled in Brahmanical lore that her husband Yajnavalkya would only speak to her when certain topics came to hand.[689] But the gradual lowering of the age at which a girl might be married often may have interfered or even prevented the pursuit of an education, and it seems indisputable that women generally held lower status. Yet we would do well to remember that not all women—or men—quietly acquiesced to the cultural norms.

As we consider gender we must be careful to keep it within a broader context of thought than merely what pertains to the conforming genders of masculinity and femininity. Gender, like sex and sexuality, manifests in different forms. We make use of the distinctions we judge to exist, but we go astray if we conclude that our distinctions ultimately matter. To overvalue male/female or masculine/feminine, as though these observed distinctions are fixed, permanent, and substantial, is to accept an illusion in place of truth. The Hindu mind seeks knowledge to overcome ignorance, which fuels the passions that create the ills that plague us.

Gender Terminology

If we would understand gender, and thus also transgender, we must grasp that while we can give names to the distinctions we perceive, those labels do not name something immutable. Indeed, the most basic term for gender reflects that it is a human judgment. In Hinduism, the key term is *linga*. Originally, this word meant simply a 'characteristic sign' or 'signifying mark.' In short, gender is a way of marking observed differences.

As in the West, this term that would come to refer to human gender first served a grammatical purpose. When applied to human beings, it attached to obvious physical differences, particularly sexual differences. Eventually, it reduced to signifying the male penis (*lingam*). It was a short conceptual step to conceive gender as tied to differences in sexed bodies (or at least the appearance of difference[690]), as the 3rd century Brahmin treatise *Mahabhasya* does in the following text:

> [Q:] What is it that people see when they decide, this is a woman, this is a man, this is neither a woman nor a man?
>
> [A:] That person who has breasts and long hair is a woman; that person who is hairy all over is a man; that person who is different from either when those characteristics are absent, is neither woman nor man.[691]

This three-fold division reflects in concrete terms the scheme found in Vedic literature (further discussed below). Gaudiya Vaishnava monk Amara Das Wilhelm observes that it sorts human beings into three types distinguished by their 'nature' (*prakriti*). He contends, "These three genders are not determined by physical characteristics alone but rather by an assessment of the entire being that includes the gross (physical) body, the subtle (psychological) body, and a unique consideration based upon social interaction (procreative status)." The resulting types are: men (*pums-prakriti*), women (*stri-prakriti*), and 'third sex' or 'third gender' (*tritiya-prakriti*). [692] Another term used both broadly and narrowly with respect to this 'third gender' is *napumsaka* (or, *napunsaka*: broadly, 'neuter'; narrowly, 'gay male').[693]

Wilhelm clarifies that *napumsaka* is a broader social category than *tritiya-prakriti* and notes that the five groups included among the *napumsaka* are characterized by a common trait: not engaging in procreation. In other words, they may either refrain from sexual activity that might lead to conception (e.g., the celibate), or are incapable of procreation (e.g., children, the elderly, the infertile), or whose sexual activity is not procreative in nature (e.g., the *tritiya-prakriti*). Wilhelm argues that all *napumsaka*, in the Vedic tradition, were considered good luck and afforded protection. Their nonreproductive role is socially valued as contributing to the overall balance of society.[694]

Before focusing on the 'third gender' with respect to what we call transgender realities, we should note also that over time a larger gender and sexual identity vocabulary has developed. Gender studies scholar Paola Baccheta points out that contemporary Indian academics and activists have proposed a number of terms to apply to various transgender identities, especially with respect to homosexual identities (because Indian languages lack a term equivalent to the Western notion of a homosexual *identity*). These include: *bhagini* ('vaginal sister'), *chay number* ('number 6'—an 'outrageous flaming gay man'), *dost* ('male friend of a male'), *gandhu* (a perjorative term for the recipient of anal penetration), *jankha* ('male transvestite' or 'effeminate gay man'), *khush* ('gay' or 'happy'), *samlingkami* ('desirous of the same sex'), *sakhi* ('woman friend of a woman'), and *zenana* ('effeminate gay man').[695] In addition to such terms there are also names applied to specific groups, such as the *Shivshakti*, the *Jogappas*, and most notably, the *Hijra* (all discussed below).

The 'Third Gender' (Tritiya-prakriti & Napumsaka/Napunsaka)

The *tritiya-prakriti*, sometimes identified as a 'third gender' and sometimes as a 'third sex,' are here considered as a 'third gender.' The Hindu texts may presume a link between sex and gender, but the latter seems intended by the manner in which the *tritiya-prakriti* are discussed. It is not their body sex that proves determinative, but their gendered identity and roles. The *tritiya-prakriti* are not all of one kind. They are further distinguishable, as the text of Vatsyayana's 4th century work, *Kama Sutra* (part 2, chapter 9) indicates:

1 People of the third sex [*tritiya prakriti*] are of two kinds, according to whether their appearance is masculine or feminine.

2 Those with a feminine appearance show it by their dress, speech, laughter, behavior, gentleness, lack of courage, silliness [*mugdha*], patience, and modesty.

. . .

6 Those who like men but dissimulate the fact maintain a manly appearance and earn their living as hairdressers or masseurs.[696]

Yashodhara's commentary (c. 12ᵗʰ century) on the *Kama Sutra* (*Jayamangala*) notes that the *tritiya prakriti* are also termed *napunsaka*. Yashodhara elaborates on their differentiation according to appearance, noting that the feminine appear with breasts while the masculine sport body hair, including moustaches.[697]

Modern efforts to differentiate the *tritiya prakriti* persist. Amara Das Wilhelm identifies a number of different terms corresponding to contemporary transgender labels. These include *Napumsaka* (homosexual males), *Svairina* (homosexual females), *Kami* (bisexuals), and *Sandha* (transgenders; more literally, 'half-man, half-woman').[698] As will be recognizable from our discussion in previous volumes (see especially the answer to Q. 20), these various terms match types of individuals embraced under the Western term 'transgender,' when that word is used in its broad sense. The term *Sandha* is given particular attention by Wilhelm and will be covered more carefully a little later.

How real is gender?

As evidenced in the foregoing material, gendered distinctions are manifold in Hindu thought. But how real is gender itself? We must step back a moment and reconsider how much weight is owed to the judgments of difference we make in gender. Masculine, feminine, and 'third gender' designations, regardless of any ties to sex differences, reflect human judgments and values. Different people at different times and in different places variously judge each gender. Similarly, transgender identities and the specific roles played by transgender behavior are shaped by the history and local religious flavors found in the varying regions under the influence of different strands of Hindu tradition. Despite the variety, though, we can say broadly that all forms of transgender reality in Hinduism are, like sex and gender in general, things that either deceive us or can help liberate us.

Brahman & Atman

In Hinduism, the ultimate and essential reality is the Unity named *Brahman*. This reality has both impersonal (*Nirguna Brahman*) and personal (*Saguna Brahman*) aspects. Brahman can name what Westerners term 'God' and as such we shall soon consider Brahman more closely. But here we must explore the Hindu vision of how we all can experience at our human level this ultimate reality. While all that exists is encompassed in Brahman, our experience of this essential unity depends on another fundamental reality: *Atman*, the 'Self' that is the universal, or world soul. This Self is in all things, a ground of unity to all reality.[699]

Atman seeks union with Brahman. By connecting to Atman within ourselves we can join Brahman. Yet the delightful, playful indulgence of Brahman in manifesting in so many diverse forms poses for us both opportunity and obstacle for achieving unity. Positively, diversity means a multitude of paths to Brahman. Hinduism prizes that so many paths exist by which Brahman reaches out to us and we may, in turn, journey one or more in pursuit of Brahman.

Negatively, though, these many paths can become ends in themselves rather than remain means to a goal. If we latch onto any forms as ultimate and abiding, or travel any path as though that path itself was all that mattered, then we will become entangled in ignorance. Fortunately, through the cycle of birth-death-rebirth we are offered more than one opportunity to realize our best destiny.

In sum, ultimate and universal reality is unified—there is no multiplicity despite what our senses insist upon. This lesson must be applied to our reckoning of gender. Gender divisions are derived and secondary features. Though convenient for discourse, they also may be treated flexibly. As Devdutt Pattanaik expresses it, "Masculinity and femininity are reduced to ephemeral robes of body and mind that ensheath the sexless, genderless soul."[700] We have already seen this to be true for divine figures.[701] It is true as well for human ones.

At the pragmatic level of social interaction these 'ephemeral robes' exercise significant influence. Human beings are labeled by sex and gender characteristics. But the perceptive Hindu sees past the obvious, as evidenced in this poem from the 10th century C.E. by Devara Dasimayya:

> If they see
> breasts and long hair coming
> they call it a woman
> If beard and whiskers
> they call it a man:
> but, look, the Self that hovers
> in between
> is neither man
> nor woman.[702]

This text is also important for revealing a sensibility about gender central to Hindu thought: the androgyny of self. The freedom from gender constraint is seen in a 12th century poem, this one by Basavanna:

> Look here, dear fellow:
> I wear these men's clothes
> Only for you.
> Sometimes I am man,
> Sometimes I am woman.
> O Lord of the Meeting Rivers
> I'll make wars for you
> But I'll be your devotees' bride.[703]

Here clothing is a matter of convention and convenience. The self is sometimes 'man' and sometimes 'woman,' and roles or activities associated with either gender are available (the 'war' of the masculine warrior, and the devotion of the feminine 'bride').

So it is *atman* in the human breast that matters, not the genitalia or the gendered roles society imposes. Because the 'true soul' is androgynous (or perhaps more accurately 'beyond gender'), the apparent gender of the mortal form is an appearance that may be manipulated. To be sure, gender crossings remain a matter not undertaken casually, not even by the gods. Yet they are always there in potentiality, for mortal and immortal alike. To better glimpse how both divine and human figures express and manipulate gender, we will soon turn to the Hindu sacred texts. But first we must linger a moment on the danger of illusion.

Sex, Gender, & Illusion (Maya)

Sex and gender deceive us, confining us to a world of illusions (*maya*, literally, 'that which is not') through a cycle of birth-death-rebirth (*samsara*), if we regard them as truly substantial and overvalue them.

As we shall consider further in a moment, the danger of *maya* is how it contributes to an ignorance (*tamas*), or lack of knowledge (*avidya*), that prevents our participation in the true unity of the universe. Practically speaking, *maya* means a sense of separateness in generating egoism, a sense of the individual self (*ahamkara*) as essential, fundamental, and true. Hindu scripture puts it this way:

> The attraction between male and female is the basic principle of material existence. On the basis of this misconception, which ties together the hearts of the male and female, one becomes attracted to his body, home, property, children, relatives and wealth. In this way one increases life's illusions and thinks in terms of "I and mine."[704]

The egoistic self, dominated by *maya*, overvalues the body, individuality, race, social status, and so forth. Rather than being seen as transient, playful manifestations of an underlying Unity, such things become valued in their own right, wrongly asserted an independence and importance that ignites passions and perpetuates a host of human inequities. So, in terms of sex and gender, a willingness to accept the sexed body as a fundamental reality that generates gender, also fixed, produces an artificial, misleading and harmful separation of people. *Maya* underlies the gender hierarchy.

Fortunately, either or both of sex and gender may be bent to the service of the truth, as we shall see has been done often enough in Hindu practice (such as the example of Sri Ramakrishna, discussed later). That truth, as we have discussed, is that an ultimate, universal Reality (*Brahman*) can be joined by means of realization of the ultimate, universal Self (*Atman*)—a process of release to freedom (*moksha*). Gender crossings—transgender realities—help expose the illusion of a binary sex and gender conception. Crossdressing can help liberate the crossdresser from artificial and restrictive identities and roles rooted in what is insubstantial. Potentially, at least, transgender offers assistance in breaking free of sex and gender limitations in order to realize true Self.

Unfortunately, while we shall further briefly explore some fundamental Hindu thinking, a comprehensive examination of this matter is beyond our scope here. Our aim will be the more modest one of indicating a little of the diversity found in Hinduism, while examining briefly a Hindu conception of the androgynous self and—especially—exploring the role of crossdressing. To accomplish this means looking at both divine and human realms. While the sheer diversity, immensity, and complexity of Hinduism is beyond adequate conveyance here, we can see enough to recognize the place transgender realities hold in the religion.

What relation do Hindu deities have to gender?

Henotheism & Gender Diversity

We must start with the Hindu godhead. The ultimate divine reality is a unity that manifests in multiplicity (sometimes referred to as 'henotheism'). Three divine forms of Brahman are primary, each representing a basic force: Brahma (creation), Vishnu (preservation), and Shiva (destruction and restoration). But a great multitude of other divine manifestations exist, expressed in a pantheon of divinities—a matter touched upon previously (cf. the answer to Q. 76).

A henotheistic model has some important advantages in terms of depicting gender. It permits an understanding of human gender, as seen in divine forms, as diverse manifestations of an underlying unity. Viewed this way, gender fluidity rather than static and fixed gender categories emerges as a basic characteristic. So it is not surprising we find gods who are gender ambiguous (Brahman, who transcends sex and gender), gender androgynous (Agni), and gender altering (Mahadeva, Vishnu-as-Mohini). There are also divine figures who are hermaphrodites (Ardhanari/Ardhanarisvara, Ayyapan). Vishnu and Shiva, in particular, often take forms that express alterations of gender. Shiva, for example, is sometimes Ardhanarisvara—the hermaphroditic unity of Shiva and his consort Parvatii—who is popularly depicted as male on one side of the body and female on the other. Shiva and Vishnu together exist in the form of Harihara (aka. Sambhu-Vishnu, or Sankara-Narayana). Yet all these are joined in an essential divine unity.

Hindu henotheism, then, offers instructive models in gender behavior. These models often inspire devotees to imitate divine behavior. So if we would understand why some folk crossdress, we must start with examining sacred stories, which include both divine and human figures, the latter mirroring divine realities. These stories display both males and females changing sex and/or gender. For example, among the many tales found in Hindu texts of female transformations are those of Shikhandini, Sariputra, and Malli. There are also tales of male transformations, like those of Riksharaja, Narada, and Vishnu. Some stories involve eunuchs. Many entail crossdressing or other behaviors we would today term transgendered.[705] Collectively, they offer insight into how transgender realities can fit within the Hindu mind.

But we won't see such gender crossings accurately unless we first grasp that multiplicity, including that of sexes and genders, is subservient to the greater reality of unity. Put in other words, masculine maleness and feminine femaleness are subordinate to the androgynous nature of reality transcending sex and gender appearances. This unity indwells and connects all forms to each other. It is as true for divine beings as for human beings.

How do Hindu scared texts help us?

Hinduism has a large, rich, and ancient sacred literature. This literature continues to exert a substantial influence on Indian culture. The breadth and complexity of the sacred tradition, which reaches beyond written to oral forms, is outside our reach to adequately expose here. What follows is merely a sampling, which means instances selected from many possibilities. While these examples are meant to be illustrative of important ideas and influential figures, we must recognize that the sheer number of possibilities means different selections might lead to somewhat different conclusions. Indeed, even with the materials selected here, not all folk agree as to how best they should be understood. As with all religious traditions the most appropriate course of study is to immerse oneself into the material and seek to understand it in its own context. This is an ongoing process, no less for us than for anyone else. The goal must be to utilize the discussion here as a startingpoint and not as an endpoint.

Hindu sacred literature includes the *Samhitas* (popularly referred to as the Vedas), comprised of four collections of which the *Rig-Veda* is the oldest, largest, and most famous. The Vedic literature stands in the first rank of Hindu sacred literature because it is *shruti*—material that discloses the divine mind. In addition to the Vedas, there are the *Upanishads*, also a diverse collection of materials. These expound upon the Vedas. These philosophical texts, like most Hindu sacred literature, occupy a place below the *Samhitas*. These lesser texts are *smriti*—wisdom that arises from the human mind in reflection on the divine mind. Rather than revelation, they constitute tradition. Thus, *smriti* (tradition) serves *shruti* (revelation), similarly as in Western religions such as Judaism.

Transgender individuals and groups that engage in transgender realities, such as the *Hijra*, look to the sacred tradition no less than do others. In the sacred texts they seek explanations for their way of being, purpose and meaning for living life, and ways to justify themselves to others. These are all common ways any religious person approaches and appropriates sacred literature. Yet, because none of us stands outside our culture and its history, all of us are influenced by these things as we interact with the very materials that have helped produce the culture and history that we are a part of. Scholars, as they try to understand both the sacred texts and the people who use them, may place greater or less influence on cultural and historical factors. In what follows, we shall attempt to integrate an appreciation of multiple factors in comprehending Hindu literature.

We have seen already that Vedic literature distinguishes three genders: men, women, and a 'third gender' that is neither man nor woman. The recognition of the *tritiya-prakriti* in this authoritative literature has meant that what we today term transgender is a reality Hinduism has constantly recognized, albeit in a wider or narrower scope depending on other factors. In continuity with the Vedic tradition, contemporary Hindus can employ a number of terms with respect to transgender people. Amara das Wilhelm identifies one such term— *sandha*—as particularly pertinent.

About the *Sandha* (a Sanskrit term), Wilhelm remarks that while it can be used to refer to anyone who is *tritiya-prakriti*, it more commonly is employed in reference to those the West terms 'transgender.' This, in turn, embraces a variety of distinctly different subgroups, including transvestites, transgenderists, and—especially—transsexuals. With this latter group in mind, Wilhelm comments that because Vedic culture discourages self-mutilation, male *Sandha* in ancient times likely would have followed a practice still found in southern India: binding up their genitals tightly against the groin. At any rate, in Vedic culture they were given liberty to live freely and openly in their gender identity.[706]

Vedic literature presents ideas about how the *Sandha* are produced. In the *Sushruta Samhita*, a presentation of Ayurvedic notions of surgical medicine, opinion is rendered that the *asekhya-sandha* (homosexual) is a male offspring of parents lacking sufficient generative fluids. On the other hand, the *Sandha* who appears and acts femininely results from a conception that occurred while the father had intercourse "as if he were a woman." Similarly, if the woman engages is sexual activity "like a man" and becomes pregnant, her female offspring will be a *Sandha* who behaves masculinely.[707]

Perhaps notable in these remarks is the preponderance of male bodies occupying *Sandha* identities. Goldman notes that throughout Hindu sacred texts there are more male transgender people than female ones. With specific reference to transsexualism, he remarks that this particular transgender reality seems deeply bound up in Indian cultural patriarchy with its ambivalent construction of women and their sexuality.[708] But, in a rather psychoanalytic interpretation, Goldman places male Oedipal issues at the heart of gender- or sex-changing episodes. He points to stories where the women are desired by both father and son, with the son thereby confronted with either facing the father's punitive act or renouncing his own sexuality, perhaps by voluntary castration. Goldman writes, "This act of degendering serves to eliminate the sexual conflict inherent in the Oedipal drama by removing the mother/woman as an object of sexual desire while pacifying the father." Among the ways one might renounce one's sexuality, says Goldman, are cultivating a gynephobia, invoking the incest taboo by regarding all women as sisters and mothers, or to abandon male sexuality and masculine gender and in some manner 'become' a woman. This last route is the one employed by transvestites and transsexuals.[709]

Certainly from a Western perspective, which shares a patriarchal framework, this kind of interpretation might make sense. Yet it is hard to understand how, if this is the case, there should develop a legitimacy to the *Sandha* as a distinct gender (*tritiya-prakriti*), side-by-side with men and women. In a patriarchal culture prizing masculinity, any paths to manhood (such as Goldman's first two ways of renunciation) would be rewarded, but any path leading away from masculinity would not. Moreover, as we have seen, Vedic literature offers alternative explanations for the *Sandha*, including those clearly so identified in the pre-Oedipal stage. At best, then, Goldman's idea can account for only a subset of 'third gender' males and leaves aside the matter of 'third gender' females.

The Bhagavad Gita

Probably the best-known Hindu work among Westerners is the *Bhagavad Gita*, a devotional work to Lord Krishna built upon a dialogue between the divine figure and Arjuna, a disciple. This dialogue is set in the wider context of a great battle, which is the concern of India's ancient epic poem, the *Mahabharata*. This poem belongs to a tradition (*Smriti*) of literature that offers commentary upon—and popularizes—the Vedic literature. One of Hinduism's most beloved stories, the *Ramayana*, also belongs to this tradition.

The *Bhagavad Gita* offers an accessible entry into the Hindu mind that will help us see why crossdressing can have a place in a world where gender itself is relatively fluid. The *Gita* extols devotion to Krishna (*B. G.* 6:13-14), envisioned here as the Universal Presence (*B. G.* 6:30), though in later Hinduism Krishna is commonly regarded as a manifestation of Vishnu. In the *Gita*, Krishna declares, "I am the father of this universe, the mother, the support and the grandsire" (*B. G.* 9:17).[710] The modern commentator, A. C. Bhaktivedanta Swami Prabhupada remarks that this reminds us that all our relations—father, mother, grandparents—are parts of Krishna, as are all living entities.[711]

Inasmuch as Krishna is a unity that transcends, and underlies, manifestations like gender, it is perfectly appropriate to name the deity by both feminine and masculine attributes. Thus, we find Krishna declaring to be seven 'feminine' riches: fame, fortune, fine speech, memory, intelligence, steadfastness and patience (*B. G.* 10:34). Disciples like Arjuna relate to Krishna in a manner that can be depicted by analogy to mundane human relations: "As a father tolerates the impudence of his son, or a friend tolerates the impertinence of a friend, or a wife tolerates the familiarity of her partner, please tolerate the wrongs I may have done You" (*B. G.* 11:45).[712] The wise and devoted disciple retains awareness of the underlying unity that is Truth and is not swept up into the secondary manifestations that seem to dominate life.

Krishna's dialog with Arjuna, set in the midst of war, underscores that loving devotion remains the superior way of attaining salvation. Such love transcends the limits imposed by sex and gender identities and roles. The warrior-god Krishna embraces feminine names and attributes, and expresses love to those devoted to him. In the larger scheme of things, reminds the *Bhagavad Gita*, the soul transcends battle, and love is without gender.

The Mahabharata

The larger context of the *Bhagavad Gita*, as mentioned before, is the great battle depicted in the *Mahabharata*. This epic poem of love and war presents notable instances of gender transformations that offer a different way of under-scoring the same truths espoused by Krishna to his disciple. Stories underscore the beauty and power of devoted love (Nala and Damayanti), or provide recognition that justice transcends the supposed limitations of time and gender, even as desire is stronger than death (Amba). And they do so with the aid of trans-gender realities.

Krishna extolled to Arjuna the superior path of loving devotion. In the *Mahabharata* the story of Nala and Damayanti, a married couple, proves its power in the midst of hardship. Their story begins in the exalted status of a king and a princess who come to love one another before they have even met. Their love proves so genuine that Princess Damayanti is able to recognize her beloved even though four demi-gods have assumed forms identical to his. Other divine beings also interfere in their lives and through their machinations cause King Nala to lose his kingdom and everything else—including the very clothes on his back—save the exception of his beloved wife. The devotion of the couple to one another, as well as the low estate to which they are reduced, are then both potently symbolized in the single act of the husband having to share with his wife her single garment, a *sari*.[713]

The *Mahabharata* also recounts the travails of the woman Amba, a victim of tragic circumstances. Although betrothed, she was kidnapped along with her two sisters by the supreme warrior Bhishma to be given as wives to others. Since Amba was promised already, she was permitted to go home—only to find her beloved no longer available, because he had perished. Bhishma, who long ago had taken a vow to remain unmarried, refused to marry her and thereby redress the injustice he had done to her. So Amba became the ultimate scorned woman, rejected by the very man who took her from her lover and who indirectly brought about his death. Understandably, she vowed revenge. After six long years of seeking in vain for a champion to oppose Bhishma and address the wrong she had suffered, the god Shiva took pity on her. He told her that in her next life she would avenge herself on Bhishma. At once Amba threw herself onto a funeral pyre.

Book 5 of the *Mahabharata* tells how Amba was reborn as the daughter of King Drupada, whose wife received Siva's promise that the child, 'born a daughter, shall become a man.' But in the meantime, the female form of her birth was not conducive to the justice the woman Amba had sought. Neverthe-

291

less, the queen acted in a manner faithful to the promise she had received. The text (5.CXCI) reads:

> And in due time, O monarch, that goddess, the queen of Drupada, gave birth to a daughter of great beauty. Thereupon, the strong-minded wife of that king, the childless Drupada, gave out, O monarch, that the child she had brought forth was a son. And then king Drupada, O ruler of men, caused all the rites prescribed for a male child to be performed in respect of that misrepresented daughter, as if she were really a son. And saying that the child was a son, Drupada's queen kept her counsels very carefully. And no other man in the city, save Prishata, knew the sex of that child. Believing these words of that deity of unfading energy, he too concealed the real sex of his child, saying,—*She is a son*. And, O king, Drupada caused all the rites of infancy, prescribed for a son, to be performed in respect of that child, and he bestowed the name of Sikhandin on her.[714]

The artifice proved a great success—at least until the time came when Sikhandin should be married. The queen insisted on a bride being found, but when the marriage had been commenced the secret of Sikhandin's sex became known. The outraged father of the bride determined to depose King Drupada for the deceit (5.CXCII). Heartsick, Drupada and his queen pondered their options, while Sikhandin, filled with shame, resolved to end her life (5.CXCIII-CXCIV). Entering a dense forest she encountered the *Yaksha* there, who took pity on her and granted her the boon of his own maleness—for a time. This resolved the crisis, with the bewildered bride rebuked for having told such a lie about an obviously masculine man (5.CXCV).

Vengeance for Amba finally was attained when Bhishma, knowing Sikhandin had been born a woman, refused to fight him (5.CXCV; 6.CXIX). Sikhandin, however, showed no such reluctance and led the force that finally slew Amba's nemesis (6.CXXff.).[715] Thus, the greatest warrior known among men was brought down by a transgendered person.

Arjuna himself, not merely devotee to Krishna but also another renowned warrior, likewise experienced transgender reality. In the fourth book of the *Mahabharata* (*Virata Parva*), Arjuna appears as a eunuch. Arjuna was one of the Pandavas (the five sons of Pandu), a group also including Bhima, whose venture into crossdressing is detailed elsewhere.[716] The Pandavas had to endure 13 years of exile, and a stipulation was that they did so in disguise. In the 13th year, Arjuna became part of the court of Virata in his guise as a eunuch. That choice for a masquerade was fitting because earlier, in spurning a sexual liaison with the nymph Urvasi, Arjuna had been cursed to become *napumsaka*—a term Lai renders as "a neutered transvestite of ambiguous sex."[717] Although this curse was modified to last but a year, for a time Arjuna truly knew this reality.

In explaining his choice of disguise, Arjuna remarked:

> O lord of the Earth, I will declare myself as one of the neuter sex. O monarch, it is, indeed difficult to hide the marks of the bowstring on my arms. I will, however, cover both my cicatrized arms with bangles. Wearing brilliant rings on my ears and conch-bangles on my wrists and causing a braid to hang down from my head, I shall, O king, appear as one of the third sex, Brihannala by name. And living as a female I shall (always) entertain the king and the inmates of the inner apartments by reciting stories. And, O king, I shall also instruct the women of Virata's palace in singing and delightful modes of dancing and in musical instruments of diverse kinds. And I shall also recite the various excellent acts of men and thus conceal myself, O son of Kunti, by feigning disguise. And, O Bharata should the king enquire, I will say that, *I lived as a waiting maid of Draupadi in Yudhishthira's palace*. And, O foremost of kings, concealing myself by this means, as fire is concealed by ashes, I shall pass my days agreeably in the palace of Virata.[718]

The disguise worked perfectly. Arjuna, under the name 'Vrihannala,' took a place at court and gave lessons in singing, dancing and playing instruments to the daughter of Virata.[719] Among the various terms ascribed to Arjuna in the *Mahabharata*, one deservedly is *tritiya-prakriti*—'third sex' (or 'third gender'). The most famous third gender people of India, the *Hijra*, regard Arjuna as one of their forebears.

The Ramayana

The *Ramayana* is the other great Hindu epic. Like the *Mahabharata*, this poem belongs to *Smriti* (tradition), literature that offers commentary upon the Vedic literature. As in the *Mahabharata*, there are startling transformations that occur in the *Ramayana*. One such is the story of Ila, a figure variously said to have been born male and become female, or born female, but raised as a son, and later transformed to a male as a boon to Ila's father, King Vaivasvata Manu.[720] At any rate, succeeding his father as ruler, King Ila set out on an adventure that led to his inadvertent encroachment on a sacred grove (*Umavana*). The place was one where Lord Shiva had love trysts with his wife Parvati. It had been enchanted by Shiva so that any male entering the space would be transformed into a female. The mortified Ila petitioned the goddess to be restored and won Parvati's favor. Yet there was a price to be paid: Ila must live as a woman part of the time, and when doing so would have no memory of being a man. During such a time, Ila was wooed by King Budha, who impregnated her; their child was Pururavas, famed ancestor of the Lunar Dynasty. Later, Ila was fully restored to permanent life as a man.[721]

How do transgender realities enter into religious matters?

Clearly, the sacred literature is replete with sex and gender transformations. But what do these mean in a religious context? First, not uncommonly, cross-dressing found in India is associated with Hindu sacred tradition. As we have seen, Indian sacred literature is replete with gender fluid deities. We should not be surprised, then, to find mortal imitation of immortal models, especially in view of the idea found often around the world that the space between genders is uniquely positioned to meet the sacred. The way in which transgender realities operate within Hinduism, however, is not uniform.

In what follows, we shall briefly examine historic movements and groups that illustrate some of the Hindu diversity and richness with respect to trans-gender realities. While doing so we should keep in mind the kind of sacred stories we have touched upon, for such provide a basis for lived realities of one kind or another. Not surprisingly, some of these center in worship of that most intimate of Hindu deities, Krishna. Widely regarded as an avatar of Vishnu, Lord Krishna enjoys popularity for a number of reasons, not least of which is his famous relationship with the woman Radha. We will begin with how this deity and this particular relationship has led to religious expressions that involve transgender realities.

Transformation in the Bengali Vaishnava Movement

Among the unique religious manifestations of Indian Hinduism is Bengali Vaishnavism (or Gaudiya Vaishnavism). Historic Bengal, now principally divided between the Indian state of West Bengal and Bangladesh, with Calcutta as its principal city, witnessed the rise of Vaishnavism in the 11th-12th centuries C.E. This movement is distinguished by its veneration of Krishna as supreme deity rather than as an avatar of Vishnu. Moreover, the focus on Krishna revolves around his relationship with his consort Radha. In the late 15th-early 16th century, the movement witnessed its most famous figure, Sri Caitanya Mahaprabhu (1486-1534). Caitanya is regarded as the incarnation of Krishna and Radha born into a single body, and thus both intimately joined and intermingled. Devotees view as their model the devotion shown by Radha and the other *gopis* ('milk-maids') who doted upon Krishna.

The manifestation of this devotion sometimes takes on gender crossing aspects. Indeed, Indian culture scholar Gerald Larson remarks that motifs of both transvestism and transsexualism are not merely present, but may be prominent in the "spiritual fantasies" of the *raganuga bhakti sadhana* (i.e., those devotees dedicated to disciplines meant to facilitate identification with the object of their worship).[722] We cannot explore this notion at any length here. Larson himself refers to, among others, the male devotees of Krishna who seek femininity in pursuit of their union with Krishna. Similarly, we have the following tale that illustrates again the sort of thing Larson is referencing.

In 16th century Greater Bengal, a conservative Brahmin named Advaitacarya headed the Gaudiya Vaishnavi community. When he died his senior wife, Sita Devi, assumed the leadership. In time she became known as Srimati Sita Devi and identified with the goddess Laksmi, consort of Krishna. An important figure in her own right, Sita Devi became the object of devotion and disciples gathered around her. A story is preserved of two men who desired to be disciples of Srimati Sita Devi. According to the tale, the men approached Sita Devi for instruction, only to be told she only taught women. However, she granted them to learn a Vaisnava meditation and encouraged them to imagine themselves as female maidservants waiting on Radha and Krishna in their love bower. The men departed. Shortly thereafter they reappeared, dressed as women. Theirs was no mere masquerade, however. Claiming that their devotion had wrought a change in their very sex, they disrobed before Sita Devi to prove it. Henceforth they were known by the feminine names of Nandini and Jangali.[723]

Bengali Vaishnavism persists into the contemporary world. Two often noted religious movements are descended from it. One is the International Society for Krishna Consciousness (ISKON), far better known simply as the Hare Krishna, once noted for their religious witnessing in the United States and elsewhere. The other is Tantric Vaishnavism (or Sahajiya Vaishnavism), which developed and elaborated the implicit erotic element in Caitanya's passion into an explicit sexuality central to belief and religious practice.[724] In Hindu Tantrism some male devotees, as an aspect of spiritual practice (*sadhana*), become like women in dress and manner, even going so far as to feign menstrual periods.[725]

The Sakhibhava Devotees of Krishna

Devotion to Krishna, as we have seen, can model itself upon the arguably most famous love relationship in Hinduism—the affection between Krishna and Radha. Given the legend that Krishna has more than 16,000 wives, and is the ultimate paramour of women, his special interest in Radha is of significant import. Since perhaps the 16th century, this relationship has been celebrated through a religious dance called the *gotipua*, performed in temples by crossdressing boys. These youth enact such Radha-Krishna poems as the Bengali *Gita Govinda* (*Song of the Cowherd*), part of the classical Vedic literature.[726]

The *Sakhibhava* sects center in the Radha-Krishna relationship. *Sakhibhava* means 'female-to-male attachment.'[727] The distinctive idea in *Sakhibhava* thinking is that Krishna preeminently embodies maleness; all other living beings play female to his maleness. Since Radha is his favorite consort, the *Sakhibhava* devotees venerate her and seek to be like her attendants. These female companions (*sakhi*), uniquely privileged as witnesses to the Krishna-Radha relationship, are thus a focus of the *Sakhibhava* sects. The male *Sakhibhava* devotees demonstrate their desire by emulation of the *sakhi*.[728] In imitation of Radha's Gopi attendants, they dress femininely, mark menstrual periods, and even occasionally undertake a femininely-assigned passive role in sexual interactions. In earlier times they also on occasion castrated themselves.[729]

The Shivshakti

Gender crossing devotees are known in other parts of India as well. The *Shivshakti* of southern India are males who come into the service of a deity through various routes. Some are given in 'marriage' to a deity while still boys. Others come as offerings from their families. A few are sold into service in response to abject poverty. By whatever motive or means they come, as *shivshakti* these biological males enact a feminine gender role, dressing and behaving as women. In this capacity they also serve sexually, and are noted for their devotion to the *shivlinga*, symbol of male and female genitalia.[730]

The Jogappas[731]

In southern India, the goddess Yellamma ('the Shameless One'; aka Holiyyamma, Jogamma, etc.), demands priestesses, called *devdassi* (temple women) as her handmaidens. Because she insists on having one such servant from every family among her devotees, where a girl (*Jogathis*) is lacking, a boy (*Jogappas* or *Jogta*) may do. Such male children dedicated to become priests to Yellamma must crossdress and enact a female gender role because the goddess will not permit touch by any male.[732] Some attribute the practice of male crossdressing as an homage to one account of the goddess, under the name of Renuka. By this account, the *Jogappas* are enacting the role of Renuka's eunuch sons. Anthropologist Erick Laurent notes that the *Jogta*, who are *not* eunuchs, are permitted to marry and have families.[733]

Originally those dedicated to Yellamma's service enjoyed high social status and performed various ritual, the most notable being sacred dance. However, these *Jogathis*, and the male *Jogappas*, became over time little more than entertainers and religious prostitutes. Their numbers today are little compared to earlier times.

The Hijras

Throughout the nation, but especially in northern India (and Pakistan) the most famous of the country's transgendered people are found—the *Hijras* (an Urdu derivation variously rendered into English, perhaps most often as 'eunuchs').[734] These people already have been considered in this work (vol. 3, answer to Q. 52), but they merit reconsideration here because of their association with Indian religious tradition. India's most famous *Hijras* are almost always anatomical males who represent a socially constituted 'third gender,' neither male nor female, though with elements of each.[735] They routinely (but not always) appear in feminine garb (*saris* or *salwar-kameez*), and, claims Lai, "all *hijras* wear a bra, which is either padded or, as is more likely, stuffed." They also assume feminine names, address each other using feminine terms (e.g., 'sister'), and adopt feminine mannerisms.[736]

Their place, historically, has been within Hinduism where they are especially associated with the female deity Bahuchara Mata,[737] who has a temple in Gujarat. These devotees of the goddess do more than just dress in female garb. Far more in the past than presently, they fulfilled a social function within society by serving as mediums for the feminine divine. They still often are found at a variety of important events and rituals with religious connotations, where their blessing is either actively sought out, or sought for fear that to not do so might bring ill fortune. Though culturally sanctioned in their religious role, some *Hijras* are also active sexually as prostitutes, a situation that poses difficulties within the larger community.[738] Their place in India was severely undercut by British colonialism and in the modern Indian state they continue to exist as a marginalized group loosely associated with Hinduism.

Historically, the *Hijras* served as eunuchs in the royal courts of Muslim rulers and thus gained influence with many adherents of Islam too. Indeed, the influence may have been reciprocal, as many *Hijras* today follow certain practices more in keeping with Islamic tradition than Hindu, such as burying their dead rather than cremating them. Some *Hijras* have become Muslim.[739] In fact, the heads of the leading *Hijra* houses typically identify as Muslim alongside their identity as Hindu.[740] Even today many Muslims, like many Hindus, believe that the *Hijras* mediate a divine ability to bless or curse; refusing them money or gifts is thought by some to bring bad luck.

The *Hijras* locate their origin in Hindu sacred literature—the *Mahabharata* and the *Ramayana*. In the former, the *Hijras* of Tamil Nadu locate their origin. The story, locally preserved, recounts how Arjuna's son Aravan nobly offered himself as a sacrifice to the goddess Kali in order to secure victory for the Pandavas in the Kurukshetra War. However, Aravan insisted he not die before he spent a night as a married man. When no woman proved willing to join him, the god Krishna assumed form as Mohini to marry him. The Tamil Nadu *Hijras* call themselves *aravanis*—descendents of Aravan.

In the *Ramayana*, the hero Rama upon his banishment bid his followers, both men and women, to turn back. In one version, a certain band of devotees, who felt excepted from Rama's injunction because they identified as neither men nor women, persisted in accompanying him. In another version, after Rama had implored the men and women following him to return to their mundane duties, he set off by himself, vanquished his foe Ravana, and after 14 years returned to the river bank at the edge of the forest where he had left his followers. There he was surprised to discover a band awaiting his return. They explained that since they are neither men nor women they were exempt from his direction and so had waited for his return.[741] In either version, these *Hijras* win Rama's favor by their exceptional devotion. He bestows upon them the power to confer blessings on special occasions (e.g., marriage, childbirth). In this story the *Hijras* locate the sanction for their practice of *badhai* (asexual ritual practice involving singing and dancing).

What connection does Sri Ramakrishna have with transgender?

One modern figure, who practiced Vaishnavism and Tantrism before finding his center in devotion to the goddess Kali, is Sri Ramakrishna Paramahamsa[742] (1836-1886). His story is both unique and *not* singular. Other prominent Hindu figures could also be used to illustrate a connection between spirituality and transgender realities, but Ramakrishna is especially appropriate because he is the best-known figure to Westerners from India's more recent past. A spiritual seeker who not only pursued the many paths of Hinduism, but also experimented with Islamic Sufism, Ramakrishna served as a priest in the temple of Dakshinewar in Calcutta.[743] Born into a poor Brahmin family, under the name Gadadhar Chattopadhyaya (or Gadadhar Chatterji), Ramakrishna in the short half-century of his life became India's most famous—and controversial—spiritual figure.

His relevance to our discussion of transgender realities stems from an unusual life that has been variously appraised. A disciple's diaries form the basis for much of what has been preserved of his life and teachings. The material reveals someone candid about the connection between sexuality and religion, and in touch with what we in the West call 'transgender' realities. Indeed, pioneering science journalist Gobind Behari Lal, the first South Asian reporter to win a Pulitzer prize (1937), extolled Ramakrishna in an appendix to Harry Benjamin's landmark volume *The Transsexual Phenomenon* (1966). Lal wrote that Ramakrishna possessed a kind of genius that permitted him to perceive the "plurality of sex patterns in every human being" and who himself sometimes played the role of 'Man-God' and sometimes that of 'Woman-God.'[744]

Indian psychoanalyst Sudhir Kakar has written that if we use the language of the modern West's psychoanalytic tradition Ramakrishna could be diagnosed as a 'secondary transsexual.' Kakar remarks:

> He would seamlessly fit in with Robert Stoller's description of the secondary transsexual as being someone who differs from his primary counterpart in that he does not appear feminine from the start of any behavior that may be classed in gender terms. Under the surface of masculinity, however, there is the persistent impulse toward being feminine, an urge which generally manifests itself in adolescence. The most obvious manifestation of these urges is the wish or the actual wearing of women's clothes. Though these urges may gather in strength and last for longer and longer periods, the masculine aspects of identity are never completely submerged. [745]

298

We shall see to what extent Ramakrishna may be characterized in such manner, but first we must provide some biographical context.

Sri Ramakrishna's Life

We shall not overly detail Ramakrishna's life, as it is fully recounted in many works, most especially through the well-known *Sri Sri Ramakrishna Kathamrta*, written by Master Mahasaya (Mahendranath Gupta, under the designation 'M.') based on his diaries, then translated by Swami Nikhilananda as *The Gospel of Sri Ramakrishna*.[746] But a brief outline is not inappropriate.[747] Despite his family belonging to the Hindu upper caste, they were poor and Ramakrishna received a perfunctory formal education. Despite this, he was known as a child of exquisite spiritual sensitivity and religious interests. He is reputed to have experienced religious trances as early as age 7. In 1852, at age 16, his family's poverty necessitated both Ramakrishna and his elder brother Ramkumar to leave their home village of Kamarpukar to seek employment in Calcutta. There, after three years as family priests, both young men found positions as temple priests in the recently completed (1855) Dakshinewar temples. At age 23, he was formally married to Sara-devi (aka. Sarada, or Sharada), then just 5 years old. The marriage was never consummated, as Ramakrishna was a dedicated celibate. However, she remained his wife until his death and she, too, was later venerated.

Ramakrishna's entrance into the service of Kali marked a turning-point. Over the next dozen years his life was characterized by an intense spiritual seeking, perhaps initiated or intensified by his brother's death in 1856. Seeking the immediate presence of Kali-Ma (Kali-the-Mother) preoccupied Ramakrishna. He gained attention for his fasting and spending the hours of the night naked, weeping and entreating Kali as he waited under an *amalaka* tree in the Panchavati garden. Months passed without a vision of Kali. In despair, contemplating suicide, Ramakrishna suddenly experienced a flood of illumination in an intense but blissful vision of the goddess.

Ramakrishna, through this 'oceanic feeling' (as Freud termed such mystic experiences), awakened. This initiated him into a new series of struggles as he practiced various *sadhanas* ('spiritual disciplines')—steps intended to facilitate an identification between the devotee and the deity. At first, his fervor and his internal ferment combined to produce some behaviors that seemed so bizarre that various observers wondered if he had lost his mind. But under the guidance of a woman *sannyasin*[748] named Bhairavi Brahmani, Ramakrishna found direction for his spiritual energies. He first accomplished tantric *sadhana*, then proceeded to Vaishnava *sadhana*. The itinerant monk Jota-puri initiated him into Vedanta (Vedic philosophy). He next moved to Advaita *sadhana*. These spiritual disciplines constituted a rigorous training that took a toll on Ramakrishna's health. Sickened by dysentery, he was for a time removed back to his native village to recuperate.

Ramakrishna continued to pursue spiritual exploration. He examined both Islam and Christianity. Together with his experience of various forms of Hinduism, these explorations persuaded him that these various religious paths were seeking a similar goal.[749] Though he understood that practitioners of different religions might view their way as the exclusively correct one, he saw deeper into a universal spirituality that championed unity in religious diversity. This conviction, alongside his own renowned passionate devotion, proved attractive to many people.

Disciples began to gather. Unlike the Western caricature of the mystic who separates from the affairs of the world, Ramakrishna engaged his world energetically. He eagerly sought young men to whom he might convey his vision. In 1879, his first disciples gathered around him. Over the remaining seven years of his life he taught them. Among these devotees his favorite was Narendra, better known to the world as Swami Vivekananda, who assumed leadership of the others after Ramakrishna's death.

Ramakrishna & Transgender Realities

To Western eyes, Ramakrishna has often seemed a bizarre spiritual eccentric whose ways ultimately prove incomprehensible. In part, this is because our Western culture feels uncomfortable seeing sexuality and religion in too close proximity. Ramakrishna's openness about such matters consternates many. Sensitive to this, the English translation of the *Kathamrta* (or, *Kathamrita*) 'sanitizes' the Indian original. However, a number of scholarly studies have sought to uncover the saint in what Western eyes often see as sin.

Religious scholar Jeffrey Kripal, in his *Kali's Child: The Mystical and the Erotic in the Life and Teachings of Ramakrishna*—a book both honored for its scholastic excellence and marked by controversy—offers English readers a different level of access to materials from the *Kathamrta*, especially those associated with the "secret sayings" (*guhya katha*) of the text, not found in the official English translation based on this work. Kripal's focus is on Ramakrishna's alleged homosexuality, which he takes as the hermeneutical key to comprehending much of Ramakrishna's life and teaching. Thus, for example, Kripal argues that Ramakrishna's crossdressing is best viewed "within the context of his homosexual orientation and the erotic mysticism such an orientation helped create."[750]

Though Kripal's work has been criticized severely by some of Ramakrishna's devotees, Gerald Larson observes that for more than a half century:

> [T]he eccentric sexual fantasies and practices of Ramakrishna have been well-known, including transvestism, transsexuality (longings to become a girl widow), oral and anal fantasies (both heterosexual and homosexual), castration fantasies of one kind or another and what psychoanalysis generally refers to as the "polymorphous sexuality" characteristic of the earliest stages of human development.[751]

Whatever one decides about Ramakrishna's sexual orientation, there remains plenty to consider with respect to transgender realities.

We have seen already psychoanalyst Sadhir Kakar's musing on the 'secondary transsexualism' of Ramakrishna. Goldman, who as we've seen locates Indian transsexualism in the Oedipal conflict of the son to his father, sees in Ramakrishna a case 'strongly reminiscent' of Freud's patient, Dr. Paul Daniel Schreber. This individual, confined to an asylum, believed he was part of a divine plan that included being transformed into a woman "by and for the enjoyment of God," as Goldman puts it.[752] Yet, if nothing else, there remains one profound difference between this Western case and Ramakrishna in the East—the former is judged someone to be put away from humankind, while the latter comes to be regarded as a great saint.

Culture exercises a decisive element. Kakar puts Ramakrishna in his cultural context—a context in which Western psychoanalytic labels may seem out of place. For example, Kakar notes that Ramakrishna grew up in a time and place where his early 'feminine identifications' were met with a greater tolerance than he would find in our contemporary West. He points out, too, that labels like 'transsexual' or 'homosexual' might obscure Ramakrishna's easy acceptance of his own femininity and, perhaps worse, lead us to view this as a sign of mental illness rather than as a token of a great human achievement. Indeed, in Kakar's view, Ramakrishna needed to draw upon this feminine identification because of its essential role in mysticism.[753]

What is important in Kakar's musings is his explicit recognition that what we call transgender realities is fundamentally important to Ramakrishna's spirituality. Those familiar with Indian religious expressions know that what Western scholars often refer to as 'religious transvestism' is a phenomenon that has been found in various parts of India over a prolonged history.[754] Ramakrishna participated in this behavior purposefully, crossdressing and imitating feminine manner as part of his praise of the *madhura bhava* ('the sweet mood')[755]—a *bhakti* devotional practice wherein the devotee is spiritually joined with the deity as a husband and wife are united in bliss.

Ramakrishna, as Lal observes, grasped that our male/female, masculine/feminine distinctions are illusory. They are rooted in an over-valuation of body distinctions, a kind of egoism that only serves to keep us separated from the essential unity of the universe. A practice dressing and living as a member of a different sex or gender facilitates overcoming this illusion, which in turn aids in overcoming the separation from Brahma.[756] By embracing femininity, then, Ramakrishna served profoundly religious ends.

With respect to his own femininity, in the *Kathamrta* Ramakrishna says:

> How can a man conquer passion? He should assume the attitude of a woman. I spent many days as the handmaid of God. I dressed myself in women's clothes, put on ornaments, and covered the upper part of my body with a scarf, just like a

woman. With the scarf on I used to perform the evening worship before the image. Otherwise, how could I have kept my wife with me for eight months? Both of us behaved as if we were the handmaids of the Divine Mother. I cannot speak of myself as a man.[757]

About this passage, religion scholar Kelley Ann Raab remarks, "The Vaishnavite mystical tenet that all humankind is female while God alone is male provides a spiritual explanation for Ramakrishna's actions."[758] Kripal, despite a different evaluation of Ramakrishna's crossdressing, acknowledges that the behavior was associated with worship, noting that Ramakrishna's comment, "At that time, while I performed the worship, I would wear silk garments and experience such bliss—the bliss of worship!" likely was in the context of his fanning the image of the goddess as a woman among other women worshipers.[759]

Raab elaborates that in this Hindu tradition another idea is that the male who comes to accept the self as feminine can thereby escape male bodily desires. Such a state elicits an awareness that the self is neither 'man' nor 'woman,' but rather 'impersonal spirit'—exactly the state capable of communion with Brahman, who is the same. [760] She also observes that crossdressing can be seen as a way to go beyond sexuality, the transcending of which constitutes a way past dualism in metaphysical thought.[761] Either viewed theologically or philosophically, crossdressing in this context is truly *trans*gender.

Ramakrishna's crossdressing is especially associated with his sometimes residence at the house of Mathur Babu, who was devoted to him. In the *Kathamrta* Ramakrishna recalls his stay at Mathur's Janbazar mansion: "While living there I regarded myself as the handmaid of the Divine Mother. The ladies of the house didn't feel at all bashful with me. They felt as free before me as women feel before a small boy or girl. I used to escort Mathur's daughter to her husband's chamber with the maidservant."[762] Kripal reports that Mathur would buy Ramakrishna women's clothes and jewelry, which on occasion elicited ecstasy and visions. Kripal notes, for example, that Ramakrishna's 'handmaid-like' vision of Radha (Krishna's favorite; see above) occurred immediately after such a gift. As Kripal tells it, Ramakrishna's crossdressing accompanied visions of other important women in Hindu tradition. For example, on one occasion after Mathur had dressed Ramakrishna in women's garments, he experienced transformation into Sita, faithful wife of Rama, hero of the *Ramayana*. [763]

Kripal is dismissive of Ramakrishna's disciple Swami Saradananda's interpretation of his master's crossdressing as "a spiritual technique that enabled the Master to realize the conditioned status of gender," an impermanent and ultimately false state. Instead, Kripal locates the meaning of Ramakrishna's crossdressing in his struggle with his own sexuality in the presence of Mathur and his young wife, Sarada.[764] While we cannot dismiss the impact of the real people around Ramakrishna, the weight of all available evidence suggests he was at least as tuned to the deities he worshipped as to the people close to him (and

Sarada he venerated as the Divine Mother). Ramakrishna was preeminently dedicated to the realization of profound religious states; his life and world were those of the mystic, not man of the flesh. Kripal's fixation on Ramakrishna's sexuality may mislead him to an overvaluation of a real issue (the very human grappling with sex and gender) and the undervaluation of the dominant force in Ramakrishna's life (mystical union with the transcendent divine).

While his crossdressing is most remarked upon, there is other evidence of Ramakrishna's transgender practices. Raab, for example, comments that he experienced "hysterical menstruation" and even offered his breast to his disciples to suckle at.[765] Both of these practices are worth examining more closely.

With regard to the former, Ramakrishna allegedly experienced bleeding for three days from the region around his pubic hair (*swadhisthanachakra*), interpreted as his 'menstruation.' In the introduction to the *Kathamrta* the context of such matters is set out as follows:

> Sri Ramakrishna now devoted himself to scaling the most inaccessible and dizzy heights of dualistic worship, namely the complete union with Sri Krishna as the Beloved of the heart. He regarded himself as one of the gopis of Vrindavan, mad with longing for her divine Sweetheart. At his request Mathur provided him with woman's dress and jewelry. In this love pursuit, food and drink were forgotten. Day and night he wept bitterly. The yearning turned into a mad frenzy; for the divine Krishna began to play with him the old tricks He had played with the gopis. He would tease and taunt, now and then revealing Himself, but always keeping at a distance. Sri Ramakrishna's anguish brought on a return of the old physical symptoms: the burning sensation, an oozing of blood through the pores, a loosening of the joints, and the stopping of physiological functions.[766]

With reference to Ramakrishna offering his breast, the *Kathamrta* relates that Ramakrishna identified with Yasoda, the woman who nursed Krishna, in his relationship with his young disciple Rakhal Ghosh (later known as Swami Brahmananda). Ramakrishna regarded Rakhal as a person like himself,[767] like a son given him by Kali,[768] and as the young Lord Krishna.[769] The affection was reciprocated. The text says: "Rakhal felt toward the Master as a child feels toward its mother. He would sit leaning on the Mother's lap as a young child leans on its mother while sucking her breast."[770] Historian Narasingha Prosad Sil cites Ramakrishna's remark about Rakhal that, "While at play, he would come running to me, sit on my lap, and suck my tits."[771]

What are we to make of such things? We may, like many Western writers, interpret them as indications of a deeply troubled man. Perhaps Ramakrishna is best understood as someone who struggled profoundly with his sexuality and his gender identity, turning to religion in an effort to manage his own experience. On the other hand, perhaps we may find credibility in his disciples' discernment that their Master's actions reflect an intense and transcendant spirituality, a realization of realities most of us do not even glimpse—in part because we shrink from seeing sexuality as something that can serve spirituality, and in part because we tend to reductionistically make all transgender realities merely sexual in character. What if transgender realities open up higher realities, subordinating sex, gender, and sexuality distinctions to a more profound unity?

Ramakrishna himself may have offered his own interpretation. According to the *Kathamrta* Ramakrishna explained, "There is Someone within me who does all these things through me"—a sentiment that seems little different than that offered by the Christian apostle Paul.[772] But this does not mean Ramakrishna leaves no room for personal agency; the human will can chain itself to higher ends. A little further on, Ramakrishna advises a young man, "A man can change his nature by imitating another's character. He can get rid of a passion like lust by assuming the feminine mood. He gradually comes to act exactly like a woman."[773] As we have seen in a previous volume (see answers to Q. 45-46), such an idea is also not entirely foreign to Western thinking.

If we are to err in how we construe Ramakrishna's acts, it seems wisest to err in the direction of trying to see such matters in his own context, and credit his own explanations. Whatever unconscious motivations might have been present remain forever a matter of speculation. But the record of how those around him viewed these things is open to public inspection. They, in deference to Ramakrishna's own perceptions, place his engagement with transgender realities squarely in the service of his spirituality. Through such participation he transcended the limits of gender and entered into a close identification with deity. There seems insufficient cause for us not to credit such thinking, especially given its manifest success in Ramakrishna's life and the fact that we have similar testimony from so many others that transgender realities can facilitate a deep spirituality.

Conclusion: A More Recent Example

Transgender realities persist in modern India, in both continuity and discontinuity with the past. The influence of colonialism, mentioned earlier, can scarcely be overestimated though we have stayed rather clear of it in the foregoing discussion. But colonialism changed India, forcing an accommodation to the West that continues today. Because of it, transgender realities have changed too, both in valuation and interpretation. Yet they persist, displaying the same remarkable resilience and strength characteristic of Hinduism itself.

As a concluding example, we shall consider the case of Nandamuri Taraka Rama Rao (1923-1995), famed first as an actor, later as a political figure. Popularly known simply by his initials (N.T.R.), Rao came from humble peasant roots, but found access to a larger world through acting. His first stage role, in the early 1940s, was crossdressed as the heroine of *Rachamullina Dautyami*. In

1960, he played the role of Lord Krishna in *Sri Venkateswara Mahatyam* and from that point began to receive veneration from fans, who regarded him as their 'living god.' After a distinguished career in films, in 1982 he formed the Telugu Desam Party, which within a year established itself as a significant force in the southern Indian state of Andhra Pradesh. Rao three times became Chief Minister of Andhra Pradesh and, among other reforms, championed amending the Hindu Succession Act to provide equal property rights for women.[774]

Rao understood and embraced Hindu religious symbolism as part of his populist politics. Exploiting his well-known portrayal of Krishna, he would dress in robes of saffron or white and encouraged the practice of his followers, who prostrated themselves, touching his feet in the traditional Hindu expression of fealty.[775] He was also capable of even more dramatic expressions. In his exploration of Hindu identities in the colonial and post-colonial periods of Indian history, Parama Roy notes Rao's employment while in political office of feminine dress, including makeup and jewelry, on one-half of his body. Roy views Rao's behavior as an apparent bid to consolidate his political/spiritual power.[776]

Cynical Westerners may be prone to see in Rao's actions purely political motives, divorced from any further or higher ends. But such a conclusion doubtless says more about the foreign observer than about Rao. Perhaps he was merely a calculating power-monger. Yet other, more appealing conclusions are possible.

In drawing upon such potent symbolism, Rao utilized transgender reality in a manner seen often in history and around the world—to bridge spheres normally kept separate. In Rao's case, this was the gulf between Hindu spirituality beloved by the people and the secular politics Rao immersed himself in. But it was also a way to position himself as a figure bridging the gulf between ordinary people and deity—a role commonly seen among shamans. It serves as one more instance of the remarkable power of transgender realities in Indian life, a power that persists despite Western prejudices against it.

Q. 80 Is Buddhism tolerant of cross-dressing?

The Short Answer. Transgendered realities are well-known in Buddhist lands. Crossdressing occurs in many countries where Buddhism is practiced and it even has a special place in the history of Buddhism. No less than other religions, Buddhism has attempted to reckon with transgendered realities, and to do so within a broader context of how it understands gender. In that respect, Buddhism presents a mixed picture. Particularly within Mahayana Buddhism there are many schools that espouse an ideal of gender equality in the pursuit of salvation. Various religious texts encourage such an ideal, especially the *Lotus Sutra*. Yet actual practice has generally failed to realize this ideal. If women, one of the two dominant genders, struggle for equality and sometimes even tolerance, how much more likely is it that transgender people, existing along the borders of conforming gender roles and identities, will enjoy acceptance? Still, there are resources that both women and transgender people can draw upon within Buddhism. Like many religious traditions, Buddhism speaks of gender-altering divine figures—one way to pattern and explain the mirroring facts of human experience. Gender-altering also serves as a way to manage ordinary religious realities in a patriarchal context. Through transgendering experience devout individuals are able to transcend hindrances, such as being assigned a subordinate gender status, in order to achieve spiritual development. Aiding this quest is the Buddhist conviction that ordinary life is beset by illusions that must be overcome to attain enlightenment. By perceiving sex and gender as illusory forms the Buddhist path permits moving between sex and gender categories along the way of transcending them—a perfect recipe for transgender experience. At the same time, in the mundane reality that occupies our daily attention, different sexual bodies and gender identities and roles call for some practical review. In this respect, Buddhists distinguish more than merely a masculine male/feminine female dichotomy. Transgender realities like intersex are recognized. Moreover, in some strands of Buddhism the dominant masculine privilege is reversed. Tantric Buddhism, for example, offers prominence for the female. But ultimately, becoming Bodhisattva on the path to Buddhahood means leaving behind the painful ties associated with sex, sexuality and gender in favor of the bliss of enlightenment.

The Longer Answer. Like any religion, Buddhism has had to reckon with sex and gender.[777] As in the modern West, Buddhism tends to find a very close connection between them. In other words, psychological gender is viewed as so closely tied to body sex that a change in the former is typically thought to require a change in the latter. Thus the stories of transformation in gender found in classical Buddhist texts are stories of changes in body sex. Still, as in other respects, we cannot assume this general tendency as a hard and fast rule. There does appear some recognition of a difference between sex and gender, thus leaving open the possibility of pairings other than feminine female or masculine male.

Like people everywhere, Buddhists are faced with sorting out not merely what gender is, and how closely it may be paired with body sex and sexual behavior, but also how important or not it is in religious matters. Not unexpectedly, like other religions, explorations and musings about sex and gender are expressed both in contemplation of divine figures as well as human ones. Although this is not an introductory text in world religions, some brief summary of the basic thrust of Buddhism seems advisable to root us in its world. In what follows we will first seek the essential philosophy of the religion, then examine its treatment of pertinent aspects of sex and gender with regard to both divine and mundane realities.

Basic Buddhism

Buddhism urges we not be distracted by the illusions that surround us. These illusions bind, blind, and wound us. Enlightenment sees through the illusory garb of what seems 'real' to reveal the enduring truth, most basically expressed in the Four Noble Truths. The first of these truths finds humanity's basic problem in suffering rooted in *karma*—acts that bring consequences either in this life or the next. The second truth tells that bad karma flows from craving—either desiring wrong things or inappropriately lusting after right things. The third truth offers a remedy: eliminate craving, which ends bad karma, and brings cessation to suffering. The fourth truth proposes an Eightfold Path as the ethical and practical way of living so as to accomplish this end.

As in other religions, various differences of thought and practice eventually created distinctly different forms of Buddhism. Two major traditions persist: Mahayana ('the Great Vessel') Buddhism and Theravada Buddhism (sometimes referred to as Hinayana, 'the Lesser Vehicle'), the older and narrower branch. But in addition to these there are a number of other Buddhist expressions. Buddhist traditions look to important texts to guide them. Buddhist *sutras* offer many discourses attributed to Buddha; different groups have elevated one or another to a higher status. Buddhist *dharma* (teaching) stresses that an individual shapes his or her own destiny. The accumulation of good karma results in rebirth to a higher state, the loftiest of which in the mortal realm is attainment of Buddha status (a *Bodhisattva* is a 'Buddha-in-the-making').

Consonant with other religions, Buddhism grapples with human experience in part by looking at divine counterparts. If transgendered realities are found in this sphere, what might be discovered among immortal or enlightened figures to explain, or at least parallel, earthly experience? Answering such a question unfolds over time and in diverse ways. For Buddhism the first problem was that the classical expression of the religion, in itself, left no explicit room for divine beings.

What role do divine beings and Bodhisattvas play in Buddhism?

While classical Buddhism can be described as devoid of deity, resembling a philosophy or psychology as much as a religion, over time many more explicitly religious features emerged, including representation of the Buddhahood in divine forms. Cynics may ascribe this development as a response to the pressure of other religions whose popular appeal stemmed in part from promoting access to divine, but highly accessible figures. On the other hand, the development of the Mahayana tradition over its first half-millennium can be seen as a logical working out of its missionary effort to extend Buddhist compassion and the path to enlightenment. Much as Christianity did, Buddhism incorporated previously existing figures (e.g., the *kami* of Shinto Japan) and developed a sense of differing degrees of saintliness among its Bodhisattvas.

Bodhisattvas

Interestingly, in Buddhism the various gods and other nonhuman figures embraced within its sphere remain subordinate to another class of beings: the *Bodhisattvas* (a 'Buddha-in-the-making' is also an 'enlightened being'). The Bodhisattvas are themselves of two kinds. There are Bodhisattvas who are devotees who attain Buddhist ideals of practice, following the Dharma correctly, living life as models of Buddhist compassion, supporting the Buddhist community—in short, to use Christian language, who 'live like Buddha would.' These compassionate figures decide, after attaining enlightenment, not to enter Nirvana, but instead remain to aid others in their spiritual quest. The other kind of Bodhisattva is a figure who comes from Buddha-land, like a savior, to offer help to earnest spiritual seekers.

East Asian religious scholar Miriam Levering observes that in Buddhist *sutras* the dominant figures are neither mere human figures, nor divine beings, but the Bodhisattvas and Buddhas. With respect to our specific concerns, both of these latter types are esteemed for having gained freedom from sexuality and for having transcended gender.[778] However, this transcendence does not mean an independence from gender identification. Rather, it means either a claim that gender itself is illusory or inconsequential for spiritual matters, or that the limitations imposed in this world upon a particular gender can be surmounted by transformation into another gender. This latter ability especially proves pivotal for women, as we shall soon see. But first we must attend to the relation between Bohisattvas and divine beings.

Avalokitesvara/Kuan-yin

Buddhist salvation—the path to enlightenment—was open not only to human beings, but to divine figures as well. A deity can become a Bodhisattva. In fact, one of the most popular figures of the Mahayana Buddhist tradition is the divine person Avalokitesvara ('the Lord who hears and sees the deepest things'), a Bodhisattva of the *Lotus Sutra.* Devotees in India, China, Tibet, Japan, and other southeastern Asian nations have venerated this divinity. Avalokitesvara can serve us as a notable instance in the way gender may be juxtaposed with salvation.

Avalokitesvara can assume many forms, but 33 have been identified as major, and 9 of these as primary. These forms may appear as male, or female, or hermaphroditic. One of the primary forms is Cundi, a female representation (the mother goddess). In China, where the worship of Avalokitesvara as Kuanyin (or Guanyin, or Kwan-yin) dates to near the beginning of the Common Era, early representations were uniformly masculine. But by the 12th century, female representations were also utilized; a popular depiction is of an attractive, middle-aged, white-robed woman. Some representations show Avalokitesvara with both male and female signs.[779]

There are various ways this variability can be assessed. Some might claim that the same being is venerated in different places as a fixed gender figure, either male or female. Seen this way, it may not be the figure that changes, but the perception of devotees. In some instances, like China, the figure was first associated with one sex, and then another, but without being viewed as a gender changing deity in the way a trickster deity might be. Or, given the existence also of hermaphroditic representations, the deity can be viewed as both masculine and feminine—or either gender at will—with the important point being that no gender confines the divine essence. In sum, there is no reason not to regard that this beloved deity displays freedom with respect to sex and gender, using either or both to reflect valued qualities.

Nevertheless, even such a remarkable figure can be subjected by society to efforts at control through interpretation. We might think that such a being shows that gender is immaterial to attaining spiritual enlightenment. Therefore, manifestation in female form would seem to offer encouragement to mortal women. But is this the case? Barbara Reed, scholar of religion and Asian studies, has explored whether Kuan-yin actually has assisted Chinese women in transcending Confucian patriarchalism or instead has tended to reinforce societal restrictions. She acknowledges that from the Sung Dynasty to the present, Kuan-yin has been looked up to by women. "For women," she writes, "this has meant a symbol of someone who would serve as their savior from all suffering, but especially from the suffering arising out of their female birth: arranged marriages, sexual attacks, the pain and stigma of both menstruation and childbirth, and the powerlessness of childlessness in a patriarchal society." Ultimately, decides Reed, Kuan-yin proves to be a figure offering women a way to ease their suffering by reconciling their lives' conflicting values: the desirability of autonomy to realize personal spiritual growth versus the value encouraged by patriarchy of nurturing family relationships.[780]

As many religions show, deities often transcend the gender distinctions and limitations common among human beings. In Buddhism this fact serves double duty. On one hand it reinforces the notion that apparent sex and gender distinctions are illusory. As such they serve as enticements to error and to suffering, though positively the appearance of gendered qualities can serve noble ends by highlighting gender-associated traits seen as admirable. On the other hand, because they are illusory the gender statuses and even the sexual bodies can be transformed and transcended—neither sex nor gender is an immutable obstacle to enlightenment. That latter truth is critical to understanding how Buddhism in practice may surmount its patriarchal system.

How does gender figure in the quest for enlightenment?

Both the long history and multiple representations of Buddhism render any short, summary statement about the religion's regard of gender differences immediately suspect. Few will quarrel with a general characterization of Buddhist practice as patriarchal. The religion traditionally has been male-dominated with an entrenched masculine privilege. Despite this, the religious philosophy inherent to Buddhism extols a perspective that is not intrinsically patriarchal. In fact, texts like the *Lotus Sutra* may offer the possibility of conceiving a significant gender equality in Buddhist thought. We shall explore this further, but we must continue our more general consideration of Buddhism's wrestling with gender.

First, while our principal interest lies in the possibilities within Buddhism for transgender realities, that interest can only be pursued by reckoning with two basic truths. One is that the dominant, conforming genders of masculinity and femininity frame all discussions of gender. Any so-called 'third genders' are mentioned in connection with these dominant ones. The other truth is that most discourse on gender focus especially on the subordinate conforming gender group: girls and women. In fact, unless we see the gender hierarchy's power and how the conforming genders grapple with it we cannot see the manner in which transgender realities emerge and exercise influence.

Second, we should note that many have remarked upon a difference between Buddhist traditions in the handling of gender, especially with respect to how women are regarded. Often the older, smaller tradition of Theravadin Buddhism is characterized as more rigid in its representation of the gender hierarchy. Commonly this is attributed to its focus on the monastic life and the inferior status of nuns to monks. In contrast, Mahayana Buddhism is typically seen as more generous in spirit. It is often seen as largely, if not entirely, leveling the gender playing field. This commonly is attributed to its openness to the possibility of any being attaining Buddhahood. The accuracy of these characterizations has been challenged by some, and of course does not address at all other specific Buddhist expressions, such as Tantric Buddhism. In considering what follows it is wise to remember that broad strokes often cover over fine lines and their important detail.

Buddhist Attitudes on Gender

Asian philosophy and religion scholar Alan Sponberg finds four distinct attitudes in Buddhism. The first he calls 'soteriological inclusiveness' and he maintains that Buddha's basic stance on gender in relation to salvation was that gender differences are insignificant. But Buddhist practice conformed to social realities, leading to the second attitude: 'institutional androcentrism.' Sponberg sees the social pressures of the time explaining why women were subordinated to men, including Buddhist nuns to priests, resulting in their marginalization. A more extreme attitude about women is found in a third attitude—'ascetic misogyny'—that Sponberg regards as an overreaction to women dedicating themselves to religious life. The final attitude he terms 'soteriological androgyny,' a Mahayana ideal offering feminine wisdom as the 'mother of all Buddhas.'[781]

Sponberg may be overly charitable in his estimation of the fourth attitude. There are abundant indications of the bifurcation between men and women that results in a gender hierarchy with men on top—and zealously protecting that status. Taiwanese Buddhist scholar Heng-Ching Shih recognizes this and points out that it is consonant with Buddhist thought to regard the difference between the sexes as an illusion, so that religiously the spirit of Buddhism is egalitarian, though actual practice in the lived world of Buddhist experience frequently falls short of that ideal. If in the mundane world the gendered order prizes masculinity, Shih maintains that the *sutras* in Mahayana present "a gradual evolution of a positive concept of women." She distinguishes four types of *sutras* with regard to women: those holding a negative view; those denying a woman's presence in Buddhaland; those accepting of woman as lower state *Bodhisattvas*; and those accepting of women as advanced *Bodhisattvas* and imminent Buddhas.[782]

Thus, one way to see Buddhism, at least with respect to the traditions of Theravada and Mahayana, is to find an evolution of thinking on gender. The older Theravadin tradition, in this view, departed somewhat from the founder's stance as a practical solution to gender issues in the developing religion. An unfortunate consequence of this was making the wider culture's gender hierarchy a power within the religion through the distinctions in status and treatment of monks and nuns. Mahayana, a wider and more popular form of Buddhism, prospered by beginning to redress the earlier gender imbalance. Over the centuries its *sutras* progressively admitted to more and more possibilities for women. The apex of this development are interpretations of the *Lotus Sutra* that accord to women the ability to become fully enlightened in their own lifetimes. To test this logic we must venture some consideration of the founder's thoughts on the subject (recognizing, of course, their preservation was by others who held their own vested interests).

Buddha on Gender

Naturally, a critical interest is in uncovering what the founding Buddha taught in regard to gender. In this respect, the material is mixed—a trait consistent with later Buddhist sources. On the one hand, well-known remarks reflect a low estimation of women and the fact of Buddha's resistance to women seeking the same kind of religious life that men did is incontrovertible. At the same time, Buddha did finally yield to the entrance of women into the spiritual community (*sangha*) as 'nuns' (*bhikkhun*). Similarly, there are comments that can be plausibly interpreted in a manner more favorable toward those who are not masculine men.

We may begin with the 'good news,' namely those materials suggesting that Buddha did not regard nonmasculine gender as an obstacle. Perhaps the words most often appealed to for the argument that Buddha regarded gender as a neutral matter in attaining enlightenment are found in the following saying with reference to the Dharma, from *Sanyutta-Nikaya* (*The Books of the Kindred Spirits*):

Upright, is the name of the path, no fear is the direction.
Not crooked is the name of the chariot with the eye of the Teaching.
Shame is the brakes and the accessories are mindfulness.
Charioteer I say is the Teaching and right view, the attendant.
If *any woman or man* goes in this direction,
He reaches close up to extinction in this vehicle [italics added].[783]

If both men and women are included, why stop there? The sense of inclusiveness may extend to those who do not identify with either gender group. A saying like this does not have to be read as applying to only the dominant genders because the idea here is less a matter of specific genders than that any *person* who adheres to the path of the Dharma may attain the sought goal. In other words, the emphasis is on '*any*' rather than 'woman or man.' There is no compelling logical reason not to view the teaching as applicable to nonconforming gender people—the so called 'third gender' or transgender folk.

Against such material is, most notoriously, the Buddha's resistance to the admission of women into a dedicated religious life as nuns (*bhikkhun*). The story of his stance is told in the *Cullavagga*, one part of the *Vinaya Pitaka*. It relates how Maha-pajapati, the nurse of the Buddha in his infancy, sought admission into the holy ranks of those who give up their mundane lives at home to serve in the religious community:

She said to the Blessed One, "It would be well, Lord, if women should be allowed to renounce their homes and enter

313

the homeless state under the doctrine and discipline proclaimed by the Tathagata."

The Buddha replied, "Enough, O Gotami! Let it not please you that women should be allowed to do so." A second and a third time Maha-pajapati made the same request in the same words, and received the same reply. Then Maha-pajapati, sad and sorrowful that the Blessed One would not allow women to enter the homeless state, bowed down before the Blessed One. Keeping him on her right hand as she passed him, she departed weeping and in tears.[784]

There is no indication in the text of the Buddha's refusal being some manner of test. Indeed, after Maha-pajapati has departed, it is not Buddha but the monk Ananda who is moved by her sorrowful state. He therefore undertakes to intervene with Buddha on her behalf—an act that is held against him by some of his colleagues. Ananda repeats Maha-pajapati's words, with exactly the same results. So he takes a different approach, inquiring whether a woman who actually does as Maha-pajapati has asked permission to do will thereby gain the hoped for spiritual benefits. To this question Buddha replies affirmatively; women are indeed capable of attaining spiritual heights. After Ananda then reminds Buddha of Maha-japati's great service to him already, Buddha at last responds that if she takes upon herself Eight Chief Rules, that act will serve as her ordination.

Now this material can admittedly be comprehended in more than one manner. While some may emphasize the resistance at the start, others may point to Buddha's susceptibility when approached in the right manner. And the text does affirm a woman's spiritual capability. Yet that acknowledgment is immediately qualified by placing on Maha-japati eight rules not imposed on monks. These might be interpreted in different ways, but it is hard not to have the impression they place any woman agreeing to them in a subordinate status. That impression is strongly reinforced immediately thereafter.

Buddha still seems resistant to the idea—or perhaps cognizant of the effect it might have on his monks. The account concludes with Buddha's rueful remark to Ananda that his concession will cut the duration of the 'pure religion and the good law' in half. In a telling illustration, Buddha says, "Houses in which there are many women but only a few men are easily violated by robber burglars. In the same way, Ananda, under whatever doctrine and discipline women are allowed to go out from household life into the homeless state, that religion will not last long."[785]

Obviously, with such material the question of whether Buddha himself actually expressed all of it, or even some, persists. The sentiments attributed to Buddha mirror the concerns the first monks expressed. Early Buddhist resistance to women centered in the perceived sexual temptation associated with their female bodies—an idea preserved, among other places, in accounts of the temptations Buddha himself had to overcome.[786] The presence of women was construed as an obstacle to progress for a monk and hence to be avoided.

From a practical standpoint, admitting women into religious community meant affording them contact with monks, for culturally women could not be left to their own devices. Thus, even after women were permitted to become nuns, Buddhists followed the conventions of the world around them in keeping women in a subordinate position. As already mentioned, Buddha's concession to permit nuns was accompanied by the enumeration of eight extra rules to govern them. These rules explicitly subordinate the nuns to the monks. This is reflected, for example, in the first rule, that even a nun (*bhikkhun*) ordained 'a hundred years' must reverence a monk (*bhikku*) ordained 'even one day.'[787] Other rules entail deference such that a monk is never reviled, abused, or even admonished by a nun—though monks could administer discipline to the nuns.

Women in the Buddhist Texts

The sheer multitude of important Buddhist texts alone prevents our examining and discussing all of them. But we can scarcely avoid some effort at making general remarks and focusing on some key texts, such as the material from the *Sanyutta-Nikaya* and *Cullavagga* a moment ago. In her influential book, *Women in Buddhism: Images of the Feminine in Mahayana Tradition*, religious studies scholar Diana Paul provides an overview of the literature, which she characterizes as revealing "a wide spectrum of views, most of which reflect male attitudes, the educated religious elite, whose views do not often reflect sexual egalitarianism." Much like the religious writings of other men in other religions, these authors, says Paul, constructed their norms for women's behavior based on their own ideals of femininity. Complicating such constructions was their own separation from women because of the strictures of devotion they had undertaken. Paul suggests that perhaps because they could not share the marginal female sphere they wrote about, some men may have devalued it.[788]

While many concur with the general depiction Paul offers, not all do. In this matter the endless gender battles continue as parties with their own interests seek to stake out a claim for legitimacy in the Buddhist texts. Some look primarily to the earliest texts. Others find later material both more agreeable and more reflective of the Buddhism they identify with in their own experience.

With respect to early Buddhist texts like the *Theragatha/Therigatha* (*Hymns of the Elders/Hymns of the Senior Nuns*), and certain Mahayanan *sutras*, religion scholar Karen Christina Lang finds two major images of women: on the one hand, they are depicted as "sensual, seductive, and capable of trapping others in the cycle of birth and death"; on the other hand, they are "compassionate, wise, and capable of enlightening others and leading them towards the divine realm."[789] She finds in the Mahayana text *Sakkapannasuttanta* (*Discourse on Sakka's Questions*) a parallel to early Gnostic teaching that to be saved women must move from a feminine mind to a masculine one. Other texts, like the *Asta-*

315

sahasrikaprajnaparamita (*Perfection of Insight in Eight Thousand Lines*), offer an oft-repeated image of a rebirth as male.[790]

It is this transformation of the woman that perhaps most fascinates scholars and lay people alike, especially today in our own conversations about gender. No matter the inadequacy of our brief look at gender in broad strokes, this transformation of sex and gender—a transgender reality—lies at the heart of our interest in this volume. So let us look more closely at it.

Gender Crossings to Become Bodhisattva

In Buddhism, those born female face the greater obstacle to enlightenment. Some males invoke such an exclusive masculine privilege in a gender hierarchy so as to deny even the possibility of a female becoming *Bodhisattva*. Even among *sutras* admitting the possibility, in many the best she can hope for is achieving one of the lower grades. This problem must be reckoned with before the solution worked out by some Buddhists can be fully appreciated.

The 4th century Buddhist teacher Asangha expresses the general view of the negative position: "Completely perfected Buddhas are not women." Asangha's reasoning was that a *Bodhisattva* is one who has abandoned the state of womanhood. "Ascending to the most excellent throne of enlightenment," Asangha continues, "he is never again reborn as a woman. All women are by nature full of defilement and of weak intelligence. And not by one who is by nature full of defilement and of weak intelligence is completely perfected Buddhahood attained."[791]

For any woman to aspire to becoming *Bodhisattva*, then, it would seem an additional step is needed—becoming male. Of course, there is always the upward cycle of rebirth whereby a woman rich enough in karma can be reborn as a male and thus one day attain *Bodhisattva*. This is the path prescribed by the Pure Land *sutras* of Mahayana Buddhism.[792] But other Mahayana *sutras*, as we shall see in a moment, may be amenable to a woman becoming *Bodhisattva* in her own life.[793] Nevertheless, it was common among Buddhists to regard women as blocked by their female bodies from attaining the kind of spiritual advancement open to male bodies. Through a 'doctrine of five obstacles' five statuses presumably unattainable to anyone born female were articulated. Chief among these is becoming a Buddha.

The Lotus Sutra

The presumed great exception to this state of affairs in Buddhist thinking is the *Lotus Sutra*. It has been especially prominent in discussions of gender in Buddhism and so may serve as a touchpoint for us. This Mahayana sacred text probably originated and was compiled progressively during a two century span from the 1st century B.C.E. through the 1st century C.E. It is commonly accepted as the best representation of the teachings of Buddha Shakyamuni, to whom it is attributed. Even today it exercises significant influence in many places, including China, Korea, and Japan (where it is central to both Tendai and Nichirin Buddhism). Despite its influence and reach, though, scholars are divided in their assessments of how the *Lotus Sutra* treats gender, or more exactly, women.

The *Lotus Sutra* Supports a Negative View of Women

Not everyone finds a rosy scenario presented for women in the *Lotus Sutra*. Religion scholar Lucinda Joy Peach observes that gender serves as an important category of analysis in the *Sutra*, providing both a means to differentiate masculine from feminine beings, and also to place them in a hierarchy. Gender in the *Lotus Sutra* also "symbolizes differences in temperament, capabilities, and virtues." But, what Peach finds most important is that gender provides a basis for evaluating the capacity for realizing full Buddhahood.[794] In that respect, her judgment is that the *Lotus Sutra* presents explicitly negative images of women and of the female sex. Further, though it seems to offer hope for women, that hope is limited. In order to attain full enlightenment they must either transform themselves into males, or await rebirth as male. In sum, argues Peach, the *Lotus Sutra* denigrates their status while bolstering a masculine-dominated gender hierarchy. Thus it does not serve the ends of social justice to eliminate oppression of women.[795]

The *Lotus Sutra* Supports a Positive View of Women

Other scholars are more positive in their appraisals. For example, Chinese scholar and philosopher Robin Wang thinks that the *Lotus Sutra* affirms the universality of the possibility of enlightenment, including for women, as illustrated in the story of the Naga King's daughter (*Devadatta* chapter; discussed in more detail later). In fact, Wang finds it reasonable to see this teaching as forming the original intent for the *Sutra*. While acknowledging that the motif of transformation from female to male is a 'compromise idea,' she argues that it is a misunderstanding of the text to see this as a mere guise for retaining the subordination of women. For Wang, the key lies in recognizing that the Naga King's daughter *already* had attained the 'stage of non-retrogression' of a Bodhisattva before transforming herself. She would have attained complete realization of Buddhahood anyway; her transformation in no way was a precondition.[796]

The *Lotus Sutra* Supports a Neutral View of Women

Buddhism scholar Bernard Faure offers another possible interpretation. For him, the *Lotus Sutra* is much more interested in promoting its own authority than in arguing for or against a beneficent view of women and their possibilities for salvation. He analyzes the *Lotus Sutra* in the context of a complex interplay between salvation and discrimination. "Although the traditional emphasis has clearly been on the Buddhahood of women," he writes, "the fact remains that the text, rather than clearly saying that the *naga*-girl is *by nature* equal to men, seems to insist on her multifaceted inferiority, which only the *Lotus Sutra* can redeem." The essential point is that a rhetorical device is used that emphasizes neither pure salvation nor pure discrimination with respect to women. Instead, the *Lotus Sutra* aims to persuade its audience that it possesses the power to redeem anyone—even women—who put their trust in it.[797]

Does the *Lotus Sutra* Support Women?

Scholars studying the *Lotus Sutra* can agree that some support of women with respect to attaining full enlightenment is proffered. The real issue is *how much* support is present? Does the text accept the wider cultural estimation of a woman's inferiority based in her female nature, or does it challenge that belief through examples like the *Naga* King's daughter? No definitive answer has been forthcoming, nor is one likely. But perhaps that is less material than the effect such ambiguity has for recent gender discussions.

As indicated when we began this brief examination of the *Lotus Sutra*, it offers a rich *possibility* for justifying contemporary efforts for gender equality on its authority. The bottom line, however gained, is that women *can* achieve full Buddhahood. It *may* be that they can do so *without* rebirth as a male, or transformation into a male. No matter the negative things said about being female, the masculine critics come into rebuke at critical points in the text. As in so many other sacred authorities, the complexity that produces ambiguity should yield a practical reticence in claiming too much certainty.

With respect to our own primary concern, the *Lotus Sutra* highlights the role gender crossings and transformations can play in spiritual pursuits. Here we have focused on how these might affect women, but there is plenty enough evidence of the same with respect to men. As in so many other religions, Buddhism struggles with gender and with gender crossings. Yet, again like so many other religions, no matter its reluctance in the world of human affairs to applaud gender crossings or transformations, it can never quite deny them. Even more powerfully, it is compelled to accord them a positive power. Through transgender realities people realize potent—even transcendent—spiritual experiences.

Tantric Buddhism

Of course, even read most favorably, the *Lotus Sutra* only offers a limited set of possible solutions to the problem posed by a gender hierarchy. Tantric Buddhism offers another solution, one that not only refrains from eradicating female sexuality and feminine gender, but may even put it in a privileged position. Long viewed as marginalizing women, Tantric Buddhism has been reappraised by Miranda Shaw. She notes that Tantric imagery is replete with the figures of female Buddhas and *dakinis* ('enlighteners'). Despite frequent Western depictions that relegate women to the margins of Tantric practice, Shaw presents evidence showing them as vital and esteemed practitioners for whom even the highest spiritual reaches are possible.[798]

Indeed, in Tantrism the ordinary gender order can be reversed on religious grounds. Shaw cites the Tantric text *Candamaharosama-tantra* (123) where the worship of Vajrayogini is mandated as follows:

"I am identical to the bodies of all women, and

There is no way that I can be worshipped

Except by the worship of women [*stripuja*]."[799]

Shaw explains that, "A man's attainment of enlightened qualities is dependent on his association with a female companion who can help him to generate these qualities in his stream of being."[800]

How does dress enter into Buddhist practice?

Perhaps, in light of what we have reviewed, we might prosper more by taking a different approach. Buddhist dress, especially the dress behavior of its monks and nuns, has long been famous. Perhaps here we may find another way to appraise gender status, gender relations—and gender crossings. In this, as in other matters, the spirit and philosophy of the Buddha has been preeminent. Anthropologist Mohan Wijayaratna, discussing the monastic practices of classical Theravada Buddhism, remarks that the Buddha wished to avoid extremes in the matter of dress. Consistent with the middle way and simplicity, Buddha sought a path in dress that would not interfere with inner progress. Since such progress relies on a spirit of detachment, members of the religious order were forbidden to decorate or color their robes, to wear ornamentation, or to accumulate more than three robes. Both men and women wore their hair short—no more than two inches long. This uniformity in dress was intended to put all members of the community, from novices to the most senior members, on an equal footing.[801]

Gender Differentiated Dress

Despite this general philosophy, traditionally Buddhists have distinguished between masculine and feminine religious apparel. The *Vinaya Pitaka* texts provide canonical rules for monastic monks (*bhikkhus*) and nuns (*bhikkhunis*), including rules for dress. Within the *sangha* (monastic community) gender differentiated dress is mandated. Chinese Buddhist monk I-Tsing, writing in the 7th century concerning Buddhist practice in India and the Malay Archipelago, elucidates at length the garments and dress practices specified in the *Vinaya*. I-Tsing touches on gender differentiation in dress while remarking on what nuns are to wear. Their prescribed garb has five garments: *sanghati* (double cloak), *uttarasanga* (upper garment), *antarvasa* (inner garment), *sankakshika* (a side-covering cloth), and skirt. I-Tsing notes that the style and rules for the first four of these are the same for nuns and monks; only a part of the skirt (an item worn by both genders) is different.[802]

Once more we can appraise this situation in various ways. On the one hand, the modest gender differentiation in dress and the similarity in hair can be said to minimize the importance of gender. On the other hand, though the difference may be modest, it is also critical. There is a clear determination to distinguish nuns from monks and, as we have seen, they are not equal in status. As it turns out, perhaps the most interesting aspect of Buddhist dress lies not in gender differentiated markers but in a garment reserved for Buddhist men.

The Saffron Robe

Easily the most distinctive part of Buddhist dress is the saffron robe worn by Buddhist monks. In both Hinduism and Buddhism the color of saffron (an orangish yellow) has special significance. This significance is often lost on outsiders; the saffron robes are sometimes regarded, predominantly by Westerners, as relatively feminine garb. Such a perception is akin to observations sometimes made about priests in both East and West: though biologically male they are not strictly masculine in the way other males might be. Their vocation sets them at some distance from traditional masculinity without rendering them feminine. In this regard we might recall the earlier observation of economist Thorstein Veblen, who used Christian priests as an example of men in apparel with feminine characteristics.[803]

Regardless of misperceptions as to the gendered nature of the garb, the saffron robe was reserved for the Buddhist monks, all of whom were male. Early on, *only* males were able to enter a full-time life as a religious devotee. The egalitarian spirit inherent in the Buddha's teaching seemed as though it had given way to the patriarchalism found throughout the culture. However, one quite remarkable woman challenged this development. She did so by employing crossdressing.

The Example of Maha-pajapati

Earlier, in examining Buddha's stance on gender matters, we mentioned his initial resistance to his stepmother Maha-pajapati. There we focused on the Buddha; now we need to continue with Maha-pajapati's story. Having been rebuffed three times by the Buddha, she took a more dramatic course of action: "Maha-pajapati cut off her hair, and put on orange-colored robes."[804] In cutting her hair and putting on a monk's robes, Maha-pajapati was crossdressing for a purpose many women in the Christian tradition would understand—to express profound devotion and dedication to a life of holy service. Although she might not be recognized for doing so, she was resolved to behave in a manner similar to the monks. As the text proceeds to relate, after much intercession on her behalf, with clever argumentation, Maha-pajapati was finally admitted to the *sangha*, though as a nun rather than as a monk, and with the stipulation that as a nun she must defer to the monks.

Though Maha-pajapati's crossdressing was calculated, and remained independent of expressing a masculine gender identity, it nonetheless made a dramatic point about gender. Despite the Buddha's reservations, women *can* practice a spiritual vocation previously thought suited only to men. Since Buddha previously had repeatedly refused Maha-pajapati's petition to enter the *sangha*, it cannot be denied that gender-crossing behavior—and not mere persistence—served to make this potent point.

An Example of Contemporary Buddhist Crossdressing

Of course, as we see in the example of Maha-pajapati, not all crossdressing reflects a transgender identity. It can occur for other reasons attached to religious occasions and purposes. For example, anthropologist Andrea Whittaker observes among contemporary Thai people situational crossdressing by some males in connection with the festivities surrounding the ordination of a young Buddhist monk. The celebration occasions a procession celebrating the monk's entrance into the *sangha*. "The procession," comments Whittaker, "is marked by its communitas, its sense of common celebration, and liminal inversive behaviours." Such behaviors include male crossdressing, without censure.[805]

What transgender realities occur in Buddhism?

As we might anticipate, the various schools of Buddhist thought and practice make it impossible to say that all Buddhists regard transgender realities in the same way. But whether within Theravada or Mahayana, Buddhism has given some recognition to such realities. Here all we can do is indicate a few strands indicative of a wider scope than we can review in this volume.

Theravada Buddhism and the Pandaka

Although the Mahayana tradition receives most of the attention in our discussion of Buddhism, we must note that Theravada Buddhism is not devoid of relevant material. Scholar Peter Jackson, in studying the Pali Canon of the Theravada tradition, remarks that he finds many references to "individuals who today would be variously identified as hermaphrodites, transvestites, transsexuals, and homosexuals."[806] However, he also notes that the imputation of such modern labels and categories on these texts scarcely does them justice since they freely combine diverse elements in the service of their own specific interests. Those interests most often have to do with the religious order of monks, rather than the common people. These monks were characterized by ascetic codes of conduct, including celibacy.

Jackson calls attention especially to the *Vinaya*, which we have seen is a sacred text regulating the lives of the *sangha*. He finds there the identification of four principal sex/gender types:

- ❑ Male;
- ❑ Female;
- ❑ *Ubhatobyanjanaka* ('a person with the signs of both genders'); and,
- ❑ *Pandaka* (a sexually different male).

The *Ubhatobyanjanaka*, thinks Jackson, refers to more than the physical hermaphrodite. Such persons include both physical *and psychological* 'hermaphrodites'—a qualification that certainly permits room for some transgender folk. The *Pandaka* are even harder to define and definitions of who qualify as *Pandaka* are diverse.[807]

The *Pandaka* present somewhat of a puzzle. Language scholar Leonard Zwilling writes that the word's origin is obscure but might be derived from *apa + anda + ka*: 'without testicles.' But he resists concluding this refers to a literal eunuch. Instead, he urges we see it as metaphorical, as in the English castigation of a certain kind of male who 'has no balls.'[808] He offers the characterization of the *Pandaka* as "one who has lost his *indriya* or masculinity principle."[809] Zwilling enumerates five types, all of which fit Jackson's general descriptor of a sexually different male. They range from one who is congenitally impotent (*napumsakapandaka*) to the male whose sexual potency depends on "some special effort or artifice" (*opakkamikapandaka*). What they have in common, he thinks, is their being *napumsaka*, 'lacking maleness.'[810]

Zwilling contends that in the *Vinaya* literature references to the *Pandaka* are almost invariably made in a sexual—especially homosexual—context. Yet he also notes, "Even as early as the period of the *Atharva Veda, pandakas* were viewed as a distinct group, different from ordinary males and females, and apparently transvestite."[811] Their differences were not merely in their sexuality; to them were also attributed a different psychological makeup, though the attributes named tend to be negative in character. Their exclusion from ordination and perhaps even as part of the laity he regards as not necessitated by Buddhist logic but rather as a concession to the social conventions then prevailing.[812]

For now, the puzzles posed by the *Ubhatobyanjanaka* and the *pandakas* must be set aside. For whatever the presumed nature of gender nonconformists, it is clear they existed. Even more pointedly, gender transformations in the context of religious concerns are subjects of Buddhist storytelling. Such tales include both females and males.

Transformation Stories: Females into Men

Mahayana Buddhism typically is represented as more favorable toward women. Most often pointed to in this regard are various transformation stories—accounts wherein a person, especially a woman, is transformed into a different gender through a change in body sex. We already have touched upon this idea above in specific connection to transformation of a female to male in becoming *Bodhisattva*.

Transformation by Change of Sex

Diana Paul offers the appraisal that Mahayana *sutras* present a dominant theme of sexual natures neither male nor female, or perhaps more positively, as both male and female. She adds, "The *sutras* refer to this as sexual transformation, that is, the capacity to transcend discriminations based upon sexual and gender distinctions (*chuan-nu-shen*), by somehow becoming the other sex.[813]" As we have seen—and Paul acknowledges—such transformations stress female-to-male changes, and in Pure Land Buddhism they mean the woman views her body sex as a hindrance and vows to be reborn as male.

Yet Paul argues that more often Mahayana *sutras* hold out the hope that a woman, in her life as a woman, can attain Bodhisattva status. Paul regards this as signifying that just as past life karma dictated the person be born as female, so karma during her life as a woman can mean a change in sexual identity through improvement in her moral behavior *in this present life*, and not merely as a reward deferred to the next life. This kind of transformation is metaphorical, not physical. The woman remains female in body, but becomes masculine in mind.[814] In this respect, Paul cites *The Sutra on Changing the Female Sex* (*Fo shuo chuan nu shen ching*), which she translates as declaring that, "If women awaken to the thought of enlightenment, then they will have the great and good person's state of mind, a man's state of mind, a sage's state of mind. . . .[815]

Gender Change without Change of Sex

Heng-Ching Shih points to the *Vimalakirti Sutra* and the *Srimala Sutra* as offering a path wherein females can attain the highest reaches of Buddhahood without changing their anatomical sex. This view follows from extending the doctrines of *sunyata* ('emptiness') and *Tathagatagarbha* ('non-duality') to their logical culmination and connecting them. This yields the realization that gender dualities, the basis for attaching masculinity to Buddhahood, are illusory mental constructions at odds with the teaching of emptiness. Gendered distinctions can be dismissed as illusory and irrelevant. Shih notes this view continues in the Chinese Buddhist Ch'an School and is preserved in the teachings of the *Bhiksuni* masters.[816]

'A Certain Goddess' Offers an Object Lesson

Levering, in examining stories from the Ch'an and Chinese Buddhist Bodhisattva tradition, draws upon these same basic Buddhist truths. Because sex and gender are not immutable, but illusory, either or both can be created or transformed. She recounts a story from the *Lotus Sutra*—the *sutra* most famous for its promise of gender equality in the hope of attaining enlightenment—in which 'a certain goddess' speaks to the Buddhist elder Sariputra. He has been puzzled why she has not transformed her body into a male one. Her response is to promptly transform *him* into female form with the challenge to change himself back to male! Then she tells him, "All women appear in the form of women in just the same way as the elder appears in the form of women. While they are not women in reality, they appear in the form of women. With this in mind, the Buddha said, 'In all things there is neither male nor female.'"[817]

The Naga King's Daughter (The Dragon Girl)

Stories depict devout females surmounting all obstacles to advance spiritually by becoming male in the present. We have seen how this might be imagined without actual physical transformation. But sometimes that act of 'becoming male' is not intended as metaphorical but is literal; the change is not just to a masculine mind but to a male body. As Levering puts it, "Women transform their bodies by an 'act of truth' into male bodies. . . ."[818] The *Lotus Sutra* story of the Dragon Girl, daughter of the *Naga* (serpent) King, illustrates this very thing: "At that time, the assembled multitude all saw the dragon girl in the space of an instant turn into a man, perfect in Bodhisattva-conduct, straightway go southward to the world-sphere Spotless, sit on a jeweled lotus blossom, and achieve undifferentiating, right, enlightened intuition. . . ."[819]

Of course, such a transformation itself constitutes proof of Bodhisattva power, for a Buddha or Bodhisattva having won freedom from the chains of illusion is able to create illusory bodies that may or may not resemble the creator.[820] Levering boils down the matter in practical terms to an equation men in a patriarchal society might comprehend: "Once a woman's sexual power is eradicated, she can be reborn as a man, from which, if she can eradicate her male sexual power, she can become a Buddha."[821]

Ambiguity

However, as Paul and others have observed, the Buddhist texts possess a certain ambiguity reflecting an inherent tension—or contradiction. On the one hand, sex and gender can be called illusory; on the other hand, they must be surmounted if one is a woman. On one side, a woman can remain female, but gain a masculine mind; on the other side, femininity remains a problem, clearly not merely subordinate to masculinity, but an obstacle to salvation. As Paul neatly puts it, "The uncomfortable 'resolution' of the *problem* of women's equality is to attain the spiritual path by not *really* being a woman."[822] Ultimately, no matter the machinations of logic, in practice being a feminine female limits a woman in spiritual attainment.

Transformation Stories: Males into Women

Bernard Faure, an expert especially on Japanese Buddhism (see the next answer), points out a number of instances in ancient Buddhist literature of transgender realities, including transformations of male bodies. For example, he records a story in the *Kii zodan* of a young male monk who after a dream of changing sex awakes to find himself transformed into a nun. The keeper of the inn where this happens is smitten, the two marry, and the former monk bears a child. For fifteen years she lives in this manner. A chance encounter with her former master leads her to confess to him what has happened. Though she has heard of females becoming males, what has happened to her is outside her knowledge and she asks if the transformation has been because of bad karma.

Her former master offers reassurance, urging her not to fear her karma and encouraging her to continue her studies.[823]

Other transformation stories are found elsewhere. From the *Wu zazu* Faure draws an account of a person who alternates between male and female forms depending on the hour. This and other like incidents are recorded also in the *Wakan sensai zue*. In some cases there is an ambiguity of gender if not of sex. In the *Mahasanghika Vinaya* (417c) Faure finds the tale of a monk who, when apprehended while sexually approaching another monk, explains to the Buddha that he/she is 'a princess,' who is 'neither man nor woman,' but who had become a monk upon hearing that they needed wives.[824]

Such stories can be seen as amusing anecdotes with little significance. Or they can be viewed as reaffirming some of the important possibilities inherent in Buddhist logic. The first story recounted above offers a counter to the presumption that males become females only because of bad karma. Though the former male is not changed back to his original sex and gender, support from his former master to continue in spiritual studies—as a woman—is offered. The tale of the monk who professes to be 'neither man nor woman' can be seen as just a clever circumvention of the problem of male same-sex sexual relations. Or it can be taken as witness to situations likely to have actually occurred where intersex or third gender people entered religious community and expressed what for them was 'heterosexual' (because the gender was different) sexuality. In sum, such stories do not have to be seen in any one way, particularly a negative way. They may provide a degree of evidence for more positive Buddhist ways to see transgender realities.

Contemporary Buddhists

Thus far our focus has been on Buddhist thought principally as found in classical religious texts and stories, with a brief nod toward clothing practice. It is important we also consider contemporary Buddhism, not merely because it is present now, but because of claims often made within it with respect to gender—and by implication, transgender. Most prominently, it is common today to find Buddhists arguing that traditional gender discriminatory practices are being overcome. If women can gain more acceptance as equals, perhaps transgender people may, too.

Toshie Kurihara, of The Institute of Oriental Philosophy, in 2005 expressed the spirit of optimism for embracing a Buddhist view of women: "In the new century, when gender equality is becoming the ethos of the age, it is important to consider a new relationship between Buddhism and women, by paying careful attention to the concept of gender equality originally embraced by Buddhism and demonstrating appreciation of women."[825] She appeals to three older sources—the Buddha, the *Lotus Sutra*, and Nichiren—linking them to the teaching of Soka Gakkai, a branch of Nichiren Buddhism founded in the late 20th century. Despite a nod at the many inequities that have plagued Buddhist women over the centuries, Kurihara believes "the genealogy of earnest women's emancipation has flowed continuously," as evidenced by her tracing of it.[826]

Certainly there is nothing objectionable in returning to venerable authorities and maintaining that these authorities, correctly interpreted, support gender equality. Reform in the name of religious ideals can be a potent force. Yet one worries at a history where the ideal has been espoused so often, while remaining always blocked by one or another momentary 'practical' concession. Kurihara hopes to attach the tradition to contemporary movements like Soka Gakkai. But her espousal of interpreting, or reinterpreting the sources "according to ones generation"[827] isn't any different from what other generations have done in finding justification for very different conclusions. Every generation has those who, in her words, "revive it [the teaching] freshly and employ it efficiently."[828] If all Buddhists are doing today is conforming to a social fashion, how can one hope for an enduring sense of gender equality?

And if the situation remains problematic for women, what about transgender people? Among Buddhists today we certainly find those who identify with one or another transgendered reality. In the United States, for example, among transgendered Asian Pacific Americans (LGBT people), Buddhism may be a particularly attractive religious identity. A 2004 conference in New York, with attendees mostly from New York and large cities on the East and West coast, found in a survey that 11% identified as Buddhist—the largest non-Christian affiliation among respondents.[829] American Buddhism appears relatively receptive to transgender people. In *The Faces of Buddhism in America*, Roger Corless provides a number of examples of Buddhist ministries to transgender people, including "an introductory meditation course' offered by Venerable Sangharakshita in San Francisco in 1995.[830]

Conclusion

In modern Buddhism, both major traditions (Theravada and Mahayana) tend toward tolerance as an ideal, though Mahayana is more vigorous in espousal of a gender ideal of equality. There is a general Buddhist view that matters of sexual orientation and gender identity are beyond an individual's control. However, this is typically conceived of as resulting from past life karma, meaning that the person in a prior life made choices resulting in the current life status. Some Buddhists thus regard transgender states as the result of *bad* karma; for example, a transsexual may have been someone who in a previous life committed adultery.[831] Fewer see it as a positive state, but some Buddhists do regard it as a kind of karmic reward. As Buddhism has gained popularity in the West it has become even more tolerant and in societies like the United States Buddhists practice a greater gender egalitarianism. In both East and West, on the whole, modern Buddhism seems generally tolerant toward transgendered people, at least in rhetoric. Yet particularly in Eastern societies where more conservative, traditional forms of Buddhism are strong, there exists a less positive appraisal.

Q. 81 Is crossdressing found in Japanese religions?

The Short Answer. Today's Japanese, though arguably more secular than their forebears, show a fascination with gender crossings. Contemporary transgender realities are a very visible and often remarked upon part of Japanese culture. Depending on one's perspective, this may either be because of modern Japan's strongly patriarchal society or in spite of it. As elsewhere in the world, as the Japanese wrestle with changing conceptions of gender the role of transgender people is being reappraised. Crossdressing serves as a signal marker to the Japanese of the presence of either gender variance or a minority sexual identity. An important partner in the ongoing cultural discussion on gender and transgender is religion. Japan has a long, rich, and complex religious heritage. In addition to the native Shinto, religions arriving from foreign soils have enriched Japanese culture. Most notable among these have been Buddhism, Confucianism, and Christianity. The first of these, in particular, has a long history of intimate coexistence with Shintoism. The religious traditions of Japan display instances of transgender realities like crossdressing that are sometimes rooted in old stories, reflect various notions about the nature of gender, and display themselves across the centuries in various public and private forms. Some of the ancient accounts of transgender realities are found in sacred texts, though not always in connection with events we might consider sacred. But their placement in such texts embeds them in a religious milieu, one in which the divine spirits are always at work. Such beings may themselves change gender, or manifest in mortals of different genders, and their human devotees may crossdress as they act out their divinely guided destinies. In that respect, while many competing religious influences merit consideration, the two most important remain Shinto and Buddhism. With respect to gender, Shinto appears to be the more flexible, although Buddhist texts can be read in such a way to promote a gender equality not always found in actual practice. Divine figures who engage in gender crossings, like the *kami* Inari, are shared by the two religions. Inari is pictured in ways that reflect gender diversity: as an old man, as a young woman, or as an androgynous boddhisatva. Both Shinto and Buddhist sacred texts include incidents of crossdressing. The latter especially includes recognition of transgender identities. More recent Japanese religious movements, such as Tenrikyo and Omoto Kyodan have particularly shown openness to gender crossings.

The Longer Answer. Japanese religion is a subject far too immense to be summarized briefly. What we need to know for our purposes is that in the long and complex religious history of Japan the religions that predominate today—Shinto, Buddhism, and Christianity—have had dynamic contact with one another.[832] The former two, especially, deserve close attention, for together they represent the religious commitments of more than four-fifths of Japan's people. The impact of Christianity, though significant, has been more limited. Its role for many Japanese is less religious than social in character. Author Patrick Drazen comments that in popular culture Church weddings have become *chic* and an old saying has been amended to include Christianity: 'Born Shinto, marry Christian, die Buddhist.'[833]

The two dominant religions remain dynamically linked despite a checkered history together. At periods, Shinto and Buddhism have been closely intertwined. At other times there has been a concerted effort to keep them separate. Regardless, the reality for most contemporary Japanese is that their personal spirituality is informed by both religions. Separating the two for the purposes of academic discussion can misleadingly suggest a bifurcation that is not as clear in lived experience. Add into the mix the influence of Confucianism, Christianity, and new religions, and the picture of religion in Japan becomes either richly textured or muddled, depending on one's perspective. In the end, the living result has always managed to be something distinctively Japanese.

In the materials included here, there is no special effort to place matters in their specific historical context to illuminate the relation at that time among the religions then present. Readers are well-advised to use the brief remarks here as a springboard to more detailed study, which will reveal the shifts across time in thought and practice on various matters. Here, our remarks are meant more generally to show that gender crossings are not unfamiliar to Japanese religion, whether such originated in this or another specific religion or at a particular time and place. In fact, transgender realities that may have originated in Shinto could easily be appropriated by Buddhist tradition. Crossdressing associated with sacred tradition should not be viewed as 'belonging' exclusively to one or another religion. What matters is that it has its place within *Japanese* culture—and that is a richly diversified complex of elements shaped by many religious influences.

As we have done elsewhere, our investigation will follow the well-worn academic path of investigating written sources as primary for our investigation. For Shinto, the distinctively indigenous religion of Japan, the principal sacred texts are the *Kojiki* (*Records of Ancient Matters*), and the *Nihongi* (or *Nihon Shoki*, the *Chronicles of Japan*), a more elaborate recounting. But there are other important texts, too, such as the *Yengishiki* (*Shinto Rituals*), the *Kogoshui* (*Gleanings from Ancient Stories*), and the *Jingiryo* (*Book of Administrative Law for the Shinto Religion*). For Buddhism, with all its diversity, there are multiple sources, including ones touched upon elsewhere in this volume, such as the *Tripitaka* and different *Sutras*. For our interests the most important of the Buddhist texts is unquestionably the *Lotus Sutra*, covered in the material on Buddhism (see the answer to Q. 80). Obviously, any number of other materials are utilized as well, especially modern scholarship drawing and remarking upon aspects relevant to our subject.

We begin our consideration of the relationship of transgender realities to Japanese religions with a more fundamental query:

How do Japanese religions regard gender?

Given the manifold nature of Japanese religious life, how do the Japanese regard gender? To get at that is not easy. Our approach will be to first begin with as broad and summary view as we can, looking at both the conforming genders and transgender realities in contemporary Japan. Then we shall devote a modest degree of attention to the prominent religions. Only after we have completed this survey will we be in a position to focus on our primary interest in the relationship between Japanese religions and transgender realities.

Conventional Gender in Japanese Society

Gender in modern Japanese culture reflects the kind of gender duality and divide common to the West. Patrilineal descent and patriarchy predominate; for example, men hold about 95% of the positions of authority in politics and business, despite being a minority of the population. Japanese Studies scholar Kenneth Henshall points out that Japanese men may be broadly categorized as *koha* ('samurai') men, who attempt to live out ideals of endurance (*gaman*), sincerity (*makoto*), and single-minded commitment in performing duties (*isshin*), and *nanpa* ('soft school') men, a label descriptive of a wide-range of masculine styles united only by being 'less masculine' than the *koha*. Yet Japenese masculinity leaves room for a kind of manliness seen as effeminate by Westerners—the *bishonen* ('beautiful young man')—who can be depicted as attaining an ideal even higher than that reached by the *koha*, a youthful purity and beauty transcending mundane gender status and sometimes depicted as semi-divine.[834]

With respect to femininity, Henshall notes that the subordinate role of women in Japanese society cannot be said to have existed from the beginning, as the exalted status of the Shinto female deity Amaterasu, the sun goddess, indicates, as well as do human models such as Himiko, Queen of Yamatai in 3rd century Japan, and Jingu, a famed warrior-leader. Various factors can be implicated in the decline of women's status, including the patriarchal influences of such other religions as Buddhism, Confucianism and Christianity. Like men, Japanese women are not all of one kind; the most famous feminine style is undoubtedly that of the *geisha* (literally, 'artistic person')—ironically, all male until 1751, when the first female *geisha* appeared. Far more common, of course, are 'good-wives/wise mothers' (*ryosai-kenbo*), and the Japanese 'new woman,' who competes in the labor force, though she does so still at a disadvantage to men.[835]

Anthropological study of contemporary Japanese popular culture, like research on other aspects of Japanese culture, finds a fixed divide between the prescribed masculine and feminine social realms, though each is regarded as instrumentally essential to social order and reality. Orientalist Dolores Martinez summarizes the situation, remarking, "It is generally held that women are associated with the inside, the private domain (*uchi*) and men with the outside, public domain (*soto*)." Yet she also notes that each gender penetrates the other's principal domain in significant ways.[836] Despite that reality, even Japanese language reflects the gender divide, not so much inherently, but by conventions of practice, with differing grammatical and lexical forms to be used by men and women. The result has been distinctively gendered literary styles and the generation of a speech style commonly called 'women's language.'[837] In short, similar to many Western societies, the Japanese daily deal with gender pressures tied to stereotypes and fixed expectations.

The socialization pressures with respect to gender identity and role performance have generated creative resistance. For example, popular fiction, especially in manga (e.g., *shonen'ai* manga) and anime—popular Japanese forms similar to our society's comic books and animation—routinely depict a gender fluidity far greater than that experienced in actuality. "In Japan," remarks sociologist Mark McLelland, "women's ficiton is a site for gender play and transformation; 'homosexuality' has become a commodity consumed by women. In Japan, homosexuality is not necessarily an anxiety-inducing 'other' but, for some women at least, it has become their most desired other."[838]

Transgender in Japanese Society

As briefly discussed in a previous volume (see the answer to Q. 52), transgender realities exist in Japan—and prompt some of the kind of confused response often seen in societies like our own. The assumed close connection among sex, sexuality, and gender leads easily to conflating separate elements in a unified, if erroneous picture. McLelland, who specializes in Japan's sexual and gender minorities, remarks that Japanese media persistently treat sexual orientation (homosexuality) and gender issues (transgender) in the same context, assuming that the former necessarily entails the latter.[839] (How American!)

In this light, McLelland observes that crossdressing has become "the main paradigm Japanese people have for non-normative sexualities." He notes that gay men (*okama*) are typically portrayed as crossdressing, effeminate males whose sexual activity is defined by anal intercourse. The connecting of crossdressing to homosexuality has carried with it the consequence that *okama* can also be applied to any male displaying any transgender reality. Lesbians (*onabe*, or more commonly *rezu*) are represented as masculine in both dress and demeanor.[840]

McLelland points to the diversity of Japanese terms coined to refer to gender and sexual minorities, many of them borrowed from the West (e.g., *gei*, 'gay'). Transvestites are *toransubuesutaito*, transgender people (in the narrow sense of those desiring to live in a different gender without sex reassignment surgery) are *toransujenda*, and transsexuals are *toransusekusharu*. The latter, of course, can be further differentiated; male-to-female transsexuals, for instance, are *nyuhafu*.[841] Transgender people, especially youth, face discrimination and bullying tied to their perceived gender deviance, such as males being seen as 'woman-like' (*onnappoi*) or 'soft acting' (*nayo nayo shite iru*).[842]

Japanese Religion & Gender: Overview

Understanding gender in contemporary Japan obviously means reckoning with more than religious influences, though those are complicated enough. As religious studies scholar Linda Edwards points out, apart from the dominant religions of Shintoism and Buddhism, one must reckon with Confucian, Taoist, new religions, and folk religious elements.[843] We need also recognize that religious influences take many forms beyond the obvious teachings of sacred texts or the ceremonies and rituals of formal religious practice. For example, popular writings often rely upon and appeal to religion.[844] While we may attempt to at least nod in as many directions as feasible, we shall concentrate on the most influential religions.

The dominant traditional religions of Shinto and Buddhism, together especially with Confucianism, all have contributed to the crafting of a gender hierarchy in which women are relegated to a lower status than men. A number of factors have been implicated in this development, including the shifting of culture in general from agricultural-based, with a reverence for fertility, to social endeavors that emphasize more the creations of men. Rather than celebrate and place female fertility at the center of appraisals of women, their monthly menstrual periods came to be seen as proofs of female pollution and weakness.

Where women in ancient Japan often filled shamanistic roles (*miko*[845]) mediating for *kami*, especially after the success of Buddhism, with its rather pessimistic appraisal of women's chances for spiritual advancement, they increasingly lost opportunities for positions of prestige. However, the proliferation of new religions in Japan, many originated and led by women, has partially redressed this imbalance. For example, the Okinawan new religion Ijun draws upon a long history of dominance in this sphere by women, based on the belief that females are spiritually superior to males.[846]

Shinto & Gender

Shintoism (or, simply, Shinto) prizes nature, family (including veneration of ancestors), cleanliness, and *kami* worship. Like other major religions, Shinto manifests in distinctive 'traditions,' or forms: the imperial Shinto (*Koshitsu Shinto*), Shrine Shinto (*Jinja*), sectarian Shinto (*Kyoha*), and folk Shinto (*Min-*

zoku). Unlike the often sharp divisions found in other major religions, the four Shinto forms exist in general harmony and Shintoism historically has been relatively content to dwell peaceably alongside other religions. This ability has proved useful. Lacking over most of its history a systematic and continuous institutional structure to unify its reach, Shinto proved vulnerable to the energetic discipline of Buddhism as it steadily exerted more and more force in Japan.

Gender Egalitarianism?

With respect to gender, Shinto arguably possesses a more relaxed attitude than its religious rivals in Japan. On the one hand, argues prominent 19th century Japanologist William George Aston, Shinto reflects the same thinking displayed in Japanese grammar, "which has practically no gender, thus showing that the Japanese mind is comparatively careless of marking the distinction between animate and inanimate and male and female."[847] Though gendered conventions in language practice developed, such emerged under the powerful force exerted by influences other than Shinto. Instead, argues anthropologist Nancy Ross Rosenberger, following Jean Herbert, Shinto views the genders as complementary in the manner of the seasons, and unified like the aspects of a tree: "Men contain the power of the tree in summer: outer, differentiating, and authoritative. Women contain the power of the tree in winter: inner, harmonizing and consolidating. . . ."[848]

On the other hand, when Shinto does employ gender in relation to deities, or when one considers the role of women, evidence still suggests a greater approach to gender egalitarianism than found in Buddhism or Confucianism. Unlike most religions found around the world, Shinto's deity (*kami*) of the sun, Amaterasu ('Great Shining Heaven'), is female. More importantly, she is the principal Shinto *kami*, and the personage from whom Japan's imperial family traces its descent. Shinto texts recount stories like that in the *Kogoshui* concerning Ame-no-Uzume-no-Mikoto, 'the Heavenly Lady of Dauntless Spirit,' sent by Divine command to confront a strange god at the crossways of Heaven, when none of the Eighty Myriads of Gods proved bold enough to do so.[849]

Women in Shinto

It is not merely female *kami* who receive veneration and praise in ways usually reserved for males, but human women also appear to have had roles and positions in Shinto not seen in androcentric religions. Most often remarked upon are figures such as the Empress Jin-go (or Jingo), in whose reign most of Korea came under Japanese sovereignty.[850] But beyond the stories there may have been real figures occupying important and instrumental roles. Although the existence of sound empirical evidence is debatable, there have been assertions based on various indications literary and archaeological, that in ancient Japan before the advent of Chinese religious influences female shamans may have been common, and the land may have had women in important positions of authority.[851] At the same time, Shinto texts are hardly devoid of the gender divisions familiar to a hierarchical patriarchy, such as the reference in the aforementioned *Kogoshui* to the separate realms for men (the public world of work) and women (private sphere of the home).[852]

Accordingly, though it remains impossible to say much about early Shinto with great confidence, it may be that gender difference was not emphasized, but was viewed in a rather egalitarian manner. Under the duress of more pronounced patriarchal ideas that presented themselves in theological dress, Shinto perhaps accommodated itself to narrower and more particular ideas. Yet even so, it may not have lost its original sense on the matter. Religion scholar Marilyn Nefsky contends that Shinto, intimately tied to Japanese daily life and devoid of a highly developed body of ideas, resisted the more patriarchal influences brought by Buddhism and Confucianism with at least some success. "Despite the institutionalization of religion," Nefsky writes, "the view of woman as compassionate and life-sustaining, continues to flow in the background as a strong undercurrent."[853]

Japanese Buddhism & Gender

Japanese Buddhism, despite its division into various 'schools,' possessed a structure and organization that the more local nature of Shinto lacked. In the convergence of Buddhism with Shinto, the latter's *kami* came to be identified as the protectors of Buddhist divine figures—a move that both joined the two religions and subtly subordinated Shinto, an outcome also seen in the relatively lesser status of Shinto priests.[854] Though the relative independence of each religion from the other has waxed and waned, Japanese Buddhism has exerted a pressure on Shinto that cannot be ignored.

One such pressure—of particular interest to us—is androcentric Buddhist patriarchalism. Since this has been addressed in an earlier answer, we shall be especially succinct here. First, let us quickly review the broader context. Mahayana Buddhism spread from China to Japan via Korea. Though a number of different Buddhist schools surfaced in Japan over the centuries, in contemporary Japan three predominate: Zen Buddhism (probably the best known in the United States), so-called 'Pure Land' (*Amida*) Buddhism, and Nichiren Buddhism (which has spawned various new religions).

Traditional Buddhist teaching enumerates five 'obstacles' (*gosho*) faced by women, including their inability to attain Buddhahood. These obstacles became joined to Confucianism's three obediences (to parents, husband, son) to buttress a strong tradition of submission for Japanese women. Nevertheless, the mere reiteration of this well-known fact scarcely covers the subject. As Bernard Faure, an expert on Japanese Buddhism, puts it after an extensive study of sexuality and gender in Buddhism, the religion is neither as sexist nor as egalitarian as many think. Simple judgments are belied by critical factors. For example, in addition to the many forms Buddhism takes, Faure points also to the fact that while Buddhism has "monopolized the afterlife and the major rites of passage—birth, death, and rebirth" it has left daily life to Shinto and Confucianism. This, he observes, has left little of relevance to women for normal life.[855]

Buddhist Rhetorics

Faure sensibly points our attention to different discourses, symbolic and narrative, on gender in Buddhism. These include various rhetorics. The 'rhetoric of subordination' (or 'rhetoric of inequality') is that of the five obstacles and three obediences mentioned above. This rhetoric maintains a gender hierarchy with masculine privilege. Seemingly on an oppositional course, the 'rhetoric of salvation and equality' promises inclusion to women in the Pure Land and Buddhahood, though still conditioned on maleness ('transformation into a man'—*henjo nanshi*). This rhetoric Faure later divides, while finding both parts complementary to the rhetoric of subordination. The 'rhetoric of salvation' appears to challenge the status quo represented in the rhetoric of subordination, but in practice reinforces it. The 'rhetoric of equality,' in the Mahayana tradition, meets the same end, though by a different path: it attempts to solve the gender problem by denying its existence in the name of nonduality.[856]

With respect to the most prominent Japanese Buddhist strands, Zen Buddhism (China's Chan Buddhism) utilizes Faure's rhetoric of equality.[857] It accepts the Mahayana doctrine of nonduality, to which is added a denial of the traditional view of karma. The Zen position, in accepting the possibility of sudden enlightenment, does not resign an individual to a position in the social hierarchy set by past life deeds. As Faure points out, at least theoretically this gender-levels the field by doing away with gradual stages, including the need for rebirth as a male, on the way to enlightenment. Yet, in practice, the ideal of gender equality has had little impact—though Faure thinks the ideal could be used to ustify various forms of female rebellion and may partly explain why Zen appeals to women.[858]

Japanese Pure Land Buddhism reflects the Mahayana discourse with its rhetoric of salvation and equality. Faure observes that traditional Mahayana thinking on salvation makes maleness mandatory to attaining Buddhahood. While, technically, by virtue of nonduality there is no ontological priority to maleness, in practice woman is secondary to man.[859] Pure Land Buddhism, through the path offered by Amida Buddha, would seem to offer an exception. It simplifies the attainment of salvation and in the process appears to make gender distinctions not only ultimately unreal, but inconsequential in practice. Faure remarks that, in time, "The belief that Amida saves *even* women developed into the idea that Amida saves women *first of all*."[860] As his phrasing suggests, Faure views the rhetoric skeptically. In his estimation, the emphasis as it came to be placed did not really highlight equality in salvation, but constitutes another view of how to transform women into men.[861]

Nichiren Buddhism likewise stands within the Mahayana tradition. Historically hostile to other Mahayana schools, Nichiren Buddhism nevertheless shares with them a professed ideal of gender equality and a longstanding practice of masculine privilege. Nichiren Buddhism is distinguished by its focus on the *Lotus Sutra*. Nichiren teaching advances the hope that any true devotee may reach enlightenment during their lifetime, regardless of sex or gender.[862] At the same time, the *Nichiren ibun* (*Writings of Nichiren*) contains passages that reflect the cultural patriarchy of the times—and thus contribute to its maintenance, wittingly or not.[863]

Contemporary Buddhism

Yet, this historic patriarchalism may or may not be indicative of the current scene. Buddhist nun Ichiu Mori, in the Nichiren-shu school, admits that the idea women must be reborn as men to attain buddhahood "remains firmly fixed in the minds of some priests."[864] Mori, though, sharply disputes the notion that such a sentiment was Nichiren's own. She points out that the section on women in the Nichiren writings is usually interpreted by male priests or scholars, and without due reference to its historical context. In her estimation, Nichiren stands out from his medieval setting by promoting the belief that women can attain Buddhahood *just as they are*; they have only to adhere faithfully to the *Lotus Sutra* throughout their lives.[865] She points to Nichiren's negation of traditional Buddhist obstacles by his words, "the three obediences will disappear in this lifetime. The five obstacles have already been dissolved."[866]

Japanese anthropologist Kyoko Nakamura concurs with Mori's admission that some contemporary Buddhist teachers remain in line with older thinking. In the mid-1990s, Nakamura observed that Buddhist notions concerning the impediments women face to spiritual advancement and an emphasis on their being submissive were even then widely believed to be disappearing from contemporary Buddhist teaching. But Nakamura points out that, first, many Buddhist teachers continue to present the traditional ideas and, second, that there may be a pronounced difference between the outer show of a professed principle and actual practice and inner feeling—a possibility buttressed by the survey results Nakamura discusses.[867]

In sum, Japanese Buddhism presents a religious influence on gender not unlike that seen in other religions: an ideal of gender equality and tolerance that in practice has been little realized. Historical struggles appear to continue, despite continuing claims of progress in gender relations. Nichiren Buddhism, in particular, is important both because of its dependence on the *Lotus Sutra*—the sacred text par excellence for the ideal—and its role in giving birth to certain of the Japanese new religions that may seem to represent a step forward in the attainment of that ideal. But do they actually realize the promise of the Buddhist gender ideal?

Japanese new religions (*shinko-shukyo*), such as Nyoraikyo, Tenrikyo, or Omoto Kyodan have exerted influence since the 19th- and early 20th centuries, but most especially since the end of the Second World War (1945). Having much common ground with pre-existing Shinto and Buddhist traditions,[868] new religions nevertheless represent significant movements that have carved out distinctive religious bodies. In the main these are notable for their origin in one or more charismatic figures, and this fact also largely accounts for the differences among them. Characteristic elements include many associated with the dominant religions, such as veneration of ancestors, purification of the souls of the departed, and dependence on established sacred texts (which may be interpreted in new ways). Additionally, new religions are typically what Westerners call 'millennarian'—espousing the ushering in of an age of peace by devotees—and attentive to things often associated with great changes, like miracles, particularly healings. Syncretistic in collecting ideas, they also tend to be less rigidly hierarchical in organizational structure.[869]

Women in the New Religions

This latter feature, together with the dependence on charismatic leadership, may help to account for the more egalitarian gender relations in many new religions. Indeed, we probably would be surprised if such gender relations were not the case, given the fact of women's involvement in these religions, and their motivations. As anthropologist Christopher Reichl rightly points out, "One striking feature of the New Religions is the high proportion of women among their founders, leaders, and followers, a phenomenon that calls for analysis of the 'social significance of female religious leaders.'"[870] While we can scarcely do such a large topic justice, we can spend a moment examining a few of the women prominent in these religions, especially since they often engaged in gender crossing of one kind or another.

Many new religions are *Lotus Sutra*-based, a Buddhist sacred text promising salvation irrespective of gender. Japanese cultural history scholar Paul Varley offers an especially pertinent comment:

> What makes the new religions most fascinating within the larger context of Japanese cultural history is the degree to which they reflect fundamental religious values and attitudes that have been held since ancient times. This can be seen perhaps most tellingly in the kinds of charismatic figures who have founded new religions, the most interesting of which are the female shamanistic types. . . . This form of divine transmission, known in Japanese as *kami* possession (*kami gakari*), is vividly described in classical works of literature such as *The Tale of Genji* and entails a process whereby, in the face of personal affliction or natural calamity, the deity believed to be responsi-

ble is invited to enter the medium, usually a girl or woman. Once the deity possesses her, the medium enters into an ecstatic, sometimes frenzied state and a voice, clearly not her own, speaks forth to indicate what must be done to placate the aroused deity.[871]

Varley offers as a prime example the person of Miki Nakayama, founder of Tenrikyo, whose story is recounted later in this answer. *Kami* possession confers upon the recipient a certain position of authority. Further sanctioned, as is often the case, by miraculous healings, this spirit possession can result in charismatic women gaining a hearing—and followers. One might reasonably expect this success at the top would be mirrored by greater opportunities for women in the ranks. In fact, as Tenrikyo developed it became common to say, 'women are pedestals,' probably a reference to the idea that the pedestal is the foundation of the religious path and that women should therefore stand at the forefront.[872]

However, an interesting irony attends the success of these new religions. Nakamura agrees that religion has been a liberating force for Japanese women, offering them a way to transcend imposed social limitations. "Yet," adds Nakamura, "even the New Religions, once established, tend not to give their ordinary rank-and-file women adherents the opportunity for the same gender-transcending self-fulfilment that their founders experienced."[873]

In sum, though the new religions with their universalistic interest and openness to new revelation have shown signs of acknowledging gender equality, the reality may not be substantially changed from older traditions. As with the dominant religions, perhaps it remains the case that for women to gain real influence in the religious sphere they must still prove some significant connection to masculinity. This might be accomplished by *kami* possession or some Buddhist transformation to maleness, but apart from the buttress of masculinity, mere femininity seems locked in a subordinate position.

What interests us is that transgender realities enter as gender-leveling ones. Through divinely guided gender crossings women may gain access to those things typically taken as masculine prerogatives. The existence of transgender realities means that gender movement of real consequence is possible in the sphere of religion. Gender crossings are sanctioned first by the example of those undertaken by divine figures themselves. These in turn pave the way for human expressions of transgender.

What divine gender crossings occur in Japanese religions?

Generally, around the world as it pertains to the realm of the sacred, gender boundaries are less rigid than in the secular world. Deities—regardless of their own gender, if they have an identifiable one—may choose to appear as masculine or feminine, and may choose a human male or female as a vehicle. Not surprisingly, then, instances of sacred gender crossings occur in Japanese religious tradition in a variety of forms, even though many sacred beings have relatively stable or fixed gender identities.

In what follows, the examples selected reflect different kinds of gender crossings. The first, concerning a powerful and popular *kami*, represents how divine beings can be assigned more than one gender, or be seen as having no gender, or more than one gender simultaneously. The second example shows how a particular deity can manifest not only in different genders, but different ways. The third example reflects the experience of divine possession of a mortal form—one common way a divine spirit can manifest in different genders. All of these examples, which overlap to some extent in their ideas, are paralleled by similar instances in other religions, and each could be multiplied by other accounts from Japanese Shinto and Buddhist traditions.

Inari

The *kami* Inari is perhaps the quintessential example of a gender-variable deity in Japan. Especially in folk Shintoism, Inari is among the most popular *kami*, being associated with agriculture and prosperity in general, and the growing of rice in particular. Inari may be pictured in a number of ways and the more prominent of these reflect gender diversity: as an old man, as a young woman, or as an androgynous boddhisatva. In each case, Inari is closely joined to the image of the fox (*kitsune*), which serves as the *kami's* servant. For example, the old man is shown with rice and foxes in attendance. Alternatively, the fox and woman may be shown as merged as one—a fox-woman. The boddhisatva is represented as carrying rice while astride a flying white fox. Within Shintoism, Inari is identified with several other *kami* (e.g., Ukanomitama no Kami), while Japanese Buddhism preserves Inari in the forms of Dakiniten (an incarnation of the Buddha), and the temple protector (chinjugami). [874]

Inari's gender—like so much else about the deity—is flexible and encompassing. Anthropologist Karen Ann Smyers writes, "Unlike other well-known Japanese deities who have unambiguous gender in anthropomorphic form, Inari is thought to be either male or female; or both; or neither." Smyers further observes that devotees, in identifying Inari as one or another gender, have their ways to justify the designation, but that no "theological orthodoxy" prevails on the question. Indeed, she points out that evidence suggests Inari originally was not gendered at all. However, Smyers suggests Inari's connections with the feminine precede those with the masculine, the latter which seem to coincide with Buddhist influences. Indeed, in investigating she encountered claims that Inari manifests in one or another mortal devotee, but typically in a woman displaying shamanic powers, who is able to speak for the *kami*. [875]

The Kasuga Deity

Mountain deities, for another example, might display both male and female manifestations. Early in the 13th century, according to tradition, the Kasuga deity manifested himself through a female medium. This deity, a local god associated with Mount Mikasa, had by this time become viewed as a representation of divine Buddhist figures. As the story goes, the famous monk Myōe Shōnin (1173-1232 C.E.) had resolved in 1202 to hazard the long journey to India to venerate the Buddha in those places where he had taught. In 1203 the Kasuga deity persuaded him not to undertake this trip by speaking to him through a 28-year-old kinswoman. Referring to himself as 'this old man,' Kasuga manifested twice over a span of three days. Instead of the proposed pilgrimage, Kasuga gave to Myōe a different sacred task, one that succeeded in extending the worship of Kasuga himself.[876]

Spirit Possession

A common way for divine figures to cross gender lines is through possession. For example, the *Kojiki* recounts the spirit possession by three male deities of the empress Okinaga-tarashi. They not only prophesied through her, but spoke directly to her as well, promising for the child in her womb a great future.[877] Whatever else such possession means, it constitutes an elevation in status; ignoring what the empress says is not without peril or consequence because it disrespects the *kami*. In a similar tale of possession in the *Nihongi*, in which the divine spirit takes both female and male forms, the *kami* Omononushi-no-kami possessed Princess Yamatototohimomoso and thereby spoke to the emperor. Upon learning who the *kami* was, the emperor offered veneration. That very night, in the emperor's dreams, Omononushi-no-kami appeared to him again, although this time as a noble man.[878] The *kami*, irrespective of the gender attributed to them, use gender crossings in possession to capture mortal attention and symbolically convey meaning.

What human gender crossings occur in Shinto and Japanese Buddhism?

Gender crossings by deities are met by gender crossings by human beings. Sometimes the two necessarily intersect, as when a divine personage associated with one gender takes possession of a human person of a different gender. In the dominant religions of Shinto and Buddhism transgender realities are multifaceted. We have set the background for them with some examination of how these religions treat gender, and by looking at some kinds of divine gender crossings. Before we press on to specific matters of transgender realities we still need to examine one more idea—androgyny, the blending or joining of masculine and feminine qualities so that neither strongly predominates over the other.

Androgeny

To comprehend human gender crossings we must first understand a long tendency in Japanese culture toward androgyny. "A taste for the androgynous," writes historian Paul Varley, "has deep roots in Japanese culture. This stems at least in part from the fact that the traditional clothing of men and women—the kimono in its various forms—has often been similar if not identical."[879] Echoing this thought is 19th century Japanese scholar Basil Hall Chamberlain's observation of early Japanese culture that the genders were not distinguished "by a diversity of apparel and ornamentation," save for a difference in the length of hair and the manner in which it was worn.[880]

We should not conclude from this that no gender differentiation in dress existed among the Japanese before Western styles became popular. Even the *kimono* is gender differentiated. Both historically and contemporaneously, Japanese clothing serves to distinguish genders. Thus the tendency toward androgyny does not foreclose acts of crossdressing, but casts them in a different light than in more polarized gender schemes. The Japanese are fascinated by gender crossings—we need look no further than the *manga* popular among Japan's youth, both boys and girls, for evidence of it—but this interest reflects a somewhat different gender sensibility than found in Western culture (despite the West's profound influence over the course of the last century).

Crossdressing in Shinto Tales

Shinto sacred texts include incidents of crossdressing. As we have learned, crossdressing is not a simple phenomenon with a uniform purpose or result. It can be used for many reasons. In heroic tales it often serves as a disguise to gain an advantage for combat. Such is the case in an explicit instance of male crossdressing found in an ancient Shinto tale.

The *Kojiki* preserves the story of Wo-usu-no-mikoto, son of the emperor Kei-Ko, who as a youth was sent by his father to vanquish two strong, but disrespectful men known as the Kumaso-takeru (or 'Kumaso bravoes'). Wo-usu, who at the time still wore his hair up on his forehead, received from his aunt a woman's upper garment and skirt. In the former he hid a small sword and set out on his journey. Arriving at his destination, he awaited a feast day. The text tells us:

> Then when the day of the rejoicing came, having combed down after the manner of girls his august hair which was bound up, and having put on his aunt's august [upper] garment and august skirt, he looked quite like a young girl, and, standing amidst the women, went inside the cave. Then the elder brother and the younger brother, the two Kumaso bravoes, delighted at the sight of the maiden, set her between them, and rejoiced exuberantly. So, when [the feast was] at its height, [His Augustness Wo-usu], drawing the sabre from his bosom, and catching Kumaso by the collar of his garment, thrust the sabre through his chest, whereupon, alarmed at the sight, the younger bravo ran out. But pursuing after and reaching him at

the bottom of the steps of the cave, and catching him by the back, [Prince Wo-usu] thrust the sabre through his buttock.[881]

It was by this deed the prince won the name of Yamato-takeru-no-miko from the younger man before Wo-usu finished dispatching him. We should note, too, that Wo-usu was not an effeminate youth; his father actually feared him because of the penchant for violence he had shown already. His act, then, is part of a heroic tradition found in both East and West of great warriors crossdressing.

Finally, there may be an allusion to gender crossing in the dress behavior of a young girl referred to in the *Kojiki*. In recounting the reign of Emperor Su-Jin, the text recounts how this maiden stood in the Pass of Hera in Yamashiro, dressed in a "loin-skirt," singing a strange song that was interpreted as a warning that the emperor's half-brother was plotting against him. Although the nature of the "loin skirt" is unknown, translator Chamberlain supposes from the nature of its mention that something contrary to custom was at hand. Perhaps the garb was martial, or otherwise masculine in character. If so, it is connected to a divine warning from a figure that immediately disappears after offering it.[882]

Gender Crossings in Japanese Buddhism

Faure observes that in its complex multiplicity of religious ideas and forms, some Buddhist texts "seem to invite, tolerate, and even cultivate 'otherness' on their margins. . . ."[883] We have seen that Japanese Buddhism can be very androcentric. Yet Faure remarks, "Like most clerical discourses, Buddhism is indeed relentlessly misogynist, but as far as misogynist discourses go, it is one of the most flexible and open to multiplicity and contradiction. In early Buddhism, for instance, genders are not fixed, but fluctuating, and cases of transsexualism seem a common occurrence."[884]

Human gender crossings in Japanese Buddhist experience can reflect the Buddhist logic that the differences perceived between males and females, men and women, is illusory. Faure refers to the early Buddhist's belief in the transient nature of gender differences and remarks, "This belief probably partly justified the practice of cross-dressing and blurring genres, paving the way to the evolution that led from the *chigo* to the *kagema* (male courtesan)."[885]

The *Chigo* (Novice)

The *chigo* (novice) needs additional notice. Faure observes that there was an idealization of boys that prompted more than one urge. On one hand, they became objects of affection, even erotic attraction. On the other hand, they could also be regarded as divine avatars. With respect to sexuality, the *chigo* was regarded like females were—as occupying the passive role.[886] Faure judges from the literature that erotic love of the *chigo* flourished especially in the late 17th-early 18th centuries.[887] But what matters to us here is the notion that the *chigo*, though always remaining male in sex, is not a 'man' in gender. He is, notes Faure, a "liminal" figure. The *chigo* can play with sexual difference only so long as remaining clearly male in body but not masculine in gender. The *chigo*, simply put, is "Transsexual, yet male." And that status reality is what provides the mystical quality that makes them suitable mediators between the sacred and the profane.[888] The novice occupies a state of gender characteristics that blur the lines a gender dualism seeks to fix firmly.

Other Examples: *Shirabyoshi, Ubhatobyanjanaka, Pandaka*

Faure also writes of an emergence in the 11th century of unisex clothing fashion and cross gender behavior such as males shaving beards and eyebrows, as well as applying makeup, while female dancers known as *shirabyoshi* dressed in masculine clothing—cultural steps that Faure contends were instrumental in "paving the way to the gender inversion that would later characterize no and kabuki."[889]

Japanese Buddhists were well aware of the classical Buddhist tradition's types of the *Ubhatobyanjanaka* (intersexed) and *Pandaka* (typically regarded as a homosexual male). The former, says Faure, were not viewed as fixed in nature—stuck between sex and gender poles—but as in movement toward one or the other end. The *Pandaka*, because they simultaneously appear both hypersexual and impotent, were either seen as threatening or were despised. Interestingly, persons we today would call transsexual were not condemned, though they were prone to being viewed as strange and somewhat pitiful.[890]

Gender Crossings in Response to Gender Inequality

But while the Buddhist logic allows us to reason that sex and gender differences are illusory, the all too common reality is that such differences have practical impacts in the world, most notably in gender inequality. Women desiring spiritual advancement have often been seen as encumbered by obstacles. To achieve enlightenment their course may mean gender alteration. For example, Jodo Shin Shu Buddhism ('True Pure Land Buddhism'), founded by Shinran Shonin in the early 13th century, espouses the need of such a transformation. In the *Larger Sukhavativyuha Vyuha Sutra* (*Sutra of Eternal Life*), Amida Buddha makes 48 vows, the 35th of which reads as follows:

> O Bhagavat, if, after I have obtained Bodhi, women in immeasurable, innumerable, inconceivable, incomparable, immense Buddha countries on all sides, after having heard my name, should allow carelessness to arise, should not turn their thoughts towards Bodhi, should, when they are free from birth, not despise their female nature; and if they, being born again, should assume a second female nature, then may I not obtain the highest perfect knowledge.[891]

Only by become masculine in nature can a woman spiritually succeed.

But as we saw in the previous answer, devout females sometimes realize transformation into males in their current lives. The story of the Dragon Girl

(The *Naga* King's Daughter) in the Devadatta chapter of the *Lotus Sutra* is perhaps the best known example. In the space of an instant, she turned into a man and attained elevated spiritual status. Nichiren, in his *Kaimoko shu* (*The Opening of the Eyes*), declares this event does not mean that she alone did so: "It means that all women can attain Buddhahood. . . . When the dragon king's daughter attained Buddhahood, it opened the way for all women to attain Buddhahood eternally."[892]

What human gender crossings occur in Japanese New Religions?

Japanese new religions, as earlier remarked, have offered more opportunities for women than generally is the case in the dominant religions. The greater prominence of women is directly associated in some instances with sacred gender crossings.

Tenrikyo

Miki Nakayama[893] (1798-1887), founder of Tenrikyo and *hinagata* ('divine model'), came from humble beginnings, born into a peasant family in the late Tokugawa Period (1603-1867). She married and had children, both matters setting the stage for a series of troubles. The marriage was an unhappy one. Her children were plagued by illness and she endured the premature death of two daughters. After her son suffered an injured foot in 1838, the stage was set for a turning point in Nakayama's life, which happened October 26th, when she was 41-years-old.

A local *yamabushi* (Japanese mountain ascetic), endowed with extraordinary powers, was summoned to give aid. But the female *miko* (shamaness) who would have acted as medium aiding the *yamabushi* was unable to come. Nakayama served in her stead. Nakayama was possessed by a male *kami* who named himself as Tsukihi ('Sun and Moon')—a name suggestive of the union of genders that the heavenly spheres symbolize. The deity proclaimed himself the 'true and original god' (aka. Tenri-O-no-Mikoto, an untranslatable name) and insisted that she yield herself to his continuing work in and through her. That work entailed transmission of the deity's revelations, the validity of which was further attested by her performing miraculous healings. Nakayama had become the 'Shrine of God'—a condition only finally and fully realized by her own family more than a quarter-century later.

Nakayama came to be called Oyasama, 'God the Parent.' The *miko* status of the foundress was recognized as well for her designated successor, her youngest daughter Kokan, born the year before her mother's transformation. Kokan's coming out as a spiritual force can be marked in 1853 when, at age 17, she spread the name of God—Tenri-O-no-Mikoto—at Dotonbori. By 1865, Kokan was sharing in the service of mediating the word of Oyasama. She was referred to as the 'Young God'; she remained forever young, dying at age 39 after an illness. Though Kokan did not completely realize her mother's ambitions for her, she does stand as another example of how this new religion made a place for women leaders.

The revelations of Tsukihi as mediated through Nakayama were set down in writing in a Tenrikyo sacred text, the *Ofudesaki* (*The Tip of the Writing Brush*), composed between 1865-1879. It espouses, as the divine will, that devotees experience 'joyous life' (*yoki gurashi*). Such a life is open to all; the *Ofudesaki* proclaims, "All people of the world are equally brothers and sisters. There is no one who is an utter stranger."[894]

Omoto Kyodan (Omoto-Kyo, Oomoto)

The creative response to social reality and Buddhist logic reached a new peak in the late 19th-early 20th centuries in Omoto Kyodan ('The Great Foundation'). We find perhaps the most interesting religious use of gender and gender crossings in this religious tradition that arose in the late 19th century. The female founder, Nao Deguchi (1836-1919), aided by her son-in-law Onisaburo Deguchi (1871-1948), introduced what scholar of Japanese religions Helen Hardacre terms a radical form of religious innovation. [895]

Similarly to the case of Miki Nakayama, Nao Deguchi's life was beset with challenges. Conceived in a time of famine, her parents contemplated whether or not the family should have another child. According to the biography accepted by devotees as the definitive account of her life, her paternal grandmother intervened, reminding her parents of the adage that a child born in such a time of distress might make a mark on the world, and that this pregnancy must exist for some unknown reason. Though spared, as a child Nao was subject to harsh treatment by her father, who often resorted to physical violence associated with bouts of drinking. His death when Nao was 9-years-old left the family destitute. It meant the girl was forced to work to help support her family. At age 16, after her mother's intercession, she was adopted by an aunt into the Deguchi family.[896]

As a girl, Nao had desired to become a Buddhist nun. Instead, through an arranged marriage, she became wife to a dissolute alcoholic and mother to eleven children, three of whom died in infancy. Her husband, whose ways had reduced the family to poverty, died when she was 53. The bad fortune, though, was about to change. On the lunar New Year of 1892, when she was 55, Nao fell under spirit possession by Ushitora no Konjin (identified with Kunitokotachi). She gained some attention as a healer, but the development of her own ideas was greatly facilitated when she met a spiritual and religiously knowledgeable man named Kisaburo Ueda. She adopted him, changed his name to Onisaburo Deguchi, married him to one of her daughters, and employed him as her *saniwa*, the male interpreter of a female shaman's trance utterances. [897]

Nao lived in a culture that kept women subordinate in social and religious roles. Her response was the idea of *henjonanshi* (or, *Henjo Nanshi*, 'Transformed Male'), the notion that women's attainment of salvation involves a transformation. The female must become male. Though this idea already existed in Buddhism, Nao placed it in a distinctive context. To buttress her idea, she constructed a mythology that placed herself as the object of a divinely ordained nature as the Transformed Male: a female with a male nature. Nao's destiny—appointed by Ushitora no Konjin at the beginning of the world—was to undergo suffering in a long cycle of rebirths in preparation for the remaking of the world. This event was to occur in the present, now revealed as the last age, in which Ushitora no Konjin completed Nao's transformation. Paralleling Nao's transformation was one by Onisaburo, through the spirit Hitsujisara Konjin, into *henjonyoshi* ('Transformed Female'). Nao declared, "I am a woman but have the nature (*shorai*) of a male, and Onisaburo is a man but has the nature of a woman." These transformations accomplished, their purpose was to work in tandem to complete a renewing of the world in which present social realities are reversed. This was work, Nao believed, that only a female accustomed to hardship and able to endure great and prolonged suffering, could accomplish.[898]

Onisaburo did not dispute that he had a male body; he merely insisted he also had a feminine gender nature. But recognizing that sex and gender are not completely severed, Onisaburo observed that even his body had female qualities: his hair was long and thick, his body soft, and his breasts large. In harmony with his perception and teaching, Onisaburo would take on the manner and appearance of Benten (a form of the goddess Benzaiten).[899]

Onisaburo echoes a positive appraisal of women in his *Divine Signposts*, where he declares, "Women are most suitable as missionaries of this way. Although they may be good, men tend to be persistent in their opinions, and there is the possibility of failing and profaning God's way."[900] This sentiment is both echoed and clarified further later in the same work. Onisaburo writes:

636. I have already written that women are more suitable as missionaries of the Divine way. This is because women possess the virtue of humility, because women are modest in all things, gentle and calm, and are by nature obedient to the Divine teachings.

637. See, then, how although the Spirit of *Mizu* or the God *Susanoo* appears majestically valiant, his spirit is female.

638. God teaches that even though one's body be male, the heart must be female, like the Spirit of *Mizu*.[901]

Ironically, by the mid-1990s, the percentage of women instructors in the religion was less than 50%.[902]

The gender crossing of the founders, though, remains recognized in the latter two of these sayings. 'His' spirit is 'female'; 'male' bodies must have 'female' hearts. Such teaching affords a continuing vein not only for equality between the dominant genders, but also for recognition of 'third gender' people. Still, transgender realities, so important to the foundation of Omoto, appear to have little if any role or place in the present. The religion also has declined significantly in numbers from its height in the mid-20th century.

Conclusion

As evidenced from the above, Japanese religions have a history of involvement with transgender realities. These, however, have served less to demonstrate actual 'third gender' identities than to modify the domineering influence of masculinity. Activities like crossdressing may serve one or another end, but most gender crossings in Japanese religion have intended a redress of patriarchy. Especially in the new religions, gender crossing has served to stake a claim for a charismatic woman to an authority usually reserved for men. By possession from a male deity, or in some other manner becoming 'like a man,' some women have succeeded in realizing spiritual advancement in ways not typically associated with women in Japanese culture.

Q. 82 Can transgender elements be found in other Eastern religions?

The Short Answer. Transgender realities of one sort or another may be discerned in many religions in addition to those already discussed. But a complicating factor arises from the profound interactions among cultures and religions over time. Today, the major world religions have largely stamped their power on indigenous religions so that the latter are commonly intermixed with elements of the larger religion. A prominent example of this is found in Chinese folk religions, a massively diverse collection of beliefs and practices claiming allegiance from millions of adherents though little discussed in the West. In such religions gender crossing figures such as Zhu Yingtai can become divine symbols of potent realities that speak to people across centuries. In other instances, in places where the major world religions have come to dominate, some strand of pre-existing indigenous religion still colors the local religious expression. For instance, the *Nat* of Burma continue to be worshipped and served by *nat kadaw*, religious figures who actively embrace what we call transgender realities. In either case, then, one can find instances where cross-gender acts and crossdressing enter in. The same is true for better known religions. In China, for example, the pervasive influence of Confucianism dominated the culture for centuries, and remains a background force even today. Though noted for its strict gender divisions and proscribed relations, Confucianism recognizes a place for gender crossing to serve its system, as seen in the habit of addressing the ruler's wife by diminutive masculine terms. Confucian society also was familiar with cross-dressing and with males exhibiting the traits we associate today with a transgender person. In India, Jainism understood that a person might have the body of a sex different from their gender. Jain thinking provides a recognition of the intersexed as a 'third sex' and 'third gender' (predicated on sex), with a corresponding sexual attraction pattern. Sikhism, a young world religion, proclaims itself the most egalitarian religion with respect to gender. Yet, in practice, as in other religions there is a struggle to reach the ideals set forth by the teaching. Transgender realities, though known, are little discussed and apparently not included in the quest for an ethical and equal gender reality. Taoism, an ancient alternative to the way of Confucianism, historically rendered an androgynous cast to its devotees. Its philosophy offers avenues to welcome transgender realities although Taoist literature does not directly address them.

The Longer Answer. Transgender realities have been discerned in every major Eastern religion—and among indigenous religious traditions, too. Descriptions of these realities have been discerned in spiritual texts, recounted in stories, and observed in religious practices. Those religions more famous in the West, such as Hinduism and Buddhism, have received more attention in English language publications, though transgender realities in the former are much better known than among the latter. But even a religion like Jainism, largely unknown among Westerners, has garnered some attention.[903] Here we will investigate major religious traditions of the East that tend to be less known among Westerners, as well as foray briefly into some indigenous religions.

Sometimes religions that have been dominant in a culture in the past have receded into the background, where they continue to exercise influence, but through less formal or obvious channels. Confucianism provides one such example. For centuries the dominant religious philosophy for millions of Chinese, it today remains a potent background force in China, Korea, and elsewhere. Sikhism, a religion born from a creative response to the tensions produced in India by the striving between Hinduism and Islam, receives little Western press though it occupies a vital place in Eastern life. Sikhs offer a distinctive stance on God, religious activities—and gender relations. Taoism, another religious tradition born in China, also has both historical significance and modern influence. These religions—all numbered among the great religions of the world—have been no more immune from transgender realities than any other religious traditions.

Alongside other major religions, Confucianism, Sikhism and Taoism continue to contribute to cultures today. But so also do a host of little known religions that have existed for centuries in particular locales, or, like Chinese folk religion, across a wide range of geography. In many places of the modern East there are indigenous religions with transgender elements, or religious expressions where the transgender element is embedded in a creative mix of indigenous religion with a major world religious tradition. The result is an astonishing variety of transgender realities, of which we can here only sample a few. Our goal is a modest one: to further document the pervasiveness of transgender expressions like crossdressing and to indicate some of the ways in which these have been responded to by religious traditions.

How do Chinese folk religions treat gender crossings?

Millions in Asia embrace Chinese folk religion (or 'religion*s*'; aka Chinese traditional religion). In a certain sense, this may be called *the* religion for many people, even though they may also consider themselves adherents of one or more of three major world religions: Buddhism, Confucianism, or Taoism. Folk religion is 'traditional' in the sense that it extends in some form as far back as Chinese religion can be traced. It is 'popular' in that it represents religion as it actually is practiced. Much like 'popular' or 'traditional' or 'folk' religions else-where in the world, Chinese folk religion mixes elements from the indigenous religion of the distant past with those from later religious traditions.

Sociologist Joseph Tamney traces its present form back to the Sung Dynasty (960-1279), with elements like shamanism and ancestor worship dating back much further. The better-defined dominant religions (Buddhism, Taoism, Confucianism) all have made their mark as well. Lacking both a central organization and a formal canon of sacred texts, folk religion remains a local spiritual expression centered in individual and family practice rather than in organized congregational worship or ritual, although there are festivals and rituals widely observed.[904] Henri Maspero, noted scholar of China and especially of Taoism, gets the situation exactly right in his remark that, "The popular religion is far from being one and the same; if certain fundamental ideas are found from one end of China to the other, the details vary infinitely from one place to another."[905]

Shamans

Across Asia, where Chinese people are found, so also is popular religion. Tamney notes that still in modern societies like Singapore more than half of the Chinese practice folk religion, which is organized around shamans. "Indeed," he writes, "the central aspect of Chinese folk religion is the performance of rituals for magical purposes."[906] In these rituals the shaman functions as the religious expert to coax from the supernatural what the supplicant desires. Shamans, who may be either male (*hsi*, or *xi*) or female (*wu*), mediate between this world and that of the spirits, typically through being possessed by a spirit. At least for a time, and in a place, it appears male and female shamans were equally valued and took equally active roles in ceremonial rituals—if we can trust the account of the 9th century B.C.E. collection of verse, the *Li-sao*.

Over the sweep of history, and under the dominance of Confucian thinking on Chinese society, the ratio of female shamans to male shamans dramatically declined.[907] Some shamans presented a gender generally conforming to what was expected for their body sex, but others did not. For example, the practice along the Chinese-Tibetan borderland of Tsinghai was for male shamans to crossdress.[908] Both the *Li-sao* (*Beset with Sorrow*) and the *Ch'un-chao ku-liang chuan* (*Spring and Autumn Annuals*) recount male shamans presenting as women.[909] Regardless of actual body sex, it was customary to refer to all shamans by the feminine *wu*. Although their manner of practice varied from one part of China to another, in general shamans for an extended period were viewed as virtuous and principled, and for a long time served a vital role in state affairs.[910]

Avalokitesvara/Kuan-yin (Guanyin, or Kwan-yin)

While Chinese folk religion, by its very nature, varies in its elements from place to place, broadly speaking we can say that populating the 'heaven' (*tien*) of these spirit beings are venerated ancestors, famed historical figures (e.g., Confucious), and a host of gods, goddesses, and demigods. As we might expect, in some instances an association exists between the power, or nature of the figure, and gender change. Perhaps the most prominent example is one we have met before (see the answer to Q. 80)—the popular deity Kuan-yin.

'Kuan-yin' is a loose translation for the Mahayana Buddhist Bodhisattva Avalokitesvara ('the Lord who hears and sees the deepest things'). This divine figure can assume many forms, with some 33 identified as major, and 9 of these as primary. These forms may appear as male, or female, or androgynous (hermaphroditic). In either sex, notes Maspero, the deity may display in a mild or severe aspect. Avalokitsevara is the male mild aspect; Ma-t'ou Kuan-yin (Avalokitesvara of the Horse's Head) the severe one. The female form in mild aspect is Pandaravasini (Kuan-yin Clad-in-White); the severe aspect is Green Tara. The form beloved of folk religion is Kuan-yin Bringing Children (Sung-tsi Kuan-yin; aka Sung-tsï niang-niang, 'The Lady Who Brings Children').[911]

The cult of Aalokitesvara spawned treatises—notably in the collections *T'o-lo-ni tsa-chi* (*Dharani Miscellany*) and *T'o-lo-ni chi ching* (*Collections of Dharani Sutras*)—describing invoking the divine figure for any number of desired ends, including gender change. One way to do so is to fast seven days, then burn incense made of sandalwood before the image while chanting the *dharani*[912] 108 times; thus focused, one chants the divine name thrice and the wish is granted.[913] Kuan-yin became particularly associated with women, and real women sometimes came to be called by the name. Among the most notable were the last empress of the Ch'en, who upon becoming a Buddhist nun received the name (7th century), and the Taoist saint Wang Feng-hsien (9th century).[914] Nevertheless, Kuan-yin has remained popular with both men and women, and could be regarded as a kind of patron divinity for transgender people.

Zhu Yingtai & Liang Shanbo

Gender changes, whether actual transformations of the body or artful disguises, are a part of popular Chinese culture and easily attached to the omnipresent religious element. A well-known example is found in the popular folk story of the 'butterfly lovers,' Zhu Yingtai and Liang Shanbo. Chinese folk literature scholar Roland Altenburger rates the tale of Zhu Yingtai alongside that of Hua Mulan (made famous in the Disney animated films) as the two most famous cases of women disguising themselves as men (or, female crossdressing—*nü ban nan zhuang*).[915] The story exists in many different forms, some shorter and others with much more detail. The gist of the story is that a young woman dons masculine dress and manner and travels afar in her pursuit of learning. On her journey she meets a man named Liang Shanbo, with whom she comes to share a room during her years of study. Liang does not discover her secret while they are living together. However, taking Zhu up on a promise to visit at Zhu's home, he discovers the truth. But it is too late for his offer of marriage to be accepted because she is promised to another. The heartbroken Liang—mourning the loss of one he had perceived as a soulmate—departs and dies not long after. Zhu, on her way to be wed, is delayed by a storm near the site where Liang is buried. Visiting his tomb, her grieving is answered by the tomb opening. Zhu disappears within it. Thus the ill-starred companions are forever joined.[916]

In at least one account—perhaps in an effort to counterbalance the attention paid to Zhu—Liang Shanbo became venerated as a lesser deity, with a temple dedicated to him. Zhu Yingtai, on the other hand, was variously appraised. Some saw in her the antithesis to the brave warrior Hua Mulan. Zhu had violated the gender rules prescribed for a woman and thus earned her demise. Others have seen in her the ultimate figure of unrequited desire. Altenburger, however, sees her as having caused "a lasting rupture in the gender order." Caught in the gender role of a man who has sworn brotherhood to another, she leaps into the tomb. "The symbolical shedding of the female gown in the very moment of disappearing in the tomb," writes Altenburger, "indicates a utopian act of negating, and thus transcending gender constraints."[917]

The magical transformation of the couple after Zhu's death into butterflies, found in some accounts, fits well with the tendencies of folk tradition. Though it is Liang rather than Zhu who is raised to divine status, it is her transformation from a woman to a man that generates the story and all its power. Many Chinese, like others around the world, yearn for the kind of transformations that might open up life's possibilities for them. Some find them in the magical transformations of more occult forms of religion. Others carve out space for themselves in more restrained religious forms.

How does Confucianism regard gender and transgender?

Perhaps no religious tradition is more restrained than classical Confucianism. Actually more a social philosophy than a religion, Confucianism makes social relations central and carefully elucidates their manner. Relationships are vertical rather than horizontal in nature. The one in the lower status is obligated to show respect to the one in the higher status, while the higher status person is obligated to exercise care for the one in the lower status. Marriage, a preeminent gender relationship,[918] exemplifies the vertical arrangement. The man in the role of husband has status over his wife. The great Confucian sage Mencius succinctly states the woman's duty: "It is the way of a wife or concubine to consider obedience and docility the norm."[919]

As in its rival Taoism, Confucian thought relies on the concepts of *yin* and *yang*. With respect to gender, *yin* (the feminine aspect) is subordinate to *yang* (the masculine aspect). As the 2nd century Confucian woman Ban Zhao (Pan Chou) reasoned, since *yin* and *yang* are of different natures, so are woman and man. The former is yielding, the latter is rigid; men are honored for strength, women for gentleness. Her famed work *Nü Jie* (*Lessons for Women*) sets out rules for correct feminine propriety and modesty in the central relations of Confucian society.[920] This way of looking at gender tends to exaggerate differences and institutionalize them in gender roles. Such rigidity in the gender system would seem to leave little room for transgender realities.

Yet Confucianism could not distance itself from the obvious occurrence of gender variance and even within its system had to develop some manner of expressing a degree of gender relativism. In its preoccupation with setting forth correct social relationships, gendered distinctions are articulated and cross-gender elements occasionally enter. When this occurs it is under the service of some relationship, as in the instance of a ruler's wife being addressed by diminutive masculine terms (see the answer to Q. 76). Altenburger explains this phenomenon as the development of a convention of understanding the bipolarity of *yin* and *yang* in a quasi-allegorical fashion. As such, *yang* came to represent the higher valued status and relationships could be expressed in relative terms. For example, relative to the Emperor (*yang*) a male official was still *yin* in status.[921] So the Emperor's wife, though female, was *yang* to the *yin* of lower status persons.

The hierarchical nature of male/female relationships and the social obligation in marriage to produce offspring would suggest that transgendered realities would be marginalized at best. In Confucian ethics, order and duty have prominence. Yet, once duty is discharged, as when a marriage yields children, other matters might be permitted. Thus, some have concluded that the activities or statuses forbidden by Confucianism do not include transgendered realities like homosexuality or transsexualism.[922] But support for that notion is scanty at best.

Dress in Social Relations

Confucian scholars understood the principal role played by clothes for social distinctions. From its earliest days proper attire, whether for ceremonial purposes or ordinary ones, was an object of attention and instruction.[923] Dorothy Ko, who has written extensively on the subject, remarks that "Correct attire—headdress, dress, and shoes—was the quintessential expression of civility, culture, and humanity, all being ramifications of *wen*. Attire played a central role in both the external and internal definitions of Chinese identities: clothing differentiated the Chinese from their (inferior) neighbors while marking social and gender distinctions within society."[924]

Confucius himself set a model example. In Book X of the *Analects* (*Lun yü*), he is "the gentleman" whose manner of dress is impeccably correct for every occasion (X. 6). Elsewhere in the *Analects* (VIII. 21) Confucius can "find no fault" in the Emperor Yü, founder of the Hsia Dynasty, a man who "wore coarse clothes while sparing no splendour in his robes and caps on sacrificial occasions."[925] Similarly, the *Book of Means*—one of the four Confucian classics—cites the *Book of Odes* in praise of a modest woman: "She covered her brocade gown with a plain robe," which is interpreted as her not wishing to show off her fine clothes.[926] The general philosophy is set forth by Mencius in a pithy analogy contrasting a virtuous emperor with an evil one: "If you wear the clothes of Yao, speak the words of Yao and behave the way Yao behaved, then you *are* a Yao. On the other hand, if you wear the clothes of Chieh, speak the words of Chieh and behave the way Chieh behaved, then you *are* a Chieh."[927]

Mencius elsewhere speaks of how one attains proper relationship through 'being true,' which is 'the Way of Heaven,' just as reflection upon it is 'the Way of man.' He describes a chain of 'being true' that leads from right relationship with one's parents all the way to being fit to rule the people. But it begins with being true to one's self. That means understanding goodness, for the true self is a morally good self. As Mencius puts it, "There has never been a man totally true to himself who fails to move others. On the other hand, one who is not true to himself can never hope to move others." [928] While Mencius did not have in mind gender variant people, is it such a stretch to include them as they are within the reach of this teaching?

Crossdressing

Indeed, in light of such sentiments we may consider a specific reference to crossdressing. The *Xunzi* of Xun Kuang (c. 310-220 B.C.E.) remarks that it is not uncommon to encounter young men who "wear striking clothing with female adornment and exhibit the blood, breath, and bearing of a young girl."[929] In the spirit of Mencius, these males *are* feminine in gender, if not female in sex. Such individuals could be regarded in more than one way in Confucian China. Chinese thinking saw the person as an organic whole, yet was dualistic in respect to distinguishing between higher internal qualities (*hun* and *shen*) and lower, body-based ones (*po*). The former matters more than the latter. In this respect, it might be argued that the feminine soul of a physical male takes priority over the body; gender means more than sex. Logically, the feminine male acting like a woman is behaving congruent to the soul. Mencius himself, we just saw, reasoned the path of success lay in the winning of trust, and traced the attainment of trust back to being true to oneself.

Yet, as already noted, Mencius conditioned the way of being true to oneself on the understanding of goodness. Mencius, like other Confucian scholars, embraced a social order in which male was above female, and shame was meant to motivate everyone to realize and fulfill their obligations. Xun Kuang, who did not share Mencius' conviction that human nature is essentially good, also saw shame as useful for reinforcing social order. His *Xunzi* represents a legalistic wing within Confucianism that advocated firmness to restrain human nature from making shipwreck of society. Religion scholar Jane Geaney observes that the above quoted text of the *Xunzi* apparently is concerned over how clothing can blur the gender boundary line and produce chaos. Indeed, the *Xunzi* contrasts those "chaotic" rulers who sanction such loss of boundaries from the "centered" (i.e., 'proper') rulers who, like all "centered" males find the behavior "shameful."[930]

353

On balance, while transgendered realities clearly existed in Confucian China, they were restricted. Social order had priority and to whatever degree a transgendered experience or expression did not promote the constructed relations and virtues of Confucianism it was shameful. In a patriarchal society a transgendered male had a particularly difficult path because it was shameful to identify and express a lower status when everything in the culture praised and supported performance of duty and seeking a higher status. The transgendered were more likely to find comfort and relief in other philosophies, like Taoism.[931]

How does Jainism treat gender and transgender realities?

Jainism, an ancient religion of India, is perhaps best known among Westerners for its doctrine of *ahimsa*, the avoidance of doing harm to any living thing, as the following sets forth: "All sorts of living beings should not be slain, nor treated with violence, nor abused, nor tormented, nor driven away."[932] Apart from this idea, most Westerners have little sense of the religion. But this venerable (arguably the oldest world religion) tradition has a fully developed view of the cosmos and our place in it, including ideas about sex, sexuality, gender and transgender.

Gender

Our primary interest lies with how Jains regard gender, and especially transgender realities. We may note first that Jainism linguistically distinguishes three genders: *pumlinga* (masculine), *strilinga* (feminine), and *napumsakalinga*. In grammar, this last term can straightforwardly be rendered 'neuter.' But what happens if it is applied to human beings? Padmanabh Jaini, scholar in both Jain and Buddhist studies, and born in a Jain (Digambara) family, reports that *napumsakalinga* with reference to gender means 'indeterminate.' Jains apply it to those whose sexed body exhibits both male and female characteristics, namely the intersexed (or as he calls them, 'hermaphrodites'). Jaini adds that this designation is not given to eunuchs because such may be made after birth. Gender is fixed to the sexed body and reflects *nama-karma*, a karma that establishes visible bodies that are clearly divine, animal, infernal or, as in these three genders, human.[933] Gender, based on sex, can in turn be matched to kinds of sexuality.

Sanskrit scholar Robert Goldman observes that Jain thinkers, perhaps alone among premodern theorists, did something akin to our modern division of sexual orientations (considered further below). But the manner in which they saw these in relation to sexual bodies and gender is more flexible than what has proved true in Western culture. Goldman notes that in the Jain perspective a male with respect to the sexed body (*dravyapurusa*) can be psychologically like a woman (*bhavastri*).[934] This recognition, as we shall see, figures into debates within Jainism over gender and 'salvation'—liberation from the cycle of birth, death, and rebirth.

Like the other dominant world religions, Jainism has developed a gender hierarchy in practice regardless of nobler sentiments that might be found within its literature or tradition. In this gender hierarchy men maintain a privileged position over others. On the face of it, Jain sacred literature preserves a rather low estimate of women. Jain monks are told, "The world is greatly troubled by women."[935] Accordingly, the advice is: "Do not desire (women), those female demons, on whose breasts grow two lumps of flesh, who continually change their mind, who entice men, and then make a sport of them as of slaves."[936]

Nevertheless, some sacred texts appear to hold out a more positive view. For instance, in the *Jaina Sutras* we find the rebirth of certain beings, who had been gods in a former existence, reborn as mortals in the Eden-like city of Ishukara. Not all of these divine beings chose rebirth as males. The text reads:

> Two males remained bachelors, (the third became) the Purohita (Bhrigu), (the fourth) his wife Yasa, (the fifth) the widely-famed king Ishukara, and (the sixth) his wife Kamalavati.
>
> Overcome by fear of birth, old age, and death, their mind intent on pilgrimage, and hoping to escape the Wheel of Births, they examined pleasures and abandoned them.[937]

Apparently, whether man or woman, an individual can become devoted to spiritual pursuits, renouncing the dangers of earthly pleasures.

Of course, the matter is not that simple. As in other religions, Jains find themselves divided into groups whose views on different matters vary. The Digambaras and the Svetambaras—Jainism's two principal groups—disagree on whether a female can attain *moksa* (liberation) from *samsara* (the cycle of birth and rebirth). Digambaras deny this possibility; Svetambaras affirm it.[938] The manner in which gender and patterns of sexual attraction may be joined provide fodder for this debate, so we must now turn to how Jains conceptualize what we today call 'sexual orientation.'

Veda

Jain thinkers, cognizant of the realities of gender and sexuality around them, came to articulate a scheme about human sexual desires (*veda*) that recognizes three distinct patterns. In the *Uttaraadhyayan Sutra* these are described as among the varieties of "pseudo-passion-related conduct-deluding karma." These pseudo-passions are regarded as "mild" and include things we might judge as positive (e.g., laughter), or negative (e.g., indulgence). *Veda*, a person's sexual attraction pattern, can be viewed either as a single pseudo-passion, or as three *vedas* (*striveda, pumveda, napumsakaveda*): "male, female and mixed."[939] Goldman explains these as, "the sexual feelings normally appropriate to a woman, a man, and a hermaphrodite respectively."[940] Jaini reminds us that regardless of gender, any given individual is capable of experiencing any of the three *vedas*.[941]

This possibility creates a point of tension that becomes clear when the different Jain camps approach the matter of *moksa*. The principal text disputed is a brief saying found in the tenth chapter of the *Tattvartha Sutra*, where the writer Umasvati lists the kinds of liberated souls with respect to their former worldly status. In doing so, Umasvati mentions *linga*, or 'gender sign.' On the face of it, the text seems to suggest a person of any human gender might attain *moksa*. Yet the Digambaras reserve such achievement to males.

Goldman and Jaini both point out that the Digambaras utilize the distinction between gender and sexual orientation to argue this Jain scripture does not envision *moksa* for females or hermaphrodites. Goldman sees their argument as that any passage apparently describing such spiritual liberation for females is really talking about males who are like women in their sexual attraction pattern—what we call 'homosexual.'[942] Jaini, instead, elaborates on the Digambara view that prefixing of *strilinga* (feminine) or *napumsakalinga* (indeterminate) to *Siddha* (a 'Perfect Being,' i.e., one who has attained *moksa*) functions "to refer not to a former woman or a former hermaphrodite but to the past state of that kind of a monk who had started to climb the spiritual ladder . . . with either a female libido (*striveda*) or hermaphrodite libido (*napumsakaveda*)." Accordingly, the use is metaphorical, not literal; only males are meant.[943]

The Svetambaras find this interpretation illogical, comments Jaini. They point out that if a male can achieve *moksa* despite having possessed a *veda*, there can be no grounds for saying that either a female or intersexed person cannot do likewise.[944] At any rate, as for biological females, Goldman observes, the principal argument of the Digambaras against their ability to achieve *moksa* lies in their very nature. Female physical anatomy and physiology presumably generates and destroys *aparyaptas*, minute living organisms which make their home in certain places on the female body, where the normal female cycle brings about their death—a profound and regular violation of *ahimsa*.[945]

Transgender Realities

In view of the Jain conception of how sex, sexuality and gender play out in individual lives, it is not hard to find in Jainism transgender realities. As we have seen, these emerge most plainly in the recognition of the intersexed as a 'third sex' and 'third gender' (predicated on sex), with a corresponding sexual attraction pattern (*napumsakaveda*). Likewise, we have seen that because gender and sexual orientation are independent and can join together in unexpected ways, the transgender realities referred to in the West as homosexuality and bisexuality are also acknowledged.

Little imagination is required to envision how other transgender manifestations might occur within Jain society. Crossdressing, for example, is one obvious way a member of one gender can claim some affiliation with another. It is not a behavior unknown among Jains. Contemporary Jain teacher Duli Chandra Jain regards transvestism as behavior refused by the Jain seeking purity in body and mind. Because crossdressing involves pleasure in the act, it represents a passion like other sensual activities, one capable of staining thoughts and feelings. "Consequently," he advises, "a rational individual sets a limit on such activities for himself/herself."[946]

But what if crossdressing is *not* a matter of sensual passion? What if the behavior reflects dress behavior analogous to that of the conforming genders? It would seem, logically, that such behavior would escape censure—at least censure along the lines offered a moment ago. Nevertheless, the dependence of gender on sex in Jain thought makes recognition of transgender people like transsexuals as difficult an idea as it is for many Westerners. In this respect, crossdressing is likely to be interpreted either in terms of a sexual fetish or as a marker of homosexuality.

How does Sikhism address gender and transgender realities?

Sikhism is a relatively young major religion. Practiced by perhaps 15-20 million devotees, mostly in India's Punjab, the religion began in the early 16th century. Sikhism from its beginnings has been a way of discipleship dedicated to following the teachings of the Guru—the holy teacher. Ultimately, God is the teacher, but within human history ten mortal men, beginning with Guru Nanak (1469-1539) have borne the honorific. So, too, does the collection of sacred teachings, the *Sri Guru Granth Sahib* (aka *Adi Granth*). A religion that privileges ethics over dogma and rite, Sikhism expresses itself concretely through *seva* (voluntary labor), the *langar* (community meal), and the *sangat* (congregation). Sikhism also offers distinctive teaching relevant to matters of sex, sexuality, gender, and transgender.

Gender & Deity in Sikhism

As is commonly the case, theology offers a starting point in gaining a perspective on why a religion adopts the position it takes on matters of sex and gender. The Sikh view of God provides a strong statement of a Being without sex or gender. As the *Sorath Mohalla* puts it, "He hath no form, or color, or outline."[947] More expressively, and reflecting the response to Hinduism and Islam, Guru Gonind Singh declares:

God is Formless, colorless, markless,
He is casteless, classless, creedless;
His form, hue, shape and garb
Cannot be described by anyone. . . .[948]

But while God's essence is sex and gender free, that does not mean God cannot be spoken about using gender language. Such an all-encompassing deity includes characteristics people typically divide along gender stereotypes into masculine and feminine. God transcends these stereotypes no less than gender itself. Thus the *Majh Mohalla* can praise God by simultaneously employing both masculine and feminine labels: "Thou art my father, thou art my mother."[949]

Contemporary Sikh scholar Nikky-Guninder Kaur Singh extols this theological lead. In her book *The Feminine Principle in the Sikh Vision of the Transcendent*, she contends that Sikh scripture gives some prominence to the feminine: the *Guru Granth* calls 'Mother' the ground of all being; God is referred to as mother as well as father, sister as well as brother. In sum, God, the Transcendent One, "is as much female as male." She quotes the scripture text which states succinctly, "It itself is man; It itself is *woman*" [italics hers].[950] Elsewhere she writes:

> The text offers a vast range of feminine symbols and imagery: the ontological ground of all existence is *mata*, the mother; the divine spark within all creatures is *joti*, the feminine light; the soul longing to unite with the transcendent One is *suhagen*, the beautiful young bride; the benevolent glance coming from the divine is the feminine *nadir*, grace.[951]

This theological perspective provides a ground for envisioning a more egalitarian social relation between men and women.

However, such efforts have remained partial and uneven—much like Sikh recognition of God's gender labels. Despite a formal recognition of the feminine alongside masculinity in speaking of the divine, in ordinary practice Sikhs have followed Western religious traditions in normally referring to God as 'he.'[952] Sikhism, then, formally grants a freedom to use masculine and feminine symbols alike to descriptions of God—a freedom we have seen in other religions that stress One God and recognize that any attribution of gender is only metaphorical, so that both genders, with all their symbolic connections, are beneficial. But in practice Sikhism still preserves masculine privilege in talking about God.

Ideology & Reality in Sikh Gender Equality

The same pertains to human affairs. Sikhism is characterized by both an ideal of gender equality and a reality of masculine privilege. These dual characteristics can be glimpsed even in the way Sikhs form their names. Sikh names, though gender neutral, affix gender markers, with males adding Singh ('lion'), and females adding Kaur ('princess'). Sikh history records the struggle between the ideal of gender equality and its imperfect implementation.

Sikh scholar Satwant Kaur Rait credits the Sikh Gurus with being ahead of their time with respect to gender equality. She finds in both the *Adi Granth* and the *Rahitnama* (Sikh Code of Conduct) authoritative support of women and equality. She says of the founder, "Guru Nanak declared that women must be respected, as they were the source of humanity's physical existence and of its entire social structure."[953] Rait argues that Guru Nanak and the early Gurus adopted a twofold approach. Negatively, they condemned the gender inequality of the religious cultures around them. Positively, they promoted an affirming attitude intended to raise the status and prestige of women and to secure their liberation from the negative attitude of these neighboring religions.[954] Rait cites lines from the *Asa di Var* (*Ballad of Hope*), originated by Guru Nanak (and later expanded), and sung each morning by the congregation in the *gurdwaras* ('gateways to the Guru,' i.e., Sikh temples):

> "Why should we call her 'inferior', who giveth birth to great men?
> A woman is born of a woman; none is born without a woman.
> O Nanak, only the Lord has no need for a woman."[955]

In many respects, from its beginnings until now Sikhism has proven more egalitarian than most other religions. Whether in the religious community, the family, or the wider society, women have enjoyed a status and recognition often not found elsewhere. Within the *sangat* women enjoy a degree of inclusion and participation that women in most other religions would marvel at. The family, a central concern to Sikhs, affords another example. Religious scholar Geoffrey Parrinder points out that Sikh marriage practices recognize women's rights and that even the wedding liturgy poetically portrays marital union as "one spirit in two bodies."[956]

Yet despite such things, no less than most other human societies, a struggle between the genders can be glimpsed. In gender relations, men still hold more power. Nikky-Guninder Singh observes wryly that, "the ideals of the Sikh gurus have been distorted because their lives and words were recorded, interpreted, and taught primarily by male elites."[957] As a result, the practical realities of gender relations among Sikhs has long entailed a creative tension between the call of the ideal set forth by the Gurus and the mundane reality of some persistent gender inequalities.

One noteworthy example of the tension between an espoused ideal of gender equality and actual social realities is the formation of the Khalsa ('the pure') community by the tenth Guru, Gobind Singh (1666-1708). The community was open to both men and women and Parrinder writes, "In the Khalsa women could be initiated and followed similar duties to men. They were neither secluded nor veiled, and worshipped with men in temples."[958] On the other hand, sociologists Inger Furseth and Pål Repstad contend that the Khalsa are best conceived of as an "elite brotherhood" and claim, "A new emphasis on masculine features was introduced, which was associated with the strongly militant character of the Khalsa."[959] In sum, this significant religious experiment in community dramatically exemplifies the struggle we have been describing—one that took a new twist with European colonial powers coming on the scene.

Religious studies scholar Doris Jakobsh, in her effort to deconstruct the socially constructed view of gender across Sikh history, contends that the impress of Victorian ideology posed a special challenge to Sikh views and practices. Traditional Sikh views of women, she argues, underwent a significant degree of modification as Sikh society sought to accommodate the presence of European power. The Singh Sabha reformers, British-educated, desired to recreate a 'pure'

Sikhism but pursued their vision through Victorian lenses. In her estimation, the Sikh 'intelligentsia,' molded as they were by the West, melded "Victorian gender constructs with hypermasculine Sikh ethos of the nineteenth and early twentieth centuries"—with profound and far-reaching effects.[960] Jakobsh's views have met with sharp criticism from some within the Sikh community, who object to her analytical framework and especially her use of Sikh holy scriptures.[961] However, her attention to the effect of a dominant Western culture on Sikhs should not be lightly set aside. However it may be explained best, the reality on the ground suggests Sikh practices felt the weight of Western expectations.

Both in Asia and in the West today Sikh gender relations retain the uneasy tension between ideals and less-than-perfect realization. Rait observes that while women have equal rights in initiation and worship participation, they remain under-represented in the management of *gurdwaras* and are especially limited with respect to participation in the management structures related directly to the concerns of women and children. She summarizes the present situation by re-marking, "Sikh women have more freedom than some other Asian women in terms of religious behavior, but the Gurus' teachings of equality have never been fully realized in practice."[962] Nikky-Guninder Singh offers a bleaker picture, pointing to inequalities at every level of Sikh life, religious and mundane, including the horrific practice of using modern technology to determine fetal sex and abort females.[963]

Transgender Realities

Given the espoused commitment to gender equality and the overall reputation for tolerance and education associated with Sikhism, we might hope for an openness to transgender realities. Given the presumptive gender duality and the apparent practiced gender hierarchy we might instead fear a situation not much different than found in the West. However, what we chiefly find is silence. Of course, this silence extends beyond transgender to most sex and gender issues.

I. J. Singh, addressing International Sikh Conferences in 2004, reflected that the reluctance of Sikhs to discuss these matters is in line with the general reticence to talk about such things found throughout India. Singh observed that on many matters, including issues like divorce, birth control, and abortion, Sikhism makes no effort to proclaim binding edicts. "The emphasis in Sikh teaching," Singh said, "is on transforming an individual into a mature, ethical being who will act in every situation in a thoughtful, non-exploitive, generous, honest, caring, responsible, and mature manner."[964]

However, this sentiment apparently does not extend to transgendered people. Though the Sikh holy texts say nothing on explicit topics related to transgender, modern Sikh authorities have not been so reticent. In 2005, Sikh leader Giani Joginder Singh Vedanti proclaimed to Canadian lawmakers considering gay marriage rights that homosexuality is contrary to Sikh religion and its code of conduct, as well as the laws of nature.[965]

While Sikhism presumes a Western-influenced heteronormativity, homosexuality and other transgender realities do occur in Sikh society. In recent years an exodus of Sikhs from India to other lands has meant some transgendered Sikhs relocating in countries like the United States. A 2004 conference focused on Asian Pacific Americans who identify as gay, lesbian, bisexual or transgender found that 2% claimed Sikhism as their religion.[966]

Few resources, either in India or elsewhere, exist for transgender Sikhs as both *transgender* and *Sikh*. As a result, many anecdotal reports found on the internet have a plaintive tone as isolated individuals reach out in the hope that other transgendered Sikhs will respond.[967] A common complaint is the deafening silence within Sikh homes about transgender realities—a silence that perpetuates ignorance. The spirit called for by I. J. Singh, so resonant with the Sikh tradition, still seems largely fallen short of in the lives of many ordinary disciples when reckoning with transgender people.[968]

How does Taoism (Daoism) regard transgender?

Taoism (or Daoism) is an ancient Chinese tradition whose principal sacred text, the *Tao Te Ching* (or *Dao De Jing*) is attributed to Lao Tzu (or Lao Tse, or Laozi), alleged to be a slightly earlier contemporary of Confucius in the 6th century B.C.E. The philosopher Chuang Tzu (4th-3rd century B.C.E.), author of a work by that same name, is also considered a primary source for the Taosit philosophy that emerged and was later given the name 'Taoist' (or *Tao-jia*, 'Way-school'). [969] It has become conventional to distinguish the older philosophical tradition from a later religious Taoism, arising early in the Common Era. By the 5th century C.E. it had become a recognized state religion.

The differences between philosophical Taoism and religious Taoism are so profound in character that many find them fundamentally irreconcilable. Noted scholar of Chinese philosophy and religion Wing-tsit Chan believes it is a great irony that the Taoist philosophy should become a popular religion so radically different from it. He contrasts the naturalism of the philosophy with the supernaturalism of the religion, where we find polytheism so pronounced that virtually everything has a deity associated with it. The philosophy's equanimity about life and death is replaced by an all-consuming quest for immortality. The teaching of simplicity is lost to an elaborate system of rituals. "In short," Chan concludes, "its basic teaching of *wu-wei* (nonaction, or rather taking no unnatural action) has been negated by a great deal of activity—idol worship, divination, geomancy, astrology, and what-not."[970] Given this state of affairs, we must sharply distinguish the earlier philosophical Taoism from its latter religious offspring.

Philosophical Taoism

Taoism, like other Chinese philosophies, speaks of the *Tao* ('Way'). In Taoism it is a natural 'way,' 'path,' or force that underlies, supports, and sustains the

Oneness of all things. Feminine titles are appropriate for the *Tao*, which is referred to as the 'mother' of all things, for it engenders all things. Feminine attributes such as a yielding nature are ascribed to it. *Tao* is the 'mysterious female' (*Shih wei hsuan p'in*), endless and energetic.[971] The *Tao Te Ching* reminds us, "In stillness the female constantly overcomes the male, in stillness takes the low place."[972] Contemporary religion scholar Russell Kirkland, a specialist on Taoism, points out that the *Tao Te Ching* can be—and has been—interpreted as under-cutting our conventional gender categories, since it "clearly warns that males who follow the attitudes and behaviors that it characterizes as 'masculine' will bring disaster to themselves and those around them."[973]

The *Tao* utilizes both *yin* and *yang*. As the 2nd century B.C.E. text *Huai-nan Tzu* (or *Huainanzi*) puts it, the *Tao* is everything, but it organizes all we know principally through two great aspects: "In the beginning, the two forces *Yin* and *Yang*, having obtained the essence of the Tao, became the central organizing powers."[974] The unifying character of *Tao* thus expressed through *yin* and *yang* when organized into human 'kinds'—or 'genders'—becomes the passive, receptive *yin* (feminine) and the active, penetrating *yang* (masculine).[975] The *Tao Te Ching* extols, "Know the male, maintain the female, become the channel of the world."[976] *Yin* is not an inferior quality to *yang* in Taoism. As contemporary *I Ching* expert Wu Wei notes, neither is greater than the other, nor are they truly opposites. "They work together to bring into being All-that-is," he writes. "Neither one can bring things into a state of being without the help of the other."[977]

Taoist articulation of *yin* and *yang* in relation to gender may offer useful insight in figuring out a contemporary Taoist logic for transgender realities. These complementary aspects not only interrelate, but penetrate each other in the constant ebb and flow of change. Yet, as *Huai-nan Tzu* makes clear, these cosmic principles remain distinct: "They are unable to co-exist identically and simultaneously in mutual contact."[978] Instead, they are each apportioned relatively in people. Human beings—whether male (*hsiung*, *ch'ien* trigram) or female (*p'in*; *k'un* trigram)—possess both *yin* and *yang*. Broadly speaking, a 'man' is a male in whom *yang* predominates, whereas a 'woman' is a female in whom *yin* predominates. But the degree or quality of *yin* and *yang* in each helps make them more or less masculine or feminine.

What, then, of intersex or gender variant people? They also have both *yin* and *yang*. Although *yin* and *yang* are associated with 'femaleness' and 'maleness' respectively, it would be misleading to see in that any strict correspondence to body sex. A Taoist might conceive of a transgendered male, for example, as one with much *yin* in him.[979] In this light, a passage from the *Chuang Tzu* (4th century B.C.E.) may be applicable:

> Those who are perfectly correct never lose the character of
> their nature and life. Therefore for them the united is not like
> joined toes, the separated is not like extra fingers, what is long
> is not considered as excessive, and what is short is not consid-

ered as deficient. Therefore although the duck's legs are short, to lengthen them would be to give it sorrow, and although the neck of the crane is long, to cut it off would be to bring it misery. Therefore what is by nature long must not be shortened, and what is by nature short must not be lengthened.[980]

Transgendered people, if seen as 'natural,' have no need to change their nature, and to try to change them would bring only sorrow. Their 'correctness' depends on faithfulness to their character. There is neither too much one thing ('long') nor the other ('short'); they are fine as is. The same text later observes that people rejoice in others being like themselves, while objecting to others being different from themselves. Chuang Tzu notes disapprovingly that such folk make friends with those like themselves in the interest of power, a desire to rise above others. Far better, he says, to look after one's own affairs than make judgments based on the opinions of others.[981]

Yet what we have said remains speculative in that our contemporary notion of transgender realities is of no interest to classical Taoist philosophy. The principal philosophical Taoist writings do not address our subject in any direct way that would help a contemporary person comprehend a Taoist stance on the subject. We are left to tease out possibilities. As such, there may be indications provided by Taoist logic like that offered above, and also by actual Taoist practice.

For example, Taoist religious orders historically rendered an androgynous cast to its devotees, whether monks (*tao-shi*) or nuns (*tao-ku*). As Livia Kohn observes, "Medieval Daoist sources make no distinction between male and female ranks, accomplishments, status, or even clothing."[982] The ordinary costume for a Taoist monk is a long gray robe with wide sleeves that are sometimes white. The hair is grown long and knotted at the top of the head.[983] On the other hand, whatever we make of this historical development among the devoted who separated themselves from the masses, we may not be able to transfer with confidence to the popular folk religion.

Religious Taoism

Religion scholar John Raines attributes the transition from Taoist philosophy to the popular religion as at least in part owing to disillusioned Taoist intellectuals becoming practiced in the art of withdrawal from politics. "As intellectuals retreated into a kind of aristocracy of the disappointed soul," he writes, "Taoism as a practice became increasingly a religion just like other religions— marketing religious capital, monopolizing the field of salvation."[984] Yet there were ways in which The Way was distinctively different from Buddhism and, especially, Confucianism.

Religious Taoism (*Tao-chiao*) particularly owes its special development to twin 2nd century C.E. sources: alchemy and utopianism. Each of these has its great sacred book—*Pao-p'u-tzu* (*He Who Keeps to Simplicity*) for the former, and *T'ai P'ing Ching* (*Great Peace Classic*) for the latter. Though these texts are principal ones, popular Taoist religion propagated a large canon.[985] In keeping with the sources of its popular life, Taoist religion became most noted for the alchemical quest for transformation to an immortal state of being and the vision of a utopian state within which health would flow from the morality of its citizens. Both sources at least offer possibilities for transgender realities.

The logic of religious Taoism starts with a nod to philosophical Taoism and then develops in its own unique way. The one *Tao* utilizes the twin complementary forces of *yin* and *yang* to divide and distinguish things. As the *Yin-chih wen* (*The Secret Accord Scripture*) puts it, *yin* and *yang* alternate and push one another ahead. As they do so, every change and every transformation is in accord.[986] Together, working naturally, they produce a complex, interacting system.

Five principal elements emerge: fire, water, wood, metal, and earth. The number 5 shows itself in a host of connections, most notably the five human relations and the five cardinal virtues. In time, eight trigrams, ten heavenly stems, and twelve earthly branches were identified. Collectively, the system aims to understand all that is, especially as each part stands in relation to every other part. Ideally, a human being should, in his or her own person and in society, manifest as a microcosm of the greater whole.

Taoist Logic & Transgender Realities

At least in principle, it should be possible to adhere to this logic and derive transgender realities. For example, we might find among humankind five sexes: male, female, and three kinds of intersex (i.e., what formerly were distinguished as 'true hermaphrodite,' 'male pseudohermaphrodite,' and 'female pseudohermaphrodite').[987] Correspondingly, it should be easy enough to find room for additional genders to match the sexes following the common custom of matching gender to sex. As such, *yin* and *yang* can be seen as correlating so as to yield alternatives to masculine male and feminine female. Contemporary sex educator Barbara Carrellas attempts this in her argument that the principles of Taoism can be applied, if we think of *yin* and *yang* in terms of hormones rather than genitals. In this respect, she writes, "People with testosterone-based bodies (whether they were born male or take testosterone as a supplement) tend to be more yang. People with estrogen-based bodies (whether they were born female or take estrogen as a supplement) tend to be more yin."[988]

This modern reading is not as far-fetched as it might seem at first blush. Taoist literature speaks often of how *yin* and *yang* interact with respect to gender.[989] For example, *Ts'an-t'ung-chi* (*Book of Changes*), traditionally ascribed to Wei Po-yang, offers basic ideas about the relation of *yin* and *yang* with reference to human genders. Both individually and socially one gender checks the power of the other. Each needs the other and both require balance through the influence of the other to be healthy. Interestingly, part of the way in which *yin* and *yang* relate is through the transformations each can undergo: thus metal (*yang*) can become water (*yang*); fire (*yin*) can change into earth (*yin*). Earth (*yin*) absorbs water (*yang*) and thus keeps it from running wild; *yin* restrains *yang*, or to put it in gender terms, the feminine restrains the masculine.[990] If one should overcome the other, both cease to exist separately and merge back into their original nature, wherein they share a common ancestry.[991] It is not hard to read in this the possibility of androgyny with the merging of male/masculinity/*yang* and female/femininity/*yin*.

Moreover, *transformations* are key in a system that finds change intrinsic to reality and believes alchemy offers ways for human beings to master changes. The *Nei P'ien of Ko Hung* (*Inner Chapters of Ko Hung*, aka *Pao-p'u-tzu*) in the 4th century speaks clearly of the possibility of all kinds of changes by people, many of which even in his own day were regarded as fantastic and implausible. He writes:

> If you claim that man, unlike other creatures, has an undeviating nature—that the destinies bestowed by August Heaven are not subject to vicissitudes—how can you account for instances where Niu Ai became a tiger, the old woman of Ch'u a tortoise, Hunchback a willow (*Chuang* 18.20), the girl of Ch'in a stone, the dead came back to life, males and females interchanged sex, old P'eng enjoyed great longevity, but a baby son died prematurely? If such divergences exist, what limits can we set to them?[992]

What limits indeed? Just a little further on the writer muses, "Why should there be any limit to the number of marvelous things that exist between sky and earth, within the vastness of Unbounded?"[993] To the master of alchemical changes almost any may seem possible. "What is it that the arts of transformation cannot do?" asks the author. "May I remind my readers that the human body, which is normally visible, can be made to disappear."[994] Still later, in speaking of a scroll entitled *Mo tzu wu hsing chi*, he says that one who has mastered its knowledge can easily change his body in an instant: "By a mere smile, a man knowing this art can become a woman."[995]

But what is touted as *possible* can pale against what proves *actual* inside a religion. In that respect, Taoists found many practical limits to the transformations they sought. Immortality proved elusive and the quest for it was eventually modified to the more modest effort to obtain a long and healthy life. If changes in sex and gender could be conceived, the question was still why would they be? For the Taoist the moral motive for a change mattered, and it was located within a certain sensibility of the way things are. A good Taoist does not strive for unnatural changes, so any transformation must be conceived in some fashion as natural.

We have seen already the possibility that transgender realities might be seen as natural. Yet the judgments of people always enter in and if *yin* and *yang* are viewed in too static a manner, if duality becomes categorized rather than seen along a continuum, then it would be easy enough to lock folks into a rigid gender system with only men and women allowed. Even in Taoist thinking a certain flexibility of vision is required when life is lived in a social reality dominated by the expectations of Confucianism. As elsewhere with other religions, Taoism produced a mixed record.

Gender Realities in Religious Taoism

Religious Taoism largely has proved not as gender egalitarian or flexible as its philosophical roots promise. As it now exists religious Taoism has a number of different sectarian traditions, most founded by men (e.g., the Zhengyi ('Orthodox Unity') sect founded by Zhang Daoling), but at least one by a woman (the Shangqing—or Sh'ang-ch'ing, 'Consummate Purity'—sect founded by Wei Huachan (or Wei H'ua-ts'un)). In most instances, religious Taoism has been male-dominated, but some branches, such as the Lung-men tradition, have a more positive record toward women.[996] Also, in some places, like among the Zhuang people of southwest China the general gender dominance of men has been modified by indigenous religious influences.[997] It is also true that Taoists have recognized exemplary women, such as Wang Feng-hsien (or Wang Fengxian), whose spiritual journey culminated in her ascension to heaven,[998] or Huang Ling-wei, the 'Flower Maid.'[999] In fact, the Taoist text *Yung-ch'eng chi-hsien lu* (*Records of the Assembled Transcendents of the Fortified Walled City*) offers a comprehensive account of both female Taoist divinities and exemplary mortal women.[1000] Nevertheless, like the wider culture and other dominant religions, for the most part men have ruled a stable gender hierarchy.

While we cannot say definitively that Taoism has a place for transgender realities, neither can we say authoritatively that they are excluded. The spirit of the Taoist philosophy permits us to read such realities as 'natural.' Indeed, it has been the flexible, yielding character of this religion that has long made it a popular alternative to the social rigidity and demands of Confucianism. As for religious Taoism, it would seem that a tradition so entranced by magic and transformations would retain a place for transgender realities, but their appraisal must reflect judgments on how Taoist ideas are interpreted and applied.

What other examples of transgender realities may be found among indigenous religions?

Around the world, indigenous people have their own religious sensibilities and ways of accounting for gender variance. We have glimpsed, in this answer and elsewhere, some of the ways these relate to transgender realities. It is neither possible nor necessary to review all indigenous religions, but at least some further accounting of them seems desirable. So we shall briefly examine a few more of better known examples. Each in its own way offers further evidence of the important ways in which transgender realities can be put to the service of a community's spiritual needs. We begin with a deity.

Bali: The Worship of Sanghyang Tunggal

Religiously, Bali is an anomaly among the islands of Indonesia. Whereas Islam predominates elsewhere in Indonesia, on Bali the ancient heritage of Hinduism remains a cultural force. Specifically, the idea of an all-encompassing Unity or Oneness is central. Accordingly, though the supreme deity is known by various names, the essential truth of this figure is the same: everything proceeds from it and is embraced by it. Anthropologist Margaret Wiener calls it the paradox of the divinity that "it is both singular and encompassing and multiple and partial."[1001] A prominent name for this deity is Sanghyang Tunggal, 'the Solitary,' 'the One who cannot be imagined,' 'the Original God.'[1002]

By whichever name, this figure is the one God of Hinduism, a deity transcending such mundane realities as sex and gender. Sanghyang Tunggal reflects time before history, when there was neither male nor female. Thus, with respect to time in history, while sex and gender divisions exist, the deity can manifest as either male or female; Sanghyang Tunggal is, metaphorically, both husband and wife, both mother and father. [1003] The devotees of Tintiya take their cue from this hermaphroditic deity. They crossdress—both men and women. Sacred dances constitute a form of ritual transvestism such as is known through other forms in cultures around the world.[1004] Where Westerners default to reductionistic thinking and assume crossdressing is low-brow secular amusement built on sexual deception, Asians have a different perspective. "In Asian aesthetics," writes Alan Heyman, "the principle of transvestism is to give the dance a higher moral quality by making it sexless.[1005]" In Bali, crossdressing is one way to express something religiously sublime and transcendent.[1006]

Burma (Myanmar): The Worship of the Nat

Burma (renamed Myanmar in 1989, though the former name remains widely used), is a land bordered by India, Bangladesh, China, Laos and Thailand. Important to the indigenous spirituality of many Burmese people is their relationship to the *Nat*, spirits whose number has been officially set at 37 since the 11th century. The *Nat* are both feared and worshipped. The origin of these spirits lies in tragedy; the spirits were once human beings who died by accident or suicide. They linger to influence the affairs of those living and they demand respect. The power of the *Nat* can be used for good or ill.

Nat Kadaw

A *Nat Pwe* is a religious ceremony conducted to stay on the good side of a *Nat*. These ceremonies are common and used in conjunction with a variety of occasions, such as weddings, to achieve business success, or for solicitation of health. A typical *Pwe* might last three days, during which a *Nat* is contacted through a *nat kadaw* ('spirit wife'). The *kadaw* is magician, entertainer, storyteller, medium, and religious figure. As among other shamans (see the answer to Q. 76), the *kadaw* might be either male or female. In the mid-1960s, anthropologist

Melford Spiro's study of Burmese supernaturalism found shamans of both sexes; later studies indicate that male shamans may be largely displacing female ones.[1007]

During a *Nat Pwe* the *kadaw* dances before an altar covered with offerings of fruit, nuts, and other goods, while music is played. Spectators, too, may experience brief possession of the *Nat* as the ceremonies proceed. In addition to the local *Nat Pwe* there is a famed celebration held yearly at Taungbyon. Each August people visit this village for the festivities, which are dedicated to two of the *Nat*. Altogether, it is easy to see why this phenomenon has been characterized by one author as Burma's 'supernatural subculture.'[1008]

Spiro observes that crossdressed male shamans in Burma have been recorded since at least the 18th century. His own observation of the same was that "with few exceptions male shamans seem to be either homosexual (manifest or latent), transvestite, or effeminate (and sometimes all three)."[1009] The *nat kadaw* costume reflects a woman because the person enacts the role of a female *Nat*. The most famous *nat kadaw* are the *acault* possessed by the *Nat* Maguedon.

Nat Manguedon's *Acault*

Some Burmese (both males and females) take their involvement with the *Nat* to an even greater level. They may be united to a *Nat* by a spiritual marriage achieved through an elaborate, and long, initiation rite. Such a union sets apart the devotee and has a marked effect on their relationships with others. This can be seen, for example, in the male *acault* who are joined to the *Nat* Manguedon.

Manguedon is a spirit connected to success and good fortune, making her welcome among people. But she is a jealous *Nat*. Those she chooses she expects to remain true to her—an expectation that for males results in a situation easily misunderstood by outsiders. When Manguedon takes possession of a biological male she changes him into someone regarded by others as no longer a masculine male, but as an *acault*—neither male nor female (but more like a female than a male). This typically occurs at an early age, though such spirit possession can happen at other times. Ceremonially wedded to Manguedon, who bestows femininity upon them, they are expected to not associate sexually with females as this arouses Manguedon's jealousy. Subsequently, the *acault* may only engage in sexual relations with other males. Yet this is not interpreted as homosexual behavior because those in the community understand that the *acault* is not a man.[1010] The *acault* stands between the sexes and genders.

In this privileged position an *acault* may be petitioned by others, with accompanying gifts, to intercede on their behalf. Should the outcome be favorable, the occasion might lead to celebrations honoring Manguedon. At such events, held in pavilions dedicated to the *Nat*, the *acault* engage in ceremonial dance while dressed in feminine clothing and cosmetics. During the dance they enter into a special state of communion with Manguedon, serving as a conduit for requests from those present.[1011]

Manguedon's association with success and good fortune ensures that an *acault* shaman holds an important position. Their occupation of religious roles fills a recognizably vital communal need. Yet this indigenous religious tradition, though supported by Myanmar's government, struggles against the influence of other powerful religious currents. Most notably, Buddhism competes for the people's devotion. This religion's influence works against the *acault*. Prevailing Buddhist beliefs, as well as the society, privilege being male; therefore, the *acault* cannot look forward to attaining salvation (in Buddhist terms) in this life but must be reborn as male. Also, some locals believe that a son's spirit possession and becoming an *acault* is a reflection on past life karma—moral failings in a previous life are interpreted as having led to the person's present condition. Such ideas help explain why families may not be favorable toward a child exhibiting the characteristics of an *acault* and may resist such development.[1012]

Korea: The Mudang and Paksu

The shamanistic tradition is well-represented in Korea by the *mudang* (female) and *paksu* (male). They are sometimes called spirit-mediums (*yeongmae*)—an apt description of what they do—though there are others who can be termed *yeongmae* who are not *mudang* or *paksu*.[1013] These shamans enact their spiritual work through the *kut*, a complex of events that ritualistically brings the shaman into contact with the spirits. A *kut* may take hours to perform and is employed for a number of reasons, including the removal of undesired spirits. One common goal is the solicitation of prosperity, especially with respect to the forthcoming crops of an agricultural people.

Most Korean shamans are women. Another name for the *mudang* reflects her spiritual prowess: *mansin*, 'ten thousand spirits'—a reference to the number of spirits she can call upon. The label particularly fits the kind of *mudang* known as *kangsin-mu* ('spirit-possessed'), who serves as a medium to give a spirit voice. A second kind of *mudang* is the *sesum-mu* ('heriditary shaman'), one who inherits her status through matrilineal descent.[1014] Crossdressing is a characteristic feature. The *mudang* wears masculine clothing freely as part of her work.

Typically, male attendants accompany a *mudang* by playing instruments while she performs the dancing crucial to the *kut*.[1015] However, as noted earlier, some shamans are male—the *paksu*. They also crossdress. As anthropologist Laurel Kendall points out, "the rare male shaman in Korea (*paksu mudong*) performs *kut* wearing women's clothing, down to the pantaloons that hide beneath his billowing skirt and slip."[1016] Like the *mudang*, the crossdressing is purposeful—the costume reflects the identity of the spirit possessing the shaman.[1017]

The *mudang* culture has persisted despite formidable pressure against it from ruling state authorities. It was suppressed during the long period of the Yin Dynasty (1392-1910),[1018] and still is in Communist North Korea, where historically it had been particularly strong. Despite this, it persists there, as well as in the South. In modern Korea much of the popularity of the shamans is attached to their proficiency with rites of healing, though as noted previously they are also sometimes asked to perform other rites, such as for the success of business.[1019]

Thailand: The Maa Khii *of the* Phi *cults*

Thailand is, arguably, the land best known for its transgender people. But when foreigners consider these folk they are almost certainly thinking of the *Kathoey* (or *katoey*, or *kathooi*) a 'third gender' group comprised of biological males. These individuals's gender reality, however, is not associated with religion *per se*. Most are Buddhist. Yet there are some who are part of a group where gender crossing is instrumental to their indigenous religion.

In northern Thailand a different, profoundly spiritual transgendered reality is known. They are the *Maa Khii* ('possessed ones'), principally women, but also sometimes men. The *Maa Khii* are associated with a spiritual tradition (the *phi* cults) in which they occupy the role of spirit mediums. In this role ancestral guardian spirits 'possess' them during an annual festival. A trance-like state, dancing and cross-gender behavior, including crossdressing, mark this possession. Outside this special spiritual role these persons enact gender-typical behavior.

Most *Maa Khii* are female. This situation is buttressed by the tradition that the ancestral guardian spirits are passed matrilineally from one generation to the next. However, male *Maa Khii* are not unknown. Some are also *Kathoey*. Like the female *Maa Khii*, these males also exhibit cross-gender behavior; in the case of the *Kathoey* this means stereotypically masculine behavior unlike what they normally exhibit.[1020]

Walter Irvine's study of the *Maa Khii* concludes that about 15% are not female. Of these, most are *Kathoey*. Irvine's explanation for why some non-females may be able to function as spirit mediums is that the *Kathoey*, like females, are viewed as 'weak-souled,' meaning they are unable to resist spirit possession like males can. He also thinks that the *Kathoey* who became *Maa Khii* do so in response to an earlier illness afflicted by a spirit (*chao*). By yielding to the *chao* and becoming possessed they can regain their health—and become spirit mediums. This choice also improves their social status since the *Maa Khii* enjoy a prestige the ordinary *Kathoey* does not.[1021]

Conclusion

As our world continues to experience the effects of global communication and transport, the survival of indigenous religions seems ever less likely. In the East, the multitude of these religions persist either by virtue of the isolation of their location or by a strategy of accommodation. A substantial part of that accommodation is with rival religions. The success of Buddhism and Islam, in particular, has meant pressure on the smaller indigenous traditions. Yet they persist, and in many of them transgender realities continue to occupy a vital part of spirituality within the community.

Q. 83 What roles do crossdressing and transgender play in African religions?

The Short Answer. Africa is a continent rich in indigenous religions as well as major world religions introduced through conquest and colonization. Often the result of the meetings between indigenous traditions and imported religions is a creative mixture. Sometimes the result is tension. But inevitably the outcome is richly diverse and complex as individuals and communities adopt distinctive religious expressions. In this material the focus is on indigenous religions, although these today almost invariably show signs of the pressure and influence from one or another world religion. For example, many indigenous religions make a place for transgender realities and utilize crossdressing behavior. But major world religions like Christianity, introduced by European colonizers, brought along European values, including a disparagement of polygyny, same-sex practices, and apparent crossdressing. Despite this, due to a number of factors, indigenous religions persist and native culture remains a vital force. African tribal peoples often hold visions of gender different from those seen by Americans or Europeans. As a result, African deities and their devotees may display gender in ways hard for outsiders to comprehend. Gender crossings of one sort or another abound. Some of these crossings are made by spirits or divine figures. Others occur by human beings, sometimes as a result of seeking contact with spirits. Spirit cults, for instance, often feature spirit possession, which may be marked by an apparent change in gender. Also important to human efforts to cope with the spirit world are shamans, who commonly display gender variant behavior. Priests and priestesses also may engage in some kind of gender crossing in their efforts to bridge the distance between the community and their deities. Many gender crossings are transient, limited to a ritual, an occasion, or a specific situation. Some, however, have a more abiding quality. They may mark an important transition in life, one that includes a change in gender status. Still, though native practices continue in the shadow of major religions, the religious officials of the dominant religions often respond with strong words of condemnation or efforts to stop native practices. Both Christianity and Islam have long histories of opposition to many indigenous beliefs and practices. These larger religions are often supported by governments wishing to prove to the Western powers their modernity. Nevertheless, the spirit of native religiosity beats vibrantly on the African continent and transgender Africans survive.

The Longer Answer. African religions include both indigenous spiritual traditions and religions brought in from other lands. Among the latter, Christianity and Islam have been especially influential. The creative dialog and tension among religions often results in mixed expressions. Thus an individual may identify as Christian and yet retain ideas, values, and practices that are derived from indigenous traditions. This reality makes anything we say subject to heavy qualification. Practiced religion rarely, if ever, conforms to what is 'officially' prescribed by religious officials or theologians.

So in answering the question as to what roles have been played by transgender realities, especially crossdressing, in African religions we must be modest in our goals. A necessary first step is recognition of African thinking about gender.

How are gender and gender crossings viewed in Africa?

The African continent provides us with supreme examples of why we must be careful about making assumptions concerning gender. The Western conception of gender has exercised extreme influence around the world, and many other cultural views of gender are enough alike in their essentials to make them readily comprehensible to Americans and Europeans. So it is seductively easy for us to assume that our way of regarding gender is basically the same as everyone else's. However, some of the tribal societies of Africa are enough different so as to pose more significant obstacles to such a naïve assumption.

Gender, we must remember, is a human social instinct pursued by sorting people into types with respect to what a given group of people regard as being both fundamental and abiding differences. Typically, gender logic has prized the place of human sex differences to determine the shape of gender schemes in society. But whether or not the difference in male and female bodies is central to gender thinking (itself a debatable proposition), there remains more than one way to conceptualize gender.

Visions of Gender in Africa

Western gender logic is body-based: it makes sex difference in human anatomy key to sorting people into two gender groups. But why does the body have to be the key? Religions often extol the higher reality of spirit—the energy that animates the body. Why not make *energy* the key to gender?

Gender Determined by Energy

At least one tribal people has done exactly that. The Dagara people of Burkina Faso (Western Africa) have decided the best way to gender people is by the energy they exhibit. Dagara shaman and scholar Malidoma Somé, who tries to explain this to Europeans and Americans, says that gender energy is independent of body sex. A male body can vibrate feminine energy; a female body can generate masculine energy. Somé maintains that gender marks a person's individuality without defining the person's social opportunities. However, the nature of the energy vibrated does motivate a person to seek out social roles and tasks that fit that energy. Masculine energy, says Somé, vibrates outward, a centrifugal force that needs expression in physically demanding work. In complementary fashion, feminine energy is centripetal, needing expression in relational roles that help hold home and community together. The Dagara conception of gender—their different choice—also gives an honored place to people who in our society are labeled homosexual or transgender, seeing in them the ability to serve as gatekeepers to realities beyond our ordinary mundane ones, realities essential to the well-being of all people.[1022] This gender choice demonstrates that people may be sorted into kinds without relying on some body feature.

Gender as Determined by Human Development

Western gender logic not only prioritizes the physical body, but also prizes a fixed determination point—birth. Whatever the apparent sex of the body at birth becomes the determiner of the person's gender. In this respect, gender is assigned as a destiny and goal. It is a status given to which an individual must learn to conform. In short, in Western culture gender is a product. But what if gender is viewed as a *developmental process* instead?

Though our Western minds love nicely drawn and stable boxes into which to put things, it is not absolutely necessary to sort people into kinds that are once and forever fixed. Some societies think a more realistic approach is to recognize how development over the course of life fundamentally changes the kind of person one is. Thus gender should sort us into kinds that recognize such change. This creates gender boxes that are stable with respect to themselves, but fluid with respect to individuals. In other words, the boxes don't change, but as people change they move from one box to another.

There are a number of ways this can be viewed. Some societies seem not to have our urgency in assigning gender; they may see infants and small children as undifferentiated, not yet exhibiting significant enough differences to be placed in any box. A child is perhaps 5 years old before the Igbo people of Nigeria assign gender, and the Mbuti pygmies of Congo—a remarkably egalitarian society—appear to find no need to do so before puberty.[1023] Or, consider the Dogon of Mali, in West Africa. They conceptualize the perfect human as androgynous. That creates an ideal gender box that depends not at all on sex difference for placement within it. Though they also link sex and gender, they do so in a way quite different from our own. An uncircumcised male child retains femininity as long as the foreskin remains; remove it and femininity flees, liberating a masculine drive to seek out a mate.[1024] In other words, a change during development (circumcision) creates a change critical to gender.

Gender fluidity may be a trait in adulthood, too. For example, among the Gabra people of Kenya older males may undergo a gender change accompanying reaching the exalted status as *D'abella* (ritual experts). They move from masculinity to femininity. What makes this transformation particularly remarkable to Westerners is not only that these males' gender identity changes, but that they are then revered in a society that denigrates females and femininity.[1025] In this society, in Western terms, the apex of a male's life happens when he becomes like a woman! Similarly, spiritual matters may be involved in other tribal societies where gender change occurs. In each instance, gender fluidity allows a society to recognize that important changes experienced in life can be fundamental to identity and role, moving them from one group ('kind') to another.

Multiple Genders

Finally, we might ask why a vision of gender must content itself with two and only two genders. Of course, the Western vision is locked in its gaze at the human body and the obvious difference between male and female. But closer inspection finds the 'obvious' is not always so obvious! Apparent sex may be different from genetic sex—a difference that may only become visible at puberty[1026] (and thereby argues for a more developmental perspective on gender). More importantly, there is abundant evidence—if we open our eyes to see it—that while there are two predominant human sexes, there are a number of less frequent ones. Only our gender logic insists on seeing these less frequent realities as aberrations rather than legitimately different sexes.

Even in a gender scheme that makes gender dependent on sex there is room for more than two genders. Some African tribal societies recognize this state of affairs. The Amhara of Ethiopia, the Igbo of Nigeria, and the Otoro of the Sudan, all allow room for intermediate, mixed, or 'third gender' expressions. Among the Basongye (Mbala) people of Central Africa there exists a distinctive gender role called *Kitesha* (pl. *Bitesha*; an unfortunately derogatory term). This role appears to be representative of a 'third gender' in which the individual—either a biological male or female—performs gender that is neither typically masculine nor typically feminine but distinctive.[1027]

Clearly these African visions of gender challenge our own. They may also disturb us. We are accustomed to assuming our cultural superiority, confusing technological and economic prowess for moral worth. These alternate visions can, if we let them, remind us of the importance of preserving human diversity and the value of cultivating humility rather than cultural hubris.

Gemder Crossings

Since much of our attention will be given to gender crossings, first with respect to divine or spirit beings, and then with regard to human beings, we may best begin by identifying a few broad points:

❑ Gender crossings for sacred purposes are sometimes made by divine figures.

- ❏ Gender crossings are sometimes used by human figures to signify a change in status with religious significance or for religious reasons.
- ❏ Gender crossings for religious purposes may be either relatively permanent (e.g., the assumption of a sacred position), or occasional (e.g., the situational and transient performance of a ritual).

These realities are experienced in a number of different ways.

What divine sacred gender crossings occur in African religions?

The relation of nonhuman spirits and divinities to gender is subject in virtually every case to some qualifying condition. In other words, the perception of gender is either nonconsequential—because the being has no intrinsic gender or can freely shift gender—or it is linked to some other perceived quality. Most often this other quality is procreative in nature, as when a divine being is seen as feminine because it is viewed as female, one-who-gives-birth. Even so, people have experienced significant freedom in mixing one sex with another's powers, as when a male deity gives birth or a female deity impregnates someone. This fluidity of gender (and sex) can be seen as capricious, or the superficial nonsense of primitive minds. On the other hand, it can be reckoned a reflection of divine realities more in tune with the way things really are than the more pristine conceptions common to some of the younger world religions like Christianity and Islam (both of which also have their share of notions about sex and gender fluidity, though these have been largely suppressed).

Gender and Deity

Given what we have learned about the different ways in which African peoples can conceive gender, it should come as no surprise to find African gods displaying remarkable gender diversity. Gender as a characteristic of deity—whether as a possession or a performance—may be incidental or intrinsic to any specific divine figure. Some deities are ambiguous in gender, others are androgynous, and still others are gender altering (see the answer to Q. 76). Examples of each of these gendered ways can be found among African deities. For example, the divine figure Cghene of the Isoko culture in Nigeria is a sexless and gender ambiguous deity. In Ghana, the figure of Nyame is gender androgynous in the sense of being depicted as either male or female. The Egyptian deity Atum proclaims 'I am that great He-She.' Another classical Egyptian deity, Ra, though normally depicted as masculine, is a gender-altering deity. In many parts of Africa the great god Leza is extolled, usually as a masculine deity, but not always.[1028] Clearly, there are many gendered realities for divine beings.

Perhaps we would do well to regard the relation of gender and deity in a somewhat different manner than we are accustomed. In the West, we think of gender as a characteristic that is stable and fixed. But if it is not, then new ways of interacting with gender become possible. Rather than try to comprehend a deity from the standpoint of a predetermined idea of what masculinity and femininity must always be, maybe we would profit from starting with what a deity shows and then figuring out what that means for gender. This instinct seems a characteristic goal of religious people around the world—first, understand the divine, then apply that knowledge to understand the world. Such a course appears imperative to understand the relation of gender and divine reality among the Yoruba people of West Africa.

The Deities of the Yoruba

To Western eyes, the gods of the Yoruba, with respect to both sex and gender, seem baffling at best. For example, Oludumare, the supreme deity, apparently has no sex and is gender ambiguous.[1029] On the other hand, Inle—noteworthy for prominence among certain groups in the Caribbean islands—is androgynous by virtue of being a hermaphroditic deity. In yet another gender twist, the deity (*orisa*) Sango is seen as masculine, yet is also called the 'wife' of the thunder deity Ara. If anything, gender seems a particularly fluid idea among the Yoruba.

Interdisciplinary scholar Randy Connor notes that as we consider different deities our notions of masculinity and femininity change. As an example, he offers the contrasting cases of the creator-god Obàtálá and the warrior figure Ògún. The former figure, regarded as both male and female, is seen as masculine in a strikingly different manner than the latter. Obàtálá is masculine in patience and compassion; Ògún is masculine in aggression and violence. Just as what is 'masculine' varies in accordance with the deity considered, so also does what is regarded as 'feminine.' The goddess Òsun (Oshun) is linked to traits easy for the Western mind to see as feminine—beauty, grace, elegance, and charm—but she is also connected to traits we do not typically see as feminine: independence, warriorhood, and rulership.[1030] The deity creates the boundaries of gender.

Gender Crossings by Deities & Spirits

To this point, our discussion has focused on deities. These often display gender fluidity, whether as a result of changing conceptions about them (i.e., as patriarchy established itself some female deities were recast as male), or because this quality is seen as intrinsic. Yet being intersexed (or bigendered), by itself, is not the same as crossing gender. Deities cross gender when they change gender, either as a quality of being or as an act of gender performance. Gender change as an aspect of being may be intentional or unintentional. As an act of gender performance, any number of reasons might motivate it, although desire for sexual contact with someone else is common.

However, it would be incorrect to suggest that carnal appetites drive all divine gender crossings. As with lesser spirits, deities may cross gender in order to make contact with their people for any number of reasons, such as prophecy, healing, or to seek some human action. A significant way to accomplish this is through possession of a human host. Typically, this is a priest, priestess, or shaman, though potentially any person may be so possessed. Using the *orisha* of the Yoruba people (and transported to Haiti) as an example, culture scholar Erik Davis points out that the identity of the possessing figure is disclosed through mannerisms, which then lead to the possessed being costumed appropriately.[1031]

Spirits also may cross gender, and in similar fashion. Their motivations also may vary, being either malicious or benevolent in character. When they desire contact with human beings, spirit possession is characteristic. Gender crossing occurs when a male spirit possesses a human female, or a female spirit possesses a human male. Such gender crossings manifest in the host as a human gender crossing, so we shall consider them next.

What human sacred gender crossings occur in African religions?

In African tribal societies the practices of indigenous religions, broadly considered, affords space for all manner of genders and gender crossings. Connor observes that generally the indigenous traditions permit both men and women to serve the community as spiritual leaders, guides, or teachers. In addition, a number of these native traditions include religious personages (shamans, proests, and priestesses) who, in Western terms, would be called 'transgender' persons.[1032] Connor rightly points out that "it is the resemblance between the gender ambiguity of these persons and the transgender or genderless nature of the gods that qualifies them as ritual specialists, who can transgress the boundaries of the mundane world."[1033] What all of these folk have in common is that for at least a time they stand at a place between the human realm and that of spirits or deities—and this place changes them. One way such change is manifested is through gender crossing, and that can be marked by crossdressing.

Sacred gender crossings occur at a boundary, or nexus point, where two sides meet. Spirits, divine or otherwise, stand on the far side, seeking contact with human beings. Likewise, humans on the near side desire to meet the deities or lesser spirits. Accordingly, with the coincidence of interest, events like spirit possession are not uncommon. Rituals and religious positions facilitate such contact. With reference to the spiritual positions of the community meant especially to meet such a need, the possessed person is likely to be a shaman, or a priest or priestess. However, many folk who are not in such a privileged position are connected to one or another spirit cult. These groups have deep roots in many societies and many still exercise influence today. They often exhibit both continuity and discontinuity with past practices. In this astounding variety the vitality of gender crossing accompanying activities like crossdressing serves to facilitate sacred contact or to indicate its occurrence.

But what do cross-gender behaviors or transgender identities signify or accomplish? In 1901, anthropologist Ferdinand Karsch-Haack concluded from his research of tribal peoples around the world that the principal purpose of crossdressing in most instances was connected to something spiritual, with the crossdresser revered by others.[1034] Yet exactly what crossdressing achieves remains a matter of conjecture and interpretation. Yoruban art historian Babatunde Lawal, with reference to the practice among the Yoruba people of Nigeria, remarks that cross-dressing within the indigenous religion possesses multiple, interrelated layers of meaning. One meaning singled out by Lawal is the idea that crossdressing may capture the "spiritual dynamics" found in male-female complementarity.[1035]

There is more than one way to approach the phenomenon of sacred crossdressing, but we shall follow a conventional path. By examining the kinds of sacred roles, or religious posts, associated with the behavior we can get at how it manifests in institutionalized religious practice. Some examples will help to also show that while similarities may exist, as is true with religion around the world, all religious experience and expression is profoundly local, with a distinctive flavor. Yet merely looking at institutional roles is insufficient. As we shall see with spirit possession cults, it is not merely designated human officials serving in a community religion who may serve as hosts for a deity or other spirit.

Shamans (& 'Witch Doctors')

Shamans around the world are commonly associated with transgender realities and behaviors (cf. the answer to Q. 76). Africa is no different; examples abound of shamans, and incredulous accounts of them by European observers go back centuries.[1036] Though there may be variations among them, they all share the role of bridging between mundane and extraordinary domains.[1037] Spirit possession of the shaman—which may come through suffering illness, through inheriting a spirit, or by another means—provides direct access to knowledge and power otherwise unattainable. The gender of the possessing spirit may be the same or different from that of the possessed person. In respect of the difference in gender, shamans commonly exhibit cross-gender behavior, including crossdressing.[1038]

The *Omasenge* of the Ovambo

A primary occupation of shamans is healing, aided by their connection to the spirits. The Ovambo culture of Namibia, comprised of eight tribal peoples (Eunda, Ombalantu, Ondonga, Ongaqndjera, Onkolonkathi, Ukualuthi, Ukuambi, and Ukuanyama), affords a well-known example. Ovambu healers (*endudu;* sing. *ondudu*) belong to one or another of several subgroups, including the *omasenge* ('not-man'; sing *esenge*)—transgendered shamans.[1039] The *omasenge* enjoy a special relationship with Kalunga, chief deity among the Ovambu and their special creator.

Occasionally, these individuals are intersexed, but much more often they are of one sex (male), yet embrace characteristics of two genders. For example, though dressed like a woman they may wear a beard like a man. Nevertheless, the overall impression they leave is of someone who is more feminine than masculine as they talk, walk, associate with, and behave like women, even adopting feminine names. Missionary Father Carlos Estermann, who set out what remains the most respected ethnography of the region, calls the *esenge* a male possessed since childhood by a female spirit. Over time this spirit draws out of the *esenge* everything masculine.[1040] The adult *esenge* puts on feminine dress and conducts tasks associated with females. The *esenge* may even marry a male who also has female wives. On certain occasions the *omasenge* engage in same-sex sexual relations as part of a ritual. As is common among shamans, an *esenge* receives the call to the spiritual vocation through a compelling dream or a spirit-inflicted illness. They enter practice as healers using herbalistic medicine, though some move beyond simple herbalism to a higher order of shamanistic practice, such as rainmaking.[1041]

The religious activities of the *omasenge* are diverse. In addition to herbalistic medicine for healing, they offer sacrifices, play a stringed instrument called the *omakola* during rituals, provide divination (chiefly through palmistry), and engage in various forms of magic.[1042] All these activities fit their unique gender. Their status as a 'third gender' is directly attributed to Kalunga. The *omasenge* see themselves as born that way, then 'called' to spiritual service in a way traditional to shamans—through spirit possession (by an illness), or a dream. Their connection with Kalunga is accepted by the community they serve, and provides them with both a social role and status.[1043]

Other Examples

Shamans are common in indigenous religions around the world. Among other examples of transgender behavior in the shamans of Africa are these:

❑ The *eshenga* of the Ndonga of Angola are gender-mixing males.[1044]

❑ The Mbunda people of Angola have shamans who are crossdressing males.[1045]

❑ Shamans who cross gender boundaries in their relation to the sacred are also found among the many Nuban peoples (e.g., Nyima and Tira).

❑ There are gender crossing shamans also among the Zulu of South Africa.

Although most of our examples are of persons the West would term transgendered males, there are biological females who cross gender boundaries for sacred reasons, too. Examples include:

❑ Female shamans in Morocco called *sahacat* have been known at least since the latter 15th century, when they were castigated by Leo Africanus because of lesbian behavior.[1046]

❑ Among the Azande there are reports of females called *adandara* ('wild cats'), who enacted transgender realities in their practice of witch-craft.[1047]

As shamans are discussed in several places elsewhere in this volume, let us move our discussion on to priests and priestesses.

Priests & Priestesses

Shamanistic functions can be joined to priestly ones, but priests and priest-esses are distinct from shamans. The priestly office is exactly that—an *office* that is part of an official religious apparatus. Priests function as *official* representa-tives, both of the deity they serve, and of the community they represent. In this dual role they mediate between the parties. On behalf of the people they offer worship, offerings, and petitions. On behalf of the deity they bestow blessings, warnings, and healings. In many places around the world it is not only larger communal groups that have priests and/or priestesses, but also families or clans.

A few examples will suffice to show how they engage in gender crossings.

The *Hogon* and the *Binukedine* of the Dogon

The Dogon people of Mali (West Africa) utilize complementary transgender roles in their indigenous religious practices. In each principal district of the Dogon there is a *hogon*, an important civic and spiritual leader. A supreme *hogon* serves the entire nation. This figure, a biological male, tangibly represents the people's sense of creation and derives authority by virtue of being the oldest direct descendant of the founder of the Dogon. Revered as holy, his person is treated as such. Among his important personal effects is a stool upon which to seat himself that bears visual representation of the male-female ancestors (*nummo*) who support him. The *hogon* serves as head of the Lebe serpent cult (one of the four principal cults of the Dogon), which is associated with the agri-cultural cycle. The *hogon* in this role is regarded as emboying the sacred femi-nine, representative of mother earth, who provides life.[1048]

In the *bulu* (Feast of Sowing) ritual the *hogon* and another sacred person, the *binukedine* (Binu priest), enact an age old fertility ritual—the symbolic acting out of the sexual act of masculine farmer (*binukedine*) impregnating the feminine earth (*hogon*) with seed. The *binukedine* is also an important figure apart from this ritual. Generally regarded as androgynous, the *binukedine* practices magic, offers sacrifices, and does divination, and serves as a healer.[1049]

The *Mugawe* of the Meru

In the traditional religion of the Meru people of Kenya certain men held a hereditary spiritual role called *mugawe* (or *mugwe*, or *muga*; pl. *agwe*). The *mugawe* served several related roles embracing priestly, prophetic, and healing functions. The chief among these seems to have been the priestly task of facilitating contact between the people and their deities. As so often found in such matters, the service of joining the tribe to spiritual realities involved transgender behavior such as crossdressing. The extent to which the cross-gender behavior occurred varied, with some *agwe* actually marrying another man.[1050] Their sexual behavior has led some observers to type the *mugawe* as homosexual, but they are more accurately seen as transgender males.[1051]

Yoruban Worship

As the previous example shows, relationship to a deity through a sacred office is life-altering. For priests in many societies it can also be gender-altering in one or another way. Perhaps the most common way this happens is in the assumption of a gendered role, as when a male priest becomes the 'wife' of a deity. For example, among the Yoruba people of Nigeria those who hold a priestly relation to the *orisa* ('deities') are termed their 'wives' regardless of their sex or gender.[1052] Their gendered relation to the deity is reflected by changes in their appearance, such as hairstyle and dress.[1053]

The worship of the Yoruban deity Sango affords an excellent example of such gender-crossing. Yoruban mythology roots Sango in human history as a human ruler who came to be revered as divine after his death. Sango is regarded as masculine, yet he also serves the role of 'wife' to Ara, another deity. Sango interacts with some of his devotees through spirit possession, entering the possessed through the head. Anthropologist Lorand Matory notes that while most Yoruban Sango priests are female, some are males, and each is a 'bride (*iyawo*) of the god.' The male Sango priests present themselves as female in dress (e.g., feminine hairstyle and outer garments), and conduct. Interestingly, Matory observes that the hierarchical nature of the relationships in which the priest is enrolled make it possible for a male priest (*elegun*) to simultaneously embody both inferior and superior social positions, as well as masculine and feminine social roles. When possessed by Sango, the priest is 'mounted' by the god (thus occupying an inferior feminine position), but while so possessed can 'mount' a woman in sexual intercourse (thus occupying a superior masculine position). No wonder, then, that Matory can call such sacred crossdressing the vehicle for "transformations of gender."[1054]

Other Examples

Examples of gender crossings involving priestly people—both males and females—abound. Other instances include:

- ❑ Among the *D'abella* (ritual experts) of the nomadic Gabra people of East Africa, male masculinity is exchanged for an honored femininity.[1055]
- ❑ The Ibo of Nigeria honor male priests of the goddess Idemili who wear clothing like the tribal women and are perceived as 'female men.'[1056]

☐ The worship in West Africa of Mammi Watain, a female water spirit, is principally a female cult administered by priestesses. Yet there are male devotees and even male priests, who feminize their presentation, sometimes by crossdressing.[1057]

☐ Among the Lugbara people of Uganda there are transgendered priests, both females presenting as male (*agule*) and males presenting as female (*ogule*).[1058]

☐ The Xhosa people of South Africa have the female *isanus* (diviner), a shamanistic priest able to 'smell out' sorceresses or others who work evil.[1059]

☐ Along the coast of West Africa in traditional societies gender roles blur in the figures of the *kosio*, 'women' who may in actuality be either male or female. The temple priests or priestesses, regardless of their sex, are 'snake-wives' (*dangbe-si*) of the serpent (*dange*) deity they serve.[1060]

This list hardly exhausts the subject.

Spirit Cults

Spirit possession cults have been a persistent aspect of African culture. They continue to exercise an often problematic influence today.[1061] Spirit possession is not a uniform phenomenon: the willingness of the possessed host may vary significantly in varying contexts, and the possessing spirit may be that of an ancestor, deity, or lesser spirit.

Tromba Spirit Cult of Madagascar

Among the best studied of the spirit cults is Madagascar's *Tromba* spirit cult. The Sakalava (people of the long valleys) bridge between past and present through spirit possession.[1062] The term *tromba* is used variously to signify the person possessed, the spiritual trance, or the possessing spirit. Socio-cultural and medical anthropologist Lesley Sharp remarks, "Tromba possession is the quintessence of Sakalava religious experience."[1063] She also notes it is key to their ethnic identity and provides historical continuity, a sense of place, and social cohesion.[1064]

Sharp writes that, ""For the Sakalava, the spirit world is inhabited by royal and common ancestors, lost souls, nature spirits, and malicious, evil spirits. Tromba, as the spirits of dead Sakalava royalty, are the most significant and influential in terms of daily interactions that occur between the living and the dead."[1065] *Tromba* spirits, though representing different lineages, fall into one or another of three distinct generations. The oldest group of spirits are the 'Grandparents' (*dadilahy*), from whom also come the most powerful spirits, associated with royal tombs. The greatest *tromba* spirits (*dadibe* or *tromba maventibe*) generally only possess the oldest mediums, typically women no younger than their late 40s. Next are the 'Children' (*zanaka*), generally appearing in women in their late 20s or 30s, followed by the youngest group of spirits, the 'Grandchildren' (*zafy*), who typically possess young women in late adolescence or early adulthood.[1066]

Most mediums for the *tromba* spirits are women (although some male mediums are also known). The *tromba* spirit is male and possession of a female medium alters her life in terms both of self-identity and social status. Raised by the spirit possession to the rank of royalty, she also gains access to knowledge. She may become a renowned healer and a central figure at religious ceremonies. Her relationship to the possessing spirit is often depicted as a marriage. Yet this is not an equal partnership; during possession the medium acts like the spirit personage. Thus, for example, those possessed by Grandchildren *tromba* may enact such masculine behaviors as smoking, drinking beer, and dancing with women.[1067]

Spirit Possession among the Swahili

A spirit possession cult with some similarities to the *Tromba* cult is found among the Swahili people of East Africa. Although spirit possession is recognized widely in Swahili society, only a small percentage of the people are active in a cult. Initiates may be either male or female, though the latter predominate. When a person has yielded to possession by a benign spirit a lifelong relationship with the possessing spirit is formed. A healer who has successfully demonstrated facility in diagnosing and treating spirit illnesses heads a local cult group. The leader may be either a man or a woman. In urban Zanzibar, along the Swahili coast of East Africa, the *Kibuki* spirits resemble the *Tromba* Grandchildren in many of their behaviors. Unlike spirit possession cults elsewhere among the Swahili, such as the *Habeshia* cult where spirit pairs are characterized by rank (e.g., a royal personage and a servant), in the *Kibuki* cult the pairs are marked by gender. Each cult initiate has one female and one male spirit.[1068]

The *'yan Daudu* of the *Bori* Cult of the Hausa

The Hausa people of Niger and Nigeria are familiar with a spirit possession cult known as the *bori* cult. Associated with the *'yan bori* (cult devotees) are *'yan Daudu* ('son of Daudu,' an honorific), crossdressing males. These individuals blur, bend, blend, and break their society's gender rules. Anatomical males, they may look like men (e.g., in hair style and dress), yet speak in falsetto, refer to themselves by female names, and perform work typically done by women. To further complicate matters in foreign eyes, *'yan Daudu* also marry women and become fathers, even while retaining their *'yan Daudu* roles. Some of them are *bori* performers and healers, but many are not. For these others, their activities occur around the performance of *bori* possession and their roles include both tasks typically assigned to females (e.g., preparing and selling food), as well as ones facilitative of the prostitution practiced by female members (*kuruwai*) of the cult (e.g., procuring customers). The *'yan Daudu* also use their freedom to live in the women's quarters to facilitate their own sexual contacts with men.[1069]

What kinds of transient ritual transgender behaviors occur?

Often transgender behaviors like crossdressing occur only for a specific ritual reason in a definite context and for a limited time. The transient transgender behaviors considered here all have in common a spiritual context, although the actual reasons can be quite varied. They include:

- ❏ *agricultural cycle ceremonies*—these reflect human dependence on the forces that govern sustenance;
- ❏ *disguises to escape harm*—these display human ingenuity to evade harmful spirits;
- ❏ *fertility rites*—these concern the basic need of reproduction, here with reference to human beings, but also connected to the earth within agricultural cycle ceremonies;
- ❏ *oracles*—these represent communication with nonhuman spirits in which the spirit speaks through the person who is displaying crossgender behavior;
- ❏ *petitions for divine relief*—these seek help from the nonhuman powers, often in a context where natural rhythms like those of the agricultural cycle have been disrupted; and,
- ❏ *rites of passage*—these mark transitions along boundaries, such as the passage from childhood to adulthood.

As these brief notations make plain, the categories are not completely independent. Significant overlap and interrelationships exist.

Agricultural Cycle Ceremonies

Agrarian people rely upon dependable cycles to plant, tend, and harvest their crops. Although no one can control the weather, spiritual means are sought to influence the forces that do control the weather. Examples of ceremonies intended to exert such influence abound, and some utilize transgender behavior.

The Nomkhubulwana Festival of the Zulu

For example, the Zulu of South Africa once held an annual ritual honoring Nomkhubulwana (or Inkosazana-ye-Zulu, 'the Princess of Heaven'),[1070] who is more than merely a fertility goddess. As goddess of the rain she is instrumental in securing life for the people; as the 'Princess Up Above' she oversees the earth as a divine guardian. She has a special relationship with females, particularly young virgins, who by virtue of their purity are efficacious in their prayers to her. During the time of the Nomkhubulwana Festival there was cross-gender behavior by both the men and the women. The men enact feminine behavior by retreating to the safety of their huts, like women might do when enemy warriors attack. In part this is a response to the boisterous, lewd behavior of the women. The women also don the accoutrements of male warriors (shield and spear), and perform the masculine task of herding cattle. Renowned anthropologist Max Gluckman believed that the Zulu women who were part of the Heavenly Princess cult succeeded during this time in gaining power normally held by men; they temporarily reversed gender status.[1071]

Fertility Festival at Ibadan

Religion scholar Geoffrey Parrinder describes a similar phenomenon at the city of Ibadan in Nigeria. There each year a festival was held honoring and petitioning the fertility goddess. Parrinder likens the occasion to Saturnalia, where normal restraints on behavior were eased and role reversals common. Although in modern times the festival has been greatly tamed by the impress of other cultures' moral values, traces of former ribaldry remain. Among the behaviors associated with the festival—one common in many such rites around the world—is the appearance of the cult's chief priest in a manner that mixes gender presentation. Though garbed in masculine dress, he wears his hair braided like a woman's.[1072]

Disguises to Escape Harm

The world is not a safe place. In addition to the all-too-familiar mundane troubles humans face, there are the malevolent forces people experience that seem to come from outside the ordinary realm of human or natural affairs. Evil spirits are something people around the world have discussed and Africa is no exception. Avoiding, or at least placating, such spirits is an important spiritual task. In the effort to escape harm the instinct to flee through an act of disguise is natural and sensible. One way of disguise is to cross the boundary of gender and temporarily find shelter in another gender. For example, among the Bangala of Congo a man might seek refuge in the dress of a woman to avoid detection and harassment by an evil spirit.[1073]

Fertility Rites

Securing the blessing of posterity is of great importance and not devoid of religious considerations. In cultures around the world and throughout history, including our own time, fertility rituals have been profoundly sacred occasions. While there is a great connection between human fertility and that of the earth, with fertility rites associated with both, our concern here is with human fertility. Sex and gender are intrinsic and transgender behaviors are common.

Already we have discussed various instances of transgender realities connected to fertility festivals and rites. A single further example will suffice, especially as it shows a somewhat different gender crossing then we have thus far considered. Among the Masai people of West Africa, fertility ceremonies feature female power that some observers have suggested represent a 'ritual of rebellion' against the normative patriarchy of the society. During this time there is an apparent gender reversal in that masculine power shifts to the women. They are able, then, to act in abusive ways toward men similar to the use of power more ordinarily exercised against them.[1074]

Oracles

It is one thing to address deities and spirits; it is another to be addressed by them. This typically comes through spirit possession, and in some instances such possession takes the particular form of an oracle. Such a person serves the role of intermediary between a petitioner and an answering spirit. Among the Ankole people of Uganda, for example, the popular guardian deity Mukasa spoke through an oracle. The Shrine of Mukasa was on Bubembe Island in Lake Victoria. The Mandwa—the leading priest or priestess—served as Mukasa's oracle, when the deity's spirit came. Inasmuch as Mukasa was a masculine gendered deity, a priestess so possessed might garb herself in masculine dress when performing as his oracle.

Petitions for Divine Relief

In less technological societies where the people rely more consciously on the natural rhythms and cycles of nature, much of religious life is organized around these rhythms and cycles. We already examined briefly some agricultural ceremonies that recognize the importance of human beings interacting in persuasive ways with the powers that control the fertility of the earth, the timely falling of rain, the proper amount of sunshine, and the harvest. But humans learned long ago that even the most beneficent of deities can be capricious. Normal religious acts may fail. In such cases, when a disturbance in the rhythms and cycles of life occur, special pleadings are needed. These petitions for divine relief sometimes utilize transgender behavior.[1075]

Zulu Gender Crossings to Petition Deities

For example, the Zulu face the problems of drought using both male and female cross-gender behavior. In the face of drought the men put on female girdles, an emasculating behavior apparently aimed at securing pity from the deities of rain. The women who serve to divine when rainfall will occur utilize the adornments of male warriors (e.g., shield and spears), and behave in loud, stereotypically masculine ways in a limited application of cross-gender behavior.[1076]

Rain Dance of the Ihanzu

Anthropologist Todd Sanders witnessed a comparable rite performed by the women of the Ihanzu people of Tanzania. In the women's rain dance (*isimpulya*) during times of drought, certain women sing and dance naked through the village. These are women who have proved fertile themselves through having borne at least one child; extraordinarily fertile women enjoy a special place while menstruating women are carefully excluded. In their ceremony the participating women are loud, offering obscene words and gestures. The men, meanwhile, generally remove themselves from the way (though certain men, such as those who have fathered twins, may join in), because a male caught is subject to lewd behavior by the women, including being stripped naked. Sanders argues that in their behavior the Ihanzu women overcome (*trans*cend?) gender dichotomy by embodying femininity (e.g., their natural "wet, fertile femininity") and masculinity (aggression, abusive and obscene behavior) simultaneously. This accomplishment of an "ultimate gendered combination" makes possible realizing an ultimate communal good—the rain the people need.[1077]

Rites of Passage

Three passages particularly mark human existence, though many other important ones might be marked. The three are: birth, moving from childhood to adult status, and death. All three are reckoned important by religions and perhaps all religions have some way to recognize them. In our previous investigation of transgender realities in Africa (see the answer to Q. 54) we examined this matter, but its pertinence here justifies reproducing some of that material. With respect to gender crossing, the transition from child to adult stands out, affording our examples.

Girls Becoming Women

The Sotho female passage into adulthood is marked by the girls putting on masculine clothing. Something similar happens among the Nandi of Kenya. However, this so-called 'ritual transvestism' can be understood in more than one way. While some scholars have seen in gender inversion a symbolic representation of the dangerous passage from childhood to adulthood, others favor more mundane explanations. The anthropological and linguistic scholars Jane and Chet Creider, for example, interpret what happens among the Nandi as a female's way of achieving equality with males. The masculine clothing girls receive is a gift from male significant others: "The apparel is given by the boyfriend to the girls as part of themselves, as something precious to them, to show the girls that they care for them, and to encourage the girls to bring honour to them (the warriors) by their brave behaviour during initiation."[1078] We need not here take a stand one way or another as how best to understand this process for the points important to us remain in any instance: there is behavior that crosses gender lines and it involves a puberty rite of passage from childhood to adulthood.

Boys Becoming Men

Transition rites for males can also involve cross-gender behaviors, although again we face the issue of Western observers applying their own filter of gender consciousness on the behavior of African people. A prime example of the issue is seen in the interpretation of certain male puberty transition rites. The Maasai of Kenya, for instance, have a rite of passage that finds boys (*ol-ayioni*) changing their appearance through dress as part of their journey to adult warrior (*ol-murrani*) status. Anthropologist Alfred Hollis, in the early 20th century, characterizes the adornment, dress and overall appearance as like that of women.[1079] More recent depictions shy away from such a judgment.

This transition for Maasai youth is a comprehensive one, entailing even where the boy lives. The Maasai live together in two kinds of enclosures (*kraals*), one including huts of families with their younger children are encircled by a fence (*enkang*), the other where circumcised males live (*manyata*). A boy's passage at puberty is but one rite of transition observed among the Maasai. Boys are circumcised at puberty (ages 11-14), after which they move out of their father's house to join the other circumcised males of the *manyata*. Their transitional status is marked by wearing a female's earrings as well as a black dress, fastened over one shoulder and cinched at the waist by cowrie shells; they will be thus clothed for several months. Only after circumcision are they permitted to engage in sexual relations with females.[1080]

Comprehending that notions of sex and gender vary culturally helps explain why certain rituals transpire. For example, in our culture male circumcision is accepted and widely practiced while female circumcision is viewed as abhorrent. Many in our culture believe female circumcision is a barbaric practice that constitutes sexual abuse and is a violation of a female's basic human rights. In Africa, both male and female circumcision are practiced in many tribal societies and for reasons other than what most of us might expect or have awareness concerning. Consider the Dogon people of Mali, for instance. As religious scholar Geoffrey Parrinder explains:

> The Dogon are said to believe that man, like the primordial beings, has two souls of opposite sexes. One lives in his body and the other lives in the sky or water. When a boy is circumcised he is freed from the element of femininity, which he had had in childhood. Similarly when a girl is circumcised or excised she is freed from the male element and her clitoris no longer prevents intercourse. At circumcision prayers are offered for the stabilization of the soul, of the boy or girl, and spiritual force is thought to be released.[1081]

For the Dogon, the transition effected by circumcision involves both sex and gender. The rite allows passage—'release' if you prefer—from childhood so that in adulthood the society's normative patterns of relationship may be pursued.

Conclusion

Despite the number of examples offered in the preceding discussion, we have scarcely brushed the surface of transgender realities connected to indigenous African religions. A much larger book than this one is required to do them justice and to more fully place them in context. Brief as our investigation has been, though, it should suffice to indicate the breadth and vitality of transgender realities in service of spiritual matters. Such matters are diverse, ranging from the personal to the communal, from healing to sacrifice, from petition to prophecy, and much, much more. Transgender realities entail purposeful gender crossings attached to the most fundamental and important aspects of human existence. Their practice, however, for these same reasons places them in conflict with rival religious systems. We shall conclude our discussion by briefly looking at how one world religion imported to Africa by European colonists has responded to some of the transgender realities among the indigenous people.

What stance do African Christians take on transgender realities?

We observed early in our consideration of African religions how Christianity came to the continent with the values and biases of Europe. Missionaries sought not merely to convert people in terms of religious belief and practice, but also with respect to culture. Monogamy was imposed on polygamous people, shamans—'witch doctors'—were condemned, and indigenous priests were replaced by Christian priests and ministers. Although Christianity's pressure succeeded in effectively ending some indigenous religions, or specific practices, for the most part this pressure merely caused the subjugated people to hide their religion or adapt it to a degree Christians could grudgingly tolerate.

Not surprisingly, given their important role in indigenous spiritual traditions, transgender people suffered from the strictures placed by Christian conquerors. Most especially, those sexual practices that appeared to Europeans as homosexual—regardless of why or how or when they occurred, or the manner in which the native people interpreted them—brought judgment, censure, and punishment to the people engaging in them. Rejecting the notion that more than two genders exist, or that gender need not be founded upon body sex, any and all forms of transgender realities were branded deviant and associated with 'primitive' people and 'superstitions.' In essence, to endorse gender crossing of any kind meant to hold on to a world and way of life that Christianity meant fully to end.

We cannot here investigate the full scope of the pain and injury brought to Africa by Europeans, almost all of it piously inflicted in the name of Christ. But we can at least acknowledge it. We should recognize as well that the influence of the religion translated into oppressive practices by the state. In post-colonial times the lingering effects of Western cultural pressure persist, ironically continuing old prejudices in Africa even as Western states themselves show signs of surmounting them. Perhaps a quick example of a single influential Christian tradition can also aid us in being more specific as to how Christians have responded to African transgender realities.

The Anglican Church came to Africa with English colonizers. Today it has a strong presence on the continent. In 1998, at the Lambeth Conference of Bishops of the Anglican Communion, world leaders of the Anglican Church gathered. In frank discussions about what should be the Church's stance on homosexuality, there were deep divisions on the matter. African bishops were strongly opposed to tolerance. The Conference concluded that homosexuality is not compatible with the teachings of the Anglican Church—a conclusion strongly endorsed by the African bishops then and since. In fact, in the early years of the 21st century, African bishops sometimes have involved themselves in the affairs of other Anglican communions, including those in the United States and England, when the issue at hand involves homosexuality.[1082]

Yet the apparent unity of the African Anglican Church may not be as pronounced as casual observation might suggest. The most strident voices against homosexuality came from Uganda and Nigeria; the communions of Southern Africa were more moderate. Kevin Ward suggests such differences reflect less issues of biblical interpretation and more matters concerning the colonial history, and contemporary social and political situations of the regions. For example, while discussions of sexuality in South Africa are framed in a context of the broader struggle for justice and human rights, in East African nations a dominant influence has been the Balokole Revival movement with its calls to holiness, including sexual abstinence and restraint from casual sex and transient cohabitation. In terms of history, until recent years homosexuality was not a substantial issue even among Christian communions, and it is commonly regarded as having been a non-issue in traditional African societies. In fact, much of the rhetoric has blamed Islamic and/or Western forces for introducing homosexual practices to Africa, though Ward points out the patent falsity of such claims.[1083]

The wider Anglican communion remains divided on many issues with respect to homosexuality and gender variance. In 1999, in response to the previous year's Lambeth Conference divisions, the Cambridge Accord was formed. By 2000, it had signees among bishops from the United States, Canada, England, Australia, New Zealand, and other nations, including South Africa. The Accord proposes that all parties recognize three essential points and to join in unity upon them: first, that homosexual persons never be denied liberty, civil rights or property based on their sexual orientation; second, that all acts of violence, oppression and degradation against them be condemned as wrong and unjustifiable by Christian faith; and, third, that all persons merit respect and dignity as created equal in the eyes of God.[1084] Yet the divisions persist; the Archbishop of Canterbury at the time did not sign, while his successor did.

The persistence, rancor, and public nature of the conflict within the Anglican Church was such that in 2007, Nobel Peace prize winner Desmond Tutu, himself formerly the Archbishop of Cape Town in South Africa, pointedly told the Anglican Church in Africa to stop its "extraordinary obsession" with homosexuality. Tutu reflected to ABC News his distress that the Church was spending so much energy on this matter at the expense of attending to such other issues as the scourge of HIV/AIDS on the continent or the continuing human rights violations in Darfur.[1085] His words fell mainly on deaf ears.

At the time of this writing tensions remain high between the most visible and outspoken African Anglican leaders and many others in the Anglican worldwide communion. The focus continues to be on homosexuality, though transsexualism has also garned attention. At the 14th Lambeth Conference (2008) in England, notable for efforts to appease the most conservative wing of the Church through proposed concessions with respect to gender and sexual minorities, some African transgender speakers were allowed at an officially sanctioned conference panel entitled 'African Voices.' A homosexual man and a transgender woman from Africa both spoke. They refuted the claims of some Anglican leaders in Africa that transgender people do not even exist on the continent. They also shared the ways in which such people suffer oppression.[1086]

Their voices were not alone, but the bishops who attended were few. At the conclusion of the Conference two groups—Changing Attitude Nigeria and Integrity Uganda—joined to issue a statement of appeal to the bishops and archbishops. Speaking on behalf of Africa's gay, lesbian, bisexual and transgender people, they asked these church leaders to listen to their stories and to let them be who they are. They also asked on behalf of people like themselves, "To bring them in and welcome them from isolation, from the margins and from loneliness. To allow them to participate and serve the Lord within their churches as much as they are able." They concluded with the reminder that those like themselves already are in their families, communities, and churches.[1087]

It remains to be seen if anyone is really listening.

Q. 84 Are transgender realities found in Native American religion?

The Short Answer. We saw in a previous volume (see the answer to Q. 59) that transgender realities are not uncommon among the indigenous people of the Americas. Ever since the first White men began encountering Native Americans there has been a fascination with them. Failing to acknowledge the possibility of more than two genders, the European visitors, and also the settlers from Europe who stayed, inevitably construed what they saw in terms of their own understanding of gender. No Indians more intrigued the Whites than the so-called *berdaches*, gender violaters in the White culture's eyes. This originally derogatory term both has been sanitized by scholarly usage and challenged by a more recent label—'two-spirit'—to name individuals who exhibit transgender realities. Either the term *berdache* or two-spirit has been applied to Indian cross-dressers (for whatever reason they crossdressed), and those with a variant sexual or gender identity. Although only some have occupied formal religious positions, there is no doubt that a close connection between being two-spirit in nature and occupying a special spiritual place within the community has been observed often enough. Part of what makes this possible is a flexibility in Indian conceptions of gender. Many tribal societies embrace multiple gender systems. In such the two-spirit people have their own gender label, gender identity, and gender role. Another aspect facilitating their recognition comes from the ways in which both Nature and divine figures are understood. As in other religions, Native Americans have looked for guidance and models from divine figures. The gender flexibility and gender crossings of such beings help make human parallels more comprehensible. Some of the sanction for two-spirit people comes from sacred stories, especially creation accounts that not only establish the presence of two-spirit people from the beginning, but also show their value to the people. The identification of two-spirit persons occasionally happens before birth, with some selected by parents to this identity. More often the identification occurs in childhood, though sometimes it is not fully recognized until adulthood. Because of their nature, seen as between the two dominant genders, two-spirit people are often viewed as uniquely positioned to serve as mediators. They may do this between men and women, but also between the community and divine figures. The most famous spiritual role they may occupy is that of shaman, a figure often popularly known as the 'medicine man' (or woman).

The Longer Answer. Native American 'religion' is not as unified a body of thought and practice as that of the major world religions, which are themselves more diversified than often credited. Although many attempts have been made to identify broad themes and common practices, the danger is that any such effort will misleadingly suggest a unity across tribal societies that never has existed. Any given American Indian tribe is likely to share certain ideas and practices with some other tribes. But that is quite different from the notion that *all* tribes believe or practice certain things. Even where some commonality among tribes exists, the valuation or weight given those things many vary. This makes it ill-advised to offer any generalization meant to apply to all tribal societies.

At the same time, there are so many tribal societies it is hardly practical to attempt covering every one of them. A common approach has been to study and report on larger and better known, or more closely studied tribes. We will use examples drawn from the literature to do exactly that. Yet it isn't entirely impossible to paint slightly larger brush strokes. For example, in broad terms it is entirely accurate to say that some tribal societies have been more welcoming of gender variant people than have others. In a previous volume (see the answer to Q. 59), dozens of tribes within which gender variant people have been identified are listed and examples are given of the language labels used for such people, as well as the relative acceptance of them. As much as we can, we shall try to use such relative but broad strokes to capture as much of a larger picture as possible with respect to transgender Indians and their indigenous religions.

How many genders do Native Americans recognize?

Our effort to get at as broad a picture as we are able must begin with the question of how many genders Native American societies recognize. Religion and Women's Studies scholar Elizabeth Currans, in her brief overview of important works on Native American spirituality, notes that many spiritual systems within tribes accept multiple genders, often also associated with variant sexuality.[1088] Exactly how many tribes recognize more than two genders is unknown.

Anthropologist Sabine Lang offers a broad characterization of these multiple gender systems. In her terms, the genders embraced by Native Americans include 'men,' 'women,' 'men-women,' and 'women-men.' She argues that the use of different language labels for these latter two groups shows their status as recognized, separate and distinct genders.[1089] While that fact in itself constitutes dubious support for her contention (consider the many terms used for transgender people in the United States without ever according them status as a gender), there are plenty of other factors that suggest people who vary from the gender conformity of male men and female women do, in fact, enjoy legitimacy as a recognized gender in many tribes. For example, Lang points out that gender assignment in many tribal cultures depends both on occupational preference (regardless of sex) and an expression of specific personality traits and mannerisms associated with each gender.[1090] We may add that members of any gender typically are expected to dress in a manner that distinguishes their gender affiliation, and they generally are permitted intimate relations with members of other genders, even if of the same sex, without these relationships being seen as homosexual.[1091]

Examples

There are too many examples of recognized gender variant people among American Indian tribes to account for them all here. In some instances, the gender variant people may be accorded 'other gender' status alongside the dominant conforming genders of masculine men and feminine women. In fact, some anthropologists suggest that 'third gender' status is the norm among tribal societies. That may be a case better argued for traditional cultures than for contemporary Indian societies long dominated by Euro-American culture. At any rate, a few examples must suffice. More detail is available in the answer to Q. 59; here we shall only briefly describe a few of the better known gender systems.

Mohave *Alyha* & *Hwame*

Anthropologist George Devereux, writing in the first third of the 20th century, distinguished four genders recognized among the Mohave (Mojave) people of the American southwest. This gender system continues to be recognized and has been remarked upon often. In addition to 'men' and 'women,' the genders include the *Alyha* and *Hwame*—both comprised of two-spirit people. The former are biological males; the latter are biological females.[1092] Mohave creation mythology recognizes that two-spirit beings have existed since the world began at the sacred mountain of Avikwame (aka Newberry Mountain). It was there that the deity Mastamho presided over the delivery of a male infant that the god prophesied would be a leader and to whom he gave the feminine name, Hatsinye-hai-kwats'ise (Little-Girl-Doctor), and whom he later clothed in a bark skirt. Mastamho also instructed this child how to lead the Mohave women in dance, which he did while also engaging in shamanistic acts.[1093] Not surprisingly, given this model, some of the *Alyha* (and some *Hwame* as well) have occupied the role of shaman.[1094]

Navajo *Nádleeh*

The Navajo (or Diné) are the largest tribe of North American Indians, found principally in Utah, Arizona and New Mexico of the southwest United States. Anthropologist Carolyn Epple notes that many Navajo see gender as situational in character.[1095] The relative fluidity of gender means traits associated with it are not static and independent but embedded in particular contexts that give rise to the meaning and assignment of 'man' and 'woman.' In traditional Navajo culture a people called *Nádleeh* (or *Nádleehí*, or *Nádleehe*; sing. *Nadle*; 'other,' 'changing one,' or 'transformed'—an alternate gender), are recognized alongside 'masculine men' and 'feminine women.' A *Nadle* might be biologically male, female, or intersexed. In fact, the *Nádleeh*, remarks anthropologist Lauren Wells Hasten, may be the closest physical manifestation of the Navajo conviction that the cyclical universal ideal is both male and female.[1096] The dual nature ('two-spirit') of the *Nádleeh* is represented in the unexpected disjunction of sex and gender; a male *Nadle* is like a woman in gender, and a female *Nadle* like a man. Accordingly, regardless of birth sex, the *Nadle* dresses like a member of the gender ordinarily associated with the opposite sex. The sanction of the *Nádleeh* by the Navajo was marked by their elevated political and social status.[1097] One noted *Nadle* was Hastiin Klah (1867-1937), both a religious leader and accomplished artist.[1098]

Teton Dakota *Winkte*

The Teton Dakota, westernmost of the tribes collectively known as 'Sioux,' are part of the Indian tribal culture most Americans think of first when they recall historic Indian life—nomadic hunters dwelling in tipis (teepees). Likewise, when many people think of transgender Indians they think first of the *Winkte* (short for *Winyanktehca*, 'to be a woman'), sometimes today translated as 'two-spirit' or 'two-souls person.'[1099] In the mid-1960s, anthropologist Royal Hassrick noted that some *Winkte* become tribal shamans, thus occupying a role of power and respect.[1100] Walter Williams, with respect to contemporary *Winkte*, finds cultural changes from even a few decades ago. Though traditionalists still see them as sacred (*wakan*) people with spiritual power, and many still engage in sacred rituals, the marks of modern American society can also be seen, including their more flexible gender presentations in dress.[1101] Today, as in the past, some *Winkte* function as *wakan* persons on behalf of their people.

Zuni *La'mana*

The Zuni, a Pueblo people of the Southwest, native to Colorado and New Mexico, also hold a multi-gender system. Anthropologist Will Roscoe observes that in the traditional worldview of the Zuni, social roles "were not biologically determined but acquired through life experience and shaped through a series of initiations."[1102] Alongside 'men' and 'women,' Zuni use the term *La'mana* ('man-woman') as a broad designation for two-spirit people who might be either male or female. They further distinguish among the *La'mana* as *ko'thlama* (male 'male-woman') and *katsotse* (female 'girl-male' or 'girl-boy'). In a 1916 report, anthropologist Elsie Parsons found various connections made among the Zuni between the *La'mana* and Zuni mythology. In these accounts the *La'mana* achieve legitimacy. Thus sanctioned, such individuals participate in events like taking the *ko'thlama* part in the *kia'nakwe* ceremonial dramatic dance.[1103] Some *La'mana* individuals have gained much respect for their spiritual contributions. For example, We'wha (pronounced 'WAY-wah', lived c. 1849-1896) was a well-known *ko'thlama*, acknowledged among the Zuni as a religious expert, in part because of a close affiliation with artistic endeavors associated with Zuni spirituality.[1104]

Gender Judgments

Regardless of how many genders might be recognized, their recognition remains a matter separate from their valuation. Tribal responses, as assessed by outside researchers, range from disapproval, even hostility (e.g., Choctaw, Eyak, Tolowa), through indifference (e.g., Achomawi, Southern Paiute, Ute, Wintu) to positive regard and support (e.g., Arapaho, Cheyenne, Cree, Eskimos, Hopi, Navajo). In some tribes, the response is varied; the two-spirit may be seen by some with indifference and by others with disapproval (e.g., Atsugewi), or the tribe may provide evidence of the entire range of responses (e.g., Crow, Dakota, Flathead, Lakota, Omaha).[1105]

Changing Gender Conceptions

Another matter also must be noted. As Social Constructionists aptly point out, gender is made within the human collective. Human minds contrive it; human minds can change. The perception of gender and transgender realities is not stable, either among Native Americans or anyone else. The passage of time interacts with other forces to modify gender schemes. Traditional gender systems among the American Indians—those prevailing prior to subjugation by White society—gradually have become contemporary gender systems that reflect to greater or lesser degree important changes that have taken place over the last two centuries.

The pressure of powerful other cultures is a major force in changing ideas of gender. For American Indians the onslaught of White culture and the subordination of Indian life to its demands brought changes in many areas, including for some tribal societies their views of gender. For example, Navajo weaver and anthropologist Wesley Thomas contends that when discussing the Navajo conception of gender, recognition must be made of distinct periods. Prior to the 1890s, he says, traditional Navajo culture recognized multiple genders. Then, from the 1890s-1930s dramatic changes came about because of Western cultural pressure, especially that exerted by Christianity. Variant genders did not disappear, but in the face of this pressure went underground.[1106] That means we can describe a multiple gender system among the Navajo, but we must recognize the manner in which it operates and is perceived today is different in substantial ways from when it was first encountered by White explorers.

Midnight Sun, a two-spirit person of the Anishnawbe people, suggests another factor at work. Using the Mohave, Navajo, and Peigan tribes as examples, she argues that their multiple gender systems determined gender with respect to modes of production. When production changes in the society, she says, gender roles, including cross gender ones, change as well.[1107] Accordingly, both internal and external pressures can produce shifts in gender systems. In fact, they often work in concert and are causally related. The external pressures imposed by White society, including forced dislocation from traditional lands, necessitated changes in modes of production. As tribal societies adjusted to new demands gender roles also accommodated the changes, especially responding to external demands to conform to a two gender model as the new ways developed.

Berdache or Two-Spirit?

In our comments thus far, we have employed the term 'two-spirit' to refer to what White culture would identify as gender variant individuals. Historically, such Native Americans have been called *berdaches*. The label has long occasioned objections because the term is derogatory in nature. It is derived from an Arabic term meaning 'sex slave boy.' The label first appears as early as late 16th century America, apparently introduced by missionaries. The Spanish, encountering crossdressing Native American people, applied their own understanding of gender and assumed they were encountering certain gender variant and sexually variant identities and behaviors that needed to be corrected. They attempted to suppress what they viewed as aberrant behavior, along with the presumed attendant identities. In this effort they enlisted the power of the Christian missions to help reform the natives.[1108] The term *berdaches* soon became especially associated with Indian *males* in female dress and role, despite the fact that some women occupied a masculine gender role.

Despite the derivation of the term, *berdaches* has become entrenched in usage. Moreover, as Roscoe points out, no readily available term exists to replace it.[1109] We should also note that today it is defined in a scholarly manner using general and inoffensive terms. For example, anthropologists Henry Angelino and Charles Shedd, in the mid-20th century, offered as a definition that a *berdache* is "an individual of a definite physiological sex (male or female), who assumes the role and status of the opposite sex, and who is viewed by the community as being of one sex physiologically but as having assumed the role and status of the opposite sex."[1110] Similarly, anthropologists Charles Callendar and Lee Kochems 'roughly' define a *berdache* as "a person, usually male, who was anatomically normal but assumed the dress, occupations, and behavior of the other sex to effect a change in gender status."[1111] That new status is intermediate between masculinity and femininity—a 'third gender.' There is no opprobrium in such modern usage.

Nevertheless, many contemporary people—including many gender variant American Indians—find the continuing use of *berdache* offensive. As a result, an alternative has surfaced: 'two-spirit' (or 'two-spirited'; sometimes 'two-souled'). The term originated within the Native American community to refer to gender variant and homosexual people; it apparently was first adopted in 1990 at the 3rd Native American/First Nations gay and lesbian conference in Winnipeg, Canada.[1112] Anthropologist Arnold Pilling says that, "'Two-spirit' refers to persons who are a blend of the feminine and the masculine, the woman and the man."[1113] However, this characterization of its meaning may be misleading in terms of the way 'two-spirit' is actually used. Gender historian Elizabeth Reis argues that using a designation like 'two-spirit people' actually distorts the past because in contemporary usage it typically refers to homosexuals.[1114] Thus, 'two-spirit' may be too narrow in its actual application to make it particularly useful when referring to gender variant persons.

In an earlier volume, after weighing the issues, the use of *berdaches* was continued, though with some reluctance. Here we shall do the opposite, using 'two-spirit,' though again with some reticence. Its use will be anachronistic in many instances. Where *berdache* is employed it will be in accordance with the material being cited. As for this terminological problem, to date a satisfactory resolution still has not been reached.

Do divine gender crossings occur in American Indian religions?

American Indian deities, like those of other religions around the world, can have a relation to gender that is assigned as masculine or feminine, or be gender ambiguous, androgynous, or gender altering. A supreme example of an ambiguous deity is Wakan Tanka of the Sioux Nation, the 'Great Incomprehensibility.'[1115] Some deities, like Awonawilona of the Zuni, contain everything, and hence are both male and female; Awonawilona is referred to as 'He-She.'[1116] On the other hand, Asgaya Gigagei of the Cherokee, deity of thunder and lightning, is a figure capable of assuming either gender, sometimes being referred to as 'Red Man' and at other times as 'Red Woman.'[1117] Yet another kind of deity is the Navajo figure Ahsonnutli, sometimes called the 'Turquoise Hermaphrodite,'[1118] and variously referred to in the literature by either gender pronoun. The different connections of divine figures to gender lead to varying ways of enacting gender. A single example must suffice to show how deities themselves cross gender or sanction the same among human beings.

Zuni Creation Accounts

The Zuni creation mythology is rich in gender crossing accounts. This stems from their worldview that characterizes 'surpassing beings' as powerful transformers of their own selves. Prominent among Zuni divine figures are Awitelin Tsita (Mother-Earth) and Apoyan Ta'chu (Father-Sky). According to the Zuni creation story, as outlined by anthropologist Frank Cushing, these beings could transform themselves at will to become what they wished: "Now like all the surpassing beings the Earth-mother and the Sky-father were *'hlimna* (changeable), even as smoke in the wind; transmutable at thought, manifesting themselves in any form at will, like as dancers may by mask-making."[1119]

The Zuni creation account also relates the origin of the ancients of the Ka'ka (dance drama people), children of the incest between siblings Siweluhsiwa and Siwiluhsitsa. This couple's twelve children were born of two natures: "From the mingling of too much seed in one kind, comes the two-fold one kind *'hla-mon*, being man and woman combined. . . ." The eldest, for example, was "a woman in fullness of contour, but a man in stature and brawn." Though a cautionary tale, the account is careful to note that this child, born of love however crazed, did not partake of her parents' 'distortions.' The younger children were "silly," but also "wise as the gods and high priests." They became the "sages and interpreters, of the ancient of dance-dramas or the Ka'ka."[1120]

The Zuni two-spirit people named *La'mana* derive their name and legitimacy from the *kachina* spirit Ko'lhamana. In the Zuni creation account this spirit plays a pivotal role. According to the story, the Zuni *kachina* spirits of farming were in conflict with enemy hunter spirits. The war was at an impasse when the enemy spirits captured Ko'lhamana. The hunters' leader was a female spirit—Warrior Woman—who provided a dress for Ko'lhamana to wear. In this newly transformed state, Ko'lhamana functioned as a mediator between the warring sides. As a result, farming and hunting were reconciled among the Zuni people. In the commemoration of this event a quadrennial ceremony occurs, in which both masculine and feminine symbols are carried to signify the bridging between differences that brought unity to the people.[1121]

Do human gender crossings occur in American Indian religions?

When we turn our attention to human gender crossings, we again find ourselves preeminently concerned with *berdache* or two-spirit persons. Will Roscoe, among the best known investigators of two-spirit people, believes it possible to identify a 'core set' of traits for them. He offers four:

- ❑ *specialized work roles* (cross-gender and unique work activities);
- ❑ *gender difference* (distinctive, 'third gender' characteristics);
- ❑ *spiritual sanction* (accepted as divine in causation); and,
- ❑ *same-sex relations* (typically, sexual relations with people who are not two-spirit).[1122]

On this last point, it should be pointed out that although the sexed bodies of the partners may be the same, the gender identities and roles are not. Therefore, use of a term like 'homosexual,' in the way our culture understands it, would be misleading. Sexual orienatation—an abominable concept at best—is more accurately applied by using gender as a standard than by relying on body sex.[1123]

Of course, our chief interest lies with the first and third traits, especially as they may converge in sanctioned religious roles. In this regard, anthropologist Italo Signorini remarks that, "supernatural powers are attributed to *berdaches*, and they have specific ritual responsibilities (funerals, conferring of secret names, warfare, and others)."[1124] A logical way to get at this matter is to ask what legitimizes their identity and social role, how such people are identified, and how all these matters reflect the intersection of religious concerns with their gender crossings.

Legitimation of Two-Spirit People

Every culture justifies its gendering (sorting into different kinds) of people. Native Americans do this in a manner familiar to adherents of other religions—by appeal to one or another authority. This can be as specific as a sacred saying, story, or text, or as broad as a cultural logic or worldview. Lang believes that the roles and statuses of 'third gender' people (men-women and women-men) are "embedded within worldviews that emphasize and appreciate transformation and change. . . . Within such worldviews, an individual who changes her or his gender once or more often in the course of her or his life is not viewed as an abnormality but rather as part of the natural order of things."[1125] Just as Nature regularly embraces changes dramatically transformative in kind (e.g., the changing of seasons, or the wandering course of rivers), so too may people.

More narrowly, but not unrelatedly, anthropologist Walter Williams locates the legitimization of two-spirit folk in various sacred accounts among tribal groups. Creation stories such as those found among the Arapaho, Mohave, Navajo, Pima, and Zuni all provide an accounting for two-spirit people.[1126] In the Navajo mythology, for example, Turquoise Boy and White Shell Girl are *Nádleeh* who are depicted as the creators of such important articles of life as axes, baskets, grinding stones, and pottery. Williams points out that this account conveys an important message to the Navajo: "The message of this story is that humans are dependent for many good things on the inventiveness of *nadle.* Such individuals were present from the earliest eras of human existence, and their presence was never questioned. They were part of the natural order of the universe, with a special contribution to make."[1127] Similarly, among the Zuni, 'changeable' ones like the *La'mana* have belonged since the beginning.

Once legitimized, such persons' gender identities—combining as they do both masculine and feminine characteristics—uniquely position them in a manner highly relevant for religious purposes. Accordingly, they can be regarded as uniquely spiritual and employed in socially important roles, especially as mediators. Their mediation has both horizontal (between men and women) and vertical (between the community and the divine) dimensions.

Identification of Two-Spirit People

Two-spirit people are identified in different ways. Broadly, the distinction is a simple one: some are identified by others; some identify themselves. However, we must consider another term in this process—'selection.' The process of *identification* of a two-spirit person can either precede or follow *selection* to this gender status. In some cases, even before birth an individual may be selected to become two-spirit and then, after birth, is so identified and treated. In other cases, something about the individual leads to an identification as two-spirit, either

401

early or late, and either by self or by others. In any event, identification and 'selection' in these cases is essentially the same. One important quality signified by the idea of 'selection' is the sense that the identification is conscious and purposeful—the latter being something we shall attend to later.

Selection/Identification By Others

Historian Richard Trexler finds that in some Indian societies the two-spirit person is consciously selected in early childhood or even before birth. He cites the historical instance of the Laches people of Colombia who permitted a family, after five boys, to "convert" one of them into a daughter (a situation echoed in the modern Artic Indian practice of permitting a girl child to be changed into a son). Other tribes have followed a similar practice of pre-selecting an unborn child to be two-spirit, although not always for the same reasons.[1128] For instance, from early in the 19th century, visitors among the Konyagas of Alaska found Kodiak Island biological males called *Achnutschik* (or *Achnuchik*), a two-spirit people. Observers noted such persons sometimes were selected before birth, and sometimes identified in early childhood. In the latter case, identification stemmed from observation of behavior, but in the former instance selection might be because parents who hoped for a daughter decided that a male child born to them would be dedicated to become *Achnutschik*.[1129]

Another example of the practice of identifying a child after birth is found among the *Alyha* of the Mohave people. Devereux observed that the *Alyha* are identified early, before puberty. The family that sees in a male child the characteristics of an *Alyha* might then plan a formal initiation ceremony, which serves both to test the youth's true nature and to introduce the child to the community in this new status. This includes a change of name as a feminine one is chosen, and a change of dress as the new *Alyha* dons a skirt. As adults, the *Alyha* occupy a sexual role like that of women.[1130]

Another instance of identification of a two-spirit person that can occur at or after birth is found among the Navajo. Gender variant individuals known as *Nádleeh* are sometimes identified as such at birth because of an intersex condition. But while an ambiguous genital presentation provides incentive to regard a child as one of the *Nádleeh*, an intersex condition is not the only causal pathway. Parents might perceive in a child a marked preference for the activities typically associated with the gender paired with the opposite sex. They might then permit the child to grow into that gendered role.[1131]

Finally, identification of a two-spirit nature may not be fully realized until after childhood. We can see this, for example, also among the Mohave in the *Hwame*, biological females who gender cross. Roscoe remarks that these two-spirit people may not emerge as such until well into adulthood. Some are not identified as *Hwame* until after they have birthed children.[1132] This does not mean no previous signs of gender variance could be detected. Whether *Alyha* or *Hwame*, such persons might give hints as to their nature as early as while still in the womb, through dreams their mothers have. As children they differentiate themselves through activities that display preference for the gender role associated with the opposite sex.[1133]

Self-Selection/Identification

Some two-spirit people are so by self-selection and identification. Anthropologist Elsie Parsons, in a 1916 report, noted that while there is never any external compulsion on a child to become one, in some households short on women a boy might be more readily permitted to become a *La'mana*. Formal recognition of the status came at about age 12. Once so recognized, the male assumed full-time the dress, manner, and roles of a woman. They could even marry men.[1134]

Other evidence suggests that in some locations or instances the individual self-identifies as gender variant even in the face of opposition. We have, for an early example, the account of German naturalist Alexander Philipp Maximilian, who between 1832-1834 visited the Great Plains and recorded his observations in two volumes.[1135] In a well-known passage, Maximilian writes of such persons: "These generally assert that a dream or some high impulse has commanded them to adopt this state as their 'medicine' or salvation, and nothing then can turn them away from their purpose."[1136] Maximilian may have misinterpreted some of the behavior he saw as oppositional, but there is no doubt that in some tribes self-identified two-spirit people do face efforts at dissuasion.

Certainly the process of self-identification occurs in today's American Indian life. For example, a contemporary *Winkte*, who holds a graduate degree in psychology, Marjorie Anne Napewastewiñ Schützer has related how she identified as a two-spirit person: "I was called through a vision, by 'Anog Ite', (Double Face Woman) from out of the womb, to be that which I am. She offered me a choice. Lakota deities never order. My gender transformation was called for by the Spirits. She blessed me with skills of a supernatural kind."[1137]

The Intersection of Religion & Gender

Native American religions are diverse in their spiritual figures, stories, and practices. But they may share some very broad commonalities. Perhaps the following characteristics are especially pertinent to our interests.

The Role of Mystery

One important quality in Native American religion is an acknowledgment of and reverence for mystery. Much around us is not easy to comprehend and such things both interest and concern us. Modern shaman Christina Pratt points to the Native American idea that the highest power can be called 'the Great Mystery.' Mysteries by their very nature seem sacred both because they stand apart from the mundane world and seem to us to mean something, even if we don't exactly know what. Pratt observes that such thinking easily extends to two-spirit people—not easily comprehended, they are mysterious and sacred. She writes, "By incorporating the Two Spirit into their societies, they can successfully use the different skills, insights, and spiritual powers of these alternate genders."[1138]

The Role of Spirit & Nature

If mystery helps set apart two-spirit people and lend to them a sacred nature or role, it does not thereby make them superior to others. Like all other things and people, two-spirit persons are spiritual and follow their given nature. Williams contends that the emphasis of American Indian religions is on the spiritual nature of all things. *Everything* is spiritual, and no spirit is superior to another by nature. Moreover, all these spiritual things have a right to exist and interrelate. As Williams puts it, "The function of religion is not to try to condemn or to change what exists, but to accept the realities of the world and to appreciate their contributions to life." As we have seen, within Nature there are transformative changes—and these are accepted as part of what is and the way things should be. Other things in Nature seem to stay much the same—and those things are accepted as well. Whether changing or stable, though, all things have a nature, all things are spiritual, and all things are connected. How they are connected and interrelate is, in part, determined by their nature.

The Role of Mediators

Because so many things present themselves as seeming opposites, or as things at different ends of a spectrum (e.g., sky and earth, or man and woman), *mediators* are essential to relate them to each other and thus keep order in the universe. Two-spirit people function as mediators—a purpose to which they are suited by their nature.[1139] Because they inhabit a space between masculine males and feminine females, two-spirit individuals are often looked to as mediators between men and women. But the idea of mediating often extends beyond being a go-between in only that one respect. When perceived as mixing masculine and feminine characteristics they may be thought uniquely able to 'see' better than either gender and so be called upon as 'seers' whose visions bridge this mundane reality with the spiritual realm. Accordingly, in some tribal societies they become shamans. As noted by many scholars, shamanistic roles are often associated with two-spirit people, and even where not specifically engaged in such a role they are often noted for their healing and spiritual prowess.

Two-Spirit Shamans

The term 'shaman' is one scholars use to cover a large range of similar-appearing social roles in indigenous cultures (see the answer to Q. 76). They are found in a number of American Indian societies.[1140] A person of any gender might become a shaman, but in some tribal societies it seems that two-spirit people in particular were either guided down such a path, or especially esteemed among the shamans of the group. Lang identifies the occupation of 'women-men' as shamans in at least 21 different Native American cultures. She elaborates:

> Women were the main practitioners in one-third of these cases, and the occupation was obviously chosen by the women-men as an aspect of their feminine gender role. Where men were the primary healers or medicine men, the women-men moved partly within the domain of the masculine gender role, both with respect to their status as medicine "men" and also with regard to acquisition of the necessary supernatural powers. Women's clothes and components of the feminine gender role appeared there as the expression of the personal "medicine" of a woman-man. In such cases, women-men were not healers in the framework of the feminine gender role, but—despite their ambivalent gender status—they were males with a special kind of supernatural power.[1141]

In some tribes either a male or female two-spirit person might be a shaman. For example, among the Mohave people either an *Alyha* or *Hwame* might fill the role. "The fact that cross gender individuals were often shamans or married to shamans or chiefs," writes Midnight Sun, "suggests not only cultural acceptance, but an association with status and prestige, as well."[1142] As indicated earlier, various factors probably contribute to their status, including recognition of their mysterious nature and how that nature places them where they might serve as mediators.

Consonant with the meaning of 'holy,' 'sacred,' and 'sanctified' in other religions, the Indian shaman is set apart from others. One aspect of this is the ritual or process by which the individual becomes sanctioned by the group as a shaman. This typically follows from signs indicating the potential to be a shaman, followed by a period of training, trial, and other preparation. This period terminates and culminates in a formal marker event whereby the new shaman is accepted by the group.

There is another way in which the shaman may be set apart from others. Lakota sacred person Lame Deer says that the *wicasa wakan* wants to be by himself, away from the crowd and everyday matters. There is a reason for this desire. Situating himself in the midst of the natural world, says Lame Deer, "He listens to the voices of the *wama kaskan*—all those who move upon the earth, the animals. He is as one with them. From all living beings something flows into him all the time, and something flows from him."[1143]

Shamanistic practice may vary in its particulars from place to place, but its essence can be characterized across different groups as involving *mediating contacts*. These may be horizontal in nature (i.e., between people, whether individuals or groups), or vertical (i.e., between our world and that of the spirits). Åke Hultcrantz, an expert on the subject, regards the central idea of shamanism as contact with the supernatural world. The shaman is a "professional and inspired intermediary" who employs ecstatic experience to bridge the gulf. Hultcrantz lists four elements to shamanism: the supernatural world and contacts with it, the shaman acting as mediator on behalf of a group, helping spirits who grant the shaman inspiration, and the extraordinary ecstastic experiences that bring all four elements together.[1144]

The nature of at least some of these shamanistic contacts is *healing*. In fact, this may be the aspect of the Indian shaman most of us think of first, especially when we use a label such as 'Medicine Man'—a designation less common today. The heart of Native American medicine lies in its close connection to—and dependence upon—the natural world. "To Native Americans," writes herbalist David Hoffmann, "health and healing are part of a way of relating to the entire world."[1145] In other words, healing is itself a process ideally suited to those who serve as mediators—in this case between sick people and their environment, or between the afflicted and whatever supernatural spirit may have made them ill. Two-spirit people, whether shamans or not, not infrequently are connected to healing in their tribal culture. This might be either by virtue of possessing healing benefit to the people or land simply by being as they are, or because they possess healing abilities.[1146]

Though shamans are culturally different from most of us, we should resist the tendency many White observers have displayed to account shamanism as reflecting mental disorder. Psychiatrist Bryce Boyer, in the middle of the 20th century, spent considerable time studying shamans among the Chiricahua and Mecalero Apache. Part of his field research included assessment of their personalities and mental health. Boyer concluded that the evidence did not suggest psychological disturbance as a characteristic of shamans.[1147] Difference does not equal disorder.

Conclusion

Two-spirit people, formerly called *berdaches*, long have fascinated non-Indian people. But they have also engrossed Indian peoples, being variously appraised among them. In some instances, the positive appraisals of an earlier period have given way to a negative one as the White man's cultural biases have been absorbed. In our consideration we have given more space to the positive appraisal, especially in connection with the intersection of gender crossings and religion. Indeed, given the state of our world today, we might well choose to echo the sentiment Julianne Cordero & Elizabeth Currans express: "Despite the homophobia that exists within both mainstream and Native communities, some Indians still view two-spirit people as signs of cultural continuity and symbols of hope for increased tolerance and spiritual and cultural renewal."[1148]

Q. 85 What role does crossdressing play in religion?

The Short Answer. As the answers to previous questions have explored, crossdressing and other transgender realities apparently occupy an important part in religions past and present, East and West. In our consideration of specific religions we have kept in mind important contexts like gender and the local character of religious experience and expression. Having looked at so many particularities we must now attempt a more general reappraisal. In asking what place crossdressing and transgender people have in religion we are seeking to paint as broadly as possible an overall picture. In one important respect this is a hopeless and foolish quest. It makes little sense to speak of 'religion' rather than 'religion*s*.' Yet in another respect the question has value if it helps us collect together our impressions and offer summary observations, however general they may be, with however many exceptions we could note. To do this task requires an appraisal of religion *per se*. This could take many forms, but our interest here is the role religion plays in culture. As a prominent force—perhaps the most prominent—religion exercises great influence on cultural conceptions, including those about gender. Simultaneously religion is also being subjected to their pressure. The principal power religion exercises lies with respect to cultural *values*. The things society esteems as meaningful, desirable, good and important are especially the object of religion's concern and typically viewed by a society's inhabitants as the proper provenance for religion. To the degree a religion succeeds in influencing a culture's values it then is motivated to serve as the conserver of those values. When a society drifts from those values, religion attempts to reform it. In some instances, though, religion finds itself called to fill a more radical role—the transformation of cultural values. Our own culture, like all cultures everywhere, is in process. The respect in which that process is most dynamic at present is with respect to gender, sex, and sexuality. New insights driven by science have called us all to a reappraisal of what we thought we knew about these matters. The lives of real people in our midst have lent an urgency, immediacy, and relevance to our wrestling with the issues. Inevitably values are involved and religion comes into play. At present, religion in our society finds itself in a tension between its desire to conserve and its desire to transform. At the very heart of this tension stand transgender realities and people.

The Longer Answer. 'Religion' is a very broad term meaning various things to different people. Thus far, we have discussed particular religions—distinct entities with definite personalities for all their diversity. But 'religion' also can be talked about in more general terms, as a particular orientation to life and reality. In this sense, religion long has been a fundamental aspect of human existence. The orientation religion presents is organized as a set of concerns. These concerns cover the most fundamental aspects of existence, including birth, life, development and purpose, work and love, dying and death. Such concerns generate questions, and religion offers answers. The entire process reflects a set of values—expressions about what are judged to be the most important things, those matters especially worthy of our attention, and those things we should esteem as good and worthwhile.

The values around which religion organizes itself are religion's principal contribution to culture. Religion has exercised a profound influence on cultures, including our own. For the most part, a culture's values are those of its most dominant religion (or religions). Societies within a culture typically embrace these values, at least as *espoused* values. The degree to which people within the society actually *practice* these values is commonly regarded as a measure of their religiosity. Having contributed values, religion then serves a set of ongoing cultural functions with respect to them. These include the inculcation of the values by various means (preaching, teaching, exhortation, religious parenting, etc.), and a kind of jurisdiction over them. Such jurisdiction means religion commonly assumes the right to pronounce judgment as to whether a society is faithfully upholding its values. If not, religion then acts, either seeking to reform the society or change it more fundamentally.

All of this can be simply represented as religion playing two very important—and seemingly contradictory—roles:

- ❑ Religion *conserves* cultural values.
- ❑ Religion *transforms* cultural values.

The former is the more accustomed, or dominant role; the latter the more dramatic one. We shall begin with what we are most acquainted.

What is the conserving role religion plays in culture—and how does crossdressing fit?

While religion has been responsible for fostering significant social upheavals and revolutionary movements, its more common role has been to conserve values a society holds near and dear to its identity. In this conserving function, religion helps construct the ethical systems and moral decision-making models that a society's citizens rely on. Drawing on a range of human resources, religion utilizes emotions, reason, and behavior to guide private and social conduct.

The conserving function of religion means that much of the time, for most of the people, religion is a bastion for preserving and supporting cultural norms.

Minority expressions in any area—the political as well as the sexual—are commonly resisted in religious terms. Whether such resistance is consistent with the best ideals (or history) of the religions involved is a source of ongoing controversy for any society, or religion's members. Thus, a significant battle is waged in the realm of religion, with advocates for minority positions appealing to the majority in the name and spirit of the religion both groups hold in common.

This is why crossdressers in our culture frequently appeal to Christian scripture and history to answer others who use those same resources to oppose them. Both sides are able to have some level of dialog through the medium religion provides. But for transgender people and their supporters the struggle is uphill. Change, when it comes, is typically slow and incremental. The conserving function of religion generally prevails over its potential ability to transform a society. In fact, this conserving function tends to produce resistance that is more than intellectual in character. The majority often finds little motivation to consider the appeal of a minority. Moreover, when made to confront a reality that reality is more likely to be seen negatively precisely because it threatens the status quo that enfranchises the majority with power and privilege. Judging a case on the merits is very difficult for most of us, most of the time.

Crossdressing, at least by males, especially challenges the status quo in our culture. Because of the connections most of us make between dress, sexuality, and gender, crossdressing often evokes negative thoughts, feelings, and behaviors by noncrossdressers. Regardless of the specific merits or demerits of crossdressing, such as whether it actually works harm, it frequently is felt as constituting a threat to the status quo—a 'harm' to social order. Crossdressing calls conventional notions into question. It thus threatens to change the way things are seen and treated, with all that may imply for the way we relate to one another. As the authors of *Sex and Morality in the U. S.* put it, "In our religiously influenced culture, then, it is no surprise that fear, disgust, abhorrence (and their correlates of fascination, temptation, and attraction) underlie many widely held sexual norms."[1149]

Presently, the dominant Christian religion within our society is struggling with its conserving role. While many Christians and Christian groups desire to preserve a status quo that includes a gender hierarchy, an inflexible dualistic sex/gender system, and heteronormativity, others are deciding such things are not truly representative of Christian values. Those who seek to conserve the social status quo with respect to gender, sex, and sexuality believe the values of this status quo fit their religion well. They seek to reform society by bringing it back to that status quo whenever and however they perceive it to be drifting away, such as in growing acceptance of same-sex marriage or tolerance of gender variant behavior. Those who find these values do not well fit Christianity are troubled by efforts to conserve the status quo. They are more likely to find in the current social upheaval an opportunity to transform society by redirecting cultural values toward Christian ideals long suppressed or unrealized.

What is the transforming role religion plays in culture— and how does crossdressing fit?

The transformation of culture by religion, whether pursued as an outside conquering force at the point of a sword, or as an inside agent of change, serves one end: to fundamentally alter the value orientation of societies. As the word itself suggests, the *form* of society is *changed*. Religion fundamentally does this through a value process, even though often enough through history it has also meant social, political, or military action in the name of the religion. This value process starts within religion as a reexamination of the fundamental questions and concerns. This leads to reappraisal. Values are reinterpreted, clarified, or reordered. Typically, this is cast as a process of recovery of the 'original' or 'true' values of the religion.

This process can produce dramatic upheaval. However, most often it is like the leaven in bread. It works slowly, gradually, incrementally, and not always evenly. Transforming values must overcome the instinct to conserve them. Therefore, tension, debate, controversy, and conflict all characterize the process. Because most of us experience this as emotionally unpleasant, we tend to shy from it. In fact, we are likely to construe the unpleasantness as a sign that the endeavor is wrongheaded. In short, even if a religion begins down the path of transformation it faces obstacles such that it has incentive to stop.

Given this state of affairs we might wonder how a religion ever musters the force to transform culture. The answer lies in the strength of the impetus to change. In our society, which treasures values such as individual liberty, justice and fairness, the rule of law, the pursuit of happiness, and truth, when all of these coincide on a particular point the resulting value pressure is enormous. That seems to be happening now with respect to gender, sex, and sexuality issues. As we learn more about the nature of transgender realities, and what these mean for our ideas of gender, sex, and sexuality, we find the emerging truths to support transgender people's claims in regard to individual liberty, justice and fairness, the rule of law, and the pursuit of happiness.

Put most simply, science seems to support the claim that gender diversity, sex diversity, and sexual diversity are all natural. Certainly their reality in our midst cannot be denied. Evidence suggests these things exist not by conscious effort, or a will to be perverse, but as a consequence of Nature, whether supported or resisted by the environment. Since our notions of moral accountability typically rest on the idea that an act can be morally judged only if freely chosen, the notion that transgender realities exist apart from acts of will casts them in a new light. If transgender people are born the way they are, then should we judge them wrong for desiring—like the rest of us—to be themselves, pursue happiness, enjoy liberty, and possess justice and fairness under the law?

Additionally, much evidence also supports that transgender realities have value for humanity. They contribute diversity and fit important social needs (e.g., for mediation between genders). Long before anyone thought to apply to them terms such as 'transgendered,' people whose sexual or gender expressions varied from the majority were notable contributors to the development of religion in their cultures.[1150] Many religions openly have sanctioned them. Even those that have not, like Christianity, possess seeds to do so. Given what we are learning about gender, sex, and sexuality, added to the compelling sense that what transgender people are asking is not unreasonable, perhaps it makes sense to reappraise the values that hold all of us back.

How do transgender people fit in religion?

A profound irony exists in the disjunction between contributions to religion made by transgender people and their acceptance today among most major religious bodies. The upheaval with respect to values and conceptions of gender, sex, and sexuality in our society today holds some promise of changing that fact. We have documented for different religions the response to transgender realities. In sum, we found that response to be mixed. Indigenous religions are more welcoming than major world religions. The most accepting major religions tend to share two characteristics: they are older and they are Eastern.

Our society embraces a Western culture whose history intertwines Christianity with Greek philosophy. The Greek logic on gender was buttressed by Christian theology. Especially with the medicalization of sex, this logic was codified in scientific language if not scientific evidence or reasoning. By the mid-20th century, the wedded bliss between Christianity and culture seemed secured by the language of science. Of course, that marriage could not account for all its children. Some—boys and men—were greatly privileged within the family. Others—girls and women—though just as numerous, were disadvantaged. Still others—transgender people—were unwelcome within the family. Those who fit our contemporary designation 'transgender' at that time had no self-affirming labels. Like unfairly castigated bastard children they sought legitimacy. In this they were inadvertently aided by the efforts of women to change the dynamics of the human family.

The latter half of the 20th century saw stress in the marriage of Christianity and culture. As the latter was challenged, the former could not help but become defensive. Nowhere were transgender people less likely to feel welcome than in churches frantically trying to conserve values under challenge. Today's transgender population are the heirs of this situation, as the research shows all too clearly. Thus, although the group of respondents to a survey administered at a 2004 conference in New York concerning transgendered (LGBT) Asian Pacific Americans is a limited sample, the experience of religion commonly reported there echoes that found in other reports: "On average, respondents said their church or religion views being lesbian, gay, bisexual, or transgender negatively. A third of respondents said their religion views LGBT people as 'wrong and sinful.'" More than half (53%) thought their religion viewed LGBT negatively;

only 19% considered their religion 'neutral' on the matter, and even fewer (16%) found their religion fully accepted LGBT people. Not surprisingly, then, most respondents also said that their church or religion was only somewhat important to them.[1151]

We might think the people of this particular research were more likely to feel this way because they also were members of a racial minority. Certainly that fact can complicate a transgender person's experience. But we cannot easily dismiss the testimony across numerous studies, others of which we considered in our earlier examination of Christianity. As people at the center of the social tumult, transgender people are apt to be the targets of hostility from frustrated proponents of a passing scene. At the same time, they are increasingly the focus of well-meaning supporters, even those who poorly understand the debate. In either instance, then, transgender people—whether they want it or not—are more in the light than previously.

Should religion in the United States exercise its role as a transforming agent of cultural values on gender, sex, and sexuality, transgender people may play a pivotal role. Indeed, if they do not, it is hard to imagine the transformation will be much beneficial to them. Queer theologians need not be the only ones trying to cultivate the seeds within Christianity capable of giving transgender people a welcome place within the Church. In fact, others—laity and ministers alike—are trying in their own ways to support change. Inevitably, such change will be one in values.

What values do we as a people want to endorse? Which ones make us stronger as a people? Which promote the development of a humanity that will prosper the world? For Christians, all the answers must be derived from the sources of the religion. Those roots, as we have seen, offer resources for a positive transformation. But in our increasingly diverse society, we ought not to lay the entire burden on this dominant religion. Other religions, and secularism too, all must contribute to the creative ferment.

That is exactly what is happening. Although perhaps incipient now, signs are that our social tumult is likely to persist for some time. Now is an exciting, interesting time in which to be a participant in the cultural conversation on gender, sex, and sexuality. Religion cannot help but be involved; religious people will determine the shape of that involvement.

May this volume contribute to their thinking, talking, and acting.

Notes

Question Set 8 Notes

[1] Clothing is examined both metaphorically and otherwise by various writers. As a single example, consider the elegantly written and insightful article by Stephanie Paulsell, "Body Lanuguage," *Christian Century*, *119* (no. 2), 18-24 (2002, Jan. 16). A brief excerpt appears in the section on Christianity.

[2] See, for example Genesis 3:21 (discussed in the Introduction), 28:20: Exodus 28:39-41; Deuteronomy 22:11; 2 Samuel 13:18; Matthew 3:4, 6:28-33, 25:36-44, James 2:15-16, etc. for various indications about dress. Metaphorical references also abound: Psalms 35:26, 104:1, 132:16; Isaiah 50:3; 59:17; Romans 13:14; I Corinthians 15:53-54, etc.

[3] Augustine (late 3rd-early 4th century), in his *City of God* (Bk. XIX, ch. 19; cf. Bk. I, ch. 10), reflects a relative indifference to dress. By contrast, Tertullian (early 3rd century) shows energetic concern in his work, *On the Apparel of Women*.

[4] See, for example, Margaret R. Miles, "Fashioning the Self," *Christian Century, 112* (no. 8), 273-275 (1995, Mar. 8).

Q. 61 Notes

[5] Tanakh—often written as TaNaKh—is an acronym for *Torah* (Law), *Nevi'im* (Prophets), and *Ketuvim* (Writings), the three divisions for the materials.

[6] Other sacred texts, like the New Testament writings that Christians include with the Old Testament as part of the Bible, or the Talmud, revered by Jews, are considered in the separate sections on Christianity and Judaism in later questions.

Q. 62 Notes

[7] The famous Old Testament theologian Gerhard Von Rad observes, "The formula 'an abomination to Yahweh' denotes cultic taboos which endanger the purity of the religion of Yahweh" (*Deuteronomy. A Commentary*. Old Testament Library (Phila.: Westminster Press, 1966), p. 141). A footnote in the Soncino Talmud at Nazir 59a (discussed in the answer to question 42) notes, "This word, '*abomination*,' is used of forbidden intercourse" (H. Freedman (Trans.), *Nedarim*. Soncino Talmud (London, Soncino Press, 1978), p. 220, fn. 3).

[8] P. J. Harland, "Menswear and Womenswear. A Study of Deuteronomy 22:5," *Expository Times, 110* (no. 3), 73-76 (1998), p. 74.

[9] The Bible is not hesitant to specify penalties so the lack of one here is quite noteworthy. In this regard, Ronald E. Clements writes, "It is significant that the prohibition against transvestism is not sanctioned by any specific punitive measures to be taken against those who contravene the demands" ("The Book of Deuteronomy," *The New Interpreter's Bible, vol. II*, pp. 269-552 (Nashville: Abingdon Press, 1998), p. 452).

[10] Cyrus H. Gordon, "A Note on the Tenth Commandment," *Journal of the American Academy of Religion, XXXI* (no. 2), 208-209 (1963), p. 209. Gordon's complete translation reads: "The instrument of a man (i.e., a man's weapon) shall not be upon a woman, nor shall a man wear a woman's clothes, for an abomination to Yahweh, thy God, are all who do these things."

[11] The esteemed commentator S. R. Driver observes of the Hebrew כְּלִי that it is "a very general term, applicable to almost any article used or worn, e.g. weapons (Gn. 27³), jewels (24⁵³), ornaments (also household objects, implements, vessels &tc.), Lev. 13⁴⁹ (a 'thing' of skin), I S. 17⁴⁰ (a shepherd's 'bag') . . ." (*A Critical and Exegetical Commentary on Deuteronomy*, 3ʳᵈ ed. (Edinburgh: T. & T. Clark, 1901), p.251.). This same character holds true in the Septuagint—the ancient Greek translation of the Hebrew text—where, as John Wevers observes, "The term σκευη/כְּלִי can refer to anything that is worn by a man, whether apparel or arms or even adornments" (*Notes on the Greek Text of Deuteronomy* (Atlanta: Scholars Press, 1995), p. 350). The *Midrash Mishlei* on Proverbs interprets *keli* as referring to 'weapons of war' and appeals to the story in Judges 4 of Jael, a woman who slew Sisera, the leader of the Hebrew people's enemies, with a tent peg (proper to a woman) rather than a sword (proper to a man) as illustration of the keeping of this commandment.

[12] K.-H. Beyse, "כְּלִי *keli*", in G. J. Botterweck, H. Ringgren, & H.-J. Fabry (Eds.), *Theological Dictionary of the Old Testament,* vol. VII, pp. 169-175, translated by D. E. Green (Grand Rapids, MI: Wm. B. Eerdmans, 1995), p. 173.

[13] The Jewish scholar Jeffrey Tigah points out that while כְּלִי is often rendered "clothing" in later Rabbinic Hebrew, in biblical Hebrew the sense is more often "implement," or "vessel" (*The JPS Torah Commentary. Deuteronomy* (Phila.: Jewish Publication Society, 1996), p. 200).

[14] The use of a simple outer covering might seem to have made telling the sexes difficult, but outer adornments and the near universal presence of beards helped keep the appearance of the sexes distinct. The difference in bodily and facial hair between the sexes enters into the arguments over this text in Rabbinic Judaism. Also among the Greeks and Romans the beard was a sign of masculinity; see, for example, the following from Athenaeus (2ⁿᵈ century):

> Hence, also, Alexis said, I believe: "If you see a man whose hair has been removed by pitch or by shaving, one or other of two things ails him: either he plainly means to 'go on a campaign' and do all kinds of things inconsistent with a beard, or else some vice peculiar to a rich man is descending upon him. For really, what harm do our hairs do us, in the gods' name? By them each one of us shows himself a real man, unless you secretly intend to do something which conflicts with them." – "Again, Diogenes, seeing a man with a chin in that condition, said: "It cannot be, can it, that you have any fault to find with nature, because she made you a man instead of a woman?' And seeing another person on horse-back in nearly the same condition, reeking with perfume and dressed in the style of clothing to

match these practices, he said that he had often before asked what the word 'horse-bawd' meant, but now he had found out.

The excerpt is from Athenaeus, *The Deipnosophists*, XIII.556, in Charles Burton Gulick (Trans.), *The Deipnosophists of Athenaeus of Naucratis*, vol. VI: Books XIII-XIV.653b (Cambridge: Harvard Univ. Press, 1993 reprint of 1937 ed. [Loeb Classical Library]), p. 53.

[15] The manner in which Jewish scholars regard these matters is looked at in a later question.

Q. 63 Notes

[16] 4Q159, fragment 2-4, lines 6-7. The text appears as follows:

אל יהיו כלי גבר על אשה כול [--]

(7) יכס בשלמות אשה ואל ילבש כתונת אשה כיא [ת]ועבה הוא

The translation is in Florentino Garcia Martinez (Ed.), *Dead Sea Scrolls Translated: The Qumran Texts in English*, 2nd ed. (Leiden: E. J. Brill, 1994), p. 86. For more on the scroll, see Francis D. Weinert, "4Q159: Legislation for an Essene Community Outside of Qumran?" *Journal for the Study of Judaism in the Persian, Hellenistic and Roman Period, 5D*, 179-207 (1974). Also see Charlotte Hempel, "4QOrd^a (4Q159) and the Laws of the Damascus Covenant," in L. H. Schiffman, E. Tov, J. VanderKam, & G. Marquis (Eds.), *The Dead Sea Scrolls Fifty Years After Their Discovery 1947-1997*, pp. 372-376 (Jerusalem: Israel Exploration Society, 2000).

[17] The Targums served an important practical purpose. Many of the listeners in the synagogue did not understand biblical Hebrew, their own language being Aramaic (Palestinian or Babylonian); a situation long familiar to Catholic Christians who heard only Latin at the Mass. The Targum not only provided a translation but with its often paraphrastic character supplied an interpretive element. Martin McNamara, Project Director for the multi-volume *Aramaic Bible*, which collects together in English translation the various targums to the Hebrew text (HT), puts the matter well: "We should never forget that the primary intention of the Palestinian Targums seems to be to render the plain meaning of the HT into Aramaic; to give the sense so that the people might understand the reading (Neh. 8:8)" (*Targum Neofiti 1: Genesis*. The Aramaic Bible, Vol. 1A (Collegeville, MN: The Liturgical Press, 1992), p. 30). This aspect reflected the understanding of the community where that Targum was used. A rough modern parallel might be the use of the *Living Bible* (1971), by Kenneth Taylor, popular among Christians as easier to read than the King James Version and, by virtue of its expansive paraphrase, often used as a guide to understand the meaning of the biblical text.

[18] Israel Drazin (Translator), *Targum Onkelos to Deuteronomy* (N. Y.: Ktav Publishing House, 1982), p. 204. This Targum, perhaps reflecting 2nd century Aramaic, ranks first in authority.

[19] Martin McNamara (Translator), *Targum Neofiti 1: Deuteronomy*. The Aramaic Bible, vol. 5A (Collegeville, MN: The Liturgical Press, 1997), p. 106. Material in italics reflects the interpretive element of the targum. Targum Neofiti, and Pseudo-Jonathan are Palestinian Targums. Cf. this older translation: "Neither fringed robes nor tephillin which are

the ornaments of a man shall be upon a woman; neither shall a man shave himself so as to appear like a woman; for every one who doeth so is an abomination before the Lord thy God." J. W. Etheridge (Translator), "The Palestinian Targum on the Sepher Haddebarim or Deuteronomy," in *The Targums of Onkelos and Jonathan ben Uzziel on the Pentateuch with the Fragments of the Jerusalem Targum from the Chaldee*, pp. 557-685 (N. Y.: Ktav Publishing House, 1968; original work published in 2 vols., 1862, 1865), p. 622f.

[20] Ernest G. Clarke (Translator), *Targum Pseudo-Jonathan: Deuteronomy*. The Aramaic Bible, vol. 5B (Collegeville, MN: The Liturgical Press, 1998), p. 60. Material in italics reflects the interpretive element of the targum.

[21] Reuven Hammer (Translator), *Sifre. A Tannaitic Commentary on the Book of Deuteronomy* (New Haven: Yale Univ. Press, 1986), p. 236 [Piska 226]. The Tannaim [sing. "Tanna"] were rabbinic scholars of the time during which Christianity arose (first two centuries of the Common Era). *Sifre* was probably edited into its final form near the end of the 3rd century C.E.

[22] Nazir 59a, in H. Freedman (Translator), *Nedarim*. Soncino Talmud (London, Soncino Press, 1978), p. 219f. This is the Babylonian Talmud. In a footnote to this passage's words "and there is no abomination here!" the Soncino editor observes, "The mere act of putting on the garments is not wrong" (p. 220, n. 4). The "Soferim" referred to are the "Scribes," or educated men of an earlier day (cf. the Scribes of the Christian New Testament).

[23] Abraham Ben Isaiah & Benjamin Sharfman, *The Pentateuch and Rashi's Commentary. A Linear Translation into English* (N. Y.: S. S. & R. Publishing Co., 1949), p. 199. "Rashi" is the common acronym for Rabbi Shlomo Yitzchaki, the French scholar of the Middle Ages whose brilliance displays itself in concise comments such as those quoted here.

[24] Maimonides, *Moreh* 3:37.

[25] Maimonides, *Mishneh Torah*; also see his *More Nebochim*. See Ronald L. Eisenberg, *The 613 Mitzvot: A Contemporary Guide to the Commandments of Judaism* (Rockville, MD: Schrieber Publishing, 2005), p. 193. Cf. Gersion Appel & Solomon ben Joseph Ganzfried, *The Concise Code of Jewish Law* (N. Y.: KTAV Publishing House, 1978), p. 287.

[26] *Sepher HaHinukh* §564. Cited in Jon-Jay Tilsen, *Cross-dressing and Deuteronomy 22:5*. Accessed online at http://www.beki.org/crossdress.html.

[27] *Shulhan Arukh, vol. 1: Orakh Hayyim*.

[28] J. H. Hertz (Ed.), *The Pentateuch and Haftorahs, vol. II. Numbers, Deuteronomy* (London: Soncino Press, 1941), p. 843.

[29] W. Gunther Plaut, "Deuteronomy," in *The Torah. A Modern Commentary* (N. Y.: Union of American Hebrew Congregations, 1981), p. 1485.

[30] Robert Alter, *The Five Books of Moses* (N. Y.: W. W. Norton & Co., 2004), p. 986.

[31] Jon-Jay Tilsen, *Cross-dressing and Deuteronomy 22:5* (n.d.). Accessed online at http://www.beki.org/crossdress.html. Tilsen is the rabbi of Congregation Beth El-Keser Israel in New Haven, Connecticut.

[32] Jeffrey H. Tigay, *The JPS Torah Commentary. Deuteronomy* (Phila.: Jewish Publication Society, 1996), p. 200. The "halakah" refers to the body of legal materials in Judaism.

Q. 64 Notes

[33] Philip Stubbes, *The Anatomie of the Abuses*, ed. F. J. Furnivall (New Shakespeare Society, 1877-1879; original work published 1583, 1585, 1595), vol. 1, p. 73. I have modernized the language somewhat by changing spellings.

[34] The *Hermaphroditi* (hermaphrodites)—today called 'intersexed'—were in some times and places of the ancient world viewed as monsters.

[35] *Geneva Study Bible* (1599). Accessed online at www.bibletechnologieswg.org; text cited accessed from http://www.bibletechnologieswg.org/cgi-bin/diatheke.pl?verse= Deuteronomy+ 22%3A5&Submit=Submit&search=&Geneva=on.

[36] Of course, there are various forms of this basic argument, but the logic remains the same: crossdressing is unnatural and sinful. As with any argument, there are rebuttals offered to this one. They will be covered later.

[37] P. J. Harland, "Menswear and Womenswear. A Study of Deuteronomy 22:5," *Expository Times, 110* (no. 3), 73-76 (1998), p. 76.

[38] Adam Clarke, *Adam Clarke's commentary on the Bible* (1825). Accessed online at various places, including www.bibletechnologieswg.org; text cited accessed from http://www.bibletechnologieswg.org/cgibin/diatheke.pl?verse=Deuteronomy+22%3A 5&Submit=Submit&search=&Clarke=on.

[39] This specific incident is covered in the answer to Q. 43. For comments on other historical incidents of crossdressing please see question set 4.

[40] Robert Jameison, A. R. Fawcett, & David Brown, *Jameison-Fawcett-Brown Commentary and Explanatory on the Whole Bible* (1871). Accessed online at http://bible. christiansunite.com/jfbindex.shtml; text cited accessed from http://bible. christiansunite.com/jfb.cgi?b=05&c=22.

[41] Please note that because the commentary offers no evidence, scriptural or otherwise, for these outcomes, the reader must either conclude that they require no evidence because they are self-evident, or that they are merely personal opinions.

[42] S. R. Driver, *A Critical and Exegetical Commentary on Deuteronomy*, 3rd ed. (Edinburgh: T. & T. Clark, 1901), p. 250.

[43] Gerhard Von Rad, *Deuteronomy. A Commentary*. Old Testament Library (Phila.: Westminster Press, 1966), p. 141.

[44] Anthony Phillips, *Deuteronomy [The Cambridge Bible Commentary]* (Cambridge: Cambridge Univ. Press, 1973), p. 145.

[45] Ronald E. Clements, "The Book of Deuteronomy," *The New Interpreter's Bible, vol. II*, pp. 269-552 (Nashville: Abingdon Press, 1998), p. 452.

[46] Ibid.

[47] Of course, this latter point can be a dangerous argument. It is all too easy to say that the original writer's theology is the same as mine, the interpreter, and thus conclude that my interpretation is solidly historical as well as doctrinally correct!

[48] F. F. Bruce (Ed.), *International Bible Commentary* (Grand Rapids: Zondervan, 1979), p. 273.

[49] John H. Walter & Victor H. Matthews, *IVP Bible Background Commentary Genesis-Deuteronomy* (Downers Grove: InterVarsity Press, 1997), p. 251. The objects mentioned at the last offer one way of understanding *keli* and *simlah*: the former referring to 'various weapons' carried by men and the latter to the 'mirror and distaff' used by women.

[50] Bruce Oberst, *Deuteronomy* (Joplin: College Press, 1968), p. 258. The connection of crossdressing to homosexuality is also a concern of Old Testament professor Terrence Fretheim, who thinks it plausible that Deuteronomy 22:5 is understood *vis-à-vis* Leviticus 18:22 in that crossdressing may be understood—for the man at least—as "a dishonorable, shaming role for the male that assumes the submissive position and confuses gender roles." See his paper, "The Old Testament and Homosexuality," excerpted in *The Lutheran* (2001, May 2), the whole text of which was accessed online at http://www. thelutheran.org/0105/page55.html.

Q. 66 Notes

[51] In fact, it could be argued it bothers highly religious folks the most. At least among Christians, dress has been viewed for a very long time as a serious indicator of virtue. Modesty in dress is thought to symbolize the same virtue in other respects, most especially sexuality.

[52] See in the Old Testament, for example, Genesis 3:21, 28:20: Exodus 28:39-41; Deuteronomy 22:11; 2 Samuel 13:18. Metaphorical references also abound: Psalms 35:26, 104:1, 132:16; Isaiah 50:3; 59:17. The New Testament also speaks of clothes both literally (e.g., Matthew 3:4, 6:28-33, 25:36-44, James 2:15-16) and figuratively (e.g., Romans 13:14; I Corinthians 15:53-54).

[53] Augustine (late 3rd-early 4th century), in his *City of God* (Bk. XIX, ch. 19; cf. Bk. I, ch. 10), reflects a relative indifference to dress. By contrast, Tertullian (early 3rd century) shows energetic concern in his work, *On the Apparel of Women*. For more, see Q. 67.

[54] See, for example, Margaret R. Miles, "Fashioning the Self," *Christian Century, 112* (no. 8), 273-275 (1995, Mar. 8).

[55] An interesting representation of the eunuch's status is that of 'exile' as in Claudius Mamertinus, *Panegyrici latini*, 11.19.4.

[56] Samual Tobias Lachs, *A Rabbinic Commentary on the New Testament* (Hoboken, NJ: KTAV, 1987), p. 327 n. 4.

[57] Gene McAfee, "Eunuch," in B. M. Metzger & M. D. Coogan (Eds.), *The Oxford Companion to the Bible*, p. 205f. (N. Y.: Oxford Univ. Press, 1993), p. 205.

[58] J. David Hester, "Eunuchs and the Post-Gender Jesus: Matthew 19:12 and Transgressive Sexualities," *Journal for the Study of the New Testament, 28* (no. 1), 13-40 (2005), p. 14f.

[59] Ibid, p. 30. Hester writes the practice was widespread among both churches of the East and West, persisted for centuries, and was found among the orthodox as well as 'heterodox' believers.

[60] See Jerome's commentary on Isaiah 56:3f. Cf. Alan Hugh McNeile, *The Gospel According to Matthew* (Grand Rapids, MI: Baker Book House, 1980 reprint of 1915 ed.), p. 276.

[61] Perhaps the teaching of Jesus is in Paul's mind in the lengthy answer he gives to the Church at Corinth after they raise the idea that "It is well for a man not to touch a woman" (I Corinthians 7:1; NSRV). Paul's reply stresses that sexual self-restraint is a gift (v. 7). Each person should "lead the life that the Lord has assigned" (v. 17; NSRV) and "remain in the condition in which you were called" (v. 20; NSRV). To unmarried virgins, though, he counsels remaining celibate because the end of days is anticipated and remaining single can facilitate single-minded devotion (vv. 25-35). Paul concludes with an echo of Jesus' teaching on marriage (v. 39). Though he never uses the word eunuch, the development of his thought is congenial to the sentiment of Jesus.

[62] Stephen J. Davis, "Crossed Texts, Crossed Sex: Intertextuality and Gender in Early Christian Legends of Holy Women Disguised as Men," *Journal of Early Christian Studies, 10* (no. 1), 1-36 (2002), p. 21.

[63] Such an application, however, does not address the fact that most crossdressing intends to express a gender identity rather than a transcending or suspension of gender identity.

[64] Interestingly, this issue also became a differentiating mark between Christianity and Judaism. In the latter, it is men who are to pray with head covered and women to leave theirs uncovered. In modern Reform and Conservation synagogues women are permitted to wear a head covering (*kippah*).

[65] A. Guillaumont, et al. (Trans.), *The Gospel According to Thomas* (Leiden: E. J. Brill, 1959), Logia 114, p. 57. See also, Elizabeth Castelli, "'I Will Make Mary Male': Pieties of the Body and Gender: Transformation of Christian Women in Late Antiquity," in Julia Epstein & Kristina Straub (Eds.), *Body Guards: The Cultural politics of Gender Ambiguity* (N.Y.: Routledge, 1991), pp. 29-49. Cf. Wayne A. Meeks, "The Image of the Androgyne: Some Uses of Symbol in Earliest Christianity," *History of Religions, 13,* 165-208 (1973-1974).

[66] For much of Church history the sentiment expressed in the Gospel of Thomas appears to have triumphed. See the answer to Q. 67 for elaboration.

[67] *Sayings of the Fathers* V.x.73 (available online at http://www.vitae-patrum.org.uk/page53.html), in the *Vitae Patrum* (available online at http://www.vitae-patrum.org.uk/index.html).

Q. 67 Notes

[68] As recently as the end of May, 2008, the Vatican publicly announced opposition to all efforts within the Catholic Church to ordain women, stating that any such so-called 'ordinations' would fetch instant excommunication. Since 2002, a movement known as Roman Catholic Womenpriests has promoted ordination of women. See Vic-

tor L. Simpson, *Vatican Says Female Priests and Those Who Ordain Them Will Incur Automatic Excommunication*, (May 30, 2008). Associated Press story accessed online at http://my.earthlink.net/article/top?guid=20080530/483f7bc0_3421_1334520080530-1884686905.

[69] Jo Ann McNamara, "Sexual Equality and the Cult of Virginity in Early Christian Thought," *Feminist Studies, 3* (nos. 3-4), 145-158 (1976), p. 145.

[70] Origen, *Homilies on the Song of Songs*, 1.2-3; quoted in Stephen D. Moore, "The Song of Songs in the History of Sexuality," *Church History, 69* (no. 2), 328-349 (2000), p. 329. Moore offers an extended analysis of Origen's comments.

[71] Peter Brown, *The Body and Society: Men, Women, and Sexual Renunciation in Early Christianity* (N. Y.: Columbia Univ. Press, 1988), p. 171.

[72] McNamara, p. 148.

[73] Although the Church employs the term 'heresy' pejoratively, it means merely the taking of a position (literally, making a choice), and in practice was applied by those who held the majority opinion against those who espoused the minority opinion. It was at various times employed against even those whose views eventually prevailed and became 'orthodoxy' (i.e., 'the right way').

[74] Clement of Alexandria, *Stromata (Miscellanies)*, III.2.6-8. Translation from John Ernest Leonard Oulton (Ed.), *Alexandrian Christianity: Selected Translations of Clement and Origen* [The Library of Christian Classics, Vol. II] (Phila.: Westminster Press, 1954). Accessed online at http://www.earlychristianwritings.com/text/clement-stromata-book3-english.html. Clement quotes from *Concerning Righteousness* the view that God implanted in the human male a sexual desire that neither law nor any other restraint could destroy; as God's decree for their nature it makes no sense to institutionalize efforts to control it.

[75] Ibid, III.6.53.

[76] Ibid, III.9.63. The Latin text reads: "Qui autem Dei creaturæ resistunt per speciosam illam continentiam, illa quoque dicunt, quæ ad Salomen dicta sunt, quorum prius meminimus: habentur autem, ut existimo, in Evangelio secundum Ægyptios. Aiunt enim ipsum dixisse Servatorem: Veni ad dissolvendum opera feminæ; feminæ quidem, cupiditatis; opera autem generationem et interitum."

[77] Cf. McNamara, p. 146.

[78] Michael Nausner, "Toward Community Beyond Gender Binaries: Gregory of Nyssa's Transgendering as Part of His Transformative Eschatology," *Theology & Sexuality*, Issue 16, 55-65 (2002), p. 58.

[79] Ibid. Gregory writes that the resurrection is "no other thing than '*the re-constitution of our nature in its original form*.'" Gregory of Nyssa, *On the Soul and the Resurrection*, in P. Schaff & H. Wace (Eds.), *Gregory of Nyssa: Dogmatic Treatises, etc.*, pp. 430-468 [Nicene and Post-Nicene Fathers, Vol. 5] (N. Y.: Christian Literature Publishing Co., 1893), p. 467.

[80] Gregory of Nyssa, *On the Creation of Man*, 16. Quote taken from Andrew Louth (Ed.), *Ancient Christian Commentary on Scripture. Old Testament, I. Genesis 1-11* (Downer's Grove, IL: InterVarsity Press, 2001), p. 35.

[81] "Thus, the end-time returns, as it were, to primordial time, to the generations of Adam before he sinned, and the primitive righteousness of Eden is at last restored. This correspondence between the beginning and the End is a frequently recurring theme in these writings." D. S. Russell, *The Old Testament Pseudepidgrapha. Patriarchs & Prophets in Early Judaism* (Phila.: Fortress Press, 1987), p.23.

[82] Ibid, pp. 59-61. Macrina is discussed on pp. 59-60; Gregory on pp. 60-61.

[83] Gregory of Nyssa: *The Life of Macrina*, trans. by W. K. Lowther Clarke, (London: SPCK, 1916), p. 18. Accessed online at http://www.fordham.edu/halsall/basis/macrina.html. Also accessed at http://www.tertullian.org/fathers/gregory_macrina_0_intro.htm. St. Macrina the Younger lived c. 330-379 C.E. The critical Greek portion reads: Γυνὴ δὲ ἦν ἡ τοῦ διη γήματος ἀφορμη, εἴπερ γυνή· οὐκ οἶδα γὰρ εἰ πρέπον ἐστὶν ἐκ τῆς φύσεως αὐτὴν ὀνομάζειν τὴν ἄνω γενομένην τῆς φύσεως.

[84] Gregory of Nyssa, *On the Soul and the Resurrection*, p. 430.

[85] Gregory of Nyssa, *The Life of Macrina*, p. 37. She is said to have become "all things" to her brother—"father, teacher, tutor, mother, giver of all good advice" (πατήρ, διδάσκολος, παιδαγωγός, μήτηρ, ἀγαθοῦ παντὸς σύμβουλος).

[86] McNamara, p. 152f.

[87] Ambrose, *Expositionis in Evangelium secundum Lucam Libri* X, PL 15. "Ambrose was well aware that sexual differences needed emphasizing by different hair and clothing styles; the only 'gender-bending' he could accept was at the spiritual level." Kim E. Power, "Ambrose of Milan: Keeper of the Boundaries," *Theology Today, 55* (no. 1), 15-34 (1998), p. 26.

[88] Table adapted from materials found in various sources, including L. L. Coon, K. J. Haldane, & E. W. Sommer (Eds.), *That Gentle Strength: Historical Perspectives on Women in Christianity*, pp. 5, 214f.; also, Elisabeth Clark (relying principally on John Chrysostom), "Ideology, History, and the Construction of 'Woman' in Late Ancient Christianity," in E. Ferguson (Ed.), *Recent Studies in Early Christianity: A Collection of Scholarly Essays*, pp. 1-30 (N. Y.: Garland Publishing, 1999), p. 13.

[89] Lynda L. Coon, Katherine J. Haldane, & Elisabeth W. Sommer, "Introduction," in L. L. Coon, K. J. Haldane, & E. W. Sommer (Eds.), *That Gentle Strength: Historical Perspectives on Women in Christianity*, pp. 1-18 (1990), p. 5.

[90] McNamara (p. 153) offers examples for some of these. 'A strong member of a weak sex' is praise found for Melania the Elder in Paulinus of Nola, *Epistola* 29. Palladius called her ἡ ἄνθροπος τοῦ δεοῦ (*he anthropos tou deou*—'the (feminine) man of God'). One who had 'gone beyond the nature of a woman' was Macrina, sister of Gregory of Nyssa, who sings her praise in his *Vie de Macrina*. 'Becoming male' is the sentiment of the famed final saying of Jesus in the *Gospel of Thomas*.

[91] Clement of Alexandria, *Paedagogus (The Instructor)*, Book II, Chapter XI ('On Clothes'), in Alexander Roberts & James Donaldson (Eds.), *Ante-Nicene Fathers, vol. II* (Grand Rapids: Wm. B. Eerdmans reprint of late 19th century work published by T. & T. Clark). Available online at http://www.ccel.org/fathers2/.

[92] Clement of Alexandria, *The Stromata, or Miscellanies*, Bk. II, ch.XVIII; in Alexander Roberts & James Donaldson (Eds.), *Ante-Nicene Fathers, vol. II* (Grand Rapids: Wm. B. Eerdmans reprint of late 19th century work published by T. & T. Clark). Available on line at http://www.ccel.org/fathers2/.

[93] Tertullian, *De Spectaculis (The Shows)*, Ch. XXIII, tr. S. Thelwall, in Alexander Roberts & James Donaldson (Eds.), *Ante-Nicene Fathers, vol. III* (Grand Rapids: Wm. B. Eerdmans reprint of late 19th century work published by T. & T. Clark). Available online at http://www.ccel.org/fathers2/. Also see Tertullian's remarks on women and dress, which emphasize modesty in appearance, in his *De Culta Feminarum (On the Dress of Women)* and *De Virginibus Velandis (On the Veiling of Virgins)*, especially XIV in the latter.

For an interesting analysis of Tertullian's thinking on women, see J. Jayakiran Sebastian, "Martyrs and Heretics: Aspects of the Contribution of Women to Early Christianity," in P. Kumari (Ed.), *Feminist Theology: Perspective and Praxis*, Gurukul Summer Institute (Chennai: Gurukul Lutheran Theological College and Reseatch Institute, 1999), pp. 135-153. Available online at http://www.religion-online.org/cgi-bin/relsearchd.dll/ showarticle?item_id=1125.

[94] Cyprian, *Epistle LX. To Euchratius, About an Actor* in Alexander Roberts & James Donaldson (Eds.), *Ante-Nicene Fathers, vol. V* (Grand Rapids: Wm. B. Eerdmans reprint of late 19th century work published by T. & T. Clark). Available online at http://www.ccel.org/fathers2/.

[95] Power, p. 15.

[96] Ibid, p. 25.

[97] Ambrose of Milan, *Concerning Virgins*, 3.3.9, with 1 Corinthians 14:33b-35 in mind. Translation of Rev. H. de Romestin. Accessed online at http://www.consecrated virgins.org/397-ambrose.pdf.

[98] Ambrose, *The Letters of S. Ambrose, Bishop of Milan, Translated with Notes and Indices* (Oxford: James Parker and Co., 1881), Epistle LXIX, §2 [italics added]. Accessed online at http://www.tertullian.org/fathers/ambrose_letters_07_letters61_70.htm#Letter 69. For original Latin text, see *Corpus Scriptorum Ecclesiasticorum Latinorum*, 82, 1:112. Letter 15 (69).

[99] Ibid, §4.

[100] Ibid. Both quotes are from §4.

[101] Ibid, §5.

[102] Ibid, §6. Both quotes are from this section.

[103] Ibid, §7.

104 Jerome, "Letter XXII. To Eustochium," §27, *The Letters of St. Jerome*, in Alexander Roberts & James Donaldson (Eds.), *Nicene and Post-Nicene Fathers, Series II, Volume VI*. (Grand Rapids: Wm. B. Eerdmans reprint of late 19th century work published by T. & T. Clark). Available online at http://www.ccel.org/fathers2/.

105 Ibid, §27.

106 Jerome, *Commentariorum in Epistolam ad Ephesio* [*Commentary on the Epistle of Ephesians*], Bk. III.5. Cf. Ronald E. Heine, *The Commentaries of Origen and Jerome on St. Paul's Epistle to the Ephesians* (N. Y.: Oxford Univ. Press, 2002).

107 John Chrysostom, *Homilies on First Corinthians*, Homily XXVI [4], in *Nicene and Post-Nicene Fathers, Series I, Volume XII*. (Grand Rapids: Wm. B. Eerdmans reprint of late 19th century work published by T. & T. Clark). Available online at http://www.ccel.org/fathers2/NPNF1-12/npnf1-12-31.htm.

108 It might not be amiss to note that while some Christians still get energized over crossdressing practiced outside the confines of a house of worship, hardly anyone gets exercised over the covering or lack thereof on the heads of parishioners worshiping inside a church.

Q. 68 Notes

109 Lynne Dahmen, "Sacred Romance: Silence and the Hagiographical Tradition," Arthuriana, 12 (no. 1), pp. 113-122. Quote is from p. 116. Cf. a similar comment by J. Herrin, "In Search of Byzantine Women: Three Avenues of Approach," in A. Cameron & A. Kuhrt (Eds.), *Images of Women in Antiquity* (Detroit: Wayne State Univ. Press, 1983), p. 179: "The monastic disguises adopted by women enabled them to simulate a holiness reserved by male ecclesiastical authorities to men only."

110 Valerie R. Hotchkiss, *Clothes Make the Man: Female Cross-Dressing in Medieval Europe* (N. Y.: Garland Publishing, Inc., 1996). Please note that one immediate complication about such accounts is that the antiquity of the stories, coupled with doubt in some cases about the facts set forth, may cause some to dismiss them. But whether the events actually happened as told seems inconsequential for our study since the record—which tells of these women dressing as men—has been preserved as part of the story. I think it obvious that if fiction, the storytellers or later Church censors surely could have expunged the crossdressing aspect had it offended them.

111 Stephen J. Davis, "Crossed Texts, Crossed Sex: Intertextuality and Gender in Early Christian Legends of Holy Women Disguised as Men," *Journal of Early Christian Studies, 10* (no. 1), 1-36 (2002). See especially p. 36.

112 Ibid, pp. 5-11.

113 Thecla's whole story can be found in the *Acts of Paul and Thecla*, easily available in many places. The translation by Jeremiah Jones (1693-1734) exists in several places on the internet; accessed online at http://www.fordham.edu/halsall/basis/ thecla.html. Also see a definitive critical rendering in R. A. Lipsius & M. Bonnet (Eds.), *Acta Apostolorum Apocrypha*, pp. 235-272 (Leipzig: Hermann Mendelssohn, 1891). For additional information, see Nancy A. Carter, *The Acts of Thecla: A Pauline Tradition Linked to Women* (2000), a webpage with links to further resources, accessed online at http://gbgm-

umc.org/umw/corinthians/theclabackground.stm. Also, for the impact of the story of Thecla on subsequent generations, see Stephen J. Davis, *The Cult of Saint Thecla* (Oxford: Oxford Univ. Press, 2001).

[114] The New Testament Apocrypha collects together a number of documents (Gospels, Acts, Epistles) that represent popular pious imagination engaged in filling in the gaps left by the documents of the New Testament.

[115] See her story in F. S. Ellis (Ed.), *The Golden Legend or Lives of the Saints* (Edinburgh: T. & A. Constable LTD, 1900; reprinted 1922, 1931). The work was originally compiled by Jacobus de Voragine, Archbishop of Genoa. It was set into English by William Caxton (1st edition, 1483). Available online at http://www.catholic-forum.com/saints/golden140.htm.

[116] Davis, pp. 17-18; cf. Stephen J. Davis, *The Cult of Saint Thecla* (Oxford: Oxford Univ. Press, 2001), chapter 4. Davis (p. 18) quotes Eugenia's confession, "I became a man for a short time, being emulous and imitating my teacher Thecla . . . ." (*Life of Eugenia* 15; translation by A. S. Lewis, *Select Narratives of Holy Women*, 21(fol. 39b) (N. Y.: Macmillan, 1900).

[117] See the discussion in John Boswell, *Same-Sex Unions in Premodern Europe* (N. Y.: Villard Books, 1994), pp. 147-155, especially p. 148. Boswell's translation of the 9th century *Passio antiquior SS. Sergei et Bacchi Graece nunc prima edita* accessed online at http://www.cs.cmu.edu/afs/cs/user/ scotts/ftp/wpaf2mc/serge.html.

[118] For more information, see "Pelagia of Antioch," in S. P. Brock & A. A. Harvey (Translators.), *Holy Women of the Syrian Orient*, pp. 40-62 (Berkeley: Univ. of California Press, 1987); see p. 58 for the account of her dressing in clothes received from the bishop. Also see Louisa Blair, "The Beardless Recluse's Passion and Daring," *Saint, 14* (no. 4), 22f. (1996, Sept./Oct.). Available online at http://gvanv.com/compass/arch/v1404/saint.html. Also see J. P. Kirsch, "Pelagia," in C. G. Herbermann, et al. (Eds.), *The Catholic Encyclopedia*, vol. XI, pp. 601-602 (N. Y.: Encyclopedia Press, 1913), p. 602. It has been claimed that this story inspired the legends of other crossdressing saints (Mary, Marina, Apollinaria, Euphrosyne, Theodora).

[119] See "St. Athanasia (2)," in Agnes B. C. Dunbar, *A Dictionary of Saintly Women*, vol. 1, pp. 87-88 (London: George Bell & Sons, 1904). Also see, Laura Swan, *The Forgotten Desert Mothers: Sayings, Lives, and Stories of Early Christian Women* (N. Y.: Paulist Press, 2001), pp. 75-76. Cf. the brief account in Vincent J. O'Malley, *Saints of Africa* (Huntington, IN: Our Sunday Visitor, Inc., 2001), p. 137.

[120] St. Euphrosyne's story is among those modern scholars tend to regard as a pious invention. For more, see Simon Gaunt, "Straight Minds/ Queer Wishes in Old French Hagiography: La Vie de Sainte Euphrosine," in L. Fradenburg & C. Freccero (Eds.), *Premodern Sexualities* (N. Y.: Routledge, 1996), pp. 155-173.

[121] For more on St. Apollonaria, see Bishop Nikolai Velimirovic, *The Prologue from Orchid* (Birmingham: Lazarica Press, 1986). Available online at http://www.westsrbdio.org/prolog/prolog.htm.

[122] For more on St. Mary, see Nicholas Constas (Trans.), "Life of St. Mary/Marinos," in Talbot (Ed.), *Holy Women of Byzantium*, pp. 1-12 (the brief quote used above is from p. 7), or chapter 13 in Mary-Ann Stouck (Ed.), *Medieval Saints: A Reader. Readings in Medieval Civilizations and Cultures*, Vol. IV (Orchard Park, NY: Broadview Press, 1998).

[123] For more on St. Hilaria, see A. J. Wensinck (Ed. and Translator), *Legends of Eastern Saints*, vol. II: *The Legend of Hilaria* (Leyden: E. J. Brill, 1913). Accessed online at http://www.tertullian.org/fathers/hilaria_01_preface.htm.

[124] For more on St. Matrona, see Jeffrey Featherstone & Cyril Mango (Trans.), "Life of St. Mary of Egypt," in Talbot (Ed.), *Holy Women of Byzantium*, pp. 13-64. Available online at http://www.doaks.org/HolyWomen/talbch2.pdf. Also see Khalifa Bennasser, *Gender and Society in Early Byzantine Monasticism: A study of the phenomenon of female ascetics in male monastic habit with translation of the life of St. Matrona*, (Ph.D Dissertation, Rutgers University, 1984). Accounts of St. Matrona's life also can be found online as part of the Medieval Sourcebook at http://www.fordham.edu/halsall/basis/ matrona.html.

[125] Gregory of Tours, *De Gloria Confessorum*, xvi. Avaliable online (in Latin) at http://www-droit.uclermont1.fr/Recherche/CentresRecherche/Histoire/gerhma/gc. pdf. Cf. the summary and assessment in Jane Tibbets Schulenburg, *Forgetful of Their Sex: Female Sanctity and Society, ca. 500-1100* (Chicago: Univ. of Chicago Press, 1998), pp. 160-161.

[126] For more on St. Mary of Egypt, see Maria Kouli (Trans.), "Life of St. Mary of Egypt," in Talbot (Ed.), *Holy Women of Byzantium*, pp. 65-93. Available online at http://www.doaks.org/HolyWomen/talbch3.pdf.

[127] For more on St. Anastasia the Patrician, see the entry in George Poulos, *Orthodox Saints*, vol. 1 (Brookline, MA: Holy Cross Orthodox Press, 1990). Available online at http://saintgeorge.org/news_and_events/church_calendar/saint_of_the_day/03mar/mar_10_st_anastasia.php. Also see Dunbar, vol. 1, p. 54f.

[128] For more details, see her story in F. S. Ellis (Ed.), *The Golden Legend or Lives of the Saints* (Edinburgh: T. & A. Constable LTD, 1900; reprinted 1922, 1931). The work was originally compiled by Jacobus de Voragine, Archbishop of Genoa. It was set into English by William Caxton (1st edition, 1483). Available online at http://www.catholic-forum.com/saints/golden224.htm.

[129] For more on St. Anna, see François Halkin (Ed.), *Bibliotheca Hagiographica Graeca*, 3rd ed. (Brussels, 1957), 2027.

[130] For more on St. Theoktiste, see Angela C. Hero (Trans.), "Life of St. Theoktiste of Lesbos," in Talbot (Ed.), *Holy Women of Byzantium*, pp. 95-116. Available online at http://www.doaks.org/ HolyWomen/talbch4.pdf. Cf. the story of St. Mary of Egypt, who similarly borrowed a garment from a man to cover her nakedness, and whose story shares other elements.

[131] This material was drawn from a number of sources, but especially Alison Jasper, "Theology at the Freak Show: St Uncumber and the Discourse of Liberation," *Theology & Sexuality, 11* (no. 2), 43-54 (2004). For a very interesting article, which might make St.

Uncumber the patron saint of those with eating disorders, see J. Hubert Lacey, "Anorexia Nervosa and a Bearded Female Saint," *British Medical Journal, 285,* 18-25 (1982, Dec.), pp. 1816-1817. Available online at http://www.philipresheph.com/ a424/study/ lacey.doc. Also, see Paul Halsall, "A Legend of the Austrian Tyrol: St. Kümmernis," Modern History Sourcebook (1998). Available online at http://www.fordham.edu/ halsall/mod/kummernis.html.

[132] Jasper, p. 48.

[133] Ibid, p. 49.

[134] Cf. Jasper, p. 50.

[135] Ibid, pp. 50-53.

[136] While the factual basis of some of the stories of crossdressing female saints has been questioned, that has not been the case for St. Hildegund. Interestingly, in artistic depictions she is portrayed as a maiden garbed in the dress of a male Cistercian novice. A brief recounting of her story is given by Toney Staley, "This Female Saint Lived the Derring-Do Life of a Man," *The Compass.* Official Newspaper of the Catholic Diocese of Green Bay (2001, April 13). Available online at http://www.thecompassnews.org/ compass/2001-04-13/01cn0413f2.htm. Also see Dunbar, vol. 1, p. 388.

[137] There have been many books written about Joan of Arc, and there are abundant resources on the internet.

[138] W. P. Barrett, *The Trial of Jeanne D'Arc Translated in English from the Original Latin and French Documents* (N. Y.: Gotham House, Inc., 1932), p. 16. Available online at http://www.fordham.edu/halsall/basis/joanofarc-trial.html.

[139] Ibid, p.62; cf. p. 118: ". . . concerning the man's dress she wears, she answered: 'Since I do it by God's command and in His service I do not think I do wrong; and so soon as it shall please God to command I will put it off.'"

[140] Ibid, p. 349.

Q. 69 Notes

[141] Valerie R. Hotchkiss, *Clothes Make the Man: Female Cross-Dressing in Medieval Europe* (N. Y.: Garland Publishing, Inc., 1996), p. 19.

[142] Elizabeth Weiss Ozorak, "The Power, But Not the Glory" How Women Empower Themselves Through Religion," *Journal for the Scientific Study of Religion, 35* (no. 1), 17-29 (1996).

[143] The story of 'Pope Joan' is not a modern invention. It can be documented as early as the 13th century C.E. For a brief account, see J. N. D. Kelly, *Oxford Dictionary of Popes* (N. Y.: Oxford Univ. Press, 1989 reprint ed.; orig. ed., 1986). An appendix (p. 331f.) covers 'Pope Joan.' For a more extended account, see Alain Boureau, *The Myth of Pope Joan,* trans. Lydia G. Cochrane (Chicago: Univ. of Chicago Press, 2001).

[144] Margot H. King, "The Desert Mothers: A Survey of the Feminine Anchoritic Tradition in Western Europe," *Fourteenth Century Mystics Newsletter, 9,* 12-25 (1983). Available online at http://www.peregrina.com/matrologia/desertmothers1.html.

[145] Ibid.

[146] See, for example, John Anson, "The Female Transvestite in Early Monasticism; The Origins and Development of a Motif," *Viator*, 5, 1-32 (1974). For more on this subject, see Vern Bullough, "Transvestites in the Middle Ages," *American Journal of Sociology*, 79, 1381-94 (1974); cf. Vern Bullough, "Transvestism in the Middle Ages," V. L. Bullough & J. Brundate (Eds.), *Sexual Practices and the Medieval Church*, (Buffalo: Prometheus Books, 1982), 43-54. Also see Rudolf M. Dekker & Lotte C. van de Pol, *The Tradition of Female Transvestism in Early Modern Europe* (N. Y.: St. Martin's Press, 1989).

[147] Margot H. King, "The Desert Mothers Revisited: The Mothers of the Diocese of Liege," *Vox Benedictina*, 5 (no. 4), 325-354 (1988, Oct.). Available online at http://www.peregrina.com/matrologia/ desertmothers2.html.

[148] For more on Jemima Wilkinson's life see Herbert Wisbey, Jr., *Pioneer Prophetess: Jemima Wilkinson, the Publick Universal Friend* (Ithica, NY: Cornell Univ. Press, 1964). Cf. the less reliable (and often hostile) work by David Hudson, *Memoir of Jemima Wilkinson, A Preacheress of the Eighteenth Century, etc.* (Bath, N. Y.: R. L. Underhill & Co., 1844).

[149] This life-turning event has been variously reported and interpreted. It is clear she became ill, though the nature of the sickness—whether physical or psychological— has been debated. The duration and seriousness of the illness likewise have been debated, with some claiming it was only a few hours and followed by a quick recovery. Other accounts say she was perceived dead, placed in a coffin, and only returned to the community of the living after someone heard her knocking on the inside of her casket. It is Jemima's conviction that she died, ascended to heaven, and returned that matters, whatever the actual facts of the case. This conviction changed her life.

[150] John H. Martin, "Jemima Wilkinson," *The Crooked Lake Review*, Issue 137 (2005, Fall). This is chapter 5 of his *Saints, Sinners and Reformers. The Burned-Over District Re-Visited*, the entirety of which was published in this online periodical. Accessed online at http://www.crookedlakereview.com/books/saints_sinners/martin5.html.

[151] Catherine A. Brekus, *Strangers & Pilgrims. Female Preaching in America, 1740-1843* (Chapel Hill, NC: Univ. of North Carolina Press, 1998), p. 90.

[152] For more on Sara Edmonds/Frank Thompson, see Seymour Reit, *Behind Rebel Lines: The Incredible Story of Emma Edmonds, Civil War Spy.* (N. Y.: Harcourt, 1991). Sara's own account can be found in Emma Edmonds, *Nurse and Spy in the Union Army: The Adventures and Experiences of a Woman in Hospitals, Camps, and Battle-Fields* (Hartford, CT: W. S. Williams & Co., 1865).

[153] Elizabeth Spearing & A. C. Spearing, "Introduction," in E. Spearing & A. C. Spearing (Translators), *Julian of Norwich. Revelations of Divine Love* (N. Y.: Penguin Classics, 1998), p. vii.

[154] Mother Julian's mystical writings have been translated; see Julian of Norwich, *Showings*, trans. Edmund Colledge & James Walsh (N. Y.: Paulist Press, 1978).

[155] Julie Bokser, "Sor Juana's Rhetoric of Silence," *Rhetoric Review, 25* (no. 1), 5-21 (2006), p. 12. There are a number of fine books on Sor Juana de la Cruz. See, for example, Gerard Flynn, *Sor Juana Ines De La Cruz* (N. Y.: Twayne Publishers, 1971). Sor

Juana de la Cruz's story also can be found online at http://www. write-page.com/others/sorjuana.htm or, at http://oregonstate.edu/instruct/phl302/ philosophers/cruz.html.

Q.70 Notes

[156] For a biography of Mother Ann Lee, see F. W. Evans, *Shakers Compendium* (1859), accessed online at http://www.bible.ca/cr-shakers.htm#CHAPXI. Cf. Lawrence Foster, *Religion and Sexuality: Three American Communal Experiments of the Nineteenth Century* (N. Y.: Oxford University Press, 1981).

[157] Nardi Reeder Champion, *Mother Ann Lee* (), pp. 126-135.

[158] Donald Cozzens, *Freeing Celibacy* (Collegeville, MN: Liturgical Press, 2006), p. 14.

[159] See "A Hymn to Inana for Iddin-Dagan (Idin-Dagan A)," lines 60-68 (ETCSL Translation: t.2.5.3.1) in Black, Cunningham, Fluckiger-Hawker, Robson, & Zólyomi, *The Electronic Text Corpus of Sumerian Literature* (1998-2005). Available from the Electronic Text Corpus of Sumerian Literature website, maintained by the Oriental Institute of the University of Oxford (2005 update). Accessed online at http://etcsl.orinst.ox.ac.uk/ cgi-bin/etcsl.cgi?text=t.2.5.3.1.

[160] Pierre Dufour, *Histoire de la prostitution chez tous les peuples du monde depuis l'antiquité la plus reculée jusqu'à nos jours* (6 vols., Paris, 1851-3; 8 vols., Brussels, 1861).

[161] Fritz Graf, "Transvestism, Ritual," in S. Hornblower & A. Spawforth (Eds.), *The Oxford Classical Dictionary*, 3rd ed. (N. Y.: Oxford Univ. Press, 1996), p. 1547.

[162] See, for example, the depiction of the priests of the Syrian goddess offered in Apuleius, *Metamorphosis*, VIII, in Jack Lindsay (Trans.), *The Golden Ass by Apuleius* (Bloomington: Indiana Univ. Press, 1962), p. 181. Also see the description of the *Enarees* in Herodotus, *The Histories* (rev. ed.), translated by Aubrey de Selincourt (N. Y.: Penguin Books, 1972), pp. 84, 292. Cf., in the Hippocratic tradition, the treatise *Airs, Waters, Places* (§§20-22), which offers a more extended consideration of the Scythian people and the Enaree (or 'Anarieis'), noting their effeminate dress; see J. Chadwick & W. N. Mann (translators), "Airs, Waters, Places," in G. E. R.Lloyd (Ed.), *Hippocratic Writings*, pp. 148-169 (N. Y.: Penguin Books, 1983), p. 166. Finally, note the portrait offered of the presiding priest of the Alcis in Tacitus, *Germania*, §43, in A. R. Birley (Trans.), *Tacitus. Agricola and Germany* (N. Y.: Oxford Univ. Press, 1999), p. 59.

[163] Jean E. Howard, "Cross-dressing, the Theater, and Gender Struggle in Early Modern England," in L. Ferris (Ed.), *Crossing the Stage: Controversies on Cross-dressing*, pp. 20-46 (N. Y.: Routledge, 1993), p. 25.

[164] Philip Jenkins, *Pedophiles and Priests: Anatomy of a Contemporary Crisis* (N. Y.: Oxford Univ. Press, 1996), p. 23.

[165] Thorstein Veblen, *The Theory of the Leisure Class* (London: Macmillan, 1911; original work published 1899), p. 181.

[166] Bettina Arnold, "'Sein und Werdern': Gender as Process in Mortuary Ritual," in S. M. Nelson & M. Rosen-Ayalon (Eds.), *In Pursuit of Gender. Worldwide Archaeological Approaches*, pp. 239-256 (Walnut Creek, CA: AltaMira Press, 2002), p. 250.

[167] Daniel Boyarin, *Unheroic Conduct: The Rise of Heterosexuality and the Invention of the Jewish Man* (Berkeley: Univ. of California Press, 1997), p. 26.

[168] Ibid, p. 142.

[169] Of course, this should not be read as suggesting either that men go into the priesthood or become monks in order to sexually prey upon others. Rather, the special gendered status accorded them helps strip away the conventional expectations and social safeguards used to regulate sexuality, making the use of the religious office for sexual improprieties easier than they might otherwise be.

[170] See Valérie Pirie, *The Triple Crown: An Account of the Papal Conclaves from the Fifteenth Century to the Present Day* (N. Y.: G. P. Putnam's Sons, 1936), p. 23f. Accessed online at Pickle-Publishing.com at http://www.pickle-publishing.com/papers/triple-crown-paul-ii.htm.

[171] See R. H. F. Scott (Trans.), *The Transvestite Memoirs of the Abbe de Choisy* (London: Peter Owen Ltd., 1973).

[172] The material here is largely reproduced from volume 3 of this work. For more information, see Charles d'Eon de Beaumont, *The Maiden of Tonnerre: The Vicissitudes of the Chevalier and the Chevalière d'Eon*, Edited and translated by Roland A. Champagne, Nina Ekstein, & Gary Kates. (Baltimore: The Johns Hopkins University Press, 2001)/

[173] Havelock Ellis, *Studies in the Psychology of Sex*, 2 vols. (N. Y.: Random House, 1941-1942; original work was published 1905-1928). See Vol. II, Part Two: 'Eonism and Other Supplementary Studies.' The work of Ellis is reviewed in the answer to Q. 95.

[174] The Beaumont Society was founded in 1966 and today claims to be the UK's "largest and longest established transgendered support group." The Society maintains a website and was accessed online at http://www.beaumontsociety.org.uk/.

[175] This volume was written by d'Eon's friend La Fortelle.

[176] For more on Chevalier d'Eon's life, see Charles d'Eon de Beaumont, *The Maiden of Tonnerre: The Vicissitudes of the Chevalier and the Chevalière d'Eon*, Eds. and trans. Roland A. Champagne, Nina Ekstein, & Gary Kates. (Baltimore: The Johns Hopkins University Press, 2001). This work provides an introduction for context, together with translations of various works by d'Eon, including his never published autobiography *La Pucelle de Tonnerre*. For an interesting theatrical treatment, see the comedic play by Mark Brownell, *Monsieur d'Eon* (Theatre Communications Group, 2001). Among numerous online sites are a biography accessed at http://www.kirjasto. sci.fi/deon.htm and the French language site http://archives.chez.tiscali.fr/eon1.html.

[177] Gary Kates, *Monsieur d'Eon Is a Woman: A Tale of Political Intrigue and Sexual Masquerade* (N. Y.: Basic Books, 1995). The Johns Hopkins University Press published a paperback edition of this book in 2001. Lest d'Eon be viewed as hopelessly disturbed in his reasoning, cf. the note in the much more contemporary account by Shere Hite: "A large part of teenage boys' 'mean and nasty' crazes are attempts by them to deal with their culturally imposed guilt; i.e., if one is 'bad' already, one might as well glorify being an outlaw, being really tough and cruel, etc. Thus, the glorification of being mean and nasty as being 'really male' (for example, as frequently seen on MTV and in children's

monster or war toy commercials) comes because men (by definition) can never be 'good.'" Shere Hite, *Women in Love. A Cultural Revolution in Progress* (N. Y.: Alfred A. Knopf, 1987), p. 689n.

[178] Gary Kates, "Introduction," in Charles d'Eon de Beaumont, *The Maiden of Tonnerre: The Vicissitudes of the Chevalier and the Chevalière d'Eon*, Eds. and trans. Roland A. Champagne, Nina Ekstein, & Gary Kates. (Baltimore: The Johns Hopkins University Press, 2001), p. ix. Concerning Joan of Arc, see her story in the answer to Q. 68.

[179] Gary Kates, "Introduction," Beaumont, *The Maiden of* Tonnerre, p. xii.

[180] Gary Kates, *Monsieur d'Eon Is a Woman: A Tale of Political Intrigue and Sexual Masquerade* (N. Y.: Basic Books, 1995).

[181] There are numerous materials available on Father Miguel. See Ann Ball, *Blessed Miguel Pro 20th- century Mexican Martyr* (Rockford: Tan Books & Publishers, 1996). Online materials were accessed at a number of sites, including http://puffin. creighton.edu/jesuit/pro/. For a brief biography, see Brother Dominic, *Padre Pro. A Modern Martyr* accessed online at http://www.catholicism.org/pages/pro.htm.

[182] For more on Lee Frances Heller's life and work, see Becky Allison, *In Memoriam. Lee Frances Heller, April 5, 1919-May 19, 2000* accessed online at http://www. drbecky.com/lee.html. Also see Rachel Miller, *Lee Frances Heller: God's Gift to the Transgendered*, accessed online at http://www.whosoever. org/v6i4/ miller.html.

[183] Lee Frances Heller and Friends, *By the Grace of God: Writings for Families, Friends, and Clergy*, edited by Julie Ann Johnson (Wheaton, IL: SPP Publications, 2001).

[184] See Christopher Morgan, *Secret TG Group Shakes Up Church* (1998, July). Available online at http://www.transgender.org/tg/tvals/tvjul98.htm as part of the Tennessee Vals Online Edition website. Tennessee Vals is a support group for transgendered people.

Q. 71 Notes

[185] For more on the history of Carnival, see Chris Humphrey, *The Politics of Carnival: Festive Misrule in Medieval England* (Manchester: Manchester Univ. Press, 2001). There is also some interesting material in Philip J. Deloria, *Playing Indian* (New Haven: Yale Univ. Press, 1998).

[186] Mikhail Bahktin, *Rabelais and His World*, translated by H. Iswolsky (Bloomington: Indiana Univ. Press, 1984), p. 7.

[187] Cf. Freud's remark about how seriously children take play; there is no reason— or evidence—to suggest festive adults are any less intense or serious. See Sigmund Freud, "The Relation of the Poet to Daydreaming," in S. Freud, *On Creativity and the Unconscious*, translated by J. Riviere (N. Y.: Harper & Row, 1958).

[188] Erik Erikson, *Identity and the Life Cycle* (N. Y.: W. W.Norton & Co., 1980; original work 1959), p. 90; cf. p. 91 on the remastering of experience.

[189] Raymond Cattell, *Personality. A Systematic Theoretical and Factual Study* (N. Y.:McGraw-Hill, 1950), p. 430.

[190] Ibid, p. 576.

[191] Ibid, pp. 430-431; cf. p. 251 on compensatory play, which is discussed similarly to Erikson's notion of play for remastering experience.

[192] So do experiences such as obtained in theater (see the answer to Q. 44).

[193] Daniel E. Burlyne, *Conflict, Arousal, and Curiosity* (N. Y.: McGraw-Hill, 1960), p. 251.

[194] Alan McGlashan, *The Savage and Beautiful Country. The Secret Life of the Mind* (N. Y.: Houghton-Mifflin, 1967). McGlashan is a Jungian analyst.

[195] Ibid. Excerpt available online at http://home.earthlink.net/~edatkeson/ Alliesart.html.

[196] Cf. Lesley Peterson, "Defects Redressed: Margaret Cavendish Aspires to Motley," *Early Modern Literary Studies, 8* (Special Issue 14), 1-30 (2004). Accessed online at http://purl.oclc.org/emls/si-14/petemotl.html.

[197] For more information, see E. K. Chambers, *The Mediaeval Stage.* 2 vols. (Mineola, NY: Dover, 1996). N.B.: The two volumes are bound together as one. Cf. Harvey Cox, *The Feast of Fools* (Cambridge: Harvard Univ. Press, 1969) for a novel application of the idea of the feast to modern times.

[198] Members of Dijon's *Mère Folle* were occasionally involved in acts of social protest with political import. For example, male members dressed in female disguise in 1576 acted to humiliate a royal official for both his personal and professional improprieties, including destroying Burgundy's forests for his own personal profit. In 1630, again disguised as women, members attacked royal tax officials.

[199] For more information, see Natalie Zemon Davis, *Society and Culture in Early Modern France* (Stanford, CA: Stanford Univ. Press, 1975). See especially pp. 124-140.

[200] Gianna E. Isreal, "Coping with the Holidays," *Gianna Israel Gender Library* (1998). Accessed online at http://www.firelily.com/gender/gianna/holidays.html.

[201] Elizabeth Pleck, "The Making of the Domestic Occasion: The History of Thanksgiving in the United States," *Journal of Social History, 33* (no. 4) 773-789 (1999), p. 776.

[202] Ibid, p. 775.

[203] Ibid. Cf. W. D. Howells, *Through the Eye of the Needle* (N.Y.: 1907), p. 49.

[204] Ibid.

[205] Ibid, pp. 776-778.

Q. 72 Notes

[206] For a brief recounting of Christian clerical reactions to acts they viewed as deviating from accepted gender roles, see David F. Greenberg, *The Construction of Homosexuality* (Chicago: Univ. of Chicago Press, 1988), chapter 6, 'Feudalism.'

[207] See Samuel Laeuchli, *Sexuality and Power: The Emergence of Canon Law at Elvira* (Phila.: Temple Univ. Press, 1972). The translation of canons 57 and 67 is from Ken Pennington's *The Council of Elvira, ca, 306* webpage, accessed online at http://faculty.cua.edu/pennington/Canon%20Law/ElviraCanons.htm.

[208] Though it is tempting to read into this prohibition some sense that clothing can be viewed as a symbolic extension and surrogate for the self, that is likely not what was behind it.

[209] *The Canons of the Holy Fathers Assembled at Gangra*, in A. Roberts & J. Donaldson (Eds.), *Nicene and Post-Nicene Fathers, Series II, Volume XIV.* (Grand Rapids: Wm. B. Eerdmans reprint of late 19th century work published by T. & T. Clark). Available online at http://www.ccel.org/fathers/NPNF2-14/2ancyra/Ganlet.htm (Letter), and http://www.ccel.org/fathers/NPNF2-14/2ancyra/Gancns.htm (Canons & Epilogue). The ancient epitome to Canon XIII states simply: "Whatever women wear men's clothes, anathema to them." To be "anathema" meant to be put out of the communion of the Church, which meant to be cut off from salvation.

[210] Anathema was a ritual 'cursing' of the offender; see Galatians 1:8, 'Let him be accursed' (*anathema*).

[211] Rather ironically, the vestments of the male priest came in time to be themselves regarded by some as effeminate. Cf. Jean E. Howard, "Cross-Dressing, the Theater, and Gender Struggle in Early Modern England," in Lesley Ferris (Ed.), *Crossing the Stage: Controversies on Cross-Dressing*, pp. 20-46 (N.Y.: Routledge, 1993), p. 25.

[212] Greenberg, p. 292f. Effeminate behavior by males was an offense far more upsetting and dangerous than females reaching upward through gender violations, though the latter merited clerical concern as well.

[213] Cited in Joan Cadden, *Meanings of Sex Difference in the Middle Ages* (N. Y.: Cambridge Univ. Press, 1993), p. 160.

[214] Kate Chedgzoy, "Impudent Women: Carnival and Gender in Early Modern Culture," *The Glasgow Review, no. 1* (1993). Accessed online at http://www.arts.gla.ac.uk/SESLL/STELLA/COMET/ glasgrev/issue1/chefgz.htm.

[215] Alan Hunt, *Governance of the Consuming Passions: A History of Sumptuary Law* (N. Y.: Macmillan, 1996).

[216] Jean E. Howard, "Cross-Dressing, the Theater, and Gender Struggle in Early Modern England," in Lesley Ferris (Ed.), *Crossing the Stage: Controversies on Cross-Dressing*, pp. 20-46 (N.Y.: Routledge, 1993), p. 21.

[217] Terry Castle, "The Culture of Travesty: Sexuality and Masquerade in Eighteenth-Century England," in G. S. Rousseau & R. Porter (Eds.), *Sexual Underworlds of the Enlightenment*, pp. 156-180 (Chapel Hill: Univ. of North Carolina Press, 1988), p. 163.

[218] John Wijngaards (Trans.), *Codex Iuris Canonici* (Freiburg: Herder, 1918). Also see, Edward Peters, *The 1917 or Pio-Benedictine Code of Canon Law in English Translation with Extensive Scholarly Apparatus* (S. F.: Ignatius Press, 2001). Canon 1262, § 2 is available online at http://www.womenpriests. org/traditio/cod_1917.htm.

[219] Pope Benedict XV, *Sacra Propediem*, §19 (1921, Jan. 6). Papal encyclical available online at http://www.papalencyclicals.net/Ben15/b15sapro.htm. Cf. the remark by Pope Pius XI a few years later: ". . . there is a sad forgetfulness of Christian modesty especially in the life and the dress of women. . . . ." Pope Pius XI, *Miserentissimus Redemptor. On Reparation to the Sacred Heart*, §16 (1928, May). Papal encyclical avaliable online at http://www.papalencyclicals.net /Pius11/P11miser.Htm.

[220] "Some Directives of the Magisterium on Christian Modesty." Part of *Our lady's Library.* (Articles, essays and stories from the pages of *The Fatima Crusader* Magazine.) Available online at http://www.fatima.org/library/cr57pg53.html.

[221] Pope Pius XII, *Counsel to Teaching Sisters*, §23 (1951, Sept. 15). Papal encyclical accessed online at http://www.papalencyclicals.net/Pius12/P12TCHRS.HTM.

[222] Pope Pius XII, "Moral Problems in Fashion Design" (speech delivered November 8, 1957 to the Congress of the Latin Union of High Fashion). The material quoted is in the following excerpt: "Yet no matter how broad and changeable the relative morals of styles may be, there is always an absolute norm to be kept after having heard the admonition of conscience warning against approaching danger: style must never be a proximate occasion of sin." This, and other comments, found in Gregory P. Lloyd, National Coalition of Clergy and Laity, *Modesty in the Light of . . . the Church's Teaching* (n.d.). Available online at http://www.veil-of-innocence.org/ modesty.html.

[223] Giuseppe Cardinal Siri, *Notification Concerning Men's Dress Worn By Women* (1960, June 12). Accessed online at http://olrl.org/virtues/pants.shtml.

[224] Ibid.

[225] Pope Paul VI, *Ecclesiae Sanctae*, §18 (1966, Aug. 6). Papal encyclical accessed online at http://www.papalencyclicals.net/Paul06/p6ecclss.htm.

[226] Bishop Antonio de Castro-Mayer, "Some Directives of the Magisterium on Christian Modesty," taken from *The Fatima Crusader* (1998, Spring/Summer). Accessed online at http://olrl.org/virtues/modcrus.html.

[227] Fr. Robert Auman, "The *ASK FATHER* Question Box," *Catholic Online Forum* (2001, May 6). The entire response accessed online at http://oldforum.catholic.org/ discussion/messages /41/16907.html?989165630.

[228] Cardinal Joseph Ratzinger, *Letter to the Bishops of the Catholic Church on the Pastoral Care of Homosexual Persons* (Vatican: Congregation for the Doctrine of the Faith, 1986), §3. Accessed online at http://www.vatican.va/roman_curia/congregations/cfaith/ documents/rc_con_cfaith_doc_19861001_homosexual-persons_en.html.

[229] Ibid.

[230] Ibid, §§8-9, 14.

[231] Cardinal Joseph Ratzinger, *Considerations Regarding Proposals to Give Legal Recognition to Unions Between Homosexual Persons* (Vatican: Congregation for the Doctrine of the Faith, 2003), §1. Accessed online at http://www.vatican.va/roman_curia/congregations/cfaith/documents/rc_con_cfaith_doc_20030731_homosexual-unions_en.html.

232 Ibid, §4.

233 Ibid, §5.

234 Ibid, §§5-9.

235 Ibid, §11. For a critique of the Church's position from a legal standpoint, see D. Ø. Endsjø, "Lesbian, Gay, Bisexual, and Transgender Rights and the Religious Relativism of Human Rights," *Human Rights Review, 6* (no. 2), 102-110 (2005), p. 107f. Endsjø (p. 108) observes of the document on same-sex unions that, "Here the Church not only clearly trespasses beyond their own rights to religious freedom by trying to enforce their values on people who are not Catholic, but, moreover, finds itself in direct opposition with the United Nations Human Rights Committee. . . ."

236 Michael Paulsen, "Pope Says Same-Sex Unions Are False," *The Boston Globe* [online] (7 June, 2005). Accessed online at boston.com news at http://www.boston .com/news/specials/gay_marriage/articles/2005/06/07/pope_says_gay_unions_are_fa lse/. Cf. the *Catechism of the Catholic Church*, Part 2, §2, Ch. 3, Art. 7, Paragraphs 1603- 1605. Accessed online at http://www.scborromeo.org/ccc/p2s2c3a7.htm#1603.

237 Boswell's work is treated briefly in the answer to Q. 74. See John Boswell, *Christianity, Social Tolerance, and Homosexuality* (Chicago: Univ. of Chicago Press, 1980). Also see John Boswell, *Same-Sex Unions in Premodern Europe* (N. Y.: Villard Books, 1994).

238 Daniel A. Helminiak, *What the Bible Really Says About Homosexuality (Millennium Edition)* (Tajique, NM: Alamo Square Press, 2000).

239 Nine priests in the Phoenix Diocese in Arizona signed a declaration affirming their stance that homosexuality is neither a sin nor a sickness. In 2004 the new bishop of the diocese, Bishop Thomas Olmsted, ordered the signers under his jurisdiction to remove their names from the document. Two previous bishops had chosen not to take any action regarding the declaration. By early 2006, six of the nine signers reported they had been forced out of their positions.

240 "Signs of the Times: Vatican Issues Norms Prohibiting Transsexuals in Religious Orders," *America. The National Catholic Weekly, 188* (no. 5) (2003, Feb. 17), accessed online at http://www.americamagazine.org/catholicnews.cfm?articleTypeID= 29&textID=2780&issueID=422. Cf. "Sex-Change Operations Ruled Invalid By Vatican," *Catholic World News* (31 Jan., 2003). Accessed online at http://www.cwnews.com/ news/viewstory.cfm?recnum=19829.

241 *Catechism of the Catholic Church*, Paragraph 2297. Accessed online at http://www. vatican.va/archive/ccc_css/archive/catechism/p3s2c2a5.htm.

242 Fr. William P. Saunders, "Straight Answers: The Morality of 'Sex Change' Operations," *Catholic Herald* (20 Oct., 2005). Accessed online at http://www. catholicherald.com/saunders/05ws/ws051020.htm.

Q. 73 Notes

243 See, for example, Wolfgang Lienemann, "Churches and Homosexuality: An Overview of Recent Official Church Statements on Sexual Orientation," *The Ecumenical Review, 50* (no. 1), 7-21 (1998). Also see B. A. Robinson, *Policies of 45 Christian Denomina-*

tions on Homosexuality (Ontario Consultants on Religious Tolerance, 1996-2003), sponsored by Religious Tolerance.org, accessed online at http://www. religioustolerance.org/hom_chur2.htm. Especially see *Report of Task Force on Homosexuality* (Council for Christian Colleges and Universities, 2001), accessed online at http://www.cccu.org/news/newsID.23, parentNav.Archives/news_past_detail.asp. For a book length treatment of various aspects, see Jeffrey S. Siker (Ed.), *Homosexuality in the Church: Both Sides of the Debate* (Louisville,KY: Westminster John Knox Press, 1994).

[244] Consider, for example, the differing stances taken by two Protestant evangelical authors: Michael Vasey, *Strangers and Friends: A New Exploration of Homosexuality and the Bible* (London: Hodder & Stoughton, 1995). Stanley J. Grenz, *Welcoming But Not Affirming: An Evangelical Approach to Homosexuality* (Louisville, KY: Westminster John Knox, 1998).

[245] For an overview, see Pim Pronk, *Against Nature? Types of Moral Argumentation Regarding Homosexuality*, translated by J. Vriend (Grand Rapids, MI: Wm. B. Eerdmans, 1983).

[246] Such authorities can range from a local elder or pastor, to the Pope or ecclesiastical conferences, councils, canons, or policy statements. On the last of these, see the references in note 1. On historical Church councils, see Derrick S. Bailey, *Homosexuality and the Western Christian Tradition* (London: Longmans, Green, 1955). Cf. John Boswell, *Christianity, Social Tolerance, and Homosexuality* (Chicago: Univ. of Chicago Press, 1980). Also cf. Bernadette J. Brooten, *Love Between Women: Early Christian Responses to Female Homoeroticism* (Chicago: Univ. of Chicago Press, 1996). Also see Paul Halsall, *Homosexuality and Catholicism Bibliography: Section 1 Basic Data* (n.d.), accessed online at http://www.fordham.edu/ halsall/pwh/lgbcathbib1.html.

[247] Fraser Watts, "Transsexualism and the Church," *Theology & Sexuality, 9* (no. 1), 63-85 (2002), p. 63.

[248] *Catechism of the Catholic Church*, Paragraph 2333. Accessed online at http://www. scborromeo.org/ccc/p3s2c2a6.htm#I.

[249] *Exegesis* is the exercise of a process using tools meant to draw out from a source its intended meaning. Reading a desired meaning into a text is disrespectful of that text and its author.

[250] George Ricker Berry, *Interlinear Greek-English New Testament* (Grand Rapids,MI: Baker Book House, 1994 printing of 1897 edition), p. 444.

[251] An example of appeal to this text is offered in the tract written by Horace F. Dean, *PANTS-SUITS and Christian Women. A Reasoned Consideration Based on the Bible.* Available online at http://www.llano.net/baptist/pantsuits.htm.
As seen in the consideration of Deuteronomy 22:5, the meaning of the text is less self-evident than many would like. When this verse is set in a larger theological context appeal is made to other scriptural texts. The success of such ventures tends to rest in the eyes of the beholder.

[252] Anonymous, "'I Was a Transsexual Male . . .': A Testimony to the Grace of God," *Journal of Biblical Counseling, 13* (no. 3), 30-35 (1995), p. 30.

253 Ibid, pp. 30-32.

254 Ibid, pp. 32-35. Cf. the testimony of Sy Rogers, *Transsexuality: My Testimony*, abridged at the affinity.org.uk website accessed online at http://www.affinity.org.uk/teams/article/transgender_and_ cross_dressing/.

255 'Anonymous' does not offer any scriptural text to substantiate his feeling these things were wrong. What he does provide, however, is interesting: scary incidents involving three male strangers on drugs and an encounter with the police lead directly to his confession of sin. Christian friends supporting a renunciation of the desires and behavior weigh in as well. There is also brief appeal to the theological argument that God as Creator meant him to be male since he was born that way, so his desire to be female was merely rebellion against God, since (presumably) God does not make mistakes. What is clear in the testimony is that feelings and circumstances triumph over any effort to provide reason and evidence. This is a common approach among Christians who prioritize experiential faith (based on feelings and desirable outcomes) over what is often seen as a secular desire to place human reasoning and dependence on science over God's revelation, which is contained in the Bible and subjectively mediated by the Holy Spirit.

256 'Anonymous' notes in passing (p. 32) that his release from police custody was predicated on the condition of counseling with the school psychiatrist. Nothing is said about whether such counseling occurred or how it went.

257 Randall Wayne, *Crossdressing and Christianity: A REAL Man's Struggle* (2003). Available online at http://www.stonewallrevisited.com/pages/randall_w.html. Or, at http://www.firststone.org/ testimonies/ Cross_Dressing/cross_dressing.htm.

258 Ibid.

259 The material used in answering this question draws on writings by the laity—Christians who are not ordained clergy or professional religious scholars. For Christian clerical and academic views relevant to the subject please see the answers to Q. 61-67, 72.

260 Ronald L. Conte Jr., "Proper Clothing for Catholic Women," *Catholic Planet*. This website is owned and edited by Conte. Available online at http://www.catholicplanet.com/women/dress.htm.

261 Ibid.

262 Daniel R. Heimbach, *True Sexual Morality. Recovering Biblical Standards for a Culture in Crisis* (Wheaton, IL: Crossway, 2004), pp. 197-198; quote is from p. 198.

263 Ibid, pp. 198-199; quote is from p. 198.

264 *Are we to love the sinner, but hate the sin?* (Got Questions Ministries, 2002-2007). Accessed online at http://www.gotquestions.org/love-sinner-hate-sin.html.

265 David H. Barlow, Gene G. Abel, & Edward B. Blanchard, "Gender Identity Change in a Transsexual: An Exorcism," *Archives of Sexual Behavior*, 6, 387-395 (1977). It is worth noting that in the mid-1970s the world of mental health professionals more

uniformly regarded transsexualism as a psychological disorder in which prevention or cure were highly desired. This sentiment is not as widely shared today.

[266] This period among evangelical Christians in the U.S. was marked by eschatological fervor, including a keen interest in demons and exorcisms.

[267] Jerry Leach, "Jerry's Credentials/Standards for Ministry," *Reality Resources* website. Accessed online at http://www.realityresources.com/credentials.htm.

[268] Jerry Leach, "Care-Givers and Crossdressers," *Reality Resources* website. Accessed online at http://www.realityresources.com/caregiver.htm.

[269] Ibid.

[270] See the True Freedom Trust website accessed online at http://www. truefreedomtrust.co.uk/.

Q. 74 Notes

[271] Robert Hamilton Simpson, "How to Be Fashionably Queer: Reminding the Church of the Importance of Sexual Stories," *Theology & Sexuality, 11* (no. 2), 97-108 (2004), p. 99.

[272] Fraser Watts, "Transsexualism and the Church," *Theology & Sexuality, 9* (no. 1), 63-85 (2002), p. 73.

[273] Wardell B. Pomeroy, "A Report on the Histories of 25 Transsexuals," *Transactions of the New York Academy of Sciences (Series 2), 29*, 444-447 (1966).

[274] Ronald E. Hellman, Richard Green, James L. Gray, & Katherine Williams, "Childhood Sexual Identity, Childhood Religiosity, and 'Homophobia' as Influences in the Development of Transsexualism, Homosexuality, and Heterosexuality," *Archives of General Psychiatry, 38*, 910-915 (1981). The authors suggest transsexualism may be a way of resolving the conflict between the individual's religious beliefs and homosexual orientation.

[275] Walter O. Bockting & Charles Cesaretti, "Spirituality, Transgender Identity, and Coming Out," *Journal of Sex Education and Therapy, 26* (no. 4), 291-300 (2001).

[276] Melissa M. Wilcox, "When Shiela's a Lesbian: Religious Individualism Among Lesbian, Gay, Bisexual, and Transgender Christians," *Sociology of Religion, 63* (no. 4), 497-513 (2002), p. 504. Also see Melissa M. Wilcox, "Dancing on the Fence: Researching Lesbian, Gay, Bisexual, and Transgender Christians," in J. V. Spickard, J. S. Landres, & M. B. McGuire (Eds.), *Personal Knowledge and Beyond*, pp. 47-60 (N. Y.: New York University Press, 2001).

[277] Suzanne H. Lease, Sharon G. Horne, & Nicole Noffsinger-Frazier, "Affirming Faith Experiences and Psychological Health for Caucasian Lesbian, Gay, and Bisexual Individuals," *Journal of Counseling Psychology, 52* (no. 3), 378-388 (2005), p. 378.

[278] L. William Countryman & M. R. Ritley, *Gifted by Otherness. Gay and Lesbian Christians in the Church* (Harrisburg, PA: Morehouse Publishing, 2001), p. 4.

[279] Ibid, p. 5.

[280] For a thorough review of the research and the issues, see Kenneth I. Pargament, *The Psychology of Religion and Coping* (N. Y.: The Guilford Press, 1997).

[281] Lease, Horne & Noffsinger-Frazier, p. 378.

[282] Ibid, p. 384. This study's participants included Christians and members of other religious groups.

[283] Wilcox, p. 500.

[284] Lease, Horne, & Noffsinger-Frazier, p. 379.

[285] Wilcox, p. 501.

[286] Ibid, pp. 503-506.

[287] Ibid, pp. 506-512; quote is from p. 511.

[288] Julie Ann Johnson, "Foreword," in J. A. Johnson (Ed.), *By the Grace of God. Lee Frances Heller and Friends: Writings for Families, Friends, and Clergy*, pp. 17-19 (Wheaton, IL: SSP Publications, 2001), p. 17.

[289] Lee Frances Heller, "Is God Against Us?" in J. A. Johnson (Ed.), *By the Grace of God. Lee Frances Heller and Friends: Writings for Families, Friends, and Clergy*, pp. 84-88 (Wheaton, IL: SSP Publications, 2001), p. 87. This book is henceforth cited as *By the Grace of God*.

[290] Wilcox, p. 504.

[291] Watts, p. 73.

[292] The alleged eunuch status of Daniel has been debated, but the weight of evidence is in favor of it. See Daniel 1:3-6 (Ashpenaz, under whom Daniel was placed, was the master of the palace eunuchs). Also see II Kings 20:18 and Isaiah 39:5-7 for pertinent information.

[293] J. David Hester, "Eunuchs and the Post-Gender Jesus: Matthew 19:12 and Transgressive Sexualities," *Journal for the Study of the New Testament, 28* (no. 1), 13-40 (2005), p. 18.

[294] Eusebius Pamphilius, *Ecclesiastical History*, VI.8.1, in P. Schaff (Ed.), *Eusebius Pamphilius: Church History, Life of Constantine, Oration in Praise of Constantine* [*Nicene and Post-Nicene Fathers*, vol. 1] (N. Y.: Christian Literature Publishing Co., 1890), p. 254.

[295] Ibid.

[296] For examples of these, and an extended discussion, see John Boswell, *Same-Sex Unions in Premodern Europe* (N. Y.: Villard Books, 1994).

[297] Stacey Schlau, "Following Saint Teresa: Early Modern Women and Religious Authority," *MLN, 117* (no. 2), 286-309 (2002), p. 287.

[298] Ibid, p. 288.

[299] We must not forget that some Christians—regardless of where they stand on the rightness or wrongness of transgender behavior—disagree with this formula by maintaining that God both hates the sin *and* the sinner. See, for example, noted Reformed

theologian John H. Gerstner's arguments at the webpage *Does God Love the Sinner and Hate Only His Sin?* (The-highway.com, 1996-2007). Accessed online at http://www.the-highway.com/lovesinner_Gerstner.html.

[300] Kenneth W. Collins, *Hate the Sin, But Love the Sinner* (1995-2007), at the www.kencollins.com website, accessed online at http://www.kencollins.com/disc-31.htm.

[301] Janet R. Jakobsen & Ann Pellegrini, *Love the Sin: Sexual Regulation and the Limits of Religious Tolerance* (N. Y.: New York Univ. Press, 2003), p. 1.

[302] Ibid, p. 14.

[303] Ibid, p. 44.

[304] Ibid, p. 45.

[305] Countryman & Ritley, p. 4.

[306] For a brief and accessible treatment by a Roman Catholic priest, see Daniel A. Helminiak, "Scripture, Sexual Ethics, and the Nature of Christianity," *Pastoral Psychology, 47* (no. 4), 261-271 (1999).

[307] Interestingly, psychologist George Weinberg in 1972 listed 'religiosity' as one of five motivations for homophobia (a term he coined); the others are reaction formation, repressed envy, threat to social values, and fear of death. See his *Society and the Healthy Homosexual* (N. Y.: St. Martin's Press, 1972).

[308] An example of this line of reasoning follows:

> The story of Adam and Eve, in the literary context in which the redaction of Genesis has given it to us, is of the greatest significance in shaping Christian thought; for there the Yahwist interest in marriage as relationship ("a man leaves his father and his mother and is united to his wife") is interpreted by the Priestly interest in sexual differentiation as creational order ("male and female he created them").

See Oliver O'Donovan, "Transsexualism and Christian Marriage," *The Journal of Religious Ethics, 11* (no. 1), 135-162 (1983), p. 141.

[309] Augustine, *Against the Manichees*, I.19.30, in R. J. Teske (Translator), *Saint Augustine on Genesis. Two Books on Genesis Against the Manicheans and On the Literal Interpretation of Genesis: An Unfinished Book* (Washington, D. C.: Catholic Univ. Press, 1991), p. 77f. Cf. Augustine, *City of God*, Bk. XXII.

[310] Daniel A. Helminiak, *What the Bible Really Says About Homosexuality (Millennium Edition)* (Tajique, NM: Alamo Square Press, 2000), p. 122.

[311] In fact, what the Fall story does say about sexual relations is entirely in terms of heterosexual consequences directed at the woman (Genesis 3:16): she shall desire her husband, who will rule over her, and she shall experience pain in childbirth. Cf. 1 Timothy 2:13-15.

[312] Phyllis Trible, *God and the Rhetoric of Sexuality* (Phila.: Fortress Press, 1978), p. 80.

313 *Apocalypse of Adam.* This Gnostic text from the Nag Hammadi library accessed online at http://www.webcom.com/gnosis/naghamm/adam.html.

314 Philo of Alexandria, *De Opificio Mundi [On the Creation]*, XXIV.75. Philo (74) argues that God's employment of assistants is necessitated by creating a being of mixed nature—one capable of doing evil. By making human beings in 'our' image, he argues (75), God gets credit for the good people do, while their evil is born by imputation to his assistants.

315 Arguably the greatest of all Christian theologians, St. Augustine, struggled to understand the purpose of Eve's creation, finally concluding it must have reference to procreation.

316 Christians should be especially open to seeing two commandments here inasmuch as elsewhere—as in interpreting the phrase 'in his image and likeness'—early commentators such as St. Augustine wrestled with the difference between two parts of a compound phrase, reasoning that each part must have a purpose or there would be no reason for their presence.

317 See, for example, *Yebamoth* 76a (cf. *Shabbat* 65a, where the characterization is 'women that rub against one another').

318 We must be cautioned again to remember that the Church Fathers had no modern sensibility about sexual orientations. The whole concept likely would have struck them as nonsense. They presumed the procreative use of genitalia as their *sole* purpose, and so all that mattered was how sexual parts fit together to yield offspring. In this light, it is the natural (i.e., procreative) use being exchanged for an unnatural (i.e., nonprocreative) use. Witness, for example, Ambrosiaster's comment on the notion of exchanging natural relations for unnatural:

> For what is it to change the use of nature into a use which is contrary to nature, if not to take away the former and adopt the latter, so that the same part of the body should be used by each of the sexes in a way for which it was not intended? Therefore, if this is the part of the body which they think it is, how could they have changed the natural use of it if they had not had this use given to them by nature?

He takes it as proven that the 'exchange' is along the lines just described. But, in our modern terms, this kind of exchange of use only matters to those who are heterosexual. Ambrosiaster, devoid of any system that classifies people by sexual orientation, applies the text to all people based on a procreative logic that applies only to some people. See Ambrosiaster, *Ambrosiastri Qui Dicitur Commentarius in Epistulas Paulinas*, edited by H. J. Vogels, in *Corpus Scriptorum Ecclesiasticorum Latinorum*, vol. 81.1 (Vienna: Hoelder-Pickler-Tempsky, 1966), p. 51. Ambrosiaster quote from Gerald Bray (Ed.), *Ancient Christian Commentary on Scripture. New Testament, VI. Romans* (Downer's Grove, IL: InterVarsity Press, 1998), p. 46f.

319 John Boswell, *Christianity, Social Tolerance, and Homosexuality* (Chicago: Univ. of Chicago Press, 1980), p. 333.

[320] John Boswell, *Same-Sex Unions in Premodern Europe* (N. Y.: Villard Books, 1994), p. 295. 'N. and N.' stand for 'name and name'—the place to insert the believer's names.

[321] Simpson, p. 102.

[322] Mel White, "Foreword," in Wayne R. Besen, *Anything But Straight: Unmasking the Scandals and Lies Behind the Ex-Gay Myth* (Binghamton, NY: Harrington Park Press, 2003), p. ix. Rev. White is the founder of Soulforce, Inc.; his biography accessed online at http://www.soulforce.org/article/11.

[323] Alison Jasper, "Theology at the Freak Show: St Uncumber and the Discourse of Liberation," *Theology & Sexuality, 11* (no. 2), 43-54 (2004), p. 47.

[324] For one example, showing how a 'queer' reading of the Bible can inform the task of preaching, see Ken Stone, "'Do Not Be Conformed to This World': Queer Reading and the Task of the Preacher," *Theology & Sexuality, 13* (no. 2), 153-166 (2007).

[325] Cf. Simpson, p. 108.

[326] Cindi Jones, *Squirrel Cage* (Mariposa, CA: Plett Stone, 2006), p. 167.

[327] Elisabeth Anne Kellogg, "Transgenderism and 1 Corinthians 6:9-10," in J. A. Johnson (Ed.), *By the Grace of God. Lee Frances Heller and Friends: Writings for Families, Friends, and Clergy*, pp. 331-336 (Wheaton, IL: SSP Publications, 2001), p. 332.

[328] Helminiak, p. 106. He is particularly caustic about the Catholic translation the *New American Bible*, which renders the Greek *arsenokoitai* as 'practicing homosexuals'—a translation conveniently consistent with Catholic teaching since the mid-1970s that it is not being homosexual that is a sin, but the practice of same-sex sexual behaviors is what is wrong. Under strong criticism for this choice, the editors of this version changed the translation to read 'sodomites.'

[329] See Henry George Liddell & Robert Scott, *A Greek-English Lexicon* (Oxford: Clarendon Press, 1996 revision of 1940 ed.), p. 1077.

[330] Fritz Reinecker, *Linguistic Key to the Greek New Testament*, edited by C. Rogers (Grand Rapids, MI: Zondervan, 1982), p. 402.

[331] Robin Scruggs argues that *arsenokoitai* originates in Helenistic Judaism and translates a rabbinic Hebrew phrase, *mishkav zakur*, 'lying with a male.' Scruggs writes, "If the *malakos* points to the effeminate call-boy, then the *arsenokoites* in this context must be the active partner who keeps the *malakos* as a 'mistress' or who hires him on occasion to satisfy his sexual desires." See his *The New Testament and Homosexuality: Contextual Background for Contemporary Debate* (Philadelphia: Fortress Press, 1983), p. 108.

[332] My brief discussion has some in common with that of Helminiak (p. 109).

[333] Discussions of these matters include both those by trained biblical scholars and by laypeople putting into their own words what they have learned in studying scholarship on the subject and then applying it in a personal way. With respect to the latter style of approach, see any number of the essays by Lee Frances Heller, such as "Self-Discrimination,' in J. A. Johnson (Ed.), *By the Grace of God. Lee Frances Heller and Friends: Writings for Families, Friends, and Clergy*, pp. 59-61 (Wheaton, IL: SSP Publications, 2001).

[334] *Sie* (like *hir*) is a contrived pronoun form for transgender people. For those who wish to stick with the pronouns 'he' (and 'him') or 'she' (and 'her') it is proper to use the pronoun matching the gender appearance of a person rather than the person's body sex.

[335] Lee Frances Heller, "God Knows We Are Crossdressers," in *By the Grace of God*, pp. 62-64. Quote is from p. 63.

[336] Lee Frances Heller, "Does God Approve of Crossdressing?" in *By the Grace of God*, pp. 65-66. Quote is from p. 65.

[337] Ibid, p. 66.

[338] Lee Frances Heller, "Where We Stand with God" in *By the Grace of God*, pp. 67-69. Quote is from p. 67.

[339] Lee Frances Heller, "Christ's Place Is in the Heart" in *By the Grace of God*, pp. 79-81. Quote is from p. 80. In a latter essay, Heller says point blank: "We were created crossdressers. We are constitutional crossdressers." Lee Frances Heller, "Unorthodoxy" in *By the Grace of God*, pp. 82-83. Quote is from p. 83.

[340] Heller, "Unorthodoxy."

[341] Heller, "Is God Against Us?" p. 86.

[342] Lacey Leigh, *Speaking of crossdressing* (2003). Available online at http://www.laceyleigh.com/ HowToOutreachII.html. Another online page along similar lines is that by Andrea James, Ph.D., *Religion and Transgenderal Behavior* (2003). Available online at http://members.tgforum.com/bobbyg/ behavior.html. Also see the *Grace & Lace Newsletter* at http://members.tgforum.com/bobbyg/tgfgnl.html.

[343] Rebecca Anne Allison, "Answered Prayers," in J. A. Johnson (Ed.), *By the Grace of God. Lee Frances Heller and Friends: Writings for Families, Friends, and Clergy*, pp. 212-215 (Wheaton, IL: SSP Publications, 2001), p. 87.

[344] Rebecca (Becky) Allison, "Self-Discovery," in *By the Grace of God*, pp. 220-223. Quote is from p. 220.

[345] Ibid, p. 222.

[346] Rebecca (Becky) Allison, "Strength Through Weakness," in *By the Grace of God*, pp. 224-226.

[347] Rebecca Anne Allison, "Sacrifice," in *By the Grace of God*, pp. 229-231.

[348] Rebecca Anne Allison, "Rest," in *By the Grace of God*, pp. 232-235.

[349] Becky Allison, "The Way We Weren't," in *By the Grace of God*, pp. 239-241. Quote is from p. 241.

[350] Becky Allison, "Cheeks," in *By the Grace of God*, pp. 267-269.

[351] Bockting & Cesaretti, p. 296f.

[352] Pope John Paul II, *On the Dignity and Vocation of Women (Mulieris Dignitatem)*, III.6 (1988). Accessed online at http://www.vatican.va/holy_father/john_paul_ii/apost_letters/documents/hf_jp-ii_apl_15081988_mulieris-dignitatem_en.html. For a consid-

eration of this letter by a sympathetic reader, see R. Mary Hayden Lemmons, "Equality, Gender, and Pope John Paul II," *Logos, 5* (no. 3), 111-130 (2002). The Pope goes on to link this text to the one in Genesis 2, which he believes "helps us to understand better what we find in the concise passage of *Gen.* 1:27-28." In his view, the latter text clarifies the essential rational and relational nature of male and female—the human need to exist in relationship. Though he uses universal language (a person "can exist only as a 'unity of two', and therefore *in relation to another human person*" [III.7]), his emphasis is clearly on the need for men and women to exist sexually together and procreate in accordance with Genesis 2:18-25.

[353] Stephanie Paulsell, "Body Language," *Christian Century, 119* (no. 2), 18-24 (2002, Jan. 16), p. 22.

[354] Vern L. Bullough & Bonnie Bullough, *Sin, Sickness, & Sanity. A History of Sexual Attitudes* (N. Y.: New American Library, 1977), p. 77.

[355] The chain of sin-sickness-sanity is not original to me (cf. Bullough & Bullough, *Sin, Sickness, & Sanity*). I believe it was an idea put forward originally and most famously by Michael Foucault.

Q. 75 Notes

[356] Melissa M. Wilcox, "A Religion of One's Own: Gender and LGBT Religiosities," in S. Thumma & E. R. Gray (Eds.), *Gay Religion*, pp. 203-220 (Walnut creek, CA: AltaMira Press, 2005). 'Transgender' here is used in the broad sense to include lesbian and bisexual women.

[357] Gerald Larue, *Sex and the Bible* (Buffalo, NY: Prometheus Books, 1983).

[358] Vanessa S., *The Cross and the Crossdresser: Personal Reflections on Crossdressing from a Christian Perspective* (King of Prussia, PA: Creative Designs Services, 1993).

[359] Vanessa S., *Cross Purposes on Being Christian and Crossgendered* (Decatur, GA: Sullivan Press, 1996). Sheridan has also written online about the experience of attending seminary as an openly transgendered person. See Vanessa Sheridan, *Happily Christian, Openly Transgendered and—A Seminary Student???* accessed online at http://www. whosoever.org/v2Issue2/sheridan.html.

[360] *Religion and Transvestism* (Waltham, MD: IFGE, 1988).

[361] Lee Frances Heller and Friends, *By the Grace of God: Writings for Families, Friends, and Clergy*, edited by Julie Ann Johnson (Wheaton, IL: SPP Publications, 2001). Heller was confirmed in the Episcopalian church slightly before her death.

[362] Pat Conover, *Transgender Good News* (Silver Spring, MD: New Wineskins Press, 2002). Conover is a member of an independent Christian congregation. She suggests that readers especially interested in the religious aspects read chapters 1, 5, and 9, plus the appendices. Chapter 9 presents 5 different approaches to Christian theology.

[363] Justin Edward Tanis, *Trans-Gendered: Theology, Ministry, and Communities of Faith* (Cleveland: Pilgrim Press, 2003).

364 Virginia Ramey Mollenkott, *Omnigender: A Trans-Religious Approach* (Cleveland: Pilgrim Press, 2001).

365 Accessed online at http://www.emergenceministries.org/indexframe.html.

366 Accessed online at http://gendertree.com/.

367 Accessed online at http://www.angelfire.com/on/otherwise/transfaith.html.

368 Accessed online at http://www.rmnetwork.org/welindex.php.

369 Accessed online at http://www.whosoever.org/index.shtml.

370 Accessed online at http://www.drbecky.com/grace.html. Information about Lee Frances Heller can be found in the answer to Q. 70.

371 Woet L. Gianotten & Harris C. A. Brautigan, "Pastoral Sexology: Guidelines for Discussion and Training," in J. H. N. Kerssemakers (Ed.), *Sex and Religion. Religious Issues in Sexological Treatment, Sexological Issues in Pastoral Care. Proceedings of the First Major Conference on the Relationship between Sex and Religion,* pp. 107-127 (Atlanta: Rodopi, 1992). Both quotes from p. 113.

372 Ibid.

373 Becky Edwards, *How Can I Be a Minister and Still Crossdress?* Accessed online at http://members.tripod.com/~Chesapeake_Tri_Ess/June2001.html.

374 See, for example, Helen Carter, "Two Go Public on Their Change of Sex," *The Guardian* (1998, Aug. 21). Accessed online at http://www.pfc.org.uk/news/1998/spouse-g.htm.

375 Christopher Morgan, "Secret TG Group Shakes Up Church," *London Sunday Times* (1998, May 31); accessed online at the Tennessee Vals Online Edition (July, 1998) website at http://www.transgender.org/tg/tvals/tvjul98.htm.

376 John Rivera, "Methodist Transgender Minister Resigns," *Baltimore Sun* (2002, July 2), 4B. Accessed online at baltimoresun.com.

377 Rev. David Horton, *Changing Channels? A Christian response to the transvestite and transsexual* (Cambridge, England: Grove Books Limited, 1994).

378 The GENDYS Network functions both for those who experience problems associated with their gender identity and for those who care for them. GENDYS produces a quarterly journal and hosts a biennial conference. The online homepage is available at http://www.gender.org.uk/gendys/.

379 Rev. David Horton, *Deuteronomy 22 verse 5—A Discussion,* version 3.4 (2003, July). Available online at http://www.gender.org.uk/gendys/journal/08hrton.htm.

380 Ibid.

381 Ibid.

382 Ibid. The Ethiopian he refers to is a eunuch, a model figure for some transgender Christians (see the answer to Q. 74).

[383] David Horton, "Evangelical Alliance Press Release of 14th May About Transsexual People," *GENDYS Journal* (2003). Available online at http://www.gender.org .uk/gendys/journal/11hrton.htm

[384] Ibid. Horton noted that since publishing his booklet *Changing Channels* he had been contacted by over 40 transgender ministers.

[385] Ibid.

[386] The objection runs along these lines: The Old Testament legal texts are replete with obligations and prohibitions routinely ignored by most Christians. In the immediate vicinity of Deuteronomy 22:5 we read, for instance, "When you build a new house, make a parapet around your roof so that you may not bring the guilt of bloodshed on your house if someone falls from the roof" (22:8, NIV), and "Do not wear clothes of wool and linen woven together" (22:11, NIV)—neither of which exercise much concern for most Christians. The reason usually given for not being bothered by such texts is that in Christ the old law is fulfilled and thus set aside as binding on Christian practice; the scripture appealed to in support of this logic starts with Matthew 5:17 (though see 5:18-20!), but often proceeds to various comments by the Apostle Paul (e.g., Galatians 2:16; 3:19; Romans 7:1-6). Yet at the same time, various texts are cited as still relevant and binding when they 'illustrate general biblical principles.' The advocates of tolerance note how such principles often conveniently reinforce current social attitudes, as when many Christians in earlier times used biblical texts—both Old and New Testament—to justify slavery. Obviously, what constitutes a 'general biblical principle' is not a self-evident matter.

I think it useful to add that such debates, with recourse to what some term 'proof-texting' (appealing to select verses to justify a position while ignoring others that might suggest a different position), are common on many subjects. For instance, in the contemporary social division over homosexuality we find Christians of all kinds of opinion appealing to various biblical texts for support of their positions. When opposing sides both appeal to different 'biblical principles' it is little wonder many Christians feel baffled, even distressed. The final result is predictable—in such chaos individual Christians simply resort to whatever belief is most comfortable. These matters are further addressed in the answer to Q. 74.

[387] David Horton, "Soapbox," in Vicky Lee (Ed.), *The Tranny Guide*, 5th ed. (1997). Article available online at http://www.wayout-publishing.com/article2.htm.

[388] This information is from the biographical press materials on Rev. Swenson's website. Accessed online at http://www.erinswen.com/personal.htm.

[389] Erin K. Swenson, *Christianity and Transsexualism*, a statement reproduced with the author's permission on the website maintained by Dr. Becky Allison. Accessed online at http://www.drbecky.com/erin.html.

[390] Ibid.

[391] Swenson, biography press material.

[392] Phyllis Randolph Frye, "Facing Discrimination, Organizing for Freedom: The Transgender Community," in J. D'Emilio, W. B. Turner & U. Vaid (Eds.), *Creating

Change: Public Policy and Civil Rights, pp. 451-522 (N. Y.: St. Martin's Press, 2000), p. 458. Accessed online at http://www.transgenderlegal.com/.

393 Lauren René Hotchkiss, "Is Transgenderism Wrong?" *Miracles Monthly, 9* (no. 1) (1995). Accessed online at http://www.miracles-course.org/display/Transgender.html.

394 Ibid.

395 Christina Hutchins, "Holy Ferment: Queer Philosophical Destabilizations and the Discourse on Lesbian, Gay, Bisexual and Transgender Lives in Christian Institutions," *Theology & Sexuality,* Issue 15, 9-22 (2001), p. 10.

396 Ibid, pp. 10-21; quoted material from p. 11.

397 Ibid, pp. 21-22.

398 Daniel Burke, "Transgender Pastor Prompts Uneasy Questions for Methodists," *USA Today* (2007, Oct. 18). Accessed online at http://www.usatoday.com/news/ religion/2007-10-18-transgender-methodist_N.htm.

399 Drew Phoenix, *Statement by the Rev. Drew Phoenix to the Plenary Session of the Baltimore-Washington Conference, May 24, 2007.* Accessed online at the St. John's of Baltimore church website, at http://www.stjohnsbaltimore.org/drewsstatement.

400 "United Methodist Court Recognizes Transgender Pastor's Appoinment," *Ekklesia* (2007, Nov. 1). Accessed online at http://www.ekklesia.co.uk/node/6064.

401 "United Methodists Decline to Act Against Transgender Clergy," *The Plain Dealer* (2008, May 2). Accessed online at http://blog.cleveland.com/lifestyles/2008/05/ methodists_decline_to_act_agai.html.

402 *Association of Welcoming & Affirming Baptists.* Accessed online at http://www. wabaptists.org/. The address is: P. O. Box 42798, Austin, TX 78704-0047. Telephone: (919) 460-7069 (Director's Office).

403 *Brethren Mennonite Council for Lesbian, Gay, Bisexual and Transgender Interests.* Accessed online at http://www.bmclgbt.org/. The address is: P. O. Box 6300, Minneapolis, MN 55406. Telephone: (612) 343-2060.

404 *DignityUSA.* Accessed online at http://www.dignityusa.org/. The address is: 1500 Mass. Ave. NW, Suite #8, Washington, D.C. 20005-1894.

405 *Gay, Lesbian and Affirming Alliance, Inc.* Accessed online at http://www.gladalliance.org/. The address is: P. O. Box 44400, Indianapolis, IN 46244-0400.

406 *Integrity.* Accessed online at http://www.integrityusa.org/. The address is: 1718 M Street NW, PMB 148, Washington, D.C. 20036. Telephone: (800) 462-9498.

407 *More Light Presbyterians.* Accessed online at http://www.mlp.org/. The address is: PMB 246, 4737 County Road 101, Minnetonka, MN 55345-2634.

408 "Open and Affirming (ONA) Program," *The Coalition. The United Church of Christ Coalition for LGBT Concerns.* Accessed online at http://www.ucccoalition.org/programs/

ona.htm. The address is: PMB 230, 800 Village Walk, Guilford, CT 06437-2740. Telephone: (800) 653-0799.

[409] "Reconciling in Christ Program," *Lutherans Concerned/North America*. Accessed online at http://www.lcna.org/ric.shtm. The address is: P. O. Box 10461, Chicago, IL 60610. Telephone: (612) 869-7471 (RIC Executive).

[410] *Reconciling Ministries Network*. Accessed online at http://www.rmnetwork .org/index.php. Quote taken from the Mission Statement. The address is: 3801 N. Keeler Ave., Chicago, IL 60641. Telephone: (773) 736-5526.

[411] *The Office of Bisexual, Gay, Lesbian and Transgender Concerns*. Accessed online at http://www.uua.org/obgltc/. The address for the Unitarian Universalist Association is: 25 Beacon St., Boston, MA 02018. Telephone: (617) 742-2100.

[412] "Reconciling in Christ Program."

[413] Scott W. Alexander, *Unitarian Universalism. A Welcoming Place for Bisexual, Gay, Lesbian, and Transgender People* (Boston: Unitarian Universalist Association, 2000). Also see Barbara J. Pescan, *Unitarian Universalism. A Religious Home for Bisexual, Gay, Lesbian, and Transgender People* (Boston: Unitarian Universalist Association, 2000).

[414] "Newsbriefs from the World," *CBMW News* (1997, June). Accessed online at http://www.cbmw.org/journal/editions/2-3.pdf. Originally reported in *Newsweek*, p. 66 (1996, Nov. 4).

[415] Ramona Faith Oswald, "Religion, Family, and Ritual: The Production of Gay, Lesbian, Bisexual, and Transgender Outsiders-Within," *Review of Religious Research, 43* (no. 1), 39-50 (2001), p. 39.

Q. 76 Notes

[416] Many scholars over the years have remarked on the role that sex and/or gender play in religions of the world. See, for example, Geoffrey Parrinder, *Sex in the World's Religions* (N. Y.: Oxford Univ. Press, 1980). Also see Joseph Runzo & Nancy M. Martin (Eds.), *Love, Sex and Gender in the World Religions* (Oxford: Oneworld Publications, 2000). In the latter volume, Christian readers may be especially interested in Karen Jo Torjesen, "Gendered Imagery in Early Christian Theologies" (pp. 203-222).

[417] Lisa Penaloza, "Crossing Boundaries/Drawing Lines: A Look at the Nature of Gender Boundaries and Their Impact on Marketing Research," *International Journal of Research in Marketing, 11* (no. 4), 359-379 (1994), p. 375.

[418] Maragaret C. Miller, "Reexamining Transvestism in Archaic and Classical Athens: The Zewadski Stamnos," *American Journal of Archaeology, 103* (no. 2), 223-253 (1999), p. 243.

[419] Ibid, p. 246.

[420] Daniel C. Matt, *The Essential Kabbalah* (Edison, NJ: Castle Books, 1995), p. 1.

[421] *Tiqqunei ha-Zohar*, 17a. Quoted in Matt, p. 50.

[422] Moses Cordovero, *Or Ne'erav*, 6:1-6 (42a-55b). Quoted in Matt, p. 45f.

[423] See, for example, the brief explanation set out by Pope John Paul II: "We find in these passages an indirect confirmation of the truth that both man and woman were created in the image and likeness of God. If there is a likeness between Creator and creatures, it is understandable that the Bible would refer to God using expressions that attribute to him both 'masculine' and 'feminine' qualities." *On the Dignity and Vocation of Women (Mulieris Dignitatem)*, III.8 (1988). Accessed online at http://www.vatican.va/holy_father/john_paul_ii/apost_letters/documents/hf_jp-ii_apl_15081988_mulieris-dignitatem_en.html.

[424] The Hebrew God—YHWH—eventually triumphed as the 'One God,' but for much of Israel's biblical history there was competition. Popular religion permitted worship of other gods. Asherah, for example, may at various times been viewed as the consort of YHWH, and as Gale Yee observes, "Veneration of the goddess Asherah was a major feature of Israelite religious pluralism . . . ." See Gale Gale A. Yee, "'She Is Not My Wife and I Am Not Her Husband': A Materialist Analysis of Hosea 1-2," *Biblical Interpretation, 9* (no. 4), 345-383 (2001), p. 366; cf. p. 352. Cf. Cf. J. A. Emerton, "'Yahweh and His Asherah': The Goddess or Her Symbol?" *Vetus Testamentum, 49* (no. 3), 315-37 (1999). For an interesting account putting the discussion into a contemporary context, see Ann Arlosoroff Vise Nunes, "The Historical Tradition of Sacral Sex and Contemporary Media Manifestations of Carnal Sex," *Studies in Media and Information Literacy Education, 4* (no. 3), article #51 (2004). Accessed online at http://www. utpjournals.com/jour.ihtml?lp=simile/issue15/nunes1.html.

[425] See Julian of Norwich, *Showings*, translated by Edmund Colledge & James Walsh (N. Y.: Paulist Press, 1978); see especially chapters 57-62. Also see Caroline Walker Bynum, *Jesus as Mother: Studies in the Spirituality of the High Middle Ages* (Berkeley: Univ. of California Press, 1982).

[426] For more on Islamic conceptions about Allah, see the answer to Q. 78.

[427] The problem posed by this situation is addressed by Rabbi Zalman Schacter-Shalomi, "God, Our Mother," *Havurah Shir Hadash* website, accessed online at http://www.havurahshirhadash.org/rebzalmanarticle1.html; for the Christian aspect of this issue, see Christian scholar Elaine Pagels, "What Became of God the Mother? Conflicting Images of God in Early Christianity," *Signs. The Journal of Women in Culture and Society, 2* (no. 2) (1976); reprinted in C. P. Christ & J. Plaskow (Eds.), *Womanspirit Rising*, pp. 107-119 (N. Y.: Harper & Row, 1979); reprinted online at *Body, Sex and Gender in the Church*, accessed at http://www.womenpriests.org/body/pagels. htm.

[428] James W. Telch, "The Isoko Tribe," *Africa, VII*, 160-173 (1934), excerpted in Mircea Eliade, *Essential Sacred Writings from Around the World* (S. F.: HarperSanFrancisco, 1967), p. 6f.

[429] Ninian Smart & Richard D. Hecht (Eds.), *Sacred Texts of the World. A Universal Anthology* (N. Y.: Crossroad, 1992), p. 348.

[430] Western theologians have often asserted the superiority of monotheism without clearly establishing why this is a better way to relate to ultimate realities.

[431] *Brihad-Aranyaka Upanishad*, I.4.1, in Robert E. Van Voorst, *An Anthology of World Scriptures* (Belmont, CA: Wadsworth, 1994), p. 32.

[432] Mircea Eliade & Ioan P. Couliano, with Hillary S. Wiesner, *The Eliade Guide to World Religions* (S. F.: Harper & Row, 1991), p. 220.

[433] *Nihongi*, Bk. 5, 7th year, in Joseph M. Kitagawa, "Religions of Japan," in W. Chan, I. R. al Faruqi, J. M. Kitagawa, & P. T. Raju (compilers), *The Great Asian Religions. An Anthology*, pp. 231-305 (N. Y.: Macmillan, 1969), p. 240.

[434] Mircea Eliade, *Patterns in Comparative Religion*, translated by R. Sheed (London: Sheed and Ward, 1958), p. 420.

[435] Mark Matousek, "The Feminine Face of God," *Common Boundary*, pp. 32-37 (1992, May/June), p. 33.

[436] Rosemary Radford Ruether, "Can Christology Be Liberated from Patriarchy?" in M. Stevens (Ed.), *Reconstructing the Christ Symbol. Essays in Feminist Christology*, pp. 7-29 (N. Y.: Paulist Press, 1993), p. 12.

[437] Elizabeth Green, "More Musings on Maleness: The Maleness of Jesus Revisited," *Feminist Theology, 20*, 9-27 (1999), p. 19.

[438] Robert Hamilton Simpson, "How to Be Fashionably Queer: Reminding the Church of the Importance of Sexual Stories," *Theology & Sexuality, 11* (no. 2), 97-108 (2004), p. 105.

[439] Steven Connor, "Men in Skirts," *Women: A Cultural Review, 13* (no. 3), 257-271 (2002), p. 261f.

[440] Lori Hope Lefkovitz, "Passing as a Man: Narratives of Jewish Gender Performance," *Narrative, 10* (no. 1), 91-103 (2002), p. 97.

[441] Stephen J. Davis, "Crossed Texts, Crossed Sex: Intertextuality and Gender in Early Christian Legends of Holy Women Disguised as Men," *Journal of Early Christian Studies, 10* (no. 1), 1-36 (2002), p. 35.

[442] Translation from Arland J. Hultgren & Steven A. Haggmark (Eds.), *The Earliest Christian Heretics* (Minneapolis, MN: Fortress Press, 1996), p.129. Also see Frank Williams (Translator), "The Panarion of Epiphanius of Salamis," in *Nag Hammadi and Manichean Studies*,vol.35 (Leiden: E. J. Brill, 1994).

[443] Hildegard of Bingen, *Liber divinorum operum* I.4.100, edited by A. Derolez & P. Dronke, CCCM 92 (Turnhout: Brepols, 1996), p. 243.

[444] Caroline Walker Bynum, *Fragmentation and Redemption: Essays on Gender and the Human Body in Medieval Religion* (N. Y.: Zone Books, 1991), p. 93.

[445] Caroline Walker Bynum, *Holy Feast and Holy Fast: The Religious Significance of Food to Medieval Women* (Berkeley: Univ. of California Press, 1987), p. 270f.; the quote is from p. 271. On Clement of Alexandria's analogy, see *Paedagogus* 1.6.

[446] Mother Julian's mystical writings have been translated; see Julian of Norwich, *Showings*, trans. Edmund Colledge & James Walsh (N. Y.: Paulist Press, 1978). Also see Thomas L. Long, "Julian of Norwich's 'Christ as Mother' and Medieval Constructions of Gender." (Paper presented at the Madison Conference on English Studies, Madison University, March 18, 1995). Accessed online at http://users.visi.net/~longt/julian.htm.

[447] Barbara Newman, "Henry Suso and the Medieval Devotion to Christ the God-dess," *Spiritus: A Journal of Christian Spirituality, 2* (no. 1), 1-14 (2002). Quotes from Suso are found in Newman, pp. 9, 4. Note the artwork described and presented in this article. Cf. Barbara Newman, *God and the Goddesses: Vision, Poetry, and Belief in the Middle Ages* (Phila.: Univ. of Pennsylvania Press, 2002).

[448] An example cited by Robert Goss, from the Swedish photographic exhibition entitled '*Ecce Homo*,' is of "a homosexual Jesus in black stiletto heels surrounded by muscular leathermen and transvestites with drag queens replacing the disciples in a ver-sion of Leonardo Da Vinci's 'The Last Supper of Christ.'" See Robert E. Goss, "Marcella Althaus-Reid's 'Obscenity no. 1: Bi/Christ': Expanding Christ's Wardrobe of Dresses," *Feminist Theology, 11* (no. 2), 157-166 (2003), p. 159. Cf. Davis, p. 33, n. 109; also see Arnfríður Guðmundsdóttir, "Female Christ-Figures in Films: A Feminist Criti-cal Analysis of *Breaking the Waves* and *Dead Man Walking*," *Studia Theologica, 56* (no. 1), 27-43 (2002).

[449] Green, p. 21.

[450] Eleanor McLaughlin, "Feminist Christologies: Re-Dressing the Tradition," in M. Stevens (Ed.), *Reconstructing the Christ Symbol. Essays in Feminist Christology*, pp. 118-149 (N. Y.: Paulist Press, 1993). Quotes are from pp. 141-142. Cf. the remark by Eisler, "[I]t is not surprising that Jesus should have been aware that the 'masculine' values of domi-nance, inequality, and conquest he could see all around him debasing and distorting human life must be replaced by a softer, more 'feminine' set of values based on com-passion, responsibility, and love." See Riane Eisler, *The Chalice and the Blade* (N.Y.: HarperCollins, 1988), p. 124.

[451] Goss, p. 360. Quote he cites is from Marcella Althaus-Reid, *Indecent Theology: Theological Perversions in Sex, Gender, and Politics* (N. Y.: Routledge, 2001), p. 114.

[452] *Coffin Texts*, I.161ff. in Eliade, *Essential Sacred Writings*, p. 25.

[453] See Betty De Shong Meador, *Innana Lady of Largest Heart: Poems of the Sumerian High Priestess Enheduanna* (Austin: Univ. of Texas Press, 2001). Note especially the sec-tion entitled 'Androgyne: Gender Crossing and Gender Ambiguity' in the discussion of the poem 'Lady of Largest Heart' at the end of ch. 9 (pp. 161-167). Also see Rivkah Harris, "Inanna-Ishtar as a Paradox and a Coincidence of Opposites," *History of Religions, 30* (no. 3), 261-278 (1991). Cf. answer to Q.38.
On the role of Inanna in contemporary pagan worship, see Paul Thomas, "Re-Imagining Inanna: The Gendered Reappropriation of the Ancient Goddess in Modern Goddess Worship," *The Pomegranate: International Journal of Pagan Studies, 6* (no. 1), 53-69 (2004).

[454] "A *Sir-namsub* to Inana," lines 16-22 (ETCSL Translation t.4.07.9), in J. A. Black, G. Cunningham, E. Fluckiger-Hawker, E. Robson, & G. Zólyomi, *The Electronic Text Corpus of Sumerian Literature* (1998-2005). Available from the Electronic Text Corpus of Sumerian Literature website, maintained by the Oriental Institute of the University of Oxford (2005 update). Accessed online at http://etcsl.orinst.ox.ac.uk/cgi-bin/etcsl.cgi?text=t.4.07.9#. Also see "A hymn to Inana for Išme-Dagan (Išme-Dagan

K)," lines 19-31 (ETCSL Translation: c.2.5.4.11). Accessed online at http://etcsl. orinst.ox.ac.uk/cgi-bin/etcsl.cgi?text=t.2.5.4.11#.

[455] "A Hymn to Inana (Inana C)," lines 115-131 (ETCSL Translation: t.4.07.3) in Black, Cunningham, Fluckiger-Hawker, Robson, & Zólyomi. Accessed online at http://etcsl.orinst.ox.ac.uk/cgi-bin/etcsl.cgi?text=t.4.07.3#.

[456] See "A Hymn to Inana for Iddin-Dagan (Idin-Dagan A)," lines 60-68 (ETCSL Translation: t.2.5.3.1) in Black, Cunningham, Fluckiger-Hawker, Robson, & Zólyomi. Accessed online at http://etcsl.orinst.ox.ac.uk/cgi-bin/etcsl.cgi?text=t.2.5.3.1#.

[457] Hans Licht, *Sexual Life in Ancient Greece* (London: Abbey Library, 1971 printing of 1932 ed.), p. 124.

[458] Ibid, p. 128f.

[459] The *dithyramb* is a choral song sung to Dionysus; the meaning of 'Dithyrambus' has long been debated and remains unsettled. My use is vis-à-vis Camille Paglia, *Sexual Personae* (N. Y.: Vintage Books, 1991), p. 89.

[460] Albert Henrichs, "Dionysus," in S. Hornblower & A. Spawforth (Eds.), *The Oxford Classical Dictionary*, 3rd ed., pp. 479-482 (N. Y.: Oxford Univ. Press, 1996), p. 479.

[461] Ibid.

[462] Oskar Seyffert, *The Dictionary of Classical Mythology, Religion, Literature, and Art* (N. Y.: Portland House, 1995 [based on Seyffert's 1882 ed.; edited and revised by H. Nettleship & J. E. Sandys]), p. 193.

[463] Paglia, p. 89. Henrichs (p. 481) noted that the older representations (pre-430 B.C.E.) showed Dionysus as bearded and older, while after he was more regularly depicted as youthful, beardless, and effeminate.

[464] The phrase translates the Greek τό ἀνδρας ὀντας μιμεισθαι γυναικας. A. M. Harmon (Trans.), "The Fly," *Lucian, vol. 1* (pp. 82-95). Loeb Classical Library (Cambridge: Harvard Univ. Press, 1913), p. 95.

[465] Macrobius, *The Saturnalia*, III.viii.2, in P. V. Davies (Trans.), *The Saturnalia* (N. Y.: Columbia Univ. Press, 1969), p. 214.

[466] Clarence J. Bulliet, *Venus Castina. Famous Female Impersonators, Celestial and Human* (N. Y.: Covici, Friede, 1928).

[467] Macrobius, §3, p. 214.

[468] As an example of the former interpretation, see Paglia, p. 87. As an example of the latter interpretation, see Robert E. Bell, *Women of Classical Mythology* (N. Y.: Oxford Univ. Press, 1991), p. 430.

[469] Bell, p. 71.

[470] Christiane Sourvinou-Inwood, "Artemis," in S. Hornblower & A. Spawforth (Eds.), *The Oxford Classical Dictionary*, 3rd ed., pp. 182-184 (N. Y.: Oxford Univ. Press, 1996), p. 183.

[471] Formerly, the bull testicles had been identified as miniature breasts, since Artemis was regarded as female and the symbolism concerned fertility.

[472] Homer, *The Odyssey*, 2.401 (and elsewhere). The translation by Samuel Butler accessed online at http://classics.mit.edu/Homer/odyssey.2.v.html.

[473] Robert Christopher Towneley Parker, "Athena," in S. Hornblower & A. Spawforth (Eds.), *The Oxford Classical Dictionary*, 3rd ed., pp. 201-202 (N. Y.: Oxford Univ. Press, 1996), p. 201.

[474] On Agdistis, see Pausanias, *Description of Greece*, 7.17.9-12. On Attis, see Catullus, *Poems*, #63; cf. answer to Q. 41. Also see R. Spencer, "The Cultural Aspects of Eunuchism," *Ciba Symposia*, 8, 406-420 (1946).

[475] Excerpts from Ovid, *Metamorphoses*, IV.287-388, in Horace Gregory (Trans.), *Ovid. The Metamorphoses* (N. Y.: Mentor Books, 1960), p. 122. A translation of the *Metamorphoses* by A. S. Kline (2000) can be accessed online at http://etext.virginia .edu/latin/ovid/trans/Ovhome.htm.

[476] Licht, p. 126.

[477] Barbara G. Walker, "Castration," *The Women's Encyclopedia of Myths and Secrets* (N. Y.: Harper & Row, 1983).

[478] Homer, *The Odyssey*, II.268, 401; XXII.206; XXIV.446, 548.

[479] *Srimad-Bhagavatam*, 8.9. Accessed online at http://www.srimadbhagavatam.org/ canto8/chapter9.html.

[480] For more on Vishnu-as-Mohini, see Devdutt Pattanaik, *The Man Who Was a Woman and Other Queer Tales from Hindu Lore* (Binghamton, NY: Haworth Press, 2002), pp. 66-76. Cf. *Bhagavata Purana Bhoothanaathopaakhyaanam*.

[481] The eminent European scholar Viktor Rydberg observed a likeness between Loki, a male, and Gullveig-Heid, a female; both used disguises and were often at the center of trouble. More interestingly, despite their gender assignment, each bent toward the 'opposite gender.' Rydberg remarked:

> The interference of both is interrupted at the close of the mythic age, when Loki is chained, and Gullveig, in the guise of Angurboða, is an exile in the Ironwood. Before this they have for a time been blended, so to speak, into a single being, in which the feminine assuming masculineness, and the masculine effeminated, bear to the world an offspring of foes to the gods and to creation.

See Viktor Rydberg, *Our Fathers' Godsaga*, translated by William P. Reaves (N. Y.: iUniverse, 2003 translation of 1911 ed.; original work published 1887). Accessed online at the Northvegr Foundation website at http://www.northvegr.org/lore/rydberg/035 .php.

[482] Eliade, Couliano & Wiesner, p. 95f.

[483] Brian Bocking, "Changing Images of Shinto: *Sanja Takusen* or the Three Oracles," in J. Breen & M. Teeuwen (Eds.), *Shinto in History: Ways of the Kami*, pp. 167-185 (Honolulu: Univ. of Hawaii Press, 2000), p. 180f.

[484] Matsumae Takeshi, "Origin and Growth of the Worship of Amaterasu," *Asian Folklore Studies, 37* (no. 1), 1-11 (1978). Quote is from p. 3.

[485] Bernard of Clairvaux, *Sermons on the Song of Songs,* 8.9. Quoted in Stephen D. Moore, "The Song of Songs in the History of Sexuality," *Church History, 69* (no. 2), 328-349 (2000), p. 343.

[486] Stanley Krippner, "Conflicting Perspectives on Shamans and Shamanism: Points and Counterpoints," *American Psychologist, 57* (no. 11), 962-977 (2002, November), p. 968. For a general introduction to shamanism, see Graham Harvey (Ed.), *Shamanism: A Reader* (N. Y.: Routledge, 2003).

[487] Ibid, p. 970.

[488] Mircea Eliade, *Shamanism: Archaic Techniques of Ecstasy,* translated by W. R. Trask (Princeton: Princeton Univ. Press, 1972 printing of 1951 ed.); see especially chapter 5. Cf. Mircea Eliade, *The Two and the One,* translated by J. M. Cohen (Chicago: Univ. of Chicago Press, 1965).

[489] M. A. Czaplicka, *Aboriginal Siberia. A Study in Social Anthropology* (Oxford: Clarendon Press, 1914). See Part III, 'Religion' (chapters VII-XIV). Accessed online at http://www.shamana.co.uk/Shamanism_in_Siberia/index5.htm.

[490] Laurel Kendall, *Shamans, Housewives, and Other Restless Spirits. Women in Korean Ritual Life* (Honolulu: Univ. of Hawaii Press, 1985), p. 27. On Korean shamanism see Tongshik Ryu, "Shamanism: The Dominant Folk Religion in Korea," *Inter-Religio, 5,* 8-15 (1984). Accessed online at http://www.riccibase.com/inter-religio/PDF/ir05.pdf.

[491] Carolyn Brewer, "*Baylan, Asog,* Transvestism and Sodomy: Gender, Sexuality and the Sacred in Early Colonial Philippines," *Intersections: Gender, History and Culture in the Asian Context, 2* (1999, May).

[492] Sabine Lang, *Men as Women, Women as Men: Changing Gender in Native American Cultures* (Austin, TX: Univ. of Texas Press, 1998), p. 167.

[493] Valentina Kharitonova, "Transvestism in Shamanism," in M. N. Walter & E. J. Neumann Fridman (Eds.), *Shamanism: An Encyclopedia of World Beliefs, Practices, and Culture,* pp. 259-262 (Santa Barbara, CA: ABC-CLIO, Inc., 2004), p. 262.

[494] Cf. John Barclay Burns, "Devotee or Deviate. The 'Dog' *(keleb)* in Ancient Israel as a Symbol of Male Passivity and Perversion," *Journal of Religion & Society, 2* (2000), accessed online at http://moses.creighton.edu/JRS/2000/2000-6.html.

[495] Tacitus, *Germania,* §43, in A. R. Birley (Trans.), *Tacitus. Agricola and Germany* (N. Y.: Oxford Univ. Press, 1999), p. 59.

[496] See Robert L. Reid, "Frey," *The Wain, 6* (1998). Accessed online at http://homepages.nildram.co.uk/~fealcen/wain6.htm. *The Wain* is "a journal dedicated to the Vanir."

[497] Dominic Montserrat, "Essay Six: Reading Gender in the Roman World," in J. Huskinson (Ed.), *Experiencing Rome: Culture, Identity, and Power in the Roman Empire,* pp. 153-182 (N. Y.: Routledge, 2000), p. 158.

[498] Richard L. Gordon, "Eunuchs," in S. Hornblower & A. Spawforth (Eds.), *The Oxford Classical Dictionary*, 3rd ed. (N. Y.: Oxford Univ. Press, 1996), p. 569.

[499] Roberta Gilchrist, *Gender and Archaeology: Contesting the Past* (N. Y.: Routledge, 1999), p. 60.

[500] Richard Valantasis, *The Gospel of Thomas* (N. Y.: Routledge, 1997), p. 11.

[501] Confucius, *Analects* XVI.14, in Arthur Waley (Trans.), *The Analects of Confucius* (N. Y.: Vintage, 1938), p. 208.

[502] Ibid, p. 251.

[503] For more on the life of Wu, see Cheng-An Jiang (illustrated by De Yuan Xu), *Empress of China Wu Ze Tian* (Monterey, CA: Victory Press, 1998).

[504] Herbert A. Giles, *The Civilization of China* (London, 1911), ch. 4. Accessed online at http://www.romanization.com/books/giles/civilization/chap04.html.

[505] Maggie Macary, "The Symbols and Structures of Initiation," *Myth and Culture* website. Accessed online at http://www.mythandculture.com/publications/initiation.html.

[506] Fritz Graf, "Transvestism, Ritual," in S. Hornblower & A. Spawforth (Eds.), *The Oxford Classical Dictionary*, 3rd ed. (N. Y.: Oxford Univ. Press, 1996), p. 1547.

[507] Paglia, p. 90.

[508] Henrichs, p. 481.

[509] Robert Christopher Towneley Parker, "Oschoporia," in S. Hornblower & A. Spawforth (Eds.), *The Oxford Classical Dictionary*, 3rd ed. (N. Y.: Oxford Univ. Press, 1996), p. 1081.

[510] John Schied, "Saturnus, Saturnalia," in S. Hornblower & A. Spawforth (Eds.), *The Oxford Classical Dictionary*, 3rd ed. (N. Y.: Oxford Univ. Press, 1996), p. 1360f.

Q. 77 Notes

[511] For a brief clarification of Maimonides' thought, see Yeshayahu Leibowitz, *The Faith of Maimonides* (N. Y.: Adama Books, 1987).

[512] For an overview, see Peter Schäfer, *Mirror of His Beauty: Feminine Images of God from the Bible to the Early Kabbalah* (Princeton: Princeton Univ. Press, 2002).

[513] Mary Joan Witt Leith, "Wisdom," in B. M. Metzger & M. D. Coogan (Eds.), *The Oxford Companion to the Bible*, pp. 800-801 (N. Y.: Oxford Univ. Press, 1993), p. 800. Also see the section entitled 'The Personification of Wisdom' (pp. 501-503) in Carole R. Fontaine, "Proverbs," in J. L. Mays (Ed.), *Harper's Bible Commentary*, pp, 495-517 (S. F.: Harper & Row, 1988).

[514] Asherah may at various times been viewed as the consort of YHWH, and as Gale Yee observes, "Veneration of the goddess Asherah was a major feature of Israelite religious pluralism . . . ." See Gale Gale A. Yee, "'She Is Not My Wife and I Am Not Her Husband': A Materialist Analysis of Hosea 1-2," *Biblical Interpretation, 9* (no. 4), 345-383 (2001), p. 366; cf. p. 352. The notion that Asherah was seen as an aspect of God, or

as a feminine expression/representation rests on slender grounds, but coupled with the handling of Wisdom and other developments in Judaic tradition is not completely implausible.

[515] Thanksgiving Hymn 18, in Geza Vermes (Ed. & Translator), *The Dead Sea Scrolls* (London: The Folio Society, 2000), p. 218.

[516] Thanksgiving Hymn 6, in Vermes, p. 186.

[517] Philo of Alexandria, *De Opificio Mundi [On the Creation]*, XXIV.76. Ironically, Philo also stands out as a preeminent example of someone opposed to gender and, especially, sexual variance. See Holger Szesnat, "'Pretty Boys' in Philo's *De Contemplativa*," *The Studia Philonica Annual, 10*, 87-107 (1998).

[518] Lori Hope Lefkovitz, "Passing as a Man: Narratives of Jewish Gender Performance," *Narrative, 10* (no. 1), 91-103 (2002), p. 91.

[519] Ibid, p. 93. She notes, too, the association of Jacob with the feminine would later contribute to anti-Semitic depictions of Jews as a feminized people. (In this connection, see p. 96f.)

[520] Ibid, p. 94.

[521] Ibid, p. 99; Lefkovitz references *Genesis Rabbah* 174.

[522] Ibid, p. 98f.

[523] Daniel Boyarin, *Carnal Israel: Reading Sex in Talmudic Culture* (Berkeley: Univ. of California Press, 1995), p.217. Boyarin's remark comes in his discussion of the androgynous figure of Rabbi Yochanan and his mentoring relationship with Resh Lakish.

[524] Daniel Boyarin, *Unheroic Conduct: The Rise of Heterosexuality and the Invention of the Jewish Man* (Berkeley: Univ. of California Press, 1997), p. 26.

[525] Flavius Josephus, *Wars of the Jews*, Bk. V, ch. IX, §10, in William Whiston (trans.), *The Complete Works of Josephus* (Grand Rapids, MI: Kregel, 1981), p. 542f. For the text, see the answer to Q. 53.

[526] Philo of Alexandria, *De Vita Contemplativa* II.52.

[527] Tova Rosen, "Circumcised Cinderella: The Fantasies of a Fourteenth-Century Jewish Author," *Prooftexts, 20* (nos. 1-2), 87-110 (2000), p. 88.

[528] Ibid. The translation is Rosen's own; the passages quoted are from various pages.

[529] Jason P. Rosenblatt, *Renaissance England's Chief Rabbi: John Selden* (N. Y.: Oxford Univ. Press, 2006), p. 54.

[530] Ibid, p. 69.

[531] Ibid, p. 73.

[532] David Shneer & Caryn Aviv, "Introduction," in D. Shneer & C. Aviv (Eds.), *Queer Jews*, pp. 3-15 (N. Y.: Routledge, 2002), p. 8.

[533] Sarah Bunin Benor, "*Talmid Chachams* and *Tsedeykeses:* Language, Learnedness, and Masculinity Among Orthodox Jews," *Jewish Social Studies, 11* (no. 1), 147-169 (2004).

[534] Shaul Magid, "Is Egalitarianism Heresy? Rethinking Gender on the Margins of Judaism," *NASHIM: A Journal of Jewish Women's Studies and Gender Issues, #8,* 189-229 (2004), p. 202.

[535] Mishnah *Yebamoth* 8.4.

[536] *Yebamoth* 63a.

[537] However, it should be noted that the eminent scholar Maimonides concluded that one born a eunuch is permitted to enter into the congregation of the Lord since the condition was an act of heaven. See *Mishneh Torah* Hilkhot Issurei Bi'a 16:9.

[538] See, for example, Jonathan Frankiel (Ed.), *Jews and Gender: The Challenge to Hierarchy* (N. Y.: Oxford Univ. Press, 2001).

[539] Alon Levkovitz, "A Halakhic Approach to Transgender," *Central Conference of American Rabbis Journal, 52* (no. 4), 84-93 (2005).

[540] Danya Ruttenberg, "*Beged Ish* or When Clothes Don't Make the Man," in R. Brodie (Compiler), *Common Threads: The Fabrics of Jewish Life,* a 'Feast' Booklet (S. F.: Bureau of Jewish Education, 2003), p. 6. *Beged Ish* means 'men's clothing.'

[541] Consider, for example, Beruriah, daughter of the renowned Rabbi Chanina ben Teradion, and wife of the even more famous Rabbi Meir. Beruriah was both learned and outspoken. She was respected by the male rabbis to the extent that she was consulted on scholarly matters (Pesachim 62b).

[542] Talya Fishman, "A Kabbalistic Perspective on Gender-Specific Commandments: On the Interplay of Symbols and Society," *AJS Review, 17* (no. 2), 199-245 (1992), p. 233f.

[543] Ibid, pp. 233-235.

[544] *Zohar* 49b in Gershom Scholem (Ed.), *Zohar* (N. Y.: Schocken Books, 1978), p. 34f. See Elliot Wolfson, *Circle in the Square—Studies in the Use of Gender in Kabbalistic Symbolism* (Albany, 1995). On the erotic connections of human beings to *Shechinah,* or of God to *Shechinah,* see Geoffrey Parrinder, *Sex in the World's Religions* (N. Y.: Oxford Univ. Press, 1980), pp. 198-200. I wonder what those who associate 'autogynophilia' (a man's love of himself as a woman) with mental disorder (cf. the answer to Q. 96) would make of this mystical notion of the masculine in God sexually yearning for the feminine aspect of deity?

[545] For relevant texts, in the Babylonian Talmud see *Yebamoth* 49a-b on characteristics of 'eunuchs' (*saris*) made by Nature; *Yebamoth* 41b and 52a on 'hermaphrodites.' (Cf. *Tosefta Yebamoth* 2:4-6, 10:2-11:2.) Also see *Shabbat* 134b, *Sanhedrin* 85b. The ανδρογυνος (*androginos*) is mentioned in *Baba Bathra* 92a, 140b. There are many scattered references to 'hermaphrodites' in the Talmudic corpus.

[546] Suzanne Baizerman, "The Jewish *Kippa Sruga* and the Social Construction of Gender in Israel," in R. Barnes & J. B. Eicher (Eds.), *Dress and Gender. Making and Meaning in Cultural Contexts*, pp. 92-105 (N. Y.: Berg, 1993), p. 103.

[547] Monford Harris, "Purim: The Celebration of Dis-Order," *Judaism*, 26 (no. 2), 161-170 (1977); quote is from p. 164.

[548] Ibid, p. 165; quote is from p. 169.

[549] Arlene Rossen Cardozo, *Jewish Family Celebrations* (N. Y.: St.Martins Press, 1982), p. 114.

[550] Ahuva Belkin, "Masks and Disguises as an Expression of Anarchy in the Jewish Festival Theatre," in S. Levy (Ed.), *Theatre and Holy Script*, pp. 205-212 (Brighton: Sussex Academic Press, 1999), p. 206.

[551] Ahuva Belkin, "Cross-dressing in Jewish Folk Theatre," in E. Tseelon (Ed.), *Masquerade and Identities: Essays on Gender, Sexuality and Marginality*, pp. 100-113 (N. Y.: Routledge, 2001), p. 101. Belkin offers a relatively full description and context for the practice.

[552] Ibid, p. 109.

[553] Ibid, pp. 110-111.

[554] *Responsa of R. Yehuda Mintz*, 16 [cited in *Mateh Moseh* 1014]; *Responsa Mahara Mintz of Padua*, 31a. Cited in Adam S. Ferziger, "Re: The Origin of Purim Costumes and 'Minhag Avoteinu Be-Yadeinu,'" *Mail. Jewish Mailing List, 31* (no. 99) (2000). Accessed online at http://www.ottmall.com/ mj_ht_arch/v31/mj_v31i99.html. For an historical analysis tracing the custom further back, see H. Pollack, "An Historical Inquiry Concerning Purim Masquerade Attire," *Proceedings of the World Jewish Congress, 7*, 217-235 (1981).

[555] See Herman Pollack, *Jewish Folkways in Germanic Lands (1648-1806)* (Cambridge, MA: M.I.T. Press, 1971), pp. 183-184.

[556] See, for example, David Shneer & Caryn Aviv (Eds.), *Queer Jews* (N. Y.: Routledge, 2002). Also see Angela Brown (Ed.), *Mentsch: On Being Jewish and Queer* (L.A.: Alyson Publications, 2004). Cf. Christi Balka & Andy Rose (Eds.), *Twice Blessed: On Being Lesbian or Gay, and Jewish* (Boston: Beacon Press, 1991 reprint of 1989 ed.).

[557] Orthodox scholars generally disapprove of homosexuality (*to'evah*), but differ in how, why, and to what extent. The most common perspective appears to be that homosexual *practice* is wrong, rather than the orientation itself. Some scholars liken the prohibition to eating non-kosher food, where others see it as a more serious moral violation. For an Orthodox perspective, see Shmuel Boteach, "Does Homosexuality Differ from Heterosexuality?" in *Moses of Oxford*, vol. 1, pp. 24-44 (London: Andre Deutsch, 1994). This tradition's objections can be found in texts such as the Talmud's *Kiddushin* 82a, *Hullin* 92a-b, *Niddah* 13b, the Midrash's *Genesis Rabbah* 26:5 and *Sifre Devarim* 318, and later, Maimonides' *Mishneh Torah* (*Hilkhot Issurei Biah 22:2*) and Rashi's remarks on *Yebamot 76*.

Conservative Judaism has taken a more moderate stance, welcoming homosexuals into the congregation but limiting their participation in some ways (e.g., as rabbinical students). See, for example, the "CJLS Consensus Statement of Policy Regarding Homosexual Jews in the Conservative Movement" EH 24.1992a" (1992, Mar. 25) adopted by the Conservative Rabbinical Assembly as a CJLS Responsum, accessed online at http://keshetjts.org/sources/CJLS_Consensus.doc. The Rabbinical Assembly has taken stances supporting civil rights for homosexuals and opposing violence toward sexual minorities, while affirming the view that homosexuals who practice same-sex behaviors are sinning. For a relatively short but thorough treatment, see Ian Silver, *Homosexuality and Judaism*, at the Congregation Beth Am website, accessed online at http://www.betham.org/kulanu/iansilver.html. For a very accepting stance, see Elliot Dorff, *This Is My Beloved. This Is My Friend: A Rabbinic Letter on Intimate Relations* (N. Y.: Rabbinical Assembly, 1995).

Reform Judaism has been more accepting still. Staunch supporters of civil protections and rights for gays and lesbians, Reform congregations welcome sexual minorities as members. Its ruling body, the Central Conference of American Rabbis (CCAR) endorsed a 1990 report by its Ad Hoc Committee on Homosexuality and the Rabbinate affirming admission of students to study for the rabbinate regardless of sexual orientation and allowing homosexual rabbis to pursue their vocation. Reform Jews have also been more accepting of recognizing same-sex unions. For more, see "Q. What Is Judaism's View on Homosexuality?" in the *Ask the Rabbi & FAQ* section of the Union for Reform Judaism website, accessed online at http://urj.org/ask/homosexuality/.

[558] T. J. Michels & Ali Cannon, "Whose Side Are You On?: Transgender at the Western Wall," in D. Shneer & C. Aviv (Eds.), *Queer Jews*, pp. 84-99 (N. Y.: Routledge, 2002).

[559] This experience is recounted in Ramona Faith Oswald, "Religion, Family, and Ritual: The Production of Gay, Lesbian, Bisexual, and Transgender Outsiders-Within," *Review of Religious Research, 43* (no. 1), 39-50 (2001), p. 43f.

[560] J. David Bleich, "Medical Questions: Sterilization of Women; Transsexual Surgery; Host-Mothers; Tay-Sachs Disease; Tay-Sachs Reexamined; Temporary Crowns; Plastic Surgery; Post-Mortem Caesareans; Autopsies with Consent of the Deceased; Medical Experimentation Upon Severed Organs," in J. D. Bleich, *Contemporary Halakhic Problems*, vol. 1, pp. 93-128 (N. Y.: Ktav, 1977); see especially pp. 100-105. Also see J. David Bleich, "Transsexual Surgery and Ambiguous Genitalia," in *Judaism and Healing: Halakhic Perspectives* (N. Y.: Ktav, 1981).

[561] See *CCAR Responsa: Conversion and Marriage After Transsexual Surgery 5750.8* (1989), at the Central Conference of American Rabbis website, accessed online at http://data.ccarnet.org/cgi-bin/respdisp.pl?file=8&year=5750. The CCAR remained "troubled" in the instance at hand because the individual in question has subsequent to surgery had a change of heart and was living as a male and desiring to marry a woman; the CCAR recommended against marriage.

[562] Information retrieved from the 'About Us' page on Congregation Beth Simchat Torah's website, accessed online at http://cbst.org/about_index.shtml.

[563] Cole Krawitz, "A Voice from Within: A Challenge for the Conservative Jewish Movement *and* Its Gay/Lesbian Activists," *NASHIM: A Journal of Jewish Women's Studies and Gender Issues, #8*, 165-174 (2004), p. 167.

[564] Ibid, p. 172.

[565] Shneer & Aviv, p. 3.

[566] But these are not *kiddushin*, sanctified marriages. See Lawrence Bush & Jeffrey Dekro, " Beyond Tolerance," *Tikkun, 15* (no. 5), 20-21 (2000).

[567] *Support for the Inclusion and Acceptance of the Transgender and Bisexual Communities* (2003, March). The full text of the document retrieved from the Union for Reform Judaism website, accessed online at http://urj.org/Articles/index.cfm?id=13462&pge _prg_id=42107&pge_id=1607.

[568] Debra Nussbaum Cohen, "Testing the Borders of Inclusivity," *The Jewish Week* (2003, Mar. 13), retrieved from The Jewish Week website, accessed online at http://www.thejewishweek.com/news/newscontent.php3?artid=7562.

[569] Jacon Anderson-Minshall, "Trans Judaism," *San Francisco Bay Times* (2006, Aug. 10), accessed online at http://cbst.org/transjudaism.shtml. Zellman joined Congregation Beth Simchat Torah in 2004 as Children's Educator and in 2005 became one of the synagogue's rabbinical interns.

[570] Information retrieved from the World Congress of Gay, Lesbian, and Transgender Jews: Keshet Ka'avah website, accessed online at http://www.glbtjews.org//. The nations listed include: Argentina, Australia, Austria, Canada, France, Germany, Hungary, Israel, Mexico, The Netherlands, Spain, Sweden, the United Kingdom, and the United States.

[571] See the view of mental health professional Judi Keshet-Orr, who writes, "According to Jewish law there are some relationships which are not sanctioned, these would include an incestuous relationship, a mixed or trans-religious relationship, adulterous relationships, a relationship with anyone who is the product of a defined forbidden relationship, and same sex relationships. Transgender or gender dysphoric work or the use of surrogates is also forbidden." Judi Keshet-Orr, "Jewish Women and Sexuality," *Sexual and Relationship Therapy, 18* (no. 2), 215-224 (2003), p. 223. Cf. the same sentiment that transgenderism is regarded as against Judaism, but argues therapists should be more involved in ending such prejudice, in Sari H. Dworkin & Huso Yi, "LGBT Identity, Violence, and Social Justice: The Psychological is Political," *International Journal for the Advancement of Counseling, 25* (no. 4), 269-279 (2003).

Q. 78 Notes

[572] Iftikhar Ahmed Mehar, *Al-Islam: Inception to Conclusion* (Charleston, SC: BookSurge Publishing, 2007), p. 6.

[573] Mohd Marmaduke Pickthall, *The Meaning of the Glorious Koran*, quoted in Hasanuddin Ahmed, *An Easy Way to the Understanding of the Qur'an* (Chicago: IQRA' International Educational Foundation, 1987), p. 9.

574 Samuel Marinus Zwemer, *Islam: A Challenge to Faith* (N. Y.: Student Volunteer Movement for Foreign Missions, 1907), p. 12. Cf. Sydney Cave, "Islam," in S. Cave, *An Introduction to the Study of Some of the Living Religions of the East*, pp. 194-240 (London: Duckworth, 1921), p. 194f.

575 See *Islam and the Divine Feminine*. Accessed online at http://www.penkatali.org/feminine.html.

576 V. A. Mohammed Ashrof, *Islam and Gender Justice. Questions at the Interface* (Delhi: Kalpaz Publications, 2005), p. 169.

Cf. the following remarks in Seyyed Hossein Nasr, *The Heart of Islam: Enduring Values for Humanity* (S. F.: HarperCollins, 2004), p. 4:

> The One God, or Allah, is neither male nor female. However, in the inner teachings of Islam His Essence is often referred to in feminine form and the Divinity is is often mentioned as the Beloved, while the Face He has turned to the world as Creator and Sustainer is addressed in the masculine form. Both the male and female are created by Him and the root of both femininity and masculinity are to be found in the Divine Nature, which transcends the duality between them. Furthermore, the Qualities of God, which are reflected throughout creation, are of a feminine as well as a masculine nature, and the traditional Islamic understanding of the Divine is not at all confined, as some think, to a purely patriarchal image.

577 Yik Koon Teh, "*Mak Nyahs* (Male Transsexuals) in Malaysia: The Influence of Culture and Religion on Their Identity," *The International Journal of Transgenderism, 5* (no. 3) (2001, July-September). Accessed online at http://www.symposion.com/ijt/ijtvo05no03_04.htm.

578 For elaboration on the idea of 'conforming genders' see G. G. Bolich, *Conversing on Gender. A Primer for Entering Dialog*, rev. ed. (Raleigh, NC: Psyche's Press, 2007).

579 Türker Özkan & Timo Lajunen, "Masculinity, Femininity, and the Bem Sex Role Inventory in Turkey," *Sex Roles. A Journal of Research, 52* (nos. 1-2), 103-110 (2005).

580 A review with respect to the issue of Islam's regard of women is found in Elizabeth Shlala Leo, "Islamic Female Sexuality and Gender in Modern Feminist Interpretation," *Islam and Christian-Muslim Relations, 16* (no. 2), 129-140 (2005).

581 Qur'an, Surah *Al-Nisah* (Women) 4:1, in N. J. Dawood (Translator), *The Koran*, 5th rev. ed. (N. Y.: penguin Books, 1994 revision of 1990 edition), p. 60. Cf. Surah *Al-Najm* (The Star) 53:43, "God created the sexes, the male and the female, from a drop of ejaculated semen, and will create all things anew. . . ." (Dawood, p. 373).

582 Qur'an, Surah *Al-Nisah* (Women) 4:2-33, in Dawood, pp. 60-64; cf. 4:126-130 (p. 74).

583 Qur'an, Surah *Al-Nisah* (Women) 4:34, in Dawood, p. 64.

584 Qur'an, Surah *Al-Nisah* (Women) 4:124, in Dawood, p. 73.

[585] An interesting glimpse into how such things were being worked out in Islamic thought can be found in *Sahih Bukhari* (7.72.734 [vol. 7, bk. 72, #734]), where a *hadith* narrated by Ibn 'Abbas presents an account of gender relations in the light of rights granted by Allah.

[586] Yvonne Yazbeck Haddad, "Islam and Gender: Dilemmas in the Changing Arab World," in Y. Y. Haddad & J. L. Esposito (Eds.), *Islam, Gender, and Social Change*, pp. 3-29 (N. Y.: Oxford Univ. Press, 1998), p. 13.

[587] Muhammed ibn Isma'il al-Bukhari, *Sahih al-Bukhari*, translated by M. M. Khan (Chicago: Kazi Publications), p. 81. Cited in Sa'diyya Shaikh, "Knowledge, Women and Gender in the Hadith: A Feminist Interpretation," *Islam and Christian-Muslim Relations, 15* (no. 1), 99-108 (2004), p. 105.

[588] Ibid, p. 97; cited in Shaikh, p. 106.

[589] I am aware that some will maintain it is better to say that men are prized *differently* than women, rather than above them. But the language of the Qur'an establishes a difference that is clearly hierarchical—and that has been and is reflected in Muslim practice.

[590] Shaikh, p. 98.

[591] Qur'an, Surah *Al-A'raf* (The Heights) 7:26, in Dawood, p. 110; bracketed material added.

[592] Ibid, 7:31-32.

[593] Abu Dawud, *Sunan Abu-Dawud*, 32.4009 [Bk. 32, #4009].

[594] In addition to describing what the Prophet liked to wear, *ahadith* also offer a few proscriptions both of kinds of garments and ways of wearing clothes. With regard to the latter, see for instance the two prohibitions in *Sahih Bukhari*: covering one shoulder while leaving the other bare, and sitting in such a manner that the genitals are not covered (Vol. 7, Bk. 72, #710-712).

[595] *Sunan Abu-Dawud*, 32.4055, 4057.

[596] *Sunan Abu-Dawud*, 32.4046; cf. #4119. With reference to gold, principally ornamentation such as gold rings is in mind (see *Sahih Bukhari*, 7.72.753-756). With reference to silk, a *hadith* in *Sahih Bukhari* relates how the Prohet gave a silk garment to Ali bin Abi Talib, who wore it, but upon seeing the Prophet's anger at this quickly bestowed it on his wives (#731). Cf. the *hadith* in the same source narrated by 'Uqba bin 'Amir: "A silken Farruj was presented to Allah's Apostle and he put it on and offered the prayer in it. When he finished the prayer, he took it off violently as if he disliked it and said, 'This (garment) does not befit those who fear Allah!'" (7.72.693); accessed online at http://www.usc.edu/dept/MSA/fundamentals/hadithsunnah/bukhari/072.sbt.html.
On the other hand, there is in the same chapter a *hadith* narrated by Aba 'Uthman An-Nahdi about a letter received from 'Umar stating that the Prophet had forbidden silk except for as much as the width of one's index and middle fingers, which was interpreted as meaning for purposes of embroidery (#718). There is also what we might call a 'medical exception' employed when the Prophet permitted Az-Zubair and 'Abdur-

Rahman to wear silk while suffering from 'an itch' (#730). Also, see #720 (and #723-726), for the Prohet's saying that those who wear silk in this world will not wear it in the next, and #722, with the Prophet's promise that gold and silk are among the rewards awaiting Muslims in the next life. Cf. *Sahih Muslim* 24.5129 [Bk. 24, #5129], #5134, #5146-5151. The *hadith* at #5150 generalizes the prohibition against silk clothing to Muslim women.

[597] *Sunan Abu-Dawud*, 32.4048.

[598] *Sunan Abu-Dawud*, 32.4089-4091, 4104.

[599] *Sahih Muslim*, 40.6840. Accessed online at http://www.usc.edu/dept/MSA/fundamentals/hadithsunnah/muslim/040.smt.html#040.6840.

[600] *Sahih Bukhari*, 7.72.815; cf. #822, #829-832. Accessed online at http://www.usc.edu/dept/MSA/fundamentals/hadithsunnah/bukhari/072.sbt.html. Cf. *Sahih Muslim*, 24.5300-5301.

[601] *Sahih Bukhari*, 7.72.716. On the use of wigs, even when the woman's hair has fallen out due to illness, see 7.72.817-818, where it is cursed by the Prophet. Cf. *Sahih Muslim*, 24.5295-5299.

[602] *Sahih Muslim*, 24.5241; the very next *hadith* retains the prohibition as a general one, presumably applying to all the obedient.

[603] *Sunan Abu-Dawud*, 32.4037.

[604] The remarks already made show the importance of dress for modesty, adornment, and religious purposes. An interesting *hadith* also suggests its use—in conjunction with modesty—as a barrier against sexual contact within same-gender groups. The *hadith* forbids men sleeping together without wearing undergarments, and declares the same for women (*Sunan Abu-Dawud*, 32.4038).

[605] Betül Ipsirli Argit, "Clothing Habits, Regulations and Non-Muslims in the Ottoman Empire," *Akademik Arastirmalar Dergisi*, 24, 79-96 (2005), p. 79. Argit writes that the traditional clothing habits were replaced by European styles in the 19th century following an 1829 law promulgated by Mahmud II.

[606] *Sunan Abu-Dawud*, 32.4020. Accessed online at http://www.usc.edu/dept/MSA/fundamentals/hadithsunnah/abudawud/032.sat.html

[607] Argit, p. 81 and p. 92, n. 11.

[608] The continual shaping of tradition, which maintains its vitality in the modern world, occurs through both commentaries on the ancient texts and through religious *fatwas* such as that by Ayatollah Ruhollah Khomeini in Iran that effectively extended the right of sex reassignment surgery from intersexed individuals to transsexuals (see the answer to Q. 53).

[609] The relation of dress to affiliation with a group is discussed in the answers to various questions found in volume 1 of this set (*Dress and Gender*).

[610] *Sunan Abu-Dawud*, 32.4087; cf. #4088, where the Prophet decries 'mannish women.'

[611] Yusuf al-Qaradawi, *The Lawful and the Prohibited in Islam* (Indianapolis: Islamic Book Service, 1982). He writes, "The evil of such conduct, which affects both the life of the individual and of society, is that it constitutes a rebellion against the natural ordering of things. According to this natural order, there are men and there are women, and each of the two sexes has its own distinctive characteristics. However, if men become effeminate and women masculinized, this natural order will be reversed and will disintegrate." Text accessed online at http://www.ymsite.com/books/lpi/ch2s2pre.htm #Concerning %20Woman%27s%20Imitating%20Man%20and%20Vice%20Versa.

[612] Brian Whitaker, "Boys Will Be Boys . . . Or Else," *The Guardian* (23 January, 2008). Accessed online at http://commentisfree.guardian.co.uk/brian_whitaker/2008/01/boys_must_be_boys.html.

[613] Some examples are provided in the answer to Q. 53 in volume 3 of this work. Also see reports offered by Amnesty Internation and Human Rights Watch.

[614] As was done in volume 2 of this work, I have chosen to capitalize the term to help highlight the reality of a distinct group and, correspondingly, hope to diminish the possibility of the term being seen pejoratively. I also, for the sake of convenience, have subsumed the terms *Mukhannis* and *Mukhannas* under *Mukhannathun*.

[615] Everett K. Rowson, "The Effeminates of Early Medina," *The Journal of the American Oriental Society, 111* (no. 4), 671-693 (1991), p. 672f.

[616] Ibid (cf. the abstract).

[617] Qu'ran, Surah *Al-Nur* (Light) 24:31, in Dawood, p. 248. Perhaps more accurately, 'lacks a man's defining skill' (i.e., his ability to impregnate). Cf. Surah 42:50.

[618] Rowson, p. 673. His coverage of these extends from pp. 673-677.

[619] *Sunan Abu-Dawud*, 32.4095. Accessed online at http://www.usc.edu/dept/MSA/fundamentals/hadithsunnah/abudawud/032.sat.html #032.4095.

[620] *Sunan Abu-Dawud*, 41.4910. Accessed online at http://www.usc.edu/dept/MSA/fundamentals/hadithsunnah/abudawud/032.sat.html #041.4910. Cf. the comment of Ibn Qudamah, with the Qur'an (Surah 24:31) in mind, who says the *mukhannath* feels no desire for women.

[621] This inability to sustain an erection (impotence) was remarked upon by Ibn 'Abbaas, with Surah 24:31 in view.

[622] Abdelwahab Bouhdiba, *Sexuality in Islam*, translated by A. Sheridan (N. Y. Routledge, 1974), p. 38, with reference to Al-Washtani, commentary by Moslem, vol. V, p. 444ff.

[623] Ibn Qudamah Al-Maqdisi, *Al-Mughni wa al-Sharh Alkabeer*, 7/463; cf. al-Sharh al-Kabeer 'ala Matan al-Muqni', 7/347-348. Accessed online at http://www. assahwah.com/discus/messages/8/951.html?1012666012; also, http://www.geocities.com/leylasuhagi/society.html.

[624] M. Muhsin Kahn (Translator), *Translation of Sahih Bakhari*, Vol. 7, Bk. 72, #773. Accessed online at http://www.usc.edu/dept/MSA/fundamentals/hadithsunnah/

bukhari/. A book translation of the *Al-Sahih* is available in English; see Muhammad Ibn Ismail Bukhari, *The English Translation of Sahih al-Bakhari with the Arabic Text*, 9 vols., trans. Muhammad Muhsin Kahn (Alexandria, VA: Al-Saadawi Publications, 1996).

The transliterated Arabic for the first text, as rendered by Faris Mailk is: *la'ana rasoolullah salla allahu 'alaihi wa sallama al-mutashabbiheena min ar-rijaali bil-nisaa'i wal-mutashabbihaati min an-nisaa'i bir-rijaali.* Accessed online at http://www.well.com/user/aquarius/Qurannotes.htm.

Cf. Vern L. Bullough, *Sexual Variance in Society and History* (N. Y.: John Wiley & Sons, 1976), p. 141.

625 Al An-Nawawi, *Riyad us Saliheen* (compiled byAl-Imam Abu Zakariya Yahya bin Sharaf An-Nawawi Ad-Dimashqi), Bk. 17, ch. 292, #1632. Accessed online at http://www.witnesspioneer.org/vil/ hadeeth/riyad/17/chap292.htm.

626 Rowson, p. 672.

627 See, for example, Malik's *Muwatta*, Bk. 37, #37.6.5. This was accessed online at http://www.usc.edu/dept/MSA/fundamentals/hadithsunnah/muwatta/037.37.6.5.

628 See, for example, *Sunan Abu-Dawud*, 32.4095, which speaks of a *mukhannath*— one "free of physical needs" (i.e., not interested in sex)—in the presence of the Prophet's wives. See the hadith online at http://www.usc.edu/dept/MSA/ fundamentals/hadithsunnah/ abudawud/ 032.sat. html#032.4095.

629 M. Muhsin Kahn (Translator), *Translation of Sahih Bakhari*, Vol. 8, Bk. 82, #820. Accessed online at http://www.usc.edu/dept/MSA/fundamentals/hadithsunnah /bukhari/082.sbt.html#008.082.820. A variant at 7.72.774 specifies that the person 'Umar turned out was a woman.

630 Rowson (p. 674) collects and comments on the sources.

631 Islamic scholars such as Imam Al An-Nawawi distinguished between *Mukhannathun* who were so by nature and others who affected the guise for immoral purposes; the former is considered blameless while the latter is regarded as a sinner.

632 See, for example, *Sahih Bakhari*, 5.59.613; accessed online at http://www. usc.edu/dept/MSA/fundamentals/hadithsunnah/bukhari/059.sbt.html#005.059.613. Cf. 7.62.162; accessed online at http://www.usc.edu/dept/MSA/fundametals/ hadithsunnah/bukhari/062.sbt.html #007.062.162.

633 Cf. Rowson, pp. 675-676.

634 Cf. Rowson, p. 679.

635 Rowson, p. 673. Ibn Maja pairs the penalty with a different false accusation—of accusing someone of taking the active (penetrating) role in same-sex intercourse.

636 *Sunan Abu-Dawud*, 4.4928. Quoted in Rowson, p. 673f.

637 Moshe Sharon, *Corpus Inscriptionum Arabicarum Palaestinae (CIAP), vol. 3: D-F* (Leiden: Brill, 2004), p. 231.

638 Rowson, p. 680.

[639] Ibid, p. 679.

[640] Habib Hassan Touma, *The Music of the Arabs*, translated by Laurie Schwartz (Portland, OR: Amadeus Press, 1996).

[641] Everett K. Rowson, "Gender Irregularity as Entertainment: Institutionalized Transvestism at the Caliph Court in Medieval Baghdad," in S. Farmer & C. B. Pasternack (Eds.), *Gender and Difference in the Middle Ages*, pp. 45-72 (Minneapolis: Univ. of Minnesota Press, 2003), p. 57. Cf. Ned Sublette, *Cuba and Its Music. From the First Drums to the Mambo* (Chicago: Chicago Review Press, 2004), p. 14.

[642] Rowson, "The Effeminates of Early Medina," pp. 692-693.

[643] Rowson, "Gender Irregularity as Entertainment," pp. 57-59.

[644] Anne Bolin, "Traversing Gender," in S. Ramet (Ed.), *Gender Reversals and Gender Cultures: Anthropological and Historical Perspectives*, pp. 22-51 (N. Y.: Routledge, 1996), p. 41.

[645] Stephen O. Murray, "The Will Not to Know: Islamic Accomodations of Male Homosexuality," in S. O. Murray & W. Roscoe, *Islamic Homosexualities: Culture, History, and Literature*, pp. 14-54 (N. Y.: New York Univ. Press, 1997), p. 45f., n. 23.

[646] *Coming Out in Dialogue: Policies and Perceptions of Sexual Minority Groups in Asia and Europe* (2005), §2.1.5 (p. 15). Research paper commissioned by the Intellectual Exchange Department of the Asia-Europe Foundation for its "Talks on the Hill" series. Accessed online at http://asef.on2web.com/ subSite/ccd/documents/ briefingpaper _001.pdf.

[647] "Kuwait Sex-Change Upheld," *BBC News World Edition* online (2004, Apr. 25). Accessed online at http://news.bbc.co.uk/2/hi/middle_east/3657727.stm.

[648] Nauman Naqvi & Hasan Mujtaba, "Two Baluchi *Buggas*, a Sindhi *Zenana*, and the Status of *Hijras* in Contemporary Pakistan," in S. O. Murray & W. Roscoe (Eds.), *Islamic Homosexualities: Culture, History, & Literature*, pp. 262-266 (N. Y.: New York Univ. Press, 1997).

[649] Yik Koon Teh, *The Mak Nyahs: Malaysian Male to Female Transsexuals* (Singapore: Eastern Universities Press, 2002).

[650] Michael G. Peletz, "'Ordinary Muslims' and Muslim Resurgents in Contemporary Malaysia: Notes on an Ambivalent Relationship," in R. W. Hefnew & P. Horvatich (Eds.), *Islam in an Era of Nation-States. Politics and Religious Renewal in Muslim Southeast Asia*, pp. 231-274 (Honolulu: univ. of Hawai'i Press, 1997), p. 240.

[651] Slamah chairs the Network of Sex Work Projects (NSWP), a global organization promoting health and human rights for sex workers.

[652] Khartini Slamah, "The Struggle to Be Ourselves, neither Men nor Women: Mak Nyahs in Malaysia," in G. Misra & R. Chandiramani (Eds.), *Sexuality, Gender and Rights. Exploring Theory and Practice in South and Southeast Asia*, pp. 98-111 (Thousand Oaks, CA: Sage, 2005), p. 99.

[653] Ibid, p. 101.

[654] Ibid, p. 101f.

655 Honey Tan Lay Ean, "Jeffrey Jessie: Recognizing Transsexuals," *The Malaysian Bar* (2005, Nov. 17). Accessed online at http://www.malaysianbar.org.my/gender_ issues/jeffrey_jessie_recognising_transexuals_by_honey_tan_lay_ean.html#_ftnref1.

656 Wong Ee Lynn, "Neither Here Nor There: The Legal Dilemma of the Transsexual Community in Malaysia,"*The Malaysian Bar* (2005, Feb. 1). Accessed online at http://www.malaysianbar.org.my/gender_issues/neither_here_nor_there_the_legal_dil emma_of_the_transsexual_community_in_malaysia.html.

657 Tom Boelstorff, "Playing Back the Nation: Waria, Indonesian Transvestites," *Cultural Anthropology, 19* (no. 2), 159-195 (2004); see esp. pp. 166-168.

658 Baudouin Dupret, "Sexual Morality at the Egyptian Bar: Female Circumcision, Sex Change Operations, and Motives for Suing," *Islamic Law and Society, 9* (no. 1), 42-69 (2002), pp. 50-51. Also see Jakob Skovgaard-Petersen, *Defining Islam for the Egyptian State. Muftis and Fatwas of the Dar al-Ifta* (N. Y.: Brill, 1997). Cf. Hamdi Rizq, "Shaykh al-Azhar yufti bi-jawaz tahwil al-jins" *(The Shaykh al-Azhar Gives a Formal Legal Opinion Permitting Sex Change). Al-Hayat* (1995, November 10), p. 24.

659 Quoted in Jakob Skovgaard-Petersen, "Sex Change in Cairo: Gender and Islamic Law," *The Journal of the International Institute, 2* (no. 3) (1996, Spring). Accessed online at http://www.umich.edu/~iinet/journal/vol2no3/sex_in_cairo.html. The *fatwa* also available under the title *Al Azhar Fatwa on Gender Reassignment*, accessed online at http://flanaganfamily.org/AlAzharFatwaSexChanges1988.html.

660 Ibid.

661 Ibid.

662 A 2002 *fatwa* issued by Al-Azhar scholar Muhammad Muhammad Abu Laylah, with respect to the possibility of a male pregnancy by scientific means, repeats the basic injunction, "Sex-change is a violation of the order set by Allah." See *Fatawa: Islam's Stance on Human Male Pregnancy* (2002), accessed at Fatwa Management System at http://infad.usim.edu.my/modules.php?op=modload&name=News&file=article&sid=8437.

663 Dupret, pp. 51-52. Sally now lives under the name of Sally Mursi. For a followup story, see Azza Hattab, "Sally's Story," *Egypt Today* (2004, July). Accessed online at http://www.egypttoday.com/article.aspx?ArticleID=1737.

664 "Sex Change for Five Saudi Sisters," *Sydney Morning Herald* (2004, June 16), found online at smh.com.au and accessed online at http://www.smh.com.au/ articles/2004/06/16/1087244946830.html.

665 Sebastian Usher, "Gender Correction for Saudi Girls," *BBC News* (2004, June 17), accessed online at http://news.bbc.co.uk/2/hi/middle_east/3814041.stm.

666 Khattab, "Sally's Story." [Please note: Minor punctuation corrections have been made to the text as it appeared in the article; these do not change either the wording or the sense of the material.]

667 Abdullah Al-faqih, *Fatawa: Operation for Sex Change* (2001; 28 Muharram, 1422); issuing authority: Islam Web. Accessed online at Fatwa Management System at http://infad.usim.edu.my/modules.php?op=modload&name=News&file=article&sid=4820.

668 Ibid, p. 53.

669 "Saudi Court Rules in Favor of Transsexual . . ." [News], *Al Bawaba* (2004, Dec. 16), accessed online at http://www.albawaba.com/en/news/178356.

670 Qu'ran, Surah 30:30, cited in Azza Khattab, "Sex Changes: Haram or Hala?" *Egypt Today* (2004, July). Accessed online at http://www.egypttoday.com/article.aspx?ArticleID=1738.

671 Abdullah Al-faqih, *Fatawa: Muslim Male, Former Female, Wants Wife* (2006; 16 Safar, 1420); issuing authority: Islam Web. Accessed at the Fatwa Management System at http://infad.usim.edu.my/modules.php?op=modload&name=News&file=article&sid=4792.

672 Abdullah Al-faqih, *Fatawa: Transsexual* (1999; 16 Safar 1420); issuing authority: Islam Web. Accessed online at Fatwa Management System at http://infad.usim.edu.my/modules.php?op=modload&name=News&file=article&sid=4813.

673 "A Fatwa for Freedom," *The Guardian* (2005, July 27), maintained on the Guardian Unlimited website, accessed online at http://www.guardian.co.uk./g2/story/0,,1536658,00.html.

674 Ibid. Also see, Frances Harrison, "Iran's Sex-Change Operations," *BBC News* (2005, Jan. 5), accessed online at http://news.bbc.co.uk/2/hi/programmes/newsnight/4115535.stm. Cf. the blog posting by 'Yosie,' "Changing Sexes, Changing Islam," *Critical Montages* (2004, August 3), accessed online at http://montages.blogspot.com/2004/08/changing-sex-changing-islam.html.

675 Nazila Fathi, "As Repression Lifts, More Iranians Change Their Sex," *New York Times* (2004, Aug. 2). With NYTimes.com membership the article can be accessed online at http://www.nytimes.com/2004/08/02/international/middleast/02iran. html?hp=&adxnnl=1&adxnnlx=1091489991-2sBf34Gerj 3nlXAaASXZcQ.

676 Bouhdiba, chapter 4 (pp. 30-42).

677 Rowson, "Gender Irregularity as Entertainment," p. 48.

678 Ibid, p. 47.

679 John Boswell, *Christianity, Social Tolerance, and Homosexuality* (Chicago: Univ. of Chicago Press, 1980), p. 195. Boswell cites an 11th century description by Ibn Shuhaid of such a female.

680 Rowson, "Gender Irregularity as Entertainment," pp. 48-49.

681 Ibid, pp. 49-51.

682 Ruth Mazo Karras, *Sexuality in Medieval Europe: Doing Unto Others* (N. Y.: Routledge, 2005), p. 111.

683 Tan Beng Hui, "Women's Sexuality and the Discourse on Asian Values: Cross-Dressing in Malaysia," in E. Blackwood & S. E. Wieringa (Eds.), *Female Desires. Same-Sex Relations and Transgender Practices Across Cultures*, pp. 281-307 (N. Y.: Columbia Univ. Press, 1999).

Q. 79 Notes

[684] Robert P. Goldman, "Transsexualism, Gender, and Anxiety in Traditional India," *Journal of the American Oriental Society, 113* (no. 3), 374-401 (1993), p. 376.

[685] Vinay Lai, "Not This, Not That: The Hijras of India and the Cultural Politics of Sexuality," *Social Text, 61*, 119-140 (1999), p. 121.

[686] Denise L. Carmody & John T. Carmody, *Ways to the Center. An Introduction to World Religions,* 4th ed. (Belmont, CA: Wadsworth, 1993), p. 107.

[687] *Subhasitaratnabhandagara,* no. 9. Quoted in Goldman, p. 377 n. 18.

[688] *Manusmerti (Laws of Manu),* V.147-151. Translated by George Büeler, *The Laws of Manu [Sacred Books of the East,* Vol. 25] (1886). Accessed at the Internet Sacred Text Archive website, online at http://www.sacred-texts.com/hin/manu/manu05.htm.

[689] S. W. Jamison & M. Witzel, *Vedic Hinduism* (1992), pp. 48, 77. Accessed online at http://www.people.fas.harvard.edu/~witzel/vedica.pdf.

[690] See volume 1 of this work (*Dress & Gender*), the answer to Q. 5.

[691] Michael J. Sweet & Leonard Swilling, "The First Medicalization: The Taxonomy and Etiology of Queerness in Classical Indian Medicine," *Journal of the History of Sexuality, 3* (no. 4), 590-607 (1993), p. 601.

[692] Amara Das Wilhelm, *Tritiya-Prakriti: People of the Third Sex. Understanding Homosexuality, Transgender Identity, and Intersex Conditions Through Hinduism* (Philadelphia: Xlibris, 2004), pp. 4-5; quote is from p. 5.

[693] See Wilhelm, pp. 5, 10. Cf. the discussion on the *napumsakalinga* in Jainism in the answer to Q. 83.

[694] Wilhelm, p. 5.

[695] Paola Bacchetta, "When the (Hindu) Nation Exiles Its Queers," *Social Text, 61,* 141-166 (1999), p. 144. In the same place, Baccheta remarks, "All these terms are still under debate for various reasons. As yet, no term has surfaced or been invented under which could be united the whole range of queer practices, lifestyles, and identities."

[696] *Kama Sutra,* II.9.1-2, 6. In Alain Danielou (translator), *The Complete Kama Sutra* (Rochester, VT: Park Street Press, 1994), pp. 183-184 (italics added). Cf. *Kama Sutra,* V.6.2-3.

[697] Yoshadhara's *Jayamangala* is included in Danielou's translation (see p. 183).

[698] Wilhelm, pp. 8-14.

[699] See, for example, the *Isa Upanishad.*

[700] Devdutt Pattanaik, *The Man Who Was a Woman and Other Queer Tales from Hindu Lore* (Binghamton, NY: Haworth Press, 2002)., p. 4.

[701] Pattanaik (p. 4) stated that the divine principle may be visualized as male (Vishnu), female (Shakti), or both (Shiva), which is the one absolute, and unfathomable. I would express it more as an essential Unity, a divine 'ground' from which springs all

appearances, and for which 'male' and 'female' are not enough by themselves to represent all-that-is.

[702] These free-verse lyrics written by Devara Dasimayya, along with others composed by South Indian Shaiva *bhaktis* (mystics devoted to the God Siva), are collected and translated in A.K. Ramanujan, *Speaking of Siva* (Baltimore, MD: Penguin Books, 1973).

[703] A.K. Ramanujan, *Speaking of Siva* (Baltimore, MD: Penguin Books, 1973). Basavanna (aka. Basaveshwara, Prince of Koodala) probably lived 1106-1167/68 C.E. The 'Lord of the Meeting Rivers' is the deity *Kudalasangamadeva* (see p. 62).

[704] *Srimad Bhagavatam* 5.5.8. Translation by A. C. Bahktivedanta Swami Prabhupada at the Bakhtivedanta VedaBase: Srimad Bhagavatam website, accessed online at http://srimadbhagavatam.com/5/5/en.

[705] See Pattanaik, who covers much ground in this text, as indicated in the opening lines of the book (p. 1):

> A god transforms into a nymph and enchants another god. A king becomes pregnant. Another king has children who call him "father," and "mother." A hero turns into a eunuch and wears female apparel. A prince discovers on his wedding night that he is not a man. A princess has to turn into a man before she can avenge her humiliation. Widows of a king make love to conceive his child. Friends of the same sex end up marrying each other after one of them metamorphoses into a woman. These are some of the tales I came upon in my study of Hindu lore.

Many of the tales involve crossdressing (chapter 3). In sum, Pattanaik collects together a larger group of stories than are found in this present text.

[706] Wilhelm, p. 12. In the discussion of *sandha* Wilhelm presents a number of variations denoted through specific compound forms. Thus, for example, *asexual* individuals—the intersexed—are designated in Sanskrit as *nisarga-sandha* (p. 13), and those whose sexual orientation the West terms *bisexual* are sometimes in Sanskrit called *paksa-sandha* (p. 15). Compound forms can explicitly connect to very narrow activities (e.g. *kumbhika-sandha* for a male who take the passive role in anal intercourse (p. 17)), or states (e.g., *sevyaka-sandha* for a man who temporarily loses his sexual potency from having exhausted himself by too much sexual activity with women (p. 117)). See Wilhelm's Appendix 3 for the 'Twenty Types of Sandha' (pp. 174-176).

[707] *Sushruta Samhita* 3.2.38, 42-43. See Wilhem, p. 130. For an English translation see Kaviraj Kunjalal Bhishagratna, *The Sushruta Samhita: An English Translation Based on Original Sanskrit Texts*, in 3 vols. in 4 parts (New Delhi: Cosmo Publications, 2006).

[708] Goldman, p. 376f.

[709] Ibid, p. 396.

[710] A. C. Bhaktivedanta Swami Prabhupada (Translator and commentator), *Bhagavad Gita as it is* (L. A.: Bhaktivedanta Book Trust, 1983), p. 477.

[711] Ibid, p. 477f.

712 Ibid, p. 590.

713 *Mahabharata*, Bk. 3, Indralokagamana Parva (§§LIIff.). Things go from bad to worse for the couple. Nala thinks to spare his wife from trouble and so deserts her, thinking she will return to her father's kingdom. The two have separate adventures before they are rejoined and 'live happily ever after.' See the translation by Kisari Mohan Ganguli, accessed online at the Internet Sacred Text Archive website, http://www.sacred-texts.com/hin/m03/index.htm. The complete text of the *Mahabharata* is available online and was accessed at http://www.sacred-texts.com/hin/maha/index.htm.

Also see John Campbell Oman, *The Great Indian Epics. The Stories of the Ramayana and the Mahabharata* (London: George Bell & Sons, 1994 reprint of 1894 ed.), p. 208.

714 *Mahabharata*, Bk. 5: *Udyoga Parva*, §CXCI, translated by Kisari Mohan Ganguli, *The Mahabharata of Krishna-Dwaipayana Vyasa*, (Calcutta: Bharata Press, 1883-1896), p. 364. Accessed online at the Internet Sacred Text Archive website, at http://www.sacred-texts.com/hin/m05/m05191.htm. Further references to this translation will be cited as 'Ganguli translation,' with page number.

715 *Mahabharata*, Bk. 6: *Bhishma Parva* (especially §§CXIXff.), Ganguli translation, accessed online at the Internet Sacred Text Archive website, at http://www.sacred-texts.com/hin/m06/m06119.htm.

716 On Bhima, see *Mahabharata* 4.15-22 ('Slaying of Kichaka'), recounted in volume 2 of this set, in the answer to Q. 43.

717 Lai, p. 125.

718 *Mahabharata*, Bk. 4: *Virata Parva*, §II, Ganguli translation, p. 3f. Available at the Mahabharat online.com website, accessed online at http://www.mahabharataonline.com/translation/mahabharata_04002.php.

719 *Mahabharata*, Bk. 4: *Virata Parva*, §XI, Ganguli translation, p. 19. Available at the Mahabharat online.com website, accessed online at

720 One version has the girl born to Vaivasvata Manu named Sudyumna upon becoming male. The name Ila is then bestowed when turned into a female because of entering the forbidden wood.

721 *Ramayana* 7.78-81 in G. H. Blatt & U. P. Shah (Eds.), *Ramayana. The Valmiki Ramayana,* 7 vols. (Baroda: Oriental Institute, 1975). Accounts and details vary. Cf. the *Gautamimahatmya* of the *Brahmapurana* (38:33-35), cited in Goldman, p. 379 n. 33.

722 Gerald James Larson, "Polymorphic Sexuality, Homoeroticism, and the Study of Religion," *Journal of the American Academy of Religion, 65* (no. 3), 655-665 (1997), p. 662.

723 Donna M. Wulff, "Radha's Audacity in *Kirtan* Performances and Women's Status in Greater Bengal," in K. L. King (Ed.), *Women and Goddess Traditions*, pp. 64-83 (Minneapolis: Fortress Press, 1007), p. 69ff. & p. 79 n. 26.

[724] June McDaniel, "Bengali Vaishnavism," *World Culture Encyclopedia* (2007), at the everyculture.com website, accessed online at http://www.everyculture.com/South-Asia/Bengali-Vaishnava.html.

[725] Philip Spratt, *Hindu Culture and Personality: A Psycho-Analytic Study* (New Delhi: Delhi Printers Prakashan), p. 237.

[726] Phil Hine, "For the Love of God: Variations of the Vaisnava School of Krishna Devotion," *Ashé, 2* (no. 4), 51-56.

[727] *Sakhabhava*, in contrast, means 'male-to-male attachment.' See John Stratton Hawley, "The Damage of Separation: Krishna's Loves and Kali's Child," *Journal of The American Academy of Religion, 72* (no. 2), 369-393 (2004), p. 386.

[728] Charles S. J. White, "Vallabhacarya on the Love Games of Krsna, by James D. Redington" [Untitled Book Review], *Journal of the American Oriental Society, 110* (no. 2), 373-374.

[729] Vern L. Bullough, "Hinduism," in E. J. Haeberle (Ed.), *Human Sexuality: An Encyclopedia* (2006; original edition published N. Y.: Garland, 1994). This electronic edition housed at the Magnus Hirschfeld Archive for Sexology, hosted by the Humboldt-Universität zu Berlin, accessed online at http://www2.hu-berlin.de/sexology/GESUND/ARCHIV/SEN/CH12.HTM. Bullough's identification of these males with India's *Hijra* has been disputed.

[730] Erick Laurent, "Sexuality and Human Rights: An Asian Perspective," *Journal of Homosexuality, 48* (nos. 3-4), 163-225 (2005), p. 172.

[731] For more see N. Bradford, "Transgenderism and the Cult of Yelamma: Heat, Sex and Sickness in South Indian Ritual," *Journal of Anthropological Research, 39* (no. 3), 307-322 (1983).

[732] Pattanaik, p. 11. However, some report *Jogappas* who retain male dress.

[733] Laurent, p. 172.

[734] For a complete account, see Serena Nanda, *Neither man Nor Woman: The Hijras of India* (N. Y.: Wadsworth, 1998).

[735] Members of this group who are female may be termed *Hijrin*.

[736] Lai, pp. 128-129. Quote is from p. 128 (italics added).

[737] Bahuchara Mata is a 'mother goddess' like Cybele. See Pattanaik, chapter 4 for her story. Cf. Will Roscoe, "Priests of the Goddess: Gender Transgression in Ancient Religion," *History of Religions, 35* (no. 3), 295-330 (1996).

[738] Serena Nanda, "The Hijras of India: Cultural and Individual Dimensions of an Institutionalized Third Gender Role. Special Issue: Anthropology and Homosexual Behavior," *Journal of Homosexuality, 11* (nos. 3-4), 35-54 (1985). Within the *Hijra* community there is some debate over engagement in sex work, which is performed by younger members. Some elder *Hijras* see this as inauthentic *Hijra* practice, while those who engage in it defend the practice as part of the *Hijra* lifecycle that culminates later in *badhai*.

See Gayatri Reddy, "Geographies of Contagion: *Hijras, Kothis*, and the politics of Sexual Marginality in Hyderabad," *Anthropology & Medicine, 12* (no. 3), 255-270 (2005), p. 260.

[739] Many *Hijra* in Pakistan, an Islamic nation, are associated with the Sufi tradition of that religion. See the answer to Q. 78.

[740] Lai, p. 122.

[741] This latter version is recounted in Lai, p. 123, who adds in a footnote (p. 136f., n. 18) that such a tale could not be found in the *Ramayana* of either Valmiki or Tulsidas, and that it likely does not appear in any of the principal versions, but is probably an oral tradition.

[742] 'Paramahamsa' is an honorific, roughly equivalent to the Western world's 'saint.'

[743] Viktor A. Van Bulert, "Hindus and Muslims in Bengal: Is Religious Experience a Unifying Factor?" in J. D. Gort, H. Jansen, & H. M. Vroom (Eds.), *Religion, Conflict and Resolution. Multifaith Ideals and Realities*, pp. 37-50 (Atlanta: Rodopi, 2002), p. 46.

[744] Gobind Behari Lal, "Appendix B: Complementarity of Human Sexes," in H. Benjamin, *The Transsexual Phenomenon* (N. Y.: The Julian Press, 1966). This volume is maintained at the website of the *International Journal of Transgenderism* and accessed online at http://www.symposium.com/ijt/benjamin/appendix_b.htm.

[745] Sudhir Kakar, *The Analyst and the Mystic: Psychoanalytic Reflections on Religion and Mysticism* (Chicago: Univ. of Chicago Press, 1991), p. 33. Cf. "The Analyst and the Mystic," in S. Kakar, *The Indian Psyche*, pp. 125-188 (New Delhi: Oxford Univ. Press, 1996), p. 157. Also see his "Ramakrishna and the Mystical Experience," in S. Kakar, *The Essential Writings of Sudhir Kakar*, ch. 12 (New Delhi: Oxford Univ. Press, 2001).

[746] M., *The Gospel of Sri Ramakrishna*, 5 vols., translated by Swami Nikhilananda (N. Y.: Ramakrishna-Vivekananda Center, 1942). An abridged edition, also translated by Swami Nikhilananda (), is available, too. Also see Narasingha P. Sil, *Ramakrishna Revisited* (Lanham, MD: University Press of America, 1998).

[747] Although a number of sources were used for compiling this brief biographical section, particularly useful was D. S. Sarma, "The Experience of Sri Ramakrishna Paramahamsa," *The Journal of Religion, 7* (no. 2), 186-203 (1927).

[748] A Hindu *sannyasin* is an individual who has renounced normal affairs to concentrate on seeking *moksha* (liberation) through spiritual practices such as meditation and prayer.

[749] Thus the front flap to *The Gospel of Sri Ramakrishna* reads, "Through the differing disciplines of Hinduism, Christianity, and Islam he reached always the single goal, realization of the one God-Consciousness."

[750] Jeffrey J. Kripal, *Kali's Child: The Mystical and the Erotic in the Life and Teachings of Ramakrishna*, 2nd ed. (Chicago: Univ. of Chicago Press, 1998). Quote is from p. xiii.

[751] Larson, p. 661f.

[752] Goldman, p. 397f. On Schreber, see Sigmund Freud, "Psychoanalytic Notes on an Autobiographical Account of a Case of Paranoia (*Dementia Paranoides*)," in S. Freud,

The Standard Edition of the Complete Psychological Works of Sigmund Frued, 12, 213-226 (London: Hogarth Press, 1958).

[753] Kakar, *The Analyst and the Mystic*, p. 33f. Kukar believes that in 'affective mysticism' women have a natural advantage and, following Donald Winnicott, proposes that the 'pure female element' of Winnicott is the 'primary femininity' essential to such mysticism.

[754] See Spratt, *Hindu Culture and Personality*.

[755] Christopher Isherwood, *Ramakrishna and His Disciples* (N. Y.: Simon & Schuster, 1965). Isherwood was a noted 20th century novelist who identified himself as a devotee of Ramakrishna, declaring his belief that Ramakrishna was "an incarnation of God upon earth" (p. 2).

[756] Lal, "Complementarity of Human Sexes."

[757] *The Gospel of Sri Ramakrishna*, 31 (p. 603).

[758] Kelley Ann Raab, "Is There Anything Transcendent about Transcendence? A Philosophical and Psychological Study of Sri Ramakrishna," *Journal of the American Academy of Religion, 63* (no. 2), 321-341 (1995), p. 332.

[759] Kripal, p. 103.

[760] Raab, p. 332.

[761] Ibid, p. 333.

[762] *The Gospel of Sri Ramakrishna*, 11 (p. 232). Entry dated Monday, June 4, 1883.

[763] Kripal, p. 105.

[764] Ibid, p. 108.

[765] Raab, p. 833. Raab references J. Moussaieff Masson, *The Oceanic Feeling: The Origins of Religious Sentiment in Ancient India* (Dordrecht, Holland: D. Reidel Publishing Co., 1980), pp. 8, 35.

[766] *The Gospel of Sri Ramakrishna*, Introduction (p. 25). Also see Swami Saradananda, *Sri Ramakrishna the Great Master*, translated by Swami Jagadananda (Mylapore: Sri Ramakrishna Math, 1952), pp. 233-234. Cf. Narasingha Prosad Sil, *Divine Dowager: The Life and Teachings of Saradamani, the Holy Mother* (Selinsgrove, PA: Susquehanna Univ. Press, 2003), p. 46. Sil adopts a Western psychiatric view to explore and explain such phenomena.

[767] *The Gospel of Sri Ramakrishna*, 8 (p. 225).

[768] Ibid, 49 (p. 934).

[769] Ibid, 8 (p. 195).

[770] Ibid, 8 (p. 185).

[771] Sil, p. 45.

[772] See Philippians 2:12-13, which reads in part: "For God is at work in you, bith to will and to work for his good pleasure." Also see Romans 15:18f., which reads in part:

"For I will not venture to speak of anything except what Christ has wrought through me . . . ." Cf. 2 Corinthians 13:3, where Paul refers to Christ speaking in him (Ramakrishna, in the same place, said, "I act as He makes me act. I speak as He makes me speak.'), and reminds the believers of Christ in them (verse 5). Also see Colossians 3:11, Ephesians 3:20, and cf., especially, Romans 9:20-21.

[773] *The Gospel of Sri Ramakrishna*, 7 (p. 176).

[774] B. M. G., "N. T. Rama Rao (1923-1995): A Messiah of the Masses," *The Hindu* (2002, Dec. 9), accessed online at http://www.hinduonnet.com/thehindu/mp/2002/12/09/stories/2002120901160200.htm. Also see John F. Burns, "N. T. Rama Rao, 72, Is Dead; Star Status Infused His Politics," *The New York Times* (1996, Jan. 19), accessed online at http://query.nytimes.com/gst/fullpage.html?res=9D03E4DE1E39F93AA25752C0A960958260.

[775] Burns, ibid.

[776] Parama Roy, *Indian Traffic. Identities in Question in Colonial and Postcolonial India* (Berkeley: Univ. of California Press, 1998). Text accessed online at http://ark.cdlib.org/ark:/13030/ft8s20097j/.

Q. 80 Notes

[777] Jose I. Cabezon, *Buddhism, Sexuality, and Gender* (Albany, NY: SUNY Press, 1992).

[778] Miriam Levering, "Stories of Enlightened Women in Ch'an and the Chinese Buddhist Female Bodhissatva/Goddess Tradition," in K. L. King (Ed.), *Women and Goddess Traditions*, pp. 137-176 (Minneapolis: Fortress Press, 1997), p. 141.

[779] For more about Avalokitesvara, see John Blofield, *Bodhisattva of Compassion: The Mystical Tradition of Kuan Yin* (London: Allen & Unwin, 1977). Also see Barbara E. Reed, "The Gender Symbolism of Kuan-yin Bodhisattva," in J. I. Cabezon (Ed.), *Buddhism, Sexuality, and Gender*, pp. 159-180 (Albany: State University of New York Press, 1992).

[780] Barbara E. Reed, "The Gender Symbolism of Kuan-yin Bodhisattva," in J. I. Cabezon (Ed.), *Buddhism, Sexuality, and Gender*, pp. 159-180 (Albany, NY: State University of New York Press, 1992). Quote is from p. 176.

[781] Alan Sponberg, "Attitdues Toward Women and the Feminine in Early Buddhism," in J. I. Cabezon (Ed.), *Buddhism, Sexuality, and Gender*, pp. 1-36 (Albany, NY: State University of New York Press, 1992).

[782] Heng-Ching Shih, *Chinese Bhiksunis in the Ch'an Tradition*, webpage on the Buddhism Today website, accessed online at http://www.buddhismtoday.com/english/sociology/026-bhikkhuni.htm. (1995), pp. 73-105.

[783] *Sanyutta-Nikaya* 1.5.6. Accessed online at the Thripitakaya Online website, at http://thripitakaya.org/thripitakaya.php?page=2Sutta-Pitaka/3Samyutta-Nikaya/Samyutta1/01-Devata-Samyutta/05-Adittavaggo-e.html. An alternate rendition: "This is the only vehicle/Be it a woman or be it a man/The one who takes this vehicle/Can reach the peace of Nibbana."

784 *Cullavagga*, 10.1.1-6, in Robert E. Van Voorst, *An Anthology of World Scriptures* (Belmont, CA: Wadsworth, 1994), p. 95.

785 Ibid, p. 96.

786 Although more than a single example of how female bodies offer temptation to Buddha could be offered, we might think preeminently of the figures of Tanha (Desire), Raga (Lust), and Arati (Discontent), the three daughters of Mara, adversary of Buddha, who are sent to distract him as he seeks enlightenment. See the *Puddhana Sutta*.

787 This instruction is the first *garudhamma* of the *Cullavaga* and is issued with respect to the ordination by Buddha of the first woman, his beloved aunt (and stepmother) Mahpajapati (Maha Pajapati) Gotami. For issues and difficulties surrounding this material see the online article by Sri Lankan *bhikkhun* Bhikkhu Kusuma, *Inaccuracies in Buddhist Women's History*, accessed online at the ASA Bikkhunni Ordination Research website, at http://bhikkhunicommittee.googlepages.com/Kusuma.doc.

788 Diana Y. Paul, *Women in Buddhism: Images of the Feminine in Mahayana Tradition* (Berkeley: Univ. of California Press, 1980; 2nd ed., 1985), pp. xix-xxi. Quote is from p. xix.

789 Karen Christina Lang, "Images of Women in Early Buddhism and Christian Gnosticism," *Buddhist-Christian Studies, 2*, 94-105 (1982), p. 94. Lang sees an interesting parallel of these images in the two groups of the title.

790 Ibid, p. 99.

791 Miranda Shaw, *Passionate Enlightenment: Women in Tantric Buddhism* (Princeton: Princeton Univ. Press, 1994), p. 27.

792 See Luis O. Gomez, *The Land of Bliss* (Honolulu: Hawaii Univ. Press, 1996), p. 170.

793 See Nancy Schuster Barnes, "Changing the Female Body: Wise Women and the Bodhisattva Career in Some Maharatnakuta Sūtras," *Journal of the International Association of Buddhist Studies, 4* (no.1), 24-69 (1981). Also see Diana Y. Paul, *Women in Buddhism: Images of the Feminine in Mahayana Tradition* (Berkeley: Univ. of California Press, 1985), especially pp. 166-216.

794 Lucinda Joy Peach, "Social Responsibility, Sex Change, and Salvation: Gender Justice in the *Lotus Sutra*," *Philosophy East and West, 52* (no. 1), 50-74 (2002), p. 50.

795 Ibid, p. 70.

796 Robin R. Wang, prefacing note to "The Story of the Dragon King's Daughter: From the Devadatta Chapter of the Lotus Sutra (*Miaofalianhua jing*)," in R. R. Wang (Ed.), *Images of Women in Chinese Thought and Culture: Writings from the Pre-Qin Period through the Song Dynasty*, pp. 278-283 (Indianapolis, IN: Hackett Publishing, 2003), p. 278f.

797 Bernard Faure, *The Power of Denial: Buddhism, Purity, and Gender* (Princeton: Princeton Univ. Press, 2003), p. 94.

798 Shih. *Contra* Shih's view, cf. Rita Gross, who contends that not only are such *sutras* few in number, their examples of *Bodhisattvas* are not representative. Gross maintains

that Buddhism views maleness as normative while females are "not full-fledged representatives of the human species." Rita M. Gross, "Anger and Meditation," in L. Fried-
man & S. Moon, *Being Bodies*, pp. 95-102 (Boston: Shambhala, 1997), p. 96.

799 Miranda Shaw, "Worship of Women in Tantric Buddhism: Male Is to Female as
Devotee Is to Goddess," in K. L. King (Ed.), *Women and Goddess Traditions*, pp. 111-136
(Minneapolis: Fortress Press, 1997), p. 118. Cf. *Candamaharosama-tantra* (32), "Wherever
in the world a female body is seen/That should be recognized as my holy body."

800 Ibid, p. 116.

801 Mohan Wijayaratna, *Buddhist Monastic Life According to the Texts of the Theravada
Tradition*, translated by C. Grangier & S. Collins (N. Y.: Cambridge Univ. Press, 1990), p.
40. See pp. 32-55 on Buddhist clothes and dress behavior.

802 I-Tsing, *A Record of the Buddhist Religion as Practiced in India and the Malay Archipelago (A.D. 671-695)*, translated by J. Takakusu (Oxford: Clarendon Press, 1896), p. 78.
The first three of those named are the elements of the *kivara*.

803 Thorstein Veblen, *The Theory of the Leisure Class* (London: Macmillan, 1911; original work published 1899), p. 181f. The text of chapter 7 of this work, "Dress as an Expression of the Pecuniary Culture," is part of the American Studies at the University of
Virginia website, and this material accessed online at http://xroads.virginia.edu/
~HYPER/VEBLEN/chap07.html. For more on Veblen's views, see the answer to Q.
4.

804 *Cullavagga*, 10.1.1-6, in Van Voorst, p. 95.

805 Andrea Whittaker, "Water Serpents and Staying By the Fire: Markers of Maturity
in a Northeast Thai Village," in L. Manderson & P. Liamputtong (Eds.), *Coming of Age in
South and Southeast Asia. Youth, Courtship and Sexuality*, pp. 17-41 (N. Y.: Routledge, 2002),
p. 23.

806 Peter A. Jackson, "Non-Normative Sex/Gender Categories in the Theravada
Buddhist Scripture," *Australian Humanities Review, 1* (1996, April-June). Accessed online
at http://www.lib.latrobe.edu.au/ AHR/archive/Issue-April-1996/Jacksonref.html.

807 Ibid.

808 Leonard Zwilling, "Homosexuality as Seen in Indian Buddhist Texts," in J. I.
Cabezon (Ed.), *Buddhism, Sexuality, and Gender*, pp. 203-214 (Albany, NY: State University of New York Press, 1992), p. 204.

809 Ibid, pp. 207, 211 n. 15.

810 Ibid, p. 205. On *napumsaka* see the extended discussion in the answer to Q. 79;
cf. the discussion of *napumsakalinga* in the answer to Q. 83.

811 Ibid.

812 Ibid, pp. 208-209.

813 Diana Y. Paul, "Buddhist Attitudes Toward Women's Bodies," *Buddhist-Christian
Studies, 1*, 63-71 (1981), p. 64.

[814] Ibid, p. 65.

[815] *Taisho shinshu daizokyo* 14.918c. 6-9, in Paul, p. 65. Cf. Paul, *Women in Buddhism*, p. 175f.

[816] Shaw.

[817] Levering, p. 150.

[818] Ibid, p. 146.

[819] Ibid, p. 147. Paul's (p. 66) version of this *sutra* more explicitly says, "King Sagara's daughter's female organs vanished, and the male organ became visible. She appeared as a Bodhisattva."

[820] Ibid, p. 145.

[821] Ibid, p. 147.

[822] Shaw, p. 67.

[823] Bernard Faure, *The Red Thread: Buddhist Approaches to Sexuality* (Princeton: Princeton Univ. Press, 1998), p. 77f.

[824] Ibid, p. 77.

[825] Toshie Kurihara, "The 21st Century Is a Century of Women—Buddhism and Women," *The Journal of Oriental Studies, 15*, 66-77 (2005), p. 67. Accessed online at the Institute of Oriental Philosophy website, at http://www.iop.or.jp/0515/kurihara.pdf.

[826] Ibid, p. 75f.

[827] Ibid, p. 76.

[828] Ibid.

[829] Alain Dang & Mandy Hu, *Lesbian, Gay, Bisexual and Transgender People: A Community Project. A Report from New York's Queer Asian Pacific Legacy Conference, 2004* (National Gay and Lesbian Task Force Policy Institute, 2004), pp. 3, 18. Accessed online at http://www.usc.edu/student-affairs/glbss/PDFS/APAstudy.pdf.

[830] Roger Corless, "Coming Out in the *Sangha*: Queer Community in American Buddhism," in C. S. Prebish & K. K. Tanaka (Eds.), *The Faces of Buddhism in America*, pp. 253-265 (Berkeley: Univ. of California Press, 1998), p. 262

[831] *Coming Out in Dialogue: Policies and Perceptions of Sexual Minority Groups in Asia and Europe* (2005), §2.1.2 (p. 10). Research paper commissioned by the Intellectual Exchange Department of the Asia-Europe Foundation for its "Talks on the Hill" series. Accessed online at http://asef.on2web.com/subSite/ccd/documents/ briefingpaper _001.pdf.

Q. 81 Notes

[832] Naming these three should not be construed as suggesting that only they have been important. Confucianism, for example, also has exercised important influence on Japanese culture, including gender ideas.

[833] Patrick Drazen, *Anime Explosion! The What? Why? and Wow! of Japanese Animation* (Berkeley, CA: Stone Bridge Press, 2003), p. 153f.

[834] Kenneth G. Henshall, *Dimensions of Japanese Society. Gender, Margins and Mainstream* (N. Y.: Palgrave Macmillan, 1999), pp. 1-8.

[835] Ibid, pp. 9-26.

[836] D. P. Martinez, "Gender, Shifting Boundaries and Global Cultures," in D. P. Martinez (Ed.), *The Worlds of Japanese Popular Culture: Gender, Shifting Boundaries and Global Cultures*, pp. 1-18 (N. Y.: Cambridge Univ. Press, 1998), p. 7.

[837] See Shigeko Okamoto & Janet S. Shibamoto Smith (Eds.), *Japanese Language, Gender, and Ideology. Cultural Models and Real People* (N. Y.: Oxford Univ. Press, 2004).

[838] Mark J. McLelland, *Male Homosexuality in Modern Japan: Cultural Myths and Social Realities* (N. Y.: RoutledgeCurzon, 2000), p. 84.

[839] Ibid, pp. 9-10; cf. p. 17. However, McLelland elsewhere comments that, "While transgender individuals have certainly been discussed in terms stressing their 'otherness,' the kind of moral and social condemnation which at times has violently erupted in English-language media has been largely absent." See his "Western Intersections, Eastern Approximations. Living More 'Like Oneself': Transgender Identities and Sexualities in Japan," in J. Alexander & K. Yescavage (Eds.), *Bisexuality and Transgenderism: InterSEXions of the Others*, pp. 203-230 (Binghamton, NY: Harrington Park Press, 2003), p. 220.

[840] Ibid, p. 8.

[841] Ibid, p. 9.

[842] Ibid, p. 195.

[843] Linda Edwards, *A Brief Guide to Beliefs: Ideas, Theologies, Mysteries, and Movements* (Louisville, KY: Westminster John Knox Press, 2001), p. 233.

[844] An example of such is the *Onna chohoki*, a popular lifestyle guide for women in 17th century Tokugawa Japan. See William Lindsey, "Religion and the Good Life. Motivation, Myth, and Metaphor in a Tokugawa Female Lifestyle Guide," *Japanese Journal of Religious Studies, 32* (no. 1), 35-52 (2005). The *Onna Daigaku* ('Greater learning for Women') of the Edo Period advised women to follow 3 Precepts of Subordination: obedience to father when young, obedience to husband when married, and obedience to so in old age. Arguably, some contemporary Japanese Manga also appeals to certain religious motifs to justify or explain various gender practices or relations.

[845] *Miko* in ancient times referred to a female shaman. More contemporaneously the term is used for female 'shrine maidens.' Broadly, *miko* ('female') has been set in contrast to *saniwa* ('male').

[846] Christopher Reichl, "The Okinawan New Religion Ijun. Innovation and Diversity in the Gender Role of the Religious Specialist," *Japanese Journal of Religious Studies, 20* (no. 4), 311-331 (1993), p. 311f.

[847] William George Aston, *Shinto, the Way of the Gods* (N. Y.: Longmans, Green, and Co., 1905), p. 21.

848 Nancy Ross Rosenberger, "Tree in Summer, Tree in Winter: Movement of Self in Japan," in N. R. Rosenberger (Ed.), *Japanese Sense of Self*, pp. 67-92 (N. Y.: Cambridge Univ. Press, 1992), p. 73. Cf. Jean Herbert, *Shinto: At the Fountainhead of Japan* (N. Y.: Stein & Day, 1967).

849 *Kogoshui. Gleanings from Ancient Stories*, 3rd ed., translated by G. Kato & H. Hoshino (Tokyo, 1926), p. 28f. Accessed online at the Internet Sacred Texts Archive, at http://www.sacred-texts.com/shi/kgsh/kgsh4.htm. 'Uzume,' remarks the text, signifies a 'strong, brave woman' (p. 21).

850 See *Kojiki* §C (Part VI) [236], in Basil Hall Chamberlain (translator), *A Translation of the "Ko-ji-ki," or Records of Ancient Matters* (Asiatic Society of Japan, 1919 reprint of 1882 ed.), p. 293. Accessed online at sacred-texts.com at http://www.sacred-texts.com/shi/kj/kj107.htm. Also see the *Nihongi*. Cf. *Kogoshui*, p. 39.

851 Sarah M. Nelson, *Gender in Archaeology: Analyzing Power and Prestige*, 2nd ed. (Walnut Creek, CA: Rowman Altamira, 2004), p. 112.

852 *Kogoshui*, p. 38. The text reads: "It was in the reign of this Emperor that regular taxes were for the first time imposed upon men and women. Men were to pay them by presenting the produce of the hunting of wild animals in the mountains and fields, whilst women were to pay by means of their home handicraft."

853 Marilyn F. Nefsky, "Liberator or Pacifer: Religion and Women in Japan," in U. King (Ed.), *Religion and Gender*, pp. 291-310 (Malden, MA: Blackwell, 1995), p. 304.

854 See Helen Hardacre, *Shinto and the State: 1868-1988* (Princeton, NJ: Princeton Univ. Press, 1989), p. 14.

855 Bernard Faure, *The Power of Denial: Buddhism, Purity, and Gender* (Princeton: Princeton Univ. Press, 2003), pp. 1-4.

856 Ibid, pp. 19, 119; cf. p. 141.

857 Faure (p. 135f.) quotes this Zen text as an example:
> What demerit is there in the fact of being a woman? What merit in being a man? There are bad men and good women. If you wish to hear the Dharma and put an end to pain and turmoil, forget about such things as male and female. As long as delusions have not yet been eliminated, neither men nor women are free from them; when they are eliminated and reality is experienced, there is no longer any distinction between male and female.

858 Ibid, pp. 127-140.

859 Ibid, p. 142; cf. p. 120-122.

860 Ibid, p. 108.

861 Faure sees Pure Land Buddhism's connecting salvation for women to Amida's 35th vow, rather than the 18th vow, colors the manner in which their view of gender develops. See pp. 108-118.

862 Mark Unno writes, "The *Lotus Sutra* is famous for Nichiren's reading that the dragon girl attains enlightenment as herself—contrary to the view of other Mahayana sutras, such as those of the Pure Land, according to which women must first be transformed into men before they can gain enlightenment." *Shingon Refractions: Myoe and the Mantra of Light* (Somerville, MA: Wisdom Publications, 2004), p. 131.

863 For examples of statements in Nichiren's writings that reflect the patriarchal spirit of medieval japan, see Ichiu Mori, "Nichiren's View of Women," *Japanese Journal of Religious Studies, 30* (nos. 3-4), 279-290 (2003), p. 284. One example: "The Chinese character for woman implies 'to depend.' The wisteria depends on the pine tree, and a woman depends on a man." (*Showa teihon Nichiren Shonin ibun* 1:858).

864 Ibid, p. 279.

865 Ibid, p. 280.

866 Ibid, p. 285 (citing *Showa teihon Nichiren Shonin ibun*, 2: 1795).

867 Kyoko Nakamura, "The Religious Consciousness and Activities of Contemporary Japanese Women," *Japanese Journal of Religious Studies, 24* (nos. 1-2), 87-120 (1997), p. 105. Nakamura (p. 106) concludes that, "a sexually discriminatory view of women still seems firmly entrencehed, but, at least outwardly, it seems to be gradually waning from people's consciousness."

868 Some new religions, like Tenrikyo or Omoto, are in a spiritual lineage principally tied to Shinto; others, like Reiyukai or its offshoot Rissho Koseikai, are descendants of Buddhism (in this case, Nichiren Buddhism). But it is better to regard all of them as having multiple forebears, including not just Shinto and Buddhism, but Confucianism, Christianity, and other religious influences.

869 For elaboration on these ideas, see Peter B. Clarke & Jeffrey Somers, "Japanese 'New' and 'New, New' Religions," in P. B. Clarke & J. Somers (Eds.), *Japanese New Religions in the West*, pp. 1-32 (N. Y.: Routledge, 1994). Also see Susumo Shimazono, *From Salvation to Spirituality: Popular Religious Movements in Japan* (Melbourne, Australia: Trans Pacific Press, 2004).

870 Reichl, p. 311.

871 H. Paul Varley, *Japanese Culture*, 4th ed. (Honolulu: Univ. of Hawaii Press, 2000), p. 335f.

872 Cf. Kaneko Juri, "Can Tenrikyo Transcend the Modern Family? From a Humanistic Understanding of *Hinagata* and Narratives of Foster Care Activities," *Japanese Journal of Religious Studies, 30* (nos. 3-4), 243-258 (2003), p. 25.

873 Nakamura, p. 87.

874 Cf. Karen Ann Smyers, *The Fox and the Jewel: Shared and Private Meanings in Contemporary Japanese Worship* (Honolulu: Univ. of Hawaii Press, 1999), p. 7.

875 Ibid, p. 8.

[876] A nice summary is provided in Royall Tyler (Ed. & Trans.), *Nō Dramas* (N. Y.: Penguin Books, 1992), pp. 142-145. Cf. Royall Tyler, *The Miracles of the Kasuga Deity* (N.Y.: Columbia Univ. Press, 1990).

[877] *Kojiki* §§ XCVI-XCVII [229], Chamberlain's translation, pp. 284-286. Accessed online at sacred-texts.com at http://www.sacred-texts.com/shi/kj/kj103.htm.

[878] *Nihongi*, Bk. 5, 7th year, in Joseph M. Kitagawa, "Religions of Japan," in W. Chan, I. R. al Faruqi, J. M. Kitagawa, & P. T. Raju (compilers), *The Great Asian Religions. An Anthology*, pp. 231-305 (N. Y.: Macmillan, 1969), p. 240. This account was mentioned also in the answer to Q. 76.

[879] Paul Varley, *Japanese Culture*, 4th ed. (Honolulu: Univ. of Hawaii Press, 2000), p. 348. The *kimono* receives special attention in the answer to Q. 52 (volume 3) of this work.

[880] Chamberlain, p. lxif. Accessed online at the sacred-texts.com website at http://www.sacred-texts.com/shi/kj/kj005.htm.

[881] *Kojiki* § LXXX [207], in Chamberlain, p. 255f. Accessed online at the sacred-texts.com website at http://www.sacred-texts.com/shi/kj/kj087.htm.

[882] *Kojiki* § LXVI [179], in Chamberlain, pp. 220, 223. Accessed online at the sacred-texts.com website at http://www.sacred-texts.com/shi/kj/kj073.htm.

[883] Faure, *The Power of Denial*, p. 2.

[884] Ibid, p. 9.

[885] Bernard Faure, *The Red Thread: Buddhist Approaches to Sexuality* (Princeton: Princeton Univ. Press, 1998), p. 277. A *chigo* is a Japanese Buddhist acolyte.

[886] Ibid, p. 217.

[887] Ibid, p. 225.

[888] Ibid, p. 277.

[889] Ibid, p. 249f.; quote is from p. 250. *Nō* and *Kabuki* theater are discussed in the answer to Q. 44 (volume 3) of this work.

[890] Ibid, p. 77.

[891] *The Larger Sukhavativyuha Sutra, or The Sutra on the Buddha of Eternal Life* (The Sutra Translation Committee of United Canada, n.d.), provided by the Ida B. Wells Memorial Sutra Library, accessed online at http://www.buddhistinformation.com/ida_b_wells_memorial_sutra_library/larger_sukhavativyuha_sutra.htm.

[892] *Showa teihon Nichiren Shonin ibun*, 1: 589-590. Quoted in Ichiu, p. 282. Cf. *Showa teihon Nichiren Shonin ibun*, 1: 335 for Nichiren's remarks on Sariputra's defamatory words about women, which Nichiren says are borrowed from 'the provisional Hinayana teachings' and are decidedly overcome by the transformation of the Dragon Girl.

[893] After some hesitation, I have opted to follow the convention of our culture for presenting names. The Japanese convention would present the name as Nakayama Miki,

and as such one will often find it in the literature. The same convention is followed in this section for other Japanese names, such as Nao Deguchi rather than Deguchi Nao.

[894] *Ofudesaki* XIII, 43. Quoted in Robert J. Kisala, "Japanese Religions," in L. Woodhead (Ed.), *Religions in the Modern World: Traditions and Transformations*, pp. 108-127 (N. Y.: Rotledge, 2002), p. 120. Cf. *Ofudesaki* IV, 62, 79; XV, 69f..

[895] Helen Hardacre, "Gender and the Millennium in Omoto Kyodan: The Limits of Religious Innovation," in M. A. Williams, C. Cox, & M. S. Jaffee (Eds.), *Innovations in Religious Traditions. Essays on the Interpretation of Religious Change*, pp. 215-240 (N. Y.: Mouton De Gruyter, 1992).

[896] This material follows the account offered at the *Nao Deguchi. A Biography of the Foundress of Oomoto* website, accessed online at http://www.oomoto.or.jp/English/ en-Kyos/kaisoden/index.html. The biography the website relies on is Sakae Oishi, *Kaiso-Den [Life of the Foundress]*, translated by C. Rowe & Y. Matsudaira (Kameoka, Japan: The Oomoto Foundation, 1982; original work published 1949).

[897] Hardacre, pp. 216-218.

[898] Ibid, pp. 218-222.

[899] Faure, *The Power of Denial*, p. 106.

[900] Onisabura Deguchi, *Divine Signposts*, translated by C. Rowe (Kameoka, Japan: The Oomoto Foundation, 1985. Original work published 1919; work written in 1904.), I.1.32. Accessed online at http://www.oomoto.jp/enSignpost/.

[901] Ibid, IV.2, 636-638.

[902] Nakamura, p. 91; see figure 1 on p. 92.

Q. 82 Notes

[903] See, for example, Leonard Zwilling & Michael J. Sweet, "'Like a City Ablaze.' The Third Sex and the Creation of Sexuality in Jain Religious Literature," *Journal of the History of Sexuality, 6* (no. 3), 359-384 (1996). Cf. Michael J. Sweet & Leonard Zwilling, "The First Medicalization: The Taxonomy and Etiology of Queerness in Classical Indian Medicine," *Journal of the History of Sexuality, 3*, 590-607 (1993).

[904] Joseph B. Tamney, "Folk Traditions," in W, H. Swatos, Jr. (Ed.), *Encyclopedia of Religion and Society*, pp. 31-32 (Walnut Creek, CA: AltaMira Press, 1998).

[905] Henri Maspero, "The Mythology of Modern China," in J. Hackin, C. Huart, R. Linossier, H. De Wilman-Grabowski, C.-H. Marchal, H. Maspero, & S. Eliseer, *Asiatic Mythology*, pp. 252-384 (N. Y.: Thomas Y. Crowell Co., 1963), p. 262f.

[906] Joseph B. Tamney, *The Struggle Over Singapore's Soul: Western Modernization and Asia Culture* (N. Y.: Walter de Gruyter, 1996), p. 41.

[907] See Vicki Noble, *The Double Goddess: Women Sharing Power* (Rochester, VT: Bear & Co., 2003), p. 93, who notes that after the Tang Dynasty female shamans were apt to be seen as witches and persecuted. Also see Christina Pratt, *An Encyclopedia of Shamanism. Volume 1: A-M* (N. Y.: Rosen Publishing Group, 2007), p. 183. Cf. Barbara N. Ra-

musack & Sharon L. Sievers, *Women in Asia: Restoring Women to History* (Bloomington, IN: Indiana Univ. Press, 1999), p. 161.

[908] Laurence Senelick, *The Changing Room: Sex, Drag and Theatre* (N. Y.: Routledge, 2000), p. 17.

[909] Karen Laughlin & Eva Wong, "Feminism and/in Taoism," in A. Sharma & K. K. Young (Eds.), *Feminism and World Religions*, pp. 148-178 (Albany: State Univ. of New York Press, 1999), p. 152.

[910] Christina Pratt, *An Encyclopedia of Shamanism. Volume 2: N-Z* (N. Y.: Rosen Publishing Group, 2007), p. 544f.

[911] Maspero, pp. 352-354.

[912] The *dharani* are summaries of sacred doctrine that help master the content of the whole teaching. Reciting a *dharani* is meritorious.

[913] Chün-fang Yü, *Kuan-yin: The Chinese Transformation of Avalokitesvara* (N. Y.: Columbia Univ. Press, 2001), p. 52.

[914] Ibid, p. 302.

[915] Roland Altenburger, "Is It Clothes that Make the Man? Cross-Dressing, Gender, and Sex in Pre-Twentieth Century Zhu Yangtai Lore," *Asian Folklore Studies, 64*, 165-205 (2005), p. 166.

[916] Ibid, pp. 174-180.

[917] Ibid, pp. 179-181; quote is from p. 181.

[918] Cf. *Mencius* V. A. 2, in D. C. Lau (Translator), *Mencius* (N. Y.: Penguin Books, 1970), p. 139.

[919] Ibid, III. B. 2, in D. C. Lau (Translator), *Mencius*, p. 107.

[920] Ban Zhao, *Nü Jie*. See Nancy Lee Swan (Translator), *Pan Chao: Foremost Woman Scholar of China* (N. Y.: Century Co., 1932), pp. 82-90.

[921] Roland Altenburger, "Androgyny in Late Ming and Early Qing Literature [Review]," *IIAS Newsletter, 35,* 30 (2004, Nov.). Accessed online at the International Institute for Asian Studies (IIAS) at http://www.iias.nl/nl/35/iias_nl35_30.pdf.

[922] *Coming Out in Dialogue: Policies and Perceptions of Sexual Minority Groups in Asia and Europe* (2005), §2.1.4 (p. 11). Research paper commissioned by the Intellectual Exchange Department of the Asia-Europe Foundation for its "Talks on the Hill" series. Accessed online at http://asef.on2web.com/subSite/ccd/documents/briefingpaper _001.pdf.

[923] James Legge (Translator), *The Sacred Books of China—The Texts of Confucianism [Sacred Books of the East*, vol. 3] (1879), while examining the text of the *The Hsiao King or Classic of Filial Piety*, observes, "the articles of dress, to be worn by individuals according to their rank, from the sovereign downwards, in their ordinary attire, and on special occasions, were the subject of attention and enactment in China from the earliest times.

We find references to them in the earliest books of the Shû (Part 11, Books iii, iv)." Accessed online at http://www.sacred-texts.com/cfu/sbe03/hsiao.htm.

[924] Dorothy Ko, "The Body as Attire: The Shifting Meanings of Footbinding in Seventeenth Century China," *Journal of Women's History, 8* (no. 4), 8-27 (1997). Accessed online at http://iupjournals.org/jwh/ jwh8-4.html.

[925] Confucius, *Confucius. The Analects (Lun yü)*, translated by D. C. Lau (N. Y.: Penguin Books, 1979). See pp. 102 (X. 6) and 95 (VIII. 21); the quote is from p. 95.

[926] Charles Muller (Translator), *The Doctrine of the Mean* (2003 updated version of 1991 translation), accessed online at http://www.hm.tyg.jp/~acmuller/contao/docofmean.htm.

[927] *Mencius* VI. B. 2, in D. C. Lau (Translator), *Mencius*, p. 172.

[928] *Mencius* IV. A. 12, in D. C. Lau, p. 123.

[929] *Xunzi* 5/15, quoted in Jane Geaney, "Guarding Moral Boundaries: Shame in Early Confucianism," *Philosophy East and West, 54* (no. 2), 113-142 (2004), p. 124. For the complete context of the passage see John Knoblock (Translator), *Xunzi: A Translation and Study of the Complete Works*, vol. 1: *Books 1-6* (Stanford: Stanford Univ. Press, 1988).

[930] Geaney, p. 124.

[931] The difficulties posed by multiple religious traditions for an individual are explored in the struggle of the Lady Wang in China's classical poem, *A Plaint of Lady Yang*. See Yan Jinfen, "A Feminine Expression of Mysticism, Romanticism and Syncretism in *A Plaint of Lady Yang*," *Inter-Religio, 42*, 3-20 (2002).

[932] Hermann Jacobi, *Jaina Sutras, Part I* [*Sacred Books of the East*, vol. 22] (Oxford: Clarendon Press, 1884), *Akaranga Sutra*, Second Lesson (5), p. 39. Accessed online at the sacred-texts.com website at http://www.sacred-texts.com/jai/sbe22/sbe2221.htm# page_38.

[933] Padmanabh S. Jaini, *Gender and Salvation: Jaina Debates on the Spiritual Liberation* (Berkeley: Univ. of California Press, 1991), p. 11.

[934] Robert P. Goldman, "Foreword," in P. S. Jaini, *Gender and Salvation: Jaina Debates on the Spiritual Liberation* (Berkeley: Univ. of California Press, 1991), p. xviii.

[935] Ibid, *Akaranga Sutra*, Fourth Lesson (3), p. 21. Accessed online at the sacred-texts.com website at http://www.sacred-texts.com/jai/sbe22/sbe2213.htm# page_21.

[936] Hermann Jacobi, *Jaina Sutras, Part II* [*Sacred Books of the East*, vol. 45] (Oxford: Clarendon Press, 1895), *Uttaradhyayana*, Lecture 8 (18), p. 35. Accessed online at the sacred-texts.com website at http://www.sacred-texts.com/jai/sbe45/sbe4510.htm# page_32.

[937] Ibid, *Uttaradhyayana*, Lecture 14 (3-4), p. 62. Accessed online at the sacred-texts.com website at http://www.sacred-texts.com/jai/sbe45/sbe4516.htm# page_62.

[938] Jaini, p. 1.

[939] *Uttaraadhyayan Sutra.* The English adaptation here is from the translation and commentary by Shri K. C. Lalwani (Calcutta: Prajnanam, 1977), provided by the Jain Study Circle website, accessed online at http://www.jainstudy.org/jsc10.98scr.htm#1.

[940] Goldman, p. xviii.

[941] Jaini, p. 11.

[942] Goldman, p. xviii.

[943] Jaini, p. 12. Italics added in quote for consistency with the main text.

[944] Ibid.

[945] Goldman, p. xviiif.

[946] Duli Chandra Jain, *Answers to Some Frequently Asked Questions* (Reprinted from A. B. Dobrin (Ed.), *Religious Ethics: A Sourcebook* (Mumbai: Hindi Granth Karyalaya, 2004), § 34. Accessed online at http://www.jainstudy.org/QAns.pdf.

[947] *Sorath Mohalla* 1, cited in *Sikh Religion* (Detroit: Sikh Missionary Center, 1990), p. 255.

[948] Ibid, p. 256.

[949] Ibid, p. 272.

[950] Nikky-Gunnider Kaur Singh, *The Feminine Principle in the Sikh Vision of the Transcendent* (Cambridge: Cambridge Univ. Press, 1993), pp. 3, 52.

[951] Nikky-Guninder Sing, "Gender and Religion: Gender and Sikhism," in L. Jones (Ed.), *Encyclopedia of Religion,* 2nd ed. (Detroit: Macmillan Reference USA, 2005), vol. 5, p. 3336.

[952] Singh, *The Feminine Principle*, p. 52.

[953] Satwant Kaur Rait, *Sikh Women in England: Their Religious and Cultural Beliefs and Social Practices* (Stoke on Trent, UK: Trentham Books, 2005), p. 47.

[954] Ibid, p. 48.

[955] *Ada di Var, Mohalla,* 475. Cited in Rait, p. 48.

[956] Geoffrey Parrinder, *Sex in the World's Religions* (N. Y.: Oxford Univ. Press, 1980), p. 68. Nikky-Guninder Singh (vol. 5, p. 3337) argues this text today has no significance.

[957] Nikky-Guninder Singh, vol. 5, p. 3335.

[958] Ibid, p. 69.

[959] Inger Furseth & Pal Repstad, *An Introduction to the Sociology of Religion. Classical and Contemporary Perspectives* (London: Ashgate, 2006), p. 182.

[960] Doris R. Jakobsh, *Relocating Gender in Sikh History: Transformation, Meaning, and Identity* (New Delhi: Oxford Univ. Press, 2003). Quoted material from p. 82. Also see her "Sikhism, Interfaith Dialogue, and Women: Transformation and Identity," *Journal of Contemporary Religion, 21* (no. 2), 183-199 (2006).

[961] See, Baldev Singh, *Relocating Gender in Sikh History: Transformation, Meaning, and Identity (Author: Doris R. Jakobsh). A Critical Analysis* (2006). This extensive analysis maintained at the SikhSpectrum.com website, accessed online at http://sikhspectrum.com/112006/doris/cover.htm. For a shorter example, see J. S. Mann & S. S. Sodhi, *Review of "Relocating Gender in Sikh History" byDr. Doris Jakobsh* (n.d.), accessed online at http://www.globalsikhstudies.net/pdf/review/Doris_R_Jakobsh_S_S.pdf.

[962] Rait, p. 51.

[963] Nikky-Guninder Singh, vol. 5, pp. 3336-3338.

[964] I. J. Singh, *What Sikhism Says About Gender and Sex.* Paper presented at International Sikh Conferences (2004). Accessed online at the Global Sikh Studies.net website, at http://www. globalsikhstudies.net/articles/iscpapers/IJ%20SINGH%20WHAT%20 SIKHISM%20SAYS% 20ABOUT%20GENDER%20 AND%20SEX.doc.

[965] Martin Cohn, "Reject Gay Bill, Sikh MPs Told," *The Toronto Star* (2005, Mar. 28), pp. A1, A10. Also see "World Sikh Group Against Gay Marriage Bill," *CBC News* (2005, Mar. 29). Accessed online at the cbc.ca website at http://www.cbc.ca/story/canada/national/2005/03/28/sikhguy-050328.html.

[966] Alain Dang & Mandy Hu, *Lesbian, Gay, Bisexual and Transgender People: A Community Project. A Report from New York's Queer Asian Pacific Legacy Conference, 2004* (National Gay and Lesbian Task Force Policy Institute, 2004), pp. 3, 18. Accessed online at http://www.usc.edu/student-affairs/glbss/PDFS/APAstudy.pdf.

[967] See, for example, the experience recounted by a young Sikh woman: Andie, *Invisibility: Without Recognition, There Is No Support.* Accessed online on the Temenos website at http://temenos.net/articles/08-06-04.shtml.

[968] Sikhs are hardly unique in the disparity between high principle enjoined by religious texts and exhorted by enlightened leaders and the actual practice of most followers. The same can be observed in all religious communities.

[969] The origins, development and dating of Taoism and Taoist texts are all debated. What is offered here reflects a common view but by no means a consensus.

[970] Wing-tsit Chan, "Religions of China," in W. Chan, I. Ragi al Faruqi, J. M. Kitagawa, & P. T. Raju, *The Great Asian Religions. An Anthology*, pp. 97-227 (N. Y.: Macmillan, 1969), p. 150.

[971] Ibid, p. 6.

[972] Ibid, p. 61.

[973] Russell Kirkland, *Taoism: The Enduring Tradition* (N. Y.: Routledge, 2004), p. 126.

[974] *Huai Nan Tzu*, Essay 1, in Evan Morgan, *Tao. The Great Luminant. Essays from Huai Nan Tzu with Introductory Articles, Notes, Analysis* (Shanghai, 1933), p. 3.

[975] Confucianism also speaks of *yin* and *yang* but the relationship between them is different when it comes to gender. In gender, *yin* is subordinate to *yang*. Thus Tung Chung-Shu (2nd century B.C.E.) declared, "Husband is *yang*, wife is *yin*. Yin is not independent. It cannot share the achievements. It is just the deputy." Quoted in Eva K. W.

Man, "Chinese Women and the Family from a Confucian Perspective," *Inter-Religio, 34,* 20-27 (1998), p. 24. Accessed online at http://www.riccibase.com/inter-religio/PDF/ir21.pdf.

[976] Lao-Tzu, *Tao Te Ching,* translated by Stephen Addiss & Stanley Lombardo (Indianapolis, IN: Hackett, 1993), p. 28.

[977] Wu Wei, *The I-Ching. The Book of Answers* (L.A.: Power Press, 2005), p. 29.

[978] *Huai Nan Tzu,* Essay 15, in Morgan, p. 212.

[979] *Coming Out in Dialogue,* §2.1.3 (p. 10f.).

[980] Chan, p. 159.

[981] See the chapter 'On Tolerance' in the *Chuang-tzu,* translated by Lin Yutang. Accessed online at http://www.clas.ufl.edu/users/gthursby/taoism/cz-text2.htm# INDEX.

[982] Livia Kohn, *Monastic Life in Medieval Daoism. A Cross-Cultural Perspective* (Honolulu: Univ. of Hawai'I Press, 2003), p. 81.

[983] Maspero, p. 257.

[984] John C. Raines, *The Justice Men Owe Women: Positive Resources from World Religions* (Minneapolis, MN: Augsburg Fortress, 2001), p. 87.

[985] Ninian Smart & Richard D. Hecht (Eds.), *Sacred Texts of the World. A Universal Anthology* (N. Y.: Crossroad, 1992), p. 291.

[986] *Yin-chih wen.* See Chan, p. 172.

[987] The contemporary biologist Anne Fausto-Sterling did exactly that in her classic article, "The Five Sexes: Why Male and Female Are Not Enough," *The Sciences, 33* (no. 2), 20-25 (1993, Mar./Apr.) Also see her "The Five Sexes, Revisited," *The Sciences, 40* (no. 4), 18-23 (2000, July/Aug.).

[988] Barbara Carrellas, *Urban Tantra. Sacred Sex for the Twenty-first Century* (Berkeley, CA: Celestial Arts, 2007), p. 85.

[989] Cf. Xinzhong Yao, "Harmony of Yin and Yang: Cosmology and Sexuality in Daoism," in D. W. Machacek & M. W. Wilcox (Eds.), *Sexuality and the World's Religions,* pp. 65-99 (Santa Barbara, CA: ABC-CLIO, Inc., 2003), p. 74.

[990] *Ts'an-t'ung-chi,* Part 2, Ch. 10. See Chan, p. 165.

[991] *Ts'an-t'ung-chi,* Part 1, Ch. 11. See Chan, p. 165.

[992] *Nei P'ien of Ko Hung,* 2.3b; in James R. Ware (Translator), *Alchemy, Medicine, Religion in the China of A. D. 320: The Nei P'ien of Ko Hung (Pao-p'u tzu)* (Cambridge, MA: M. I. T. Press, 1966), p. 37.

[993] *Nei P'ien of Ko Hung,* 2.3b; in Ware, p. 38.

[994] *Nei P'ien of Ko Hung,* 16.2a; in Ware, p. 262f.

[995] *Nei P'ien of Ko Hung,* 19.7b; in Ware, p. 316.

⁹⁹⁶ Kirkland, p. 25. In the pages following he offers a generally positive appraisal of the status and opportunities for women in Taoism, particularly in contrast to Buddhism and Confucianism. Also see Laughlin & Wong.

⁹⁹⁷ See James Wilerson, "Negotiating Local Tradition with Taoism: Female Ritual Specialists in the Zhuang Religion," *Religion, 37* (no. 2), 150-163 (2007).

⁹⁹⁸ See Suzanne Cahill (Translator), "Biography of the Daoist Saint Weng Fengxian by Du Guangting," in S. Mann & Y.-Y. Cheng (Eds.), *Under Confucian Eyes: Writings on Gender in Chinese History,* pp. 17-30 (Berkeley: Univ. of California Press, 2001). Cf. Kirkland, p. 135.

⁹⁹⁹ See Kirkland, p. 137f.

¹⁰⁰⁰ Ibid, p. 139.

¹⁰⁰¹ Margaret J. Wiener, *Visible and Invisible Realms: Power, Magic and Colonial Conquest in Bali* (Chicago: Univ. of Chicago Press, 1995), p. 51.

¹⁰⁰² Other names include Acintya, Sang Hyang Kawi, Sang Hwang Widhi, Tijinitja, Tintiya, and the particularly apt name Sang Hyang Licin ('the Slippery one').

¹⁰⁰³ Vern L. Bullough, *Science in the Bedroom. A History of Sex Research* (N. Y.: Basic Books, 1995), p. 159. Cf. Vern L. Bullough, *Sexual Variance in Society and History* (N. Y.: John Wiley & Sons, 1976), p. 24.

¹⁰⁰⁴ See J. Emigh & J. Hunt, "Gender Bending in Balinese Performance," in L. Senelick (Ed.), *Gender in Performance. The Presentation of Difference in the Performing Arts,* pp. 207-216 (Hanover, NH: University Press of New England, 1992).

¹⁰⁰⁵ Alan C. Heyman, *Dances of the Three-Thousand League Land* (Seoul: Dang A., 1966), p. 32; cited in Judith Lynne Hanna, *Dance, Sex, and Gender* (Chicago: Univ. of Chicago Press, 1988), p. 59.

¹⁰⁰⁶ That does not mean crossdressing cannot also be used for other purposes, including popular entertainment.

¹⁰⁰⁷ Melford E. Spiro, *Burmese Supernaturalism* (Englewood Cliffs, NJ: Prentice-Hall, 1967), p. 220. Cf. Eli Coleman, Philip Colgan, & Louis Gooren, "Male Cross-Gender Behaviour in Myanmar (Burma): A Description of the Acault," *Archives of Sexual Behavior, 21* (no. 3), 313-321 (1992). Also see Michael G. Peletz, "Transgenderism and Gender Pluralism in Southeast Asia Since Early Modern Times," *Current Anthropology, 47* (no. 2), 309-340 (2006), pp. 318-320.

¹⁰⁰⁸ Yves Rodrigue, *Nat-Pwe: Burma's Supernatural Subculture* (Gartmore: Kiscadale Publications, 1992).

¹⁰⁰⁹ Spiro, p. 220.

¹⁰¹⁰ See Stephen O. Murray, *Homosexualities* (Chicago: Univ. of Chicago Press, 2000), p. 335. Cf. Coleman, Colgan, & Gooren, p. 317.

¹⁰¹¹ Coleman, Colgan, & Gooren, p. 316. For more information on the *acault* see the answer to Q. 52.

[1012] Coleman, Colgan & Gooren, pp. 315-316. Cf. Vern L. Bullough & Bonnie Bullough, *Cross Dressing, Sex, and Gender* (Phila.: Univ. of Pennsylvania Press, 1993), p. 15.

[1013] Chongho Kim, *Korean Shamanism. The Cultural Paradox* (Burlington, VT: Ashgate Publishing Ltd., 2003), p. 32.

[1014] James Huntley Grayson, *Korea—A Religious History* (N. Y.: Routledge, 2002), p. 218.

[1015] Christina Pratt, *An Encyclopedia of Shamanism. Volume 1: A-M* (N. Y.: Rosen Publishing Group, 2007), p. 132.

[1016] Laurel Kendall, *Shamans, Housewives, and Other Restless Spirits. Women in Korean Ritual Life* (Honolulu: Univ. of Hawaii Press, 1985), p. 27.

[1017] "Mudang," in Keith Pratt & Richard Rutt, with additional material by James Hoare, *Korea. A Historical and Cultural Dictionary* (N. Y.: Routledge, 1999), p. 296.

[1018] Kim, p. 156.

[1019] For more on contemporary Korean shamanism, see S. A. Mousalimas (Ed.), *Christianity & Shamanism: Proceedings of the First Seoul International Consultation (25-30 June 2000, Seoul, Korea)*, accessed online at http://www.OxfordU.net/seoul (2001). See especially Cha Ok Soong, "Korean Shamanism," chapter 2 of the *Proceedings*.

[1020] Kittiwut Jod Taywaditep, Eli Coleman, & Pacharin Dumronggittigule, "Thailand," in R. T. Francoeur (Ed.), *The International Encyclopedia of Sexuality*, Vols. I-III (N.Y.: Continuum, 1997). Accessed online at http://www2.rz.hu-berlin.de/sexology/GESUND/ARCHIV/IES/THAILAND.HTM#7.%20GENDER%20CONFLICTED%20PERSONS. See §7. Gender Conflicted Persons.

[1021] Walter Irvine, *The Thai-Yuan 'Madman' and the Modernizing, Developing Thai Nation as Bounded Entities Under Threat: A Study in the Replication of a Single Image*. Ph.D. dissertation (London: University of London, 1982).

Q. 83 Notes

[1022] Burt H. Hoff, "Gays: Guardians at the Gates. An Interview with Malidoma Somé," *MEN Magazine* (1993, Sept.), accessed online at http://www.menweb.org/somegay.htm.

[1023] See Edwin S. Segal, *Gender Transformation in Cross Cultural Perspective*. Paper prepared for presentation at Women's Worlds 99, the seventh International Interdisciplinary Congress on Women, Program Section II: New Constructions of Gender, session 2, Friday, June 25, Tromsø, Norway, June 20-26, 1999. Accessed online at http://www.skk.uit.no/WW99/papers/Segal_Edwin_S.pdf.
On the Mbuti, cf. Colin Turnbull, "Sex and Gender. The Role of Subjectivity in Field Research," in T. Larry & M. E. Conaway (Eds.), *Self, Sex, and Gender in Cross-Cultural Fieldwork*, pp. 17-27 (Urbana, IL: Univ. of Illinois Press, 1987).

[1024] Mircea Eliade & Ioan P. Couliano, *The Eliade Guide to World Religions* (S. F.: HarperSanFrancisco, 1991), p. 16.

[1025] See John Coleman Wood, *When Men Are Women. Manhood Among Gabra Nomads of East Africa* (Madison, WI: Univ. of Wisconsin Press, 1999).

[1026] Consider, for example, the *machi-embra* (or *Guevedoche*), 'male-female' of the Dominican Republic, a 'thrid gender' population. These intersex individuals appear female at birth and are gender assigned to be rasied as girls. However, these genetic males at puberty manifest male secondary sex characteristics. Some reassign themselves to masculinity; others retain their feminine gender assignment. See Zachary Nataf, "Whatever I Feel, That's the Way I Am," *New Internationalist*, pp. 22-25 (1998, Apr. 1). On the debate within medicine over whether hormones contribute decisively to the adoption of gender identity, see both Juliane Imperato-McGinley, R. E. Peterson, T. Gautier, & E. Sturla, "Androgens and the Evolution of Male Gender Identity Among Male Pseudo-Hermaphrodites," *New England Journal of Medicine, 300* (no. 22), 1233-1237 (1979), and Jean D. Wilson, "The Role of Androgens in Male Gender Role Behavior," *Endocrine Review, 20* (no. 5), 726-737 (1999).

[1027] Alan P. Merriam, *An African World: The Basongye Village of Lupupa Ngye* (Bloomington: Indiana Univ. Press, 1974). See Stephen O. Murray & Will Roscoe (Eds.), *Boy-Wives and Female Husbands: Studies in African Homosexualities*, pp. 144-146. Cf. Louis A. Berman, *The Puzzle. Exploring the Evolutionary Puzzle of Male Homosexuality* (Wilmette, IL: Godot Press, 2003), p. 186.

[1028] On Leza, see Geoffrey Parrinder, *Sex in the World's Religions* (N. Y.: Oxford Univ. Press, 1980), p. 129.

[1029] Oyeronke Oyewumi, *The Invention of Women: Making an African Sense of Western Gender Discourses* (Minneapolis: Univ. of Minnesota Press, 1997). Oyewumi (p. 140) contends that reference to Oludumare by the masculine pronoun is an effect of colonization and Christian influence.

[1030] Randy P. Connor, "Sexuality and Gender in African Spiritual Traditions," in D. W. Machacek & M. M. Wilcox (Eds.), *Sexuality and the World's Religions*, pp. 3-30 (Santa Barbara, CA: ABC-CLIO, 2003), p. 7.

[1031] Erik Davis, "Trickster at the Crossroads," *Gnosis*, issue no. 19, pp. 37-45 (1991, Spring).

[1032] Connor, p. 6.

[1033] Ibid, p. 19.

[1034] Ferdinand Karsch-Haack, "Uranismus oder Päderastie und Tribadie bei den Naturvölkern" ["Uranism or Pederasty and Tribady Among Primitive Peoples"], *Jahrbuch für sexuelle Zwischenstufen, III*, 72-202 (1901; reprinted in 1983).

[1035] Babatunde Lawal, "Orilonise: The Hermeneutics of the Head and Hairstyles Among the Yoruba," *Tribal Arts, 7* (no. 2) (2001/2002). Accessed online at http://www.tribalarts.com/feature/lawal/.

[1036] Consider, for example, the 1732 report by Dominican missionary Jean Baptiste Labat, who resided for a time among the Giagues people of the Congo. Labat wrote of the *Ganga-Ya-Chibanda*, a male who crossdressed and was reverently addressed as

490

'Grandmother.' See Stephen O. Murray, "Appendix II: Organizations of Homosexuality and Other Social Structures in Sub-Saharan Africa," in Murray & Roscoe, pp. 283-298 (N. Y.: Palgrave, 1998), pp. 163ff.

[1037] For an outstanding, brief introduction with reference to Africa, see Jessica Erdtsieck, "Encounters with Forces of Pepo: Shamanism and Healing in East Africa," *Tanzanet Journal, 1* (no. 2), 1-10 (2001). Accessed online at http://tanzanet.org/int/journal/Tanzanet%20Journal-JErd122001.pdf. Also see I. M. Lewis, "Trance, Possession, Shamanism and Sex," *Anthropology of Consciousness, 14* (no. 1), 20-39 (2004). Cf. S. F. Nadel, "A Study of Shamanism in the Nuba Mountains," *Journal of the Royal Anthropological Institute, LXXVI* (no. 1), 25-37 (1946).

[1038] Anthropologist Janice Boddy calls attention to the importance of the fact that it is female deities who possess the crossdressing possessed males of Kahartoum and Omdurman in Sudan. See Janice Boddy, *Wombs and Alien Spirits. Women, Men, and the Zar Cult in Northern Sudan* (Madison: Univ. of Wisconsin Press, 1989).

[1039] See Edwin M. Loeb, "Kuanyama Ambo Magic 2. Kuanyama Doctors," *Journal of American Folklore, 68* (no. 268), 153-168 (1955), p. 154. Loeb has the peculiar Western preoccupation of the period with the same-sex sexual connections observed that lead him to characterize (erroneously) the *omasenge* as 'homosexuals.'

[1040] R. P. Carlos Estermann, *Ethnography of Southwestern Angola, vol. 1: The Non-Bantu Peoples, the Ambo Ethnic Group*, edited and translated by G. Gibson (N. Y.: Africana, 1976), p. 197.

[1041] Gwyneth Davies, *The Medical Culture of the Ovambo of Southern Angola and Northern Namibia* (Canterbury: Univ. of Kent doctoral dissertation, 1994). Accessed online at http://lucy.ukc.ac.uk/ csacpub/Davies_thesis/. See especially chapter 4, 'Indigenous Specialists: Recreators of Health and Harmony.' Davis identifies the *omasenge* as a 'third gender.'

[1042] Connor, p. 19.

[1043] Davies, ch. 4, p. 13.

[1044] Murray & Roscoe, pp. 147, 281.

[1045] W. D. Hambly, *Source Book for African Anthropology* (Chicago: Field Museum, 1937).

[1046] Edward Carpenter, *Intermediate Types Among Primitive Folk. A Study in Social Evolution* (London: George Allen & Co., Inc., 1914), p. 39. Accessed online at http://www.sacredtexts.com/lgbt/ itp/itp05.htm.

[1047] Connor, p. 19.

[1048] Denise Paulme, *Organisation sociale des Dogon (Soudan francais) [Social Organization of the Dogon (French Sudan)]* (Paris, Editions Domat-Montchrestien, F. Loviton et Cie., 1940), p. 109. Also, Connor, p. 20.

[1049] Connor, p. 20.

[1050] Rodney Needham, "The Left Hand of the Mugwe: An Analytical Note on the Structure of Meru Symbolism," in R. Needham, *Right and Left Essays on Dual Classifications*, pp. 109-127 (Chicago: Univ. of Chicago Press, 1973).

[1051] Cf. Randy P. Connor with David Hatfield Sparks, *Queering Creole Spiritual Traditions. Lesbian, Gay, Bisexual, and Transgender Participation in African-Inspired Traditions in the Americas* (N. Y.: Haworth Press, 2004), p. 38. On the characterization of them as homosexuals—a depiction commonly followed in the literature that is derived from this source—see David F. Greenberg, *The Construction of Homosexuality* (Chicago: Univ. of Chicago Press, 1988), p. 60.

[1052] For more on Yoruban religion and gender, see J. D. Y. Peel, "Gender in Yoruba Religious Change," *Journal of Religion in Africa, 32* (no. 2), 136-166 (2002).

[1053] Lawal.

[1054] J. Lorand Matory, *Sex and the Empire That Is No More: Gender and the Politics of Metaphor in Oyo Yoruban Religion* (Minneapolis: Univ. of Minnesota Press, 1994). See especially p. 170; quote is from p. 175. Cf. Judith Perani & Norma H. Wolff, *Cloth, Dress, and Art Patronage in Africa* (N. Y.: Berg, 1999), p. 36.

[1055] See John Coleman Wood, *When Men Are Women. Manhood Among Gabra Nomads of East Africa* (Madison, WI: Univ. of Wisconsin Press, 1999).

[1056] Ifi Amadiume, *Male Daughters, Female Husbands: Gender and Sex in an African Society* (London: Zed Books, 1987), p. 53.

[1057] Keith Nicklin, "The Mermaid and the Snake Charmer: Mammi Watain in West Africa," *Raw Vision,49* (2004/2005,Winter). Accessed online at http://www. rawvision.com/rawvision/current/wata/ wata.html.

[1058] Leslie Feinberg, *Transgender Warriors: Making History from Joan of Arc to Dennis Rodman* (Boston: Beacon Press, 1996), p. 45.

[1059] Cf. Connor, p. 19.

[1060] See both Sir James Fraser, *Adonis, Attis, Osiris: Studies in the History of Oriental Religion* [Part IV of *The Golden Bough*] (London: Macmillan, 1906), p. 60, and Parrinder, p. 132.

[1061] See Heike Behrend & Ute Luig, *Spirit Possession, Modernity, and Power in Africa* (Madison: Univ. of Wisconsin Press, 2000).

[1062] For a comprehensive, contextual history and analysis, see anthropologist Michael Lambek, *The Weight of the Past. Living with History in Mahajanga, Madagscar* (N. Y.: Palgrave Macmillan, 2003). Cf. Lesley A. Sharp, "Exorcists, Psychiatrists, and the Problems of Possession in Northwest Madagascar," *Journal of Social Science and Medicine, 38* (no. 4), 525-542 (1994). Also cf. Janice Boddy, "Spirits and Selves in Northern Sudan: The Cultural Therapeutics of Possession and Trance," *American Ethnologist, 15* (no. 1), 4-27 (1988).

[1063] Lesley A. Sharp, *The Possessed and the Dispossessed: Spirits, Identity, and Power in a Madagascar Migrant Town* (Berkeley: Univ. of California Press, 1993), p. 115.

[1064] Ibid, p. 19.

[1065] Ibid, p. 115.

[1066] Lesley A. Sharp, "Playboy Princely Spirits of Madagascar: Possession as Youthful Commentary and Social Critique," *Anthropological Quarterly, 68* (no. 2), 75-88 (1995).

[1067] Ibid. Also see Sharp, *The Possessed and the Dispossessed*, pp.171ff.

[1068] Linda L. Giles, "Sociocultural Change and Spirit Possession on the Swahili Coast of East Africa," *Anthropological Quarterly, 68* (no. 2), 89-106 (1995). Cf. Linda L. Giles, "Possession Cults on the Swahili Coast: A Re-examination of Theories of Marginality," *Africa, 57*, 234-258 (1987). Also cf. chapter 9, 'Swahili Experience of Jinn-Possession,' in Caleb Chul-Soo Kim (Ed.), *Islam Among the Swahili in East Africa* (Nairobi, Kenya: Acton Publishers, 2004).

On the important connection between health and spirituality, see T. J. Sordas, "Health and the Holy in African and Afro-American Spirit Possession," *Social Science Medicine, 24* (no. 1) 1-11 (1987).

[1069] Renee Pittin, "Houses of Women: A Focus on Alternative Life-Styles in Katsina City," in C. Oppong (Ed.), *Female and Male in West Africa*, 291-302 (Allen & Unwin, 1983). Cf. Susan O'Brien, "Pilgrimage, Power, and Identity: The Role of the *Hajj* in the Lives of Nigerian Hausa *Bori* Adepts," *Africa Today, 46* (nos. 3-4), 11-40 (1999). Also cf. Fremont E. Besmer, *Horses, Musicians and Gods: The Hausa Cult of Possession Trance* (South Hadley, MA: Bergin and Garvey, 1983).

[1070] The festival, complete with virgin testing of young women, was revived in the mid-1990s.

[1071] Max Gluckman, *Custom and Conflict in Africa* (Oxford: Blackwell, 1955), Lecture Five. Also see Max Gluckman, "Rituals of Rebellion in South-East Africa," in M. Gluckman, *Order and Rebellion in Tribal Africa: A Functionalist Approach*, pp. 110-136 (London: Cohen and West, 1963). Even earlier, Gluckman had published an article on the subject entitled, "Zulu Women in Hoeculture Ritual," *Bantu Studies Journal* (1935).

[1072] Edward Geoffrey Parrinder, *Religion in an African City* (N. Y.: Oxford Univ. Press, 1953). Cf. Parrinder, *Sex in the World's Religions*, p. 142.

[1073] Max Gluckman, "Rituals of Rebellion in South-East Africa," in M. Gluckman, *Order and Rebellion in Tribal Africa: A Functionalist Approach*, pp. 110-136 (London: Cohen and West, 1963).

[1074] Paul Spencer, *The Maasai of Matapato: A Study of Rituals of Rebellion* (Bloomington, IN: Indiana Univ. Press, 1988).

[1075] On Buganda's indigenous religion, see B. Nsimbi, "Traditional Religion in Buganda," *Bulletin of the Pontifical Council for Interreligious Dialogue, 28-29*, 159-163 (1975). For a more accessible source, which discusses Mukasa, see *Buganda's Indigenous Religion* on the bugnada.com website, accessed online at http://www.buganda.com/eddiini.htm.

[1076] Roberta Perkins, "Cross-Dressing Magic, Intersexuals & Female Husbands," *Polare 9* (1995) at the Gender Centre, Inc. of Sydney, Australia website, accessed online at http://www.gendercentre.org.au/ 9article7.htm.

[1077] Todd Sanders, "Rains Gone Bad, Women Gone Mad: Rethinking Gender Rituals of Rebellion and Patriarchy," *Journal of the Royal Anthropological Institute, 6* (no.3), 469-486 (2000).

[1078] Jane T. Creider & Chet A. Creider, "Gender Inversion in Nandi Ritual," *Anthropos, 92* (no. 1), 51-58 (1997), p. 56.

[1079] Alfred Claud Hollis, *The Maasai: Their Language and Folklore* (Oxford: Clarendon Press, 1905). Hollis draws a similar conclusion about the circumcision rituals involving Nandi boys. Cf. A. C. Hollis, *The Nandi: Their Language and Folklore* (Oxford: Clarendon Press, 1909).

[1080] See S. Bagge, "The Circumcision Ceremony Among the Naivasha Maasai," *Journal of the Anthropological Institute*, 167-169 (1904). Joy Adamson, *The Peoples of Kenya* (N. Y.: Harcourt, Brace & World, 1967), p. 224. Cf. Joseph Lemasolai-Lekuton & Herman Viola, *Facing the Lion: Growing Up Maasai on the African Savannah* (Washington, D. C.: National Geographic Society, 2003), which though aimed at young adults offers a friendly entry into the subject.

[1081] Geoffrey Parrinder, *Sex in the World's Religions* (N. Y.: Oxford Univ. Press, 1980), p. 130f. Cf. Aud Talle, "Transforming Women into 'Pure' Agnates: Aspects of Female Infibulation in Somalia," in V. Broch-Due, I. Rudie, & T. Bleie (Eds.), *Carved Flesh/Cast Selves. Gendered Symbols and Social Practices*, pp. 83-106 (Oxford: Berg, 1993). Talle explains how infibulation (removal of clitoris and labia minora, followed by stitching) constructs body sexuality by further emphasizing the differences between male and female.

[1082] Kevin Ward, "Same-Sex Relations in Africa and the Debate on Homosexuality in East African Anglicanism," *Anglican Review, 84* (no. 1), 81-111 (2002).

[1083] Ibid. See especially the discussion under the heading 'Homosexuality and Christianity in Africa: Some Historical Perspectives.'

[1084] House of Bishops Group on Issues in Human Sexuality, *Some Issues in Human Sexuality: A Guide to the Debate* (London: Church House Publishing, 2003), p. 298. For the full text of the Cambridge Accord, see http://www.wfn.org/1999/10/msg00103.html.

[1085] Amy Bourke, "Tutu Tells Church to Stop Obsessing About Gays," *PinkNews* (2007, May 29), accessed online at http://www.pinknews.co.uk/news/articles/2005-4507.html.

[1086] Cameron Partridge, "In a Rising Storm, African Voices," *TransEpiscopal* (2008, July 29), accessed online at http://transepiscopal.blogspot.com/2008/07/in-rising-storm-african-voices.html.

[1087] Colin Coward, *Lambeth Conference 2008: African LGBT Anglicans Appeal to Bishops and Archbishops* (2008, July 29), accessed online at http://www.changingattitude.org.uk/news/newsitem.asp?id=375.

Q. 84 Notes

[1088] Elizabeth Currans, "Native American Spirituality," in T. Murphy (Ed.), *Reader's Guide to Lesbian and Gay Studies*, pp. 413-414 (Chicago: Fitzroy Dearborn Publishers, 2000), p. 413.

[1089] Sabine Lang, "Lesbians, Men-Women and Two-Spirits: Homosexuality and Gender in Native American Cultures," in E. Blackwood & S. Wieringa (Eds.), *Female Desires: Same-Sex Relations and Transgender Practices Across Cultures*, pp. 91-116 (N. Y.: Columbia Univ. Press, 1999), p. 92.

[1090] Ibid, p. 95f.

[1091] This situation pertains where sexual relationships are sanctioned based on differences in *gender* rather than differences in *sex*. Where the former is made dependent on the latter, then the judgments are different.

[1092] George Devereux, "Homosexuality Among the Mohave Indians," *Human Biology, 9*, 498-597 (1937), esp. p. 516.

[1093] Will Roscoe, *Changing Ones: Third and Fourth Genders in Native North America* (N.Y.: Palgrave Macmillan, 2000), pp. 137-138.

[1094] Midnight Sun, "Sex/Gender Systems in Native North America," in W. Roscoe (Ed.), *Living the Spirit: A Gay American Indian Anthology*, pp. 32-47 (N. Y.: St. Martin's Press, 1988), p. 39. Cf. A. L. Kroeber, "Two Myths of the Mission Indians of California," *Journal of the American Folk-Lore Society, XIX* (No. LXXV), 309-321 (1906), p. 315.

[1095] Carolyn Epple, "Coming to Terms with Navajo *Nádleehí*: A Critique of Berdache,'Gay,' 'Alternative Gender,' and 'Two Spirit'," *American Ethnologist, 25* (no. 2), 267-290 (1998). Cf. the much earlier work, W. W. Hill, "The Status of Hermaphrodite and Transvestite in Navaho Culture," *American Anthropologist, 37*, 273-279 (1935).

[1096] Lauren Wells Hasten, *In Search of the 'Berdache': Multiple Genders and Other Myths* (1998). Accessed online at http://www.laurenhasten.com/berdache.htm#navaho.

[1097] Midnight Sun, p. 41.

[1098] Will Roscoe, "We'wha and Klah: The American Berdache as Artist and Priest," in G. D. Comstock & S. E. Henking (Eds.), *Que(e)rying Religion: A Critical Anthology* (N.Y.: Continuum, 1997), pp. 89-106.

[1099] See Marjorie Anne Napewastewiñ Schützer, *Winyanktehca: Two-souls Person* (1994). Paper presented to the European Network of Professionals in Transsexualism, August, 1994. Found at the gender.org website and accessed online at http://www.gender.org.uk/conf/trilogy/winkte.htm.

[1100] Royal B. Hassrick, *The Sioux: Life and Customs of a Warrior Society* (Norman: Univ. of Oklahoma Press, 1964), pp. 121-123.

[1101] Walter L. Williams, "Persistence and Change in the Berdache Tradition Among Contemporary Lakota Indians," in L. D. Garnets & D. C. Kimmel (Eds), *Psychological Perspectives on Lesbian and Gay Male Experiences*, pp. 339-347 (N. Y.: Columbia Univ. Press, 1993), pp. 343-344.

[1102] Roscoe, "We'wha and Klah," p. 91. In Zuni terms, one is born 'raw' and must be 'cooked' throughout life.

[1103] Elsie Parsons, "The Zuni La'mana," *American Anthropologist, 18* (no. 4), 521-528 (1916), p. 523.

[1104] *The Zuni Man-Woman* (2005). Article posted on SantaFe.com. Accessed online at http://www.santafe.com/history/zuni_man-woman.html. For much more detail, see Will Roscoe, *The Zuni Man-Woman* (Albuquerque: Univ. of New Mexico Press, 1991). For a briefer account, see Roscoe, "We'wha and Klah."

[1105] Sabine Lang, *Men as Women, Women as Men: Changing Gender in Native American Cultures* (Austin, TX: Univ. of Texas Press, 1998), Table 10, pp. 314-318.

[1106] Wesley Thomas, "Navajo Cultural Constructions of Gender and Sexuality," in S-E. Jacobs, W. Thomas, & S. Lang (Eds.), *Two-Spirit People: Native American Gender Identity, Sexuality, and Spirituality*, pp. 156-173 (Champaign, IL: Univ. of Illinois Press, 1997), p.p. 156-157.

[1107] Midnight Sun, p. 47.

[1108] John D'Emilio & Estelle B. Freedman, *Intimate Matters. A History of Sexuality in America* (N. Y.: Harper & Row, 1988), p. 91.

[1109] Roscoe, *Changing Ones,* p. 19; cf. his discussion pp. 17-19.

[1110] Henry Angelino & Charles L. Shedd, "A Note on Berdache," *American Anthropologist, 57*, 121-126 (1955).

[1111] Charles Callendar & Lee M. Kochems, "The North American Berdache," *Current Anthropology, 24* (no.4), 443-456 (1983), p. 443. With comments, the article extends to p. 470.

[1112] Sue-Ellen Jacobs, Wesley Thomas, & Sabine Lang, "Introduction," in S.-E. Jacobs, W. Thomas, & S. Lang (Eds.), *Two-Spirit People: Native American Gender Identity, Sexuality, and Spirituality*, pp. 1-18 (Chicago: Univ. of Illinois Press, 1997), p. 2.

[1113] Arnold R. Pilling, "Cross-Dressing and Shaminism Among Selected Western North American Tribes," in S-E. Jacobs, W. Thomas, & S. Lang (Eds.), *Two-Spirit People: Native American Gender Identity, Sexuality, and Spirituality*, pp. 69-99 (Champaign, IL: Univ. of Illinois Press, 1997), p. 69. In the same volume, Lang (p. 100) makes clear that the term is meant to replace *berdaches*.

[1114] Elizabeth Reis, "Teaching Transgender History, Identity, and Politics," *Radical History Review, 88*, 166-177 (2004), p. 170.

[1115] Raymond J. DeMallie (Ed.), *The Sixth Grandfather. Black Elk's Teachings Given to John G. Neihardt* (Lincoln: Univ. of Nebraska Press, 1984), p. 81. Black Elk was an Oglala holy man.

[1116] Jamaka Highwater, *The Mythology of Transgression: Homosexuality as Metaphor* (N. Y.: Oxford Univ. Press, 1997), p. 81.

[1117] Egerton Sykes (Revised by Alan Kendall), *Who's Who in Non-Classical Mythology* (N. Y.: Routledge, 1993), p. 18.

[1118] Ibid, p. 5.

[1119] F. H. Cushing, "Outlines of Zuni Creation Myths," *Thirteenth Annual Report*, pp. 325-447 (Washington, D.C.: Bureau of Ethnology, 1896), p. 380.

[1120] Ibid, p. 401.

[1121] See Roscoe, "We'wha and Klah," p. 105. Also see Walter L. Williams, *The Spirit and the Flesh: Sexual Diversity in American Indian Culture* (Boston: Beacon Press, 1992), p. 18.

[1122] Roscoe, *Changing Ones*, p. 8.

[1123] In other words, a 'heterosexual orientation' is a relatively fixed erotic attraction pattern that has as its object members of a different *gender*, regardless of the person's *sex*. Similarly, a 'homosexual orientation' is a relatively fixed erotic attraction pattern toward members of the same gender. Reliance on body sex is far less accurate, though given the absolute uselessness of the concept in relating to one another we all would be better off without the idea at all.

[1124] Italo Signorini, "Comment" on Callendar & Ketchum, "North American Berdache," *Current Anthropology, 24* (no.4), 443-456 (1983), p. 463. With comments, the article extends to p. 470.

[1125] Lang, "Lesbians, Men-Women and Two-Spirits," p. 93.

[1126] Kroeber notes the fundamental similarity in nature of the mythologies of the Mohave, Navajo, Sia, and Zuni peoples. A. L. Kroeber, "Preliminary Sketch of the Mohave Indians," in Frederica de Laguna, *American Anthropology 1888-1920: Papers from the American Anthropologist*, pp. 484-491 (Lincoln: Univ. of Nebraska Press, 1960), p. 490. [Paper originally published in 1902.]

[1127] Williams, p. 19. Interestingly, the contribution can literally be a salvific one. Turquoise Boy and White Shell Girl ultimately save the people from a great flood and bring them to the present world of the Navajo (Williams, p. 20).

[1128] Richard C. Trexler, "Making the American Berdache: Choice or Constraint?" *Journal of Social History, 35* (no. 3), 613-636 (2002). Trexler, in surveying the literature of Latin American records at the time of the Spanish Conquest finds no instances of an individual self-selecting this place in society. Moreover, this general situation pertains to later times. In his estimation, even the notion of a 'test' to determine a child's 'true gender' is contrived; adult authorities construe the gender they want.

[1129] Edward Carpenter, *Intermediate Types Among Primitive Folk. A Study in Social Evolution* (London: George Allen & Co., Inc., 1914), p. 37. Accessed online at http://www.sacredtexts.com/ lgbt/itp/itp05.htm.

[1130] Devereux.

[1131] Sabine Lang, "Various Kinds of Two-Spirit People: Gender Variance and Homosexuality in Native American Communities," in S-E. Jacobs, W. Thomas, & S. Lang (Eds.), *Two-Spirit People: Native American Gender Identity, Sexuality, and Spirituality*, pp. 100-118 (Champaign, IL: Univ. of Illinois Press, 1997), p. 105.

[1132] Roscoe, p. 141.

[1133] Cf. Devereux, p. 501-506.

[1134] Parsons, pp. 526-527.

[1135] Prince Alexander Philipp Maximilian, *Reise in das innere Nord-America in den Jahren 1832 bis 1834*, 2 vols. (*Travels in the Interior of North America, 1832-1834*), excerpts of which are offered in an English translation by D. Thomas & K. Ronnefeldt (Eds.), *People of the First Man: Life Among the Plains Indians in Their Final Days of Glory* (N. Y.: Dutton, 1976).

[1136] Maximilian, *Reise in das innere Nord-America*, II, p. 133; cited in Carpenter, *Intermediate Types Among Primitive Folk*, p. 43.

[1137] Marjorie Anne Napewastewiñ Schützer, *Winyanktehca: Two-souls Person* (1994). Paper presented to the European Network of Professionals in Transsexualism, August, 1994. Found at the gender.org website and accessed online at http://www. gender.org.uk/conf/trilogy/winkte.htm.

[1138] Christina Pratt, *An Encyclopedia of Shamanism. Volume 2: N-Z* (N. Y.: Rosen Publishing Group, 2007), p. 522.

[1139] Williams, *The Spirit and the Flesh*, pp. 21-22; quote is from p. 21.

[1140] On the connection of the idea of 'shamanism' with Native Americans, see Andrei A. Znamenski, "General Introduction—Adventures of the Metaphor: Shamanism and Shamanism Studies," in A. A. Znamenski (Ed.), *Shamanism*, vol. 1, pp. xix-lxxxvi (N.Y.: Routledge, 2004), pp. xxxiv-xxxv.

[1141] Lang, "Various Kinds of Two-Spirit People," p. 167. Cf. Lang, "Lesbians, Men-Women and Two-Spirits," p. 95.

[1142] Midnight Sun, p. 39.

[1143] Lame Deer, quoted in Mary Pat Fisher, *Living Religions*, 3rd ed. (Upper Saddle River, NJ: Prentice Hall, 1997), p. 54.

[1144] Åke Hultcrantz, "The Specific Character of North American Shamanism," in A. A. Znamenski (Ed.), *Shamanism*, vol. 2, pp. 15-36 (N. Y.: Routledge, 2004), p. 16.

[1145] David Hoffmann, *The Herbal Handbook: A User's Guide to Medical Herbalism* (Rochester, VT: Healing Arts Press, 1998), p. 12.

[1146] Cf. Gilbert H. Herdt, *Same Sex, Different Cultures: Gays and Lesbians Across Cultures* (Boulder, CO: Westview Press, 1997), p. 94.

[1147] See, among other works, L. B. Boyer, "Remarks on the Personality of Shamans with Special Reference to the Apache of the Mescalero Indian Reservation," in W. Muensterberger & S. Axelrad (Eds.), *The Psychoanalytic Study of Society*, vol. 2, pp. 233-254 (N. Y.: International Universities Press, 1962). Also see L. B. Boyer, "Comparisons of the Shamans and Pseudoshamans of the Apaches of the Mescalero Indian Reservation: A Rohrshach Study," *Journal of Projective Techniques and Personality Assessment*, 28, 173-180 (1964). Also see L. B. Boyer, "Shamans: To Set the Record Straight," *American Anthropologist*, 71, 307-309 (1969).

[1148] Julianne Cordero & Elizabeth Currans, "Gender, Sexuality, and the Balance of Power in Native American Worldviews," in D. W. Machacek & M. M. Wilcox (Eds.), *Sexuality and the World's Religions*, pp. 31-64 (Santa Barbara, CA: ABC-CLIO, Inc., 2003), p. 58.

Q. 85 Notes

[1149] Albert D. Klassen, Colin J. Williams, & Eugene E. Levitt, *Sex and Morality in the U. S.*, H. J. O'Gorman, Ed. (Middletown, CT: Wesleyan Univ. Press, 1989), p. 270f.

[1150] For a wide-ranging, scholarly, and compelling portrait of such contributions, including crossdressers but extending beyond them, see Randy P. Conner, *Blossom of Bone: Reclaiming the Connections Between Homoeroticism and the Sacred* (S. F.: Harper, 1993).

[1151] Alain Dang & Mandy Hu, *Lesbian, Gay, Bisexual and Transgender People: A Community Project. A Report from New York's Queer Asian Pacific Legacy Conference, 2004* (National Gay and Lesbian Task Force Policy Institute, 2004), p. 18f. Accessed online at http://www.usc.edu/student-affairs/glbss/PDFS/APAstudy.pdf.

Author/Person Index

[Individuals listed with surname first are authors cited in text. Other names are listed in the manner they appear in the text and may signify a subject and/or author. Divine figures are not included.]

A

'Abbada, 268

Abraham Joshua Heschel, 248

Allison, Becky, 183-184

al-Qaradawi, Yusuf, 261

Altenburger, Roland, 350, 351, 352

Alter, Robert, 37

Althaus-Reid, Marcella, 218

al-Tirmidhi, 267

Ambrose of Milan, 69, 73-75

Amba, 291, 292

Ananda, 314

Anastasia the Patrician, 90

Angelino, Henry, 398

Anna of Constantinople, 91

Abu 'Ubayd, 262

Abu Dawud, 265

al-'Arabî, Ibn, 255

Albertus Magnus, 126

al-Bukhari, 258, 264

al-cAsqalani, 272

Al-faqih, Abdullah, 273, 274, 275

al-Khalil b. Ahmad, 262

Apollonaria, 85, 86, 95

Argit, Betül Ipsirli, 260

Arjuna, 290, 291, 292, 293, 297

Arnold, Bettina, 108

Ashrof, V. A. Mohammed, 255

Aston, William George, 332

Athanasia, 84-85, 90, 95

Augustine, 73, 167, 418 n. 3, 440 n. 315

Aviv, Caryn, 243

Ayatollah Ruhollah Khomeini, 275

Azizah Abdul Rahman, 277

B

Baccheta, Paola, 283

Baizerman, Suzanne, 247

Bakhtin, Mikhail, 116, 119

Ban Zhao, 351

Basavanna, 285

Belkin, Ahuva, 249

Benjamin, Harry, 298

Bernard of Clairvaux, 216, 225

Bhima, 292

Bishop Antonio de Castro-Mayer, 131

Bleich, David, 251

Bocking, Brian, 224

Bockting, Walter, 153, 184

Boelstorff, Tom, 271

Boswell, John, 133, 173

Bouhdiba, Abdelwahab, 263, 276

Boyarin, Daniel, 108, 240

Boyer, Bryce, 406

Brautigan, Harris, 193

Brekus, Catherine, 102

Brown, Peter, 65

Bullough, Bonnie, 187

Bullough, Vern, 187

Burlyne, Daniel, 118

Butler, Judith, 59, 211

Bynum, Caroline Walker, 216

C

Caliph al-Amin, 276

Caliph Sulayman, 268

Callendar, Charles, 398

Cardinal Joseph Ratzinger
   See Pope Benedict XVI

Carrellas, Barbara, 364

Castle, Terry, 127

Catherine of Siena, 216

Cattell, Raymond, 117

Cesaretti, Charles, 153

Chamberlain, Basil Hall, 340, 341

Chan, Wing-tsit, 334, 361

Chedgzoy, Kate, 127

Chevalier d'Eon, 105, 110-112, 162

Christina Hutchins, 198

Clarke, Adam, 39, 42-44

Religious Texts Index

Buddhist Texts

Chinese Traditional Religion

Christian Texts
(also see Tanakh in Jewish Texts)

Taoist Texts

Subject Index

A

B

C

V

Vaishnavism, 294-295, 298
Values, 407-408
Vatican II, 92, 123, 130
    See Second Vatican Council

Wakan sensai zue, 325
Wakan Tanka, 399
Waria, 271
Welcoming Ministries, 192, 200
Winkte, 396, 403

Yan Daudu, 383
Yellamma, 296

Zen Buddhism, 333-334

Venus, 36, 42, 220, 242, 255
    Also See Aphrodite
Vishnu, 209, 223, 232, 287, 290, 294

W

Wisdom, 58, 169, 210, 216-217, 237, 238
Women, 29, 41-42, 55, 59, 61-62, 69, 71f.,
    73-76, 79-104, 126-131, 246-247, 257-
    260, 280-282, 312-318, 329-337, 351-
    352, 356, 358-360, 362, 387, 394

X-Y

Yin/Yang, 230, 310, 351-352, 362,
    364-365

Z

Zubayda, 276

Crossdressing in Context.
Dress, Gender, Transgender, and Crossdressing.

Table of Contents for 5 Volume Set

Q. 16   What do people find entertaining about crossdressing?

Q. 17   Why do some homosexuals crossdress?

Q. 18   What is 'transvestism'?

Q. 19   What is 'transsexualism'?

Q. 20   What does 'transgender' mean?

Question Set 3: What causes crossdressing?

Q. 21   Is crossdressing 'natural'?

Q. 22   Is crossdressing learned behavior?

Q. 23   Is crossdressing developmental (i.e., "just a 24phase")?

Q. 24   Is crossdressing caused by sexual abuse?

Q. 25   Is crossdressing a choice?

Question Set 4: What is it like to be a transgendered crossdresser?

Q. 26   How do crossdressers describe themselves?

Q. 27   What is the profile of a 'typical' crossdresser?

Q. 28   When does crossdressing usually start?

Q. 29   What is childhood and adolescence like?

Q. 30   What is adulthood like for a crossdresser?

Q. 31   Does crossdressing lead to a sex change operation?

Q. 32   Is crossdressing harmful?

Q. 33   What is involved in crossdressing?

Q. 34   Where do crossdressers find support?

Q. 35   Are all crossdressers homosexual?

Question Set 5: How are transgender realities regarded by others?

Q. 36   What is the legal status of crossdressers?

Q. 37   How are crossdressers treated in public?

Q. 38   How do partners handle the crossdressing of their significant others?

Q. 39   How does crossdressing affect families?

Q. 40   Why does society tolerate crossdressing?

Volume 3: Transgender History & Geography

Volume 4: Transgender & Religion

Q. 64   What do Christian commentators say?

Q. 65   What constitutes a 'reasonable' position to take?

Question Set 9: What does Christianity say about crossdressing?

Q. 66   What does the New Testament say?

Q. 67   What did the Church Fathers say?

Q. 68   Are there crossdressing saints?

Q. 69   Are there notable crossdressing Christian women?

Q. 70   Are there notable crossdressing Christian men?

Q. 71   Are there Christian festivals where crossdressing is accepted?

Q. 72   Has the Church said anything "officially" about crossdressing?

Q. 73   What do Christians today who oppose transgender realities say?

Q. 74   What do transgender Christians and their supporters today say?

Q. 75   Are there resources for transgender Christians?

Question Set 10: What do other religions say about crossdressing?

Q. 76   How did crossdressing figure in ancient and pre-modern religions?

Q. 77   What stance does Judaism take on crossdressing?

Q. 78   What role has crossdressing played in Islam?

Q. 79   How does Hinduism regard crossdressing?

Q. 80   Is Buddhism tolerant of crossdressing?

Q. 81   Is crossdressing found in Japanese religions?

Q. 82   Can transgender elements be found in other Eastern religions?

Q. 83   What roles do crossdressing and transgender play in African religions?

Q. 84   Are transgender realities found in Native American religiosity?

Q. 85   What role does crossdressing play in religion?

Volume 5: Transgender & Mental Health

Reader's Notes

Lightning Source UK Ltd.
Milton Keynes UK
UKHW010919271120
374179UK00001B/6